ADMINISTRATION AND LEADERSHIP IN STUDENT AFFAIRS
ACTUALIZING STUDENT DEVELOPMENT IN HIGHER EDUCATION

EDITORS

Theodore K. Miller, Ed.D.
Roger B. Winston, Jr., Ph.D.
William R. Mendenhall, Ph.D.

CONTRIBUTORS

Margaret J. Barr
David T. Borland
Suzanne S. Brown
Richard B. Caple
D. Stanley Carpenter
Robert K. Conyne
Michael J. Cuyjet
David A. DeCoster
Dwight O. Douglas
Steven C. Ender
Donald D. Gehring
Daniel A. Hallenbeck
Patricia A. Hollander
Phyllis Mable
Sue Saunders McCaffrey
William R. Mendenhall
Theodore K. Miller
Fred B. Newton
Robert F. Rodgers
Louis C. Stamatakos
Wilbur A. Tincher
Roger B. Winston, Jr.
D. Parker Young
FOREWORD Robert H. Shaffer

Editors Consulting Editor
Jenny W. Best

ACCELERATED DEVELOPMENT INC.
Muncie   Indiana

ADMINISTRATION AND LEADERSHIP
IN STUDENT AFFAIRS

Actualizing Student Development In Higher Education

Library of Congress Number: 82-73318

International Standard Book Number: 0-915202-35-2

Publications Coordinator: Cindy Lyons

Associate Editor: Colleen Wolowski

Technical Assistants: Nell Young
                      Sarah Middleton

Cover: Larry Spangler

Printed in the United States of America
First Printing December, 1982
Second Printing January, 1984
Third Printing April, 1986
Fourth Printing February, 1988

 **ACCELERATED DEVELOPMENT INC.**
3400 Kilgore Avenue
Muncie, IN 47304

Tel. (317) 284-7511

FOREWORD

These times are an especially propitious period for releasing a new book on the administration of student affairs. The environment of higher education for the next two decades will force every institution to reexamine its relationship with its students and the way it meets their needs. Not only will goals and specific purposes be reexamined, redefined, and restated, but also the organizational structure and functions will be evaluated and redesigned to attain greater effectiveness. These steps will be taken in the midst of such countervailing forces and confusion as to create suspicion, fear, antagonism, and perplexity. What was long considered good and proper may be challenged as no longer even being worth doing!

In one sense, the situation on campuses across the country mirrors the confusion surrounding the social, economic, and political problems of American life in general. In another sense, however, the situation reflects the self-doubt and failing leadership of institutions of higher education. After all, higher education is generally regarded as contributing mightily to the amazing technological and social progress that has characterized the country since World War II. Many individuals now wonder where the leadership of colleges and universities is today and what it is doing to prepare citizens for the problems plaguing the country. Definitely the situation calls for self-examination and skilled response, instead of self-doubt, lack of confidence, unresponsiveness, and indecision.

A book emphasizing administration and leadership in student affairs focused on actualizing student development is particularly valuable. It provides important guidelines for making significant contributions to the institution's own developmental process. Failure on the part of student affairs administrators and other professionals to engage forcefully, competently, and knowledgeably in their institution's deliberations is an abdication of professional responsibilities.

A number of forces and trends contribute to the need for reexamination of present programs and practices. The massive budget cuts already occurring in many states coupled with predictions of continued financial stringency in both public and private institutions force intensive scrutiny of all expenditures. Student affairs is particularly vulnerable because traditional academic policies and procedures protect the faculty to a great extent, and union, civil service, or system personnel procedures protect clerical and maintenance staff. Student affairs practitioners are often in limbo and, therefore, more vulnerable even though they enjoy traditional popular support. These budget crunches are coming on many campuses at the very time that new and extended services are being required to meet needs of older, handicapped, minority, and other non-traditional students.

Stringent finances, however, are not the only reason institutions are being required to take a closer look at themselves. The great diversity of students arriving on campuses and changed relationships in society are challenging some basic assumptions underlying traditional practices in the various areas of student affairs. What should be the institution's role in shaping life styles, contributing to value formation, and challenging traditional beliefs? Has the concern of some institutions for total individual development undermined the emphasis upon intellectual development? The growing legalistic relationship with students emphasizing a seller-consumer posture, or at least a narrow contractual agreement, challenges the concern of student affairs professionals for a broader institutional commitment and contribution to students. Each institution must ask itself if an essentially legalistic relationship between institution and student is the best paradigm for fostering educational growth and individual development.

One of the most obvious implications of current trends and forces is the inescapable realization that student affairs practitioners need to be true professionals in their work and in their relationships within the total institutional environment. They must be thoroughly knowledgeable about the theoretical foundations of their work, not only as theory underlies specific practices, but also as it supports the educational efforts of institutions. Thus, when institutional practices are at variance with or even contradictory to sound theory, professionals must be forthright, confident, and sound in their opposition to such practices.

The first two parts, 11 chapters, of this book represent the theoretical foundations and the parameters of professional practice in all aspects of student affairs. The professional response to problems and issues is to utilize relevant theory and sound practice to define the problem as precisely as possible and assess those factors relating to the problem as it affects the achievement of personal, professional, and organizational objectives. Then the student affairs professional must be instrumental in initiating appropriate responses to policies, practices, and events within the setting to reduce interference with the desired and agreed upon outcomes. It is not professional nor productive to merely bemoan economic and social trends or to view with alarm or castigate critics and challengers.

A second implication of trends and issues in higher education is the need to understand that the particular organizational and environmental context of each institution will determine to a major extent the essential nature of that institution's responses to problems. This is particularly true of the institution's student affairs structure and administration. Solutions to complex problems and issues cannot be applied in general and without regard to specific institutional goals, constituencies, self images, and unique settings. Several chapters introduce the readers to organizational theory and development that should contribute to an understanding of the organizational context within which a practitioner works. Related to this understanding are skills involved in institutional and student needs assessment and in the effective, continuous evaluation of practices. Doing better what has always been done may not be an adequate response to the challenges and demands posed by a changing society!

Another significant implication of the environment of the 80's and 90's for the administration of student affairs is the need for effective interpretation of student affairs and services. Often this is best accomplished on a continuous basis through visibly efficient administration. Part Three of the book entitled, "Strategies for Administration and Leadership," consisting of nine chapters, provides practical application strategies for day-to-day student affairs administration by merging the theory and practice outlined in the first two parts.

No one book will change practices and solve all complex issues facing student affairs in postsecondary education today. However, editors Miller, Winston, and Mendenhall have made a significant contribution not only through their own chapters but also through those written by the outstanding practitioners recruited by them to be authors. These authors represent different philosophical orientations and institutions and yet the book provides a holistic, in-depth view of student affairs administration and leadership.

Improved administrative practices comprise an important first step in meeting the challenges posed by contemporary issues and circumstances in higher education in the years immediately ahead.

Robert H. Shaffer
Indiana University
Bloomington, Indiana

Robert H. Shaffer of Indiana University received his master's degree from Teachers College, Columbia University, and the Ph.D. from New York University. He is now professor emeritus of Education and Business Administration. Among the positions he held over a 40 year span at Indiana University were Director of Counseling, Dean of Students, and Chairman, Departments of College Student Personnel and Higher Education. He has held major offices in a number of student affairs asociations including the Presidency of the American Personnel and Guidance Association, Chairmanship of the Council of Student Personnel Associations, Editorship of the *NASPA Journal,* Associate Editorship of the *Personnel and Guidance Journal,* and service on the editorial boards of other journals. He has authored, edited, or contributed to a number of books and monographs.

CONTENTS

FOREWORD iii
Robert H. Shaffer

LIST OF FIGURES xiv

LIST OF TABLES xv

INTRODUCTION xvi

PART I   THEORETICAL FOUNDATIONS

1   **HUMAN DEVELOPMENT AND HIGHER
     EDUCATION** 3
     Theodore K. Miller, Roger B. Winston, Jr.,
     William R. Mendenhall

     HISTORICAL PERSPECTIVE   4
     *DEVELOPMENTAL RATIONALE FOR STUDENT
       AFFAIRS*   10
     *STUDENT DEVELOPMENT AND STUDENT AFFAIRS
       ADMINISTRATION*   18
     References   25
     Suggested Readings   29

2   **ORGANIZATIONAL FOUNDATIONS OF
     ADMINISTRATION** 31
     David T. Borland

     ORGANIZATIONAL THEORY DEVELOPMENT   32
     ORGANIZATIONAL ANALYSIS   39
     *ORGANIZATIONAL ALTERNATIVES FOR STUDENT
       AFFAIRS*   44
     CONCLUSION   48
     References   49
     Suggested Readings   50

3 ORGANIZATION DEVELOPMENT: A BROAD NET INTERVENTION FOR STUDENT AFFAIRS...............................53
Robert K. Conyne

DEFINING ORGANIZATION DEVELOPMENT 54
OPEN-SYSTEM: A FRAMEWORK FOR OD 54
ACTION RESEARCH AS A CHANGE PROCESS 58
CLASSIFYING AND USING OD INTERVENTIONS 62
SELECTED OD INTERVENTIONS 64
OD IN HIGHER EDUCATION 69
*STUDENT AFFAIRS AS AN OD NUCLEUS IN HIGHER
    EDUCATION* 71
USING OD IN STUDENT AFFAIRS 76
References 78
Suggested Readings 80

4 MANAGERIAL LEADERSHIP 83
Fred B. Newton, Richard B. Caple

*HISTORICAL PERSPECTIVE ON MANAGEMENT
    THEORY* 85
LEADERSHIP 92
*NEW WAYS FOR VIEWING MANAGERIAL
    LEADERSHIP* 97
APPLICATIONS TO STUDENT AFFAIRS 99
A PERORATION 105
References 106
Suggested Readings 108

PART II PARAMETERS OF PROFESSIONAL PRACTICE

5 USING THEORY IN PRACTICE 111
Robert F. Rodgers
CONTINUUM FOR UNDERSTANDING THEORY 113
THEORY-TO-PRACTICE APPROACH 116
A CASE STUDY 125
SUMMARY 137
References 140
Suggested Readings 144

6 THE STUDENT AFFAIRS PROFESSION: A DEVELOPMENTAL PERSPECTIVE 147

D. Stanley Carpenter

THE EMERGENCE OF STUDENT AFFAIRS PROFESSIONALS 148
MODEL OF PROFESSIONAL DEVELOPMENT IN STUDENT AFFAIRS 154
PROFESSIONAL IMPLICATIONS OF A DEVELOPMENTAL MODEL 159
SUMMARY 163
References 163
Suggested Readings 165

7 ETHICAL PRACTICE IN STUDENT AFFAIRS ADMINISTRATION 167

Roger B. Winston, Jr., Sue Saunders McCaffrey

ETHICS: A DEFINITION 168
ETHICS, LAW, SOCIETY, AND THE PROFESSION 171
VALUES AND THE STUDENT AFFAIRS PROFESSION 175
ISSUES AND PRINCIPLES 177
A MODEL OF ETHICAL DECISION MAKING 178
APPLICATION OF ETHICAL DECISION-MAKING MODEL 182
RESPONSIBILITIES OF ALL STUDENT AFFAIRS PROFESSIONALS 185
RECOMMENDATIONS TO IMPROVE ETHICAL CONDUCT IN THE PROFESSION 186
References 189
Suggested Readings 191

8 STANDARDS FOR PROFESSIONAL PRACTICE 193

Phyllis Mable, Theodore K. Miller

FOUNDATIONS OF ACCREDITATION 197
RATIONALE FOR PROFESSIONAL STANDARDS IN STUDENT AFFAIRS PRACTICE AND PREPARATION 199
USE OF STANDARDS 206
References 209
Suggested Readings 211

9 LEGAL ISSUES IN THE ADMINISTRATION OF STUDENT AFFAIRS 213
  Donald D. Gehring

  WHY STUDY LEGAL ISSUES 213
  THE STUDENT-INSTITUTION RELATIONSHIP:
   PUBLIC V. PRIVATE 214
  CONSTITUTIONAL PARAMETERS 216
  CONTRACTUAL RELATIONSHIP 226
  REGULATORY RELATIONSHIPS 228
  SUMMARY 231
  Case Citations 233
  Suggested Readings 237

10 LEGAL ISSUES AND EMPLOYMENT PRACTICES IN STUDENT AFFAIRS 239
  Patricia A. Hollander, D. Parker Young

  THRESHOLD QUESTIONS 240
  EMPLOYMENT ISSUES 242
  LEGAL LIABILITY 253
  CASE CITATIONS 260
  References 261
  Suggested Readings 261

11 THE IMPACT OF COLLECTIVE BARGAINING: PROFESSIONAL DILEMMA OR PANACEA? 263
  David T. Borland

  HISTORICAL DEVELOPMENT 264
  BARGAINING PROCESSES 268
  IMPACT ON STUDENT AFFAIRS 275
  CONCLUSION 281
  References 281
  Suggested Readings 283

PART III STRATEGIES FOR ADMINISTRATION AND LEADERSHIP

12 MANAGING HUMAN RESOURCES: STAFFING, SUPERVISION, AND EVALUATION 285
  Roger B. Winston, Jr., William R. Mendenhall,
  Theodore K. Miller

THE STUDENT AFFAIRS STAFF 285
STAFFING THE STUDENT AFFAIRS DIVISION 289
FILLING POSITION VACANCIES 294
SUPPORT STAFF POSITIONS 307
ROLE OF THE PERSONNEL OFFICE 310
STAFF SUPERVISION 311
STAFF EVALUATION 315
SUMMARY 318
References 319
Suggested Readings 321

13 **STUDENTS AS PARAPROFESSIONALS** 323
   Steven C. Ender

A RATIONALE 324
ROLES, GOALS, AND LIMITATIONS 326
IMPLEMENTING PARAPROFESSIONAL PROGRAMS 329
EVALUATION 333
SPECIAL ISSUES 335
SUMMARY 336
References 337
Suggested Readings 339

14 **STAFF DEVELOPMENT: PERSONAL AND
   PROFESSIONAL EDUCATION** 341
   David A. DeCoster, Suzanne S. Brown

PHILOSOPHICAL FOUNDATION 341
COMPONENTS OF STAFF DEVELOPMENT 345
SUPERVISION AND PERFORMANCE EVALUATION 351
ISSUES AND IMPLICATIONS FOR THE FUTURE 365
References 370
Suggested Readings 373

15 **FISCAL RESOURCE MANAGEMENT:
   BACKGROUND AND RELEVANCE FOR
   STUDENT AFFAIRS** 375
   Dwight O. Douglas

BUDGETS AS MANAGEMENT TOOLS 377
FINANCIAL STATEMENTS AS MANAGEMENT TOOLS 379
TYPES OF BUDGETS 385

LONGITUDINAL FISCAL MANAGEMENT 390
BEYOND THE FORMULA, ALLOCATION, OR
   BUDGET 392
DETERMINING THE PLANNING BACKGROUND 394
RECAPITULATION 396
References 397
Suggested Readings 397

16 STUDENT AFFAIRS ADMINISTRATOR AS
    FACILITIES MANAGER....................399
    Daniel A. Hallenbeck

CREATION OF ENVIRONMENTS 399
MANAGEMENT OF PHYSICAL FACILITIES 401
STRUCTURING OF FACILITIES 404
PRACTICAL ASPECTS OF FACILITY MANAGEMENT 405
SUMMARY AND CONCLUSION 414
References 416
Suggested Readings 417

17 TIME MANAGEMENT AND PLANNING FOR
    STUDENT AFFAIRS PROFESSIONALS 419
    Wilbur A. Tincher

EFFECTIVE USE OF TIME 420
DECIDING WHAT NEEDS TO BE DONE 435
A RECAPITULATION 442
References 444
Suggested Readings 445

18 PROGRAM DEVELOPMENT AND
    IMPLEMENTATION 447
    Margaret J. Barr, Michael J. Cuyjet

THEORY AND PRACTICE IN PROGRAM
   DEVELOPMENT 448
A MODEL FOR PROGRAM PLANNING 451
SUMMARY AND IMPLICATIONS 469
References 473
Suggested Readings 475

19 MAXIMIZING OPPORTUNITIES FOR SUCCESS 477
Louis C. Stamatakos

PROFESSIONAL PREPARATION 477
ENTERING THE PROFESSIONAL WORKWORLD 487
BEING PROFESSIONAL 494
THE IMPORTANCE OF A MENTOR 497
References 500
Suggested Readings 501

20 ROLES AND FUNCTIONS OF STUDENT AFFAIRS PROFESSIONALS.........................503
William R. Mendenhall, Theodore K. Miller,
Roger B. Winston, Jr.

VIEWS OF MANAGEMENT IN HIGHER EDUCATION 504
ROLES 505
ACCOUNTABILITY FOR ROLES AND FUNCTIONS 519
PROFESSIONALS IN ORGANIZATIONS 522
References 528
Suggested Readings 532

APPENDIX A....................................534

APPENDIX B 540

APPENDIX C 546

NAME INDEX 559

SUBJECT INDEX 566

ABOUT THE EDITORS 578

LIST OF FIGURES

2.1 The matrix pyramid 47

3.1 Organization assessment model: Six organizational
     processes (dimensions) of the open system model 57

4.1 Conceptualization of the four major managerial
     functions 88

4.2 The academic administrator grid 95

5.1 Examples of defined direction of process variable:
     Managing emotions in Location 3 114

5.2 Chickering's (1969) seven vectors in chronological,
     directional, and age-related order 116

5.3 Schematic of person-environment interaction: Degree
     of challenge and support 121

6.1 Four steps and related developmental tasks of student
     affairs professionals 156

7.1 The context of professional ethics 172

7.2 Paradigm of ethical decision-making process 181

12.1 Selection and analysis form: Used by
     interventions to systematize the analysis of
     candidate's qualifications 300

12.2 Permissible and impermissible interview
     questions 302

14.1 Self-assessment model for staff development related
     to career objectives 348

14.2 Functional roles within professional
     relationships 356

15.1 Monthly operations statement for a residence
     hall 381

15.2 Residence hall statement of operations
     (February FY '99) 382

15.3 Residential hall statement of operations
     (June FY '99) 386

16.1 Illustration of a facility equipment and furnishings
     record that contains date acquired or date when last
     maintained and life expectancy for each item 412

16.2 Five-year replacement and renovation program for
Douglas Hall 413

17.1 Time management weekly log 425

18.1 Dimensions of intervention for student affairs 451

LIST OF TABLES

2.1 Examples of Goal Analysis and Classification of Goals
for Higher Education 43

3.1 Definitions of Organization Development
Summarized According to Authors and Elements
of OD Process 55

5.1 Selected Developmental and Related
Theories 117

5.2 Currently Available Procedural and Process Models
and Source Theorists 124

5.3 Students Data: Actual Behavior and Outcome
in Roommate Conflict Situations 130

5.4 Resident Advisor Data: Actual Behavior and
Self-evaluation in Conflict Situations....................131

5.5 Brainstorm on Possible Interventions in Roommate
Conflict Situations 135

5.6 Design of Resident Advisor Workshop on
Roommate Conflict Resolution 138

7.1 Levels of Ethical Codes 170

17.1 The Fifteen Leading Time Wasters......................423

17.2 Six-month Review Questions...........................435

17.3 Planning as a Management Function 437

EDITORS' INTRODUCTION

Administration of student affairs programs requires a broader base of knowledge than do many other types of organizational enterprises because of the unique educational goals and purposes of student affairs. Although management techniques are extremely important to effective administration of student affairs programs, techniques alone are not enough to accomplish required tasks. Likewise, human development principles that can guide the design and implementation of important educational and organizational activities are not in and of themselves sufficient to carry out an effective student affairs operation. In effect, basic principles of both management and human development so essential to successful practice in student affairs are, when taken individually, insufficient as either a theoretical or pragmatic base. Only when principles, functions, techniques, and basic premises are integrated into a dynamic whole can the professional practice of student affairs administration become a reality. The integration of theory, technique, philosophy, and technology is essential to effective professional student affairs practice.

Student affairs administration is an unique specialty within the context of higher education and requires more than either good management or good facilitative practice alone to accomplish its mission. With this proposition as a foundation, the editors have sought to bring together both management and student development theory and philosophy in order to demonstrate that these concepts are not antagonistic and that they, in fact, complement each other. The approach emphasized throughout the book, therefore, is application of management theory and principles in higher education settings from a student development point of view.

This book was written by and for student affairs leaders, as well as for future practitioners. Contributor selection was based upon both professional expertise and comprehension of student affairs administration. Both theoretical conceptualizations about and practical solutions to issues and problems faced by entry and mid-management level student affairs practitioners are presented. This book was written as a response to a need for a text about administrative issues and concerns in student affairs that recognized the importance of student development as a goal for the profession.

Works in the student affairs area have tended to take three distinct forms. These included (1) books on management of higher education organizations, (2) books articulating the context and philosophy of student affairs practice, and (3) books outlining intervention process models and approaches to the education and development of college students. Although important and often seminal in nature, these books tend to view student affairs practice as (1) a special form of counseling, or (2) a collection of student services, or (3) a form of educational administration, or (4) a philosophical position for educating students. They also tend to be written from a functional or descriptive approach to student services; a higher education/student affairs issues approach; a process model approach; or a collection of readings approach. In contrast, the intent of this book is to begin the process of identifying student affairs as a unique and essential component of higher education. Its purpose is the intentional development of students who are aided in realizing their potential in the intellectual, social, aesthetic, moral, and physical areas of their lives. Students are consequently more effective human beings who can cope successfully in an increasingly complex world and whose quality of life is enhanced by participation in the higher education process.

The book is organized into three parts, each of which is designed to present an essential aspect of student affairs administration and leadership, and all of which are essential to the totality. In Part I is presented *philosophical and theoretical foundations* intended to give the reader a cursory understanding. This section should peak readers' interests and stimulate them to pursue this area in greater detail. Professionals must understand both presuppositions and theoretical underpinnings of student affairs practice within the larger context of higher education.

Part II consists of seven chapters designed to articulate *issues, concerns, and restrictions that define practice in student affairs*. This part defines issues that practitioners must consider when offering student services and developmental programs. Specific issues addressed include application of theory to practice, elements of professionalism such as standards for professional practice and ethics, legal parameters regarding students and staff, and collective bargaining.

Part III consists of nine chapters and provides *practical strategies for day-to-day student affairs administration*. Human, fiscal, facility, and programmatic resources are emphasized; alternative ways and means through which student affairs practitioners can better implement their professional responsibilities are presented. Specific strategies for managing these resources are suggested along with the rationale for their use. The two final chapters are designed to focus attention directly upon the student affairs administrator as he/she seeks to grow both professionally and personally. In addition, in the appendices are included an ethical and professional standards statement, an introduction to legal research, and a standards statement for the professional preparation of student affairs practitioners.

TERMINOLOGY

As Crookston (1976) noted, the field is still unsettled about what terms to use to describe itself. *Student personnel, student affairs, student services, and student development* are often used interchangeably. In order to introduce some order into the confusion, the editors have followed the advice of Crookston throughout this book.

Student personnel is an anachronistic term that is no longer a suitable description; it appears only in quotations.

Student affairs is used to describe the organizational structure or unit on a campus responsible for the out-of-class education of students. Its administrative head usually has the title of Dean of Students (Affairs) or Vice President for Student Affairs. *Student affairs administration or practice* is viewed as a professional field.

Student services are specific activities designed to support the educational mission of the institution, but are not designed to contribute directly to the education of students. Examples of student services include making and controlling ID cards, maintaining transcripts, and processing financial aid applications. They are critically important to the effective functioning of the institution, but are not educational in themselves; they may be thought of as the tracks that allow the train of education to move ahead.

Student development is both a theory base and a philosophy for education and student affairs practice; it is the application of human development principles to students in higher education. "Student development" is not used in titles for individuals or administrative units. On the other hand, *student development programs* are used to describe activities designed to stimulate self-understanding, and/or to strengthen skills, and/or to increase knowledge.

Terminology regarding organizational structure varies considerably from campus to campus. For consistency the following schema was adopted. The basic administrative unit is referred to as the *student affairs division;* it is divided into *departments,* such as housing, student activities, or financial aid. Departments may be composed of units called *offices*, such as married student housing, student organizations, and work-study program. Professional practitioners are referred to inter-changeably as student affairs administrators, student affairs profes-sionals, and student affairs staff members. Finally, *college* is used as a general term to refer to any postsecondary educational institution.

ACKNOWLEDGEMENTS

Many people have contributed to making this book a reality. The editors wish to thank three hard-working secretaries for puzzling through the sometimes illegible handwriting and retyping countless drafts. Specifically, sincere thanks are extended to Cynthia Turner and Jean Wheat in the Office of the Vice-President for Student Affairs and Marian Burgess in the Department of Counseling and Human Develop-ment Services. Suzanne Royal, Department of Student Activities, is also thanked for her work on the graphics.

Special appreciation is expressed to many people at the University of Georgia, especially to Dwight O. Douglas, Vice-President for Student Affairs, who lent the editors both moral and staff support. Students in the Student Personnel in Higher Education Preparation program must be thanked for giving honest reactions to ideas and drafts.

The contributors to this volume have in all cases been extremely cooperative, have indulged the editors in their preferences for style, and have been thorough and diligent in making revisions. Without their ex-pertise and hard work this book would not have been possible.

Finally, the editors express their admiration and gratitude to Jenny W. Best for her dedicated copy editing. She has made subjects and verbs agree, mended the fractured syntax, and deleted the jargon. Her work has been very professional and invaluable.

Theodore K. Miller
Roger B. Winston, Jr.
William R. Mendenhall
University of Georgia
August, 1982   *Athens, Georgia*

REFERENCES

Crookston, B. B. Student personnel: All hail and farewell! *Personnel and Guidance Jour-nal*, 1976, *55*, 26-9.

PART I
THEORETICAL
FOUNDATIONS

Theodore K. Miller is Professor of Counseling and Human Development Services at the University of Georgia, where he is coordinator of the Student Personnel in Higher Education Preparation Program and Director of the College of Education Center for Student Development.

For additional information please refer to the last section of the book entitled "About the Authors."

Roger B. Winston, Jr. is Assistant Professor in the Student Personnel in Higher Education Program in the Department of Counseling and Human Development Services and Director of the Student Development Laboratory at the University of Georgia.

For further information please refer to the last section of the book entitled "About the Authors."

William R. Mendenhall currently serves as Associate Vice-President for Student Affairs at the University of Georgia, and he has had seventeen years experience in successive levels of student affairs administration.

For additional information please refer to the last section of the book entitled "About the Authors."

Chapter 1

HUMAN DEVELOPMENT AND HIGHER EDUCATION

Theodore K. Miller
Roger B. Winston, Jr.
William R. Mendenhall

American higher education, as all social institutions, develops neither in a vacuum nor in a fashion unrelated to the culture which surrounds, nurtures, and guide its progress. As Brubacher and Rudy (1976) so aptly noted, European traditions, when merged with native American conditions and augmented by the growth of American democracy, have resulted in a truly unique system of higher education. The student affairs area, an important component of that system, is the result of philosophical presuppositions about the nature of humankind; theoretical postulations about how people grow, learn, and develop; and the intuition of practitioners over the years who have sought to create environments that would nurture the growth of higher education. Both the ideas and the actions of philosophers, theorists, and practitioners have created the student affairs area. Today, human development theory has merged with the student personnel point of view to create an effective foundation for the area. Integrating the principles of developmental theory with the presuppositions of this point of view has much utility for student affairs.

Developmental theory and the basic principles that underly that theory have great utility for those student affairs leaders who view their role as active participants in the education of students. This book is predicated on the belief that student affairs administrators of the future will be successful, not because they are good people, but because they are competent professionals who comprehend their roles and responsibilities as being founded upon a set of theoretical principles that guide their everyday efforts. Human developmental theory is an appropriate foundation upon which to build. The intent in this chapter is to present both an historial perspective and a rationale for development and future expansion.

HISTORICAL PERSPECTIVE

As with all dynamic entities, higher education in America has been in transition since its inception. Higher education has, in other words, been growing, changing, and developing over the past 350 years in this country. The same social, cultural, and environmental influences that have sculpted the nation have had impact on higher education. Much can be learned from observing and interpreting the passages of higher education over the years, and this knowledge can be beneficial to those responsible for guiding the institutional life cycle of higher education in the years ahead.

Just as it is possible to understand better the growth and development of an individual by observing the challenges that a person faces and responses made to those challenges, so too is it possible to obtain a better understanding of the dynamics of higher education through an examination of its historical development. Lippitt and Schmidt (1967) postulated three stages of development through which organizations typically move as they become mature. They named the stages *Birth,* during which creation of the new organization and survival as a viable system are critical; *Youth,* when gaining stability, achieving reputability, and developing pride are of the essence; and *Maturity,* where critical concerns are to achieve uniqueness and adaptability and to contribute to society. Examining the development of higher education in America from this three-stage perspective is enlightening especially as that development is reflected in the way institutions have related to their student clientele and their organizational responses to challenges faced over the years. This perspective also is helpful for visualizing how the field of student affairs developed.

Birth

The first three institutions of higher learning founded in America—Harvard, William and Mary, and Yale—were more closely related in both conception and government to the then contemporary academies, gymnasia, and independent grammar schools of Elizabethan England than they were to medieval universities. William and Mary, in fact, was for the first 36 years of its operation a grammar school for Indian boys and local children. Also notable is the fact that these founding institutions served a colony-wide public and were not limited to a single local community's origin or control. These institutions were funded initially by trusts from public monies and their initial government was by appointed boards of trustees (Herbst, 1974).

Since religious objectives tended to dominate early colonial institutions, the early years of higher education in America largely reflect a picture of cohesiveness and unity concerning student life, educational goals, and institutional missions. Students themselves, however, represented more diverse socioeconomic backgrounds than often is recognized in historical literature. Students were not all of the social elite—some came from ordinary farming families, and most were relatively young (many in their early teens). The poor but ambitious youth also had the opportunity to attend college and thus elevate himself (only males were in attendance) into the professional classes (Brubacher & Rudy, 1976). Even in colonial times commonly some financial support was available for students of limited means, usually in the form of petty work positions.

The Collegiate Way of Life. Because most of the early colleges were founded outside the confines of urban communities of the day, the need for lodging students at or near the college was necessary. The decision to create "dormitories" in which students must live in order that they could be better supervised and thereby controlled reflects clearly the philosophy of paternalism that prevailed. Herein lies a major distinction between early American higher education institutions and universities of Europe. Rudolph (1962), as well as Brubacher and Rudy (1976), recognized the collegiate way of life with its emphasis upon concern for all aspects of the student's life as being a major factor in the unique development of higher education in America. What the student did before, after, and between his academic studies was viewed as important, perhaps even paramount, to the educational mission involved. This philosophical concept contributed to the formation of student affairs units.

Motives of the founding fathers of many early colleges included concern for good citizenship, good moral conduct, and the capacity to meet basic vocational needs of the New World. The collegiate way of life seemed most appropriate for such aims and purposes, especially in light of the pioneer conditions that existed. By extending their supervisory role into all areas of student life, institutions were able to replace much of what, in the Old World, would have been the responsibility of the young men's families. For instance, many rules and regulations existed to guide student conduct and the consequences for even minor infractions were often quite severe, including public floggings and confessions in the presence of the assembled faculty and students (Leonard, 1956).

Although the president and faculty were responsible for supervising the moral training and behavior of students, peer pressure was often more influential. At its worst, the collegiate way of life restrained intellectual potential, prolonged adolescent behavior, and promoted excessive paternalism. At its best, however, it offered a vehicle for providing susceptible young students with community support, social consciousness, better tastes, higher aims, and a mature intellectual and moral capacity (Rudolph, 1962). Even today remnants of this style of the collegiate way of life can be found in institutions of American higher education.

Student Activities. During the course of the first 200 years of higher education in America, the increasing influence of students can be seen through their often spontaneous and sometimes systematic progress toward creation of what became known as the "extracurriculum." The first organized student activities grew out of the traditional college class structure in which upperclassmen, especially sophomores, initiated new students into the college community. As informal hazing declined, it was often replaced by an institutionalized activity called "rush" in which the sophomore class would wage an organized struggle such as wrestling matches with the freshman class to see who persevered. If the freshmen won, then they would be accorded certain privileges not otherwise awarded them (Brubacher & Rudy, 1976). Some of these traditions carried on well into the 20th century.

Soon literary societies flourished and brought with them intellectual debate and oratory, literary magazines, and even libraries. In their beginnings, literary societies commanded passionate student loyalties and even serious rivalries, for usually at least two literary societies were organized on most campuses (Brubacher & Rudy, 1976). In large part, the literary society can be viewed as one of the first instances of organized student activity—activity organized and largely controlled by students themselves, that is. As one might expect, before long institutional leaders became aware of the immense popularity and influence these societies had upon students, and sought to gain some control over them.

Other types of student clubs and organizations became evident by the late 18th and early 19th centuries. College students were obviously manifesting certain personal and social needs not readily being met by the organized college curriculum and related programs of the day. Amateur dramatics and students' singing clubs were not uncommon by the turn of the 19th century, and the Greek-letter fraternity movement, with its purpose to change the focus to present-day worldly events rather than to the "hereafter" was soon forthcoming (Rudolph, 1962). The fraternity appeal to many college students was very powerful because it offered them an outlet not available within the formal framework of colleges in which they studied. In some ways, the advent of these secret societies within the college communities may have heralded the completion of the first stage of organizational development of student affairs in American higher education.

Just as earlier student rebellions had given evidence of the colleges' failure to provide adequate outlets for the normal exuberance of youth (Rudolph, 1962), so too does the initiation of secret societies show that students' needs were not being met. These organizations, along with the need for physical exercise and athletics, provided the foundation for movement into the next stage of development for American higher education.

Youth

As so often occurs within a life cycle, the point at which it appears that things are stable is very likely to be followed quickly by the unexpected and possibly most challenging new circumstances to be faced for some period of time. In other words, just when all seems well with the world, it may be the most likely time for that world to turn upside down.

As the young country developed in complexity during the 1800s, so did its educational institutions. Coeducation in its earliest form grew from the establishment of Oberlin College in Ohio in 1833. Soon thereafter colleges established for women only came into being: first in the South in 1836 with the Wesleyan Female College of Macon, Georgia, and later in the north with Rockford College in Illinois in 1849 (Brubacher & Rudy, 1976).

During the first half of the 19th century reform ran rampant throughout the land. One result was more egalitarian and utilitarian approaches to education. A primary example of the practical application emphasis of higher education during this time was the establishment of land-grant colleges. These colleges, committed to agricultural and mechanical education, were the recipients of some of the earliest federal aid to higher education upon passage of the Morrill Act of 1862.

Student Activities. As changes occurred throughout higher education, so did they take place in regard to student collegiate life as well. Secret society and Greek-letter fraternity organizations, whose seeds had been planted during the first half of the 19th century, came into full blossom during the second half of the century.

Early in the 20th century students were becoming increasingly influential in those areas of college life not directly linked to academic disciplines and rigors of the classroom. American higher education was indeed moving through a transition that demanded alterations of programs and processes involved. Somehow, for American higher education to survive as a viable force, the college student's out-of-class life needed to be reinstitutionalized as an integral part of the higher education enterprise.

By the early 1920s American higher education was facing consequences of rapid growth, extensive change, and impersonalization. In a harbinger of things to come three decades later, colleges were both expanding in size and faced with an increasingly divergent student clientele.

Maturity

The student personnel services movement blossomed during the first half of the 20th century. Student housing, always an influential feature in American higher education, shifted from an emphasis upon the small, close-knit, English residential college approach to a residence hall approach for housing larger numbers of single students as well as an increasing number of apartment-style facilities for married students (Schneider, 1977).

Student health programs were also on the increase, for World War I had pointed out the physical limitations of young Americans, and there were several epidemics that concerned both college administrators and government leaders. Another major indicator of the post World War I emphasis on individualizing the college campus was the advent of counseling bureaus. Vocational counseling, along with the testing movement, resulted in many colleges hiring counselors to help students make decisions about their educational and vocational plans. Closely related to this was the area of graduate placement. More and more students were seeking higher education as a way for advancing their careers. With the Great Depression of the 1930s came the understanding that a college degree was no assurance of employment. Colleges responded by increasingly offering students counseling in their search for post college jobs.

In the more advanced stages of organizational development, according to Lippit and Schmidt (1967), the organization seeks to achieve uniqueness and adaptability and to make a significant contribution to society as a whole.

Following World War II there was again a burst in student enrollment and an increase in diversity. The Federal Government was becoming increasingly involved in higher education, and student services functions were being increasingly organized within divisions of student affairs, which led to increased need for student affairs administrators. By 1966 the U.S. Department of Health, Education, and Welfare had identified 17 student service administrative functions common to most institutions of higher learning for which the student affairs office was primarily responsible. These included: (1) recruitment, (2) admissions, (3) nonacademic records, (4) counseling, (5) discipline, (6) testing, (7) financial aid, (8) foreign students, (9) nurse-care services, (10) medical services, (11) residence halls, (12) married student housing, (13) job placement, (14) student union, (15) student activities, (16) intramural athletics, and (17) religious affairs (Ayers, Tripp, & Russel, 1966).

Obviously, by the middle of the twentieth century the student personnel movement had matured into an emerging profession. The second quarter of the century had produced not only descriptive studies of the field (Cowley, 1936; Hopkins, 1926; Maverick, 1926), but also philosophically founded statements of student personnel work, *The Student Personnel Point of View* (American Council on Education, 1937, 1949). These seminal documents articulated four basic assumptions concerning college students and the responsibilities of higher education institutions in relation to those students. Miller and Prince (1976) stated these assumptions as

(1) the individual student must be considered as a whole; (2) each student is a unique person and must be treated as such; (3) the total environment of the student is educational and must be used to achieve his or her full development; (4) the major responsibility for a student's personal and social development rests with the student and his or her personal resources. (p. 4)

Implicit within these assumptions is a philosophical position that undergirds what has, in recent years, come to be viewed as the "student development movement."

The essence of intentional student development is the interaction between the student and the educational environment so that all aspects of the student's life are attended to and the environmental resources both challenge the student and give the support needed to meet these challenges so that more advanced levels of development result.

Whether history will record that the student development movement was a critical and significant influence upon American higher education during the second half of the twentieth century is yet to be determined. However, in the years ahead the thrust of this movement very likely will be felt to as great an extent as any other educational philosophy. Not only has the field of student affairs been emerging as a professional entity, but its practitioners have benefitted from the human development theory. The field has moved rapidly from offering student services to intentionally facilitating holistic development of students as an integral part of their formal education.

A DEVELOPMENTAL RATIONALE FOR STUDENT AFFAIRS

Student affairs is in transition. This transition basically reflects the ways professionals view their primary missions, their primary responsibilities, and the ways they should structure organizations and implement programs.

Student affairs is currently viewed by increasing numbers of professionals in the academic community as parallel to formal instruction as an essential part of the overall educational program (Wrenn, 1968).

Developmental Theory as a Foundation

For the past two decades an increasing trend toward the student development movement has existed. This school of thought quickly captured the imagination of a number of student affairs professionals as a way of adding credibility and validity to the work of administrators and practitioners responsible for organizing, guiding, and facilitating the out-of-class education and development of college students.

The professional student affairs practitioner of the future must know and understand human development theory as it applies to the life cycles of the students served. Student affairs administrators must understand the theory that underlies the work of the staff whom they supervise because without such understanding, conflicts and even adversary relationships may develop among staff, administrators, and supervisors. All professionals need not necessarily agree on what is the best theoretical view or the most effective way of implementing theory in practice. But all professionals must have a basic understanding of what is involved, or communications will become so snarled that failure likely will result. At the very least, an understanding of the basics and a general agreement need to be established on the part of all concerned on a campus as to how to proceed.

Schools of Thought. At least three major schools of thought have been identified as important to guiding student affairs. These include (1) the cognitive theories concerned with intellectual and moral development, (2) the psychosocial theories concerned with personal and life cycle development, and (3) the person-environment interaction theories that focus attention upon the ecology of student life.

The intellectual and moral development theories represented in the work of Piaget (1952), Perry (1970, 1981), and Kohlberg (1969) focused attention primarily upon process. How people learn, think, reason, make decisions, establish ethical positions, and make meaning out of available information are the key elements in most cognitive theories. Cognitive theorists are not particularly concerned with *what* people learn. Rather they are concerned with *how* people learn. Most of these theorists recognize the existence of a number of *stages* that people move into, through, and beyond to more advanced levels. Perry, however, uses the concept of *phases* instead, a way of looking at development that may have more validity. Most theorists of this school of thought view the stages as being *sequential* and *invariant* in nature. That is, not only does a *hierarchy* of stages exist in which each advanced stage incorporates what has been learned in the preceding stages, but the individual moves through stages in a relatively prescribed order. The implication is that if a person has not progressed through a particular intermediate stage, then he/she will not be able to move to a more advanced stage. Likewise, cognitive developmental theorists hold that cognitive and moral development is *universal* in nature and that persons from all cultures probably experience similar processes, stages, and sequences. Rather definitive *qualitative differences* exist between stages in which the new learning is not simply additive in nature, but rather reflects change in the basic characteristics or qualities of the reasoning processes from those apparent in earlier stages.

Of equal importance to student affairs practitioners is the second group of theories, the developmental theories espoused by those representing the psychosocial school of thought. Theorists with this frame of reference include Erikson (1963, 1968), Havighurst (1953, 1972), Chickering (1969, 1981), Sanford (1967), and Sanford and Axelrod (1979) as well as many of the adult life cycle theorists. Psychosocial theories focus more attention upon the *what,* or the content, involved in the developmental processes than upon the processes themselves. The concept of developmental stages is prevalent in the thinking of these theorists, and they often tend to correlate stages with chronological age. In this concept, stages are viewed as being sequential, but not necessarily invariant. One progresses from one stage to another by accomplishing a number of related developmental tasks (Havighurst, 1972) or vectors (Chickering, 1969) or by successfully resolving developmental crises (Erikson, 1963). Most theorists agree that the content involved in development at one stage, for example, establishing mature interpersonal relationships, developing autonomy, achieving identity, resolving the child-parent relationship, can and often does reappear in a later stage of development, usually in an altered form. Psychosocial theorists are greatly concerned with life transitions and the development of life-coping skills.

The third school of thought particularly viable for student affairs professionals is person-environment interaction theory. This theoretical approach is represented in the work of Moos (1979), Holland (1973), Pace (1979), Banning (1978), and Huebner (1979, 1980) and is based upon the principle that behavior is a direct function of the relationship between the individual and the environment (Lewin, 1936; Stern, 1970)—a simple but powerful idea. Many implicit behavioral elements are involved; effects of environmental stimuli on individual responses can be seen readily. The establishment of a healthy student environment is viewed as an important consideration, and the ability to assess that environment is basic to the success of this approach. As a result, a number of environmental assessment techniques have been developed to determine the effect the institutional environment has upon both the perceptions and the behavior of its students.

Principles of Student Development. A number of basic principles derived from developmental theories can be very helpful to student affairs practitioners wishing to facilitate development in students. These principles can help professionals as they seek to implement developmental theory. First, *human development is both continuous and cumulative in nature.* That is, individuals are constantly and continuously in the process of transition. Although the direction one's life development takes is influenced by life experiences, development will continue in some form no matter what attempts are made to diminish it. Development is also cumulative in nature because what has been learned and experienced in the past influences the form future development takes. People and situations experienced, decisions made to act or not to act, attitudes and perceptions of those to whom one is exposed, the type and amount of stimulation available, and the support or lack of support experienced all have the capacity to influence the character of one's development and growth. One is, to a large extent, the result of what one has experienced in the past.

Development is also a matter of movement from the simpler to the more complex. Sanford (1967) stated that most essentially, development is defined as the organization of increasing complexity, and that it is this directional movement toward greater complexity and competence that distinguishes development from growth. Growth is defined as simply an expansion or enlargement of what already exists. For the student affairs practitioner this principle is particularly important because it suggests that one's energies and activities need to be guided by the idea that an individual student can best be served by being aided to move from where he/she is at the moment to a slightly higher level of complexity. Plus-One, a concept originating with Kohlberg (1969) that can be used by student affairs practitioners, reasons that a challenge offered to a student that is just slightly more complex in concept, reasoning, or acquired skill may result in a slightly more complex level of response on the part of the student. Challenge that does not stimulate a higher level response or that requires response at a much higher level will very likely fail to stimulate development and, in fact, may retard it. As Heath (1968) and Chickering (1969) noted, the first "law" of human development is that development results through cycles of differentiation and integration. Student affairs practitioners who intentionally wish to promote development in those with whom they work must be concerned about creating stimulating and challenging environments.

Another principle of human development is that it tends to be orderly and stage related. The stage concept, however, should not be literally or too narrowly interpreted because a great deal of variability exists in human development. Because of this variability and to avoid false assumptions often associated with stage theory approaches, some authorities strongly suggest that thinking about developmental phases, as opposed to stages, would be wiser and more descriptively accurate (Montagu, 1981; Perry, 1970). Montagu suggested that a stage implies discontinuity whereas a phase implies continuity with the developmental changes passing imperceptibly into one another as a normal process. In other words, practitioners and theorists alike have tended to set arbitrary limits to the phases of development and called them stages. Research with the Student Developmental Task Inventory, for example, confirms that age alone is not a good predictor of the developmental status of traditional aged college students (Winston, Miller, & Prince, 1979). For student affairs practitioners, this suggests that seeking to establish group norms or similar expectations for all students is not desirable. Rather, the more that the developmental milieu can be individualized the better; it can stimulate and support students as they progress through their own unique developmental processes.

A Process Model for Student Development

Although a fundamental purpose of theory is the plausible explanation of observed phenomena, its primary value to student affairs professionals is as a guide to practice. In this regard, several student development models have been created that have enhanced the profession's capacity to implement programs of intentional student development. These include the Ecosystem Model (Aulepp & Delworth, 1976), Developmental Instruction (Knefelkamp, 1974), the Cube Model (Morrill & Hurst, 1980), the Grounded Formal Theory Process Model (Rodgers & Widick, 1980), the Student Development Education Model (Rippey, 1981), and the Seven-Dimensional Model of Student Development (Drum, 1980) among others. Such models are not intended to be initiated or copied intact, rather they have utility to be used as prototypes for creating programs, organizations, or approaches on one's own campus. Because every institution is unique, all programs of student development need to be especially created with that uniqueness in mind.

During the 1970s two parallel projects resulted in creation of a definitive model for intentional student development programming. In 1972 the Council of Student Personnel Associations (COSPA) proposed a student development model for use in student affairs programs (Cooper, 1972). In that same year the American College Personnel Association (ACPA) sponsored a monograph entitled *Student Development in Tomorrow's Higher Education: A Return to the Academy* (Brown, 1972). These two documents stimulated rapid movement toward a "student development point of view." When the book *The Future of Student Affairs* (Miller & Prince, 1976) was published as Phase II of the ACPA project, many of the basic concepts and principles reflected in both the COSPA statement and the Brown monograph were integrated into the Tomorrow's Higher Education (THE) Student Development Process Model. This model represents one viable approach for those seeking to apply informal theory in a planned, timely, and organized fashion.

The model postulates four primary functions essential to implementation of an intentional student developmental approach. These are (1) goal setting, (2) assessment, (3) procedural strategies for change including instruction, consultation, and environmental resource management, and (4) program evaluation. The translation of these components into practice allows for the creation of a substantive student development program.

The Goal Setting Function. Often students have not taken the time or had the opportunity to identify carefully why they are in college and what they hope to accomplish in college and in life. Setting goals and determining specific objectives can help students find the kind of structure they need for achieving the more complex behavior essential for advancing their development. Goal setting, therefore, is viewed as one of the primary survival skills needed in life, and most students can benefit from expanding their capacity to use this strategy. Student affairs practitioners can help students acquire goal setting skills.

Goal setting, from a Model perspective, involves collaboration between students and developmental facilitators and is intended to help students identify the specific behaviors and life situations toward which they wish to strive. The more tangible the desired outcomes and the more they are based upon students' felt needs, the more viable they will be. Without predetermined goals, assessing developmental progress or the effectiveness of a given strategy is all but impossible. The practitioner who regularly and systematically introduces and educates students to the use of this important skill is making a developmental difference that will benefit the recipient throughout life. Noteworthy, however, is the fact that students must learn this skill for themselves; practitioners setting goals for students will diminish the opportunities for students to accomplish this important learning. Helping students to move from vague, general goals through a clarification process to an attainable goal is an excellent method for facilitating planned development as a normal part of one's learning experience.

The Assessment Function. Assessment has the capacity to help students determine their present developmental status as well as what remains to be accomplished. It represents a general sequence of interlocking relationships. These include (1) an initial profile of students' developmental needs, (2) specification of their educational and personal goals and objectives, (3) an inventory of current levels of behavior or accomplishment, (4) creation of a plan using available change strategies and resources to achieve the desired outcomes, (5) continuous assessment of performance as the plan is being implemented, and (6) evaluation of movement toward the identified goals and their final achievement. This process is cyclical in nature, as the final step of one phase can serve as the initial assessment for the next.

Procedural Strategies for Change. The THE Process Model identified three primary strategies that planners can use to good advantage. These strategies encompass intervention approaches that are most appropriate and available within higher education to facilitate developmental growth. They include *instruction,* which is concerned with the teaching-learning function; *consultation,* which emphasizes counseling and advising functions; and *environmental resource management,* which focuses upon the establishment of climates conducive to development and learning. Although other strategies may be used, conceptionally, they would appear to be included within one of these three.

In the developmental planning phase of these processes, special competence and expertise on the part of practitioners are paramount. *Setting goals and assessing* developmental status are meaningful only to the extent that they identify human developmental needs and circumstances that require attention. Developmental action plans require both accurate information about needs and knowledge about how they may be met. Knowledge of available resources is essential, as is the ability to create innovative approaches when necessary.

The *instructional strategy* fits easily into educational settings. Collaboration between student affairs practitioners and faculty members is essential to the establishment of developmental task achievement under the instructional mode. In some instances creating instructional opportunities (courses, workshops, training sessions) not otherwise available on campus for personal development purposes may be necessary.

The *consultation strategy* calls for one person to engage with another person, group, or organization to identify needs and capabilities, and then to plan, initiate, implement, and evaluate action designed to meet or develop those needs and capabilities (Lanning, 1974). As a change strategy, this approach is of particular value when practitioners establish collegial relationships with the goal of collaboratively serving the developmental needs of greater numbers of students than they could serve individually.

Environmental resource management is somewhat more complex than is either instruction or consultation. In this approach pertinent resources are organized within both the institution and the larger community to shape the environment in ways designed to maximize human development. In this instance, practitioners act as both managers of the learning environment and experts in structuring climates that will promote healthy development. The ultimate intent is to design a learning environment that is planned carefully to build systematically upon the existing competencies and accomplishments of individuals and to create an environment to which exposure increases growth in appropriate facets of development. The term "resource" refers to all human, physical, and fiscal support systems with which the student interacts. The term "management" is not synonomous with control. Rather, it recognizes that students, practitioners, faculty, and administrators are all shareholders in both the educational process and its outcomes. Students must become active participants in structuring their environments because their lives and development are to be affected especially.

The Program Evaluation Function. In addition to implementing the action strategies as noted, evaluating the programs which result to assure that they are both effective and viable is essential. The evaluation process should begin with an examination of how program goals and activities relate to participants' goals and objectives and the influence the former has upon the latter. Evaluation provides the best means for clarifying both individual and program objectives and thereby provides a sound basis for modification and future planning.

Application of the THE Student Development Process Model does not call necessarily for reorganization of the student affairs structure, although its application may well lead to new and different associations and alliances being established. Freedom and encouragement to develop new and different linkages result usually in more viable programming with more involvement evidenced on the part of all concerned. Cooperative endeavors of an informal nature which may blossom into comprehensive programs, or which can be withdrawn if evaluated as being ineffective, represent an excellent method for using human resources.

STUDENT DEVELOPMENT AND STUDENT AFFAIRS ADMINISTRATION

The historical perspective, theoretical constructs, and the developmental process models noted are prologue to the paramount issue in student affairs administration: the education of individual students. Those in student affairs, whether parent-surrogates, teachers, or deans, have always sought to aid students in growing up and gaining a meaningful education. Student affairs practitioners must appreciate the wealth of knowledge, much of it gained through trial and error in the early years, that is their professional heritage. From a modern perspective many of their approaches, while well intended, were only partially effective because they were developed *ad hoc* without an extensive theoretical underpinning, and often required a charismatic personality to be made effective. However, they laid a foundation that the current generation of professionals can build upon. The responsibility of the professional student affairs staff is to use all available resources to both maintain and enhance the educational environments and opportunities available to students.

Professional practitioners must consider at least four important issues when seeking to carry forward the developmental mission of student affairs: (1) the role and function of theory in practice, (2) the relationship between student development and student affairs administration, (3) the influence of the institutional context on practice, and (4) the designation of responsibility for intentionally applying theory in the educational setting.

Using Theory in Administration

One of the most misunderstood, and probably most debilitating, problems faced by the student affairs profession concerns the theoretical underpinnings that essentially guide professional practice. Too often those who espouse developmental theory as a foundation for student affairs practice are charged with being idealistic, "blue sky dreamers" who are impractical, importunate, and quixotic in the eyes of those responsible for administering student affairs programs. Many with day-to-day administrative responsibilities have an administrative style that views attempts to initiate new or different functions, programs, or procedures as irritations that can be avoided. Practitioners who seek to administer programs primarily to avoid conflict, to overcome present crises, and to maintain the status quo cause those who espouse developmental theory to wring their hands and pull their hair because of those administrators' apparent insensitivity to students' developmental needs. Somehow, for the good of higher education, leaders, practitioners, and theoreticians must be brought together so that they can collaboratively create better and more effective growth enhancing environments.

Student development represents a theoretical foundation, not a formula, for student affairs practice. In many ways, student development reflects an informal theory upon which student affairs practice can be based. Student affairs administration, on the other hand, represents an action element, a pragmatic approach to solving problems and achieving goals and is only as good as the theory upon which it is based and for which it is intended. Appleton, Briggs and Rhatigan (1978) challenged the essential connection between theory and practice by setting them off, one against the other when they noted "one must eventually move from statements of ideals, however, to the essentials of practice" (p.22). Such statements appear to deny that practitioners should view theory and practice as coordinate parts of a larger whole so that the practice of student affairs reflects directly the theory upon which it is founded. Only as this important principle becomes better understood and integrated will the evolution of the student affairs profession move to more effective processes and procedures that will ultimately lead to more advanced cycles of professional development.

Without question colleges are responsible for influencing the personal development of students. The question then is not whether student development is an assigned mission of higher education, and logically of student affairs, but how student affairs is going to accomplish that mission. Student development theory seems to be the best available foundation for organizing this effort. As Hurst (1980b) noted, "it serves as the core construct around which goals are identified, programs developed, agencies organized, and interventions evaluated" (p. 151).

Those in student affairs prior to the emergence of student development theory as a foundation viewed their work as building and maintaining an administrative structure that could efficiently provide students with services and supports ordinarily provided by family.

With the emergence of student and environmental resource development, the emphasis is changing toward educators operating within the administrative and academic structure to teach and provide students with the skills, attitudes, and resources necessary for them to maximally utilize the educational environment and fully develop their individual potential. (Hurst, 1980a, p. 321)

Student Development and Student Affairs

Not unlike the difficulty the profession has had in understanding the distinction between developmental theory and practice, so too its understanding of the differences between student development and student services has been problematic. Riker (1977), for instance, viewed the term "student development" as nothing more than a new appellation assigned to the earlier term "student personnel." Others (Appleton, Briggs, & Rhatigan, 1978) take the position that both deans of men and women and "personnel workers" of the past had the development of their students in mind as a primary purpose for their work, and therefore, the idea and ideals of student development are neither new nor fundamentally different from years gone by. What these authors seem to be suggesting is that the whole concept of student development is largely a reflection of some of today's professionals trying to put old wine into new bottles, or new labels on old bottles. This thinking is at best a misconception of the developmental theories and their testing and at worse a conscious attempt to deny the theoretical breakthroughs that have occurred recently. The fact that arguments abound concerning whether or not student affairs work is a profession; that some practitioners do not understand it; that the future is tenuous; or that someone is usually working to reorganize, reevaluate, reshape, or rename the field (Appleton, Briggs, & Rhatigan, 1978) does not, in and of itself, belie the evolutionary processes involved.

Much of the controversy about "student development," as it relates to "student affairs," may be attributed to a semantic confusion. "Student development" has been and continues to be used in at least four distinct ways. First, "student development" refers to a body of knowledge, both theoretical and data-based, that describes how persons in higher education settings behave. The focus may be on the content of development (for example, career decision making, autonomy formation, interpersonal relations with peers) or on the process of development (such as cognitive processes, moral reasoning, stimulus-response). This has been called "formal theory" by Rodgers (Chapter 5) and Widick, Knefelkamp, and Parker (1980). Its value is to describe the phenomena of higher education (that is the participants, the environments and the interaction between the two), but it does not dictate what one should do as a student affairs professional. Administrators who argue that "student development" is academic, not practical, are viewing formal theory as if it were applied technique.

Second, "student development" also has been used to describe a wide variety of behavioral and social science-based interventions, some relatively new such as ecosystem intervention and some quite old such as individual counseling, that have been used by student affairs practitioners with students. Disciplines of psychology, sociology, education, and management have all contributed techniques used by student affairs professionals. This bag of tools is diverse and sometimes based upon incompatible philosophical positions. No distinct set of techniques can be called "student development techniques." For this reason it has been difficult for many to distinguish those devoted to student development from those hostile to it by looking at the day-to-day practice of professionals. What makes an intervention "student development" is not the approach, but the purpose for which the approach is intended. The final test is whether the intervention enhances the quality of students' educational experiences and facilitates their accomplishment of developmental tasks.

A third use of "student development" has been to describe the purpose or outcome desired as a result of a student's attendance at college. Miller and Prince (1976, p.3) described "student development" as a goal that *"everyone involved* [in higher education] . . . *master increasingly complex developmental tasks, achieve self-direction, and become interdependent."* While the language is different, that goal is not dissimilar to what the 1937 *Student Personnel Point of View* espoused. From this perspective, it is not difficult to see why some professionals assume that "student development" is little more than a new term for old ideas.

Finally, in some instances the term "student development" has been used to replace "student affairs" or "student services" in position titles. In many cases this change has been cosmetic at best and has not influenced in any significant way either organizational structures or daily contact with students. This has been an inappropriate use of the term and has added greatly to the confusion in understanding the term.

What the field of student affairs needs now are more divergent thinkers who can identify new and creative ways for doing better what has always been the intent of the field, namely education that will enhance the quality of students' lives. Student developmental theory holds greater potential for aiding student affairs professionals in conceptualizing their work.

Whether or not practitioners over the years were developmentally facilitative is not at issue; on many occasions they were! The question is one of how to do better what has been to varying degrees the purpose of the field from the beginning. That early deans and "personnel workers" were less effective than they could have been had they possessed the current body of knowledge and experience upon which to base their work is not the issue. What is at issue is how well today's administrators and practitioners can accomplish their more clearly defined developmental goals and purposes using the skills and knowledge currently available. Student development reflects theories of human growth and environmental influences as applied to student affairs practice. Student affairs administration reflects the structuring and managing of the goals of student development. The goals of student development are not new, but many of the objectives, methods, and approaches for achieving them are. Student development is not "student personnel" revisited.

The Context for Student Development

As Cyert (1980) noted when identifying the problems faced by those responsible for institutions of higher learning, management problems are in part a function of both the type and location of the institution. Funding sources (public-private), endowments (miniscule-ample), size (large-small), type (residential-commuter), sex (single sex-coed), and location (rural-urban), among others, are factors that differentially influence the nature and character of the student affairs administrative approaches used.

Institutional Size and Type. Although there are many factors that influence the nature and scope of student affairs practice, both the size and the type of the institution are extremely important variables. Institutional size, therefore, becomes an important factor in both the type and quality of experience available to students. Although larger institutions probably have more resources available, the very fact that more students are seeking to take advantage of them decreases their potential for impact. "As the number of persons outstrips the opportunities for significant participation and satisfaction, the developmental potential of available settings is attenuated for all" (Chickering, 1969, p. 148).

Growth and development are largely a result of the quality of the interaction between the individual and his/her environment, and although programs of student development may not be feasible on a campus-wide basis in larger institutions, the various components and subunits are appropriate settings. In other words, the larger the campus, the greater is the need for breaking down developmental programming efforts to smaller, more manageable organizational units. Whereas on a campus of 2,000 or less, initiating a campus-wide program of student development may be quite feasible; on a campus of 20,000 or more, initiating many coordinated, but individualized, efforts to the same end may be necessary. The key to success is the availability and easy access to campus and community resources designed to facilitate developmental growth and change. Large institutions need concurrent programs within different units and settings throughout the campus community. In some instances academic divisions are working with student affairs leaders to create student affairs components within instructional units to enhance and augment existing campus support and service systems. Size makes a difference, but it is not, in and of itself, a deterrent to the developmental programming for students. One advantage large institutions have is more staff who possess a greater variety and depth of intervention skills.

Institutional type also influences developmental outcomes of students. The traditional resident institution where many students spend most of their time on campus has greater influence on student's total development than does the predominantly nonresident, commuter institution (Chickering, 1974). Residential students have more contact with faculty, perform better academically, and are more satisfied with their undergraduate experience than commuters. Residents are also more likely to aspire to graduate or professional degrees (Astin, 1973, 1975, 1978; Chickering, 1974).

Obviously student affairs administrators can communicate with resident students more conveniently than with students living off campus. Still much can be done with commuter students to enhance their development. The more student affairs administrators can make available opportunities for commuters to establish campus related reference groups, the more commuters will tend to identify with the campus on a personal and individual basis. The key issue is that all students have developmental life cycle needs, and the educational enterprise is more than an intellectual supermarket. Personal development is equally important, and higher education will do both students and society a disservice if it does not seek diligently to make experiences of quality equally available to all.

Responsibility for Student Development

The building of personal and organizational territory, turf, or property is evident in most institutions of higher learning. This is not surprising because in many ways American society is founded on competition and individual freedom to a much greater extent than it is upon mutuality and cooperation. In the educational enterprise, teamwork and collaboration must be encouraged and emphasized when developing the total student, for no single individual, program, or institutional subunit can do the job alone. Quality education and development result from the interaction of the individual with a comprehensive environment and not bits and pieces thereof. All involved in education and development of students must realize this important fact and use it as a guide in their work with students. This is as true for student affairs administrators as it is for faculty members or other institutional staff members.

The intentional development of college students is not the private domain of student affairs practitioners and administrators, even though it may sometimes seem that way in the eyes of many on the college campus. If student development is indeed the application of human development principles in a college environment, then all responsible parties need to be involved. In this sense, student development theory is integrative in nature. It has the potential to bring all elements of the campus community into a goal-oriented focus designed to create growth-engendering environments. Integration implies mutuality, equality, cooperation, and collaboration among all parties concerned. Student affairs professionals must not become caught in the territorial trap, for this promotes adversary relations and divisive environments that are not conducive to healthy development. This does not mean that student affairs administrators seek to give over to others their power to make a developmental difference in the lives of students, but it does mean that collaboration as an educational doctrine should be the cornerstone of practice. Higher education is a system that is influenced by all people, structures, technologies, and tasks involved and belongs to no single individual or organizational entity. Student affairs professionals must take leadership in seeking to effect this type of educational environment for the task of those dedicated to the development of the total student goes far beyond the limited perspectives of any single group. Student development is the domain of all those involved. Just as no student should be denied access to resources and support services needed, neither should any part of the educational enterprise view itself as the ultimate authority or the sole responsible agent for the development of students everyone serves.

As Shaffer (1980) stated, an integrated approach can work only if based on a careful, systematic analysis of the specific institutional setting. "Constraints need to be identified and weakened by specific, consciously planned steps. Support strengths located in given situations need to be further strengthened by specific, consciously planned steps" (p. 311). The task of student affairs administration, then is to find ways to realize goals of student development.

REFERENCES

American Council on Education. The student personnel point of view. American Council on Education Studies (Series 1, Vol. 1, No. 3). Washington, DC: Author, 1937.

American Council on Education. *The student personnel point of view* (Rev. ed.). American Council on Education Studies (Series 6, Vol. 13, No. 13). Washington, DC: Author, 1949.

Appleton, J. R., Briggs, C. M., & Rhatigan, J. J. *Pieces of eight: The rites, roles, and styles of the dean by eight who have been there.* Portland, OR: NASPA Institute of Research and Development, 1978.

Astin, A. W. Impact of dormitory living on students. *Educational Record,* 1973, *54,* 204-10.

Astin, A. W. *Preventing students from dropping out.* San Francisco: Jossey-Bass, 1975.

Astin, A. W. *Four critical years: Effects of college on beliefs, attitudes, and knowledge.* San Francisco: Jossey-Bass, 1978.

Aulepp, L., & Delworth, U. *Training manual for an ecosystem model.* Boulder, CO: Western Interstate Commission on Higher Education, 1976.

Ayers, A. R., Tripp, P. A., & Russel, J. H. *Student services administration in higher education* (OE-53026 Bul. 1966, No. 16). Washington, DC: U.S. Government Printing Office, 1966.

Banning, J. H. (Ed.). *Campus ecology: A perspective for student affairs.* Cincinnati: National Association of Student Personnel Administrators, 1978.

Brown, R. D. *Student development in tomorrow's higher education: A return to the academy.* Washington, DC: American College Personnel Association, 1972.

Brubacher, J. S., & Rudy, W. *Higher education in transition: A history of American colleges and universities, 1636-1976* (Rev. ed.). New York: Harper & Row, Publishers, 1976.

Chickering, A. W. *Education and identity.* San Francisco: Jossey-Bass, 1969.

Chickering, A. W. *Commuting versus residence students: Overcoming the educational inequities of living off campus.* San Francisco: Jossey-Bass, 1974.

Chickering, A. W., & Associates. *The modern American college: Responding to the new realities of diverse students and a changing society.* San Francisco: Jossey-Bass, 1981.

Cooper, A. C. Student development services in higher education. Report from Commission on Professional Development, Council of Student Personnel Associations, 1972.

Cowley, W. H. The nature of student personnel work. *Educational Record,* 1936, *17,* 198-226.

Cyert, R. M. Managing universities in the 1980s. In C. Argyris & R. M. Cyert (Eds.), *Leadership in the '80s: Essays on higher education.* Cambridge, MA: Institute for Educational Management, 1980.

Drum, D. J. Understanding student development. In W. H. Morrill & J. C. Hurst (Eds.), *Dimensions of intervention for student development.* New York: John Wiley & Sons, 1980.

Erikson, E. H. *Childhood and society* (2nd ed.). New York: W. W. Norton & Co., 1963.

Erikson, E. H. *Identity: Youth and crisis.* New York: W. W. Norton and Co., 1968.

Havighurst, R. J. *Human development and education.* New York: Longman's, 1953.

Havighurst, R. J. *Developmental tasks and education* (3rd ed.). New York: McKay, 1972.

Heath, D. *Growing up in college: Liberal education and maturity.* San Francisco: Jossey-Bass, 1968.

Herbst, J. The first three American colleges: Schools of the reformation. *Perspectives in American History, 1974, 8,* 7-52.

Holland, J. L. *Making vocational choices: A theory of careers.* Englewood Cliffs, NJ: Prentice-Hall, 1973.

Hopkins, L. B. Personnel procedure in education. *The Educational Record Supplement,* 1926, *7(3).*

Huebner, L. A. (Ed.). *New directions for student services: Redesigning campus environments* (No. 8). San Francisco: Jossey-Bass, 1979.

Huebner, L. A. Interaction of student and campus. In U. Delworth & G. R. Hanson (Eds.), *Student Services: A handbook for the profession.* San Francisco: Jossey-Bass, 1980.

Hurst, J. C. Challenges for the future. In W. H. Morrill & J. C. Hurst (Eds.), *Dimensions of intervention for student development.* New York: John Wiley & Sons, 1980(a).

Hurst, J. C. The emergence of student/environmental development as the conceptual foundation for student affairs and some implications for large universities. In D. G. Creamer (Ed.), *Student development in higher education: Theories, practices, and future directions.* Washington, DC: American College Personnel Association, 1980(b).

Knefelkamp, L. L. *Developmental instruction: Fostering intellectual and personal growth.* Unpublished doctoral dissertation: University of Minnesota, 1974.

Kohlberg, L. Stages and sequences: The cognitive-developmental approach to socialization. In D. P. Goslin (Ed.), *Handbook of socialization theory and research.* Chicago: Rand McNally, 1969.

Lanning, W. An expanded view of consultation for college and university counseling centers. *Journal of College Student Personnel,* 1974, *15,* 171-6.

Leonard, E. A. *Origins of personnel services in American higher education.* Minneapolis: University of Minnesota Press, 1956.

Lewin, K. *Principles of topological psychology.* New York: McGraw-Hill, 1936.

Lippitt, G. L., & Schmidt, W. H. Crises in a developing organization. *Harvard Business Review,* 1967, *45,* 102-12.

Maverick, L. A. *The vocational guidance of college students.* Cambridge, MA: Harvard University Press, 1926.

Miller, T. K., & Prince, J. S. *The future of student affairs: A guide to student development for tomorrow's higher education.* San Francisco: Jossey-Bass, 1976.

Montagu, A. *Growing young.* New York: McGraw-Hill Book Co., 1981.

Moos, R. H. *Evaluating Educational Environments.* San Francisco: Jossey-Bass, 1979.

Morrill, W. H., & Hurst, J. C. (Eds.). *Dimensions of intervention for student development.* New York: John Wiley & Sons, 1980.

Pace, C. R. *Measuring outcomes of college: Fifty years of findings and recommendations for the future.* San Francisco: Jossey-Bass, 1979.

Perry, W. G., Jr. *Forms of intellectual and ethical development in the college years.* New York: Holt, Rinehart and Winston, 1970.

Perry, W. G., Jr. Cognitive and ethical growth: The making of meaning. In A. W. Chickering and Associates (Eds.), *The modern American college: Responding to the new realities of diverse students and a changing society.* San Francisco: Jossey-Bass, 1981.

Piaget, J. *The origins of intelligence in children.* New York: International Universities Press, 1952.

Riker, H. C. Learning by doing. In G. H. Knock (Ed.), *Perspectives on the preparation of student affairs professionals.* Washington, DC: American College Personnel Association, 1977.

Rippey, D. *What is student development?* Washington, DC: American Association of Community and Junior Colleges, 1981.

Rodgers, R. F., & Widick, C. Theory to practice: Uniting concepts, logic, and creativity. In F. B. Newton & K. L. Ender (Eds.), *Student development practices: Strategies for making a difference.* Springfield, IL: Charles C. Thomas, 1980.

Rudolph, F. *The American college and university: A history.* New York: Random House, 1962.

Sanford, N. *Where colleges fail.* San Francisco: Jossey-Bass, 1967.

Sanford, N., & Axelrod, J. (Eds.). *College and character.* Berkeley, CA: Montaigne, Inc., 1979.

Schneider, L. D. Housing. In W. T. Packwood (Ed.), *College student personnel services.* Springfield, IL: Charles C. Thomas, 1977.

Shaffer, R. H. Analyzing institutional constraints upon student development activities. In D. G. Creamer (Ed.), *Student development in higher education: Theories, practices, and future directions.* Washington, DC: American College Personnel Association, 1980.

Stern, G. G. *People in context: Measuring person-environment congruences in education and industry.* New York: John Wiley and Sons, Inc., 1970.

Widick, C., Knefelkamp, L., & Parker, C. A. Student development. In U. Delworth, G. R. Hanson, & Associates (Eds.), *Student services: A handbook for the profession.* San Francisco: Jossey-Bass, 1980.

Winston, R. B., Jr., Miller, T. K., & Prince, J. S. *Assessing student development: A preliminary manual for the student developmental task inventory (Rev. 2nd ed.) and the student developmental profile and planning record.* Athens, GA: Student Development Associates, 1979.

Wrenn, C. G. The development of student personnel work in the United States and some guidelines for the future. In M. J. Minter (Ed.), *The student and the system.* Boulder, CO: Western Interstate Commission on Higher Education, 1968.

SUGGESTED READINGS

Brown, R. D. *Student development in tomorrow's higher education: A return to the academy.* Washington, DC: American College Personnel Association, 1972.

Brubacher, J. S., & Rudy, W. *Higher education in transition: A history of American colleges and univerities, 1636-1976* (Rev. ed.). New York: Harper and Row Publishers, 1976.

Chickering, A. W., & Associates. *The modern American college: Responding to the new realities of diverse students and a changing society.* San Francisco: Jossey-Bass, 1981.

Creamer, D. G. (Ed.). *Student development in higher education: Theories, practices, and future directions.* Washington, DC: American College Personnel Association, 1980.

Delworth, U., Hanson, G. R., & Associates. *Student services: A handbook for the profession.* San Francisco: Jossey-Bass, 1980.

Knefelkamp, L. L., Widick, C., & Parker, C. A. (Eds.). *New directions for student services: Applying new developmental findings,* No. 4. San Francisco: Jossey-Bass, 1978.

Miller, T. K., & Prince, J. S. *The future of student affairs: A guide to student development for tomorrow's higher education.* San Francisco: Jossey-Bass, 1976.

Morrill, W. H., & Hurst, J. C. (Eds.). *Dimensions of intervention for student development.* New York: John Wiley and Sons, 1980.

Newton, F. B., & Ender, K. L. (Eds.). *Student development practices: Strategies for making a difference.* Springfield, IL: Charles C. Thomas, 1980.

David T. Borland is Consultant and Arbitrator, Dispute Resolution Services, Lansing, Michigan. He formerly served in various faculty and administrative roles at Miami University (Ohio), Indiana University, Ferris State College (Michigan), and North Texas State University, receiving NTSU's Distinguished Teaching Award. He served in various leadership roles of the American College Personnel Association, including that of President (1981-82).

Borland has consulted with over 40 professional, public service, industrial, penal, health care, and educational institutions and has presented over 75 workshops, training and professional institutes. Currently in providing resolution services for differing personal, professional, and employment disputes, he serves in the roles of negotiator, mediator, factfinder, arbitrator, and consultant for several dozen clients. He serves on the National Labor Panel of Arbitrators of the American Arbitration Association, the Roster of Arbitrators for the Federal Mediation and Conciliation Service, and is listed on the panels of arbitrators with the Michigan Employment Relations Commission. He has authored more than 35 professional publications in higher education and labor relations.

Chapter **2**

ORGANIZATIONAL FOUNDATIONS OF ADMINISTRATION

David T. Borland

The popular myth that modern organizations are either self-operating or can be operated well by anyone who is given the appropriate authority has been discredited by the growing body of organizational literature. Various theories have been postulated, tested, reformulated, and synthesized to provide a systematic basis for the study of effective management both in private business and industry and in public service organizations. While some individuals still believe that administrators/leaders "are born, not made," realities of contemporary technological society require leaders with specific skills. Abilities, foresight, and sensitivity of successful administrators have been analyzed by the many disciplines now researching organizational behavior. This research has led to verification of qualities that can lead to effective management of organizations. Concurrent with research into the environmental context of administrative behavior, an organizational base for the administrative process has been identified.

Organizational Foundations of Administration   31

The interface between factors within the environment and the organizational structure designed to meet environmental goals (macroorganizational factors) and factors within the organization and attitudes, skills, and personalities (microorganizational factors) of those charged with the responsibility of managing the organization often becomes obscured when observations of daily functions are made. The focus of this chapter is on the macroorganizational factors (Gibson, Ivancevich, & Donnelly, 1979); the concepts of management, leadership, and organization development are discussed in following chapters.

ORGANIZATIONAL THEORY DEVELOPMENT

Concern about management of human work behavior can be traced to ancient times in such sociological units as villages, families, religions, and later in unions or guilds. The primary focus of concern shifted to a collective perspective as the pervasive effects of the Industrial Revolution during the 19th Century began to have an impact on these individual units. The development of research and theory into work behavior and its relationship to society can be viewed from three perspectives—economic, behavioral, and integrated.

Economic Theory of Organizations

The base for the development of industrial organizations was that a specialized division of labor and a mass production potential was economically efficient. Skill in a trade required much time and funds for development and could be accomplished for only a small number of people concurrently. A cheaper and more abundant labor force of unskilled or semiskilled workers was available, if the tasks to be performed were simple. The shift from a craft orientation where trade workers could manufacture an entire product themselves to a mass production orientation where one product could be assembled by several semiskilled or unskilled workers, each performing a specialized task, solved one problem but created another need.

After unskilled and semiskilled workers replaced the master craft worker, the questions of who made decisions about the product; who controlled work flow; and who had responsibility for coordination and direction of the large, unskilled work force were left unattended. In small enterprises these coordinating functions were performed by owners; however, the industrial workplace with hundreds and later thousands of employees required an assigned and shared managerial function throughout the organization.

As the practice and development of supervisory techniques continued, it became clear, even before the Civil War, that if cost and time efficient methods were to be emphasized, a need for clear organization of the jobs to be performed was as crucial as the performance of the jobs themselves. The concept of the organization as a rational decision maker to replace the control provided earlier by the craft workers, therefore, became the central theme for industrial organization. As a separate entity, the organization became the object for efficient consumption of resources which included capital, raw materials, and people. The transferral of the cognitive image of unskilled workers as machines who must be organized and controlled for efficiency of use was a somewhat easy and often unconscious conclusion evidenced in daily practice.

Scientific Managment

Managerial understanding could be improved if facts about jobs and organizations could be quantified, compared, and improved. These conclusions led to the first organized attempts to study, synthesize, and disseminate the principles of managing a work force within an organizational context. This classical organizational doctrine, embodied in the writings of Taylor (1911), came to be referred to as "scientific management."

Taylor emphasized measurement of the tasks and of the tools by which industrial jobs were accomplished. Having the information to design job operations properly, he then emphasized the formal organizational structure as the means by which planned and coordinated efforts of the workers would lead to maximum efficiency.

Central to Taylor's work was the concept of division of specialized labor and the physical capabilities of the worker who was motivated by economic rewards. The forms of the "science" behind appropriate managerial planning was as varied as the approaches taken by Taylor and his contemporaries. Taylor himself introduced time studies to the cause of efficient organization. Gantt (1916) developed incentive pay systems and charting techniques for scheduling work flow. Gilbreth (1911) introduced the concept of motion study to organizations. Later,

Fayol (1929), Mooney and Reiley (1939), and Urick (1944) attempted to synthesize these writings and industrial practices into the 14 "Universal Principles of Management."

Universal Principles of Management. Basic to these efforts was an authoritarian and mechanistic approach to organizational work, regulated by specific principles of managerial behavior. These principles provided a rational and consistent basis for the understanding of organizational effort. A scalar and centralized chain of command provided unity and direction in the rules for the organization and resolved conflicts legitimately. The principles provided for delegation of authority and responsibility for the discipline, order, equity, initiative, stablity of tenure, accountability, and morale of the work force. These principles, many of which are followed *currently* in organizations, brought such concepts to organizational study as hierarchy of authority, line-staff relationships, and span of control, which are basic to organizational interactions.

Behavioral Theory of Organizations

Analysis of the various principles of scientific management from a sociological perspective exposed many voids in knowledge about organizations and their pervasive effects on people. The concept of division of labor; for example, provided a blueprint of production processes, but could not explain the problems of worker isolation, fatigue, monotony, and anonymity that were being expressed which were discovered at the Western Electric Company, Hawthorne Works (Roethlisberger & Dickson, 1939). The concepts of structure, hierarchy of authority, and span of control were lacking in analysis of the problems of overlapping authority, line-staff conflicts, proper delegation and span of control conflicts, and correlated authoritarianism with low morale.

Investigators such as Mayo (1933), Lewin (1938), and various university research groups began to provide the concepts and evidence to support the basic premise of the behavioral perspective of organizational interaction, usually referred to as "human relations." The premise was that organizational behavior could be understood fully only when the behavior of individual workers was viewed as they grouped together naturally in response to social needs. While occupational similarity and assignment within the organization might influence those social factors, they alone could not often overcome the significant influences of social pressures. The major emphasis for these human relations proponents, then, was to analyze the informal organizational structure to which workers were attracted and establish working conditions that would lead to satisfied workers. Organizational effectiveness, therefore, would be implemented through the efforts of satisfied workers, rather than through the competitive environment basic to scientific management's concept of the man-machine model.

The primary difference between these two schools of organizational theory was that the physiological emphasis of scientific management was contrasted with the psychological and sociological perspectives of human relations. The discovery that informal groups were agents of social control with independence from the formal structure led to investigation and formulation of new concepts. The terms of communication, status, motivation, coordination, and leadership became significant to the full comprehension of organizational behavior. The discovery of the informal structure's influence through independent communication, resistance, and leadership networks on such primary industrial concerns as productivity provided the basis for change in the management process.

Integrated Theory of Organizations

While the development of each of these schools of organizational inquiry occurred historically, various aspects of each exists currently in the practice of organizational interaction. Competitive proponents of each perspective defended those views as the truly accurate perspective of effective organizational and administrative process. Dissatisfaction with each viewpoint as the exclusive doctrine leading to full comprehension of organizational interaction led to a synthesis of the two perspectives into a "structuralist school" (Etzioni, 1964).

The social psychologists of the structuralist school synthesized the significant contributions of both the scientific management and human relations perspectives into a full understanding of organizational behavior. First, this school of thought recognized that an inevitable strain exists within organizations between the personal needs of its members (human relations) and the needs of the organization itself (scientific management). Second, in order to achieve maximum organizational effectiveness, neither set of needs can be ignored, but their mutuality must be recognized and achieved. Finally, as Etzioni (1964) suggested, the achievement of effectiveness in an ever-changing competitive environment is not in searching for the perfectly organized structure (scientific management) or for the happiest workers (human relations), but in searching for a rational organizational environment and process that has the best chance for a successful effort to move toward effectiveness. Two concepts of integrated theory, systems theory and bureaucracy, are discussed as requisite for a basis for contemporary administration of organizations.

Systems Theory. Several contributors, such as Homans (1950); Katz and Kahn (1978); and Trist, Higgin, Murray, and Pollack (1963) led to development of the concept of the systems theory. A system is a series of interrelated and interdependent parts, referred to as subsystems, such that the interaction of these subsystems affects the entire system. The focus of concern here is the continuous organizational system that exists within an environmental system and is composed of various human systems. An organization has the capacity to interpret demands from the environment and to utilize and transform human, material, and other resources into a problem solving entity primarily by differentiating and integrating human activities (Lawrence & Lorsch, 1967).

Because organizations are interdependent, an understanding of the interaction among their subsystems is essential for effective administrators. Because organizations exist both formally and informally in a sequential interaction with other systems, they are considered to be open to complex influence from changes in other systems. These changes may be created independently of consideration of the effects on the other organizations. For example, if inflation rates are determined by the government to be excessive, certain economic decisions will be made that may increase unemployment. Unemployment traditionally has meant a source of new students to institutions of higher education. If those same economic conditions result in a loss of funds for financial aid from government sources, the organizational strain for administrators in colleges and universities with larger numbers of students to serve and less funds becomes evident.

In order to remain aware of the varying interactions that might affect the organization, a comprehensive organizational communication process must be available. The communication system must receive input from the external environment and from internal subsystems; must process that input; and must provide output to the environment and to its own subsystems. After output is processed by other systems and the organization's own subsystems, changes may occur that will be funneled through feedback mechanisms to the organization's input mechanism again. In this manner the organization's communication cycle is established and self-corrected. To continue the previous example, the input for the potential increase of new students and for decreased governmental funds must be processed by the admissions office, financial aid office, and the development office on campus in order to allow for admission of more students and increased efforts at private fund raising. As new input is fed back to institutional subsystems, more input about needs for increased funds and staff in these offices might be communicated by each of them back into the system's decision-making channels.

If a larger group of students than usual has been admitted to the institution, resources will be strained and the environment within the institution will be changed which will activate behaviors to achieve *organizational balance.* In any organization over a period of time, two conflicting forces exist: one is for the initiation of change and growth; another is for maintenance of the status quo; and both are in dynamic struggle for resolution. If the status quo is maintained when the external environment is changing rapidly or if constant change leads to anarchy, the organization will be damaged.

To avoid damage to the organization, administrators not only must understand the inevitable strains toward balance, but also the multiplicity of goals that exist in any organization. If the institution is striving toward excellence, is in financial difficulty, or is striving toward a select group of students, its admissions decision on potential new students would be different than if the institutions's goals were to include universal access to educational opportunity. The difficulty for administrators is that the one-goal organization seldom exists, so that goals among systems or within the organization's subsystems may conflict. That conflict requires that the communication and balance mechanisms process the information. As a result of that processing the organization's goals may be clarified and organizational activity made more efficient and effective. Goal conflict, then, is not always nonproductive. The productivity of goal conflict resolution depends instead on the methods used for resolution in meeting both the formal (organizational) and the informal (individuals') needs, which exist in an organizational "psychological contract" (Schein, 1980).

In summary, then, characteristics of a system are that they (1) have integrated parts, (2) are open to environmental influence, (3) create and utilize communication, (4) are constantly striving for balance, (5) possess a multiplicity of goals, and (6) have both formal and informal components. Full comprehension of these characteristics of systems, their ebb and flow in organizational functioning, and the appropriate strategies and tactics to make full use of their potential in managing organizational behavior is mandatory if a student affairs administrator is to become effective, and the student development concept is to become reality in the experiences of students on college campuses.

Bureaucracy. No organizational concept has such universal suspicion as does bureaucracy. This structuralist concept, conceived by Weber (1947) prior to World War I, maintained that an organization can maximize efficiency and effectiveness while reducing unhappiness. Equally true is the observation that no social organization has affected people so pervasively or significantly as has bureaucracy, even though as it exists in contemporary society it primarily is an embodiment of the misuses of the concept's tenets.

The first characteristic of a bureaucracy is that it is a large scale organization with a definite social function. Although size is a flexible criterion, a bureaucracy must be large enough to have sufficient resources to meet its social functions.

The second characteristic of the bureaucratic form of social organization evidences a division of labor into specialized functions. Cultural conditions underlying this division are a money economy, which provides the resources to be used as rewards for work, and the initiative and self-interest of the people in the bureaucracy.

The third tenet of a bureaucracy is that it is regulated by written rules that are operational presentations of the organization's goals. Rules are constructed to regulate the behavior within an organization, so that consistent and efficient progress toward the accomplishment of goals can be facilitated. Exceptions to rationally conceived and effectively administered rules are intended to be rare, lest they create confusion. The flexibility to permit exceptions to written rules increases only as individuals achieve higher positions within the bureaucracy.

A hierarchy of authority in incremental levels is the fourth criterion of bureaucracy and reflects the right to issue orders from the top levels and an accepted obligation of the lower levels to obey the orders. Weber (1947) emphasized, however, that this authority has limits in that all persons, regardless of bureaucratic level, must follow the established rules, and the attitudes of the lower levels in the organization dictate the limits to which that authority will be accepted. Finally the authority is legitimate only within the bureaucracy.

The final criterion in Weber's (1947) analysis is that interaction among those in the bureaucracy must be impersonal. The authority and staff must be detached, and staff must be viewed as equal. Any concessions to individuals gives substance to feelings of illegitimate interaction that may be unfairly discriminatory. A lack of emotional involvement with staff reinforces the feeling that all will be treated the same according to the rules.

The implications for an administrator of the influence of bureaucracy affect managerial behavior. As an office holder or authority of the formal structure, one must realize that personal commitment and loyalty to the organization are expected of administrators in return for the personal and professional security the organization provides.

Merton (1968) indicated, therefore, that roles performed in bureaucratic positions should lead to a high degree of reliable and consistent behavior. He cautioned, however, that devotion to duty and to a sense of one's own authority and competence that results from this basic discipline in a bureaucracy also may lead to a devotion to rules as absolutes, which can interfere with the adaptive and spontaneous behavior needed when existing conditions are not facilitated by the rules.

Because the administrative process is an individually derived one, knowledge about bureaucratic theory and practice is a base which must be established. Future decisions or regulations and any subsequent exceptions to those theories and practices must be accepted with their attendant consequences.

ORGANIZATIONAL ANALYSIS

With at least a brief background in the historical and conceptual development of organizational theory, an administrator in a contemporary organization, regardless of the level of administrative authority, can understand the need for becoming an efficient and effective organizational analyst. The information gathered from periodic analysis can provide the rational base from which to make decisions that are as effective and consistent as prevailing conditions will allow. The components recommended for this analysis contain three major emphases—structures, interdependence, and goals.

Strategic Structures in the Organization

A valid knowledge of the components of a particular organization subsystem that one is to manage is essential for success. Pertinent information about the structure of an organization can be analyzed within the framework of the following five components: (1) individual's characteristics, (2) physical environment, (3) administrative structure, (4) roles of each position, and (5) informal structure.

Individuals' Characteristics. First, the characteristics of the individuals within the subsystem must be determined. Information such as who they are, how they respond to varying conditions, why they have chosen to work there, and what their nonemployment interests are is essential.

Physical Environment. The second component concerns the physical environment in which these individuals are working: attention to the details of space allocation, comfort and ease to facilitate work, and the relative significance of these working conditions for each individual.

Administrative Structure. After the individual's place in the work environment has been determined, the third essential component in the analysis is the knowledge of the administrative structure within which each individual has been assigned in the organization. Knowledge of the official chain of command within which this particular system is expected to function is basic to parameters within which administrative alternatives may be implemented.

Roles of Each Position. Flowing from the formal structure are the roles of each position that have been determined as required for organizational success. This fourth component of work role and its subsequent status among the workers must be analyzed to determine the types of conditions necessary to facilitate success of the subsystem most effectively.

Informal Structure. Finally a specific and detailed analysis of the informal structure of the subsystem within its surrounding formal structures must be performed. Just as analysis of the formal structure identifies where the influential individuals and powerful groups are designed to be, the analysis of the informal structure may yield information that actual influence rests in unexpected places, such as with a particular administrator's secretary or handball partner who holds a position within another subsystem of the organization. For administrators to attempt to manage a subsystem without these five essential bases of organizational knowledge, periodically gathered and analyzed, is to relegate them to a career of poor performance and their own occupational dissatisfaction.

Interdependency of Organizational Structures

Using these five components as the base, effective administrators must compare and contrast the components in order to determine conflicts among them and to discover the points at which collaborative efforts for mutual success might be attempted. For example, after determining the structure and status of the formal structure, analyzing the independent and often conflicting informal structure may initiate different administrative strategy than a more superficial analysis would have prompted.

Once comparison is made of the status and roles expected of workers, a more successful strategy of motivation may be attempted than one of simply demanding that job requirements must be met to maintain one's employment. A study of both formally expected and actual informal organizational communication patterns may reveal that the reason for a morale problem exists with other subsystems, organizations, or external individuals, even though the formal structure indicates the most efficient structure. Concern about turnover and its effect on organizational balance and on motivational efforts and rewards to keep individuals or groups satisfied cannot compensate for a poorly designed job that encourages sabotage rather than efficiency.

These examples are attempts to analyze the various linking processes that bring workers and organizations together as a conscious effort and agreement by both to produce for mutual benefit. The role of the successful administrator is to continue the mutuality of benefit efficiently and effectively within the societal mission of the organization.

Goals of the Organization

The final link of any structure is with the society that supports the organization. This link is represented in the organization by its goals, whether they are formal or informal, or internally or externally directed.

The most general type of goal is classified as a *societal goal,* which defines the direction society wishes to pursue as related to this particular type of organization. The second class of goals is the *output goal,* which defines specific directions pursued by this particular organization to contribute to the comprehensive societal goals. The survival of an organization is dependent on its *system goals,* which direct such elements as the specific growth, stability, and control features of an enterprise. A fourth class of goals is the *product goal,* which specifies the characteristics of the product or service offered in terms of quantity or quality. *Derived goals* are tangential to the organizational mission, where power from within the organization is used to pursue other goals in general society.

Within this classification of goals, Perrow (1961) also provided a dual concept of goal analysis as essential to understanding an organization. He identified *official goals* as those statements of intended future affairs, expressing the general purposes of the organization as evidenced by charters, annual reports, and public statements, such as in higher education—teaching, research, and service. Perrow (1961) indicated that these statements are purposely vague and general. In terms of understanding human behavior within organizations, however, these official or formally stated goals do not indicate the direction of alternative decisions, the priority of multiple goals, or the individual or subsystem goals being pursued.

The second portion of Perrow's (1961) analytical concept is operative goal. *Operative goals* indicate the missions of an organization through actual operating policies and decisions within the organization. For example, while the official goal of an institution of higher education may be what seems to be the egalitarian concept of "teaching, research, and service," the operative and significant goal may be evidenced in faculty rewards systems where publication of research activities leads to quicker and higher levels of salary or academic rank. Accepting superficial statements of goals without real analysis of the operational goals affecting one's own subsystem can be a behavior fatal to the potential success of an administrator. Table 2.1 gives an example of goal classification and analysis.

Analysis needed to determine successful administrative behavior concerns goals of higher education. Gross and Grambsch (1964) and Borland (1974) indicated that incongruence between stated mission and operational policies required specific organizational analysis by administrators to determine appropriate methods available for success. While the often stated goal of "teaching, research, and service" is

Table 2.1

Examples of Goal Analysis and Classification
of Goals for Higher Education

GOALS	OFFICIAL (Formal)	OPERATIVE (Informal)
SOCIETAL	Educating people	To provide employment for individuals
OUTPUT	Production of college graduates	To produce a top 10 rated athletic team
SYSTEM	Tuition and credit hour plan for degree progress	To solicite actively student financial aid sources
PRODUCT	Minimum number of graduates or quality of their work	To produce a Rhodes scholar or active alumni association
DERIVED	100% employee participation in charitable contributions	To have a student lobby on campus that affects environmental legislation

acknowledged, faculty and administrators may not see that goal as operational either in the rewards system or in the roles performed. These operational goals may be personal and professional goals of the faculty.

Concern of faculty for interaction with students and for the undergraduate curriculum may be clear, but subordinate to professional academic goals. For student affairs administrators, then, a perspective on alternative approaches to management must be analyzed and implemented for the particular circumstances existing at one's own campus. The administrative approach must not only be related to one's own personal skills and personality strengths, but also must be adaptive to the particular organizational factors and opportunities available.

ORGANIZATIONAL ALTERNATIVES FOR STUDENT AFFAIRS

Collegial Community of Scholars

Brown (1972) has advocated a "return to the academy" as an organizational model facilitating the comprehensive development of students. The existence of this bucolic model in an increasingly urban society with increasingly complex bureaucracies would seem to be impossible if viewed superficially. While few institutions are organized solely on the principles of collegiality, these principles can be implemented in varying ways within current institutions.

The major criterion for success of the contemplative life seems to revolve around the residential environs of a campus. Although some campuses have established somewhat autonomous residential colleges, others have offered a more modest program of residential classes. The appeal of offering this alternative to the ever increasing heterogeneity of students must be implemented through sound administrative planning, based on knowledge of organizational parameters (Borland, 1971). Planning such a program without considering the constraints on faculty interaction or the threats to the institution itself represented by such a structure can bring failure, either by dissolution or by attrition. The potential that exists in such a structure, however, also must be analyzed and administered as an attempt to bring together campus resources for mutual benefit.

Bureaucratic Models

The predominant organizational structure in society is in the bureaucratic form, which extends into the world of higher education as well. No matter the vehement denials to the contrary, colleges and universities operate and respond as do other bureaucracies, notwithstanding some of their unique characteristics. The traditional organizational charts with their lines and boxes representing positions and formally acceptable communication paths provide the effective administrator with information to be used for successful implementation of plans and programs.

If an administrator chooses to violate the structure or employ some of the "creative" administrative techniques described below, it must be attempted only with full understanding that negative consequences from that formal structure are possible. The full impact of legitimate power within the bureaucratic hierarchy of authority can be viewed as a negative deterent or a powerful ally in support of new approaches to student development.

Within student affairs, whether the organization chart is presented in its traditional vertical shape or in an overlapping radial configuration, its formal positions and channels of authority must be comprehended. Informal structure may not be represented on such a chart, but it does exist *within the context* of the formal structure.

Political Models

Modern institutions of higher education with their ever-changing economic, political, and sociological influences might be viewed best by administrators as political mechanisms (Baldridge, 1971). Alternative structures for administrative processes from this perspective range from formal collective bargaining mechanisms to modified representational structures, through both formal and informal organizational strategies for change. Three examples of these alternative structures follow.

One political strategy used by a group of individuals in an organization who believe their individual influence over crucial matters to be less than the current structure will permit is the *collective bargaining* process. Through collective action, goals of shared decision making can be facilitated by employees from a position approaching an equal level with the bureaucracy. While this process for administrators is discussed specifically in Chapter 11, the significant point is that collective bargaining exists as a formal and powerful mechanism, representing effective communication. Specific approaches, techniques, and legal considerations must be comprehended for effective administration under the collective bargaining approach.

A modified bureaucratic form was proposed by Borland (1977) as a *matrix pyramid*. In this organizational foundation for administration are recognized the bureaucratic form of organization and the need for change to satisfy those who support institutions of higher education.

The matrix pyramid in Figure 2.1 provides a flattened bureaucratic chain to facilitate the integration of collegial, bureaucratic, and political components in institutions of higher education. The divisions at the base of the pyramid represent a range of the educational activities of an institution, which may be altered as the needs of students and staff change over time. With the matrix pyramid model the administrator must develop the skills of organizational analysis and facilitate the political process (Borland & Thomas, 1976). While student affairs personnel have viewed themselves primarily as human relations advocates, they now must become organizational advocates, not in competition but in symbiotic relationship, with human development goals.

In a similar manner *organizational change strategies* reject competitive approaches in attempting to meet both individual and institutional goals. The formal process of organization development as proposed for student affairs administrators by Borland (1980) is based on a valid organizational analysis as the approach to integrate the needs of the institution and the individual. A five-step program including clarification of goals, assessment of the environment, selection of the appropriate strategy, planning the specific tactics, and measuring the results of the process for feedback into the system is proposed in detail to bring student development programs into existence with a valid opportunity for success.

A more direct advocacy role in bringing change into an organization, primarily in informal manners has been suggested by Alinsky (1971). Alinsky's approach employs an analysis of current conditions, assets and liabilities, and potential tactics by "doing what you can with what you have!" This role is dependent on correct assessment of changing conditions because organizational office holders learn how to neutralize the effect of change agents.

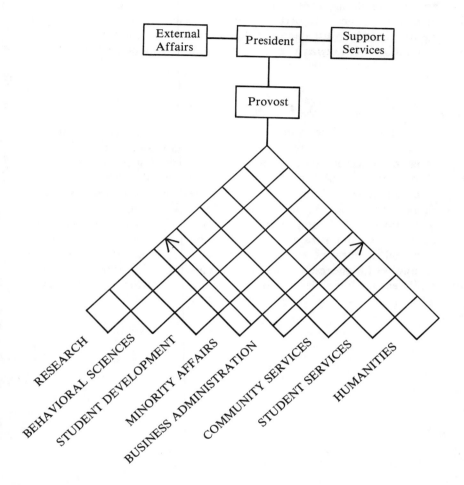

Figure 2.1. The matrix pyramid.

Note. From "Aggressive neglect, matrix organization, and student development implementation" by D.T. Borland, *Journal of College Student Personnel,* 1977, *18,* 452-61. Copyright 1977 by American College Personnel Association. Reprinted by permission. No further reproduction authorized without ACPA permission.

Basic to utilization of change strategies by administrators is the knowledge of organizational balance. If organizational forces for change are predominating, another move for change may bring anarchy and its debilitating effects. An organization at the static stage of reinforcing the status quo will resist change (Chamberlain 1970) and cause a misappropriation of energies and resources because of poor timing.

CONCLUSION

Analyses of organization information reveal the intense complexity of the administrative process in contemporary organizations. They also provide, however, rational bases for the administrator aspiring to become effective both professionally and personally. The use of leadership techniques or administrative processes external to their organizational context invites failure in influencing organizational behavior toward the goal of comprehensive student development. Success by student affairs administrators in pursuing the goal of student development is crucial for them personally, for the student affairs profession, for institutions of higher education, and most importantly, for the student currently enrolled in colleges and universities and for those yet to come.

REFERENCES

Alinsky, S. D. *Rules for radicals.* New York: Random House, 1971.

Baldridge, J. V. *Power and conflict in the university.* New York: John Wiley & Sons, 1971.

Borland, D. T. Faculty participation in university residence hall classes. *NASPA Journal,* 1971, *9,* 62-70.

Borland, D. T. Faculty roles and academic rewards. *Intellect,* 1974, *102,* 246-9.

Borland, D. T. Aggressive neglect, matrix organization, and student development implementation. *Journal of College Student Personnel,* 1977, *18,* 452-61.

Borland, D. T. Organization development: A professional imperative. In D. G. Creamer (Ed.), *Student development in higher education: Theories, practices, and future directions.* Washingon, DC: American College Personnel Association, 1980.

Borland, D. T., & Thomas, R. E. Student development implementation through expanded professional skills. *Journal of College Student Personnel,* 1976, *17,* 145-9.

Brown, R. D. *Student development in tomorrow's higher education: A return to the academy.* Washington, DC: American Personnel and Guidance Association, 1972.

Chamberlain, P. C. Obstacles to change in the university. *NASPA Journal,* 1970, *8,* 29-34.

Etzioni, A. *Modern organizations.* Englewood Cliffs, NJ: Prentice-Hall, 1964.

Fayol, H. *General and industrial management.* (Translated by J. A. Conbrough). Geneva: International Management Institute, 1929.

Gantt, H. L. *Industrial leadership.* New Haven: Yale University Press, 1916.

Gibson, J. L., Ivancevich, J. M., & Donnelly, J. H., Jr. *Organizations behavior, structure, processes.* Dallas: Business Publication, 1979.

Gilbreth, F. B. *Motion study.* New York: Harcourt, Brace and World, 1911.

Gross, E., & Grambsch, P. V. *University goals and academic power.* Washington, DC: American Council on Education, 1964.

Homans, G. C. *The human group.* New York: Harcourt, Brace, and World. 1950.

Katz, D., & Kahn, R. L. *The social psychology of organizations* (2nd ed.). New York: Wiley, 1978.

Lawrence, P. R., & Lorsch, J. W. *Organization and environment: Managing differentiation and integration.* Boston: Harvard University Press, 1967.

Lewin, K. *The conceptual representation and the measurement of psychological forces.* Durham, NC: Duke University Press, 1938.

Mayo, E. *The human problems of industrial civilization.* New York: Macmillan, 1933.

Merton, R. K. *Social theory and social structure* (2nd Edition). New York: Free Press, 1968.

Mooney, J. D., & Reiley, A. C. *Onward industry.* New York: Harper, 1939.

Perrow, C. The analysis of goal in complex organizations. *American Sociological Review,* 1961, *26,* 854.

Roethlisberger, F. J., & Dickson, W. J. *Management and the worker.* Boston: Harvard Business School, 1939.

Schein, E. H. *Organizational psychology.* Englewood Cliffs, NJ: Prentice-Hall, 1980.

Taylor, F. W. *Principles of management.* New York: Harper, 1911.

Trist, E. L., Higgin, G. W., Murray, H., & Pollack, A. B. *Organizational choice.* London: Tavistock Publications, 1963.

Urick, L. *The elements of administration.* New York: Harper, 1944.

Weber, M. *The theory of social and economic organization* (A. M. Henderson & T. Parsons, trans.). New York: Free Press, 1947.

SUGGESTED READINGS

Alinsky, S. D. *Rules for radicals.* New York: Random House, 1971.

Birenbaum, W. M. *Overlive power, poverty, and the university.* New York: Delta, 1969.

Caplow, T. *How to run any organization.* New York: Holt, Rinehart and Winston, 1976.

Etzioni, A. *Modern organizations.* Englewood Cliffs, N.J.: Prentice-Hall, 1964.

Gibson, J. L., Ivancevich, J. M., and Donnelly, Jr., J. H. *Organizations: Behavior, structure, processes.* Dallas: Business Publications, 1979.

Hersey, P., & Blanchard, K. H. *Management of organizational behavior: Utilizing human resources.* Engle Cliffs, N.J.: Prentice-Hall, 1977.

Schein, E. H. *Organizational psychology.* Englewood Cliffs, NJ: Prentice-Hall, 1980.

Robert K. Conyne was educated at Syracuse University and Purdue University and received postdoctoral training at the University of California-Berkeley and the University of Michigan. For ten years he worked at Illinois State University as Coordinator of Consultation in the Counseling Center and as Professor of Counselor Education. He is currently employed at the University of Cincinnati as Associate Vice Provost for Student Life and Programs and as Professor of Counselor Education. In 1979, he was appointed Editor of the *Journal for Specialists in Group Work* and recently he was elected Chair of the American Personnel and Guidance Association Council of Journal Editors. He is a Licensed Psychologist in two states. His book (with Clack), *Environmental Assessment and Design,* addresses an area of special professional interest.

Chapter 3

ORGANIZATION DEVELOPMENT: A BROAD NET INTERVENTION FOR STUDENT AFFAIRS

Robert K. Conyne

The purpose of this chapter is twofold: *to provide the reader with a basic framework for conceptualizing organization development (OD) and to explore potential uses of OD for student affairs administrators in higher education.* The first goal is addressed by examining important conceptual and practical dimensions in OD, such as definitions, the open-system model, and intervention typologies. Application of OD strategies by student affairs administrators is perhaps of more interest to readers of this volume. Despite recent contributions by Borland (1980), who views OD work done by student affairs staff as an "imperative," the current state of the art still requires that a tentative, if not primarily heuristic, treatment be given this topic. The second section of this chapter contains general directions for such activity.

DEFINING ORGANIZATION DEVELOPMENT

Organization development has been defined by many theorists in a variety of ways. French, Bell, and Zawacki (1978) have organized much of the material according to author, using the following critical components to analyze the definitions: (1) nature and scope of the effort, (2) nature of activities/interventions, (3) targets of intervention/activities, (4) knowledge base, and (5) desired goals, outcomes, or end states of organization development effort. Table 3.1 presents a definitional summary that results from this scheme.

What does all this mean? Very simply, OD consists of a broad net of applied behavioral science techniques. Following careful diagnosis, any of these techniques might be used in a planned process for change to benefit both the organization and its members.

OPEN-SYSTEM:
A FRAMEWORK FOR OD

Potential uses to which organization development approaches can be put are dependent, in part, on the organizational model adopted. That is, OD needs to be implemented within an appropriate conceptual (as well as situational) context. It is important to identify what models of organizations are well suited for conducting OD.

The open-system model (Katz & Kahn, 1966) has been shown to be especially useful for conceptualizing about organizations (Huse, 1975; Seiler, 1967), and it has proven to be of heuristic value in generating appropriate organizational assessments (Kast & Rosenzweig, 1970; Weisbord, 1978), and organizational design interventions (Huse & Bowditch, 1973; Weisbord, 1978). Basically, an organization viewed from the open-system model of Katz and Kahn (1966) is comprised of five mutually influencing dimensions: (1) *input,* or the importation of energy (e.g., personnel, money, equipment, etc.), (2) *throughput,* or the transformation process (e.g., information flow, purposes, leadership, etc.) used by the organization to convert input into products, (3) *external environment,* the influence exerted on the organization from outside its boundaries (e.g., legislation, economic conditions, community demands, etc.), (4) *output,* or the products (e.g., courses by an academic department, counseling for a counseling center) produced by the organization and exported to the environment, and (5) *feedback,* or information that is made available to the organization to keep it on course.

Table 3.1
Definitions of Organization Development Summarized According to Authors and Elements of OD Process

Author	Focus of Effort	Elements of OD Process		
		Activities/Interventions	Targets	Desired Goals
Beckhard	Planned, organization-wide, managed from top.	"Organizational Process" planned interventions	Total organizations processes	Improved organization, effects.
Bennis	Response to change using complex educational strategy	Change-Oriented educational strategy	Beliefs, attitudes, values, and structures of organizations	Increased capacity to adapt to change, new technologies markets, and challenges.
French & Bell	A long-range effort	Change agent is used to help design a more effective, collaborative management of organizational culture	Culture of organization, formal work teams; organizational problem solving and renewal processes	Increase organize problem solving renewal processes
Lawrence & Lorsch	A series of sequential stages	Educational, structural, transactional change strategies	Organization-Environment interface	Better fit between organization and environment and organization and its members.
Schmuck & Miles	A planned and sustained effort	Reflexive, Self-analytic methods are used to apply behavioral science for system improvement.	Total Organization	System improvement

Note. Based on and modified from French, Bell, and Zawacki, 1978, p. 8.

The open-system concept underscores the position that an organization and its external environment are mutually permeable (Emery & Trist, 1960). That is, they are continually interdependent and, therefore, are always subject to turbulence and change arising from the organization-environment interface, as well as from interfaces occurring within the organization itself—among groups, between the employee and the organization, and between employees—(Lawrence & Lorsch, 1969). By contrast, a misplaced reliance on a closed system perspective leads, as Katz and Kahn (1966) have indicated, to a disregard for the nature of organizational interdependency with its environment and to excessive concern with internal functioning. Such imbalanced attention threatens organizational survival.

The open-system model for understanding how an organization functions also is useful for understanding OD. It provides a general, systemic framework that comfortably accommodates qualities of dynamism and interdependence that are closely associated with OD interventions. Further, the open-system framework provides such flexibility and coherence that concrete organizational models have been generated from it. One illustrative model is in Figure 3.1, "a six-box model" of Weisbord (1978).

The six boxes in Weisbord's (1978) organizational assessment model refer to six organizational processes in the throughput dimension of the open-system model. These six organizational processes are involved in transferring inputs, or imported energy and resources (such as ideas and money), into outputs (such as human relations workshops or concerts); as well, these six processes are involved in negotiating continual pushes and pulls of the external environment, such as a sudden change in a college's administrative direction, and incorporating these outcomes into the transformation process.

Weisbord (1978) labeled the six processes as follows:

Purposes: What is the organization's mission?

Structure: How is the organization assembled to perform necessary tasks?

Relationships: How effectively do employees, work groups, and employees and their technologies (equipment) interrelate?

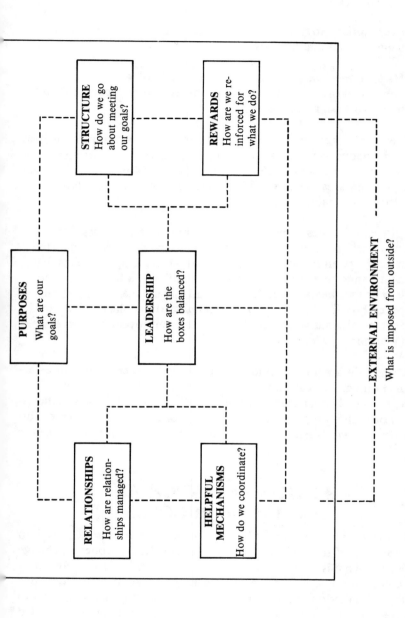

Figure 3.1. Organizational assessment model: Six organizational processes (dimensions) of the open system model.

Note. Based on and modified from M. Weisbord, 1978.

The diagram contains the following boxes:

STRUCTURE
How do we go about meeting our goals?

REWARDS
How are we re-inforced for what we do?

PURPOSES
What are our goals?

LEADERSHIP
How are the boxes balanced?

RELATIONSHIPS
How are relation-ships managed?

HELPFUL MECHANISMS
How do we coordinate?

EXTERNAL ENVIRONMENT
What is imposed from outside?

Rewards: Are there proper incentives and reinforcement for doing what needs to be done?

Leadership: How well does the leader keep all the processes balanced and maintained?

Helpful mechanisms: Are adequate technologies used (e.g., policies, agendas, planning, budgeting, socializing space) to promote work and staff needs?

Weisbord suggested that use of six boxes in organizational diagnosis can be analogous to use of a radar screen by air traffic controllers. Appearance of a blip in any of the six boxes indicates a potential organizational problem area. Thus visualizing the six interconnected boxes as a radar screen, he stated,

> "Process" issues show up as blips in one or more boxes, blocking work on important tasks. Air controllers use radar to manage relationships among aircraft—height, speed, distance apart—and to avoid heavy weather. Similarly, a blip in any one box cannot be managed independently of its relationship to the other boxes. However, six potential starting places give you several alternatives when choosing an improvement strategy. (Weisbord, 1978, p. 8)

Once blips are identified in an organization's internal and/or external functioning, inauguration of an OD program may be in order. Or, it could very well be that the organizational diagnosis itself marked the inception of such a program. Regardless, a broad net of OD intervention strategies, evolving directly from the open-system model, is available for use.

ACTION RESEARCH AS A CHANGE PROCESS

Organization development interventions, to be discussed in detail in a later section of this chapter, are undertaken within a coherent change framework. That is, while the nature of the interventions themselves may vary considerably (e.g., a physical structure change in office locations versus a consultation about staff communication patterns), they tend to be lodged within a change process wherein the internal structure is guided by a series of interlocking steps.

This last phrase, "guided by a common series of interlocking steps," suggests that change can be *managed*. In fact, as has been implied, OD is a long-term, planned, and sustained effort that is centered on an overall strategy. It is a form of managed change (Huse, 1975), as compared with the incessant, inevitable, uncontrolled change that occurs in and around organizations as a natural function of life itself.

A few important managed-change approaches exist for use in organization development activities. Among them are the intervention theory and method of Argyris (1970); the linkage model of Havelock (1969); the research, development, and diffusion model of Clark and Guba (1965); the utilization-focused evaluation approach of Patton (1978); and, perhaps especially, the planned-change model of Lippitt, Watson, and Westley (1958). However, the action-research model (Collier, 1945; Corey, 1953; Frohman, Sashkin, & Kavanagh, 1978; Huse, 1975; Lewin, 1946) to managed change in organization development will be given attention. Action research is selected as a template because assumptions underlying its use are highly compatible with those that support OD. Both sets of assumptions endorse: (1) a planned, systematic approach to change arising from collaboration between change agent and client system, (2) an emphasis on solving current organization problems through specific attention to process issues, and (3) client system members gaining the working knowledge and skills necessary to use and adapt an OD innovation in the future.

Beyond these direct compatibility areas between OD and action research, the action-research model offers substantially attractive evaluation and research capacities that are not shared by all other change models. Action and research occur simultaneously through a project. Thus, the managed-change process is couched within an evaluation context, with evaluative feedback used planfully to guide and modify actions. Further, and of particular note, a successful action research project generates from its research activity new knowledge that addresses broader concerns than the specific interests of the client system itself (such as intervention effects, client system amenability to OD, or general process issues). If worthwhile, these research findings can be disseminated for the scientific and professional community at large, thus adding to the reservoir of knowledge in the public domain.

Action research as a generic change process within OD has been described previously as an OD form (Frohman, Sashkin, & Kavanagh, 1978). According to them, action-research OD involves data collected together by an OD practitioner and a client. Working collaboratively, they obtain information enabling them jointly to conceive and conduct action plans in the client system, evaluate the effects of these plans, and implement further action plans.

Frohman, Sashkin, and Kavanagh (1978) discussed eight phases of action-research OD that result from the product of action research. More subtly, perhaps, these phases can be seen as extending to OD expanded variations of Lewin's (1946) three-phases social system change method (unfreezing, moving, refreezing) and of Lippitt, Watson, and Westley's (1958) planned-change approach (developing a need for a change, establishing a change relationship, working toward change, generalizing and stabilizing change, and achieving a terminal relationship).

The eight phases of action-research organization development are summarized briefly in the next eight headings along with a continuing example.

Scouting

A *research* function used by the OD practitioner to decide whether to enter an organization is called scouting. For instance, Dr. Brown, the OD consultant from the Psychology Department, evaluates information at her disposal to determine if she should seek to become involved with the Student Life Department.

Entry

Entrance into the program is an *action* function used by the OD practitioner to establish a collaborative working relationship with members of the client system. Steps to be conducted include initial problem identification and determining procedures for data collection and feedback. Once Dr. Brown decides tentatively to proceed, she begins talking with the Student Life Director and staff about existing needs and how best to acquire assessment information.

Data Collection

A *research* function in which suitable data collection methods are selected and/or developed, followed by data collection is the next step. Dr. Brown may interview selected staff and students, examine archival sources, observe relevant groups in action, or conduct a survey to implement data collection procedure that was developed.

Data Feedback

Data feedback is an *action* function in which data are shared with the client system members through any number of means, such as a group meeting. Data gathered are organized by the consultant and communicated personally to Student Life staff members for their discussion. In this case, a series of total staff group meetings was held.

Diagnosis

Diagnosis is a *research* function clearly illustrated by the collaboration between OD practitioner and client system members. The intent is to develop a mutually derived understanding of the state of the organization, its problems, and its strengths. Dr. Brown works closely with staff members, helping them to develop their own understanding of the information and to draw their own conclusions. For instance, they may identify a primary problem of low staff morale resulting from a lack of staff development activities.

Action Planning

As the name implies, action planning is an *action* function in which the OD practitioner assists the client to create specific action plans, based on results obtained through the preceding phases. This includes deciding what will be done, by whom, when, and how evaluation will be accomplished. The Student Life staff may work with Dr. Brown to design a staff development program emphasizing a variety of skill training components, such as in working with groups.

Action Implementation

Action implementation is an *action* function that implements the conceived plan through a wide range of OD interventions that relate directly to the current situation. In this example, the detailed plan describing how a staff skill training program would be conducted is carried out by colleagues of Dr. Brown, under her immediate supervision.

Evaluation

Evaluation is a *research* function designed to determine the effects and effectiveness of the action implementation, resulting (1) in recycling to a previous phase and continued change efforts, or (2) in terminating the project. The staff training program in this example is evaluated by the staff at several points. Their mid-program evaluation requested greater emphasis on task, as compared with human relations groups, and the remainder of the program was restructured successfully.

Action-research OD serves to articulate the generic action research mode of change found in many organization development models. It is but one of several change models that can be used to provide a kind of conceptual map for conducting OD action interventions. However, it seems especially useful for conducting OD action interventions within organizations of higher education by student affairs practitioners because of its emphasis on collaboration.

CLASSIFYING AND USING OD INTERVENTIONS

According to French, Bell, and Zawacki (1978), the term "OD interventions" refers to the range of planned, sequential activities in which clients and consultants alike participate during an organization development program. They observed that these are mostly diagnostic and problem-solving activities that ordinarily would occur with the assistance of an external OD practitioner, and that the client system adopts and integrates many of the activities as a successful OD process evolves.

A substantial number of OD interventions are available for use. Important ones include: team building (Reilly & Jones, 1974), process consultation (Schein, 1969), survey feedback (Hausser, Pecorella, & Wissler, 1977), grid OD (Blake & Mouton, 1976), life planning (Kirn & Kirn, 1978), T-groups (Bradford, Gibb, & Benne, 1964), and physical setting change (Steele, 1973). Likewise, a variety of OD classification schemata have been developed to assist in bringing increased order to all of this diversity. French and Bell (1973), French, Bell, and Zawacki (1978), and Huse (1975) are among those who have offered summaries of these several schemata. Four of these classification approaches are examined briefly in this chapter.

Organization-Environment Interface

Lawrence and Lorsch (1969) based their schema on diagnosed mismatches that are revealed in the transactions of an organization with its external environment. Interventions are selected based on nature and size of the identified mismatch between actual and desired states. These interventions may include a range of structural and procedural changes, such as altering formal communication and control procedures, changing division of labor and authority system, or changing selection criteria. A variety of educational designs have been employed, also, including sensitivity and human relations training and the case study method of instruction.

Depth of Intervention

Harrison (1970) differentiated OD interventions according to the depth of emotional involvement tapped. The deeper the intervention, the greater the potential positive or negative impact on individuals. He has suggested that two criteria be used for determining the appropriate depth of any OD intervention. The first consideration is that the intervention be no deeper than is needed to produce enduring solutions to the presenting problems. The second consideration is that the intervention depth should be consistent with the energy and resources that the client can commit to problem solving and change. Harrison's analysis indicated that OD interventions become successively deeper as they move from *systemwide* approaches such as survey feedback, to *individual/organizational interfaces* (e.g., job design), to *concern with personal work style* such as team building, to the deepest level, *intrapersonal analysis and relationships* (e.g., encounter groups).

Individual-group and Task-process

French and Bell (1973) have classified OD interventions based on how much they placed relative emphasis on individual versus group phenomena, such as learning, insight, skill building, and on task or process issues, where task represents what is being done (skills are being developed, jobs are being redesigned) and process represents how these events are occurring (through training, consultation, T-groups, education, etc.). OD interventions are classified, with natural overlap, into quadrants produced by these dimensions: *individual-task* (e.g., career planning), *group-task* (e.g., intergroup activities), *individual-process* (e.g., coaching), and *group-process* (e.g., process consultation).

Target Groups

French and Bell (1973) offered a classification schema of OD interventions that is based on the size and complexity of the target group.

That is, interdependencies and complexity increase as OD interventions are targeted progressively at *individuals,* through coaching, or role analysis, etc., to *dyads/triads* (e.g., interviews, third-party peacemaking, to *teams and groups* (e.g. team building, process consultation, etc.), to *intergroup relations* (e.g., organizational mirroring, subgrouping), and to the *total organization,* through survey feedback, strategic planning, etc. As with the previously described classification schema, interventions in this system can overlap different target levels depending on the situation. Although this may be confusing, it nevertheless reflects the real life of uses to various interventions.

SELECTED OD INTERVENTIONS

Four representative and frequently used OD interventions are presented here because they are particularly well suited for use by student affairs administrators. For instance, when recalling the "six boxes" of Weisbord (1978) (i.e., purposes, structure, relationships, rewards, leadership, and helpful mechanisms) these four interventions could be applied to seek improvement in any of those areas. However, this does not mean that all interventions can be expected to be equally effective in all situations. Team building, for instance, is particularly well designed for relationship and less so for structural interventions. Yet, these four interventions can be viewed as being broadly applicable to meet a range of organization development purposes.

The objective of this section is to provide a sense of what OD interventions are like. It is meant *to describe their nature rather than to prescribe when they should be used.*

Sensing Interview

Jones (1973) has labeled a certain form of face-to-face diagnostic OD interviewing as the "sensing interview." This interview has three main purposes. (1) The interview process allows for the generation of subjective, intuitive data that is a useful expansion of objective survey data. (2) The sensing interview allows the opportunity for OD consultants to clarify objective data generated by checking consultant perceptions with those of the client group. (3) The personal, involving format of the sensing interview encourages interviewees to increase their ownership in the diagnosis, with the potential for their greater ownership of the complete OD program itself.

The sensing interview can nonthreateningly explore many content areas. Those proposed by Weisbord (1978) represent appropriate examples. Argyris (1970) has offered another list of content areas, including roles, goals, the job itself, the organization, interpersonal relations, interpersonal perceptions, the work team, necessary changes, and the here-and-now of the interviewee. The "nonthreatening exploration," sensing interview process, includes important helping techniques such as appropriate probing and leading through open-ended questions, general and follow-up leads, demonstration of interviewer understanding through restatement, paraphrasing, reflection, and summarization, and communication of interviewer support through sharing, consoling, and expressed caring. An appropriate blending of content and process in a sensing interview can lead to a collaborative effort to produce the sum of the information that is needed to produce internal change in the system.

Sensing interviews are highly compatible with human relations emphasis common to many student affairs programs. Therefore, their potential as an organizational assessment method for student affairs is high. Sensing interviews are commonly used by OD practitioners not only to gather information needed, but also to enrich the consultative relationship.

Survey Feedback

Bowers and Franklin (1974) and Hausser, Pecorella, and Wissler (1977) considered survey feedback to be a comparatively complex guidance method that uses the questionnaire survey to improve the change process in a social organization by making it more complete, rational, and sufficient. As a method, survey feedback is sometimes set in the broader paradigm of "survey-guided development." In addition to survey feedback, the more inclusive procedure includes the following steps:
- goal setting,
- survey administration to organizational members,
- diagnosis of present organizational functioning,
- feeding back survey data to work groups that generated data,
- planning and implementing action steps at the work-group level,
- feedback of survey data about the entire organization to its leaders,
- planning and implementing action steps at the organizational level, and
- re-administration of the survey

Thus, both assessment and action phases overlap and together constitute survey-guided development (Hausser, Pecorella, & Wissler, 1977). Embedding survey feedback in this sequential and cyclical process clearly extends it far beyond "a sheet of tabulated data" (Bowers & Franklin, 1974, p. 1) to become an important element in an ongoing change process. While survey feedback has been used with some frequency by OD practitioners in student affairs, it has less often been successfully implanted within an ongoing change process. All too commonly, the OD expert gathers survey information, submits a report, and leaves. This kind of approach is contrary to the intervention discussed, which is quite closely related to OD action research. It represents a direction of choice for OD work in student affairs.

Team Building

Many organization development writers regard team-building activities as the most important single class of OD interventions. According to Reilly and Jones (1974), team building aims at improving the problem-solving ability among team (work group) members by providing means for working through task and interpersonal issues that may impede a team's functioning. Beckhard (1967) has identified four general purposes for team building, and he further suggested that one purpose should be designated as primary for a given project in order to avoid a misuse of energy. These team building purposes are to (1) establish goals and/or priorities, (2) analyze or assign the way work is conducted, (3) examine how a group works, and (4) explain relationships among workers.

Reilly and Jones (1974) identified the purposes for team building as being to: (1) promote a better understanding of each member's role in the work group, (2) develop a better understanding of the team's overall role in the total functioning of the organization, (3) increase communication among team members about issues affecting group efficiency, (4) enhance group member support, (5) increase group process understanding, (6) find effective ways of handling task and interpersonal problems that the team faces, (7) become more able to use conflict constructively, (8) promote collaborative team functioning over a competitive style, (9) increase the group's ability to work effectively with other groups in the organization, and (10) enhance interdependence among group members.

The OD consultant's role in team-building activities is that of "process facilitator." In this intervention, the consultant's responsibility is to develop the process awareness (Reilly & Jones, 1974) team members need in order to realistically assess both task accomplishments and group maintenance. Illustrations of process interventions in task accomplishment include helping a group convert an issue to a problem statement, or suggesting to the group that members evaluate their functioning during a designated work time. Examples of process interventions in group maintenance include reinforcing positive member behaviors like gatekeeping, and encouraging the giving and receiving of feedback.

Attention to process issues is given considerable importance in team building. This intervention has been used frequently in student affairs. For instance, team building activities are offered on many campuses to student organizations to develop member skills in planning tasks, leading meetings, working together, and communicating with others in the group. Rarely is team building in student affairs a part of a concerted, long-range, planned OD effort however.

Process Consultation

Schein (1969) has written the basic treatise on process consultation and its role in OD. Process consultation is "a set of activities on the part of the consultant which help the client to perceive, understand, and act upon process events which occur in the client's environment" (Schein, 1969, p. 9). As French and Bell (1973) have stressed, process consultation nearly exclusively emphasizes the diagnosis and management of personal, interpersonal, and group processes. Schein (1969) has identified the human processes that are most critical for effective organizational performance as: (1) communication (e.g., who talks to whom?); (2) member roles and functions in groups (e.g., initiator, harmonizer); (3) group problem solving and decision making; (4) group norms and growth (e.g., conflict is to be avoided at all costs); (5) leadership and authority (e.g., democratic vs. autocratic); and (6) intergroup cooperation and competition.

As in team building, process consultation is used to increase awareness of human processes, the consequences of these processes, and how they might be changed. A critical difference between the two OD interventions is found in their respective scopes. Where team building is restricted to a work team focus, process consultation takes a total organizational perspective and occurs within the stages of a general consultative model that includes: (1) establish contact, (2) define work relationships, (3) select a setting and method of work, (4) gather process data, (5) intervene, (6) evaluate, and (7) disengage. Process consultation is, then, a complete consultation program that is undertaken to improve the human processes throughout an organization. Team building, for instance, could become a part of process consultation at the intervention stage, or it could stand alone.

A range of process consultation interventions is available for use. These interventions have been organized by Schein (1969) into four categories.

Agenda Setting Interventions. Procedures are used to generate agenda for potential later action, such as in process-analysis periods at the end of every work meeting.

Feedback of Data Generated. Feedback can be given by consultants during process analysis, regular work time, and/or to individuals following such events. Guidelines for providing feedback include being descriptive rather than evaluative, and specific as opposed to general. The intent of the consultant in giving feedback is to promote acceptance and understanding of the data so that corrective action can effectively result.

Coaching or Counseling Individuals or Groups. The consultant often needs to work with individuals or groups following feedback. The purpose of this activity is to assist, concretely and supportively, the client in effectively processing and attributing his/her own meaning to the feedback, hopefully leading to problem solving.

Structural Suggestions. Such areas as work allocation, authority lines, and committee organization are used far less frequently in process consultation than the above interventions, because these kinds of suggestions are more in line with an "expert model" of consulting than with a process model. However, Schein (1969) observed that structural suggestions such as these may be occasionally offered, if appropriate.

A student affairs example of process consultation may be interesting. A counseling center contracted the services of an outside consultant in order to improve the functioning of the agency. The consultant, after working with the staff for a while, suggested that one reason the agency was floundering may be because of the way meetings were conducted—they were unstructured, fun but vague, and were usually left without closure. The consultant's suggestion that all future meetings include ten minutes of process observation at their end, in order to analyze what had worked and what had not, was accepted and used later to good advantage.

OD IN HIGHER EDUCATION

Institutions of higher learning typify organizational environments that present distinct barriers for successful organization development efforts. Borland (1980) has identified several of them, including resistance to change, improper analysis of the problem, and improper strategy choice, among others. As Bennis (1973) has observed, OD has been successful in organizations, primarily business and industrial, that are

> self-contained, large, rich, and where the product is easily identifiable and *measurable*. . . . In the university, . . . [one is] not dealing with a family group face-to-face; . . . [one is] dealing with a large, heterogeneous, pluralistic, professional, and political set of constituencies. (p. 390)

Likewise, Boyer and Crockett (1973) suggested that colleges, when compared to industry, (1) have more diverse goal structures, (2) are pluralistic subsystems, (3) present difficulty in measuring the quality of their products, and (4) are more dependent on their external environment, such as state legislatures, federal agencies, foundations, parents, alumni, or community groups. Moreover, teaching and research tend to promote norms of individualism and autonomy in higher education that counter the cooperative norms encouraged by OD practice. These authorities conclude that problems of power and conflict abound in higher education institutions.

These analyses of college organizational life imply that unique challenges face the effective conduct of OD. Any one college organization (such as an academic department or a student affairs unit) is confronted with an internal institutional environment that is characterized by autonomy and low interdependence, and an external environment that is highly changeable. Taken together, these two general conditions mean that college organizations are often isolated entities, cut off from one another and at the behest of outside forces. To use a metaphor drawn from the field of primary prevention, they are organizations *at risk* for not only their future growth and development but for their very survival.

The larger institutions of which these organizations are a part are themselves in trouble. Many smaller schools have been forced to close and many more are threatened, to varying degree, by that prospect. During the 1980s, lowered enrollment, decreased funding levels appropriated for higher education by state legislatures, reductions in federal funds for education, and rampant inflation all illustrate forces in the external environment that combine synergistically to produce not only *at risk organizations* within institutions but, even more critically, *at risk institutions* themselves.

Most higher education institutions during the coming decade are going to be stressed by these (and other) very harsh, inhospitable external environmental factors. These stressors will strain colleges and their internal organizations. Decreased resources will force the direct confrontation of uncomfortable issues. For instance, which institutional programs will be retained and which limited or dropped? Which target populations get served and which do not? Can current staffing patterns be continued or will a decrease in staff positions be necessary? How is staff morale maintained in times of uncertainty and adversity? Can other more effective and efficient organizational patterns be adopted? This pattern of stress and strain promises to be both naggingly pervasive and difficult to address satisfactorily. For some institutions it may be cataclysmic, while for others it may prove to yield adaptive and useful innovations.

New ways are needed for educational institutions to tackle this crisis head-on or, better yet, before it reaches crisis proportions. Methods must be found to prevent the failure of sound institutions and their organizational entities. As OD evolves to include a systemic emphasis and to expand its techniques, it becomes one potential means to use in protecting and in some cases promoting the continued development of higher education.

A Future for OD in Higher Education

Organization development as an intact intervention area has been in existence for only about 25 years, used mostly in business and industry. However, OD has found its way into other settings, including higher education (Alderfer, 1977). What appears to be happening is that OD has been garnering increasing attention in higher education (Astin, Comstock, Epperson, Greeley, Katz, & Kauffman, 1974; Borland, 1980; Boyer & Crockett, 1973; Miller & Prince, 1976). Its use in higher education will grow in direct proportion to two interrelated factors: the forecasted retrenchment that faces postsecondary education and the emergence of college staff members who are committed to finding ways to cope creatively with the strains that are inevitably produced.

By all signs it seems clear that hard times will increase in the immediate future. That reality implies many potential strategies for staff and faculty including, of course, leaving the field of higher education. From another perspective, one may view this crisis as a challenge to be struggled and experimented with so as to produce innovative and adaptive mechanisms that serve to more ably secure and advance higher education. There is utility in the belief that OD as a broad net of interventions has something significant to offer higher education. However, in order for OD to be used effectively and maintained over time, a sanctioned campus group needs to assume responsibility for offering a campus organization development program. Student affairs divisions could provide such a home base.

STUDENT AFFAIRS AS AN OD NUCLEUS IN HIGHER EDUCATION

Adoption of a system view to college life easily allows one to see that issues related to student welfare and development are involved closely with issues related to a host of other populations and conditions, both internal and external to the campus. Everything seems interconnected. A policy enacted by a governing body in July regarding tuition costs and payments has certain effects on students the entire next year; faculty members undergoing severe psychological problems may be unable to prevent their debilitating effect on classroom teaching; civil service employees who feel underpaid and overworked may make life uncomfortable for faculty and students alike; and so on. Student affairs divisions that recognize the high degree of interdependence present in higher education (and the baffling reluctance of this phenomenon to be directly addressed) could begin to interpret themselves as a group whose mission, at least in part, becomes one of promoting greater integrity of the components in the system.

OD provides a conceptual model and a broad net of interventions that could be used in this effort. Three basic strategy levels are available for use by student affairs divisions that would adopt this approach: (1) internal OD work within individual student affairs departments, (2) network generator of division-wide OD work, and (3) OD to the college community.

Level 1: Internal OD Work

"Charity begins at home." This homily suggests that perhaps the most realistic point to initiate an OD project in the student affairs division is within the individual departments themselves. Thus, a housing department might inaugurate its own OD project, the counseling center might do the same, and so on. The OD consultant could be a skilled within-agency-staff member, be drawn from the division central office, or be imported from outside the college. The critical questions faced by these student affairs departments are how to review and evaluate, and whether and how to change? Failure to effectively resolve these and other important issues at the agency level can expose the organizations to risk factors that begin consistently to outstrip available resources; one outcome of such a process is organizational death.

OD can be instituted within hospitable agencies in order to avoid stagnation, and perhaps death, and to promote organizational health (Fordyce & Weil, 1971). In a healthy organization:

1. Objectives are shared widely by members and energy is devoted to executing them properly.

2. Members point out difficulties with the expectation that they will be solved effectively.

3. Problem solving is very pragmatic, unconfined by status, territoriality, or fearing what the boss might think. Ample nonconforming behavior is accepted.

4. Who makes what decisions is not rigidly predetermined. It is flexibly determined, a function of information availability, skills, sense of responsibility, work load, and so on.

5. Members mobilize their resources to respond to crisis situations.

6. Conflicts are viewed as useful for organizational growth and they are encountered openly.

7. Risk is accepted as a consolation of growth and change.

Miller and Prince (1976) have attempted to convert notions associated with a healthy organization into organization principles of an ideal "student development organization." They suggested that goals set and decisions made should be consistent with the collegiate mission. Because all system parts are interdependent, planners must be certain that all members understand and are committed to the purposes of the proposed change. Following goal support, attention can be given to the means for change. All available physical, financial, and human resources should be integrated so that the student affairs staff can respond effectively to present demands as well as to anticipate future needs. Throughout the change effort, decision makers must maintain an open communication system so that each participant can give and receive timely and accurate information and so that continuous evaluation procedures can be implemented. Finally, Miller and Prince (1976) emphasized that the healthy student affairs division should have a climate that encourages and rewards personal and professional development by all its members.

In a grand design, OD programs might begin at the individual student affairs department level and then be generalized across the entire division. The notion here is that once the individual parts are strengthened, attention can then be given more fully to strengthening the whole body.

Level 2: Division-wide OD Work

Sarason and colleagues (Sarason, Carroll, Maton, Cohen, & Lorentz, 1977) have provided a model called "resource exchange" that holds promise for division-wide OD work in student affairs.

The concepts of "resource exchange" and "networking" build from the conviction that people and organizations can sometimes do together what each is unable to do individually. This collaborative stance conflicts with dominant interorganization behaviors of competitiveness, standoffishness, and narrow self-interest and self-reliance; productive mutuality may be an espoused value, but it is rarely enacted, especially in the rugged individualist world of the academy.

Student affairs departments function within a formally constructed organizational system. Most typically, these separate agencies exist in parallel form, reporting directly and independently to the division's central office administrator. Although the capacity for an interorganizational network (Baker & Schulberg, 1970; Turk, 1970) is present, seldom is it activated; agencies function autonomously from each other. A Level 2 OD strategy represents the infusion of an OD program throughout the student affairs division. It is toward this end that the concepts of resource exchange and of interorganizational networking can be useful.

Collaboration, the give-and-get exchange of resources, and the sense of psychological connection can emerge from these processes. A critical variable is that these activities are conducted around a *real life* set of tasks or demands that requires the combined participation of all agencies to obtain satisfaction. When the tasks are accepted as important and agencies begin to collaborate on their accomplishment through joint action, conditions can be created that support implementation of a division-wide OD project. The proximal goal for Level 2 OD in student affairs should be to design ways to put departments in contact with each other in order to solve important problems. It is here that resource exchange, for instance, can contribute directly. Once connections begin to solidify among agencies around important tasks or goals, then they can be capitalized on by implanting an appropriately shaped OD program that would continue to strengthen the collaborative activities clearly underway while attributing meaning to them from a divisional perspective.

An illustration may be useful. A resource-exchange network at a midwestern college (Conyne, 1980) was formed. The program emerged from a four-year campus environmental assessment project (Conyne, 1975, 1978) that had developed a considerably large body of student-environment fit data. A "project team," comprised of student affairs staff and administrators (plus some individuals from outside student affairs), was formed to develop a collaboratively based change program derived from selected aspects of these data. A benignly neglected group was targeted, students who were new to the university (freshmen and transfers who lived off campus). The interdependence that was demanded in creating joint interventions that spoke to this group led to the mutual pooling of resources, to a developed sense of community among project team members, and to setting the climate for subsequent OD activities.

Level 3: OD to the Institutional Community

The general procedure of a resource-exchange network can be applied, also, to a total university focus, although OD at Level 3 becomes a very complex process. OD becomes increasingly intricate at this level because of the size and diversity of the institution itself. One aspect of the diversity dimension, values, provides an example of this complexity. Consider the question, "What values are espoused by the institution?" If one thinks about it for a moment, one soon realizes that, phrased in this manner, the question is largely unanswerable. While a college of liberal arts, for instance, purports to value the generation and dissemination of artistic, scientific, and cultural knowledge, a college of agriculture is said to value applied, technical knowledge and practice; within the two colleges diversity can be easily found in terms of values. For instance, the physics and English departments in liberal arts differentially support mathematics and literature as avenues to knowledge. The combination of diversity and size suggests that conceptualizing the entire institution as an organization amenable to OD may be, not only overly ambitious, but also unrealistic.

Rather, targeting organizations *within* the institution and *external* to student affairs seems to be a more manageable Level 3 approach. Offering OD consultation to academic departments, central administration, civil service, and to student organizations represents a means by which student affairs can put itself in the position of having a significant impact on the institution. As Miller and Prince (1976) have indicated in regard to student development, *collaboration* among student affairs staff, faculty members, and students is essential to success. Becoming known on campus as a credible nucleus for conducting OD interventions available to other campus organizations would provide the student affairs division with an important function, especially in times of constricted resources.

Several examples of OD exist in the campus community that could constitute models for student affairs to consider. Three such activities will be described briefly. The first example is focused on academic departments; the second on change teams comprised of volunteer students, faculty, and administrators; and the third illustrates progressive involvement from training to OD in an academic department.

Bolton and Boyer (1973) reported an OD project for academic departments that has been conducted by a staff unit at the University of Cincinnati. Academic departments were selected as a change focus because of their ubiquity in higher education and because they have a major influence on the nature of the teaching and learning processes. A basic assumption underlying their work is that enhanced departmental effectiveness will yield adaptive departmental changes demonstrated, in part, by departmental capacities to better meet the needs of students it serves. A four-phase action research process was used (consultant-client relationship development, data collection, feedback and discussion, and follow-up) to address such adaptive activities in departments as organizational planning, environmental analysis, innovation, and experimentation. Success in enhancing the effectiveness of these activities is seen as furthering the development of the total institution.

Another instance of OD in the college community is the use of campus change agent teams (Sikes, Schlesinger, & Seashore, 1973). These teams are comprised of volunteers, sanctioned by a key campus administrator, and they avail themselves of external consultation during their existence. A team defines a problem area, such as improvement of student participation in institutional decision making, and uses an action research model to seek change in the practice of the institution relative to the focal problem. This process is similar to the resource exchange model noted earlier except that external consultation is a critical addition. Sikes and others (1973) reported that the campus teams with whom they have worked have been able to develop the skills in group process and planned change necessary for producing valuable campus innovations that exceed the capacity for innovation that is possible by individual change agents.

A final illustration of OD in the college community is a project conducted for one academic department by a counseling center staff (Conyne, Rapin, & Berger, 1980; Rapin, Conyne, & Berger, 1980). This project began in the form of a training request to advance the group facilitation skills of student discussion group leaders in a large undergraduate course (N=480) in the department. This training continued over a three-year period, leading to an expansion of the involvement beyond (but including) the training element to a focus on the total discussion group program itself. The initial training contract was renegotiated with program planners to include assessing the ideal and real social climates of 12 discussion groups (as perceived by students, facilitators, and program planners), followed by feedback sessions, and program-centered administrative consultation to the program planners, aimed at program redesign. This project nicely demonstrated how a counseling center staff can become engaged in OD activities with an academic department program that evolved from an initial training involvement.

USING OD IN STUDENT AFFAIRS

Crisis theory holds that emergency situations provide critical leverage points for significant advancement or decline in the organism experiencing the crisis. At such times the assistance of a skilled helper such as a crisis intervenor can intensify advancement opportunities. This analogy can be applied nearly directly to higher education today.

As has been indicated, higher education is in a state of crisis. Campuses, some more so than others, need their own skilled crisis intervenors. Student affairs divisions can begin to conceptualize ways to become an important crisis intervention source for the campus community. It is at this point that a range of OD interventions can be of use both within the division (Levels 1 and 2 OD strategies) and outside with other campus organizations (Level 3).

Building an "OD nucleus" within student affairs that can be drawn upon by the campus at large can give student affairs an essential and critically important new mission to benefit the institution. Doing so, of course, is no small task and needs to be considered in respect to a panoply of local factors. However, if the decision is "go," then the challenges and potential rewards would be many.

REFERENCES

Alderfer, C. Organization development. In M. Rosenzweig & L. Porter (Eds.), *Annual Review of Psychology*, 1977, *28*, 197-223.

Argyris, C. *Intervention theory and method*. Reading, MA: Addison-Wesley, 1970.

Astin, A., Comstock, C., Epperson, D., Greeley, A., Katz, Jr., & Kauffman, J. *Faculty development in a time of retrenchment*. New Rochelle, NY: Change, 1974.

Baker, F., & Schulberg, H. Community health caregiving systems. In A. Sheldon, F. Baker, & C. McLaughlin (Eds.), *Systems and medical care*. Cambridge, MA: MIT Press, 1970.

Beckhard, R. The confrontation meeting. *Harvard Business Review*, 1967, *45*, 149-55.

Bennis, W. An OD expert in the cat bird's seat: An interview with Warren Bennis. In R. Boyer & C. Crockett (Eds.), *Organizational development in higher education*, 1973, *44*, 389-98.

Blake, R., & Mouton, J. *Consultation*. Reading, MA: Addison-Wesley, 1976.

Bolton, C., & Boyer, R. Organizational development for academic departments. In R. Boyer & C. Crockett (Eds.), Organizational development in higher education (Special Issue), *Journal of Higher Education*, 1973, *44*, 352-69.

Borland, D. Organization development: A professional imperative. In D. G. Creamer (Ed.), *Student development in higher education: Theories, practices, and future directions*. Washington, DC: American College Personnel Association, 1980.

Bowers, D., & Franklin, J. Basic concepts of survey feedback. In J. Pfeiffer & J. Jones (Eds.), *The 1974 annual handbook for group facilitators*. La Jolla, CA: University Associates, 1974.

Boyer, R., & Crockett, C. Organizational development in higher education: Introduction. *Journal of Higher Education,* 1973, *44,* 339-51.

Bradford, L., Gibb, J., & Benne, K. (Eds.). *T-group theory and laboratory method: Innovation in re-education.* New York: John Wiley, 1964.

Clark, D., & Guba, E. *Innovation in school curricula.* Washington, DC: The Center for the Study of Instruction, National Education Association, 1965.

Collier, J. United States Indian administration as a laboratory of ethnic relations. Social Research, *1945, 12,* 275-6.

Conyne, R. Resource networking on the campus: A prospective for prevention. *Journal of College Student Personnel,* 1980, *21,* 573-4.

Conyne, R. An analysis of student-environment mismatches. *Journal of College Student Personnel,* 1978, *19,* 461-5.

Conyne, R. Environmental assessment: Mapping for counselor action. *Personnel and Guidance Journal,* 1975, *54,* 150-5.

Conyne, R., Rapin, L., & Berger, R. Consulting with academia using a collaborative research approach. Paper presented at the annual meeting of the American College Personnel Association, Boston, April, 1980.

Corey, S. *Action research to improve school practices.* New York: Bureau of Publications, Teachers College, Columbia University, 1953.

Emery, F., & Trist, E. Socio-technical systems. In C. Churchman & M. Verhulst (Eds.), *Management sciences models and techniques* (Vol. 2). London: Pergamon Press, 1960.

Fordyce, J., & Weil, R. *Managing with people.* Reading, MA: Addison-Wesley, 1971.

French, W., & Bell, C. *Organization development.* Englewood Cliffs, NJ: Prentice-Hall, 1973.

French, W., Bell, C., & Zawacki, R. (Eds.). *Organization development: Theory, practice, and research.* Dallas: Business Publications, 1978.

Frohman, M., Sashkin, M., & Kavanagh, M. Action-research as applied to organization development. In W. French, C. Bell, & R. Zawacki (Eds.), *Organization development: Theory, practice, and research.* Dallas: Business Publications, 1978.

Harrison, R. Choosing the depth of organizational intervention. *Journal of Applied Behavioral Science,* 1970, *6,* 181-202.

Hausser, D., Pecorella, P., & Wissler, A. *Survey-guided development II: A manual for consultants.* La Jolla, CA: University Associates, 1977.

Havelock, R. *Planning for innovation.* Ann Arbor, MI: Center for Research on Utilization of Scientific Knowledge, Institute for Social Research, 1969.

Huse, E. *Organization development and change.* St. Paul, MN: West Publishing, 1975.

Huse, E., & Bowditch, J. *Behavior in organizations: A systems approach to managing.* Reading, MA: Addison-Wesley, 1973.

Jones, J. The sensing interview. In J. Pfeiffer and J. Jones (Eds.), *The 1973 annual handbook for group facilitators.* La Jolla, CA: University Associates, 1973.

Kast, F., & Rosenzweig, J. *Organization and management: A systems approach.* New York: McGraw-Hill, 1970.

Katz, D., & Kahn, R. *The social psychology of organizations.* New York: Wiley, 1966.

Kirn, A., & Kirn, M. *Life work planning* (4th ed.). New York: McGraw-Hill, 1978.

Lawrence, P., & Lorsch, J. *Developing organizations: Diagnosis and action.* Reading, MA: Addision-Wesley, 1969.

Lewin, K. Action research and minority problems. *Journal of Social Issues,* 1946, *2,* 34-46.

Lippitt, R., Watson, J., & Westley, B. *The dynamics of planned change: A comparative study of principles and techniques.* New York: Harcourt, Brace, & World, 1958.

Miller, T. K., & Prince, J. *The future of student affairs: A guide to student development for tomorrow's higher education.* San Francisco: Jossey-Bass, 1976.

Patton, M. *Utilization-focused evaluation.* Beverly Hills, CA: Sage, 1978.

Rapin, L., Conyne, R., & Berger, R. Consultation and collaborative research: A new direction for counseling centers. Paper presented at the annual meeting of the American Psychological Association, Montreal, Canada, September, 1980.

Reilly, A., & Jones, J. Team Building. In J. Pfeiffer & J. Jones (Eds.), *The 1974 annual handbook for group facilitators.* LaJolla, CA: University Associates, 1974.

Sarason, C., Carroll, C., Maton, K., Cohen, S., & Lorentz, E. *Human services and resource networks.* San Francisco: Jossey-Bass, 1977.

Schein, E. *Process consultation: Its role in organization development.* Reading, MA: Addison-Wesley, 1969.

Seiler, J. *Systems analysis in organizational behavior.* Homewood, IL: R. D. Irwin-Dorsey Press, 1967.

Sikes, W., Schlesinger, L., & Seashore, C. Developing change agent teams on campus. *Journal of Higher Education,* 1973, *44,* 399-413.

Steele, F. *Physical settings and organization development.* Reading, MA: Addison-Wesley, 1973.

Turk, H. Interoganizational networks in urban society: Initial perspectives and comparative research. *American Sociological Review,* 1970, *35,* 1-19.

Weisbord, M. *Organizational diagnosis: A workbook of theory and practice.* Reading, MA: Addison-Wesley, 1978.

SUGGESTED READINGS

Alderfer, C. Organization development. In M. Rosenzweig & L. Porter (Eds.), *Annual Review of Psychology,* 1977, *28,* 197-223.

Borland, D. Organization development: A professional imperative. In D. Creamer (Ed.), *Student development in higher education: Theories, practices, and future directions.* Washington, DC: American College Personnel Association, 1980.

Boyer, R., & Crockett, C. Organizational Development in Higher Education: Introduction. *Journal of Higher Education,* 1973, *44,* 339-51.

French, W., & Bell, C. *Organization development.* Englewood Cliffs, NJ: Prentice-Hall, 1973.

French, W., Bell, C., & Zawacki, R. (Eds.). *Organization development: Theory, practice, and research.* Dallas: Business Publications, 1978.

Huse, E. *Organization development and change.* St. Paul, MN: West Publishing, 1975.

Katz, D., & Kahn, R. *The social psychology of organizations.* New York: Wiley, 1966.

Lawrence, P., & Lorsch, J. *Developing organizations: Diagnosis and action.* Reading, MA: Addison-Wesley, 1969.

Schein, E. *Process consultation: Its role in organization development.* Reading, MA: Addison-Wesley, 1969.

Weisbord, M. *Organizational diagnosis: A workbook of theory and practice.* Reading, MA: Addison-Wesley, 1978.

Fred B. Newton is presently Director of the Counseling Center and Associate Professor in the Department of Administration and Foundations, College of Education, at Kansas State University. His previous experience includes both teaching and administrative positions at Duke University, University of Georgia, and Sinclair Community College in Dayton, Ohio. Dr. Newton received his master's degree in student personnel in higher education at The Ohio State University. He received his doctorate in counseling and student personnel services from the University of Missouri-Columbia. He is an editor of *Student Development Practices: Strategies for Making a Difference* and author of numerous journal articles.

Richard B. Caple is Professor of Counseling Psychology in the Department of Educational and Counseling Psychology and is a Counseling Psychologist in the Counseling Center at the University of Missouri, Columbia. He received his B.A. from Cornell College and his M.A. and Ed.D from Teachers College, Columbia University. He has had previous experience in counseling and administration at New Mexico State University and Northwestern State College, Oklahoma.

Dr. Caple has had a long term interest in value theory and its meaning for human behavior. This led to his special interest in new paradigms and models that conceptualize human beings and their environments holistically. During the time he was serving as Chief Student Affairs Officer, he began to study and use general systems theory and has continued to use it as a foundation for work in group therapy, and organizational and community development.

Chapter **4**

MANAGERIAL
LEADERSHIP

Fred B. Newton
Richard B. Caple

In 1970 Alvin Toffler wrote about the phenomenon of "future shock"—the reaction to a period of technological innovation, accumulation of knowledge, and access to information which has occurred so rapidly that the people and systems of society are overwhelmed and under stress to make adjustments and accommodation. Science and technology have daily opened new boundaries but at the same time created dilemmas that tax the environment, test the flexibility of institutions, and present conflicts of priority for individuals. Communication, trade, and all manner of interlocking alliances by business, government, and individual entrepreneurs connect corners of the world in an instantaneous reaction with startling and unpredictable consequences for economic, political, and social impact.

A glance at the headlines of the eighties confirms the point that "future shock" was not only applicable to the seventies, but continues to be a present-day reality. How have people and institutions of society responded to this phenomenon of our times?

Old models of change through deliberate study and gradual adjustment are criticized as too inefficient to respond to the rapidity and complexity of change that are now occurring. Priogogine, a physical chemist, has proposed and demonstrated a theory of cellular change that also has been applied to social change. This theory postulates that when a perturbance becomes so great that the old system is disrupted, a higher level of organization is forced into being to prevent chaos (Ferguson, 1980).

Kuhn (1962) in the *Structure of Scientific Revolutions* noted new paradigms, explanatory models that more effectively explain phenomena, were at first met with resistance. As the more powerful idea gained ascendance, however, a shift occurred as if the old model were suddenly replaced in a revolutionary manner. Perhaps a paradigm shift is now occurring. Ferguson (1980) discussed the presence of an "aquarian conspiracy," people from all walks of life who are linking together in networks of support to use a greater level of their potential to develop new life styles, rearrange priorities, and lead a quiet revolution to achieve a new level of human existence. As tensions and dissonance caused by change stimulate the opportunity for new ways of acting upon the world, they also frighten people to withdraw into a protective stance trying to hold on to the security of the old way of living and resisting with a last gasp the familiar and seemingly safe world. A recent compilation of Carnegie Reports on today's college student illustrated this point. Levine (1980) described many students as having a "lifeboat mentality"—"The world is going to hell, but I'll be OK." Persons who exhibit this behavior express a belief in personal survival by old standards in spite of seeing and feeling the perturbance around them.

Indeed, a world that is undergoing transformation rather than maintenance is in need of an extraordinary form of leadership: the type of leadership that is able to inspire and create new processes of social existence. Leaders are needed who are similar to those leaders that shaped the beginnings of this country—leaders with a broad range of knowledge, a sense of courage, a belief in a strong set of ethical and moral principles, and a creative, imaginative mind capable of identifying many potentials. In a world, in a country, and specifically on campuses, can leaders manage resources and develop human processes to move toward a qualitatively higher level of society?

In this chapter theories of management that have been prominent during the past fifty or more years are reviewed, and present trends are emphasized. Evolving research and descriptions of leadership are presented in a separate section. Applications of managerial leadership as designed for student affairs administration in institutions of higher education are illustrated with vignettes. The focus in the applications section is upon current trends in higher education and how the propositions for effective management and leadership may be applied.

Leadership and Management: A Definition

Leadership, according to Burns, is "the exercise of those with power potential, to engage, mobilize, induce, and transform followers to act for certain goals which represent the values and motivations—the wants and the needs, the aspirations *of both leaders and followers*" (1978, pp. 18-9). The leader is powerful but not a power wielder. The leader takes initiative creating links for communication. The leader is moral, raising the level of human conduct and ethical aspiration. The leader is "transforming" as followers proceed to higher levels permitting the relationship to change. The extent of the quality and power of the leader is measured by the actual accomplishment toward promised change.

The process of getting things done within any organization, institution, or system by using material resources and human resources in a purposeful way to achieve stated outcomes is called management (Stoner, 1978). Leadership is one aspect of the management process; Moyers (1980) indicated it is the crucial part that inspires and directs the human element of enterprise.

HISTORICAL PERSPECTIVE ON MANAGEMENT THEORY

The Classical School

Development of an organized body of knowledge on management began around the turn of the century. Prior to that time the general belief was that a person with authority and responsibility was more or less born to that station in life. Taylor (1911), often called the father of management as a discipline, suggested that the key to greater output and efficiency was to have the right person specialized to a specific task. A familiar early example of this approach was the development of the assembly line. Henry Ford applied this technique to the making of automobiles, and what happened is well known. Taylor's ideas also became the basis for time and motion studies to determine the most efficient use of effort and piece work pay to link worker performance to output. The manager's role was to develop the efficient organizational process and fit the worker into that process at the right place.

Human Relations and Organizational Behavior School

In 1924 researchers at the Western Electric plant in Illinois began some efficiency studies to determine the effects of illumination on the production of assembly line workers. This study, started in the best tradition of the classical school, resulted in new conclusions and established the importance of human factors in production. Researchers were surprised to find that no matter what level of illumination was used, work production still managed to increase. Mayo and his associates scratched their heads about the increases—as lights were dimmed to such minimal levels that lanterns were brought from home by the workers and reversed to such brightness that visors were worn—and still production increased. The answer came when the young women workers in the study themselves disclosed in follow-up interviews how pleased they had been that someone was interested in what they could do, thus the phenomenon known as the Hawthorne Effect was hypothesized. In the same plant a similar study was conducted with male assemblers who performed a team task under variant conditions of temperature. This time, no matter how warm or cold the temperature, the production remained exactly the same. Again the explanation came from workers who disclosed informally to a researcher that an unwritten agreement existed between production teams about what an adequate day's work would be. Anybody that underproduced was admonished as a slacker, or he was slapped on the knuckles if he tried to work faster. Thus, the implication of sociological influence also was discovered.

Since that time, the study of individual and social psychology within the workplace has proliferated through efforts of people interested in group dynamics and industrial psychology. McGregor (1960) postulated the manager's role in terms of human factors of production. He saw two major attitudinal perspectives that managers might take in regards to people as workers which he designated Theory X and Theory Y. Theory X held that managers are responsible for organizing elements of production: materials, equipment, directing people's efforts by controlling their behavior to fit into the organizational purpose. People by nature were considered as passive, indolent, and self-centered; and therefore, workers must be persuaded by whatever means possible to perform—which was the manager's task. Theory Y still held the manager responsible for production, but considered people able to assume responsibility and direct their own behavior toward an organizational goal. People are motivated by needs that seek continually higher levels progressing from safety to social, then ultimately to self-actualization. Maslow's (1954) classic study of full-functioning people provided support for Theory Y. The manager's responsibility was to make possible for individual needs and goals to be achieved while organizational objectives were met. According to McGregor (1960), people following Theory Y were found to be the more effective managers. He therefore concluded that what a manager thinks about people becomes a self-fulfilling prophesy in terms of the resultant style of managing the behavior of the worker in response to that style.

Following McGregor's lead, Argyris (1971) found that behavior as well as attitude was important to the actual management approach followed. He postulated two behavior patterns often exhibited by managers. One was pattern A, which reflects behavior expected from one holding Theory X assumptions such as being directive, controlling, and closely supervising subordinates. The other was pattern B, which is representative of Theory Y assumptions and behaviorally reflects responsiveness to others, openness to feelings, and an experimental posture. Argyris noted that, although most managers follow an XA or a YB approach, under certain conditions the Theory X leader may behave in open and noncontrolling ways while the Theory Y person may act in a directive fashion. Argyris argued, therefore, that situational factors may influence leaders to behave in one way even though their basic assumptions about people are not parallel to that behavior. In effect, sometimes by necessity, immediate action is taken without consultation and involvement with others even in a democratic atmosphere. The wise administrator, however, will seek to function in a thoughtful and consistent fashion as leadership responsibilities are being implemented.

Managerial Process School

This school can best be identified by the general texts of the field during the sixties that attempted to outline the principles, functions, resources, and responsibilities of management. Figure 4.1 is an example of the typical conceptualization of the management process, including some elaboration on the four major functions of planning, organizing, leading, and controlling (Stoner, 1978). Resources feeding into the pro-

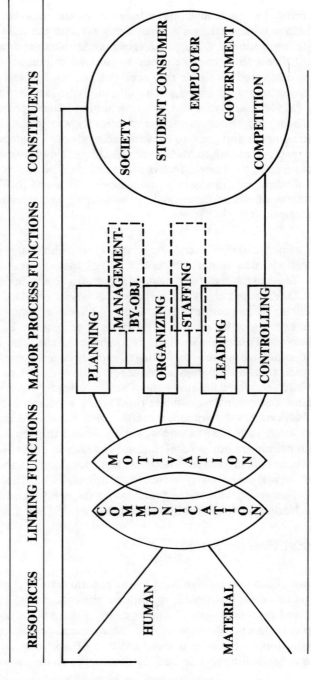

Figure 4.1 Conceptualization of the four major managerial functions.

cesses of production include the inanimate material and the human. A description of each of the major functions identified by this process school provides a helpful description of management dynamics from input of resources to constituent consumers. Essential during each of the phases of production are the permeating ingredients that tie the processes together, effective communication and motivation.

Planning. The process starts with the planning phase. Planning includes a clarification of goals, determination of assets and obstacles, description of decision-making and problem solving processes, and the steps or activities to be taken. Drucker (1954) was the first to promote a process whereby managers actively would identify objectives for their work and plan the manner in which these objectives would be met. This process he labeled management by objectives (MBO). These ideas have been refined by Odiorne (1979) into a systematic process for entire organizations to determine objectives and make plans to meet them. In MBO, objectives are set in performance terms which clearly define individual and unit responsibilities. Clarity, openness, flexibility, and adaptability are characteristics necessary to the planning stage. The identification of key results that may be assessed for attainment at increments and outcome points are crucial factors in making MBO more popular than other planning processes.

Organizing. The second phase in the management process, organizing, includes a consideration of the work environment, the delegation of line and staff authority, and the structural method in which change and conflict will be accommodated. Organizing is often the key to success as the structure may significantly impact the two catalysts of the total process, communication and motivation. Whyte's (1948) example of structure in the restaurant business illustrated this phase. Whyte was asked by restaurant owners for consultation on a problem that continually eluded attempts to resolve conflict between employees. The artistic chefs seemed to be resentful of the interaction with unappreciative waiters. One of Whyte's resolutions was to structurally separate the two groups from direct interaction by cutting a hole in the wall between the kitchen and order area and suspending a bicycle wheel from the top of the opening to which orders could be attached by clothes pins and rotated to each area minimizing the objectionable contact but maintaining essential communication. Most people probably have seen this adaption built into the structure of many restaurants today.

Staffing. Staffing initially was seen as a part of the organization phase. Staffing involves matching the right person to the right job and includes the process of attraction, recruitment, selection, and placement. Mistakes in the staffing procedure are often seen as the employee being underemployed—has too much experience and capability for the job—or being overemployed—is advanced to a level for which employee is incapable or unprepared a la the Peter Principle (Peter & Hull, 1969). Responding to changing needs and new stimuli for employees has implications for new staffing techniques that may include team management, flexible staffing, parallel systems, in-service training, and rotated responsibilities. Some of these responses are discussed in the application section.

Leading. The third phase of management process is one of directing, or the leadership function. This aspect is mentioned to indicate its place in the process school and is discussed in more detail in the next section.

Controlling. The final function of management is controlling. While often unpopular as the watchdog evaluator of production, it is nonetheless essential. Control provides the standards for which one measures the performance of the organization. A manager, in the controller's role, is responsible for providing rewards and merits as well as the confrontation and sometimes release of employees. The latter becomes the uncomfortable aspect of many managers' jobs. If accountability measures are determined clearly in the planning phase, however, control becomes a point of information that identifies one's progress toward a goal and becomes a significant point of reward for the work investment.

Quantitative School

The Quantitative School has emphasized the use of scientifically controlled study and mathematical formulation to delineate the process of management as a science of laws and principles. The difficulty of this approach has been to identify these principles with certainty, mainly due to the fluctuation and complexity of human behavior which tends to confound an approach that seeks lawfulness.

Some studies have shown sufficient evidence to question the proposition that managers go through reflective scientific methods of planning. Mintzberg (1975) reported that the typical managerial activity is better described as brief, varied, and discontinuous with one study of foremen showing that they were involved with over 500 activities during the single working day. Information processes follow "soft" sources of communication such as conversation and casual oral communication rather than formal networks. Similarly, decisions, scheduling, and the like rely more on processes that could be better described as intuitive rather than systematic judgment.

Summary Regarding Schools of Managerial Theory

These four major schools of theory discussed have all in some way influenced the state of management theory today. Elements of each may be found in most work situations. Tenets of the classical school of thought have waned in favor of the human relations approach. Managers are presently seen more as enablers than enforcers. Communication processes are recognized as the key to positive and productive human interaction. The process management school of thought has provided a framework that continues to be influenced and altered by new suggestions, processes, and knowledge that develop into more elaborate systems and even matrix configurations. In a matrix or parallel organizational system, traditional lines of authority may be maintained for certain aspects of the job, while special projects or temporary tasks are organized around decentralized matrix units that include employees across the organization.

Attempts to quantify management into exacting principles continue, but usually within very definable aspects of the management discipline. It is now generally recognized that management of people is not as easily reduced to a simple formula as once thought. New paradigms of understanding human behavior, human consciousness, and the nature of reality form the basis for the beginning of new ways of thought.

Contemporary Management Practices

Job rotation, job enrichment, and job enlargement are examples of contemporary management practices used to improve individual satisfaction with the work role (Butteriss & Albrecht, 1979). Job rotation permits the movement of workers among many tasks avoiding the monotony of repetitive performance and providing the opportunity for new challenge. This process also is called flexible staffing and may involve only a part of the workers' time during peak seasons or for special tasks. Job enrichment expands the variety of tasks an employee might perform. Job enlargement would give added responsibilities to an employee which might include coordination or direction of a program or a task force for someone who otherwise would not be considered on the management level.

Another practice that allows a worker more autonomy and control over the job situation is the use of flexible time. In "flex time" the employee may be responsible for certain job functions and the commitment to a total number of hours over a given time period; however, the person may come and go as he/she pleases. A typical modification of this plan holds the employee responsible on the job for certain core times, but may accomplish other tasks of the job with individualized scheduling. An established example of this has been the practice of faculty to meet classes and maintain some specified office hours, while the rest of their time for preparation and research may be determined individually. The delegation of more responsibility to all levels of employment is also seen in the rise of participatory management practices. In many institutions, some policy and procedure decisions enlist the opinions of front line workers, consumers, and managers with equal voice.

A final practice to be mentioned includes the use of more rigorous accountability practices. Likert (1967) described a human resource accountability system. The system attempts to quantify the relationship of personal variables (motivation, attitude, leadership) to production variables to show cost effectiveness. An example of this is the implementation of program planning budgeting systems. The cost of attaining specified program objectives is identified in terms of materials, equipment, space utilization, and staff time. Student affairs units may soon be asked to justify which programs are the most effective based upon this type of approach.

LEADERSHIP

Leadership has been a topic of widespread interest throughout much of recorded history from Plato's discussion of the "philosopher king" and Machiavelli's description of the "Prince" to countless modern day biographies of American presidents, generals, and world leaders in nearly every walk of life. Management science programs require courses in leadership, political scientists research the nature of individual impact, and sociologists and social psychologists study the interface of individual and group dynamics. Still leadership in many ways remains an enigma, a much discussed but little understood phenomenon (Burns, 1978).

Fiedler (1967) reviewed many of the diverse descriptions of leadership enumerating phrases such as the exercise of authority and responsibility, the making of decisions, the initiation of acts leading to purposeful group solutions, the creation of change, and the direction and coordination of task relevant group activity. Leadership also has been viewed as a relationship of leader to follower; an ability to understand human behavior, to listen, understand and respond to human need. The relationship potentially can be one of transaction, an agreement between two levels: transformation, encouraging followers to greater potential; and transcendence, which elevates followers to leaders (Burns, 1978). The following historical development of leadership theory will provide some perspective for the present status of this complex and sometimes controversial subject.

Twentieth Century Leadership Theory

Two major explanations were used as models for the description of leadership 50 years ago. One was commonly referred to as the "Great Man" theory which described qualities of superiority that were ascribed as the domain of certain elite that became leaders because of a natural tendency for "the cream to rise to the top." A counter theory, the Zeitgeist, explained leadership as a result of the situation with factors of time, place, and circumstance as preeminent determinants for the emergence of leader behavior. In the 1930s and 1940s, early research on group dynamics attempted to isolate the behaviors and qualities that identified leadership. The White and Lippitt (1968) study of democratic, autocratic, and laissez-faire behaviors exemplified research that isolated leader behavior and its impact upon the group.

In the 1950s, a study of specific characteristics of leaders seen as effective by subordinates was carried out by researchers at The Ohio State University. This study was the first to identify two sets of variables that became the focus for leadership study during the sixties. The first of these variables followed a dimension that has been variously called maintenance, relationship, likeability, or process. The second dimension was described as task, structure, initiation, or production (Hershey & Blanchard, 1977). Studies of relationships between variables in the leader behavior and the performance or effectiveness of the group led to the subsequent emphasis on the interaction of a situation with the leader's behavior.

The "contingency model" was an outcome of style and situation research. Fiedler (1967) took three variables: (1) the group atmosphere—measure of the leader-group relationship, (2) the task structure—the specificity of goals, and (3) the leader power position—the authority over group members. He concluded that the favorableness of leader behavior was contingent upon the situation. Task-oriented leaders performed best in less favorable situational structure, and relationship-oriented leaders functioned best in moderately structured settings. Thus the leader must either adapt to the situation, or the appropriate leader must be matched to the situation (Fiedler, 1967). Subsequent research has considered variations on this theme.

Tannebaum (1973) emphasized that a person with qualities of sensitivity, insight, and flexibility is more able to adapt and have a higher batting average in successfully assessing appropriate behavior for the setting. House and Mitchell (1974) reasoned that a leader's choice of behavior is related directly to the awareness of subordinate motivaton and the influence the leader has in influencing the work goals and personal goals on a personally satisfying path.

Hershey and Blanchard (1977) took the relationship and task dichotomies and added a "life cycle" or time maturity dimension. The life cycle theory demonstrates the relationship of task and maintenance functions to the level of group or follower developmental maturity. As the level of maturity of the group increases, the leader behavior requires less structure and support.

Herzberg (1968) emphasized the leader's need to understand what really motivates followers. He said that the commonly thought means of directing action (money, benefits) are "hygiene" factors that do not motivate or satisfy workers, although they are means for causing dissatisfaction. Herzberg hypothesized that the true motivators are individual responsibility, achievement, internal recognition, growth, advancement, and learning.

A discussion of the leader-situation interaction applied to the higher education setting has been provided by Blake, Mouton, and Williams (1981) (Figure 4.2). They hold that by considering two functional aspects of leadership—concern for institutional performance and concern for people—as horizontal and vertical scaled continua (ranging from low 1 to high 9), an administrator's leadership style may be described as coordinates of a grid. One, one administrators are called "caretakers"; they exert the minimum amount of effort required to meet minimum work expectations and demand little from subordinates. One, nine administrators are characterized as "comfortable and pleasant" and are concerned primarily with creating satisfying relationships and a pleasant work tempo. They display little concern for production and reaching institutional goals. Administrators whose emphasis is on efficiency in

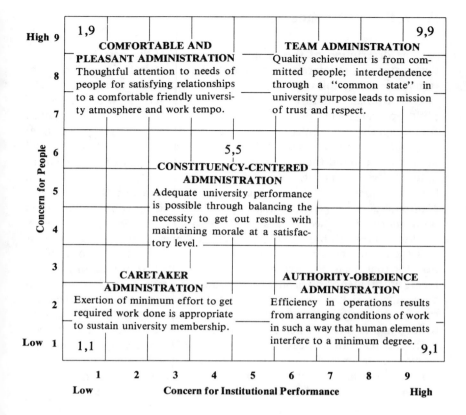

Figure 4.2. The academic administrator grid.

Note. From *the academic administrator grid,* by R.R. Blake, J.S. Mouton, and M.S. Williams, San Francisco, Jossey-Bass, 1981, p. 12. Copyright 1981 by Jossey-Bass. Reprinted by permission.

operations with little regard for the feelings of staff are 9, 1 on the grid. They concentrate on getting results by the use of power and authority, and demand unquestioning obedience from subordinates. Leaders who subscribe to a "constituency-centered" approach (5, 5 on the grid) attempt to balance the needs of the college to get results while maintaining good morale among the staff. The "team administrator" (9, 9 on the grid) has equally high concern for institutional performance and people. This style leader encourages staff to achieve at high levels and attempts to motivate them by gaining their commitment to the college's goals.

A Synthesis of Leadership Theory

The description of theory and research over the past 50 years has demonstrated the interaction of variables such as style, behavior, situational structure, follower maturity, motivation, and adaptability. The inter-disciplinary nature of leadership has left a wide range of philosophical, social, psychological, and political perspectives with need for a synthesizer. Burns (1978), a political scientist, presidential biographer, and ardent student of leadership theory across all disciplines, offered the most complete dynamic theory of leadership to date. He described leadership as a reciprocal and interactive relationship between leader and follower. It is a dynamic interaction that involves a continual dialectic give and take. Burns based his ideas of leadership on both motivation theory (Maslow, 1954) and developmental theory (Erikson, 1968; Kohlberg, 1981). Maslow's hierarchy of needs explains how the attainment of a lower level of need depletes the drive or motivation for that need. For example, once people feel secure in an environment, unthreatened by arbitrary or punitive intervention, they may then be willing to risk more open relationships with associates. The leader's role is to recognize continually and facilitate the follower's striving toward higher levels of personal fulfillment. Developmental theories are used to explain the process of crisis and equilibrium people go through leading to higher levels of personal competence and confidence in achieving potentials and moral commitment. People mature through stages in life in which personal issues are confronted and resolved and tasks mastered before advancing. Burns uses extensive case evidence of famous world leaders of the century—Churchill, Mao, Gandhi, and several American presidents—to assess and identify qualities of leadership.

Burns' analysis of leadership types in the world today found the "transactional" leader to be the most common. The transactional leader mobilizes various economic or political resources to realize goals which may be independent or mutually held by followers and leaders. Goals may be quite different between leaders and followers but are interrelated so that the tradeoff or exchange is made which will allow both to reach their ends. A politician is continually trading favors of influence in legislation for votes or financial campaign support. Values of transactional leadership relate to the manner of this exchange with emphasis on honesty, responsibility, honoring of commitments, and fairness (Burns, 1978).

A higher form of leadership is the "transforming" leader. An example is a person like Gandhi who shaped, altered, and elevated goals of followers. Instead of bargaining for separate goals based upon individual need, the transforming leader seeks the common goal of personal development of leader and follower, each wanting to move to a higher level of potential. The role of leadership may become educational as a means of modeling or demonstrating the way to elevation. The value of this type of leadership relates more to ends than means with liberty, justice, equality, and morality as the measuring rods. Burns considered this type of leadership sorely lacking during our present era, a time which may need the transformer more than ever before. He cites the example created by a Roosevelt or Kennedy who elicited strong feeling and reactions from people, in some cases anger, which had impact to inspire and elicit greater levels of achievement and moral direction from many followers (Burns, 1978).

NEW WAYS FOR VIEWING
MANAGERIAL LEADERSHIP

Paradigms or models are tools that help conceptualize and explain certain aspects of reality. In one sense they become maps that help to explore unfamiliar territory and act as guides that permit individuals to look beyond present positions. But paradigms and models are always incomplete and invite generalizations that go beyond their original purpose. They are restrictive, too, because people tend to become accustomed to their perceptions and will not give up an old framework until circumstances demand it. This leads to the creation of new paradigms.

To provide a more integrative and comprehensive system for leadership management, general systems theory can be utilized. Von Bertalanffy (1968) saw all nature, including human behavior, as interconnected. Nothing can be understood in isolation. Everything must be seen in context. Variables in a system interact with each other so fully that cause and effect cannot be separated linearly. Thus, general systems theory provides the most holistic model presently available. Currently the state of the art relies on mechanistic or cause and effect concepts emphasizing structure rather than process. A more appropriate perspective emphasizes process over structure, the exchange of energy over its containment and flexibility over stability. Structure, then, is simply the result of interacting processes utilizing energy to maintain connections. This relationship can be likened to water that flows within a riverbed; the water and the earth are part and parcel of a system interacting fully with one another. It is a matter of perspective and the perspective is relational.

In general, open systems theory involves a continuous exchange of energy with the environment. The continuous flow of energy through a system creates fluctuations. Change, therefore, for any system is never in isolation. When a system reaches beyond itself, it becomes creative; in isolation from its environment, it can only evolve toward decay.

Groups, organizations, and institutions, like human beings, are partially open systems (Katz & Kahn, 1966). The more complex the system (the more connections involved) the more energy that is needed to maintain all of the connections. Because the system is sustained by a constant flow of energy, it is always in process and subject to fluctuation, nonequilibrium, and change. If one is to participate in managing more responsiblity, an understanding of how the change occurs in an open system context is necessary.

Managing becomes planning. To be effective, planning must occur at several levels. The objective of *short-range level* planning is the efficient and economic realization of a specific and relatively clearly recognized product within a rigid structure of planning and action. This is primarily tactical or operational planning. Further along is the *strategic level* where a variety of options is imagined, tested, and prepared for realization. Strategic planning creates a mental nonequilibrium with fluctuations introduced purposely to create further evolution. Even further along is the *policy level* where the dynamics of the system are appraised in the context of all the sociocultural dynamics. A policy establishes the direction and momentum a dynamic system takes: for example, growth, profit, dominance are old traditional policy objectives. Policy established by corporate groups will create fluctuations that in turn help produce society's policy. Concern with this dynamic is concern with the concept of "industry as a planner of society." Jantsch (1980), for example, asks, whether it is the proper role of industry to pump cars into cities or is industry's role to invent and plan for entire urban transportation that will fully enhance urban life.

An even higher level of planning is the *level of values* that always operates in a decisive and guiding role. Valuing is not a completely rational process; values may get reversed from one level to another. Open planning, Jantsch (1980) believed, is never a purely rational process. Each level is inseparable from the others and provides feedback to other levels. The systems approach does not eradicate uncertainty and remove all frustration and confusion. But it leads to uncertainty, frustration, and confusion at successively higher levels. Moving ahead perturbs a system to evolve toward new connections and parts reorganize into a new whole. The system transforms into a higher order of functioning creating second order changes (Watzlawick, Weakland, & Fisch, 1974). This evolution occurs without the system being able to predict exactly how the changes will look or feel. This approach requires multilevel management. Lower levels need administrators that are dependable to handle first order change (Watzlawick et al., 1974) where minor fluctuations are absorbed and adjusted to by the system without altering its structural integrity. Normally it is easier to think in a concrete, short-range view or in a general, long-range manner. The higher art of management is to think and feel at several levels simultaneously. One form emphasizes a safe, static, and unchanging work environment, and the other promises an unpredictable, ever changing dynamic process. The one emphasizes structure while the other focuses on process. In process oriented management the manager is a catalyst encouraging processes that promise to be creative and discouraging those that seem static.

Process planning in an evolving, second order change paradigm eliminates the dualism that exists between the various levels, between the planner and the environment. Planning becomes a means of integrating all levels into an evolving process. Colleges and universities are open systems like government and industry. They are both unique in some respects and alike in others; some survive and a few perish. In open systems with an evolving spirit, creative processes ought to be permitted to interact freely and find their own order of evolving structure. The emphasis shifts from structure that attempts to preserve what is, to managing a process that creates what is to be without knowing precisely how it will be.

APPLICATIONS TO STUDENT AFFAIRS

The beginning of a new decade has led many in the area of student affairs administration to speculate on trends and possible challenges in the years ahead. Recent monographs written by practitioners, including those by Tilley, Berezet, Katz, and Shanteau (1979) and Lynch (1981), have identified key issues they anticipate will soon, if they have not already, confront the management of student affairs divisions. Management strategies to cope with these anticipated demands of the eighties are presented. These brief vignettes are offered as examples and stimuli to practitioners in adapting an effective leadership style and management process.

Vignette 1: Financial Exigency

Student affairs divisions including all component units are faced with an institutional plan for economic retrenchment. Cutbacks of 10, 25, even 50 percent are made in operating budgets. In many places development budgets have ceased to exist. Concurrent with reductions is increased demand from student consumers representing a greater range of age groups, educational background, socioeconomic level, language and cultural differences. Students, themselves under more stress because of present atmosphere of societal frustration and economic gloom, are seeking to use student services more frequently.

Some typical responses made by administrators of higher education, including chief student affairs officers, follow the principle of maintaining the old form but trimming it down. Examples of these responses include staff reductions through replacement and hiring freezes, elimination of travel and professional development expenses, and across the board percentage cutbacks in operation expenses which usually mean the fixed overheads remain the same while telephone, postage, paper, and pencil are cut 50 percent.

This response is the usual response of a system that attempts to maintain itself by adjusting without altering its structural integrity (first order change). Without realizing it, this effort may result in system pseudo-equilibrium leading eventually to decline and even death. Some institutions, some departments, some programs within institutions may flourish and then be phased out or even abruptly cut.

Simon (1980) described the situation that occurred when the New York City budgets were cut in 1975 as a "vicious circle" from the resulting fallout of the anxiety ridden campus. Tension and apprehension spread to all levels, including students. The institutional response created an inverse reaction, a greater need for services that were being cut.

A more creative management response to the problems of austerity would be to use the crisis perturbance as an opportunity to work cooperatively with all levels of staff to develop new models and structures of efficient yet purposeful service delivery that might even include income generating alternatives. This approach would operate on the premise that more motivation in recreating or developing a new, efficient, and perhaps scaled down model facilitates better than living with a starved elephant. The key is that a planning and reconstruction system would need to be implemented to foster cooperative redevelopment rather than established political alliances or expedient personal criteria for distinguishing the have and have-nots by seniority, tenure, and quotas.

The manager has a key role in modeling an acceptance of fluctuations that may occur. The leader can choose to view austerity as an opportunity to reorder the priorities and activities of one's job (to achieve new connecting points in the system). Flexible staffing, a concept which permits staff to shift responsibilities to more relevant roles, may be one response. The old order that perceived a position as permanent or static unless promoted would be replaced by a higher order concept in which staff would see the value of a less stable and more flexible job role that can keep pace with necessary changes.

For student affairs positions, flexible staffing would mean breaking down the lines and barriers between separate office units with differential functions. Staff would be encouraged to make new connections. They may shift efforts toward specific needs and services that follow a more seasonal peak such as orientation during the summer, advisement and career planning at the beginning of a term, and placement counseling during the recruitment season. This is not a new concept to smaller institutions of higher education whose staff members have had to learn to wear many hats. In flexible staffing the specialty staff of each office provides the structure and information service with necessary training for the seasonal supplement; they in turn become the supplement for the special interests of another staff during other times of the year. Another concept to replacing the functional mode would be the use of staff members in consortia or *ad hoc* task forces that tackle specific situations, problems, or new goals identified for a given period of time and are then dissolved. Toffler (1980) mentioned the need for developing "adhocracies" to replace the cumbersome methods of the predominant "bureaucracies."

Johnson (1978) indicated that the easy times are over and that the time of scarcity is upon us. No matter how hard people will attempt to maintain the old ways, a disequilibrium will occur that will force change and adaption, that is the biological way. He wrote also that people will muddle toward frugality, a word in its Latin origin that means becoming useful and productive.

Vignette 2: *Raison D'Etre*

Accountability, a key word for the past decade, continues to take on new meaning as federal and state governments seek to eliminate unnecessary programs, duplications, and wasteful spending. Additionally, consumers of education, representing a wider range of personal backgrounds, age, and aspiration levels, arrive on campus with pragmatic goals to receive specific services. Accountability for these constituencies means more than head counts. Student affairs administrators are asked to provide leadership in finding qualitative measures that demonstrate how certain programs or services relate to the educational mission of the institution.

How does a manager facilitate better controls? What are indicators of impact, quality, or satisfaction of services rendered? The first step in demonstrating accountability would be to establish a planning system that not only permits, but also systematically seeks evaluations from several directions and outlines in specific terms intent and responsibilities. More services will adapt processes such as MBO (Odiorne, 1979). This method has subunits that identify goals and objectives indicating the target result areas for routine, problem, and innovative service needs. This format necessitates the identification of measurements that directly measure progress toward the specified goal. The clarity of this approach makes it quite possible to issue "consumer reports" that identify the activity, direction, and accomplishment of a person, subunit, department, and division within the mission of the greater institution. Communication of unit goals relating to other departments, students, or administrative offices helps to decry myths and stereotypes of how others may view a unit's function. Also the communication may serve to define the interaction with outside units and specific constituents.

A note of caution is in order, however; the difficulty with this particular strategy is that emphasis on specific measurable outcomes may lead to neglect of the process involved in reaching them, and tools of measurment become more important for the production of quantitative data than their appropriateness to what is being measured. In other words, the clarity and objectivity sought by this approach may quickly become more myth than reality. Care should be given in using this approach so as to apply it only when appropriate and useful, rather than in a blanket manner, to a whole system.

Another step in the process of developing more responsive and accountable divisions is to set up means for a constant flow of information.

The promotion and use of an information system encourages, even forces, second order change within the organizational unit. Goals and activities toward those goals that prove through the feedback system to be ineffective or nonessential can be eliminated as an act of responsiveness rather than defended as an out-of-date vestige that justifies one's existence.

Finally, an accountability system would need to have a method for making the responsive changes that are necessary. In industry this system is called the research and development component. A discussion of methods for creating and adapting to change are provided in Vignette 3.

Vignette 3: Change, the Necessity of the Future

Higher education is faced with the same dilemma as the greater society—a need to develop faster and more efficient processes to adapt to and cope with rapid change. On an institutional level, established structures and procedures of operation often become cumbersome obstacles to change. For example, at one institution to make a simple adaptation of a new course requires approval of eight different offices or committees. Turbulence, sudden and dramatic shifts predicted for the future, will not be effectively met by this slow deliberate linear problem-solving process of present bureaucracies (Stein & Kanter, 1980).

On the individual level, students are confused and uncertain about how to prepare themselves for a changing future. Members of a campus club of agricultural mechanization majors were recently asked what changes they could expect in the next 10 years. Without hesitation, one student asserted that within that time, the diesel and internal combustion engine will become nearly obsolete, along with most of the training these students were now receiving in their classes. It was obvious to these students that the content of their education would not be lasting, and they would need to adapt quickly to new learning.

Institutions will, out of necessity, develop systems that will respond more quickly to at least some crises that occur. It is not likely that old structures will be easily replaced, which leads to Stein and Kanter's (1980) suggestion for a parallel organization. Parallel organizations are

flexible, but formal problem-solving and governance organizations that serve to supplement bureaucracy and exist side-by-side with it, not to replace it. . . . The parallel organization is an attempt to institutionalize a set of externally and internally responsive, participatory problem-solving structures . . . provides a means for managing change and providing flexibility and responsiveness [while] the conventional line organization . . .carries out routine tasks. (Stein & Kanter, 1980, pp. 371-2)

The parallel organization in effect uses process to replace the more static structure of the hierarchial system.

Methods of problem solving that permit the forming of new perspectives and ideas that foster an escape from the set way of viewing a situation are necessary for the adaptive unit. One method coming out of the "think tank" invention process in industry is the "synectics" approach. Gordon (1961) developed this combination of linear problem solving (analysis and deduction) with the more creative process (metaphor and analogy). Application of the synectics model to human services may prove just as effective as its application to finding a better "pop-top" can.

Preparing students to cope with change and to become problem solvers may become the most essential education that colleges can provide. Presently, higher education has focused the majority of attention on the acquisition of data and the use of analytical deductive processes. This, in effect, results in educating only "half the brain" as development of creative, intuitive, holistic processes (the essential ingredients for overcoming limited perspectives) have been badly neglected (Samples, 1976). Recent improvements in understanding the functions of the brain and the nature of consciousness that have integrated with long established notions from the Eastern psychologies have afforded many new possibilities for expanding the use of the mind. Already, researchers have demonstrated that learning processes integrating the rhythm of the physical body with right and left hemisphere operations of the brain have increased the acquisition of language vocabulary from four to ten times the usual rate and have dramatically improved the performance of athletes (Ostrander & Schroeder, 1979). *Student affairs practitioners may well be the central educators of the future, calling upon and developing their own training to facilitate the skills of creative thinking, and the use of affective intuitive components of one's self in developing a more efficient, more effective learner.*

Vignette 4: Moral Leadership

Boards of directors, presidents, and faculty lament a situation in which a "liberal education" is no longer valued or understood by the consumer. Education of the whole person, as citizen, as carrier of the culture, as a searcher for the meaning of life seems abstract to someone looking for economic security. Who will espouse the cause of liberal education and of educating the whole person? Perhaps student affairs divisions, having identified with the theory and application of student development (an approach that considers the whole person), will find themselves the champions and architects of liberal education. Can the age old purpose of higher education be fashioned to take on new meaning for the consumers in a new stage?

It does not seem too grandiose to say that the purpose of student affairs professionals, and perhaps all personnel in higher education, is to assist the student in the process of learning to live in harmony with the world and to proceed toward a higher order of existence that connects the person and the environment. This would require the highest form of moral leadership. How would this leadership be accomplished?

The direct living experience of morality is expressed in the form of ethics. Ethics express the structure for moral living. Ethical information is retrieved and applied as a moral process to actual life situations. This permits a process that continuously makes complexity available to life, but thereby generates new complexity. What is being sought is a level that will ensure the fullest development and evolvement of the individual. Statements of rights tend to maintain a static and defensive structure-oriented approach, but creative involvement in designing new condition requires responsibility (Vickers, 1973). The development of one's world (environment) and of the mind are two aspects of the same process and form a complementary interaction. What is being sought is to stimulate a process that will help students learn how to utilize new information in order to recreate continuously the process for themselves. What is being learned about the behavior of the total central nervous system may help this process grow.

A PERORATION

In this chapter has been emphasized the fact that no simple answers are formulated to challenges the future holds for those who propose to assume leadership in society, and higher education in particular. While no easy answers stand forth, the future depends upon leaders who have the courage to ask the difficult questions and who encourage others to do the same.

The 1980s require transforming leaders, those who can raise the aspiration levels of followers. Administrators who are catalysts for generating creative solutions to society's concerns and who have the fortitude to resist self-serving, status quo solutions are higher education's hope during the projected difficult times of declining enrollments and receding resources. The future need not be gloomy. With leadership that can set into motion the forces that can lead to higher forms of existence, the future can indeed be bright.

REFERENCES

Argyris, C. *Management and organizational development: The path from XA to YB.* New York: McGraw-Hill Book Co., 1971.

Blake, A.R., Mouton, J.S., & Williams, M. S. *The academic administrator grid: A guide to developing effective management teams.* San Francisco: Jossey-Bass, 1981.

Burns, D.M. *Leadership.* New York: Harper and Row, 1978.

Butteriss, M., & Albrecht, K. *New management tools.* Englewood Cliffs, NJ: Prentice-Hall, Inc., 1979.

Drucker, P.F. *The practice of management.* New York: Harper and Row, 1954.

Erikson, E. *Identity, youth and crisis.* New York: W.W. Norton, 1968.

Ferguson, M. *The aquarian conspiracy: Personal and social transformation in the 1980s.* Los Angeles: J.P. Tarcher, Inc., 1980.

Fiedler, F. *A theory of leadership effectiveness.* New York: McGraw-Hill, 1967.

Gordon, W.W.J. *Synectics: The development of creative capacity.* New York: Harper and Brothers, 1961.

Hershey, P., & Blanchard, K. *Management of organizational behavior: Utilizing human resources.* Englewood Cliffs, NJ: Prentice-Hall, 1977.

Herzberg, F. One more time: How do you motivate employees? *Harvard Business Review,* January/February 1968, *46*(1), 53-62.

House, J., & Mitchell, T.R. Path-goal theory of leadership. *Journal of Contemporary Business,* Autumn 1974, *3*(4), 81-98.

Jantsch, E. *The self-organizing universe.* New York: Pergamon, 1980.

Johnson, W. *Muddling toward frugality.* Boulder, CO: Ahambhala Publications, Inc., 1978.

Katz, D., & Kahn, R. *The social psychology of organizations.* New York: Wiley, 1966.

Kohlberg, L. *The philosophy of moral development: Moral stages and the idea of justice.* New York: Harper and Row, 1981.

Kuhn, T. *The structure of scientific revolutions.* Chicago: University of Chicago Press, 1962.

Levine, A. *When dreams and heroes died.* San Francisco: Jossey-Bass Inc., 1980.

Likert, R. *The human organization—Its management and value.* New York: McGraw-Hill, 1967.

Lynch, M.L. *Student affairs in the 1980s: A decade of crisis or opportunity?* Ann Arbor, MI: ERIC Counseling and Personnel Services Clearinghouse, 1981.

Maslow, A.H. *Motivation and personality.* New York: Harper and Row, 1954.

McGregor, D. M. *The human side of enterprise.* New York: McGraw-Hill, 1960.

McGregor, D.M. The human side of enterprise. In W. Eddy et al. (Eds.), *Behavioral science and the manager's role.* Washington, DC: NTL Institute for Applied Behavioral Science, 1969.

Mintzberg, H. The manager's job: Folklore and fact. *Harvard Business Review,* July/August 1975, *53*(4), 49-61.

Moyers, B. Campaign report –8. *Bill Moyers' Journal.* New York: Educational Broadcasting Corporation, October, 1980.

Odiorne, G.S. *MBO II: A system of managerial leadership for the 80s.* Belmont, CA: Fearon Pittman, 1979.

Ostrander, S., & Schroeder, L. *Super-learning.* New York: Dell Publishing Co., 1979.

Peter, L.J., & Hull, R. *The Peter principle.* New York: William Morrow & Co., 1969.

Samples, B. *The metaphoric mind: A celebration of creative consciousness.* Reading, MA: Addison-Wesley, 1976.

Simon, N. The changing economy and its effect on services, professions, and students: A cautionary note. In D. G. Creamer, (Ed.), *Student Development in Higher Education.* Washington, DC: American College Personnel Association, 1980.

Stein, B.A., & Kanter, R.M. Building the parallel organization: Creating mechanisms for permanent quality of work life. *The Journal of Applied Behavioral Science,* 1980, *16*(3), 371-85.

Stoner, J. *Management.* Englewood Cliffs, NJ: Prentice-Hall, 1978.

Tannebaum, R., & Schmidt, W.H. How to choose a leadership pattern. *Harvard Business Review,* May/June 1973, *51*(3), 162-75.

Taylor, F.W. *The principle of scientific management.* New York: Harper and Row, 1911.

Tilley, D.C., Berezet, L.T., Katz, J., & Shanteau, W. *The student affairs dean and the president: Trends in higher education.* Ann Arbor, MI: ERIC Counseling and Personnel Services Clearinghouse, 1979.

Toffler, A. *Future shock.* New York: Bantam Books, 1970.

Toffler A. *The third wave.* New York: Bantam Books, 1980.

Vickers, G. *Making institutions work.* London: Associated Business Programmes, 1973.

Von Bertalanffy, L. *General system theory: Foundations applications.* New York: Braziller, 1968.

Watzlawick, P., Weakland, J. H., & Fisch, P. *Change.* New York: Norton, 1974.

White, R., & Lippitt, R. Leader behavior and member reaction in three social climates. In D. Cartwright & A. Zander (Eds.), *Group dynamics: Research and theory.* New York: Harper and Row, 1968.

Whyte, W.F. *Human relations in the restaurant industry.* New York: McGraw-Hill, 1948.

SUGGESTED READINGS

Blake, A. R., Mouton, J. S., & Williams, M. S. *The academic administrator grid: A guide to developing effective management teams.* San Francisco: Jossey-Bass, 1981.

Burns, D. M. *Leadership.* New York: Harper and Row, 1978.

Hershey, P., & Blanchard, K. *Management of organizational behavior: Utilizing human resources.* Englewood Cliffs, NY: Prentice-Hall, 1977.

Jantsch, E. *The self-organizing universe.* New York: Pergamon, 1980.

Odiorne, G. S. *MBO II: A system of managerial leadership for the 80's.* Belmont, CA: Fearon Pittman, 1979.

Ouchi, W.G. *Theory Z.* New York: Avon, 1981.

PART II
PARAMETERS
OF
PROFESSIONAL
PRACTICE

Robert F. (Bob) Rodgers is Associate Professor of Education and Psychology at The Ohio State University where he teaches and conducts research in the area of college student development theory and practice and serves as Director of the Student Personnel Assistantship Program. Rodgers received his Bachelor of Science degree in systems engineering from Texas Tech University, his M.A. in counseling psychology from The Ohio State University, and his Ph.D. in higher education from The Ohio State University. He came to his faculty position in 1970 after serving as a residence hall director, assistant dean of students, and associate vice-president for student affairs at The Ohio State University. He has been very active in the Council for the Development of Standards for Student Services/Development Programs.

Chapter 5

USING THEORY
IN PRACTICE

Robert F. Rodgers

This chapter examines a general approach to using theory in the practice of student affairs administration. The essential character, general assumptions, and operating principles are presented along with specific examples of theory in practice.

That the use of theory in practice is *good* is assumed in the content of this chapter. Not all student affairs practitioners share this assumption. Essentially, the issue turns upon the questions of whether the practice of student affairs is best served by professionals using applied social and behavioral sciences or craftsmen and amateurs using disciplined intuition and common sense. Is student affairs a professional field or more of a practical and commonsense field of endeavor?

Following are some criteria common to many definitions of a professional field (Larson, 1977):

•A profession bases its practice and interventions on a systematic body of knowledge.

•A profession has authority over the interventions it uses, and standards of minimum competence exist for the services and practices offered.

•A profession has standards for accrediting professional preparation programs and for licensing or certifying personnel, and it has the means to implement both accreditation and certification processes.

•A profession has a regulative code of ethics to control abusive use of knowledge, interventions, or standards.

•A profession has a culture of shared values, norms, and symbols which is learned through a common socialization process.

Arguments in this chapter are as follows:

1. Student affairs can meet criteria for being a field which bases its practice and interventions on a systematic body of knowledge; that is, student affairs practice can and should be based upon applied social and behavioral sciences. Given recent cooperative work among professional associations on standards for accreditation and codes of ethics, all of these criteria except for licensure of individuals are characteristics of student affairs.

2. If content mastery (for example, mastery of knowledge or skills taught in a class, workshop, living context, or other college-related experience), student satisfaction with their experiences, and well-rounded development of personality are desired outcomes of higher education, then the field is better served by professionals who use theory in practice than by nonprofessional craftsmen or amateurs.

3. For the young professional, no substitute exists for having an in-depth knowledge and understanding of specific student development theories and intervention methodologies. To proceed on the basis of common sense or a superficial knowledge of theory or interventions is not adequate.

4. Finally, although young professionals cannot be expected to know all of the theories available in student affairs, they can be expected to have intimate knowledge and understanding of selected theories and to work continuously to broaden their repertoire of competence. Recommendations of useful theories to initiate a professional repertoire will be made later in this chapter.

All four points will be defended through a detailed description of the theory-in-practice approach and a case study. The third point concerning the need for in-depth knowledge and understanding of theories, however, needs further differentiation.

CONTINUUM FOR UNDERSTANDING THEORY

In order to understand the degree of in-depth knowledge of theory needed in order to use theory in practice, examining various degrees of depth and richness with which a construct may be understood is useful. These degrees of understanding can be viewed on a continuum. Four locations can be described and related to using theory in practice:

Location 1

This is an amorphous, almost distinctionless understanding of a construct. For example, a person may have just heard or read the terms "managing emotions" (Chickering, 1969) and may be inclined to wonder, "What is that?" The person may only recognize the name of the construct but not know the definition. This degree of knowledge and understanding is *not* sufficient for using theory in practice.

Location 2

At this location the construct has more meaning. *A person is able to recognize or give a brief description or definition of the construct.* For example, a person is able to indicate that "managing emotions" means a developmental task of young adults between the ages of 17 and 25 in which the control of emotions moves from control by external rigid rules of one's heritage through external control by the rules of the primary peer group to internal flexible control. This degree of knowledge and understanding also is *not* sufficient for using theory in practice.

Location 3

A person at Location 3 has achieved a greater degree of knowledge and understanding of the construct than at locations 1 and 2. For example, the person knows that the concept "managing emotions" focuses on the emotions of *sex* and *aggression* in the 17 to 25 age range and that it involves a process variable (see Figure 5.1) that has defined direction.

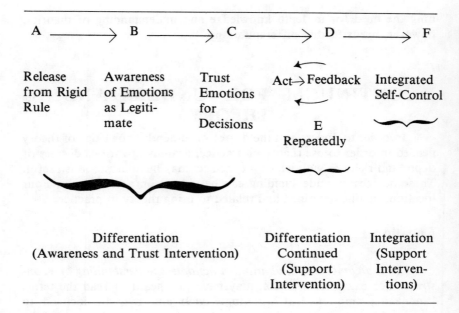

Figure 5.1. Example of defined direction of process variable:
Managing emotions in Location 3

Managing of emotions of sex and aggression moves through the following phases: (A) release of rigid controls over emotions by the external
rules of one's heritage or peer group; (B) achievement of an awareness
and acceptance that these emotions are legitimate and normal; (C) trust
in one's feelings as a basis for action—that is, appropriate action is often
an integration of logic and these emotions; (D) acting on these emotions,
both vicariously and realistically and receiving feedback; (E) acting and
receiving feedback repeatedly; and (F) reflecting on one's experience
with sex and aggression and integrating and internalizing personalized
control.

Phases A, B, and C involve awareness, trust, and differentiation
tasks, while phases D, E, and F involve both differentiation and integration of tasks. Programs which respond to phases A, B, and C should
reflect awareness, trust, and differentiation. Programs responsive to
phases D, E, and F should reflect support as a person lives through new
behaviors and learns their meaning.

Finally, a person at Location 3 knows that the movement previously described proceeds from the external rules of one's primary peer group to internalized, flexible control regardless of peer group norms or rules of heritage. In Location 3 the person's knowledge and understanding of "managing emotions" are no longer amorphous or superficial. The concept has taken on shape, structure, and meaning. This degree of knowledge and understanding of the construct is almost sufficient for using theory in practice.

Location 4

This is the location on the continuum where the degree of understanding and knowledge is sufficient for using theory as a basis for practice. This is the level of knowledge and understanding possessed by professionals in the field. In this case, a professional person not only knows the construct as defined in Location 3, but also knows the intimate and detailed relationships between "managing emotions" and all of the other constructs in the general theory of which it is part. That is, the professional knows the relationships between managing emotions and the other six vectors (establishing competence, autonomy, establishing identity, freeing interpersonal relationships, establishing purpose, and developing integrity, Figure 5.2) of Chickering's theory (1969). These relationships are known in sufficient detail so that a person is able to reconstruct "managing emotions" within the general developmental themes of values and moral development, intimacy, sexuality, and in career and vocational growth. A person at Location 4 can easily relate any one vector to any of the others in diagnosing a problem or in designing an intervention. This person also is familiar with and experienced in using the various means of measuring all the constructs in the theory. The person also is able to discuss advantages and disadvantages of each method of measurement.

In summary, a professional at Location 4 has (1) intimate familiarity with the constructs covered by a theory and the interrelationships among the constructs and subconstructs of the theory; (2) knowledge of how developmental change takes place in terms of the constructs of the theory; and (3) an intimate familiarity with the means of measuring the constructs and the advantages and limitations of each. This is the level of in-depth knowledge and understanding of selected social and behavioral science theories that the professional needs to achieve in order to use theory in practice.

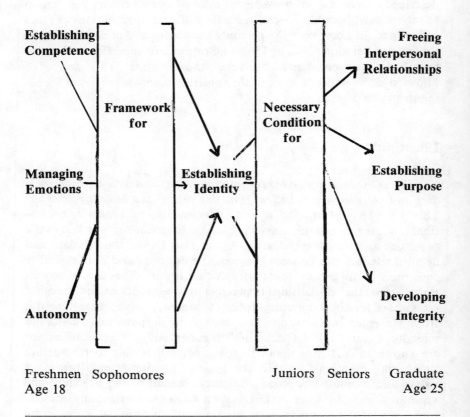

Figure 5.2. Chickering's (1969) seven vectors in chronological, directional, and age-related order.

THEORY-TO-PRACTICE APPROACH

The theory-to-practice approach to student development programs is potentially applicable to a broad range of areas of practice that are often in a professional's position description. The essential character of the approach can be summarized as follows: *formal theories plus procedural process models can lead to more professionalized practice.* The theory-to-practice formula can be written as follows:

Formal Theory + **Procedural or Process Models** ⟹ **Professional Practice**

Formal Theory

The term formal theory in the formula refers both to content and developmental, formal, scientific theories and the research that has been derived from the theories. "Content" refers to theories about and associated research on a given problem or area of practice. For example, if one were working on a career development project, then career development theories and research would be content. If one were working on conflict resolution problems among roommates in a residence hall, then theories of conflict resolution would be the content.

"Developmental" refers to theories and associated research applicable to the specific levels or stages of the population. Several general reviews of development theory and research have been published recently (Drum, 1980; Rodgers, 1980).

Professionals should become aware (Locations 2 and 3) of the wide array of theories listed in Table 5.1 and, based on Rodgers' (1980) classification of theories, develop in-depth knowledge and understanding (Location 4) of selected theories.

Table 5.1

Selected Developmental and Related Theories

Psychosocial	Cognitive Developmental	Person-Environmental Interaction
White (1966)	Harvey, Hunt, & Schroeder	Levin (1936)
Sanford (1967)	(1961)	Clark & Trow (1960)
*Erikson (1968)	Piaget (1965)	Pace (1966)
*Heath (1968)	*Perry (1970)	Newcomb (1967)
*Chickering (1969)	*Kohlberg (1971)	Pervin (1967)
Keniston (1970)	Loevinger (1976)	Astin (1968)
Havighurst (1972)	Kegan (1977)	Barker (1968)
Sheehy (1974)	Selman (1980)	Stern (1970)
Neugarten (1975)	Fowler (1981)	Chickering (1972)
Vaillant (1977)	Kitchener & King (In Press)	*Holland (1973)
Gould (1978)		*Moos (1979)
Levinson (1978)		

* Recommended for initial in-depth knowledge and understanding.

Psychosocial Theory. Psychosocial theories and research are especially useful in helping student affairs professionals understand developmental tasks of people throughout the life cycle. This knowledge and understanding can provide the basis for many applied responses. For example, if given an assessment of a population, appropriate developmental tasks can be identified; these, in turn, become content and criteria for mapping and evaluating the appropriateness of past programs and services and for planning appropriate future programs, services, and environmental designs. Designing interventions and evaluating outcomes, uses of psychosocial theory in mapping, and evaluating past programming are presented in the next few pages. Then later in the chapter a case study is presented to illustrate their uses. In this section Chickering's (1969) theory is used to map and evaluate past programming in a residence hall.

Figure 5.2 presents Chickering's vectors in chronological, directional, and age-related order. Briefly, many freshmen and sophomores are developmentally involved with resolving the first four vectors, while many juniors, seniors, and graduate students are involved with the last three. Within a given vector, the beginning content of the vector often can be differentiated from advanced levels. A residence hall director, therefore, can use Chickering's vectors as a map for locating the programs offered during a previous year and determining which vectors were emphasized and to what degree they were addressed. Then, given an assessment of the population, a director could evaluate the appropriateness of both the content and the variety of programs offered. A residence hall director at The Ohio State University, for example, mapped his previous year's programs. Because the residence hall housed predominately 18 to 19 year old freshmen, programs that seemed to be appropriate developmentally were the programs categorized under Developing Competence (77 percent of the total). The incongruent programming was the 23 percent that dealt with the developmental tasks of Freeing Interpersonal Relationships, Developing Purpose, and Developing Integrity. These programs were probably developmentally inappropriate for many in this freshman population.

Before the hall director congratulated himself, however, he analyzed his omissions and the scope and variety of the 77 percent of the programming that seemed to be appropriate developmentally. Omissions were obvious. No deliberate efforts had been made to offer programming consistent with the developmental vectors of Managing Emotions, Developing Autonomy, or Establishing Identity. Only two percent of the programs dealt with intellectual competence. The analysis of the scope and variety of the programming was also revealing. The variety and scope of athletic and other physical-manual programming were excellent. In the area of social-interpersonal competence, programming was limited in scope. Even though a large number of social programs were sponsored (30 percent), opportunities to learn and use a variety of social-interpersonal competencies were not provided. Basically, the social programming required students to use the same social skills over and over again. The director summarized the situation himself when he exclaimed, "We didn't expand the social competence of our students! Instead of offering programs that taught different social competencies, our social calendar called for one set of skills repeated 10 or 20 times."

Cognitive Developmental Theory. The second family of developmental theories that is useful in student affairs practice is cognitive developmental theories. These theories are useful in planning how student affairs practitioners should package programs and services. That is, persons who reason or make meaning in different cognitive developmental stages apparently learn and develop best in different kinds of environments. Information on how cognitive-structural developmental change takes place provides cues and criteria for designing appropriate environments for different students. In the Perry (1970) scheme of intellectual and ethical development, for example, students reasoning in positions of dualism apparently learn best, are more satisfied, and develop their intellectual structures more quickly if their environments provide encounters with moderate degrees of diversity (in terms of content) through highly structured and experiential learning processes. These encounters need to be followed by analytic processing with an emphasis on differentiation. Finally, all of these processes need to take place in a warm, personal atmosphere (Widick, Knefelkamp, & Parker, 1975). Students making meaning in the positions of relativism may learn best, however, if their environments provide encounters with many points of view on a subject through abstract learning processes. Having extensive degrees of freedom to influence both the content to be learned and the process to be used is helpful to students. Similar to dualistically reasoning students, an environment that is warm and personal is also helpful (Widick et al., 1975).

Person-environment Interaction Theory. The third family of theories relevant to the theory-in-practice approach is person-environment interaction theories (see Table 5.1). These theories require student affairs staff to focus on three questions:

•Who are the students and what are relevant ways to conceptualize their characteristics?

•What is the nature of the environment or social setting in which the students live or learn, and what are the relevant ways to conceptualize the environment?

•How do the student and the environment interact? Congruence? Incongruence? To what extent?

These questions can be applied to a variety of person-environment settings in order to better understand the situation and intervene to change the environment, the student, or both (Banning & McKinley, 1980; Paul, 1980). In the in-depth case study that follows these questions and person-environment models provide a basic framework for examining the problem of roommate conflicts in a residence hall and for designing an effective conflict resolution program.

Finally, in explicating the role of formal theories in the theory-to-practice equation, concepts of challenge and response (Rodgers, 1980; Sanford, 1967) need to be examined.

Concepts of challenge and response are helpful in understanding developmental change across many developmental and person-environment theories. They are useful concepts for diagnosing person-environmental interactions and designing interventions.

Briefly, a person can be thought of as having a range of dissonance that is developmentally appropriate. This is illustrated in Figure 5.3.

Location and range of developmental dissonance of a person are functions of the challenge-support ratio of the person-environment interaction in a given setting (see Figure 5.3). Three cases will illustrate this point.

The person-environment interaction may be characterized as balanced. The degree of challenge and support falls within the range of developmental dissonance of a person. Typically some tension and anxiety exist, therefore, the person is challenged to develop new skills, insights, differentiations, ways of making meaning, and is supported to deal with difficulties and anxieties created by these experiences. This is a developmental person-environment interaction.

This interaction may be characterized as too challenging. The degree of challenge in the environment compared to support for the person is over-balanced in favor of challenge. As a result, the person's range of

Developmental Dissonance

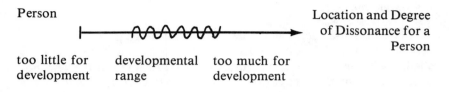

Person

too little for developmental too much for
development range development

Location and Degree
of Dissonance for a
Person

Balanced Person-Environment Interaction

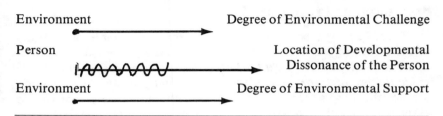

Environment — Degree of Environmental Challenge

Person — Location of Developmental Dissonance of the Person

Environment — Degree of Environmental Support

Too Challenging Person-Environment Interaction

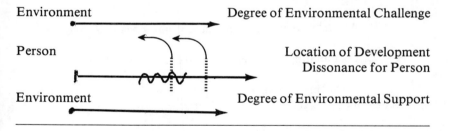

Environment — Degree of Environmental Challenge

Person — Location of Development Dissonance for Person

Environment — Degree of Environmental Support

Too Supportive Person Environmental Interaction

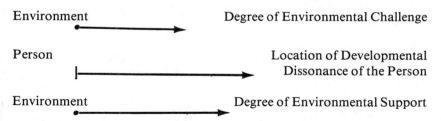

Environment — Degree of Environmental Challenge

Person — Location of Developmental Dissonance of the Person

Environment — Degree of Environmental Support

Figure 5.3. Schematic of person-environment interaction: Degree of challenge and support.

developmental dissonance shrinks and shifts downward. Typically the person polarizes, hardens his/her position, tries to flee the environment, and experiences high tension and anxiety. This challenge-support ratio is not developmental.

The person-environment interaction may be characterized as too supportive. The degree of support in the environment compared to challenge is over-balanced in favor of support. As a result, the demands of the environment never challenge the person to develop. Typically the person may be complacent or even bored and may develop elitist attitudes. This challenge-support ratio is not developmental either.

Procedural or Process Models

Procedural or process models are the second element in the formula of the theory-to-practice approach. *These terms refer to alternative sets of steps developed by student affairs professionals, that can be used to guide the use of theory in student development practice.* These models are not theories; rather, they are rules of thumb or steps that can be taken when theory is to be used in practice. For example, the Council of Student Personnel Associations (COSPA) (Cooper, 1971) process model outlined 10 steps that should be taken when designing and implementing student development programs.

1. Assessing behaviors the student has already developed.

2. Formulating the student's behavioral objectives.

3. Selecting college programs that build on existing behaviors to accomplish the student's objectives.

4. Fostering student growth within the context of his own cultural background and encouraging his appreciation of the cultural backgrounds of the educational institution and of other students.

5. Developing physical environments, human groups, institutional organizations, and financial resources most conducive to the student's growth.

6. Integrating concurrent experiences outside the institution with the student's educational program as an aid in achieving the student's objectives.

7. Modifying existing behaviors that block the further growth of the student.

8. Giving visibility to a value system that enables the student to judge the worth of behavior patterns.

9. Recording the student's progress as a means of facilitating his growth.

10. Identifying appropriate environments for continued development before and after the student leaves his present educational setting. (pp. 2-3)

These steps do not provide a definition of development, information on how development can be assessed, how developmental change takes place, or criteria for determining whether environments are developmentally appropriate. Only theories can provide this information. Models, however, can provide student affairs professionals with a structure and a set of steps for defining "what one should do" and "the order in which one should do it" as student developmental programs are created.

Table 5.2 contains references for procedural and process models. Professionals are encouraged to learn all of these models because different models may be useful in different programmatic or environmental settings.

The symbol $\Longrightarrow$ represents the phrase "can lead to" in the theory-to-practice formula. This is an important phrase because many people in student affairs are seeking fool-proof recipes for student development programs. Such recipes do not exist. This symbol $\Longrightarrow$ is deliberately used because the combination of formal theories with process models does not automatically result in a positive solution. The design cues and criteria provided by content and developmental theories may be more or less specific, and often a creative interpretation is required in order to translate the cues and criteria of the theory into dimensions of a given setting. In addition, multiple interventions can be generated for the same problem and setting using the same theories and design criteria. One *correct* intervention for each student development problem does not exist; multiple solutions, many of which may be equally valid in principle and similar in empirical outcome, do exist.

Table 5.2

Currently Available Procedural and Process Models and Source Theorists

Name of Model	Source Theorists
Model for Behavioral Change	Blocker & Shaeffer (1971)
COSPA-I Model	Cooper (1971)
Deliberate Psychological Education	Mosher & Sprinthall (1971)
Model for Creating a Democratic Society	Crookston (1974)
BPE Analysis	Hunt Sullivan (1974)
Deliberate Psychological Instruction	Widick, Knefelkamp & Parker (1975)
Ecosystems Model	Aulepp & Delworth (1976)
Eco-mapping Model	Huebner & Corazzini (1976)
THE Student Development Model	Miller & Prince (1976)
Developmental Transcripts	Brown & Citrin (1977)
Multiple Perspective Model	Paul & Huebner (1978)
Seven-Dimensional Model	Drum (1980)
Conceptual Model of Intervention Strategies	Morrill & Hurst (1980)
Grounded Formal Theory Model	Rodgers & Widick (1980)

Professional Practice

Finally, the phrase "professional practice" in the formula refers to the intervention or student development program actually selected for implementation from an array of possible programs. The term "professional" is used because the theory-to-practice approach is logically consistent with criteria for defining professional activity, and the term serves as a reminder that no substitute for an in-depth knowledge and understanding of theories, process models, and interventions exists if student affairs staff members are to practice professionally.

A CASE STUDY

This case study concerns roommate conflicts in a university residence hall and how a developmental response was created that achieved effective conflict resolution, student satisfaction, and enhanced development of the students involved. The Grounded Formal Theory (Rodgers & Widick, 1980) process model was used, and through its phases the person-environment interaction approach was selected as a basic framework for understanding and defining the problem. Conflict resolution theories also were used in defining the problem and planning an intervention.

Phases in the Grounded Formal Theory (GFT) model are

Phase I	Focus on a problem, a context, and a population
Phase II	Select useful and useable formal theories to enlighten or define the problem in principle
Phase III	Ground the formal theories in the context with the population(s)
Phase IV	Formulate goals and objectives
Phase V	Design interventions or programs
Phase VI	Evaluate the intervention/program

Problem Area, Context, and Population

Phase I in the GFT model directs staff to develop a commonsense description of the problem, context or setting, and population under consideration. Purposes of this phase are to provide a data base for selecting relevant content and developmental theories for use in the process and to begin to define and understand the problem and the realities in which it operates.

The Problem. *Roommate conflict is a common problem faced by almost every professional who works in a residence hall. Like the common cold, this problem has not received the attention it deserves. A systematic application of the GFT approach to roommate conflict has been developed.*

The Population. *A residence hall staff at The Ohio State University identified roommates who were having difficulty. Thirty-two pairs (16 female pairs and 16 male pairs) or 64 persons were randomly selected from the total pool of subjects and agreed to participate in Phases I and III of the GFT process. The sample was composed of 70 percent freshmen and 30 percent sophomores; their ages ranged from 18 to 20. The mode was 18. The group was 10 percent Black and 90 percent white. The group was culturally diversified, with 50 percent coming from metropolitan centers (15 percent from inner cities and 35 percent from suburbs), 20 percent from rural homes, and 30 percent from moderate to small towns. Five percent came from families earning more than $50,000 per year, 25 percent between $30,000 and $49,000; 50 percent between $20,000 and $29,000; and 20 percent less than $19,000.*

The second population relevant to this problem was the Resident Advisors (RA) who served as floor staff members. At Ohio State, these staff members are undergraduate juniors and seniors, ranging in age from 20 to 23. In this case, 5 percent were Black and 95 percent were white. The group included 60 percent juniors and 40 percent seniors. The modal age was 21. Sixty percent were from large metropolitan centers (5 percent from the inner cities and 55 percent from suburbs), 35 percent from moderate to small towns, and 5 percent from rural areas.

The Setting. *All the students lived either in double rooms (70 percent) or triple rooms (30 percent). The RA-student ratio was 1 to 40. The community unit was a floor with rooms on both sides of the hall. The halls involved were coed with men on one side of the hall and women on* *the other. The general population of these halls was 50 percent freshmen, 30 percent sophomores, and 20 percent juniors and seniors.*

Select Theories

Phase II focuses on defining and understanding the problem in terms of content and developmental theory. The task is to select relevant content and developmental theories and to apply them in principle to the problem, setting, and population.

In the residence hall example, the staff examined the work of Deutsch (1969), Eiseman (1977), Thomas (1976), Jones and Banet (1976), Pfeiffer and Jones (1981), Porter (1981), Sherwood and Glidewell (1973), and Kurtz and Jones (1973). Finding criteria for discriminating among these content theories was difficult without adding the insights of developmental theory. In this case, Perry (1970) (cognitive development) and Chickering (1969) (psychosocial) were used to analyze the situation and to derive criteria for evaluating the models of conflict resolution.

In terms of Perry's (1970) scheme, if the students involved in roommate conflicts reason primarily in dualistic ways, then the method or processes used in conflict resolution would need to be characterized by the following: (1) high degrees of structure, (2) limited degrees of freedom to change the purpose(s) or process(es) used, (3) an agenda controlled and facilitated by an authority figure or by the structure, (4) encounter with the other person's point of view followed by structured processing that focuses on awareness and differentiation, and (5) an atmosphere as warm and personal as can be created under the circumstances (Knefelkamp, Widick, & Parker, 1975).

When these criteria are applied to different theories and models of conflict mediation, Walton (1969), Pfeiffer and Jones (1981), and Porter (1981) were found to be more compatible with the criteria in principle than were other models.

If students reason in relativistic ways, however, criteria alter radically. In this case, processes used would need to be characterized by the following: (1) moderate and then low degrees of structure, (2) higher degrees of freedom to alter the process or agenda, (3) encounter with the point of view of the other, (4) generation of alternatives to control or solve the problem areas, (5) a commitment to a program of control or resolution, and (6) a personal environment (Knefelkamp et al., 1975). These criteria were more characteristic of Eiseman's (1977) and Jones and Banet's (1976) models than other theories or models.

In terms of Chickering's theory (1969), if students are dealing with the first four vectors, then they may not have developed the social skills necessary for unaided interpersonal negotiation, and may not be emotionally autonomous enough to handle interpersonal conflict resolution on their own. In addition, emotions of anger and aggression could be aroused, and the student might still be managing emotions through external rules of heritage or peer group. If so, winning the conflict in order to save face, rather than negotiating in order to solve a problem, may be more important from the student's perspective. If an appropriate environment for conflict resolution can be designed and used, conflicts can become the medium for helping students learn these new skills and perhaps resolve the tasks of these first three vectors.

In contrast, if students are dealing with the last four vectors, then they probably already have developed interpersonal skills, emotional autonomy, and sense of self to handle interpersonal conflict without the aid of resident advisors.

Combining analyses of the problem from points of view of both Perry (1970) and Chickering (1969) and applying their theories to the three questions of person-environment interaction, the following can be hypothesized in principle: If the students are primarily dualistic (Perry) and working on the first four vectors (Chickering), then the person-environment interaction would be congruent. Current resolution practice of RAs and students are consistent with the Perry and Chickering criteria for defining a developmental environment if students are dualists and are involved in developing competence, managing emotions, and developing autonomy. The interaction would be partially to totally incongruent if current RA and student behaviors vary more or less from the criteria.

If, on the other hand, students are primarily relativistic and operating on the last three vectors, then the person-environment interaction would be congruent if current practice of RAs and behaviors of students are consistent with Perry and Chickering criteria for relativists and persons involved with freeing interpersonal relationships and developing purpose and integrity. The interaction would be partially to totally incongruent if practices and behaviors vary much from the criteria.

Given these two hypotheses, in order to determine which applies in this case, RA practices and student behavior need to be assessed. Perry and Chickering levels of both groups also need to be determined. Actual practices and behaviors of both RAs and students classified in terms of both Perry and Chickering criteria would be a developmental assessment of the conflict resolution environment. Similarly, personal development levels of the RA and the student would be an assessment of persons in the environment. The assessment of the persons would determine which of the two hypotheses applies to the setting, either dualistic and vectors one through four or relativistic and vectors five through seven. The degree of congruence or incongruence between the persons and the environment is determined by comparing personal development levels of students with assessed characteristics (in terms of Perry and Chickering) of the actual conflict resolution environment.

Ground the Formal Theories in the Context

Phase III of GFT Model generates a data base for selecting an interpretation of the problem in terms of the hypotheses developed in Phase II. Both RAs and students involved in conflicts were assessed on the Perry scheme (1970) and on Chickering vectors (1969), and they were interviewed concerning their real behaviors in roommate conflicts and also how they thought they should behave in these situations.

Student Data. Data provided by students on how they behaved in roommate conflicts are outlined in Table 5.3. Most students do nothing, and the situation either stabilizes at a given level of conflict or gets worse. Some of the students appealed to their RAs to solve problems or applied for room or hall changes. The RAs usually refused to get involved until students had tried to resolve their conflicts on their own. Students reported that they usually did nothing after being told to try to resolve their conflicts on their own. Hence, the RA usually did not see the students again and may have assumed that conflicts were resolved when they were not. A few students tried to confront roommates and to solve conflict problems. Most behaviors described would be called "win-lose" rather than "win-win" (Wiley, 1973), and the situation in their rooms usually got worse rather than better. For a few, conflicts were apparently resolved.

The students lacked empathy and assertiveness. They described a defensive behavior where "I try aggressively to prove that I'm right and you are wrong."

Table 5.3

Students Data: Actual Behavior and Outcome
in Roommate Conflict Situations

Actual Behavior in Conflict Situations	Frequency of Behavior	Outcome
1. I avoid the conflict and do nothing.	usually	Things get worse or stay at the same level of conflict.
2. I appeal to my RA to solve the problem. It's his/her job, isn't it?	sometimes	RA usually refuses and then tells the student to try to settle the conflict on his/her own first. If the student tries and it does not work, then the student is told to see the RA. After hearing this from the RA, students usually do nothing.
3. I confront my roommate and we try to work out our conflicts.	rarely	A few students try to resolve their conflicts on their own. They report behaviors that would be called WIN-LOSE, and the situation tends to get worse.

All of the students were assessed as reasoning in positions of *dualism* on the Perry scheme (1970). On Chickering vectors (1969), 90 percent were still coping with vectors one through four. They were not yet autonomous, and they worried about peer group impressions of themselves. They could not manage aggressive emotions autonomously; they were still developing interpersonal skills of empathy, assertiveness, and negotiation.

Resident Advisor Data. The RAs espoused a philosophy that room-mates should not avoid their conflicts. The best method of resolution was to have students deal with their conflicts themselves. Preferably the RA will not become involved until students have tried to settle their own conflicts.

The RA's behavior was sometimes inconsistent with his/her espoused ideal as shown in Table 5.4. In 60 percent of the cases, the behavior matched the espoused ideal; however, in 40 percent of the conflict situations, the RA took charge and told students what to do to solve their problems. In the former case, the RAs felt satisfied and thought they had taken the proper and expected action. In the latter case, they felt guilty for taking charge and violating the system's expected behavior for RAs in roommate conflicts; however, they also felt powerful because they had influence over the people in the situation.

Table 5.4

Resident Advisor Data: Actual Behavior and
Self-evaluation in Conflict Situations

Self Report Action Taken	Frequency	Feelings and Evaluation
1. I make them deal with each other first.	60%	*Satisfied* that I did what is best, and this is what I was taught to do.
2. I step in, listen to them separately, and then tell the students what to do, and we solve the problem.	40%	*Guilty* for taking responsibility for the situation, and powerful because I did something important and had influence in the situation.

On the Perry (1970) scheme, RAs were more advanced in intellectual and ethical development than students involved in roommate conflicts, with 30 percent being dualistic, 65 percent multiplistic and 5 percent relativistic.

In terms of Chickering's vectors (1969), 60 percent of the RAs were assessed as being involved in resolving the last three vectors, while 40 percent were still involved with the first four.

If student data and environmental data are compared, the person-environment interaction in this setting of roommate conflict resolution is basically incongruent. Students reason in dualistic ways and are resolving tasks of vectors one through four. The environment for resolving roommate conflicts, on the other hand, is basically relativistic, and, hence, such an environment assumes that students already have achieved skills, competence, and attitudes of vectors one through four. That is, the RAs ask students to try to solve their problems themselves. This would require relativistic reasoning and competencies of vectors one through four in order to have a reasonable probability of success. In fact, students who tried to resolve their conflicts without help usually failed, and often they perceived their situations as getting worse. The "successes" seemed to be the occasions where the RAs took charge and told students what to do. This would be consistent with students' levels according to Perry and Chickering but would not offer an opportunity for development as well. What is needed is a procedure for conflict resolution having a reasonable probability for successfully resolving conflicts that would not rob students of the opportunity to advance their cognitive and psychosocial development.

These last two assertions require a more detailed comparative analysis of the current and apparently "successful" method (RA tells them what to do) of conflict resolution and the desired environment as defined by criteria for dualists and vectors one through four.

Design criteria for dualists once again are as follows: high degrees of structure, low degrees of freedom to restructure the processes and content involved, encounters with moderate diversity through experiential learning activities if possible, analytical processing of the encounter with an emphasis on empathetic awareness and differentiation, and a personal atmosphere. In terms of challenge and support, the conditions for challenge are encounters with diversity followed by analytic processing and experiential learning activities. High degrees of structure, limited degrees of freedom, and personal atmosphere are conditions of support.

In the situations in which RAs took charge and told students what to do to resolve their conflicts, the RA structured the situation, and the students could not alter the process or content of the situation. Because of the rapport and respect among students and RAs, a trusting, personal atmosphere existed in these sessions. On the other hand, this method did not involve encounters with another person's point of view or the processing of such an encounter. No opportunity to experience the other person's version of the problems *per se* existed.

In Chickering's (1969) terms, when the RA takes charge, students do not have the opportunity to experience and to learn assertion, negotiation, control of aggression, and emotional and instrumental autonomy.

Hence, a highly supportive environment is created for students who reason in dualistic ways when the RA solves the roommate conflict, but it does not contain the challenge necessary to help foster development. The resolution may be effective, but it probably is not developmental. Further, telling students to solve their own conflicts is too challenging in that students encounter a high degree of diversity but without the support they need. That is, the environment of "doing it on your own" is not highly structured, does not limit freedom to alter the agenda or processes used, and does not use an outside authority who keeps emotions within acceptable limits and who controls the atmosphere. For the few who tried this last method, it usually was not effective or satisfying. It may be the worst of all environments for students.

The desired environment would contain elements of both support and challenge. It would be structured, limit freedom, involve encounter with diversity through experiential activities, process the encounter, and be personal. It would model and teach assertion and negotiation, be an experience with controlling anger and aggression, and help to develop emotional and instrumental autonomy.

Formulate Goals and Objectives for an Intervention

Phase IV focuses on setting both content and developmental goals and objectives using data generated in the previous Phase.

Goals in the case study were as follows: (1) to control or resolve roommate conflicts, (2) to achieve student satisfaction with the processes used in the conflict management process, and (3) to foster psychosocial and cognitive structural development through the conflict management process.

Content objectives were to control or resolve 50 percent of the roommate conflicts and to have students report satisfaction with the process used 70 percent of the time.

Developmental objectives were as follows: (1) to design a conflict management process to meet both challenge and support criteria for defining a developmental environment for dualists, (2) to help to teach negotiation skills in the process, (3) to help to learn to control emotions of anger and aggression, and (4) to help to develop emotional and instrumental autonomy.

Design Intervention

In order to design an intervention, the student affairs staff used the goals and objectives (Phase IV) and information about the general political and organizational realities in which these specific residence halls operated (Phase I of GFT Model) and they also sought to identify interventions (Phase II) characteristics of which would be consistent with the developmental levels of students (Phase III).

The staff began by brainstorming the following questions: What should be done with whom? When? And why? As indicated, many interventions are logically consistent with the goals, objectives, and realities of a setting. Quality and variety of interventions generated depend upon the repertoire of professional interventions known to a staff and the quality of their creativity. In the case study, a partial list of interventions generated in the brainstorm session is listed in Table 5.5. Three interventions ultimately were used by the staff; however, only one program will be described. This program focused on teaching RAs to use Walton's (1969) model of third party mediation in dealing with roommate conflicts, and, through use of Walton's model, to achieve goals and objectives outlined in Phase IV.

Walton's (1969) model of third party conflict mediation was selected because its characteristics are consistent with dualistic challenge and support criteria for environmental design and skills taught in the process are consistent with those needed to resolve the tasks of vectors one through four. Organizational realities also provided opportunities to teach this

Table 5.5

Brainstorm on Possible Interventions in Roommate Conflict Situations

Who	When	What	Why
all students on floor	hall orientation	roommate conflict lecturettes on data from processes 1 through 4 and then an appeal to use RA if needed to mediate conflicts. Explain procedures RA will use.	preventative maintenance create expectation of using the RA
all students on floor	after first big conflict	human relations lab on lifestyle differences and conflict resolution skills	first big conflict provides motivation and readiness for internalizing awareness and skills learned in such a lab
all students on floor	monthly floor meetings	reinforce the skills, norms, and expectations of human relations lab mentioned above	behavior change takes repeated experience and reinforcement
students in conflict	as conflicts occur	use Walton's model of third party conflict mediation	Walton's model is consistent with the goals and objectives; is teachable to RAs; is useable by most RAs
RAs	Spring course or Fall orientation	conflict resoltuion workshop to teach Walton's model	to teach RAs to use Walton's model and explain *why* changing from "have them do it" to Walton's third party mediation
RAs	Spring course	teach RAs to design and facilitate human relations workshops	so RAs can do workshops for entire floor
RAs	in-service training	assertion workshop	so RAs can develop assertion skills and have a basis for calling on senior staff to do a similar workshop for the floor, if needed

model to RAs. All new RAs take a course to prepare them for their positions during the spring before their service in the fall, and all RAs participate in two weeks of training immediately before service in the fall. Walton's model and associated skills could be taught on either or both occasions. Hence, Walton's model logically seemed to be consistent with all goals: that is, control or resolution of roommate conflicts, a higher level of student satisfaction than the level expressed by the students who were assessed in Phase III, opportunities to learn interpersonal negotiation skills, control of emotions of anger and aggression, emotional and instrumental autonomy, and an environment appropriate for dualists.

Two days during the fall orientation were used in order to teach RAs the Walton model. Objectives of the workshop were (1) to learn Walton's model and skills needed to use it, (2) to learn Chickering's vectors well enough to understand *why* most students with roommate problems lack social skills, autonomy, and ability to control emotions needed to resolve these conflicts on their own, (3) to learn Perry's scheme and environmental design criteria well enough to understand *why* a third party mediator and a method like Walton's may be needed when helping students who reason primarily in dualistic ways, (4) to design the training consistent with the dualistic and multiplistic developmental levels of the majority of the RAs, and (5) to help those RAs dealing with the first four vectors to accomplish developmental tasks of these vectors.

The Rodgers, Bryer, and Hollingsworth (1976) teaching-learning model was used to teach the Walton model.

1. Provide Cognitive Understanding: (a) define the model or skill including both what it is and what it is not, and (b) relate the model and the needs of the persons who are in conflict and the mediator's role.

2. Model the Process and Skills: (a) model appropriate use of the model and skills needed to use it, and (b) model inappropriate uses of the model and skills.

3. Practice Using the Model and Skills: (a) practice using the model and skills in a structured skill-building setting and (b) receive positive and corrective feedback from observers.

4. Evaluate Level of Achievement using Behavioral Criteria and Give Feedback on Level of Achievement.

This teaching-learning model is structured and experiential, introduces moderate to high degrees of complexity, and processes interactions through feedback and evaluation. Hence, the method is consistent with the dualistic and muliplistic levels of most of the RAs. In addition, learning Walton's model and skills needed to use it would, in itself, help to develop interpersonal competence and autonomy for RAs who have not yet resolved these vectors. The design of the workshop is outlined in Table 5.6.

Evaluate Outcomes

In Phase VI instructions are given to young professionals to evaluate the use of the intervention designed in Phase V.

In this case a pilot study would involve teaching a random sample of RAs to use the Walton model and then monitoring the RA's use, modifications, or failure to use the model. These steps would be followed by obtaining data on resolution outcomes, students' levels of satisfaction with the process, and post-test Perry and Chickering levels. These data would then be compared to the data obtained in the grounding (Phase III) in order to determine if intended objectives have been achieved.

In a pilot evaluation involving live modeling rather than videotapes, the Walton trained RAs used the Walton method 80 percent of the time during the Fall Quarter. Twenty percent of their behavior in roommate conflicts was not consistent with Walton's model. Control or resolution of conflicts was achieved in 67 percent of the cases using Walton's method compared to 25 percent for a comparison group using regular methods. Similarly, student satisfaction with the Walton process was significantly higher than for regular practices. No significant differences were found in Perry levels between the two groups of students at the pre or post-test. Differences in favor of the Walton group occurred in both negotiation and assertion.

SUMMARY

As illustrated in the case study the theory-to-practice approach to student development has practical applicability. The approach emphasizes the use of procedural or process models as the guiding structures for using theory in practice. The approach also uses formal social and

Table 5.6
Design of Resident Advisor Workshop on
Roommate Conflict Resolution

Objectives	Activities
1. to model three approaches to roommate conflict resolution to inform RA's on *why* a new conflict resolution approach is being adopted	1-1 Introduce videotapes of three approaches and outcomes. (5 min) Materials: psychodrama videotapes of the three models and results developed originally by residence hall staff using staff as actors 1-2 Approach #1 (a) "do it yourself first" with result that students do nothing or they try and WIN-LOSE make matters worse; (b) discuss and analyze; (c) present data from Phases I to III of the GFT applicable to this approach (10 min) 1-3 Approach #2 (a) "do it for them" with result of control or resolution but no development; (b) discuss and analyze; (c) present data from Phases I to III of GFT applicable to this approach (30 min) 1-4 Approach #3 (a) "Walton's method" with result of control or resolution and some progress on developmental goals; (b) discuss and analyze; (c) compare Walton's model and other two approaches (45 min)
2. Break	2-1 Break and refreshments (20 min)
3. to learn Chickering's vectors with concentration on one through four	3-1 Lecturette on Chickering's vectors, especially one through four and related behaviors in videotapes to Chickering's vectors. [transparencies, screen, overhead projector, and handouts] (30 min)
4. Eat and Free Time	4-1 Lunch (2 hours)
5. to learn the basics of Perry's scheme and environmental design criteria for dualists	5-1 Lecturette on Perry's stages and design criteria and relate criteria to behaviors in videotapes [transparencies, screen, overhead projector, and handouts] (50 min)
6. to learn elements of Walton's model and to identify skills required to use it	6-1 Lecturette to describe the model, what it is and is not, skills needed to use it [transparencies, screen, overhead projector, and handouts] (30 min)

Table 5.6: Continued

7. to model the process in appropriate and then in "common errors" ways	7-1 Re-play videotape of Walton's model or another videotape of a second person using Walton's model (45 min.) 7-2 Play videotape of an RA making common errors in using Walton's model 7-3 Analyze, discuss and relate to Chickering's and Perry's criteria [videotape player, screen] (20 min)
8. Break	8-1 Break (15 min)
9. to practice using Walton's model and skills it requires	9-1 Role play and feedback (three RAs and one senior staff person work together—there are three role play situations involving an RA and two roommates—each RA serves once as the RA. The other RAs play the students. The senior staff person acts as coach to the RAs preparing to be the RA in the role play and gives feedback on positive and corrective behaviors 9-2 After one role play, dismiss for the day. [role play materials, semi-private space] (1 hr role play)
10. Warm-up and introduction	10-1 Some ice breaker and brief lecturette on previous day's and current day's activities (15 min)
11. to practice using Walton's model and skills continued	11-1 Same three RAs and 1 senior staff member do the two remaining role plays as described in 9 above. [role play materials, semi-private space] (2 hr.)
12. Eat and Free Time	12-1 Lunch and break (1½ hr)
13. to practice and to evaluate the level of competence in using Walton's model	13-1 Rotate and use a different set of three RAs with a different senior staff member. Do three more role plays. Each RA serves as RA in a role play once. Senior staff evaluate performances and gives positive and corrective feedback. [role play materials, semiprivate space] (3 hr)
14. to reinforce use of the model in actual practice	14-1 Closing assembly and lecturette by director of training to reinforce the purpose of the workshop (15 min.)

behavioral science theories, research on theories and various means of measuring theories in order to give substance to steps in the process models. Initially, formal theories provide a basis for defining and understanding the problem in principle. When the theory is made actual with real people involved, a data base is generated that provides a concrete basis for defining and understanding the problem in the real setting, and provides a basis for defining appropriate content and developmental goals and objectives. Finally, theories also provide criteria for designing developmentally appropriate interventions and for defining and measuring outcomes.

Both *process models* and *formal theories* are needed in order to use theory in practice. Neither can do the job without the other.

Finally, this approach requires professionals to have an in-depth (Location 4) understanding and knowledge of (1) process models, (2) selected content and developmental theories, and (3) means for measuring persons and environments relative to the theories. It requires professional competence.

REFERENCES

Astin, A. W. *The college environment.* Washington, DC: American Council on Education, 1968.

Aulepp, L., & Delworth, U. *Training manual for an ecosystem model: Assessing and designing campus environments.* Boulder, CO: Western Interstate Commission for Higher Education, 1976.

Banning, J. H., & McKinley, D. L. Conceptions of the campus environment. In W. H. Morrill & J. C. Hurst (Eds.), *Dimensions of intervention for student development.* New York: John Wiley & Sons, 1980.

Barker, R. G. *Ecological psychology: Concepts and methods for studying the environment of human behavior.* Stanford, CA: Stanford University Press, 1968.

Blocker, D. H., & Shaffer, W. F. Guidance and human developmemt. In D. R. Cook (Ed.), *Guidance for Education in Revolution.* Boston, MA: Allyn & Bacon, 1971.

Brown, R. D., & Citrin, R. S. A student development transcript: Assumptions, uses and formats. *Journal of College Student Personnel,* 1977, *18,* 163-8.

Chickering, A. W. Undergraduate academic experience. *Journal of Educational Psychology,* 1972, *63,* 134-43.

Chickering, A. W. *Education and identity.* San Francisco: Jossey-Bass, 1969.

Clark, B. R. & Trow, M. *Determinants of college student subcultures.* Berkeley: Center for the Study of Higher Education, 1960.

Cooper, A. C. A proposal for professional preparation of the college development educators. Report from the Commission of Professional Development, Council of Student Personnel Associations, 1971.

Crookston, B. Design for an intentional democratic community. In D. A. DeCoster & P. Mabel (Eds.), *Student development and education in college residence halls.* Washington, DC: American College Personnel Association, 1974.

Deutsch, M. Conflicts: Productive and destructive. *Journal of Social Issues,* 1969, *25,* 7-41.

Drum, D. Understanding student development. In W.H. Morrill & J.C. Hurst (Eds.), *Dimensions of intervention for student development.* New York: John Wiley & Sons, 1980.

Eiseman, J. W. A third-party consultation model for resolving recurring conflicts collaboratively. *Journal of Applied Behavioral Science,* 1977, *13,* 303-14.

Erikson, E. *Identity, youth and crisis.* New York: Norton, 1968.

Fowler, J. *Stages of faith.* San Francisco: Harper & Row, 1981.

Gould, R. *Transformations.* New York: Simon and Schuster, 1978.

Harvey, O. J., Hunt, D. E., & Schroeder, H. M. *Conceptual systems and personality organization.* New York: John Wiley & Sons, 1961.

Havighurst, R. J. *Developmental tasks and education* (3rd ed.). New York: McKay, 1972.

Heath, D. H. *Growing up in college: Liberal education and maturity.* San Francisco: Jossey-Bass, 1968.

Holland, J. L. *Making vocational choices: A theory of careers.* Englewood Cliffs, NJ: Prentice Hall, 1973.

Huebner, L. A., & Corazzini, J. G. Ego-mapping: A dynamic model for intentional campus design. (Student Development Staff Papers.) Fort Collins, CO: Colorado State University, 1976.

Hunt, D. E., & Sullivan, E. V. *Between psychology and education.* Hinsdale, IL: Dryden Press, 1974.

Jones, J. E., & Banet, A. G. Dealing with anger. In J. W. Pfeiffer & J. E. Jones (Eds.), *Annual Handbook for Group Facilitators.* La Jolla, CA: University Associates, 1976.

Keagan, R. Ego and truth: Personality and the Piaget tradition. Unpublished doctoral dissertation, Harvard University, 1977.

Keniston, K. Youth: A "new" stage of life. *American Scholar,* 1970, *39,* 631-54.

Kitchener, R. S., & King, P. M. Reflective judgment: Concepts of justification and their relationship to age and education. *Journal of Applied Developmental Psychology,* in press.

Knefelkamp, L., Widick, C., & Parker, C. A. *New directions for student services: Applying new developmental findings* (No. 2). San Francisco: Jossey-Bass, 1975.

Kohlberg, L. From is to ought: How to commit the naturalistic fallacy and get away with it in the study of moral development. In T. Mischel (Ed.), *Cognitive development and epistemology.* New York: Academic Press, 1971.

Kurtz, R. R., & Jones, J. E. Confrontation types, conditions and outcomes. In J. W. Pfeiffer & J. E. Jones (Eds.), *Annual handbook for group facilitators,* La Jolla, CA: University Associates, 1973.

Larson, N. S. *The rise of professionalism: A sociological analysis.* Berkeley, CA: University of California Press, 1977.

Levinson, D. J., Darrow, C. N., Klein, E. S., Levinson, M. H., & McKee, B. *The seasons of a man's life.* New York: Knopf, 1978.

Lewin, K. *Principles of topological psychology.* New York: McGraw-Hill, 1936.

Loevinger, J. *Ego development.* San Francisco: Jossey-Bass, 1976.

Moos, R. H. *Evaluating educational environments: Procedures, measures, findings, and policy implications.* San Francisco: Jossey-Bass, 1979.

Morrill, W. H., & Hurst, J. C. (Eds.). *Dimensions of intervention for student development.* New York: John Wiley & Sons, 1980.

Mosher, R. L., & Sprinthall, N. A. Psychological education: A means to promote personal development during adolescence. *Counseling Psychologist†,* 1971, *2,* 3-82.

Neugarten, B. Adult personality: Toward a psychology of life cycle. In W. C. Sze (Ed.), *The human life cycle.* New York: Jason Aronson, 1975.

Newcomb, T. M., Joenig, K. E., Flacks, R., & Warwick, D. P. *Persistence and change: Bennington College and its students after 25 years.* New York: John Wiley & Sons, 1967.

Pace, C. R., & Baird, L. L. Attainment patterns in the environmental press of college subcultures. In T. M. Newcomb & E. K. Wilson (Eds.), *College peer groups.* Chicago: Aldine, 1966.

Paul, S. C. Understanding student environment interaction. In W. H. Morrill & J. C. Hurst (Eds.), *Dimensions of intervention for student development.* New York: John Wiley & Sons, 1980.

Paul, S. C., & Huebner, L. A. Persons in their contextual systems of consumers in the market place. A paper presented at the annual convention of the American College Personnel Association, Detroit, MI, 1978.

Perry, W., Jr. *Intellectual and ethical development in the college years.* New York: Holt, Rinehart & Winston, 1970.

Pervin, L. A. Satisfaction and perceived self-environment similarity: A semantic differential study of student-college interaction. *Journal of Personality,* 1967, *35,* 623-34.

Pfeiffer, J. W., & Jones, J. E. Intergroup meeting: An image exchange. *Structured Experiences for Human Relations Training.* LaJolla, CA: University Associates, 1981.

Piaget, J. *The moral judgment of the child.* New York: The Free Press, 1965.

Porter, L. C. Intergroup clearing: A relationship building intervention. In J. W. Pfeiffer & J. E. Jones (Eds.), *Annual Handbook for Group Facilitators,* La Jolla, CA: University Associates, 1981.

Rodgers, R. F. Theories underlying student development. In D. G. Creamer (Ed.), *Student development in higher education: Theories, practices, and future directions.* Washington, DC: American College Personnel Association, 1980.

Rodgers, R. F., & Widick, C. Theory to practice: Uniting concepts, logic and creativity. In F. B. Newton & K. L. Ender (Eds.), *Student development practices: Strategies for making a difference.* Springfield, IL: Charles C. Thomas, 1980.

Rodgers, R. F., Bryer, J., & Hollingsworth, R. *Helping skills for paraprofessionals* (3rd ed.). Columbus, OH: Office of Student Services, 1976.

Sanford, N. *Where colleges fail.* San Francisco: Jossey-Bass, 1967.

Selman, R. L. *The growth of interpersonal understanding.* New York: Academic Press, 1980.

Sheehy, G. *Passages: Predictable crises of adult life.* New York: Dutton, 1974.

Sherwood, J. J., & Glidewell, J. C. Planned renegotiation. In J. W. Pfeiffer & J. E. Jones (Eds.), *Annual handbook for group facilitators.* LaJolla, CA: University Associates, 1973.

Sprinthall, N.A. A curriculum for schools: Counselors as teachers for psychological growth. *School Counselor,* 1973, *20,* 361-9.

Stern, G. G. *People in context.* New York: John Wiley & Sons, 1970.

Thomas, K. Conflict and conflict management. In M. D. Dunnette (Ed.), *Handbook of industrial and organizational psychology.* Chicago: Rand McNally, 1976.

Vaillant, G. *Adaptation to life.* Boston: Little, Brown & Co., 1977.

Walton, R. E. *Interpersonal peace making: Confrontation and third party consultation.* Reading, MA: Addison Wesley, 1969.

White, R. W. *Lives in progress* (2nd ed.). New York: Holt, Rinehart, & Winston, 1966.

Widick, C., Knefelkamp, L. L., & Parker, C. A. The counselor as a developmental instructor. *Counselor Education and Supervision,* 1975, *14,* 286-96.

Wiley, G. E. Win/Lose Situations. In J. W. Pfeiffer & J. E. Jones (Eds.), *Annual handbook for group facilitators.* LaJolla, CA: University Associates, 1973.

SUGGESTED READINGS

Knefelkamp, L., Widick, C., & Parker, C. A. *New directions for student services: Applying new developmental findings* (No. 2). San Francisco: Jossey-Bass, 1978.

Moos, R. H. *Evaluating educational environments: Procedures, measures, findings, and policy implications.* San Francisco: Jossey-Bass, 1979.

Rodgers, R. F., & Widick, C. Theory to practice: Uniting concepts, logic and creativity. In F. B. Newton & K. L. Ender (Eds.), *Student development practices: Strategies for making a difference.* Springfield, IL: Charles C. Thomas, 1980.

Walton, R.E. *Interpersonal peace making: Confrontation and third party consultation.* Reading, MA: Addison Wesley, 1969.

Widick, C., Knefelkamp, L. L., & Parker, C. A. The counselor as a developmental instructor. *Counselor Education and Supervision,* 1975, *14,* 286-96.

D. Stanley Carpenter, a native of Texas, received his bachelor's degree in mathematics from Tarleton State University (Texas) and a master's degree in student personnel and guidance from East Texas State University. He worked in residence halls at Oglethorpe University (Georgia) before moving to the University of Georgia where he received the Ph.D. in counseling and student personnel services. His dissertation on professional development in student affairs earned the dissertation of the year award from the National Association of Student Personnel Administrators. He served as Dean of Students at the University of Arkansas at Monticello before assuming his present position as Assistant Director of Development at Texas A&M University.

Chapter 6

THE STUDENT AFFAIRS PROFESSION: A DEVELOPMENTAL PERSPECTIVE

D. Stanley Carpenter

This chapter takes a comprehensive look at professionalism and professional development in the field of student affairs administration, and briefly traces the development of the profession historically and the place of professional development therein. To avoid confusion, a few definitions are important. First, the term profession is used in a sociological sense. That is, a generalized continuum exists with some jobs classified as occupations (at one end of the continuum) and some as professions (at the other end) with all other jobs classified somewhere in between. The location of a particular job on the continuum is dependent upon criteria such as feeling of community, formal and informal sanctions, and enforced codes of ethics (Pavalko, 1971). Based upon these criteria, the term student affairs is seen as being on the profession end of the continuum.

Second, professional development is considered to be a universal process analogous to human development with many of the same elements involved. It is not narrowly defined as simply in-service education or professional association activity. Rather, it includes developmental aspects such as developmental tasks and stages common to student affairs professionals, and a case will be made in this chapter for use of a developmental model to make such assertions about professional growth. In addition, one conception of such professional growth is offered, and the implications of professionalism and professional development for the field are examined.

THE EMERGENCE OF STUDENT AFFAIRS PROFESSIONALS

The English Influence

In the earliest colleges in America, nearly everyone had some type of student affairs responsibility. The colleges were imitations of the English residential model and by definition had to be concerned with extracurricular activities. One has only to consider the histories of such cities as Athens (Georgia and Ohio); Cambridge, Massachusetts; Oxford (Ohio and Mississippi); and numerous other college communities to deduce that the founders of early colleges were interested in insulation and isolation from the outside world. Colleges were largely self-contained units in terms of residence, food, and social life. Religious and moral developments were as important as cognitive development—often more important. Students were typically quite young, often as young as 11 (Rudolph, 1962). The president, the faculty, trustees, and all other college officials took an active hand in the control and guidance of students (Leonard, 1956). For control it was. Often one of the most important duties of the president was his series of moral lectures to seniors.

The legal doctrine of *in loco parentis,* while not truly established as law until 1913 (*Gott* v. *Berea College,* 161 S.W. 204. Court of Appeals of Kentucky, 1913) was not a debated abstraction, but a useful paradigm. Care must be taken in generalizing because, as Appleton, Briggs, and Rhatigan (1978) pointed out, *in loco parentis* is an incomplete and often inaccurate way to look at total educational practice in early colleges. There was what would today be termed developmental concern, but it was of a directive and judgmental nature and involved very little student volition.

The English model predominated until about the Civil War when the pendulum began to swing. New forces were shaping higher education.

Curricula, and indeed entire colleges, began to be secularized. Science and technology began to be legitimized as fields of study. The land grant movement aided the proliferation of "nonreligious" institutions.

The German Influence

In the middle of all this change, an aberration appeared. During the 19th century, more and more faculty members completed formal study in Germany, and the influence of German university thinking spread throughout American higher education. The German system was viewed by many as being the best in the world with its emphasis upon scholarship, graduate education, and research and thus thought worthy of emulation. The best minds in higher education began to take the attitude that students' behavior out of class was of no concern to the institution. This laissez-faire attitude was reinforced by faculty reaction to the old control model of their youth (Cowley, 1964). Also, faculty and administrators were having too many other demands put on their time to continue 24-hour a day surveillance and concern with students.

The Emergence of Student Affairs Administrators

When these factors were added to the increasing presence of women students (who educational leaders believed needed additional supervision) and the burgeoning of extracurricular activities, such as fraternities, literary societies, and sports activities, the stage was set for the entrance of the student affairs officer. Just as the German movement was in part a reaction to the earlier emphazied English model, the proliferation of student affairs officers was a response to the 30-year German influence. Obviously these time periods were not sharply defined. Historians agree that the positions of Dean of Men and Dean of Women increased rapidly on American campuses during the period from 1870 to 1910. During the latter part of this time period, vocational counseling, mental hygiene, and psychological testing were gaining credence on campuses, also. During the early 20th century, the increased emphasis upon student services contributed to student affairs administration as a field (Lloyd-Jones, 1954).

Interesting to note is that only in America did the Dean of Men/Women movement surface. Even then, deans were nearly always appointed from the teaching faculty, which often resulted in a confusing and sometimes humorous lack of specific duties for early appointees. The first academic course in student affairs was conducted at Columbia University in 1915 (Appleton, Briggs, & Rhatigan, 1978).

Formal associations for student affairs practitioners were established and gained strength during the first quarter of the 20th century. Groups such as the National Association of Deans and Advisers of Men and the National Association of Women Deans were formed as were organizations for college physicians, college union directors, appointment secretaries (placement directors), and vocational guidance personnel. These fragmented organizations provided identity for practitioners in specific areas, but a more generalized and comprehensive conception of student affairs administration was coming. In 1937, the American Council on Education published the "Student Personnel Point of View" and revised it in 1949. These statements made three basic assumptions: (1) each student is unique; (2) each student is an integrated whole and the development of this whole person is mandatory; and (3) all development begins at the individual student's level and not at some mythical mean. This introduction of areas of development other than cognitive and the necessary tailoring of developmental experiences for different students implied out-of-class education conducted by knowledgeable professionals. Student affairs practitioners now had a philosophy to guide their work with students.

The "Profession" Controversy

Given the diversity of student affairs practice and the more or less peripheral structure of student affairs on many campuses, it is not surprising that consensus among practitioners on the efficacy of the "Student Personnel Point of View" did not accrue overnight. The post World War II period has been characterized by active disagreement among the authorities in the student affairs literature. Many authors engaged in breast-beating and moaning about the state of student affairs. Wrenn (1949) analyzed student affairs administration from a sociological perspective and concluded that it did not meet the criteria for being a profession. Shoben (1967) chided the field for being essentially contentless and urged it to stay out of areas belonging to other fields such as counseling. Koile (1966) was disappointed that student affairs had neither a clear body of knowledge, skills, and ethics, nor a central place in American higher education. Penney (1969) pointed out that student affairs had had time to prove itself as a profession and had not done so. He was concerned with the housekeeping emphasis apparent in much of the student affairs literature and the failure of the literature to promote areas of exclusive practice for the field. For some of these authors there appears to have been an apologetic or *mea culpa* attitude concerning the very existence of student affairs.

Fortunately, other authors challenged these negative viewpoints. Williamson (1958) left little doubt that he considered student affairs administration to be an identifiable field with its own preparation and professional characteristics. Miller (1967) called for an increased awareness of the student affairs practitioner as an educator, implying the professionalization of the field. He further proposed that practitioners should function as scholar-administrators with the creation of total learning environments as one of their primary tasks. Penn (1974) assumed he was writing to a professional field in calling for more collegial control of preparation programs. Bloland (1974) suggested that the personal development of students should be viewed as a major point of unity for the field. Trueblood (1966) made a case for the exclusivity of student affairs preparation and practice, and Nygreen (1968) noted that student affairs had many aspects of a profession and should be so amended in the future. A growing acceptance of human development theory as a foundation for practice (Miller & Prince, 1976), increasing emphasis upon professional preparation programs (Knock, 1977), and concern with the nomenclature of the field (Crookston, 1976) are more recent examples in the literature of powerful, positive influences toward greater professionalism.

During this time of professional controversy, the 1960s and early 1970s, the entire higher education establishment was in ferment. While initially being criticized for not controlling student dissent, student affairs practitioners often came to be viewed as the only persons on campus truly able to deal with the student disaffection. As the liaison between students and administrations, student affairs professionals often gained much respect. Further, the educational reforms that resulted from student demonstrations and the humanizing of the college environment necessitated by the student demands were often carried out by the student affairs staff.

Also during the 1960s came the formal death of the *in loco parentis* doctrine as a cornerstone of student control. With the new legal requirements of due process for students and the lowering of the age of majority nationwide came a necessity for a new relationship with students. Colleges could (and can) still require certain behaviors, but the new emphasis was upon collaboration with adults (rather than control of children) to maintain and enhance the educational community. Student affairs practitioners have been at the forefront in negotiating and administering this new relationship.

This brief historical review has traced the development of student affairs administration from a series of parental oriented chores to a complex set of educational responsibilities involving difficult academic, psychological, and legal issues. Student affairs professionals increasingly are filling the role of valued partners with the faculty in an evolving educational mission of intentional student development. Professionalism, then, is an essential ingredient of both preparation and practice in the field of student affairs.

PROFESSIONALISM AS DEVELOPMENT

The specific application of principles of human development as articulated in Chapter 1 requires a knowledge of both the culture and community within which the individual lives and works. Human development theory, of course, has value in analyzing the comprehensive psychosocial, cognitive, and psychomotor development of individuals. However, it also can be applied to modular portions of total development, if such modules are defined by a community. Developmental principles, for example, may be applied specifically to the content and process of career development. This component of total development may be examined in light of its unique developmental tasks and stages that can be identified, verified, and discussed as separate units. Similarly, an even smaller area of human growth, development as a professional, can be profitably analyzed if a community can be defined within which such development occurs. Student affairs administration, like any profession, represents such a community (Carpenter, Miller, & Winston, 1980).

A professional community may be largely defined by three main sets of commonalities. First, *a group of professionals must share goals and objectives.* For student affairs professionals, the most common goal is the structuring of a campus environment in which students may maximize their growth in all possible ways. Ways to influence this environment or developmental milieu range from the most mundane services such as food and shelter to the most esoteric sensitivity training, but all are means to the common end. Student affairs staffs and programs exist to promote student development.

A second attribute of professional community is *the existence of formal and informal sanctions.* That is, certain practices are rewarded and others are punished. For example, consider resumes. While resumes vary in style and content, most are expected to conform to relatively narrow norms. Generally, they should be neat, succinct, and honest. Deviations are punished by the simple expedient of not being hired or not being interviewed. On the positive side, persons who publish their work in books or professional journals are rewarded with respect, consulting jobs, and sometimes increased chances for better jobs or promotions, especially in professional preparation programs. Willingness to participate in and contribute to professional association activities is usually rewarded by the opportunity to assume more responsibility and leadership.

In the future, the profession will need a code of ethics, and at least one codification has been adopted (ACPA, 1981). If such a code and attendant enforcement procedures take root, a flexible but more formal set of sanctions will evolve.

Any community must *attend to socialization and regeneration,* the third set of processes considered. Socialization has both formal and informal forms. Informally, the lore of student affairs is communicated by more experienced professionals to new and less experienced ones. Proper ways to work with students, to communicate appropriately orally and in writing, to behave at conventions, to obtain or change positions, and many other things are taught by example, dialogue, and experience. Many of these same professional traits or activities are dealt with more formally in professional preparation programs, professional literature, and periodic job performance evaluations. An example of such formal codification of the field is Packwood's (1977) descriptive book that examines the basics of the profession.

Regeneration is related closely to socialization in that certain of the processes are quite similar. However, the focus is more upon the actual bringing of individuals into the field. In order to continue to be vital, the profession must have new blood and the new blood should share the values, goals, and skills of the field after a brief orientation or preparation period. Therefore this preparation period needs to be a relatively common or similar experience for all the new recruits. Assurance of this commonality of training is the responsibility of practitioners and educators alike and is accomplished informally through communication and formally through accreditation, research, and professional association guidelines for training. The most promising recent development in this area is the formation of the Council for the Advancement of Standards for Student Service/Development Programs (CAS). CAS is composed of representatives of the major student affairs generalist associations as well as a host of more specialty oriented organizations. The standards produced by CAS are intended to gain widespread use by higher education accrediting agencies, thus further defining student affairs work as a profession (Miller, 1980).

MODEL OF PROFESSIONAL DEVELOPMENT IN STUDENT AFFAIRS

Accepting that the student affairs profession is a community with shared goals, sanctions, and socialization/regeneration criteria, and believing that principles of human development have direct application to professional development, Miller and Carpenter (1980) suggested five propositions for consideration.

1. Professional development is continuous and cumulative in nature, moves from simpler to more complex behavior, and can be described via levels or stages held in common.

2. Optimal professional development is a direct result of the interaction between the total person striving for positive professional growth and the environment.

3. Optimal professional preparation combines mastery of a body of knowledge and a cluster of skills and competencies within the context of personal development.

4. Professional credibility and excellence of practice are directly dependent upon the quality of professional preparation.

5. Professional preparation is a lifelong learning process. (p. 84)

These propositions have many implications and offer a number of testable hypotheses. One such hypothesis, the existence of developmental stages, can be derived from Proposition One. Four stages have been proposed: Formative, Application, Additive, and Generative. These four stages provide the basis for the postulation of the developmental tasks of student affairs professionals (Carpenter, 1979). These tasks were formulated on the basis of Pavalko's (1971) profession-occupation continua

•Knowledge of theory and levels of skill.
•Clarification of motivation and relevance to society.
•Decisions regarding preparation and career.
•Autonomy of professional behavior.
•Developing a sense of professional community (professional association activity and colleague relationships).
•Activities related to professional publications.
•Developing a sense of ethical practice.

The tasks were sorted by expert judges and are listed by stages in Figure 6.1. A factor analysis of responses to an instrument created from these tasks yielded four professional development factors (Carpenter & Miller, 1981):

1. Contributions to the professional community
2. Institutional leadership and practice
3. Professional preparation
4. Career awareness

A Composite Career Path

A good way to synthesize all this stage, task, continuum, and factor information is to look at a career ladder composite for the student affairs professional.

Consider a hypothetical college student—John Johnson. He or his counterpart Jane Johnson (J.J.) probably became aware of student affairs administration as a career option through a positive relationship with one or more professionals. Maybe J.J. was a resident assistant, active in student government, a student activity board member, an orientation assistant, or filled some other paraprofessional role. Usually, as J.J. considers a student affairs career, the next step is to enter a master's degree program in counseling, student affairs practice, student development, or higher education administration. J.J. concurrently gets a graduate assistantship in housing, student activities, or some other area as a financial and experiential supplement to his/her education. Parenthetically, it is possible to enter the student affairs field without a master's degree, usually at smaller institutions, but this is becoming rare.

During the *Formative Stage,* J.J. is accomplishing several specific tasks related to acquiring knowledge of the field of student affairs administration. Course work, books, and journals are all used to gain knowledge, and supervised practice is used to gain necessary skills. Students begin to become more committed to the values of the student affairs field (if they decide to stay with their studies) as their learning increases. Professional associations are seen primarily as placement vehicles. Standards for knowledge, skills, practice, ethics, career awareness, and all other facets of professionalism are derived from and dependent upon the views of the instructors and practicum/internship/assistantship supervisors.

Stage 2
Application

1. Beginning to apply the skills and competencies involved with student affairs practice.

2. Learning to take responsibility for professional decisions.

3. Attaining the respect of the campus community.

4. Making a firm commitment to student affairs as a profession.

5. Applying established ethical standards in direct contact work with students.

6. Contributing to newsletters that report on current practices in specific student services.

7. Taking part in inservice education, workshops, and other methods of gaining knowledge and skills to aid performance in one's current position.

Stage 1
Formative

1. Getting enough education and/or skill training to obtain and hold a position in students affairs.

2. Tailoring learnings and experiences to meet the criteria and expectations of my teachers or supervisors.

3. Attaining a knowledge of the theory and skills necessary for facilitating the development of students.

4. Reading journals and other professional publications in order to learn about the field and become aware of basic approaches.

5. Internalizing the values of student affairs professionals.

6. Attending regional and national conferences to make contacts and obtain a position.

Figure 6.1. Four stages and related developmental tasks of student affairs professionals.

**Stage 3
Additive**

1. Creating and devising new approaches to student development.

2. Taking responsibility for the professional activities and ethics of one's administrative subdivision and the professionals one supervises.

3. Contributing to professional publications in order to share current thinking and practice techniques.

4. Interpreting the rationale of student affairs to the larger community.

5. Encouraging younger professionals to take responsibility for their own professional efforts, while still providing them with support, input, and feedback.

6. Helping to welcome and orient young professionals to the field by "showing them the ropes" and encouraging the continued professional development of all colleagues.

7. Consulting with, directing, and/or supervising those responsible for accomplishing practical student development goals.

8. Taking part in the leadership of local, regional, and national professional associations.

**Stage 4
Generative**

1. Judging the merits of, and otherwise criticizing new student development/student affairs theories.

2. Contributing broad-scale "think pieces" concerning current and future student development theory and student affairs practices.

3. Sharing one's wealth of experience in student affairs with the profession as a whole.

4. Being heavily involved in the upper level leadership of and helping to shape the direction of professional associations.

5. Encouraging involvement of and being a mentor to less experienced student affairs workers in professional association leadership.

The *Application Stage* begins with the first professional position. Possible job titles include Head Resident or Resident Director, Programming Assistant, Counselor, Career Counselor, or sometimes (usually at smaller schools) Assistant Dean of Students, Assistant Director of Housing, Assistant Director of Student Activities, and so forth. J.J. still has much to learn. Education and training continue through in-service workshops, conference sessions, informal consultations with colleagues, journals and newsletters, and supervisors. However, the best teacher in this stage is experience. The budding professional is able to (indeed required to) test theories and practice skills with students. J.J. finds that student affairs practice is idiosyncratic in some ways and that personal style contributes a part. Gaining respect from colleagues, students, and the academic community is important. Ethics are tested—and sometimes altered.

On the career front, J.J. needs to decide whether to change jobs and campuses after two or three years in an initial position. Should central office or specific service area work be a goal? Also, a decision must be made about continuing in student affairs as a career as J.J. moves into the later Application Stage (after three to five years in the field). If a student affairs career is to be pursued, then J.J. must either decide to seek more formal education, or middle-management positions with increasing responsibility. These activities reflect the transition to the next stage.

The *Additive Stage* is not as easily or sharply defined. It can be said to start when J.J. obtains a policy-making position, although senior-level counseling and staff positions exist that are very influential without having final decision power. Sample position titles include Dean of Students, Vice-President for Student Affairs, Director of Housing (or Career Planning and Placement, Student Activities, Counseling, Financial Aid, Recruitment and Orientation), Counseling Psychologist, Coordinator for Minority Programs, or Associate Vice-President or Director. Additive Stage professionals are generally quite knowledgeable, highly skilled people who are in a position to supervise others. As such, they are creative and take a holistic view of student affairs. J.J., in such a position, must take responsibility for the ethical practices of the staff members of that administrative sub-unit as well as be accountable for achieving its goals and purposes. Additionally, the Additive J.J. will often take leadership in regional and national professional associations and will contribute to professional journals, books, and convention programs. J.J. is seen more and more as a role model and leader in the campus and community by colleagues as evidenced by consulting opportunities, and particularly by younger staff members who look to J.J. for guidance. J.J. will usually have made a decision about continued practice as an administrator or moving into the teaching ranks by the early Additive Stage. (This hypothetical composite career is based upon an administrative practitioner, but fits a teacher with minor modifications such as substituting students for subordinates.) J.J. as an Additive professional is a leader by example, by job description, by activity, and by temperament.

If J.J. stays in student affairs administration through a long and productive career, passing appropriately through the previous stages, the time will come when achievement of the pinnacle of professional practice, the *Generative Stage,* will be within reach. In this stage, J.J. has earned the professional respect of others and is frequently called upon for consulting activities, invited presentations, broadranging articles or books charting the future of the field, and top association leadership, task force, and editorial positions. There are relatively few Generative professionals and their titles are often those of Vice-President, full Professor, Executive Director, or they may even have emeritus status. J.J. as a Generative professional would be an assertive and able elder spokesperson for the profession and function as a mentor and guide to many of the more youthful professionals. Note that often difficulty occurs in distinguishing between the advanced Additive and the Generative professionals as many of the behaviors and characteristics of the two stages tend to be somewhat similar. In many instances, the years of service and the recognition factors reflect the greatest distinction.

PROFESSIONAL IMPLICATIONS OF A DEVELOPMENTAL MODEL

Perhaps the most important concept in this developmental framework of professional growth is that there are different levels of tasks in each area of professionalism. That is, the crises or growth points for a beginning professional in the areas of ethical practice or association activity (for example) are different from those of the seasoned practitioner. However, if earlier tasks are not mastered, later ones are impossible. Once again, development is cumulative and continuous.

Career Implications

It is possible to get "too much, too soon" in student affairs work. Some evidence has been presented in this chapter that development in practice-related knowledge and skills is a process occurring over time, as is professional association leadership. It seems clear that persons who take on professional or associational positions beyond their capabilities or beyond their developmental level are likely doomed to failure or at least mediocrity of performance. This implies that individuals must keep a developmental awareness of the consequences of professional activities as they move up the ladder in responsibility of position in practice and in associational participation. While it is true that some people experience professional growth more rapidly than do others, care must be taken to accomplish tasks and gain skills in a timely fashion. Taking a position totally disparate from one's skills and abilities will result in frustration, disappointment, and stalled growth. Similarly, failure to advance to positions of greater responsibility when they are appropriate is to cease developing. The knowledge of when career moves are or are not appropriate comes from assessing and actively working on one's own professional development.

For at the base of it, professional development is the responsibility of the individual. The profession and the employer should provide systematic opportunities, but the practitioner must take advantage of such opportunities. Professionals should engage in continual clarification of values. If two-year college administration is a goal, then appropriate academic or workshop education and proper experience should be obtained. If practitioners feel inadequately prepared to work with budgets, then certain books, courses, or supervised experiences may be indicated. Appropriate professional growth is possible only through stringent self-assessment, goal setting, and action. All position or responsibility shifts should be made with an eye toward professional growth.

This is not to say that all ambition is bad, that individuals can know everything about the future, or that professional growth is mechanistic. However, very few newly minted masters degree recipients are ready to be chief student affairs officers. Careful, individualized, and planned professional development is crucial to any successful career.

Professional Preparation Implications

Separate and apart from personal career considerations, developmental aspects of professionalism in student affairs require a rethinking of professional preparation. If developmental principles can be applied to student affairs professional growth, then such growth *must* be recognized as continuous and cumulative. That is, from the time that a person decides to enter student affairs, there begins a process of continual upgrading in skills, knowledge of student development theory, and personal/professional awareness. While initial preparation (masters or paraprofessional level) is not the end of preparation by any means, it is the basic foundation. (See Appendix C for a comprehensive statement of essentials related to professional preparation). Student affairs professional educators, then, have an enormous responsibility. Professional development is best facilitated if it takes place in an environment in which change is planned and anticipated. Initial preparation should, therefore, concentrate not only on skills needed for meeting the needs of entry-level professional positions, but also upon an awareness of professional development stages and tasks and factors of professional development that come into play as careers continue. Rather than being nebulous or too narrowly focused, masters (and even doctoral) programs should identify developmental tasks and stages (those suggested and others) and endeavor to increase student knowledge and awareness of them. Further, systematic, developmental-based continuing education in the form of workshops, courses, and publications must become a focus for professional associations, preparation programs, and practitioners alike.

Professional preparation is a career-long process. If one stops intentionally growing and preparing, then more complex and higher-level developmental tasks will be impossible to accomplish or master. What must be recognized by the student affairs profession is that continuous preparation and education at all levels are too important to be left to chance or whim and must be addressed systematically.

Professional Practice Implications

Professional awareness in preparation should be mirrored in practice. Apparently the ability to perform ever more complex duties in student affairs positions is related to professional development level. At the beginning of their careers, new professionals need careful supervision and mentors to aid them in beginning their career-long development auspiciously, so as not to get in over their heads immediately. As experience and professional development increase, student affairs practitioners are able to take more and more responsibility for their activities and decisions as well as for those of their administrative subdivisions and subordinates. The responsibility of both individual practitioners and their supervisors is to create and maintain an environment encouraging professional growth.

The importance of personal mentors at all levels cannot be overemphasized as a key component of continued professional development. Without support, encouragement, help, and role modeling, stagnation and retarded development will occur. Professionals, then, are responsible not only for their own development, but also for that of less experienced practitioners.

Professional Association Implications

Professional associations have a major responsibility to the profession of student affairs if a developmental model is accepted as a paradigm for professional growth. If professional preparation is to be considered career-long and hierarchical in nature, then associations must take a much more serious approach to their instructional function than has heretofore been apparent. Workshops and interest sessions at national and regional conferences, while given importance currently, are not offered with anything approaching regularity or singleness of purpose. The American College Personnel Association (ACPA) focuses upon new professionals with content sessions and encouragement of involvement as do several other associations. Also, ACPA cosponsors or sanctions numerous campus-based skill-building workshops and conferences designed to address various levels of concern. The National Association of Student Personnel Administrators has for years sponsored a summer program for new chief student affairs officers and is moving toward a "level" concept in conference content sessions. Most professional associations are doing an increasingly effective job of placement and career orientation for their members. However, these halting steps are not enough. Many instructional avenues have gone unexplored to date. Modular instruction, for example, with specific goals and objectives over a long term is only one way to approach "leveled" instruction. Specific "tracks" based upon strong research could be offered at both annual conferences and year-round locations in such areas as budgeting, personnel management, theory intensive service delivery, ethical practice, and many other topics at each of the four professional stage levels. Such goals will not be met by adopting standards for masters programs alone, however, but must be tied into a continuing education format by professional associations with appropriate recognition and reward systems. Obviously, in order for such a scheme to be functional, the associations must first lead the way in research and reeducation concerning professional development.

Additionally, and more specifically, a developmental process occurs with respect to associational leadership and publication activity. However, systematic effort is made by few professional associations to induce, encourage, and develop younger and lower-level professional leadership. While some attempts are made in this area, they are relatively irregular and disorganized. In a very real sense the persons who need the least help, the higher level professionals, find it far easier to participate in associational leadership, while those lower-level persons who could best benefit are often discouraged by the seeming impenetrability of the bureaucracy. This is not to say that experience is unnecessary in association leadership, but rather that there are appropriate levels of leadership for persons in all stages of development, and that consistently using only high level professionals for all leadership is expedient but ultimately damaging to everyone concerned, including the association. Some efforts are being made in this area, but these efforts are neither widespread nor consistent. Professional associations must lead the way in an organized, systematic fashion, and younger professionals must take advantage of available opportunities (see Chapter 19).

SUMMARY

Consequences of continuing to ignore the developmental nature of professional growth are significant. If individual professionals ignore their personal growth, they will stagnate and become ineffective, thereby hurting their employing institutions and the profession of student affairs as well as the students they serve. If institutions, associations, and preparation programs do not systematically and energetically set about insuring professional development, the entire profession will suffer, and indeed in an era of cutbacks and retrenchment, may not survive. And, if student affairs administration as a profession falters, weakens, or perishes, then higher education, all college students, and, at the risk of sounding melodramatic, the nation will have lost valuable resources. The growing understanding about the nature of professional development and the individual's responsibilities and opportunities inherent therein will enhance the profession of student affairs administration in the years ahead.

REFERENCES

American College Personnel Association statement of ethical and professional standards. *Journal of College Student Personnel,* 1981, *22,* 184-9.

American Council on Education. *The student personnel point of view.* American Council on Education Studies (Series 1, Vol. 1, No. 3). Washington, DC: Author, 1937.

American Council on Education. *The student personnel point of view* (Rev. ed.). American Council on Education Studies (Series 6, Vol. 13, No. 13). Washington, DC: Author, 1949.

Appleton, J.R., Briggs, C.M., & Rhatigan, J.S. *Pieces of eight: The rites, roles and styles of the dean by eight who have been there.* Portland, OR: NASPA Institute of Research and Development, 1978.

Bloland, P.A. Professionalism and the professional organization. In T.F. Harrington (Ed.), *Student personnel work in urban colleges.* New York: Intext Educational Publishing, 1974.

Carpenter, D.S. *The professional development of student affairs workers: An analysis.* Unpublished dissertation, University of Georgia, 1979.

Carpenter, D.S., & Miller, T.K. An analysis of professional development in student affairs. *NASPA Journal,* 1981, *19*(1), 2-11.

Carpenter, D.S., Miller, T.K., & Winston, R.B., Jr. Toward the professionalization of student affairs. *NASPA Journal,* 1980, *18*(2), 16-23.

Cowley, W.H. Reflections of a troublesome but hopeful Rip Van Winkle. *Journal of College Student Personnel,* 1964, *6,* 66-73.

Crookston, B.B. Student personnel—All hail and farewell. *Personnel and Guidance Journal,* 1976, *55,* 26-9.

Knock, G.H. (Ed.) *Perspectives on the preparation of student affairs professionals.* Washingon, DC: American College Personnel Association, 1977.

Koile, E.A. Student affairs: Forever the bridesmaid. *NASPA Journal,* 1966, *4,* 65-72.

Leonard, E. *Origins of the personnel services.* Minneapolis, MN: University of Minnesota Press, 1956.

Lloyd-Jones, E. Changing concepts of student personnel work. In E. Lloyd-Jones & M.R. Smith (Eds.)., *Student personnel work as deeper teaching.* New York: Harper & Brothers, 1954.

Miller, T.K. Agenda for the eighties: Professionalism challenges and opportunities for the American College Personnel Association. (Report to the ACPA Business Meeting). Mimeograph, 1980.

Miller, T.K. College student personnel preparation: Present perspective and future directions. *NASPA Journal,* 1967, *4,* 171-8.

Miller, T.K., & Carpenter, D.S. Professional preparation for today and tomorrow. In D.G. Creamer (Ed.), *Student development in higher education: Theories, practices and future directions.* Washington, DC: American College Personnel Association, 1980.

Miller, T.K., & Prince, J. *The future of student affairs: A guide to student development for tomorrow's higher education.* San Francisco: Jossey-Bass, 1976.

Nygreen, G.T. Professional status for student personnel administrators. *NASPA Journal,* 1968, *5,* 283-91.

Packwood, W.T. *College student personnel services.* Springfield, IL: Charles C. Thomas, 1977.

Pavalko, R.M. *Sociology of occupations and professions.* Itasca, IL: F.E. Peacock, Inc., 1971.

Penn, J.R. Professional accreditation: A key to excellence. *Journal of College Student Personnel,* 1974, *15,* 257-9.

Penney, J.F. Student personnel work: A profession stillborn. *Personnel and Guidance Journal,* 1969, *47,* 958-62.

Rudolph, F. *The American college and university: A history.* New York: Random House, 1962.

Shoben, E.J. Psychology and student personnel work. *Journal of College Student Personnel,* 1967, *8,* 239-44.

Trueblood, D.L. The educational preparation of the college student personnel leader of the future. In G.J. Kloph (Ed.), *College student personnel in the years ahead.* Washington, DC: American College Personnel Association, 1966.

Williamson, E.G. Professional preparation of student personnel workers. *School and Society,* 1958, *86,* 21-3.

Wrenn, C.G. An appraisal of the professional status of student personnel workers, Part I. In E.G. Williamson (Ed.), *Trends in student personnel work.* Minneapolis: University of Minneapolis Press, 1949.

SUGGESTED READINGS

American College Personnel Association statement of ethical and professional standards. *Journal of College Student Personnel,* 1981, *22,* 184-9.

Appleton, J.R., Briggs, C.M., & Rhatigan, J.S. *Pieces of eight: The rites, rules and styles of the dean by eight who have been there.* Portland, OR: NASPA Institute of Research and Development, 1978.

Crookston, B.B. Student personnel—All hail and farewell. *Personnel and Guidance Journal,* 1976, *55,* 26-9.

Leonard, E. *Origins of personnel services in American higher education.* Minneapolis, MN: University of Minnesota Press, 1956.

Miller, T.K., & Carpenter, D.S. Professional preparation for today and tomorrow. In D.G. Creamer (Ed.), *Student development in higher education: Theories, practices and future directions.* Washington, DC: American College Personnel Association, 1980.

Nygreen, G.T. Professional status for student personnel administrators. *NASPA Journal,* 1968, *5,* 283-91.

Pavalko, R.M. *Sociology of occupations and professions.* Itasca, IL: F.E. Peacock Inc., 1971.

Roger B. Winston, Jr. is Assistant Professor in the Student Personnel in Higher Education Program in the Department of Counseling and Human Development Services and Director of the Student Development Laboratory at the University of Georgia.

For further information please refer to the last section of the book entitled "About the Authors."

Sue Saunders McCaffrey is the Associate Director of the Division of Developmental Studies, University of Georgia. She received her doctorate in counseling and student personnel services from the University of Georgia. Her bachelor's degree in journalism and master's degree in counseling are from Ohio University. She has worked in residence halls and counseling and placement centers as well as in academic administration positions. Dr. McCaffrey's research interests include investigation of career decision-making processes and inquiry into the non-intellective factors related to academic success.

She is co-author of *Students Helping Students: A Training Manual for Peer Helpers on the College Campus* and has contributed chapters on mentoring in academic advising, student development theory as related to advising and student affairs program development. She was a member of the Task Force that coordinated development of the American College Personnel Association Statement of Ethical and Professional Standards.

Chapter 7

ETHICAL PRACTICE IN STUDENT AFFAIRS ADMINISTRATION

Roger B. Winston, Jr.
Sue Saunders McCaffrey

If student affairs administrators are to be justified in being considered professionals, as many have argued (Carpenter, Miller, & Winston, 1980; Miller & Carpenter, 1980; Stamatakos, 1981; Trueblood, 1966; Wrenn & Darley, 1949), then they must possess commonly recognized ethical standards that are clearly defined and backed by sanctions. Without such functioning guidelines and canons, the profession is open to the justified criticism that it, especially in its culpable professional organizations, is "much more concerned about the welfare of its membership than the protection of those whom the profession is to serve" (Stamatakos, 1981, p. 201). The student affairs profession, when compared to more established fields such as law and medicine, is still in its infancy with regard to establishing and enforcing standards of professional behavior.

However, the field has not been without its attempt to promulgate standards. As Stamatakos (1981) stated, a number of statements have been proposed in the past 20 years. For example, the American Personnel and Guidance Association adopted its first statement in 1961 which was primarily directed at counselor-client relationships. The National Association of Student Personnel Administrators (1960) adopted a rather narrow statement without enforcement mechanisms. The American College Personnel Association adopted a statement of standards related to working with students in groups (1976) and a more general statement of ethical and professional standards designed to address the broad range of student affairs practice (1981), both of which presently lack sanctioning procedures. A number of specialized student affairs associations such as the College Placement Council, Association of College and University Housing Officers, National Association of Foreign Student Advisors, Association of College Unions-International, and National Association of Campus Activities have standards statements that are at various levels of sophistication and specificity. The area of admissions, records, and student recruitment has received considerable attention as reflected in the *Joint Statement on Principles of Good Practice in College Admissions and Recruitment* (Amercian Association of Collegiate Registrars and Admissions Officers, College Entrance Examination of Collegiate Registrars and Admissions Officers, College Entrance Examination Board, National Association of College Admissions Counselors, and National Association of Secondary School Principals, 1979) and in statements on fair practices by the Carnegie Council (Policy Studies in Higher Education, 1979). Without question issues of ethical and professional practice will receive more attention in the decade of the 1980s.

This chapter offers schemata for viewing professional ethics in the student affairs field from both theoretical and historical perspectives. A paradigm for ethical decision making is presented, along with some vignettes depicting application of an ethical decision-making process. Finally, recommendations are offered for enhancing ethical practice in student affairs.

ETHICS: A DEFINITION

For most student affairs administrators the idea that they should be *ethical* is often accepted as a given, but is seldom analyzed and only vaguely understood. "Ethics" from a philosophical point of view is concerned with determining what acts or behaviors are "right," or "ought to be done/not done," as well as determining the epistemological justifications for ethical statements or assertions. From the philosophical perspective, the first sense of ethics is normative in that the concerns are in specifying rules or principles which can guide individual decisions about conduct. The second sense of ethics has to do with asking questions about what does it mean to say "one ought to" or "that is good" and is known a metaethics. "Ethics" is also used to describe the activity of specifying how and why some particular group of people decide a given behavior is right or wrong and then acts upon these decisions. This sense of ethics is descriptive of human behavior and seeks to find empirical explanations for such conduct. This area is typically thought the province of anthropology, psychology, and sociology (Bruening, 1975). The concern in this chapter is with normative ethics, that is, what behaviors fit within a code of professional ethics for student affairs administrators.

Bruening (1975) has proposed a broad framework that specifies four different levels of ethical codes (See Table 7.1). Levels 1 and 2 are based either on some fundamental philosophical principles—such as the utilitarian principle of *promote the greatest good for the greatest number* or the egoistic hedonism principle of *in the present moment I should always do what will give me the most pleasure* (Hospers, 1972)—or some religious tenet or doctrine (such as, *do unto others as you would have them do unto you)* which is sanctioned by appeal to some supernatural authority. These two levels are of interest primarily to philosophers and theologians. While these considerations are both interesting and important and need to be more thoroughly investigated in relationship to the student affairs profession, for the purposes of this chapter attention will be focused on identifying some of the commonly shared philosophical values and underpinnings of the profession, but shall not attempt to formulate them into any principles or laws.

Level 3 is the category in which one would place codes of professional ethics. Student affairs administrators, to paraphrase Golightly's (1971) comment about counselors, are professional makers of value judgments and ethical decisions within a given social context. In other words, they are concerned with application of Level 3 ethical codes. They are asking questions such as what are the rules; do they apply here; can there be a justification for violating the rules? For many years the student affairs profession has struggled because a comprehensive statement of ethical rules was lacking. Practitioners have been required to construct their own set of standards and then repeatedly to justify and defend them against challenges from other members of the academic community or the general public, generally without support or guidance from their professional associations.

Level 4 overlaps with law in that many ethical rules have been felt to be critical to the protection of the public and, therefore, governmental bodies have given them the added sanctioning power of the state's judicial system. (This overlap of ethics and law will be explored later.)

Table 7.1
Levels of Ethical Codes

LEVEL 1: ULTIMATE MORAL PRINCIPLE(S)

Characteristics of this level are (a) the principle(s) always hold(s) and always apply(ies) and (b) there is usually only one principle, but if there are more, then they can never conflict.

EXAMPLE: Promote the greatest good for the greatest number.

LEVEL 2: ETHICAL LAWS

Characteristics of this level are (a) the laws always hold, but do not always apply and (b) they cannot conflict with the ultimate principle(s) or with other ethical laws.

EXAMPLE: Lying is wrong.

EXAMPLE: Degrading the worth or dignity of any person is wrong.

LEVEL 3: ETHICAL RULES

Characteristics of this level are (a) the rules usually hold, but do not always apply, (b) violation must justified, and (c) the rules cannot conflict with either laws or ultimate principles.

EXAMPLE: Lying is wrong.

EXAMPLE: Revealing information about a student received in confidence is wrong.

LEVEL 4: LEGAL RULES/LAWS

Characteristics of this level are (a) the rules usually hold, but do not always apply, (b) violation must be justified, and (c) the rules cannot conflict with either laws or ultimate principles.

EXAMPLE: One should honor copyright restrictions.

Note. Based on and modified from Bruening, 1975.

With this framework in mind, it can be seen that professional ethics is a set of rules devised through a consensus of the profession that guides or specifies the parameters of the conduct of members of the profession when fulfilling professional responsibilities and roles. Ethical codes have three different functions: (1) protecting the clientele from incompetent, unfair, or exploitive practices, (2) protecting professionals from unwarranted intrusion from others within and outside the higher education community, and (3) protecting the profession from practices that could result in condemnation or ridicule. A code can fulfill these functions by

•establishing standards of practice specific enough so that a professional can decide what he/she should do when situations of conflict arise;

•specifying the professional's responsibilities to his/her clientele and providing sanctions when the professional fails to fulfill them;

•delineating practices detrimental to the profession and its general goals and aims;

•providing guarantees to the public that the professional will demonstrate sensible regard for the social codes, moral expectations, and legal prescriptions of the community in which he/she works;

•offering the professional a basis for safeguarding his/her integrity and the integrity of services or programs provided (McGowan & Schmidt, 1962).

ETHICS, LAW, SOCIETY, AND THE PROFESSION

Professional ethics cannot be discussed in a social vacuum. Codes of professional ethics are intimately intertwined with social mores, professional norms, and law. What then are the connections among these different ideas and social entities?

Social Mores and Values

Any given society shares a collection of moral attitudes or mores, that is, some generally accepted beliefs defining right and wrong conduct (See Figure 7.1). For example, in this country it is a generally accepted belief

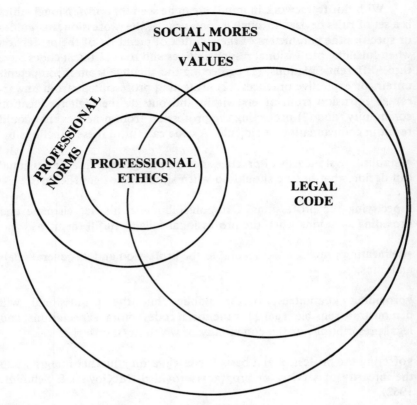

Figure 7.1.   The context of professional ethics.

that it is wrong to kill another person or to steal something belonging to another. Likewise, it is considered wrong for a professional to take advantage of or to fail to provide reasonable service to his/her clients who are depending on the professional for expertise. Society then can be seen to have certain expectations of those who label themselves as "professionals." Generally, the public expectation is that professionals in higher education will provide nurturant care to students, even though they appear to be mature and are legally classified as adults. Despite the legal burial of *in loco parentis*, student affairs professionals reason that

> most college students are still searching for their life goals and are steadily forming personal values and beliefs. Consequently, many students are susceptible to exploitation, abuse, manipulation, or simple neglect by college personnel who . . . remain powerful role models for young minds. (Chambers, 1981, p. 2)

Professional Norms

A profession can be thought of as a community within the larger society that has influence and sanctioning power, both formal and informal, over its members. This professional community exercises influence through selection, training, and socialization of new members. It establishes norms of behavior for its members, violations of which may be classified as either "unprofessional" or "unethical." A behavior can hence be called "unprofessional," but not "unethical," but all unethical conduct is by definition unprofessional. For example, failure to extend common courtesies such as returning fellow professionals' telephone calls, appearing promptly for appointments, or failure to support to one's full capacity the endeavors of the employing institution is unprofessional conduct, but may not be unethical. Typically, violations of professional norms are sanctioned informally through social ostracism and by withholding rewards such as membership in professional societies or offices or recognitions within those societies. Formal sanctioning often occurs at the institutional level by reducing or withholding salary increments, transferring the offender to a menial position, or terminating employment.

Ethical Code

The existence of a regulative code of ethics is a common attribute of any profession (Greenwood, 1957; Wilensky, 1964). Rather universal standards of ethical behavior in all professions include (1) maximum competence, (2) lack of self-interest as a motivator, (3) colleague relationships characterized as cooperative, egalitarian, and supportive, and (4) sharing new information rather than using it to gain a competitive edge as in business (Greenwood, 1957).

Professional associations can perform a valuable and necessary function by serving as the formal mechanisms for enforcement of the ethical code. Their ultimate sanction is to exclude an individual from membership. Informally, members of the profession can and should apply social pressure to assure conformity to the ethical code.

The student affairs field lacks an ethical code that is both generally accepted throughout the field and has sanctioning mechanisms in place. This lack of a code is one of the reasons the student affairs field must be classified as an emerging profession (Carpenter, Miller, & Winston,

1980). At this writing the American College Personnel Association is developing a sanctioning procedure for its ethical standards statement, and discussions are occurring of the idea of a broad-based ethical standards statement to be adopted through the Council for the Advancement of Standards for Student Services/Development Programs. Should these efforts bear fruit, the student affairs field will have made major strides toward becoming a true profession.

Professional Ethics and the Law

Law may be thought of as a subset of ethical practice that society, through its governmental bodies and agencies, has decided is so important to community welfare that the coercive power of the state is required to maintain it. No exact dividing line exists between legal and ethical principles, however. Governments are always writing new laws that redefine boundaries. Nevertheless, "an illegal act is, within the context of the given society, an unethical act" (Chambers, 1981, p. 4). However, in the narrow sense of professional ethics, much of the law is only distantly related; for example, driving 56 miles per hours down an interstate highway is a violation of the 55 miles per hour speed limit, but would not be classified as unethical professional behavior. On the other hand, for a residence hall director to divulge a student confidence without a compelling reason would generally be considered unethical, but not illegal since no statute requires the protection of that confidence.

From a more pragmatic point of view, Fargo (1981) has observed that government has moved into the province of professional ethics when the profession has acted in its own self-interest rather than the public interest. "Law fills ethical vacuums. When . . . [a profession] insists on acting on the basis of self-interest," Fargo (1981, p. 73) asserts that "law is the responsive social mechanism that mediates . . . conflicts." An excellent example is Title IX of the Education Amendments of 1972 (PL 92-318) which prohibited sex discrimination in higher education. The government decided to influence this area of higher education because professional administrators had been unable or unwilling to change age-old, unfair attitudes and practices toward women. El-Khawas (1981) has argued that if colleges wish to maintain their autonomy and minimize governmental regulation, then they must take seriously self-regulation, which includes well defined and enforced codes of ethical conduct that assure fair and equitable treatment for all of higher education's constituencies.

VALUES AND THE STUDENT AFFAIRS PROFESSION

Before one can hope to establish a code of professional ethics, one must seek to identify values that the profession holds consensually (Peterson, 1970). However, with a few exceptions, the student affairs profession has not been introspective, nor analytical, concerning its philosophy and values. Generally speaking, student affairs professionals have been "doers," not "thinkers." As a consequence no first-rate philosophical analysis of the field's assumptions, beliefs, and values has yet appeared. Three documents have served as basic statements of values and philosophy: (1) *The Student Personnel Point of View* (American Council on Education, 1937), (2) *The Student Personnel Point of View,* Revised Edition (American Council on Education, 1949), and (3) "Student Development Services in Post Secondary Education" (Council of Student Personnel Associations in Higher Education, COSPA, 1975). Four diverse philosophical traditions—holism, humanism, pragmatism, and individualism—are woven throughout the profession's fundamental literature (Appleton, Briggs, & Rhatigan, 1978; Saddlemire, 1980).

Holism means, in the words of the 1937 *Student Personnel Point of View,* that colleges have

the obligation to consider the student as a whole—his intellectual capacity and achievement, his emotional make-up, his physical condition, his social relationships, his vocational aptitudes and skills, his moral and religious values, his economic resources, his aesthetic appreciation. . . . [This philosophy] puts emphasis . . . upon the development of the student as a person rather than upon his intellectual training alone. (p. 1)

This commitment to dealing with the person in the totality of her/his selfhood was reaffirmed in the COSPA (1975) statement with the added dimension of advocating a developmental perspective for conceptualizing students and for designing interventions. Some student development advocates (Brown, 1972, 1980; Ender, Winston, & Miller, 1982; Miller & Prince, 1976) have applied the concept of holism to the institution by asserting that the whole college—students, faculty, administrators, and other student affairs staff—must collaborate in creating a positive learning environment.

Humanism makes three basic assumptions about the nature of humankind: (1) belief in human rationality, (2) possibility of human perfectibility, and (3) insistence on the importance of self-awareness and self-understanding (Appleton, Briggs, & Rhatigan, 1978). Belief in rationality and belief in human perfectibility are cornerstones of education; without these assumptions there is no point to the education enterprise. The student affairs field has its historical roots in vocational guidance, which emphasized the necessity for students to identify their aptitudes and skills and then to match them to an occupation. As the COSPA (1975) student development statement asserts, "the potential for development and self-direction is possessed by everyone. Education is a way of assisting in developing these potentials" (p. 525). One very important result of a humanistic view is a basic optimism about the profession's clientele—students—and its setting—the college environment.

Pragmatism, the "American philosophy," first expressed itself in higher education through the shift from classical and liberal arts education to more vocational and technical-scientific training. As Saddlemire observed

> Dewey's position that knowledge is a consequence of combining thought and action provided a solid theoretical base for the evolution for a student services approach to involving students in many campus roles. (1980, p. 26)

Student affairs administrators have always been viewed as the persons whose responsibility it is to make things work—whether through control and discipline or through facilitating the institution's meeting the needs of students. *The Student Personnel Point of View* (1937, 1949) assigned student affairs professionals the roles of interpreter of the institution and its policies, coordinator, facilitator, counselor, supervisor, institutional researcher, record keeper, disciplinarian, cheerleader (maintainer of morale), and employer.

Individualism is another philosophical cornerstone.

> Human beings express their life goal as becoming free, liberated, self-directed, and they seek it through a process variously called self-actualization, full functioning, and behavioral development. (COSPA, 1975)

The touchstone of the student affairs profession is a recognition of individual differences in backgrounds, abilities, interests, and goals (American Council on Education, 1949). Only through recognizing these differences and then taking appropriate action to meet the diversity of needs can a college provide quality education; otherwise it is simply broadcasting information. Student affairs historically has seen as its mission identification of individual uniqueness and provision of individualized attention.

As the Preamble of the ACPA Statement of Ethical and Professional Standards stated, the profession is

> dedicated to the worth, dignity, potential and uniqueness of each individual and thus to the service of society. [Professionals] . . . are committed to protecting individual human rights, advancing knowledge of college student growth and development and to promoting effectiveness in student affairs organizations and operations. (1981, p. 184)

The profession values service to individuals and society. The conflict for student affairs professionals comes when individuals and institutions differ. Brown (1977) suggested three value conflict areas repeatedly encountered by student affairs professionals: (1) dissonance between individual liberty and social responsibility, (2) conflict between hedonistic needs/desires and altruism, and (3) search for meaning to human existence. Ethical codes are needed by the profession, not to solve these problems, but to lay out the parameters of acceptable solutions.

ISSUES AND PRINCIPLES

Although a historical understanding of the philosophical underpinnings of the student affairs profession is a necessary prerequisite to defining a clear set of ethical principles, it is also necessary to identify ethical questions faced by student affairs professionals and ways in which these issues may be resolved. While general ethical issues are covered, ethical standards references will be to the ACPA Standards (1981) for simplicity sake. (A copy of the ACPA Ethical and Professional Standards can be found in Appendix A.)

Ethical standards, such as those cited in this chapter, define behaviors which ought to or ought not be performed by student affairs professionals. Although standards are essential and helpful as guides to behavior, they do not solve all individual ethical problems (Van Hoose & Kottler, 1977). In writing about the ethics of counselors/therapists, Barclay (1968) stated that the ultimate safeguards for ethical practice are individual professionals' sense of integrity and responsibility. This statement may well apply to student affairs professionals as well. Wrenn (1966) stated that although many professionals have established codes of ethics, the application of such principles may require courage and depth of conviction as well as a reliance on the "great values and principles of the human race" (p. 135). Oftentimes, the entering professional is faced with ambiguous, nonspecific standards and also lacks a clear understanding of his/her personal values in relation to professional issues and situations. Therefore, because ethical issues are not usually resolved in a simplistic, "cookbook" fashion, in this chapter is explored a process model for ethical decision making.

A MODEL OF ETHICAL DECISION MAKING

Apparently no clear answers exist to all of the various ethical and professional behavior issues faced by student affairs professionals. Also, the process that the individual practitioner uses to make ethical decisions is based on a variety of complex and interrelated factors, such as previous training, ethical behavior of significant mentors, general moral and ethical values of the practitioner, theoretical orientation, the situation being considered, and so forth. In order to conceptualize a model of ethical decision making, it is necessary to understand the ethical orientation of practitioners, thus enhancing the understanding of rationales related to the individual decision-making process. How, then, does one conceptualize the ethical orientation of practitioners?

Relying on the work of Kohlberg and Piaget, Van Hoose and Paradise (1979) have proposed conceptualizing the ethical orientation of counselors along a developmental continuum. Their five-stage model begins with the *Punishment Orientation* in which decisions are based on rules and standards (all external to the counselor): criteria for judgment are the physical consequences of behavior. The second stage in this model is the *Institutional Orientation* in which the guiding principles for ethical judgments are the rules and policies of institutional or agency authorities. *Societal Orientation* is the third stage. It is characterized by concern for society's laws and community welfare, but with little concern for the individual. In the fourth stage, *Individual Orientation*, the counselor's ethical judgments are made with concern primarily for the needs of the individual, while avoiding violation of the rights of others. Individual principles and internalized ethical standards form the basis of judgments in the fifth stage, *Principle or Conscience Orientation.* In this stage, there is little regard for legal, professional, or societal consequences; concern for the individual is paramount.

This ethical orientation model is directed to counselors whose primary responsibility is to the treatment of individual clients, rather than to organizations or to institutional programs. Student affairs staff members, because their responsibilities involve concern for individuals, organizations, and programs alike, are faced with more complex and intricate ethical dilemmas. For example, when a student affairs professional disciplines a student, the prescribed disciplinary action specified by the institution may not enhance the development of the individual student. However, that disciplinarian is not likely to be at a less advanced stage of ethical development than a student affairs professional who regards individual rights as primary.

The Preamble of the American College Personnel Association Statement of Ethical and Professional Standards (1981) highlights the dual responsibilities of student affairs professionals to individual students and institutions. Therefore, this statement validates the notion that the student affairs professional, in order to make ethical decisions, must be able to evaluate a particular ethical dilemma and to find an appropriate balance between needs for individual growth, needs of organizations, and integrity of institutional programs.

The student affairs professional operating at the more advanced levels of ethical development has a clear understanding of his/her ethical principles. Ethical decisions reflect an internal orientation rather than immediate and automatic responses to external pressures and demands. These higher levels of ethical development should, for the student affairs professional, reflect cognizance of consequences for organizations, for the institution, and for society at large, as well as for individuals.

In light of the difficult dilemmas and conflicting demands on a student affairs staff, what would be an appropriate process for practitioners to use in making ethical decisions? As stated earlier, ethical judgments reflect the individual decision-maker's past experiences, current conflicts, and personal values. Another difficulty faced by student affairs practitioners is that oftentimes, there is not sufficient time to analyze adequately a given situation in terms of the complex factors involved, the possible ramifications, and consequences. Given these limitations and individual differences, it is plausible to create a general process model for use in making ethical judgments. A model was constructed by Van

Hoose and Kottler (1977) for use by counselors, and an adaptation for student affairs practitioners is presented in Figure 7.2.

The effective use of the decision-making model is dependent on the practitioner's willingness and ability to (1) confront personal values related to ethical decisions, (2) tolerate ambiguity and a lack of clear external directives, (3) analyze ethical standards, institutional rules, legal principles, (4) assess results of ethical judgments in a nondefensive manner, and (5) take positions that may be unpopular or that may be detrimental to career advancement.

Particularly for beginning professionals, it is often confusing and anxiety producing to be thrust into situations that require quick and competent resolution of an ethical dilemma. It is possible through personal questioning and confrontation to enhance development of a personal style of ethics. Answers to the following questions adapted from Van Hoose & Kottler (1977) may help one to develop confidence with complex ethical decisions.

•How congruent are ethical standards and institutional rules with personal values? How does one confront incongruities?

•What criteria would one use to decide about ambiguous ethical problems, such as divulging confidential material, sharing test results, confronting an unethical colleague, or deciding what constitutes a significant contribution to research?

•In which situations might one provide services in which he/she has not had adequate training?

•With what types of students and colleagues is one most effective?

•What personal "payoffs" (such as prestige, power, responsibility, helpfulness, money) does one receive from work and how important are each of these rewards?

•What criteria does one use to evaluate the effectiveness of one's work and professional development?

These questions obviously have no clear and universal answers. The purpose of such questions is to help professionals assess their values—a first step toward ethical development.

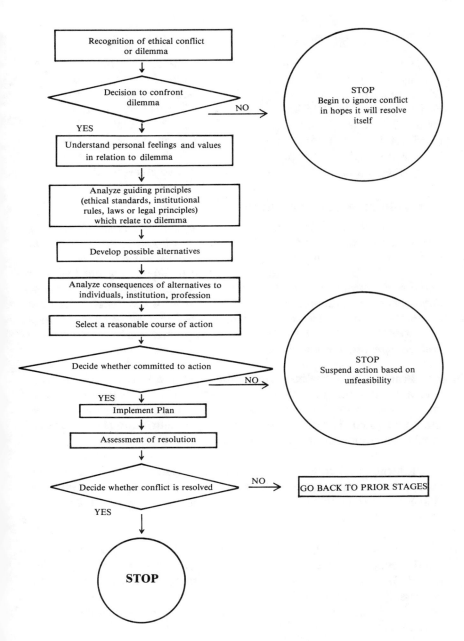

Figure 7.2.   Paradigm of ethical decision-making process.

Note.   Based on and modified from Van Hoose & Kottler, 1977.

APPLICATION OF ETHICAL DECISION-MAKING MODEL

Perhaps the most effective way to understand ethical decision-making principles is to identify hypothetical ethical problems and to apply the ethical decision-making model. This section focuses on the application of the ethical decision-making model in three hypothetical situations. The reader should be forewarned that the alternative resolutions listed herein do not constitute a complete, or, in fact, a recommended list. Each student affairs professional can use these examples as stimuli for further questioning, rather than as definitive answers.

The Dilemma of Jane Smith

Jane Smith was in her second year as a residence hall director. During that time she had written a research study investigating the relationship of hall activities to academic performance. The housing director, Dr. Jones, had helped Jane gather information by contacting the Registrar and by informing Jane of the institution's educational record policy. Jane conceived, designed, and wrote the study. When Jane showed the completed study to Dr. Jones, he demanded that he be included as a coauthor because he had made the essential contacts with the appropriate college officials. How might Jane respond to this situation?

Practitioner's Feelings and Values. Jane Smith has experienced several heated disagreements with Dr. Jones and wants to smooth over any conflicts with him. Jane believes that any and all collaboration should be noted. However, she defines major contributions as those that involve collaboration in the design and writing of research.

Ethical Conflict. Should Dr. Jones be included as a coauthor, even though his contribution was not nearly as significant as Jane Smith's? Was Dr. Jones' contribution major, and was it, in fact, essential to completion of the study?

Guiding Principles. ACPA Ethical and Professional Standards (1981) Section F, Number 9, states: "Members acknowledge major contributions to research projects and professional writings through joint authorships, with the author who made the principal contributions listed first. Contributions of a professional and technical nature are acknowledged in footnotes or introductory statements."

Alternative Actions. Actions open to Jane include (1) Jane tells Dr. Jones that he will not be included as a coauthor because his contributions were minor; (2) Jane informs Dr. Jones that his assistance will be noted in a footnote, but that he will not be listed as a coauthor; (3) Jane agrees to include Dr. Jones as a coauthor.

Evaluation of Alternatives. In this particular situation, two criteria should be used to evaluate alternatives: (1) the consequences of a particular action for Jane's relationship with her supervisor and (2) the consequence of the action chosen for Jane's sense of professional integrity.

The Dilemma of Bill Brown

Bill Brown is a new dean of students on a small, private college campus. Shortly after his arrival in July a vacancy occurs in a residence hall, and Bill is named chairperson of the search committee to find a replacement before the beginning of the fall term. The screening committee receives applications and one applicant appears far superior in terms of education and experience and is invited for an on-campus interview. After a poll of all interviewers, the consensus was to offer the applicant the position. Bill sought the president's approval to offer the position and was refused. When pressed, the president stated that although he had not interviewed the candidate, he felt that a Black person from a public school background could not project the kind of image the college should have.

Practitioner's Feelings and Values. Bill is committed to anti-discriminatory practices in all aspects of higher education. Furthermore, Bill feels that the candidate chosen by the committee would serve as an excellent role model for minorities. Because Bill is new to his job, he is uncertain of the most effective ways to voice disagreements. Also, Bill is too new to his position to have amassed much political support.

Ethical Conflict. How can one be certain whether or not this action was, in fact, based on racial discrimination? How can one most effectively work to modify discriminatory practices?

Guiding Principles. The ACPA Statement of Ethical and Professional Standards (1981), Section B, Number 5, states: "Members perform in a fashion that is not discriminatory on the basis of race, sex, national origin, affectional/sexual preference, handicap, age or creed, and they work actively to modify discriminatory practices when encountered" (p. 185).

Alternative Actions. Actions available include the following: (1) Bill would contact the candidate directly, inform the candidate of the racial bias used in decision making, and encourage the candidate to take legal action. (2) Bill would confront the president directly, ask for a clear-cut explanation of the decision, share reasons for wanting to hire the candidate, and encourage the president to reverse his position. (3) Bill would accept the decision, say nothing and immediately begin seeking another candidate.

Evaluation of Alternatives. In this particular situation, three criteria should be used to evaluate alternatives: (1) What will be the effect of the action on the institution's programs, students, and integrity? (2) How will the action taken affect Bill's sense of upholding standards of professional behavior? (3) How will the action affect Bill's future effectiveness at the institution?

The Dilemma of Pat Martin

Pat Martin is responsible for the orientation and admission of transfer students at a small, regional university. Pat possesses a M.A. in counseling, but she has not worked in a counseling capacity for five years. After leading an orientation seminar for several weeks, Pat is contacted by one of the women students enrolled in the seminar. The young woman, Sheila, shares that she is lonely and homesick and wants to drop out. Pat and Sheila spend much time talking about Sheila's adjustment difficulties. At the end of the first term, Sheila starts to become verbally abusive with Pat. She also begins talking about past violent behavior and her hostility towards her roommate. As time progresses, Sheila's hostility becomes more intense, and she threatens to push her roommate out of the window.

Practitioner's Feelings and Values. Pat is aware that Sheila regards her relationship with Pat as a counseling or therapeutic one. Sheila has opened up to Pat about a variety of deep personal issues and says that she has not exposed herself like this before. Pat feels that her counseling skills are somewhat rusty and is concerned about her ability to deal with the intense nature of Sheila's problem. Pat is also aware that Sheila is likely to stop talking to her if the hostility is exposed to a third party.

Ethical Conflict. Should Pat break confidentiality in light of the threats made against the roommate?

Guiding Principles. The ACPA Statement of Ethical and Professional Standards (1981) Section A, Number 4 states: "Members respect the student's right to privacy and share information about individuals only in accordance with institutional policies, or when given permission by the student, or when required to prevent personal harm" (p. 184).

Alternative Actions. Actions available include: (1) Pat would contact the campus psychologist for consultation and would refer Sheila to the psychologist. Pat would also inform Sheila that unless she sees the psychologist, Pat will take further action. (2) Pat would inform Sheila's resident director of the situation and recommend that Sheila's roommate be changed. (3) Pat would contact campus security with the information she possesses. (4) Pat would take no action and continue to keep what is said strictly confidential. (5) Pat would inform the roommate she may be in danger.

Evaluation of Alternatives. In this particular dilemma, the following criteria should be used to evaluate alternatives: (1) the effect of Sheila's threats on the roommate and other residents, (2) the effect of disclosure on Sheila's personal development, (3) the possible physical harm which could occur, and (4) the effect of this intense relationship on Pat's effective performance as orientation director.

RESPONSIBILITIES OF ALL STUDENT AFFAIRS PROFESSIONALS

The fundamental responsibility of all student affairs professionals is to be knowledgeable of the existing ethical standards statements and to assess their conduct in relation to those standards. As part of the assessment, student affairs professionals must become aware of the implications of their behavior and be reflective and introspective about their motivations in working with students and community members. Ethical behavior is contingent upon a high level of self-awareness.

Each student affairs staff member has a primary responsibility to model high levels of ethical and professional conduct for fellow professionals and students alike. With the sometimes lamented demise of *in loco parentis,* some have argued that the traditional charge to higher education for responding to the character development of students has been abandoned. This is true to a large extent when viewed from a prescriptive perspective. However, student affairs staff members probably can have a much greater impact on students' ethical development by modeling a concern for and adherence to a set of publicly owned standards than they ever could have when prescribing rigid rules for students. Other powerful techniques for enhancing the ethical development of students include (1) student affairs professionals directly confronting students about conduct that has ethical implications when it occurs and (2) stimulating dialogue and critical analysis of situations that present ethical or moral questions, whether in response to issues related to campus activities or to societal concerns.

Chief Student Affairs Administrator Responsibilities

All student affairs administrators bear responsibilities in the area of professional and ethical conduct. However, the chief student affairs administrator has some additional responsibilities by virtue of his/her leadership position.

The chief student affairs administrator has the responsibility to assure that staff members are aware of ethical standards. This may be most effectively addressed by insisting that ethical standards are given regular attention in staff development activities. At least once a year every staff member should be reminded about ethical concerns and assisted in examining his/her behavior. Even more importantly, ethical behavior should be one category addressed in the formal staff evaluation process. If ethical behavior is a serious concern of the profession, then simply giving lip service is inadequate. Ethics must be directly applied to the day-to-day operations with students and staff.

Another major responsibility of the chief student affairs administrator is to monitor, either personally or through assignment to a specific staff member, the institution's policies, procedures, and practices as they relate to the profession's statements of ethical standards. When violations or inconsistencies are recognized, the institution's leadership should be informed. Only when student affairs professionals are willing to confront unethical behavior (particularly when institutionalized) will the field in fact become a true profession. By placing concern for its clientele (students) and protection of the public interest ahead of personal gain or loyalty to individual institutional leaders, the profession will preserve its integrity and will gain the respect from other members of the academic community that it has often felt lacking.

RECOMMENDATIONS TO IMPROVE ETHICAL CONDUCT IN THE PROFESSION

Two areas require attention in order to improve ethical practice in the profession: professional association activities and professional preparation programs.

Professional Associations

Profession-wide Statement of Standards. A statement of ethical standards that addresses student affairs practice in a generic or general sense and that has the approval of all or most student affairs professional associations is badly needed. Once adopted, such a statement would require wide dissemination and a vigorous educational campaign. Workshops, newsletter columns, a standards casebook, and convention programs could all be used in the educational effort.

Support and Consultation. Professional associations need to develop task forces or commissions that will provide consultation to members in dealing with questions about ethical conduct. There is also the need to provide support to members who elect to take action against either individuals or colleges who are unethical in their treatment of students and/or staff.

Sanctioning Mechanisms. Ethical standards that have no consequences if violated have limited value for a profession. Some would argue that such standards are only a facade, designed to give student affairs practitioners a cosmetic appearance of being professionals. Professional associations, either in concert or independently, need to establish processes through which alleged violations of ethical standards can be quickly investigated and sanctions applied when violations have been established. A process for admonishing higher education institutions that disregard or refuse to alter practices found to violate principles of ethical practice is also needed.

Professional Preparation Programs

Student affairs preparation programs bear a heavy responsibility for improving ethical practice in the profession. Graduate students need to become very familiar with the statements of ethical standards. During practicum and internship supervision sessions, preparation program faculty should help students examine their behavior, as well as that of the professionals in the setting, for ethical implications. Even before students enter practicum sites they should have spent time discussing potential ethical dilemmas. Without having time to reflect on how one might deal with an ethical problem before it is encountered, because of the press of time and circumstances, one may take an unethical course of action that could have been avoided.

One question that students need to consider carefully before the practicum placement is the distinction between the ethics in counseling and other student affairs functions. As a counselor, one's primary responsibility is to the individual receiving attention, provided the actions are not dangerous to themselves or others. What is said in the counseling session is confidential, and the counselor's attention and concern are focused on the welfare of that individual student. However, in settings outside the counseling session, the student affairs practitioner has a major responsibility to the institution, as well as to the student. In some senses this issue can be seen as a matter of accountability. In a counseling relationship, the counselor is primarily accountable to, or responsible to, his/her client; however, in the student activities office or housing department, for instance, the student affairs professional has a responsibility to protect the integrity of the institution and the best interests of all students and must therefore work with individual students within that context. This issue is further complicated by the fact that hall directors who possess counseling skills may establish counseling relationships with residents. (All counseling does not occur in the counseling center, nor should it.) Graduate students and professionals alike need to consider carefully these issues before being thrust into the middle of them and to develop a set of personal guidelines, within the boundaries of the established ethical standards statements, that can be used to guide their conduct in such situations.

Preparation program faculty members must model appropriate ethical behavior, instruct students about ethical standards, create a climate that evidences a concern about ethical issues, and provide stimulation and support to students as they explore ethical issues. However, faculty cannot accomplish the task alone; practitioners as they have contact with students in preparation programs have a responsibility to help students confront the ethical issues of the profession.

A concern for the ethics of student affairs practice in a formal sense is relatively recent. Whether the profession chooses to accept the challenge to deal with these important issues will determine whether student affairs will move beyond its emerging professional status to become a true profession.

REFERENCES

American Association of Collegiate Registrars and Admissions Officers, College Entrance Examination Board, National Association of College Admissions Counselors, & National Association of Secondary School Principals. *Joint statement on principles of good practice in college admissions and recruitment.* Authors, 1979.

American College Personnel Association. The use of group procedures in higher education: A position statement by ACPA. *Journal of College Student Personnel,* 1976, *17,* 161-8.

American College Personnel Association. American College Personnel Association statement of ethical and professional standards. *Journal of College Student Personnel,* 1981, *22,* 184-9.

American Council on Education. *The student personnel point of view.* American Council on Education Studies (Series 1, Vol. 1, No. 3). Washington, DC: Author, 1937.

American Council on Education. *The student personnel point of view* (Rev. ed.). American Council on Education Studies, (Series 6, Vol. 13, No. 13). Washington, DC: Author, 1949.

American Personnel and Guidance Association. Ethical standards. *Personnel and Guidance Journal,* 1961, *40,* 206-9.

Appleton, J.R., Briggs, C.M., & Rhatigan, J.J. *Pieces of eight: The rite, roles, and styles of the dean by eight who have been there.* Portland, OR: NASPA Institute of Research and Development, 1978.

Barclay, J. *Counseling and philosophy: A theoretical exposition.* Boston: Houghton Mifflin, 1968.

Brown, R.D. *Student development in tomorrow's higher education: A return to the academy.* Washington, DC: American Personnel and Guidance Association, 1972.

Brown, R.D. Professional development and staff development: The search for a metaphor. In R.P. Wanzek (Ed.), *Staff development.* DeKalb, IL: Northern Illinois University, 1977.

Brown, R.D. Student development and the academy: New directions and horizons. In D.A. DeCoster & P. Mable (Eds.), *Personal education & community development in college residence halls.* Washington, DC: American College Personnel Association, 1980.

Bruening, W.H. Ethics and morality. In W.R. Durland & W.H. Bruening (Eds.), *Ethical issues: A search for the contemporary conscience.* Palo Alto, CA: Mayfield Publishing Co., 1975.

Carnegie Council on Policy Studies. *Fair practices in higher education: Rights and responsibilities of students and their colleges in a period of intensified competition for enrollments.* San Francisco: Jossey-Bass, 1979.

Carpenter, D.S., Miller, T.K., & Winston, R.B., Jr. Toward the professionalization of student affairs. *NASPA Journal,* 1980, *18*(2), 16-22.

Chambers, C.M. Foundations of ethical responsibility in higher education administration. In R.H. Stein & M.C. Baca (Eds.), *New directions for higher education: Professional ethics in university administration* (No. 33). San Francisco: Jossey-Bass, 1981.

Council of Student Personnel Associations in Higher Education. Student development services in post secondary education. *Journal of College Student Personnel,* 1975, *16,* 524-8.

El-Khawas, E. Self-regulation: An approach to ethical standards. In R.H. Stein & M.C. Baca (Eds.), *New directions for higher education: Professional ethics in university administration* (No. 33). San Francisco: Jossey-Bass, 1981.

Ender, S.C., Winston, R.B., Jr., & Miller, T.K. Academic advising as student development. In R.B. Winston, Jr., S.C. Ender, & T.K. Miller (Eds.), *New directions for student services: Developmental approaches to academic advising* (No. 17). San Francisco: Jossey-Bass, 1982.

Fargo, J.M. Academic chivalry and professional responsibility. In R.H. Stein & M.C. Baca (Eds.), *New directions for higher education: Professional ethics in university administration* (No. 33). San Francisco: Jossey-Bass, 1981.

Golightly, C.L. A philosopher's view of values and ethics. *Personnel and Guidance Journal,* 1971, *50,* 289-94.

Greenwood, E. Attributes of a profession. *Social Work,* 1957, *2,* 45-55.

Hospers, J. *Human conduct: Problems in ethics.* New York: Harcourt Brace Jovanovich, 1972.

McGowan, J.F., & Schmidt, L.D. *Counseling: Readings in theory and practice.* New York: Holt, Rinehart & Winston, 1962.

Miller, T.K., & Carpenter, D.S. Professional preparation for today and tomorrow. In D.G. Creamer (Ed.), *Student development in higher education: Theories, practices, and future directions.* Washington, DC: American College Personnel Association, 1980.

Miller, T.K., & Prince, J.S. *The future of student affairs: A guide to student development for tomorrow's higher education.* San Francisco: Jossey-Bass, 1976.

National Association of Student Personnel Administrators. Statement of principles and ethical practices of student personnel administrators. Portland, OR: Author, 1960.

Peterson, J.A. *Counseling and values: A philosophical examination.* Scranton, PA: International Textbook Co., 1970.

Saddlemire, G.L. Professional developments. In U. Delworth, G.R. Hanson, & Associates (Eds.), *Student services: A handbook for the profession.* San Francisco: Jossey-Bass, 1980.

Stamatakos, L.D. Student affairs progress toward professionalism: Recommendations for action. *Journal of College Student Personnel,* 1981, *22,* 105-12, 197-207.

Trueblood, D.L. The educational preparation of the college student personnel leader of the future. In G.J. Klopf (Ed.), *College student personnel in the years ahead.* Washington, DC: American Personnel and Guidance Association, 1966.

Van Hoose, W.H., & Kottler, J.A. *Ethical and legal issues in counseling and psychotherapy.* San Francisco: Jossey-Bass, 1977.

Van Hoose, W.H., & Paradise, L.V. *Ethics in counseling and psychotherapy: Perspectives in issues and decision making.* Cranston, RI: Carroll Press, 1979.

Wilensky, H.L. The professionalization of everyone? *American Journal of Sociology,* 1964, *70,* 137-58.

Wrenn, C.G. The ethics of counseling. In R. Bernard (Ed.), *Counseling and psychotherapy.* Palo Alto, CA: Science and Behavior Books, 1966.

Wrenn, C.G., & Darley, J.G. An appraisal of the professional status of personnel work. In E.G. Williamson (Ed.), *Trends in student personnel work.* Minneapolis: University of Minnesota Press, 1949.

SUGGESTED READINGS

Carnegie Council on Policy Studies. *Fair practices in higher education: Rights and responsibilities of students and their colleges in a period of intensified competition for enrollments.* San Francisco: Jossey-Bass, 1979.

Golightly, C.L. A philosopher's view of values and ethics. *Personnel and Guidance Journal,* 1971, *50,* 289-94.

Stein, R.H., & Baca, M.C. (Eds.). *New directions for higher education: Professional ethics in university administration* (No. 33). San Francisco: Jossey-Bass, 1981.

Van Hoose, W.H., & Kottler, J.A. *Ethical and legal issues in counseling and psychotherapy.* San Francisco: Jossey-Bass, 1977.

Van Hoose, W.H., & Paradise, L.V. *Ethics in counseling and psychotherapy: Perspectives in issues and decision-making.* Cranston, RI: Carroll Press, 1979.

Phyllis Mable has been involved with college students, student affairs services and programs, and higher education for over twenty years and has provided leadership promoting change from student adjustment themes to human development themes. Professional involvement has been primarily with the Division of Housing at the University of Florida in Gainesville and with the Division of Student Affairs at Virginia Commonwealth University. She is now Vice-President for Student Affairs at Longwood College (Virginia). Mable has co-edited two publications supporting student development, residence education, personal education, and community development in college residence halls.

During the past several years, she has been involved with the broader aspects of student affairs. A publication dedicated to understanding students, co-edited with David A. DeCoster, was recently published as part of the Jossey-Bass "New Directions for Student Services" series. During most of her professional years, she has been actively involved with the American College Personnel Association and served as its President in 1979-80.

Theodore K. Miller is Professor of Counseling and Human Development Services at the University of Georgia, where he is coordinator of the Student Personnel in Higher Education Preparation Program and Director of the College of Education Center for Student Development.

For additional information please refer to the last section of the book entitled "About the Authors."

Chapter 8

STANDARDS FOR PROFESSIONAL PRACTICE

Phyllis Mable
Theodore K. Miller

The practice of student affairs can be traced back to the earliest days of higher education in America (Leonard, 1956; Rudolph, 1962). Yet, both those concerned about and those responsible for personal aspects of student life have had no clearly defined criteria to judge the quality of their efforts and activities. This lack of minimum standards for both the practice and the preparation of its member practitioners has limited seriously the establishment of student affairs as a recognized profession (Larson, 1977).

Although a number of authorities have focused attention upon the importance of standards for preparation program accreditation, little attention has been given to standards for practice (Penn, 1974). As Penney (1969; 1972) strongly implied, the field of student affairs has lacked congruence and consistency of practice essential to the existence of a profession. Thus, even though the lack of professional standards has caused concern, relatively little activity has been designed to establish standards of practice or preparation for the field.

Certain terms and concepts are basic to understanding and communicating professional standards in student affairs. Although some terms occasionally are used interchangeably, the professional practitioner must be able to distinguish their varied meanings and nuances.

Accreditation

Accreditation represents both a concept and a process used throughout postsecondary education in the United States. The *concept of accreditation* is defined as the formation of voluntary groups of institutions, practitioners, or educators that encourage and assist institutions or their specialized subunits such as colleges, schools, departments, or programs in evaluating and improving their educational endeavors. These groups publish the names of institutions or programs that meet or exceed acceptable standards of educational quality. The *process of accreditation* is defined as a periodic evaluation of the educational activities of an institution or its subunits and is therefore an independent judgment by peers, specialists, or other professionals that determine whether or not the institution has achieved its stated educational mission. This process typically involves a concise statement of educational objectives, a self-study to examine the extent to which those objectives have been met, an on-site peer review, and a judgment by the accrediting body. Accreditation is applied to institutions and their educational programs, not to individuals. Accreditation functions for the benefit of the public as a check on the quality of services rendered to the public. According to the Council on Postsecondary Accreditation (COPA) (1981), accreditation at the postsecondary level may be said to

•foster excellence in postsecondary education through the development of uniform national criteria and guidelines for assessing educational effectiveness;

•encourage improvement through continuous self-study and review;

•assure the educational community, the general public, and other agencies or organizations that an institution or program has clearly defined and appropriate objectives, maintains conditions under which their achievement can reasonably be expected, appears in fact to be accomplishing them substantially, and can be expected to continue to do so; and

•provide counsel and assistance to established and developing institutions and programs; and endeavor to protect institutions against encroachments which might jeopardize their educational effectiveness or academic freedom. (p.3)

Accreditation Standards and Guidelines. Standards reflect criteria established by an accrediting body to articulate its expectations of an accreditable institution or specialized program. Standards provide a frame of reference or context within which the accreditation process can be implemented. Other terms such as "criteria," "requirements," or "essentials" are sometimes used in lieu of the term "standards" by some accrediting bodies. Because standards reflect requirements, auxiliary verbs *shall* and *must* are used in their wording.

Guidelines are used to explain and amplify standards and frequently provide examples of flexible interpretations that are acceptable to the accrediting body. Auxiliary verbs used when wording guidelines are *should* and *may*.

Presently, at least two of the six regional accrediting associations have published standards or guidelines related to the practice of student affairs on their member campuses. The Commission on Colleges (1977) of the Southern Association of Schools and Colleges has issued Standard Seven, Student Development Services; the Northwest Association of Schools and Colleges has prepared guidelines for evaluation committee members. In addition, the Association of Independent Colleges and Schools recognizes student services in its standards.

Credentialing

Institutions of higher learning, whether accredited or not, typically issue credits upon completion of academic and technical work. When the specified number and type of credits are earned, a diploma or degree is granted as evidence of successful mastery of required knowledge and skills. These requirements are based upon professional standards for preparation and ethical practice and represent the minimum criteria established for entrance into a particular field or endeavor. Resulting "credentials awarded by institutions gain 'legitimacy' for third parties through their value in the marketplace and through accreditation by nongovernmental institutional and specialized accrediting agencies" (Miller & Boswell, 1979, p. 219). Noteworthy in relationship to these factors is the fact that whereas accreditation is applied to institutions and programs, credentialing is applied to individuals.

In addition to institutional endorsements by diplomas and degrees, at least three other major forms of endorsement are common to many professions: certification, licensure, and registry. At present these alternative endorsements usually do not directly influence employment practices in institutions of higher learning.

Certification. This type endorsement can take several forms but basically involves a process by which an authorizing agency or organization officially certifies that an individual, voluntarily seeking such recognition, has met certain predetermined qualifications specified by that authorizing body. In addition to formal academic preparation requirements and supervised practice, satifactory performance on examination also may be required. Certification is usually monitored on a regular basis by the authorizing body.

State certification of elementary and secondary school teachers, counselors, and administrators are familiar examples of this procedure, although not all certifying agencies are governmentally sponsored or limited to a localized area. Two examples of non-governmental agencies that grant certification on the national level are the Commission on Rehabilitation Counselor Certification and the National Academy of Certified Clinical Mental Health Counselors.

Licensure. Professional licensure is a process by which an agency of government, usually on the state level, grants permission to individuals who meet predetermined qualifications to engage in a specified profession or occupation and/or to use a particular title (for example: counselor, psychologist). Through licensure, governments legally define and regulate the practice of a variety of professions. Licensure legislation sets standards of training and practice to protect the public from unqualified practitioner and better assures practitioner protection under the law in the application of skills.

Registry. Through a national register of professional practitioners, individual practitioners are endorsed as being especially competent to render professional service to members of the public at large. A national registry establishes standards not unlike those involved in state licensure legislation, although its existence need not be legislated as such. Being listed on a national register is especially beneficial to those living and working in states that currently do not have professional licensure in their area of expertise. Similar to other forms of certification, registry may involve some form of examination.

Peer Endorsement

In student affairs practice, formal endorsement procedures such as certification, licensure, or registry are emphasized much less than endorsement and sponsorship by peers.

Publications, presentations, consultations, and professional leadership activities are key elements in establishing a professional reputation. The recognition by peers of quality performance, dependability, productivity, and the resulting endorsement or lack thereof is as much a part of one's credentials as are the more formal certifying processes and procedures.

FOUNDATIONS OF ACCREDITATION

Higher education exists within the context of a larger community. To be viable, higher education must be responsive to everchanging social realities. The nongovernmental, voluntary accreditation process is the means by which the U.S. higher education community seeks to assure viability over time. Two critical developments have challenged accreditation and guided its existence in recent years according to Thrash (1979): (1) the reliance of the federal government on nongovernmental accrediting agencies as reliable authorities in determining the eligibility of schools and colleges to participate in federal education assistance programs and (2) the exploding educational universe that has caused higher education to expand its program offerings, its missions, and its accessibility to nontraditional student populations. Federal government influence has been increasingly obvious since World War II. The Veterans' Readjustment Assistance Act of 1952 (Korean GI Bill) and the parallel establishment of the Division of Eligibility and Agency Evaluation (DEAE) within the U.S. Office of Education brought about a unique triad of two governmental agencies and one nongovernmental entity concerned with the quality of postsecondary education institutions throughout the nation. As the federal government pressed to assure that funds designated for veterans' education would go to institutions offering quality educational experiences, the DEAE was faced with making judgments about institutional eligibility. The voluntary accrediting agencies became the vehicle for DEAE to carry out its mission. As the years passed and the federal government increased its involvement in higher education, the importance of a more highly organized accreditation system to assure quality education grew as well.

Nongovernmental Accrediting Agencies

Initially a number of independent accrediting bodies offered institutional or academic program accreditation with little or no coordination among the groups. In 1949, seven national organizations that accredited higher education merged and created the National Commission on Accrediting (NCA). This commission both recognized and monitored the various groups that awarded accreditation to specialized educational programs (e.g., academic schools, colleges, divisions, and departments). In 1964, the Federation of Regional Accrediting Commissions of Higher Education (FRACHE) was organized to coordinate the work of the postsecondary commissions of the six regional accrediting associations. These two bodies represented, on a national basis, both the regional and programmatic accreditation bodies then in existence. In addition, four other national groups were concerned with the accreditation of over 1000 specialized institutions such as Bible colleges, independent colleges and schools, trade and technical schools, and home study institutions. The Council on Postsecondary Accreditation (COPA) was organized early in 1975 as the result of a merger of FRACHE, NCA, and the four national groups accrediting specialized institutions. With this merger, COPA became the lead agency for establishing policies and practices in postsecondary accreditation (COPA, 1981).

Accrediting Student Affairs Practice

Accreditation is important to professional student affairs practitioners as it concerns both professional practice within institutions of higher education and formal academic preparation of practitioners. However, only two of the regional accrediting associations and one of the specialized institutional accrediting bodies have specifically addressed student affairs, student services, or student development in their published accreditation standards. At best a great inconsistency exists in the criteria used to judge the effectiveness and quality of these programs. This lack of uniform standards for practice has hindered the professional growth and recognition of student affairs programs throughout the country.

Special Program Accreditation. Several specialty program areas of student affairs practice have established accreditation bodies. The International Association of Counseling Services (1978) created criteria and implemented accreditation procedures for student counseling centers, while the American College Health Association (1977) provided accreditation for student health centers. The trend for specialty areas to have standards and to be accredited by an appropriate authorizing body tends to fragment the field of student affairs and could well cause territorial conflict and even adversary relationships to occur. Without a concerted effort to establish coordinated accreditation standards and procedures for the field as a whole, accreditation on a specialized or programmatic basis certainly will increase. If student affairs is to function as an integrated whole, then efforts must be made to deal with its practice in a holistic fashion. This is a key issue that needs immediate and increased attention by all members of the profession.

Accrediting Preparation Programs

A similar problem exists in the area of student affairs preparation. Although an initial set of standards for professional preparation has been adopted by the American College Personnel Association (1979), and are included in Appendix C, currently no accreditation body seeks to accredit the full range of student affairs preparation programs including those housed in academic departments of administration, departments of counselor education and others. Recently, the Council for Accreditation of Counseling and Related Educational Programs (CACREP) was established under the sponsorship of the American Personnel and Guidance Association. Although this agency potentially could evaluate and accredit programs of student affairs preparation that are housed in departments of counselor education, those whose academic homes are elsewhere may be left in nonaccreditable situations. Likewise, although the National Council for Accreditation of Teacher Education (NCATE) has the capacity to evaluate and accredit programs of school counselor preparation, it is neither organized nor qualified to accredit preparation programs designed to educate those who will practice in postsecondary education institutions, including student affairs practitioners. As a result, currently no procedures are available or are agencies qualified to accredit preparation programs for student affairs in higher education. This creates a major void in the professional qualifications in the field of student affairs, a void that needs immediate and increased attention.

RATIONALE FOR PROFESSIONAL STANDARDS IN STUDENT AFFAIRS PRACTICE AND PREPARATION

Importance of Standards

Only recently the importance of standards has been realized by student affairs practitioners, primarily because professionals and others in leadership positions have exercised judgments based largely on instinct, intuition, and conventional wisdom. As a result, the increase or decrease in student affairs services and programs has depended largely on institutional values, priorities, finances, and felt needs. Further, professional preparation programs have often focused on three levels of training: (1) counseling, (2) student and organizational development, and (3) administrative knowledge and skills (Rodgers, 1977). These programs, according to many practitioners, are too far removed from the actual practice of student affairs and consequently fail to influence the quality of student life as an educational priority. Stamatakos stated that

> student affairs professional associations exist for a number of good reasons, among which is the responsibility for providing creative, courageous, and assertive leadership that constantly challenges accepted assumptions, sets professional standards and goals, ventures into unchartered waters, elevates the thinking and operational levels of preparation and professional practice, and demands outstanding performance of its members. (1981, p. 199)

Unfortunately, the profession has not educated itself or acted responsibly through professional associations in establishing the educational quality and integrity of student affairs programs. Professional standards for student affairs practice must be established for three reasons.

First, professional standards provide uniform reference points for student affairs practitioners and institutional leaders in (1) evaluating the quality of student services programs, (2) evaluating staff members, and (3) giving direction for creating new and better programs of intentional development. Standards represent the criteria that are used to assure quality of both program and staff.

Second, a direct relationship exists between the process and procedures utilized by student affairs practitioners and the quality of students' out-of-class educational experiences (Astin, 1977; Feldman & Newcomb, 1969). Concisely defined professional standards for student affairs assure higher quality staff and programs, they also assure higher quality experiences for students involved.

Finally, written standards provide consistent criteria for institutional and academic accreditation in student services and student developmental areas. Young explained that accreditation currently focuses on two concerns: *educational quality,* defined and interpreted within the context of the institution or program's statement of its own scope and purpose as compared with similar institutions and programs; and *institutional integrity,* viewed from the perspective that the institution or program is what it says it is and does what it says it does educationally, at any given point in time. (1979, p. 134)

Concisely defined criteria are essential to implement accreditation processes wherein institutions may assess and improve their educational endeavors and assure the public that the educational endeavors meet or exceed commonly accepted standards of educational quality.

Alternatives Facing the Profession
Regarding Standards and Accreditation

Most professionals believe that the coming decades present unique opportunities to affect a basic change in the human development themes of American higher education. Leaders in both the academic and larger communities argue that the quality of higher education must be improved. It is becoming increasingly necessary for human development themes to permeate the higher education enterprise. The alternatives are obvious. If professionals are educated about standards and leaders are given concise directions, standards, and procedures to guide and influence institutional priorities and policy making, then higher education will become responsive to human development needs. Failure by the profession to establish professional standards and accreditation procedures will result in limitations on its professional aims, conduct, and quality and in a continued inability to improve and identify exemplary student affairs programs.

Responsibility for Standards
Development and Implementation

Eighteen professional associations representing the interests of student affairs practice and preparation are working together to develop standards for professional practice. The Council for the Advancement of Standards for Student Services/Development Programs (CAS) began with 12 associations in 1979. The Council, according to its by-laws, has these purposes:

the Council for the Advancement of Standards for Student Services/Development Programs . . . is a non-profit corporation organized for the purposes generally of improving and advancing student services/development programs, and educational opportunities in institutions of higher education; and of promoting cooperative interassociation efforts to improve the quality of services offered to students by establishing, adopting, and/or recommending professional standards for student services/development programs, and by establishing, adopting, and/or recommending standards for preparing professionals for these fields . . . (p.1)

CAS was formed as a consortium of professional associations each reflecting its own constituency. CAS reflects an attempt at professional collaboration, an awareness that the professsion was and is much more than the sum of its collective parts.

Members of CAS are American College Personnel Association (ACPA); Association of College and University Housing Officers (ACUHO); Association of College Unions-International (ACU-I); Association of Fraternity Advisors (AFA); Association on Handicapped Student Services Programs in Postsecondary Education (AHSSPPE); Association for School, College, and University Staffing (ASCUS); College Placement Council (CPC); National Academic Advising Association (NACADA); National Association of College Admissions Counselors (NACAC); National Association of Student Personnel Administrators (NASPA); National Association for Women Deans, Administrators, and Counselors (NAWDAC); National Clearinghouse for Commuter Programs (NCCP); National Council on Student Development (NCSD); National Association of Campus Activities (NACA); National Intramural-Recreational Sports Association (NIRSA); National Orientation Directors Association (NODA); National University Continuing Education Association (NUCEA); and Southern Association of College Student Affairs (SACSA).

CAS is preparing standards for both student affairs practice and preparation programs. Specific areas of practice for which standards are being prepared include academic advising, professional preparation, admissions, career planning and placement, chief student affairs office, college unions, commuter and adult student services, counseling and testing services, social fraternities and sororities, handicapped student services, intramurals and recreational programs, lecture/concert programs, orientation programs, paraprofessional programs, religious programs, services for special populations, student activities, student housing, student life research/evaluation, student judicial/legal affairs, and learning assistance programs.

A participatory democratic approach to dealing with and resolving profession-wide issues and concerns is not easy. The logistics are mind boggling, particularly because some professional associations focus attention upon only one or two facets (specialty areas) whereas others are more general in nature and seek to respond to nearly all specialty areas. For such a consortium to be cooperative, supportive, open to reexamination of past thinking, and occasionally willing to compromise, professional dedication is essential.

The CAS process for developing standards of professional practice and preparation for student development programs take the following form (Rodgers, 1981).

•Development of standards in areas of practice and/or preparation by individual member associations.

•Consolidation and unification of standards prepared by individual associations into a single standard statement for each area.

•CAS adoption of the unified standard statement in each area and dissemination to member associations' membership for feedback and endorsement.

•Development and approval of operational versions of the officially adopted standards in each area.

•Administration of standard statements in field testing situations with pilot institutions for evaluation purposes.

•Provide COPA, regional accrediting association, and appropriate specialty accrediting agencies (e.g., CACREP, NCATE) with standards and operational versions.

•Provide training for professionals to use standards in institutional and specialty program area accreditation review processes.

•Conduct audits to determine if CAS approved standards are being used by accreditation associations and in self-studies.

Once the professional standards are developed, endorsed, and adopted they are disseminated throughout the profession by both CAS member associations and the Council's publication of professional standards statements. Although a primary function of the standards is to assure quality through the accreditation process, each institution and each practitioner has access to a concisely defined and readily available set of standards to guide their practice. Paramount to the evolution of the profession is the need for practitioners, both individually and collectively, to be well informed about the existence of standards, to understand how to interpret and use them, and to be held accountable by their institutions, colleagues, and professional associations for using the standards in everyday practice. Ultimately, the profession will need to establish a monitoring process with appropriate sanctions for those who fail to be guided by the intent or spirit of the standards. For institutions this occurs through the process of accreditation; for individuals it occurs through peer judgments and under the auspices of their professional associations.

Components Essential For Standards

Operational versions of standards should include interpretations and guidelines to aid practitioners in their use. Such addenda might include examples for comparison purposes but should also allow for flexibility and diversity by users in various settings and under differing circumstances. Some type of introduction or preamble which outlines the preconditions under which the standard is designed to be used should lead off the statement. This section delineates the intent for which the standards were created and the context within which they should be used. Obviously, the more specific and limited the content to be included, the more narrowly the standards can be applied. This section should also delineate between *essentials* and *guidelines*. The following categories should be incorporated into standard statements to aid practitioners.

Human Resources. Program officers and administrative staff members; instructional staff and faculty; program coordinators and supervisors; other professional and paraprofessional full and part-time staff members; and technical, secretarial, and clerical staff members all reflect the human resources needed or recommended to carry out the program goals and objectives. This section should include criteria concerning minimal competencies and/or training required along with specific skills and competencies essential to implement the program.

Financial and Physical Resources. Other resources must be adequate and available to achieve program purposes and to support the number of students admitted. Financial resources for continuation of the program must be assured as well as the essential facilities, equipment, and supplies. For academic programs, library facilities are of the essence as they may be for certain student affairs programs such as career planning and development that require published information. Some programs need special equipment such as computer terminals for study skills or programmed learning approaches. Similar equipment may be needed for record keeping processes that are involved in nearly any student service program. Many student affairs services or programs could not exist without adequate financial and physical resources especially intended or designed for their use (e.g., residence halls, intramural equipment and grounds, financial aid programs).

Programs, Services, and Activities. A necessity is for student affairs divisions to identify and to specify essential functions and student services required to meet needs of students on their particular type of campus. Likewise, describing the essential criteria for specific programs or academic departments housed within a sponsoring student affairs division is important. The *Standards of the College Delegate Assembly* of the Southern Association of Colleges and Schools (Commission on Colleges, 1977), for example, lists administration, counseling and guidance, extra-class activities, student participation in institutional government, student discipline, student records, student financial aid, student housing, health services, and athletics among the student development services outlined in the illustrations and interpretations section of Standard Seven, Student Development Services. Specific functions and programs indentified in such standards reflect the minimal essential service areas required by the profession to achieve goals and objectives of the program or area of practice under consideration.

Relationships with Allied Professionals and Other Support Groups. Student affairs professionals must seek support from others who also are concerned with the welfare, growth, and development of college students. To think that any one individual, program, department, division, or larger administrative or service unit can meet developmental needs of all students is unrealistic. Not only should professional standards outline minimum staff competencies and resources required within a given component, they also should identify the importance of support personnel and agencies that student affairs practitioners and program implementers call upon for aid in accomplishing their missions. The value of strong relationships with other segments of the campus and larger community that allow for collaborations and cooperative programming efforts to benefit the intentional development of students cannot be overlooked if quality services and programs are to result. The total educational environment is involved, and all resources must be utilized.

Evaluation and Ethics. The standard statement must identify not only the criteria to be used to assess value, credibility, and effectiveness of the programs under consideration, but also must include recognition of periodic evaluative self-studies that are undertaken. Evaluation, to be effective, must be an integral part of the total program. Likewise, the ethical behavior of all persons involved is of the essence for any profession. Not only should professional ethical standards be promulgated, they should be monitored similarly to the other standards of professional practice and preparation that guide the behavior and operations of practitioners throughout the field.

USE OF STANDARDS

Impact of Standards
on Practice and Preparation

Standards make a difference only when individuals understand them, promote them, use them, practice them, and uphold them. At present a question exists concerning practitioners' interest in establishing and maintaining substantial and widespread programs in student development, liberal learning, and practical competence. Practitioners are, to some extent, held together by an immensely intricate network of mutual obligation. Assumptions, promises, agreements, plans, and contracts are made, and they remind practitioners of their obligation and of the human context of their calling. Practitioners must learn to view standards as acts of will and intelligence that shape the future of student affairs as a profession.

How can practitioners come to this important awareness? Impact will come as professional associations wage educational campaigns with depth, scope, and vision. A high quality of student life requires programs of intentional student development with goals that enhance the student's life in cognitive, affective, and practical ways. Student affairs programs support the main ingredients of higher education: sciences and humanities, student satisfactions and enjoyments, self-discovery, career choice and job opportunities, and institutional and student financial support. Practitioners will gain more from consistent student affairs programs with standards that have consistent definitions and designs than they will from innovations, operations, and procedures that change every year. In the words of Stamatakos, "the task before us is to accept and respond cooperatively, systematically, and vigorously to the constant challenge of becoming a profession" (1981, p. 202).

Using Standards in Everyday Work

The presence of standards significantly affects student affairs programs as rising productivity and increased excellence combine to enhance the quality of student life and diminish the losses to institutions from student attrition and budget cuts. As Young (1979) stated, higher education is "moving into a time when institutions, for their own purposes (survival) as well as for socially induced reasons (accountability, consumer information), will engage in a continuing process of self-evaluation" (p. 136). As a result of this evolutionary process, students will be able to know precisely what to expect because institutional communications about their services and programs will be increasingly accurate, reliable, and valid according to their stated missions and objectives.

Specifically, practitioners should use professional standards to assess the present quality of student affairs administration, services, and programs; to set goals consistent with the quality level expected of professional practice; to alter, discard, and innovate with services and programs to meet those goals; and to educate and persuade higher education planners to work together as professionals in implementing standards.

Practitioners must be both pragmatic and visionary in their needs. They must favor the political power and processes as they work to reshape student affairs programs. They must set goals that do not simply preserve present programs or correct deficiencies; they must set goals that affect the way student affairs is conceived and perceived throughout higher education.

Implication of Standards
for the Profession

With deepening economic problems, priorities in higher education may shift from offering many different programs to providing fewer but higher quality programs. As compromises are hammered out between planning and budgeting committees, student affairs can gain credibility, especially as professionals articulate their needs, values, and requirements.

Given the pecuniary pinch and realignment of priorities that confront all educational institutions, student affairs, however, must be assertive and creative in determining its rightful place in higher education during the decades ahead. It cannot afford to wait for "outsiders" to develop and force upon it unacceptable models for evaluation and assessment. It is the task and responsibility of its collective associations to assure the profession that it will be assessed or evaluated on its own, not upon others' philosophies or terms. (Stamatakos, 1981, p. 200)

Management of standards for the profession must be regarded as even more important than standards themselves. Professionals who are competent managers with savvy political sense can fuel the development of the profession by sorting out the possible winning service and program designs from those that will almost certainly fail. By engaging in the use of standards for service and program implementation and evaluation, these professionals can open whole new areas of influence, involvement, and innovation. Professionals who find and foster the standards' intent will design new student affairs programs that provide increased opportunities for meaning and purpose in students' lives and increase productivity in the student affairs services and programs of the twenty-first century.

Standards for professional practice are a major tool for assuring the integrity of institutions of postsecondary education. Outlining this program of standards is one thing; selling it is something very different. The impact of standards for professional practice is subtle and hard to detect by even those members of the Council for the Advancement of Standards and associations who are writing and influencing standards. Interest in standards has expanded, respect for the profession has deepened, and liking for the task has grown. Basic to standards for professional practice is the ability and willingness of student affairs and the professional to engage in continuing self evaluation. Standards for professional practice will support Young's assertion that "colleges and universities will be expected to ask and answer what it is, specifically, that they are about as educational institutions, and how they know they are achieving their objectives" (1979, p. 136). Professionals expect and demand that standards for professional practice keep purpose high, preserve hope and honor, and ignite learning.

REFERENCES

American College Health Association recommended standards and practices for a college health program (3rd ed.). *Journal of American College Health Association,* 1977, *25.*

American College Personnel Association standards for the preparation of counselors and other personnel services specialists at the masters degree level. Washington, DC: Author, 1979 (mimeographed).

Anderson, G. V. Professional standards and training for college personnel workers. *Educational and Psychological Measurement,* 1948, *8,* 451-9.

Astin, A. W. *Four critical years: Effects of college on beliefs, attitudes, and knowledge.* San Francisco: Jossey-Bass, 1977.

Council for the Advancement of Standards for Student Services/Development Programs. By-laws for the Council for the Advancement of Standards for Student Services/Development Programs. Washington, DC: Author, 1979.

Commission on Colleges. *Standards of the college delegate assembly.* Atlanta: Southern Association of Colleges and Schools, 1977.

Council on Postsecondary Accreditation. *The balance wheel for accreditation.* Washington, DC: Author, 1981.

Feldman, K. A. & Newcomb, T. M. *The impact of college on students* (2 vols.). San Francisco: Jossey-Bass, 1969.

Greenwood, E. Attributes of a profession. *Social Work,* 1957, *2,* 44-55.

Hullfish, H. G. Advising a graduate student who wants to be a dean of men. *Proceedings of the 23rd Conference of the National Association of Deans and Advisers of Men,* Cincinnati, 1941.

International Association of Counseling Services. *Documents pertaining to the evaluation and accreditation of counseling services.* Washington, DC: Author, 1978.

Larson, N. S. *The rise of professionalism: A sociological analysis.* Berkeley: University of California Press, 1977.

Leonard, E. A. *Origins of personnel services in American higher education.* Minneapolis: University of Minnesota Press, 1956.

Miller, J. W., & Boswell, L. E. Accreditation assessment, and the credentialing of educational accomplishment. *Journal of Higher Education,* 1979, *50,* 219-25.

Pavalko, R. M. *Sociology of occupations and professions.* Itasca, IL: F.E. Peacock, Inc., 1971.

Penn, J. R. Professional accreditation: A key to excellence. *Journal of College Student Personnel, 15,* 257-9.

Penney, J. F. *Perspective and challenge in college personnel work.* Springfield, IL: Charles C. Thomas, 1972.

Penney J. F. Student personnel work: A profession stillborn. *Personnel and Guidance Journal,* 1969, *47,* 958-62.

Rodgers, R. F. Student personnel work as social intervention. In G. H. Knock (Ed.), *Perspectives on the preparation of student affairs professionals.* Washington, DC: American College Personnel Association, 1977.

Rodgers, R. F. Process for developing standards for student services development programs: Practice and professional preparation. Washington, DC: Council for the Advancement of Standards for Student Services/Development Programs (3rd rev. ed.) June 5, 1981 (mimeographed).

Rudolph, F. *The American college and university: A history.* New York: Random House, 1962.

Stamatakos, L. C. Student affairs progress toward professionalism: Recommendations for action (Part 2). *Journal of College Student Personnel,* 1981, *22,* 197-207.

Thrash, P. A. Accreditation: A perspective, *Journal of Higher Education,* 1979 *50,* 115-20.

Williamson, E. G. Professional preparation of student personnel workers. *School and Society,* 1958, *1,* 3-5.

Young, K. New pressures on accreditation. *Journal of Higher Education,* 1979, *50,* 132-44.

SUGGESTED READINGS

Greenwood, E. Attributes of a profession. *Social Work,* 1957, *2,* 44-55.

Penn, J. R. Professional accreditation: A key to excellence. *Journal of College Student Personnel,* 1974, *15,* 257-9.

Thrash, P. S. (Ed.). *Journal of Higher Education,* 1979, *50,* 115-232.

Donald D. Gehring is Associate Professor of Higher Education at the University of Louisville. He was awarded the B.S. degree in industrial management from Georgia Institute of Technology, the M.Ed. in mathematics education from Emory University, and was the first graduate of the doctoral program in higher education at the University of Georgia.

He has held numerous administrative positions in higher education including Director of Student Activities, Director of Housing, Assistant to the Dean of Men, and Dean of Student Development. He has authored several articles dealing with legal issues in higher education. Currently he edits all state higher education cases for the *School Law Reporter* and annually has written the chapter on students in *The Yearbook of Higher Education Law*. Dr. Gehring is co-author and co-editor of *The College Student and the Courts*.

Chapter **9**

LEGAL ISSUES IN THE ADMINISTRATION OF STUDENT AFFAIRS

Donald D. Gehring

WHY STUDY LEGAL ISSUES?

Student affairs professionals must have a basic understanding of the law as it affects their relationships with students. Programs, policies, and practices that are well grounded in developmental theory, but fail to take into consideration legal rights of students can result in personal liability suits and create adversarial relationships with students.*

Student affairs professionals need not be lawyers, but an understanding of the legal aspects of their work and their relationships to students can be helpful. They will be better able to recognize circumstances and situations that raise legal questions and that need to be brought to the attention of the institution's counsel. Because these lawyers are not usually familiar with every policy or practice of the institution, they appreciate administrators who can spot the warning flags and raise legal questions with them before an action is taken that could be filled with potential liability.

---

*Appendix B, An Introduction to Legal Research, provides an explanation of how to read legal citations and to locate and use legal sources in research.

Another reason for studying legal issues is that administrators need to consider students' basic rights as they develop institutional policies, procedures, and practices. Student affairs can assist in educating and sensitizing other policy groups on campus to the rights and responsibilities of students. This may even be an area in which student affairs professionals, by exhibiting expertise where faculty need help, may gain recognition from the faculty. Interpreting the legal rationale underlying institutional policy to the college community and external constituents also can be facilitated by a basic knowledge of the law. It is not unusual for policies to be called into question by faculty, other administrators, trustees, and external constituents. The student affairs administrator can respond to the legitimate concerns of other members of the community.

One of the most important reasons for understanding legal relationships that exist between the institution and the student, and knowing the legal rights and responsibilities of each is that the student affairs professional is in a better position to provide students the information they need to make decisions. Developmentally, young adult college students are at a period where they are confronting a whole series of questions concerning values, relationships to others, and careers. These questions must be answered in the context of a society that affords certain rights and imposes certain responsibilities. However, most students are not taught these concepts. The student affairs staff member has an excellent opportunity to provide developmental education in this respect.

Finally, the student affairs professional has a responsibility to learn the basic legal aspects of the profession in order to guard against potential liability. This responsibility is not only to protect the individual, but also to protect the institution as one's employer.

THE STUDENT-INSTITUTION RELATIONSHIP: PUBLIC v. PRIVATE

Relationships students have with institutions define individual rights. Thus, it is imperative for student affairs professionals to understand various legal relationships that exist between students and institutions they attend. These relationships are determined by the facts and circumstances of each situation, but generally can be classified as constitutional, statutory, and contractual.

Public Colleges and the Constitution

The Constitution of the United States provides in its amendments certain rights that guarantee citizens protection against certain actions by the government or its agencies. Most state constitutions provide similar protections. State supported colleges and universities are agencies of the government and, therefore, students have a constitutional relationship to these institutions. This means that in its dealings with students, a public college or university must afford the rights guaranteed under the federal and state constitutions. While that may not be very revolutionary, it has been accepted practice only for the past twenty years *(Dixon v. Alabama State Board of Education)*. Prior to that time, colleges and universities generally took the attitude that students only had the rights that the institution gave them. If students did not agree, then they were free to attend another institution. Those days have passed, and the United States Supreme Court has decided that students do not shed their constitutional rights when they enter a college *(Tinker v. Des Moines)*.

Private Colleges and Contracts

Students attending private institutions, however, do not enjoy protections of the Constitution in their relationships with colleges and universities. The Constitution only protects citizens against actions by the government or its agencies but "erects no shield against purely private conduct" *(Shelly v. Kraemer)*. If a private institution is found to be closely linked to the state, then it could be required to provide constitutional guarantees. This concept of a private institution being involved in "state action" has seldom been applied to a private college by the courts. Examples of factors that have been used in unsuccessful attempts to show that private institutions have been engaged in state action include: receipt of state money that did not constitute a significant proportion of operating funds *(Torres v. Puerto Rico Junior College)*; receipt of federal funds *(Grossner v. Trustees of Columbia University)*; contracts with the state *(Powe v. Miles)*; tax exempt status *(Browns v. Mitchell)*; serving a public function *(Counts v. Voorhees College)*; being chartered by the state and being granted powers of *eminent domain (Blackburn v. Fisk University)*; use of local police as campus security *(Robinson v. Davis)*; state approval of courses *(Rowe v. Chandler)*; and state accreditation *(Berrios v. Inter American University)*. The Supreme Court has said that only by "sifting facts and weighing circumstances" can the imperceptible involvement of the state in the affairs of a private institution be determined *(Burton v. Wilmington Parking Authority)*. Thus, "state action" is very elusive and will be determined by the facts of each case. Courts, however, have found state action in business involving racial discrimination *(Hammond* v. *Tampa).* Although private institutions are not required to provide constitutional safeguards for students, it seems antithetical to the purpose of a liberal education to deny such rights. Only where religious tenets would preclude granting constitutional rights should they be denied.

CONSTITUTIONAL PARAMETERS

The constitutional relationship that students have with their institutions emerges in many student affairs functions. The relationship is given expression for students primarily as a result of three constitutional amendments—the First, Fourth, and Fourteenth. Courts have provided a series of decisions giving guidance to the administrator in the application of each of these amendments on the campus.

First Amendment

The First Amendment includes several clauses that directly affect the operation of various student development programs. As stated in the Amendment:

> Congress shall make no laws respecting the establishment of religion or prohibiting the free exercise thereof; or abridging the freedom of speech or of the press; or the right of the people peaceably to assemble; and to petition the Government for a redress of grievances.

The first two clauses are generally referred to as the Establishment Clause and the Free Exercise Clause. Taken together, they constitute the concept of separation of church and state so fundamental to this country's social system.

Separation of Church and State. In higher education, the concept of separation of church and state applies to a whole range of internal and external activities. The Supreme Court has supplied a test to serve as a guide in determining if particular activities or actions violate the separation concept. The test seeks to ascertain whether the law, program, policy, or practice (1) reflects a clearly secular legislative purpose; (2) has a primary effect that neither advances nor inhibits religion; and (3) avoids excessive government entanglement with religion *(Lemon v. Kurtzman)*. Most often the test is applied to situations in which state or federal financial aid is being provided to private, church related institutions or to the students who attend them. Where such financial assistance is not used for sectarian purposes and does not violate other specific provisions of state or federal constitutions, courts have found the aid programs to be permissible *(Tilton v. Richardson; Roemer v. Board of Public Works; Americans United v. Rogers).*

Financial assistance programs are not the only activities affected by the concept of separation of church and state. The use of state college facilities by religious groups has also been litigated, but with differing results. In Delaware the state supreme court held a university prohibition against the use of a residence hall lounge for religious services to violate the free exercise clause *(University of Delaware v. Keegan).* A similar university prohibition at the University of Missouri-Kansas City was recently upheld by a federal district court, but reversed on appeal *(Chess v. Widmar).* The Supreme Court has agreed to hear this controversy. Campus regulations of this type should be reviewed thoroughly by institutional counsel. Whether to permit the distribution of religious material on campus is another issue that is affected by the Establishment Clause. Recently, Ohio State University was temporarily enjoined from restricting the distribution of a religiously oriented publication on its campus *(Solid Rock Foundation v. Ohio State University).*

Speech and Expression. The First Amendment prohibition against abridging freedom of speech or press can become an issue in a variety of student development programs. Campus lecture series, student newspapers and other media, individuals who speak out on topics of interest, and groups banded together to advocate a particular position are all activities protected by the First Amendment. While no absolute right exists to engage in such activities, once an institution opens its doors to one group, establishes a newspaper, or provides a forum for one individual, then all others must be treated under constitutionally valid principles.

One constitutional principle that applies to speech, expression, or advocacy is definite—such occasions may not be regulated based upon the content of the message. The editor of the student newspaper cannot be terminated simply because the administration does not like the editorials. Students cannot, under the First Amendment, be denied the right to invite controversial speakers based on the fact that the administration does not like what the speakers will say or have said, or on their political or idealogical positions. The same principle is also true for other student media and student organizations. In one instance a graduate student was suspended from a public university for distributing a newspaper on campus that included a picture of policemen raping the Statue of Liberty, the Goddess of Justice, and which also contained allegedly obscene language. The basis for the suspension was violation of a university rule prohibiting indecent conduct or speech. The United States Supreme Court, however, noted that while public institutions are free to enforce reasonable rules, governing student conduct consistent with their mission, they "are not enclaves immune from the sweep of the First Amendment" *(Papish* v. *Board of Curators of University of Missouri)*. The Supreme Court further pointed out "that the mere dissemination of ideas—no matter how offensive to good taste—on a state university campus may not be shut off in the name alone of 'conventions of decency.'" The student was dismissed because of disapproved "content" of the publication, and such action violated rights guaranteed by the First Amendment.

No absolute rights exist, and if an expression in any form, including symbolic expression, would "materially and substantially disrupt the work and discipline of the school," present a clear and present danger, or exhort others to imminent violence, only then may the expression be regulated *(Tinker* v. *Des Moines)*. However, those attempting to regulate expression have a heavy burden to show convincing evidence that a danger exists. The mere speculation that the expression will present danger is not enough. A Federal District Court upheld the disciplining of one student who spoke to a large gathering of his classmates urging them to make it "costly" for the university to erect a particular fence. The court said that "utterances in a context of violence, involving a definite and present danger can lose [their] significance as an appeal to reason and become part of an instrument of force . . . unprotected by the Constitution" *(Siegel* v. *Regents of the University of California)*.

Student Organizations. "While the freedom of association is not explicitly set out in the [First] Amendment, it has long been held to be implicit in the freedoms of speech, assembly, and petition. No doubt denial of official recognition, without justification, to college organizations burdens or abridges that associational right" *(Student Coalition* v. *Austin Peay State University)*. With this statement, a federal district court held invalid a decision of a university to deny recognition to a group organized to promote gay rights. Student organizations, deriving their right of association from the First Amendment, are protected in ways similar to those already mentioned. While no absolute right exists to be granted official recognition, once one organization has been so recognized or registered all others must be accorded similar privileges under constitutionally valid principles. Official registration or recognition, however, does not mean that the organization gains any new rights *(National Strike Information Center* v. *Brandeis)* nor that the institution takes on any new responsibilities to assist the organization in exercising its constitutional rights. The Fourth Circuit Court of Appeals noted this principle when the student chapter of the Maryland Public Interest Research Group, a recognized campus organization, challenged the university policy of withholding activity funds from organizations that would use the money to pay litigation expenses. Students charged that the policy violated their First Amendment rights, but the court said, "there is no affirmative commandment upon the university to activate Mary Pirg's exercise of First Amendment guarantees; the only commandment is not to infringe their enjoyment" *(Maryland Public Interest Research Group* v. *Elkins).*

An institution cannot withhold recognition simply because it disagrees with the organization's philosophy. That would be a type of impermissible censorship *(Healy* v. *James).* An institution may, however, require the organization to provide a statement of purposes, names of officers, and an assurance that the group will comply with reasonable and valid rules of the college *(Eisen* v. *Regents; Merkey* v. *Board of Regents).* The Supreme Court of Washington has also pointed out that the constitutional right of association carries with it a corresponding right to not associate. That court had "no hesitancy in holding that the state, through the university, may not compel membership in an association, such as ASUW [the student government type of organization], which purports to represent all the students at the university" *(Good* v. *Associated Students).*

Activity Fees. Activities such as lecture series, campus newspapers, and organizations that sponsor these activities are generally funded by fees assessed all students. Challenges have been made regarding the assessment, collection, and use of these fees. Some students have argued that they are forced to pay activity fees that are used to support speakers and media whose philosophies are repugnant to their own. This, they argue, is a violation of their own right to free speech and association. Courts have disagreed and permitted the assessment of mandatory activity fees to provide a forum for the expression of political and personal opinions *(Veed* v. *Schwartzkoph).* Fees may not, however, be used to support only one particular philosophy, and equal access to the fees should be provided.

Assembly Rights and Demonstrations. The final clause of the First Amendment that emerges as an area of concern to the student affairs administrator is "the right of the people peaceably to assemble." Campus demonstrations still take place, and like other activities protected by the First Amendment, they cannot be regulated on the basis of the message to be conveyed. Reasonable time, place, and manner restrictions may be imposed, and prior registration may be required for scheduling purposes. However, prior restraint is impermissible *(Sword* v. *Fox; Bayless* v. *Martine).* Disruption of the ongoing functions of the university may be prohibited *(Esteban* v. *Central Missouri).* A good example of the line drawn between time, place, and manner restrictions and prior restraint arose at Mississippi State University. Regulations at the University required that students receive authorization for demonstrations, rallies, or parades at least three days prior to the event, and only those activities of a "wholesome nature" would be approved. The court held the regulation to be an impermissible prior restraint on First Amendment freedom. The prior notice aspect of the regulation was acceptable to the court, but the "wholesome nature" language was unacceptable. The court said, "the point of this language converts what might have otherwise been a reasonable regulation of time, place, and manner into a restriction on the content of speech. Therefore, the regulation appears to be unreasonable on its face" *(Shamloo* v. *Mississippi State Board of Trustees, Etc.).*

Fourth Amendment

Application of the law concerning the Fourth Amendment rights of students on campus is controversial *(Morale* v. *Grigel).* This Amendment guarantees, in part, "the right of the people to be secure in their persons, houses, papers, and effects against unreasonable searches and seizures shall not be violated, and no warrants shall be issued but upon probable cause. . . ." The controversy surrounding search and seizure on campus concerns whether college officials are required to obtain a warrant before a search of a student's room can be conducted. Several courts have argued that if college officials had "reasonable cause to believe" that activity was taking place in a student's residence hall room that was in violation of college regulations, a warrantless search could be conducted. The basis for this rationale was that a search to maintain good order and discipline on campus was considered a *reasonable* search because criminal prosecution was not contemplated—thus the application of a "reasonable cause" standard as opposed to the "probable cause" standard required by the Fourth Amendment *(Moore* v. *Troy State; United States* v. *Coles; Keene* v. *Rodgers).* However, where police have sought evidence for a criminal prosecution rather than a mere disciplinary proceeding, courts have required a warrant and held that college administrators could not delegate their lower "reasonable cause" standard to the police *(Piazzola* v. *Watkins)*. Subsequently, the "reasonable cause" standard was rejected by another federal district court *(Smythe and Smith* v. *Lubbers)*. Thus, until the Supreme Court provides guidance with respect to the applicable standard to be used, administrators would be well advised to review their search and seizure policy with institutional counsel.

The "plain view" and "emergency" doctrines are still legally sound. In essence, the plain view doctrine holds that any contraband that is in plain view may be seized. Thus, where entry to a room has been made legally, such as maintenance checks either requested by the occupant or carried out as an announced routine, and an illegal substance is seen in plain view, it may then be seized and used for disciplinary purposes *(State* v. *Kappes)*. Plain view means exactly that—if something must be moved or opened to see the substance, then it is not in plain view. An "emergency" does not demand a warrant to search. If someone credible reported in good faith that there was a bomb in locker 319 in the university student center, to attempt to obtain a warrant would be ridiculous. Once that locker is legally opened, as in the case of an emergency, anything illegal that is in plain view may be confiscated *(People* v. *Lanthier)*.

Finally, several courts have interpreted the privacy rights contained in the Fourth Amendment to support a denial of door-to-door canvassing or voter registration in the residence halls *(National Movement* v. *Regents; Brush* v. *Penn State University; American Future Systems, Inc.* v. *Penn State)*. The upper floors of a residence hall have been held to be private living quarters, and prohibiting door-to-door registration and canvassing is not a Fourth Amendment violation where other alternatives exist.

Fourteenth Amendment

Due Process. Two clauses of Section 1 of the Fourteenth Amendment, the Due Process Clause and the Equal Protection Clause, have particular significance for the student affairs professional. The due process clause was the basis for one of the most significant decisions in higher education. The *Dixon* case set forth the principle that students attending state colleges or universities were entitled to due process. A natural question that arises, however, is "What process is due?" The answer lies in an understanding of due process as a flexible concept rather than a fixed standard. Due process is fundamental fairness, and therefore, depends upon individual circumstances. A fair summary of due process is that the greater the right sought to be deprived, the greater the process due. Thus, a deprivation of some social privileges would not demand the degree of procedure required for an expulsion. Both the *Dixon* decision and *General Order on Judicial Standards of Procedure and Substance in Review of Student Discipline in Tax Supported Institutions of Higher Education* provide excellent guidelines for the administrator involved in disciplinary affairs. Courts have held consistently that college discipline is not a criminal procedure, and thus, is not required to conform to the rules of criminal jurisprudence.

Courts have stated that three general standards must be met in order to satisfy the minimum requirements of due process in instances of student discipline: students must be given adequate notice and an opportunity for a hearing, and decisions must be based upon substantial evidence. The Supreme Court has recently held that academic dismissals do not, however, require the same procedural safeguards demanded by disciplinary dismissals *(Board of Curators* v. *Horowitz)*. Over the years the standards of notice, hearing, and decisions based upon substantial evidence have been refined by the courts and are summarized:

1. Notice:

Students charged with infractions should be provided with a notice that (a) is written *(Esteban* v. *Central Missouri State College);* (b) contains the charges against them in enough detail to permit the preparation of a defense against the charges *(Esteban* v. *Central Missouri)*. The regulations the students are charged with violating should also be specific enough to give a reasonable person notice of what is prohibited *(Soglin* v. *Kauffman);* (c) includes the nature of the evidence supporting the charge *(Dixon* v. *Alabama State Board of Education),* and (d) provides a time, date, and place of hearing in enough time after delivery of the notice that the student can prepare a defense *(Dixon* v. *Alabama State Board of Education)*. Reasonable efforts to deliver the notice are all that are required, and the student cannot frustrate this process by moving or failing to accept mail *(Wright* v. *Texas Southern University)*.

2. Hearing:

The hearing should provide an opportunity to hear both sides of the controversy. (a) The hearing is to be conducted by an impartial person or persons *(Dixon* v. *Alabama State Board of Education)*. That a panel or board conduct hearings is not a general requirement. One person may conduct the hearing so long as that individual is impartial. (b) The student must be provided with an opportunity to present a defense against the charges, including presenting witnesses and oral, written, or physical evidence *(Dixon* v. *Alabama State Board of Education)*. (c) The hearing process must be fair and impartial. For example, allowing the student an attorney is not a general requirement *(Dixon* v. *Alabama State Board of Education)*, however, if the institution is represented by an attorney or if the student faces similar charges in criminal court, then it would be only fair to allow the student to have counsel *(French v. Bashful)*. Similarly, there is no absolute right to cross-examine witnesses *(Dixon* v. *Alabama State Board of Education)*, but where there are real questions or witness credibility, cross examination of witnesses might be essential to a fair hearing *(Blanton v. State University of New York)*.

3. Evidence:

Decisions in student disciplinary cases must be based upon "substantial" evidence, and if the hearing is not conducted by the decision-making body, then "the results and finding of the hearing should be presented in an open report to the student's inspection" *(Dixon* v. *Alabama State Board of Education)*.

These due process requirements may seem cumbersome, but they are designed to ensure that each student is accorded "a day in court" without being too legalistic. The procedures do take time; in most instances this is beneficial because time has a way of adding a measure of objectivity. However, one cannot always take the time required by these standards when a possible rapist, arsonist, or other offender, who constitutes a threat to self, to property, or to others remains on campus. This individual must be dealt with immediately. In instances in which a student's continued presence on the campus poses a threat to the welfare of the student, property, or others, an interim suspension may be imposed. The student could be suspended immediately, with a hearing set at a later time *(Gardenhire v. Chalmers)*. This is a very serious action, however, and should be reserved for actual threats.

Two final aspects of due process of interest to the student affairs administrator involve double jeopardy and proceeding with campus hearings before civil or criminal charges are settled in court. If a student has been charged by civil authorities, the on-campus hearing need not wait until the case has been settled in court. The Supreme Court of Vermont decided a case where a student, charged with burglary, attempted rape, and simple assault and whose campus hearing preceded his criminal prosecution, alleged that his due process rights were violated. The court upheld the right of the college to proceed first.

> Educational institutions have both a need and a right to formulate their own standards and to enforce them; such enforcement is only coincidentally related to criminal charges and the defense against them. To hold otherwise would, in our view, lead logically to the conclusion that civil remedies must, as a matter of law, wait for determination until related criminal charges are disposed. *(Nzuve* v. *Castleton State College)*

Equal Protection. The Fourteenth Amendment also contains equal protection guarantees that apply to a variety of student development programs. Equal treatment under the law does not necessarily mean that everyone must be treated exactly the same. For example, many states have laws that permit an 18 year old to drink beer, but require that one be 21 to drink liquor. This is not a violation of the equal protection clause, yet citizens are being treated differently on the basis of age. Similarly, colleges and universities may treat different classifications of students differently, but institutional officials must be prepared to bear the burden of showing that the classifications so established are justified.

The courts generally apply either a "strict scrutiny" or a "rational relationship" test to situations in which some people are treated differently based upon a particular classification scheme. The test used is determined by the rights being deprived by the classification used. If the classifications create a "suspect" class—one based on race, alienage, or national origin, then the court will demand "strict scrutiny" to determine if a "compelling state interest" will be served by the classification. Thus far the Supreme Court has not chosen to specify sex as a suspect category. The "strict scrutiny" test also will be applied if one of the classes created will be deprived of a fundamental right. A college education is not a fundamental right *(Mauclet* v. *Nyquist),* nor is the pursuit of a graduate degree *(Purdie* v. *University of Utah).* Living in college housing also has been held not to be a fundamental right *(Bynes* v. *Toll).* However, voting, interstate travel, marriage, procreation, and freedom from wealth distinctions in criminal prosecution have been held to be fundamental rights. Thus, a deprivation of any of these rights would require that a "compelling state interest" exist.

If the classifications are not suspect and if no fundamental rights are involved, then the courts apply a less demanding standard called the "rational relationship" test, which requires that a rational relationship be shown to exist between the classifications established and the legitimate interests of the state.

The two tests, while certainly not restricted to these areas, are often applied to athletic eligibility, admissions, and housing. An excellent example of the "strict scrutiny" test involved a hockey player who was declared ineligible at Boston University under a National Collegiate Athletic Association (NCAA) rule holding ineligible any student who "participated as a member of the Canadian Amateur Hockey Association's major junior A hockey classification . . ." *(Buckton v. NCAA).* The court first found that both the NCAA and Boston University were involved in "state action" in declaring the players ineligible, thus bringing these two private corporations under the jurisdiction of the Constitution. Once this threshold question was answered, the court pointed out that resident aliens were guaranteed the same constitutional rights of equal protection as those afforded American citizens. The violation arose out of classifying students on the basis of alienage: Canadian boys who played for Canadian major junior A teams were ineligible, whereas American boys who played, under scholarship or otherwise, for American college or prep teams were not. Because the NCAA rule treated resident aliens differently from their American counterparts, the "strict scrutiny" test was applied. The NCAA could not overcome its burden of showing a "compelling state interest" in classifying athletes on the basis of alienage. The rule was thus held to violate the equal protection clause of the Fourteenth Amendment.

The "rational relationship" test has also been applied to athletic rules of the NCAA. To be academically eligible to participate in intercollegiate athletics, freshmen must have a 1.60 predicted grade point average. Because students are classified on the basis of grades, which is not a "suspect" criterion and fundamental rights (participating in intercollegiate athletics) are not involved, the "rational relationship" test has been applied to this rule. The statement by the Ninth Circuit Court of Appeals showed how the NCAA met the burden of the test.

> The evidence of the NCAA reveals that NCAA adopted the 1.60 Rule in order to reduce the possibility of exploiting young athletes by recruiting those who would not be representatives of an institution's student body and probably would be unable to meet the necessary academic requirements for a degree. *(Associated Students, Inc. v. NCAA).*

The rational relationship was thus established between the classification and the legitimate interests of the organization.

Frequently equal protection challenges to on-campus living regulations have been made. Those students required to live in college residence halls complained that they were discriminated against by being required to pay rents to amortize loans on the buildings. Because classifications were usually based upon academic class (freshmen and sophomores required to live in residence halls), which is not suspect, and no fundamental rights were involved, the "rational relationship" test was applied in these cases. In one instance all women students, but only male freshmen, were required to live on campus because that was the number required to fill the residence halls. The institution failed its "rational relationship" test *(Mollere* v. *Southeastern Louisiana College)*. While the court would not uphold such an arbitrary classification without some rational relationship, it pointed out that an institution might require all or certain categories of students to live on campus to promote the education of those students. That hint did not go unnoticed. A year later an institution defended successfully its required on-campus residence regulation on the basis of the educational benefits to be derived from on-campus living *(Pratz* v. *Louisiana Polytechnic Institute)*. Courts have since held that even where one of the reasons behind the regulation may be amortization of loans on the buildings, "so long as the stated purpose upholding a statutory class is legitimate and non-illusionary, its lack of primacy is not disqualifying" *(Schick v. Kent State University)*.

Admissions also can be fertile ground for equal protection suits. The Supreme Court of Utah found no rational relationship to exist between the legitimate interest of the state and the age of a 51 year old applicant to a graduate program. She had been denied admission because the department to which she applied preferred younger students *(Purdie* v. *University of Utah)*. Finally the fact that even constitutionally valid rules may be implemented in ways that offend the Constitution must be realized *(Cooper* v. *Nix)*. For this reason practices, procedures, programs, and policies should be reviewed systematically with legal counsel.

CONTRACTUAL RELATIONSHIP

The discussion of relationships has focused on those rights of students that are derived from the constitutional relationship of the student to the college or university. It has also been pointed out that only students at public institutions have such a relationship with their institutions, unless "state action" can be shown. However, students also have contractual rights and the exercise of those rights derived from the contractual relationship with the institution is often referred to as educational consumerism. In essence, the students and the college enter into a contract in which the institution offers certain educational services and a degree and the student agrees to abide by the rules and regulations and pay a specified tuition. This relationship between the student and the institution applies equally at public and private colleges and universities. The college catalog, student handbook, and the variety of brochures published by an institution of higher education all constitute part of the terms of the contract. The Illinois Supreme Court provided a good example of the contractual relationship when it said,

> the description in the brochure containing the terms under which an application will be appraised constituted an invitation for an offer. The tender of the application, as well as the payment of the fee pursuant to the terms of the brochure, was an offer to apply. Acceptance of the application and fee constituted acceptance of an offer to apply under the criteria the defendant (medical school) had established. *(Steinberg* v. *Chicago Medical School)*

The court also held that the $15 application fee was sufficient consideration to support the agreement. Contracts are not chipped in concrete, and with proper notice, terms can be modified *(Jones* v. *Vassar; Pride* v. *Howard)*, even to the extent of substantially increasing tuition *(Eisele* v. *Ayers)* or making changes in academic requirements. The latter point was concisely stated by the Fifth Circuit in a case involving a graduate student who was notified that a change in requirements for the master's degree would require that she take a final comprehensive exam. She was first notified of this requirement six weeks prior to completion of her course work and two weeks before the exam was to be administered. The exam was not mentioned as a requirement in the catalog. The student alleged that requiring the exam breached the "implied contract" she had with the institution. The court, concluded that "implicit in the student's contract with the university upon matriculation is the student's agreement to comply with the university's rules and regulations, which the university definitely is entitled to modify so as to properly exercise its educational responsibilities" *(Mahavongsana* v. *Hall)*.

Some terms of the contract are not explicitly stated, but rather are implicit understandings. An Ohio court stated that students have an implied contractual right to receive accredited instruction *(Behrend* v. *State)*. Once the student fulfills the reasonable requirements set forth by the institution, the degree must be awarded *(Tanner* v. *Board of Trustees)*. Students also have contractual arrangements with the institution for housing, meals, and other services. These contracts should be examined by an institutional counsel before they are executed by the institution and should be reviewed every few years to keep abreast of changing conditions. In recent years, suits, based upon contractual obligations, both expressed and implied, have surpassed in number those based on civil rights violations in the student area.

REGULATORY RELATIONSHIPS

In recent years, the federal government has enacted several laws or statutes specifically designed to aid students. These statutes have generally prohibited discrimination by recipients of federal financial assistance. Because almost every college and university receives some form of federal aid, these statutes apply to both public and private institutions. The aid can be made directly to the college or given directly to the student for the school to qualify as a recipient. Thus, student affairs administrators at both public and private institutions need to become familiar with the rights students derive from this statutory relationship. In some instances, statutes and regulations implementing them set higher standards than do constitutional rights. For example, a curfew for female students without a corresponding restriction for men was upheld under the "rational relationship" test for equal protection under the Fourteenth Amendment *(Robinson* v. *Eastern Kentucky University)*. This same rule, however, would violate a student's statutory rights, as defined by federal regulations, under Title IX (34 *C.F.R.* 106).

Primary federal statutes affecting student affairs administration are Title VI, Title IX, Section 504, and the Buckley Amendment. Title VI of the Civil Rights Act of 1964 (42 *U.S.C.* 2000d) prohibits discrimination on the basis of race, color, or national origin in any educational program or activity receiving federal financial assistance. Title IX of the Education Amendments of 1972 (20 *U.S.C.* 1681) was modeled after Title VI and prohibits discrimination on the basis of sex. Section 504 of the Rehabilitation Act of 1973 (29 *U.S.C.* 794) is also modeled after the language of Title VI but prohibits discrimination on the basis of a handicap.

Statutes provide general guidance, but specific regulations are issued to effectuate the intent of statutes. Regulations for Title IX can be found in Title 34 of the *Code of Federal Regulations* at part 106; Section 504 regulations also can be found in Title 34 but at part 104. Title VI regulations appear at 34 *C.F.R.* 100. These regulations contain detailed specifications of policies, practices, and procedures permitted and precluded by law. These laws and their implementing regulations cover everything from pre-admission inquiry to placement services.

Although Title VI was originally designed to benefit minority students, it also is being used to prevent reverse discrimination. The constitution of the student government association at the University of North Carolina-Chapel Hill specified that a specific number of minorities must be elected to the Campus Governing Council. It also stated that student defendants had the right to demand four of the seven honor court justices be of their race or sex. These sections of the constitution were challenged under Title VI and found to be in violation *(Uzzell* v. *Friday)*. The admissions area has also been held up to Title VI scrutiny. Probably the most famous case in postsecondary education since *Dixon* was the *Bakke* case, which held that an admissions quota specifically reserved for minorities violated Title VI. The Supreme Court did state, however, that colleges and universities may consider race or ancestry factors in the selection process to obtain diversity in the student body *(Regents* v. *Bakke)*. Two institutions that have since given consideration to race in their admission process have been upheld by their respective state supreme courts *(McDonald* v. *Hogness; DeRonde* v. *Regents of University of California)*.

Title IX also has provided a graduate admissions case. In *Cannon* the Supreme Court was asked to decide whether an applicant who alleged that she was being denied admission on the basis of her sex had a private right of action *(Cannon* v. *University of Chicago)*. The Supreme Court answered affirmatively. Because Title IX and Section 504 are both modeled after Title VI, all three statutes probably allow a student to bring suit directly against the college without going through the federal administration procedures outlined in the regulations. Title IX also has significant application to student organizations, housing, counseling, and placement, but these areas have not been tested judicially.

Making physical changes to facilities would seem to have been the most significant aspect of Section 504. However, two other areas have had greater impact. Several courts have ordered colleges to provide sign language interpreters for deaf students under the Section 504 regulations

(Barnes v. *Converse College; Crawford* v. *University of North Carolina).*
This requirement is under "auxiliary aids" section of the regulations.
One most interesting case involved a controversy between Illinois Institute of Technology and the Illinois Department of Rehabilitative Services over who would pay the interpreter's salary; the institution was willing to provide an interpreter but believed that the Department of Rehabilitative Services had primary responsibility to pay the interpreter's salary. The court agreed with the college when it found the Department was not precluded from paying for the service and the intent of the federal government when it promulgated the regulations was "that the bulk of auxiliary aids will be paid for by the state and private agencies, not colleges or universities" *(Jones* v. *Illinois Department of Rehabilitation Services).*

Another Section 504 decision involved admissions and held that the regulations implementing the Section may not be interpreted to require curricular modifications. In this instance, a licensed practical nurse was denied admission to a nursing education program on the basis that her hearing loss would make it impossible to participate safely in the program *(Southeastern Community College* v. *Davis).*

The fourth federal statute involving student affairs programs is the Buckley Amendment, formally known as the Family Educational Rights and Privacy Act of 1974 (20 *U.S.C.* 1232g). Regulations implementing the act appear in 34 *C.F.R.* 99. This law and its regulations guarantee students access to their educational records and, with a few exceptions, prohibit release or review of those records to anyone without the student's written consent. The law has not been interpreted to mean that students who leave the institution owing money must be furnished copies of the official transcripts. However, if students who attended state institutions discharge their outstanding debts in bankruptcy, the institution may not withhold transcripts *(Handsome* v. *Rutgers).* Private institutions, on the other hand, may withhold transcripts under similar circumstances *(Girardier* v. *Webster College).* Finally, under the Buckley Amendment disciplinary hearings must be closed unless the defendant student waives that right *(Marston* v. *Gainesville Sun).* To prohibit students access to their records, if the disciplinary hearings of the institution were open to the college community, would be illogical. The regulations also require that each institution have a written policy concerning specific points outlined in the regulations and students receive annual notification that such policy exists and where to find it.

SUMMARY

A basic understanding of the law related to postsecondary education is a necessity for student affairs practitioners at every level as this knowledge can benefit the practitioner in policy development, in relations with internal and external constituents, in facilitating students' educational and personal development, and in avoiding personal and institutional liability. With the average age of students increasing, a lowered age of majority, and economically hard times, the amount of litigation brought against administrators and institutions they represent will continue to increase. Through a better understanding of the relationships that exist between students and institutions, the student affairs practitioner can prevent time consuming and financially draining legal battles.

These relationships depend, first, upon whether the student is attending a public or a private institution, and to what extent the state is involved in its affairs. Students at public colleges or universities have been recognized to be full beneficiaries of the rights guaranteed by the United States Constitution. The rights most frequently exercised on campus are embodied by the First, Fourth, and Fourteenth Amendments—religion, speech, press, assembly, association, search and seizure, due process, and equal protection. Aspects of one or more of these rights are involved in almost every student development program.

Students at public as well as those at private institutions generally have a relationship to their college or university that is based upon a series of public laws or statutes enacted during the past two decades. These statutes and the regulations designed to implement them essentially guarantee students the right to be free from discrimination based upon race, sex, national origin, and handicap in educational programs and activities. Privacy rights of students and their records also are a subject of statutory and regulatory control that must be fully understood by the practitioner.

Finally, the student affairs practitioner needs to understand the contractual relationship between the student and the institution. These contractual rights apply to both public as well as private institutions and are generally defined by terms contained in the catalog and other official publications. Oral agreements may also bind as implicit understandings. To know what has been promised and to fulfill those obligations is therefore most important. Students, too, may be held to their part of the contract; and when they breach terms of the agreement, the contract may be set aside or considered invalid.

Understanding these basic legal relationships can provide a firm foundation for creating student affairs programs. The adversarial relationship, so common to criminal law, is antithetical to the purposes of higher education. Through professional study and understanding of the law as it affects the work of student affairs practitioners, adversarial relations may be eliminated and programs that facilitate educational and personal development may be enhanced while maintaining the rights of all.

CASE CITATIONS

American Future Systems, Inc. v. *Penn. State,* 618 F.2d 252 (3rd Cir., 1980).

Americans United v. *Rogers,* 45 L.W. 3429 (1976).

Associated Students, Inc. v. *NCAA,* 493 F.2d 1251 (9th Cir., 1974).

Barnes v. *Converse College,* 436 F.Supp. 635 (D. S. C., Spartnaburg Div., 1977).

Bayless v. *Martine,* 430 F.2d 873 (5th Cir., 1970).

Behrend v. *State,* 379 N.E. 2d 617 (Ct. App. Oh., Franklin Cty., 1977).

Berrios v. *Inter American University,* 535 F.2d 1330 1st Cir., 1976).

Blackburn v. *Fisk,* 443 F.2d 121 (6th Cir., 1971).

Blanton v. *State University of New York,* 489 F.2d 377 (2nd Cir., 1973).

Board of Curators v. *Horowitz,* 46 L.W. 4179 (1978).

Browns v. *Mitchell,* 409 F.2d 593 (10th Cir., 1969).

Brush v. *Penn State University,* 414 A.2d 48 (Pa., 1980).

Buckton v. *NCAA,* 366 F.Supp. 1152 (D. Mass., 1973).

Burton v. *Wilmington Parking Authority,* 365 U.S. 715 (1961).

Bynes v. *Toll,* 512 F.2d 252 (2nd Cir., 1975).

Cannon v. *University of Chicago,* 99 S.Ct. 1946 (1979).

Chess v. *Widmar,* 480 F.Supp. 907 (W.D. Mo. W.D., 1979); *rev'd* 635 F.2d 1310 (8th Cir., 1980).

Cooper v. *Nix,* 496 F.2d 1285 (5th Cir., 1974).

Counts v. *Voorhees College,* 312 F.Supp. 598 (D.S.C. Charleston Div., 1970).

Crawford v. *University of North Carolina,* 440 F.Supp. 1047 (M.D.N.C., Durham Div., 1977).

DeRonde v. *Regents of University of California,* 172 Cal. Rptr. 677 (Ca., 1981).

Dickson v. *Sitterson,* 280 F.Supp. 486 (M.D., N.C., 1968).

Dixon v. *Alabama State Board of Education,* 294 F.2d 150 (5th Cir., 1961); *cert. den.* 386 U.S. 930 (1961).

Eisele v. *Ayers,* 381 N.E. 2d 21 (App. Ct. Ill., 1st Dist., 3rd Div., 1978).

Eisen v. *Regents,* 75 Cal. Rptr. 45 (Ct. App., 1969).

Esteban v. *Central Missouri State College,* 277 F.Supp. 649 (W.D. Mo., 1967).

Esteban v. *Central Missouri,* 415 F.2d 1077 (8th Cir., 1969).

French v. *Bashful,* 303 F.Supp. 1333 (E.D. La. No. Div., 1969).

Gardenhire v. *Chalmers,* 326 F.Supp. 1200 (D.Ks., 1971).

General Order on Judicial Standards of Procedure and Substance in Review of Student Discipline in Tax Supported Institutions of Higher Education, 45 FRD 133 (W.D. Mo., 1968).

Girardier v. *Webster College,* 563 F.2d 1267 (8th Cir., 1977).

Good v. *Associated Students,* 542 P.2d 762 (Wa., 1975).

Grossner v. *Trustees of Columbia University,* 287 F.Supp. 535 (S.D.N.Y., 1968).

Hammond v. *Tampa,* 344 F.2d 951 (5th Cir., 1965).

Handsome v. *Rutgers,* 445 F.Supp. 1362 (D. N.J., 1978).

Healy v. *James,* 92 S.Ct. 2338 (1972).

Jones v. *Illinois Department of Rehabilitation Services,* 504 F.Supp. 1244 (N.D. Ill. E.D., 1981).

Jones v. *Vassar,* 299 N.Y.S. 2d 283 (S.Ct. Dutchess Cty., 1969).

Keene v. *Rodgers,* 316 F.Supp. 217 (D. Me. N.D., 1970).

Lemon v. *Kurtzman,* 403 U.S. 602 (1971).

McDonald v. *Hogness,* 598 P.2d 707 (Wa., 1979).

Mahavongsana v. *Hall,* 529 F.2d 448 (5th Cir., 1976).

Marston v. *Gainesville Sun,* 341 So. 2d 783 (Dist. Ct. App. FLA., 1st Dist., 1976).

Maryland Public Interest Research Group v. *Elkins,* 565 F.2d 864 (4th Cir., 1977).

Mauclet v. *Nyquist,* 406 F.Supp. 1233 (W.D. N.Y., 1976); aff'd. 97S.Ct. 2120 (1977).

Merkey v. *Board of Regents,* 344 F.Supp. 1296 (N.D. FLA., 1972).

Mollere v. *Southeastern Louisiana College,* 304 F.Supp. 826 (W.D. Ark., Fayetteville Div., 1969).

Moore v. *Troy State,* 284 F.Supp. 725 (M.D. Ala N. Div., 1968).

Morale v. *Grigel,* 422 F.Supp. 988 (D. N.H., 1976).

National Movement v. *Regents,* 123 Cal. Rptr. 141 (Ct. App. 2nd Dist., Div. 1, 1975).

National Strike Information Center v. *Brandeis,* 315 F.Supp. 928 (D. Mass., 1970).

Nzuve v. *Castleton State College,* 335 A.2d 321 (Vt., 1975).

Papish v. *Board of Curators of University of Missouri,* 93 S.Ct. 1197 (1973).

People v. *Lanthier,* 97 Cal. Rptr. 297 (CA., 1971).

Piazzola v. *Watkins,* 442 F.2d 284 (5th Cir., 1971).

Powe v. *Miles,* 407 F.2d 73 (2nd Cir., 1968).

Pratz v. *Louisiana Polytechnic Institute,* 316 F.Supp. 872 (W.D. La., 1970); *cert. den.* 401 U.S. 1004 (1971).

Pride v. *Howard,* 384 A.2d 31 (D.C. Ct. App., 1978).

Purdie v. *University of Utah,* 584 P.2d 831 (Ut., 1978).

Regents v. *Bakke,* 98 S.Ct. 2733 (1978).

Robinson v. *Davis,* 447 F.2d 753 (4th Cir., 1971).

Robinson v. *Eastern Kentucky University,* 475 F.2d 707 (6th Cir., 1973); *cert. den.* 416 U.S. 982 (1973).

Roemer v. *Board of Public Works,* 96 S.Ct. 2337 (1976).

Rowe v. *Chandler,* 332 F.Supp. 336 (D. Ks., 1971).

Shick v. *Kent State University,* (74-646 (N.D. Oh. E.D., 1975).

Shamloo v. *Mississippi State Board of Trustees, Etc.,* 620 F.2d 516 (5th Cir., 1980).

Shelly v. *Kraemer,* 334 U.S. 1 (1947).

Siegel v. *Regents of the University of California,* 308 F.Supp. 832 (N.D. Cal., 1970).

Smythe and Smith v. *Lubbers,* 398 F.Supp. 777 (W.D. Mich., 1975).

Soglin v. *Kauffman,* 418 F.2d 163 (7th Cir., 1969).

Solid Rock Foundation v. *Ohio State University,* 478 F.Supp. 96 (S.D. Oh. E.D., 1979).

Southeastern Community College v. *Davis,* 99 S.Ct. 2361 (1979).

State v. *Kappes,* 550 P.2d 121 (Ct. App. Az., Div. 1 Dept. A, 1976).

Steinberg v. *Chicago Medical School,* 371 N.E. 634 (Ill., 1977).

Student Coalition v. *Austin Peay State University,* 477 F.Supp. 1267 (M.D. Tenn., Nashville Div., 1979).

Sword v. *Fox,* 446 F.2d 1091 (4th Cir., 1971).

Tanner v. *Board of Trustees,* 363 N.E. 2d 208 (App. Ct. Ill. 4th Dist., 1977).

Tilton v. *Richardson,* 403 U.S. 627 (1970).

Tinker v. *Des Moines,* 393 U.S. 503 (1969).

Torres v. *Puerto Rico Junior College,* 298 F.Supp. 458 (D. P.R., 1969).

United States v. *Coles,* 302 F.Supp. 99 (D.Me. N.D., 1969).

University of Delaware v. *Keegan,* 349 A.2d 14 (Del., 1975); *cert. den.* 424 U.S. 934 (1975).

Uzzell v. *Friday,* 591 F.2d 997 (4th Cir., 1979).

Veed v. *Schwartzkoph,* 353 F.Supp. 149 (D. Neb., 1973); aff'd. 478 F.2d 1407 (8th Cir., 1973); *cert. den.* 414 U.S. 1135 (1973).

Wright v. *Texas Southern University,* 392 F.2d 728 (5th Cir., 1968).

SUGGESTED READINGS

Alexander, K., & Solomon, E. *College and university law.* Charlottesville, VA: Michie Co., 1972.

Appenzeller, H., & Appenzeller, T. *Sports and the courts.* Charlottesville, VA: Michie Co., 1980.

Bender, L. *Federal regulation and higher education.* Washington, DC: American Association of Higher Education, 1977.

Bickel, R., & Brechner, J. *The college administrator and the courts.* Asheville, NC: College Administration Publications, 1978.

Edwards, T., & Nordin, V. D. *Higher education and the law.* Cambridge, MA: Institute for Educational Management, Harvard University, 1979.

Hammond, E., & Shaffer, R. *The legal foundation of student personnel services in higher education.* Washington, DC: American College Personnel Association, 1979.

Hollander, P. *Legal handbook for educators.* Boulder, CO: Westview Press, 1978.

Kaplin, W. *The law of higher education: Legal implications of administrative decision making.* San Francisco: Jossey-Bass, 1978.

Kaplin, W. A. *The law of higher education 1980.* San Francisco: Jossey-Bass, 1980.

Weistart, J., & Lowell, C. *The law of sports.* Charlottesville, VA: Michie Co., 1979.

Young, D. P. *The law and the student in higher education.* Topeka, KS: National Organization on Legal Problems of Education, 1976.

Young, D. P. (Ed.). *The yearbook of higher education law.* Topeka, KS: National Organization on Legal Problems of Education, 1980.

Young, D. P., & Gehring, D. *The college student and the courts* (2nd ed.). Asheville, NC: College Administration Publications, 1977.

Patricia A. Hollander, an attorney in Buffalo, New York, is General Counsel of the American Association of University Administrators. She was Visiting Professor at the University of Virginia where she taught a doctoral course on Legal Aspects of College Administration, and served as both an administrator and faculty member at the State University of New York at Buffalo. Annually she conducts many seminars and workshops, and addresses national and regional meetings, on higher education law. Hollander has written numerous articles in the field, and is author of *Legal Handbook for Educators.*

D. Parker Young is Professor of Higher Education in the Institute of Higher Education at the University of Georgia teaching doctoral courses in college law and the two-year college. He has had extensive experience as an administrator and faculty member and is a nationally known scholar in the field of college law. He conducts many conferences each year concerning higher education and the law. In addition, he has written and edited many books, monographs, and articles. He is also co-editor of the *College Student and the Courts 2d* and *The College Administrator and the Courts.* Young is in frequent demand to address and chair sessions of state, regional, and national groups.

Chapter 10

LEGAL ISSUES AND EMPLOYMENT PRACTICES IN STUDENT AFFAIRS

Patricia A. Hollander
D. Parker Young

Student affairs administrators frequently will make decisions relating to staff employment, tort liability, and civil rights liability. In order to make effective and appropriate decisions, they need to understand the legal parameters within which these decisions must be made.*

Administrators may be expected to deal with staff employment practices such as determining job descriptions and job qualifications; recruiting candidates for positions; interviewing; negotiating salaries; and making recommendations or decisions regarding appointments, promotions, tenure or continuing appointment, or about nonrenewal or dismissal. Employment issues concerning evaluation of staff, appropriate review and due process procedures for termination of staff from the institution, and handling the consequences of financial exigency also need to be considered in light of legal requirements and pertinent court decisions.

---

*Appendix B, An Introduction to Legal Research, provides an explanation of how to read legal citations and to locate and use legal sources in research.

Student affairs administrators also should be aware that their actions may lead to claims based upon tort liability, as for negligence or defamation, and civil rights liability, as may arise if staff are deprived of constitutional rights.

THRESHOLD QUESTIONS

A number of threshold questions must be explored by student affairs administrators in order to make appropriate decisions relating to staff. Among the most important are (1) Is the institution private or public? (2) What are the essential employment and tort liability concepts that apply to each type institution? (3) What is the chief student affairs officer's job description, including authority to hire and fire staff? (4) Are student affairs staff positions administrative, faculty, or a combination of both? What are their job descriptions and qualifications?

Private-Public Distinction

At both private and public institutions, sources of employment rights of student affairs administrators and their staff members may be found in statutes, contracts, policies of governing boards, faculty or staff handbooks, college catalogues, and customs and practices at the institution. In addition, professional standards promulgated by groups such as the American Association of University Professors and the American Association of University Administrators are considered by many courts to be appropriate standards to which institutions should adhere. However, at public institutions the federal and/or state constitutions are additional sources of employment rights. In other words, employees at private institutions have employment rights and obligations based principally on statutes and contracts, while employees at public institutions are affected additionally by constitutional rights, such as freedom of expression and due process.

Tort Liability

Regarding tort liability, employees at private institutions need to be concerned about negligence and defamation, and employees at public institutions, in addition to negligence and defamation, must be aware of constitutional torts that may occur in connection with violations of constitutional protections, such as constitutionally impermissible dismissals from employment. Student affairs administrators often function as Vice-Presidents or Deans of Student Affairs and report to the President or Executive Vice-President of the institution. They may have delegated to them the authority to hire and fire their own staffs, particularly if their staff members do not receive concurrent faculty appointments. In the latter case, the faculty apppointment would normally be subject to peer scrutiny by faculty committees, as well as ultimate approval by the top hiring authority of the institution.

Delegation of Authority

Kinds of staff positions that student affairs administrators generally are authorized to fill include the following: admissions, positions related to student disciplinary codes, veteran services, foreign student programs, student financial aid, services for the handicapped, student activities and programs, student testing and research, personal counseling of students, career planning and placement, student publications, student housing, and student records. Sometimes medical services may be included, but at large institutions these may be placed under the jurisdiction of an office of business affairs or health services. Basically, the kinds of staff positions for which a student affairs administrator is responsible are those involving student matters after a student has been admitted to the institution and which do not relate to a student's academic program. A number of clerical, graduate or undergraduate assistantships, and other miscellaneous support positions also may be the responsibility of a student affairs administrator.

Classification of Positions

The various student affairs staff positions may be filled by persons classified only as administrators, only as faculty, or as a combination of both. How the job is classified is crucial to knowing what legal rights and responsibilities are involved. For instance, if a position is one classified purely as administrative, the person hired for that position may or may not have a written contract, be hired for a definite period of time, serve at the pleasure of his/her supervisor, be periodically evaluated, have a right to review of decisions regarding employment, have a right to some stated period of notice prior to nonrenewal or termination, or have a clearly stated job description.

By contrast, some members of the student affairs staff are also faculty members assigned certain administrative duties, such as publications advising or supervising athletics. The assignment may be on a voluntary basis that can be discontinued at the pleasure of either the board or the chief administrator to whom the employee reports. These purely faculty positions usually carry with them normal faculty employment conditions, such as peer review prior to hiring, written contracts of appointment for a certain length of time with a stated period of notice prior to nonrenewal, regular evaluation, and an opportunity for career advancement in their disciplinary departments.

A third classification is the position that may be part-time administrative and part-time faculty. For example, the job may involve implementing the student disciplinary procedure as the administrative part of the position, and an appointment as a tenured faculty member in journalism with teaching duties as the faculty part of the position. Each of these positions confers different rights and obligations regarding employment, as has been presented.

EMPLOYMENT ISSUES

Employment issues normally relate to the following: deciding upon job descriptions and qualifications, advertising for the position, interviewing candidates, hiring, setting salaries, evaluation, promotion, and termination.

At a private institution employment practices generally are affected by very few statutory constraints. The employment statutes that affect private institutions the most are those that prohibit certain specific employment practices such as discrimination based on race, sex, or religion. These statutes apply to public institutions as well. They have nothing to do with the fact that the employer is an educational institution, but cover many employers in the country. Exceptions would be employers with very few employees or those who may be covered by a similar state law rather than a federal law.

Public institutions, in addition to statutes and contract law, are usually considered to be units of government. Therefore, those who act on behalf of public institutions may be considered to be public officials. As such, their actions are subject to certain constraints set forth in the U.S. Constitution. Public officials may not refuse to hire persons, nor may they terminate persons, for constitutionally impermissible reasons, such as exercising their rights under the First Amendment protection of free speech.

Selection, Appointment, and Retention of Staff

Selection of staff should be done according to a standard set of procedures adopted in advance that take into account the job description developed for the position and the job qualifications set forth as requirements to meet the job description. All applications should be processed in a similar and nondiscriminatory fashion.

A critical issue, from the standpoint of preventing legal challenges, is that a strong rationale be presented for whatever job qualifications are set. For example, a position of program director of a student center may be advertised as requiring three years experience in administration and supervision related to student activities or a student center. Under Title VII of the Civil Rights of 1964, a court may be asked to examine the qualifications required by other colleges for similar positions in their student centers and determine whether in fact the requirement of three years experience was job-related.

Appointment procedures should be made absolutely clear, especially with regard to who has the authority to hire. If in a college handbook the governing board authority to hire is stated clearly, an applicant for employment may be expected to know that the authority to hire has been placed in that particular body and, therefore, has no right to rely on statements of anyone else, such as an associate dean. Only rarely have courts recognized that past custom and practice may clothe someone other than the designated individual or group with apparent authority to hire or promote.

Retention problems often may be the result of a lack of mutual understanding about the basic terms of the appointment that occurred between parties at the very beginning of the employment relationship. A clear understanding is made definite about the following matters: Is the person being hired as an administrator, a faculty member, or a combination of both? Is a written contract involved? Is it for a definite term, such as one year or three years? Is there a possibility of continuing appointment or tenure thereafter?

First of all, the employment contract may consist of more than the basic document itself. By implication or by reference, other institutional documents may be incorporated as part of the contract, including policies of the governing board, the administrator or faculty handbook, the college catalogue, and the institution's customs and practices.

At a private institution, if a contract is breached, the injured employee may sue for breach of contract and recover lost wages. This is true also at a public institution. However, a public institution as a unit of the government is bound also to recognize constitutional rights of employees.

In *Board of Regents* v. *Roth* the U.S. Supreme Court held that where a faculty member was hired on a one-year contract and notified of nonrenewal during the appropriate period, there was no requirement under the Fourteenth Amendment Due Process Clause of the Constitution that Roth be given notice of a reason for the nonrenewal or an opportunity for a hearing.

A companion case to *Roth* was decided differently. In *Perry* v. *Sindermann* the U.S. Supreme Court held that the faculty handbook and the state system guidelines at a Texas college were sufficient to create the possibility of *de facto* tenure. The faculty member, therefore, was to be given the opportunity to prove such *de facto* tenure. If he were able to do so, then he would have a property interest entitled to Constitutional protection, and would have a right to be told the reason for nonrenewal, and given the opportunity for a hearing to rebut the charges.

Regarding nonrenewal decisions, in two kinds of situations an appropriate form of due process should take place: first, where the institution, in connection with the nonrenewal, makes some publicly known charge, such as dishonesty or immorality, that imposes a stigma on the individual and forecloses other employment opportunities, or that seriously damages the individual's reputation, or standing in the community; second, where statutory, or contractual law, or the existing rules or practices of the situation create a mutual understanding between the employee and the institution regarding an expectation of continued employment.

The form of due process required in a nonrenewal situation usually should consist of some appropriate process that provides the individual with notice of the reason for the nonrenewal and an opportunity for a hearing to rebut charges. If a tenured individual, or person on a continuing appointment, is being dismissed, more formal procedures are required. In *Ferguson* v. *Thomas* the Fifth Circuit Court of Appeals set forth a minimal procedural process to be provided in a tenured termination hearing for cause:

•The teacher be advised of the cause or causes for termination in sufficient detail to fairly enable teacher to show any error that may exist.

•The teacher be advised of the names and the nature of the testimony against him/her.

•At a reasonable time after such advice, the teacher must be accorded a meaningful opportunity to be heard in his/her own defense.

•A hearing should be held before a tribunal that both possesses some academic expertise and has an impartiality toward the charges.

Evaluation. Evaluation of student affairs administrators and staff for purposes of contract or appointment renewal, promotion, and salary increases is a process that only recently has become one for research and study. Faculty evaluation has a long history and tradition associated with promotion and tenure; evaluation of administration has little history to serve as a guide. Courts have routinely held that faculty evaluations made by peers, according to accepted standards and in a nonarbitrary and nondiscriminatory manner, should not be tampered with by the courts.

Standards for evaluating administrators have only recently been developed. The American Association of University Administrators (AAUA) adopted "Professional Standards for Administrators in Higher Education" in 1975 (Hollander). These standards specify that

an administrator has the right to be free from arbitrary or capricious action on the part of the institution's administration or governing board, especially in those decisions affecting continuation or termination of office. . . . An administrator has the right, under conditions established by the institution's board, to regular and formal evaluation of job performance, to participation in the evaluation process, and to receipt of timely knowledge of the results of such evaluation. (Stein & Baca, 1981, p.90)

Other associations of administrators also have developed professional standards. One of these is the ethical standards statement concerning employment practices of the American College Personnel Association listed in Appendix A.

The purpose of an evaluation must be clear. Evaluation may be principally for the purpose of assisting administrators and faculty in improving performance and becoming more skilled and valued members of an academic community. What also must be emphasized, however, is that evaluation may be done by institutions on two levels. One level has to do with the performance of the individual. The other level has to do with the needs of the institution. Thus, it may happen that an individual may receive a positive personal evaluation, yet be dismissed because the institution no longer has a need for the services of an individual with this particular set of skills.

An institution also may change its evaluation criteria from time to time. Persons hired under the new criteria should expect to be measured by them rather than by any earlier criteria.

Those who are asked to do the evaluations usually are protected from defamation suits, even when they communicate information that is false, so long as there is no proven malice or ill will.

Separation. Separation of student affairs staff members from employment at an institution raises various legal issues related to the kind of appointment the person had, whether the institution was private or public, and whether the person allegedly was deprived of any constitutional rights.

Where a student affairs administrator or staff member was serving at the pleasure of the employer, generally there would be no right to notice, a reason for dismissal, or a hearing. Many employers have believed that this arrangement gave them great freedom and flexibility. However, now the realization is that this so-called freedom also may lead to unnecessarily high costs associated with turnover, new hiring, and new training periods. The American Association of University Administrators reacted to this concern about better management of human resources by including the following in its 1975 Professional Standards for Administrators in Higher Education:

> an administrator has a right to a written statement of the conditions of employment, including, but not limited to, statements on salary and fringe benefits, term of office, process of review, date of notification of action regarding renewal or continuance, and responsibilities of the position. (Stein & Baca, 1981, p. 89)

Where an employee has a contract for a specified term, the employment relationship ceases at the end of the contract period. If the employer chooses to dismiss the employee during the contract period, the employer would have to show just cause or else the employee could sue for breach of contract.

Where an employee has a continuing contract or tenure, some form of just cause for dismissal has to be shown and the employee may have a right to a pre-termination or post-termination hearing. Lack of just cause could result in reinstatement and/or back pay.

If the employer were a public institution, or if a private institution were sufficiently involved in "state action" (see Chapter 9), and an employee could show an expectancy of continued employment by statute, contract, or custom, most employment decisions could be subject to challenge by the employee on the ground that the action was not based on job-related performance, but on the employee's exercise of some constitutionally protected activity. For example, in *Mt. Healthy City School District Board of Education* v. *Doyle,* the U.S. Supreme Court held that where a dismissed teacher claimed his conduct was protected by the First and Fourteenth Amendments (he had made a telephone call to a radio station about school business), but his employer claimed that he was dismissed for other permissible reasons (among them, making obscene gestures to students in the school cafeteria), the trial court should determine whether the employer had shown by a preponderance of the evidence that the employee would have been dismissed even if there had been no constitutionally protected conduct.

Without question, public employees have a right to free expression protected by the First Amendment. But it is not an absolute right. In *Pickering* v. *Board of Education,* the U.S. Supreme Court was asked to decide a case involving a public school teacher who was dismissed after writing a letter to a newspaper in which he spoke out against a school bond issue. He was dismissed on the ground that a teacher's relationship to a school superintendent is so close that by taking a position in opposition to the superintendent he had destroyed their working relationship. The Supreme Court's decision was in favor of the teacher and became known as the "Pickering Rule." The Supreme Court held that a teacher could not be dismissed for making public statements upon matters of public concern in the exercise of First Amendment rights, unless the statement could be shown to (1) impede the teacher's proper performance of classroom duties, (2) disrupt substantially the regular operation of the school, (3) violate an express need for confidentiality, or (4) undermine the effectiveness of the working relationship between the superior and the subordinates. In the *Pickering* case the Supreme Court felt that there was enough distance between the teacher in the classroom and the superintendent in the central school district office building that no undermining of their working relationship would take place.

Financial Exigency. Bona fide financial exigency has been upheld by courts as just cause for separation of employees on term contract as well as those on continuing contracts or tenure. Sometimes the financial crisis may affect the whole institution, only one school or program within an institution, or just one department. Assuming the financial crisis to be valid, courts usually have sustained layoffs so long as there was proof that the decision as to which specific employees were to be dismissed was reached in some rational fashion. In the case of public institutions, once again, the principal reason would have to be financial distress and not the employee's exercise of some constitutionally protected right. Where a bona fide budgetary exigency exists, a tenured faculty member may be terminated and a nontenured person kept on the payroll. For instance, accreditation may be lost in the tenured person's area, and growth may be occurring in that of the nontenured faculty member.

Legal Implications of Nondiscrimination Statutes. Prominent among statutes that may affect both private and public institutional employers are nondiscrimination statutes, such as (1) Title VII of the 1964 Civil Rights Act, 42 *U.S.C.* A. Sec. 2000, as amended by the Equal Employment Opportunity Act of 1972, the Pregnancy Discrimination Act of 1978, and the Equal Employment Opportunity Commission (EEOC) Regulations of 1980 regarding Sexual Harassment; (2) the Equal Pay Act of 1963, 29 *U.S.C.* A. Sec. 206(d); (3) the Age Discrimination in Employment Act of 1967, 29 *U.S.C.* A. Sec. 621, as amended in 1978; and (4) the Rehabilitation Act of 1973, 29 *U.S.C.* A. Sec. 701 as amended.

Title VII of the 1964 Civil Rights Act affects such employment practices as hiring, upgrading, salaries, fringe benefits, and training opportunities. Title VII prohibits employers from discriminating in employment on the basis of race, religion (except religious institutions regarding a particular religion), national origin, and sex. The first cases to arise under Title VII often alleged discrimination on the basis of race. Many of those cases did not involve educational institutions, but decisions in the cases certainly applied to colleges and universities as employers. For instance, where a job candidate is given a test, or must meet stated job qualifications, the test or the qualifications must be related to the job. It is not enough that the test of qualifications measure the candidate in the abstract, they must measure in relation to criteria needed to do the job *(Griggs* v. *Duke Power Company).* Racial discrimination may be proved in a *prima facie* sense by producing statistics showing a substantial lack of minorities in the employer's labor force *(McDonnell Douglas Corporation* v. *Green).* An employer then may rebut such statistical evidence by articulating some legitimate, nondiscriminatory reason for the rejection of the candidate *(Furno Construction Company* v. *Waters).* In a significant case involving an allegation of sex discrimination at a college, regarding nonpromotion on a timely basis, the female faculty member proved to the court's satisfaction that the college's reasons for the delay were based on pretext and were discriminatory. The Court ordered back pay for the period of delay regarding the promotion *(Sweeney* v. *Board of Trustees of Keene State College).*

Title VII was amended to include the Pregnancy Discrimination Act of 1978. EEOC's final guidelines for this act will be found in 44 *Federal Register* 13278, March 9, 1979. The Pregnancy Discrimination Act makes it a violation of Title VII for an employer to discriminate on the basis of pregnancy, childbirth, or related illnesses in employment opportunities, health or disability insurance programs, or sick leave plans. Under this act pregnancy-related conditions must be treated the same as any other disability. Health insurance that covers pregnancy-related conditions of male employee dependents also must cover pregnancy-related conditions of female employees. This act is meant principally to affect attempts by employers to terminate pregnant employees rather than giving them leaves of absence, to refuse to reimburse an employee's pregnancy costs under health or disability income insurance plans, or to penalize a female employee returning from pregnancy leave by denying her access to her former position at her regular pay.

Sexual harrassment regulations under Title VII were published by EEOC on November 10, 1980, in 45 *Federal Register,* at page 25024. These rules generally apply to all employers, including colleges and universities, having more than 15 employees. In the past, courts tended to distinguish between what were referred to as unfortunate personal encounters as compared to sexual harrassment by persons of authority where refusal to comply could affect adversely one's terms and conditions of employment. One of these early cases was *Fisher* v. *Flynn.* It involved an assistant professor of psychology, who was terminated at Bridgewater State College. She filed suit in Federal District Court claiming a violation of Title VII based in part on her refusal to accede to alleged sexual advances of her department chairman. In essence, the Court found that insufficient evidence existed to establish that her chairman had influence on the decision to terminate her. Therefore, the Court found that this was a purely personal sexual advance, without employment repercussions, and consequently not actionable under Title VII.

By comparison to the *Fisher* case, the 1980 EEOC Sexual Harrassment Regulations appear to be broader in scope. The language of the regulations mentions employers' being responsible by preventing hostile and harrassing working environments, *Bundy* v. *Jackson.* This may be interpreted to mean that the regulations cover not only behavior of persons with authority to affect hiring, salaries, or terminations, but also the behavior of co-workers, and, in some instances, nonemployees. Generally, sexual harrassment has been found where there is evidence of repeated offenses corroborated by witnesses.

The Equal Pay Act affects not only an employee's initial hiring salary, but rates of pay for subsequent promotions as well. It provides that females and males employed in the same establishment receive equal pay for substantially equal work. Legal challenges by females usually allege that the work they are doing is substantially equal to the work being done by males, but that their pay is not. One of the earliest cases based on the Equal Pay Act was *Corning Glass Works* v. *Brennan,* in which the U.S. Supreme Court held that equal work will be rewarded by equal wages. The defense raised by employers in most cases is that the particular job being performed by a female is not in fact equal to the job to which it is being compared and for which a male is being paid a higher wage. More specifically, the Act requires that men and women employed in the same establishment receive equal pay, including fringe benefits, for jobs that involve substantially equal skill, effort, and responsibility, and are performed under similar working conditions. Comparison of actual job content, not job titles, determines whether the work is substantially equal. Four exceptions are permitted by this Act. They are unequal payments based on other factors, specifically: (1) a seniority system, (2) a merit system, (3) a system that measures earnings by quantity or quality of production, or (4) a differential based on any factor other than sex.

Equal pay cases turn on the facts and evidence in each case. The burden of proving that two jobs are substantially equal is a heavy one. For example, different pay scales have been found appropriate for female custodians doing lighter cleaning work than that done by males. Similarly, the initial salary of a male faculty member may be higher than that of a female hired at the same time for an equal job, where the male had other job offers at a higher starting wage, and the institution merely was meeting market conditions.

Comparable worth is a concept that looks beyond equal pay for equal work. Comparable worth deals with sex-based wage discrimination under Title VII in instances when the jobs typically assigned to men and women, though not the same, arguably could be classifed as comparable regarding skill or worth. For example, secretarial jobs in an organization may have been assigned typically to women. Where the secretarial job pay scale is less than that of the janitorial job, a Title VII claim might allege that an analysis of two jobs would show that the secretarial job required as much or more education, experience, and skill as the janitorial job, and that the sole reason for its lower pay scale was that it was typically held by women. An employer can defend Title VII claims concerning wage differentials on the basis of the same four exceptions set out in the Equal Pay Act, namely, seniority, merit, quality or quantity of production, or any other factor other than sex.

The Age Discrimination in Employment Act of 1967, as amended in 1978, is one of the most critical new statutes with which educational institutions must deal. The Age Discrimination in Employment Act prohibits discrimination in employment for persons in the age group 40 to 70 years of age. A statutory exception for higher education institutions permitted them to continue to terminate tenured faculty and administrators at age 65 until July 1982. This Act affects hiring, promotion, fringe benefits, and termination, among other employment conditions. Several examples may be instructive relative to this Act. For instance, a *prima facie* case of age discrimination may be proved by showing that the complainant is in the protected age group, that his/her job performance meets appropriate expectations of employers, that someone else was hired to perform the same work after the complainant was terminated, and that age was shown to be the determining factor in the termination decision.

The question of what remedy is available to persons who believe they have been discriminated against in employment on the basis of age has been litigated in the courts for some time. Generally, the appropriate remedy is the repayment of lost wages, including lost minimums and overtime, but not damages for pain and suffering or punitive damages.

The Rehabilitation Act of 1973 (Section 504) prohibits covered federal contractors from discriminating in employment against qualified handicapped persons. Employment practices covered by this Act include recruiting, hiring, compensation, job assignment, classification, and fringe benefits. Employers must make affirmative efforts (Section 503) to employ and advance in employment qualified persons with handicaps. Structural barriers must be modified as well.

Employers are expected to make reasonable accommodations for qualified handicapped employees, such as modification of work schedules, use of ramps, and the shifting of some nonessential duties to other employees. Employers are not expected to make accommodations that would be an undue hardship, based on business necessity. Persons handicapped by alcohol or other drugs are covered by this Act, but institutions may take into account the actual behavior of handicapped individuals in deciding whether they are qualified in spite of such handicap.

Employers are urged to make employment decisions regarding persons with handicaps on a case by case basis, taking care to make a fair determination whether the individual is qualified in spite of the handicap. If an employer requires medical exams of handicapped applicants or employees, exams must be required for the nonhandicapped as well.

A person with only one kidney generally would be found qualified. A taxi driver with only one arm, but with a past record of safe driving in spite of the handicap, may be qualified. However, a person with a severe hearing loss who applied for employment as a school bus driver most likely would not be considered qualified.

Affirmative Action

The principles involved in affirmative action came into vogue in the 1970s. The guiding priciple behind affirmative action plans is to provide opportunities for members of minority groups and women who have been previously deprived of equal opportunity. Much controversy and debate has arisen from implementation of affirmative action plans, with opponents claiming that affirmative action is often synonymous with reverse discrimination.

Educational institutions that qualify as federal contractors or subcontractors are subject to Executive Order 11246, as amended. The institution's attorney should be consulted as to whether the college must adhere to this Executive Order. If so, the essential purpose of this Executive Order is to prohibit discrimination in employment on the basis of race, color, religion, sex, and national origin in hiring, upgrading, salaries, finge benefits, training, and other conditions of employment.

The institution generally is required to analyze its work force to see if minorities and women are being underutilized. If they are, the employer is to create an affirmative action plan setting forth a timetable within which goals of hiring certain numbers of minorities and women are set. The employer then is obligated to make a good faith effort to reach the goals within the timetable.

The legality of affirmative action has been challenged often. However, two recent U.S. Supreme Court decisions regarding affirmative action in employment have supported the basic concept. They are *Weber* v. *Kaiser Aluminum Co.* and *Fullilove* v. *Klutznick.* The *Weber* case involved a legal challenge to private, voluntary affirmative action plans. The *Weber* opinion upheld a collective bargaining agreement that reserved for Black employees 50 percent of the openings in an in-plant craft training program until the percentage of Black craft workers in the plant was commensurate with the percentage of Blacks in the local labor force. A white employee, Brian Weber, challenged the plan. The Supreme Court found that employers and the unions in the private sector were free to take such voluntary race-conscious steps to eliminate manifest racial imbalance in traditionally segregated job categories. The Court specifically noted that the plan did not necessarily trammel interest of white employees; the plan was a temporary measure and was not intended to maintain race balance, but simply to eliminate a manifest racial imbalance.

The *Fullilove* case upheld the provisions of the Public Works Employment Act of 1977. That Act provides that 10 percent of all federally funded public works projects shall be awarded to minority contractors.

The emphasis given to affirmative action is subject to change due to the changes in philosophy of different national government administrations and the philosophy of administrators who enforce civil rights laws. Because of these periodic shifts in governmental philosophy, student affairs administrators need to be aware continually of parameters governing affirmative action issues.

LEGAL LIABILITY

Student affairs administrators often are faced with two major kinds of legal liability—tort liability and civil rights liability. Tort liability refers to most wrongful, civil, injurious acts that occur between individuals, except for acts involving contracts or crimes. Civil rights liability arises when government, through public officials, causes an injury by deprivation of Constitutional or statutory rights.

Tort

Four elements generally must be present for tort liability to exist. First, there must be a duty to use due care under the circumstances to prevent an unreasonable risk of harm. Second, there must be a breach of that duty. Third, there must be proved a direct, causal relationship between the behavior and the alleged injury. Fourth, there must be proof that an actual injury occurred. Common examples of torts include negligence, such as an injury to an employee that is caused by ice allowed to remain on the steps of a campus office building, and defamation, such as an injury to an employee's reputation that is caused by a news story in the college paper falsely and knowingly accusing him/her of theft of funds.

Sovereign Immunity. One defense against tort liability available to some public institutions is based on the premise that a government may not be sued without its consent. This defense is referred to as sovereign or governmental immunity. However, the concept of sovereign immunity has been abrogated by statute in some states and by judicial decisions in others. Student affairs administrators should not rely upon sovereign immunity as a defense without checking carefully with their attorneys. Also, even where the public institution itself may be protected by sovereign immunity, an individual administrator may not be.

Proprietary Functions. Even when sovereign immunity ordinarily might be available—as in the case of a public university in a state where such immunity still exists—the particular behavior that caused the injury may be characterized as a proprietary function rather than a governmental function, and sovereign immunity may not apply. For example, courts have found in some instances that jobs performed by doctors and nurses at public university hospitals did constitute proprietary rather than governmental functions, because they were the same jobs as those performed by doctors and nurses in private practice. Big time college football, similarly, has been held a proprietary function.

Negligence. Student affairs administrators must know that negligence may consist of either doing an act or failing to do an act, such as neglecting to remove snow and ice from stairs and walks. Generally the institution itself is liable for damages caused by torts if the individual administrator who caused the injury was acting within the scope of employment. Even then, however, the administrator may be sued as well and will be protected only if he/she can show no lack of reasonable care. If an administrator acts outside the scope of employment, the individual administrator alone may be liable.

Assumption of the risk is a defense against a claim of negligence. For instance, staff members who are employed as athletic coaches or assistant coaches would be expected to have assumed the normal risks attendant to employment duties associated with their particular athletic activities. Probably no remedy for negligence is available to them if they are injured at work. There may be a basis for relief under Workers' Compensation Laws, however.

Contributory negligence is another defense against liability for negligence. If a student affairs staff member were aware, for example, that his/her office door handle was loose and then was injured when the handle fell off and broke a toe, the staff member may be found contributorily negligent. In such a situation, the injured party may recover only part of the costs of the damages suffered.

Defamation. Defamation is a false and injurious statement about another person. If the statement is an oral statement, it is called slander. If it is written, broadcast, or televised, it is called libel. There are a number of defenses against a charge of defamation, such as that the statement is true, that the statement is privileged, or that the injured person is a "public figure" in which case malice must be proved. In order for a statement to be found slanderous or libelous, it must be communicated to some one, not merely to the complaining party. Where a third party overhears or reads a statement, communication has taken place.

Some communications to others about a person are considered to be privileged. The nature of privilege may be absolute, as in the case of judges' communications from the bench, or qualified, as in the case of persons authorized to perform a certain function and making otherwise defamatory statements in the course of performing that function. In an academic setting a person chairing a personnel committee deciding whether or not to continue staff members' employment may be in such a situation.

If a person is a "public figure," he/she must prove malice in an action for defamation. A well-known case that arose in an academic setting involved an adjunct professor at Western Michigan University. He received the notorious "Golden Fleece Award" from U.S. Senator William Proxmire and thereafter was adversely affected as to employment and research funding. He sued Senator Proxmire for defamation. Ultimately the U.S. Supreme Court held that a U.S. Senator is not immunized from suit for allegedly defamatory statements that he makes in press releases and newsletters, in contrast to actions and statements made on the floor of the Senate. More to the point of this discussion, the Supreme Court also ruled that Hutchinson, the professor, was not a public figure merely because he received public grants for research and published his work in professional journals. Hutchinson and Proxmire then reached an out of court settlement. Basically, Proxmire was to pay Hutchinson $10,000 damages out of personal funds and issue a public apology to Hutchinson on the floor of the Senate and through the same media and newsletters intially used to disseminate the falsehoods *(Hutchinson* v. *Proxmire)*.

Civil Rights Liability

Civil rights liability generally refers to the liability that emanates from guarantees of due process in the U.S. Constitution, particularly from an implementing statute referred to as 42 *U.S.C.* Sec. 1983 that provides

> every person who, under color of any statute, ordinance, regulation, custom or usage, or any State or Territory, subjects or causes to be subjected, any citizen of the United States or other person within the jurisdiction thereof to the deprivation of any rights, privileges, or immunities secured by the Constitution and laws, shall be liable to the party injured in an action at law, suit in equity, or other proper proceeding for redress.

Civil rights liability also may refer more broadly to a whole range of liabilities arising under civil rights statutes such as Title VII. The discussion here will be confined largely to liability under 42 *U.S.C.* Sec. 1983, which seeks to redress acts by public officials *who knew or should have known* that their actions would deprive persons of their constitutional rights without due process *(Wood* v. *Strickland)*. Public officials may be personally liable in such situations. Where a procedural due process requirement is violated and no actual financial loss is proved, a nominal award, such as one dollar, may be ordered *(Carey* v. *Piphus)*.

42 *U.S.C.* Sec. 1983 protects administrators, faculty, and other staff members at public institutions who allege they were suspended or disciplined or terminated without due process for exercising a constitutional right, such as participation in political activities.

In addition to claims for violations of constitutional rights, 42 *U.S.C.* Sec. 1983 has been recently interpreted by the U.S. Supreme Court to encompass claims based solely on statutory violations of federal law, such as the Social Security Act *(Maine* v. *Thiboutot).*

Award of Attorneys' Fees. The Civil Rights Attorneys' Fees Awards Act of 1976, 90 Stat. 2641, 42 *U.S.C.* Sec. 1988 is one of some 50 statutes that give courts discretionary or mandatory power to award reasonable attorney's fees to prevailing parties in suits filed under federal statutes. Other such statutes are Title VII, the Fair Labor Standards Act, the Employees Retirement Income Security Act (ERISA), the Age Discrimination in Employment Act, and the Equal Pay Act. Under Title VII, for example, prevailing plaintiffs' attorneys may submit their bills to courts, and the courts examine them carefully regarding time and labor required, difficulty of the legal questions, skill required, and other criteria to determine the award of attorney's fees that may be approved. Occasionally, a prevailing defendant's attorney may be awarded fees where the plaintiff's suit was shown to be vexatious, in bad faith, and characterized by abusive conduct or attempts at harrassment. Amounts of fees awarded range widely. Prevailing attorneys have been awarded as much as $160,000 based on actual hours spent by the attorney in the office and in court.

The first step for an attorney seeking the awarding of fees from a public employer is, as has been suggested already, to overcome the doctrine of sovereign immunity under the Eleventh Amendment of the Constitution that would prohibit paying damages from public funds without some express language from Congress in the pertinent statute permitting such payment. The trend appears to be to permit such awards in accordance with a Supreme Court decision in a Title VII case *(Fitzpatrick* v. *Bitzer).* Attorney's fees also may be awarded to a party who prevails through settlement rather than through judicial determination *(Maher* v. *Gagne).*

Guidelines for Student Affairs Administrators

1. Student affairs administrators should familiarize themselves with an institution's corporate and organizational structure as it affects

employment matters, that is, whether it is a private or public institution, and what employment-related constitutional and statutory mandates apply to it at both the federal and state levels.

2. Official documents of the institution should be read and understood. These include policies of the governing board; various faculty, staff, and student handbooks; and college catalogues and bulletins. In addition, the institution's past practices and customs regarding employment should be reviewed.

3. Each individual student affairs administrator should reach a mutual understanding with the proper hiring authority at the institution regarding term and conditions of his/her own employment. This understanding preferably should be in writing. The understanding should be clear about all employment responsibilities and rights, including the following:

- Job description:
  administrative or faculty
  part-time or full-time
  authority to hire or terminate subordinates
  authority regarding budget

- Salary

- Fringe benefits, including sabbatical and leaves of absence

- Term of office

- Process of evaluation

- Date of notification of action regarding promotions, renewals, or continuance

- Due process procedures regarding review of institutional actions affecting employment

- Other relevant employment-related issues, such as: attendance at professional meetings; personal rights to free expression, privacy, and outside activities; assistance in seeking new employment in cases of reallocation of institutional resources; permissible outside employment; and seeking funds for research.

4. Student affairs administrators should ascertain what are institutional policies regarding risk management: what insurance coverage or other mechanisms exist for handling tort, civil rights, or statutory claims, particularly costs of defense of claims and payment of court or other awards?

CASE CITATIONS

Board of Regents v. *Roth*, 408 U.S. 564 (1972)

Bundy v. *Jackson*, 49 U.S.L.W. 2453 (1981)

Carey v. *Piphus*, 98 S. Ct. 1042 (1978)

Corning Glass Works v. *Brennan*, 417 U.S. 188 (1974)

Ferguson v. *Thomas*, 430 F. 2d 852 (1970)

Fisher v. *Flynn*, 598 F. 2d 663 (1979)

Fitzpatrick v. *Bitzer*, 427 U.S. 445 (1976)

Fullilove v. *Klutznick*, 100 S. Ct. 2758 (1980)

Furnco Construction Company v. *Waters*, 98 S. Ct. 2943 (1978)

Griggs v. *Duke Power Company*, 401 U.S. 424 (1971)

Hutchinson v. *Proxmire*, 99 S. Ct. 2675 (1979)

Maher v. *Gagne*, 100 S. Ct. 2570 (1980)

Maine v. *Thiboutot*, 100 S. Ct. 2502 (1980)

MacDonnell Douglas Corporation v. *Green*, 411 U.S. 792 (1973)

Mt. Healthy City School District Board of Education v. *Doyle*, 429 U.S. 274 (1977)

Perry v. *Sindermann*, 408 U.S. 593 (1972)

Pickering v. *Board of Education*, 391 U.S. 563 (1968)

Sweeney v. *Board of Trustees of Keene State College*, 604 F. 2d 106 (1979)

Weber v. *Kaiser Aluminum Co.*, 99 S. Ct. 2721 (1979)

Wood v. *Strickland*, 420 U.S. 308 (1975)

REFERENCES

Hollander, P.A. *Legal handbook for educators.* Boulder, CO: Westview Press, 1978.

Stein, R.H., & Baca, M.C. (Eds.). *New directions for higher education: Professional ethics in university administration* (No. 33). San Francisco: Jossey-Bass, 1981.

SUGGESTED READINGS

Bickel, R.D., & Brechner, J.A. *The college administrator and the courts* (and quarterly updating supplements). Asheville, NC: College Administration Publications, 1978.

Hollander, P.A. Higher education and the handicapped: Current status and future prognosis. In D.P. Young (Ed.), *Higher education: The law and the 1980s in perspective.* Athens, GA: University of Georgia Institute of Higher Education, 1979.

Hollander, P.A. *Legal handbook for educators.* Boulder, CO: Westview Press, 1978.

Hollander, P.A. Legal liability of administrators: Civil rights laws and actions in tort. In D.P. Young (Ed.), *Higher education: The law and constructive change.* Athens, GA: University of Georgia Institute of Higher Education, 1975.

Hollander, P.A. A mediation service for administrators. In J. McCarthy (Ed.), *New directions for higher education: Resolving conflicts for higher education* (No. 32). San Francisco: Jossey-Bass, 1980.

Hollander, P.A. Personal liability of administrators under civil rights law. In D.P. Young (Ed.), *Higher education: The law and administrative responsibilities.* Athens, GA: University of Georgia Institute of Higher Education, 1977.

Young, D.P., & Gehring, D.D. *The college student and the courts* (and quarterly updating supplements). Asheville, NC: College Administration Publications, 1977.

Young, D.P. (Ed.). *Yearbook of higher education law.* Topeka, KS: National Organization on Legal Problems of Education, 1977-1981.

David T. Borland is Consultant and Arbitrator, Dispute Resolution Services, Lansing, Michigan. He formerly served in various faculty and administrative roles at Miami University (Ohio), Indiana University, Ferris State College (Michigan), and North Texas State University, receiving NTSU's Distinguished Teaching Award. He served in various leadership roles of the American College Personnel Association, including that of President (1981-82).

Borland has consulted with over 40 professional, public service, industrial, penal, health care, and educational institutions and has presented over 75 workshops, training and professional institutes. Currently in providing resolution services for differing personal, professional, and employment disputes, he serves in the roles of negotiator, mediator, factfinder, arbitrator, and consultant for several dozen clients. He serves on the National Labor Panel of Arbitrators of the American Arbitration Association, the Roster of Arbitrators for the Federal Mediation and Conciliation Service, and is listed on the panels of arbitrators with the Michigan Employment Relations Commission. He has authored more than 35 professional publications in higher education and labor relations.

Chapter 11

THE IMPACT OF COLLECTIVE BARGAINING: PROFESSIONAL DILEMMA OR PANACEA?

David T. Borland

The goal of the student affairs profession is to enhance the comprehensive development of college students. Because this goal must be accomplished through cooperative efforts of an institution's personnel and because collective bargaining increasingly has affected higher education, student affairs practitioners need to understand the issue of collective bargaining and its impact on professional activities.

Student affairs professionals are becoming more involved in employee relations processes, both on the labor and the management sides of the issue, at both public and private institutions, and at both the senior and community/junior college levels. However, knowledge about collective bargaining and its impact on professionals, staff, and students varies greatly. Many colleagues in the nearly 700 college and university campuses with collective bargaining have an understanding of issues involved in the collective bargaining process. Perhaps a majority of the remaining approximately 3,500 higher education institutions are either unsure about the issues, have ignored the trend toward collective bargaining, or mistakenly have viewed collective bargaining as significant only for faculty. Other university personnel have been competitive in self representation without unifying under collective bargaining management.

Confusion often results when attempting to apply a trade union model of employee relations, designed primarily for employees in the private sector of the economy, to the specific needs of personnel employed by governmental or educational agencies (public sector), and more particularly, to institutions of higher education with traditions of staff involvement in personnel decisions. This confusion has led some administrators to see a disaster for the current system of higher education, while faculty and other professional employees tend to view collective bargaining as a cure for all employment problems.

Although neither extreme view—disaster nor panacea—is accurate, both sides agree on one conclusion: collective bargaining in the public sector is a reality. While that reality is less evident in the South and the West (Borland, 1976a), increasing pressure for collective bargaining in public agencies does exist in these regions as well (Borland, 1975). With the increase in the past decade in the number of higher education institutions utilizing collective bargaining mechanisms for employee/employer employee/employer relations, in addition to the intensive efforts of national bargaining agents to attract more members, clearly student affairs professionals and the students they serve will be affected significantly.

HISTORICAL DEVELOPMENT

Private Sector

Until 1962 the collective bargaining process was utilized only in private companies and by their employees. In that year President Kennedy signed Executive Order 10988, which extended collective bargaining to some federal employees and to most private institutions of higher education. The National Labor Relations Board (NLRB) then asserted its jurisdiction over private colleges and universities in its 1970 Cornell University decision. Although NLRB jurisdiction over private universities has been challenged several times since then, a decision in the Yeshiva University case by the Second Circuit of the United States Court of Appeals during the summer of 1978 overruled for the first time an NLRB position on faculty bargaining in higher education. In February,

1980, the United States Supreme Court upheld the Appeals Court decision, stating that faculty held so much authority in institutional and academic policies and procedures that they were operating the institution substantially in a manner that would be considered managerial in any other enterprise (Watkins, 1980). Even though both courts limited their rulings to Yeshiva University's situation, a few institutions of higher education immediately following the issuance of the decision suspended their negotiations and submitted petitions to the courts for a similar ruling in their own situations. Even though the NLRB has extended or withheld its authority only on an individual case basis so far this decade, the exact impact of these rulings is still unknown.

Public Sector

Using the NLRB as a model and Executive Order 10988 as the authority, several employees in governmental and educational agencies sought authority and structure for collective bargaining in their respective states through the legislative process. Legislation, however, is not required legally, even in states with "right-to-work" statutes. These statutes, which exist in 20 states, are viewed by management as protecting rights of employees, while unions believe they were designed to inhibit labor organizations' security (Borland & Birmingham, 1981). Such legislation facilitates effective (good faith) bargaining, however, contracts are negotiated by public employees in states where legislation is nonexistent.

At this time 24 states, generally including the North and the East and excluding most of the South and many states in the West, now have varying degrees of enabling legislation. Enabling legislation in each state, modeled after existing federal legislation, establishes rules and designates the state agency to administer collective bargaining for various public employees. These agencies are similar in scope and authority to the NLRB.

Specifically in higher education according to an article in *Chronicle of Higher Education* (July 7, 1980), the number of campuses with collective bargaining increased from nine in 1968 to 681 in 1980. The more than 130,000 faculty and staff employed by these institutions represent over 20 percent of college faculty and staff members in the country—all of this involvement having come about in a span of about one decade. About 90 percent of the institutions with collective bargaining are publicly supported, with two-thirds being two-year colleges (Borland, 1977).

Essential for student affairs professionals is awareness that efforts to gain collective bargaining rights by faculty, custodians, librarians, food service employees, and secretaries on their own campuses will have an impact on their own employment relationships (Latta, 1979). Student affairs has become an integral part of the contemporary labor relations scene.

Bargaining Agents

Bargaining is organized by persons, either internal or external to an institution, who sense some sentiment or conflict that could benefit from the use of a bargaining process. A bargaining agent is an organization that represents employees in their relations with management. It is a labor group. The agent may be a national organization associated with employees outside of higher education such as the Teamsters, the United Auto Workers (UAW), or the American Federation of State, County, and Municipal Employees (AFSCME). Often these unions are criticized for being ineffective in colleges and universities because they are unaware of particular characteristics of employment relationships in higher education. However, while groups outside higher education have organized primarily in private industry and more recently in higher education among classified (support) employees, AFSCME has organized 12 campuses in the Connecticut community college system successfully, and the TOPS (Technical, Office, and Professional Services) Division of the UAW now represents student affairs personnel at Eastern Michigan University.

Educational associations active as agents in higher education include the American Federation of Teachers (AFT), the American Association of University Professors (AAUP), and the National Education Association (NEA). While the AFT always has aligned itself with the trade union movement in philosophy, organization, and tactics, the NEA and the AAUP have considered themselves as organizations of professional educators separated from trade unions. As collective bargaining has become accepted increasingly in higher education, various pressures and experiences have eliminated many distinctions among these three organizations.

A bargaining agent also may be a state organization or even a local independent group. Generally, greater strength and technical assistance are available in national organizations, but local groups have more independent control.

Factors Contributing to Unionization

Individuals at different institutions will vote for a bargaining agent in a representation election for various reasons, whether in the public or the private sector. Staff members generally have four basic problems that union organizers use as the reasons for voting for collective bargaining in higher education.

Economics. When funds supporting higher education are constricted through declines in support, as inflation continues to rise, and as declining institutional budget support becomes more visible to student affairs employees, power to determine fiscal priorities with management is seen as desirable by employees. While results are varied in institutions and states, generally higher salaries and benefits do result at institutions with bargaining powers as compared to similar institutions without collective bargaining.

Structural Complexity. As institutions have grown larger and as they have become organizationally more complex, communication distance is perceived by employees as too great, and effective staff input into the institution's decision-making processes is lost. Once organizational distance is formalized, the movement by employees toward a power mechanism in order to regain effectiveness is perceived as a logical step.

Security. As these structurally complex bureaucracies come under intensive attack from financial supporters, as demands for accountability increase, and as enrollments decline, administrators must search for more efficient operations. This often means a reduction in the staff or a change in the working environment. Often a situation develops where staff members desire a share of the effective decision-making authority in personnel matters.

Conflict Resolution. The pressure of economics, complexity of structure, and need for security create situations for potential conflict and increase the employee perception that the administration and the employees have mutually exclusive goals. In such an atmosphere any disagreement with administrative decisions is perceived by employees as requiring formal resolution of the resulting conflict.

Basically, personnel want better pay and working conditions, more objectivity and due process in management practices, and equal power with administrators and governing boards in the determination of professional considerations.

This general overview of elements and current status of collective bargaining in higher education provides the basis for further analysis and application to the student affairs profession. This new employee relations process has consequences for every phase of campus life and the potential for changing significantly campus relationships for student affairs practitioners.

BARGAINING PROCESSES

Collective bargaining is defined as a process where representatives of employers and employees determine wages, hours, and conditions of employment, and results in a written contract for a specified duration. It is an adversary process by tradition and law, and a power tactic in practice. Collective bargaining also has been defined as a forced system of communication.

Many individuals believe that the collective bargaining process is involved primarily with exchanging proposals and counterproposals across the bargaining table. Coe (1973a) described a process in which the actual table process itself is a very small portion of the entire planning and preparation sequence necessary for successful bargaining. Significant stages in the total collective bargaining process are represented by the following questions: (1) how does collective bargaining come to a campus; (2) who is included in the bargaining process; (3) who represents employees in this process; and (4) how is a contract negotiated and administered?

Initiation of Collective Bargaining

The enabling legislation, regulating bodies, and formal procedures affect the internal relationships of a campus when collective bargaining processes are initiated. The process depends on the specific law. The following is presented as a composite of many state statutes and NLRB interpretations, as well as personal experiences with the process from both sides of the bargaining issue.

The interest of campus personnel must be determined formally as a first step. Generally before initial discussions of collective bargaining on a campus take place, a history of employee complaints has existed concerning a variety of matters. When these matters are left unresolved by administrators or are of such a nature that administrators believe they cannot or should not implement what employees desire, the law requires that these complaints be consolidated in a formal manner by a significant proportion of these employees. The requirement of formal action is designed to prevent minor complaints existing in any employment environment from creating major problems.

This formal process, the second step, is accomplished through a petition type of process. This sometimes is a lengthy process that usually results in an election. The first prospective bargaining agent who wishes formal recognition must gather the signatures of at least 30 percent of proposed bargaining unit members. Once this is verified by appropriate state labor relations board for publicly supported institutions or by the NLRB for private colleges and universities, an election will be held. Thereafter, any prospective agent who wishes to appear on the ballot must gather signatures of at least 10 percent of proposed bargaining unit members. Once the informal complaints have been verified by this formal petition process, the collective bargaining process has begun, and the remaining stages eventuate automatically in most cases.

Representation Elections

Once a bargaining agent has organized the staff and once the bargaining unit has been determined, a campaign, which usually results in an election, is begun to promote the advantages of the various bargaining agents. All bargaining agents certified by the appropriate labor relations board will appear on the ballot along with a "no union" choice.

Many institutional leaders mistakenly believe that either they have no right to present views opposing collective bargaining; or on the other extreme, they might take an aggressive stance in an effort to destroy the union. While aggressive institutional overreaction actually may convince the staff that they need the protection of a bargaining agent, no institutional response at all may mislead the staff into believing that collective bargaining actually is endorsed by the particular college or university.

Bargaining Unit Determination

After the petition for recognition is made by the potential bargaining agents, a hearing is held by the NLRB for private institutions or by the state labor relations board for public institutions to determine which employees will be in the bargaining unit. The process of unit determination potentially affects all staff whether or not they want to be included as a part of the bargaining unit. Generally, bargaining agents want as many members as possible in the bargaining unit including members who are not in the institutional management structure and members who oppose bargaining.

Decisions of these boards as to bargaining unit membership generally are based on four factors. First, they attempt to avoid fragmentation of personnel, an undue burden on an institution, by constructing the largest possible units. Second, the members must share a "community of interest," such as work, education, or criteria for evaluation. Third, any individual or group of employees, over whom no disagreement exists between the administration and those representing employees as to their inclusion will be accepted by the labor relations board. Finally, all employees in a supervisory position will be excluded from the provisions of appropriate statutes, as determined primarily by functions in which one serves rather than by titles alone.

Given the fact that student affairs practitioners are accountable to students, the institution, the student affairs profession, and the staff, determination of the bargaining unit is crucial. Each of these constituencies may require conflicting loyalties from student affairs professionals on varying issues. The appropriate bargaining unit for each situation, therefore, differs in relation to the structure and environment on each campus.

Some units are composed solely of student affairs professionals, while other units contain all nonteaching personnel. Others contain classified staff in the student affairs areas, and some contain all professional nonsupervisory employees, including faculty with student affairs staff. Aaron (1975) found that at 73 percent of the campuses analyzed, student affairs professionals were included in the faculty unit. Studies by Fisher and Packwood (1975) and Borland (1979b) indicated that these staff members preferred this type of unit. Phelan's (1977) study confirmed the desire of student affairs staff to be included in the faculty unit, but also found that faculty and students opposed their inclusion. Although specific differences existed between two-year and four-year campuses, Kellett (1976) found that a majority of both union leaders and chief student affairs officers believed that student affairs staff were included with faculty in bargaining units because of common teaching functions and the greater strength of the larger bargaining unit.

Aaron's (1975) analysis of contracts further indicated, however, that student affairs staff members were virtually silent on concerns of the student affairs profession. If student affairs professionals are included with the faculty unit, therefore, they will tend to have a minority voice within that unit. If the student affairs staff is organized in a separate unit, the question of generating the required power necessary to back demands is raised. The evidence of this power factor is scarce because of the current unit determination trends. A strike by the administrative unit, including the student affairs staff, at Eastern Michigan University, may provide some insight that the power can be generated by such a unit (Borland, MacLean, White, & Scott, 1979). Finally, the alternative of including all nonteaching professionals in the same unit seems to lack the common professional bond for current student affairs professional issues.

Borland (1979a) discussed several factors in detail that should be considered by student affairs profession as an institutional plan for bargaining unit determination. These factors are preferences of staff, needs of students, concerns and roles of the profession, and the political, organizational, and administrative environment in which the formalization of employee relationships is taking place. In addition, the complex factors considered in determining the composition of the bargaining unit from the view of labor relations boards must be included in the formal planning. As student affairs practitioners consider all of these factors, the maximization of institutional, student, staff, and professional objectives must be mediated in constructing strategies for appropriate bargaining units.

Union Approaches. The approach to staff by bargaining agents in organizing a local bargaining group, whether affiliated with a national organization or not, and in conducting an election campaign, is basically similar. The most effective appeals of bargaining agents to staff have been appeals to human dignity and the recognition of the potential pressure that organized employees can bring to campus issues (Braun, 1972). Institutional leaders may be surprised by this approach and often may find themselves in agreement with the formal positions of bargaining agents on those issues.

Strategy and specific tactics differ in conducting a campaign, depending on a variety of factors, such as previous staff-institution relationships, degree of unionization in that geographic region, degree of access to campus facilities, attitudes of staff toward the labor movement, and condition of current personnel policies and practices.

In preparing for the election itself, a bargaining agent attempts to demonstrate to employees in the bargaining unit that (1) collective bargaining is the preferable alternative to institutional authority; (2) it is better able to represent them than are any of the other prospective agents; and (3) gains made by that particular agent at other campuses are superior to achievements of competing agents. Overt actions to create membership and gain support to win elections will be made through such efforts as literature in campus mail boxes, personal letters, possible home visitations, coffee hours, lunches, parties, and professional seminars. Although general visibility must be maintained by bargaining agents, private meetings and efforts aimed at particular individuals or small groups help to avoid revealing a particular agent's position or tactics to its competitors.

Institutional Approaches. Once the petition for recognition is filed with the appropriate labor relations board, institutional response will come under scrutiny of statutory provisions and interpretations. The right of an institution to respond to an effort for formalization of staff relationships, however, is definite (Sullivan, 1974). The National Labor Relations Act (NLRA) in Section 8c provides what has been referred to as the "Free Speech Proviso" for institutions, the essence of which also is contained in most state labor legislation for the public sector. This statute provides guidelines for fair labor practices by colleges and universities, which if violated can lead to immediate certification of a bargaining agent.

While specific acts are subject to review, a lack of action tends to commit employees to requirements of bargaining when no majority for the process may have existed. While a response to bargaining agents by student affairs professionals must be made within the total institutional context, the response should reflect needs of their student, professional, and staff constituencies. Borland (1979a) has provided specific suggestions for administrative response during a representation election. These suggestions, include continuous preparation, knowledge of rules, availability to staff and students, and organization of a strategy.

Election Results. A winner is declared by a simple majority of those voting; if no majority is obtained, a run-off election is held for two choices with the most votes. Although specific tactics may change, the significant difference would be negotiations between losers in the original election and choices on the run-off ballot. While that negotiation is legal among agents, it would be an unfair labor practice for institutional representatives to be involved in such discussions.

If the campaign results in the election of an exclusive bargaining agent, administrative conduct should reflect that the institution will continue to work with staff in response to the desires of the majority. If the election results in selection of "no union", preparations for another election should begin immediately. Depending on the vote and the resources of the bargaining agents, the NLRA requires only that one year pass before another election may be called.

Once an exclusive bargaining agent has been selected through this process, all unit members are represented by the exclusive agent, even if they are not members of that labor organization, or have not voted for that agent, or did not vote at all. Comparatively few elections (82 of the 763 elections held in higher education) have resulted in defeat of a bargaining agent *(Chronicle of Higher Education, 1980)*. Also, once an agent is selected, rarely will it be decertified. Decertification is a process used to dismiss a bargaining agent; but in higher education, it is usually done to replace the particular agent, rather than to eliminate the collective bargaining process itself. Two exceptions in higher education at this writing occurred at New England College and at Jamestown College, when the "no union" choice won the decertification election.

Just as prior planning and positive action can facilitate meeting both institutional and employee objectives in bargaining unit determination, these two elements also are essential in providing the base from which an assertive institutional plan can be made in response to the campaign by bargaining agents for the exclusive right to represent employee interests. Once faced with the requirement of a formal personnel petition for representation, student affairs staff must prepare themselves in detail for the new employment environment that will exist during a campaign and an election for representation.

Negotiations. After an exclusive agent has been selected, work on the contract begins. The biggest problem with table bargaining in higher education is that few campus staff members or administrators are prepared for it. Even industrial negotiators are not prepared unless they have had experience in the public sector generally and in education particularly.

The collective bargaining process has many stages, each of which is crucial to effective campus employment relations programs for student affairs practitioners (Coe, 1973b). The first step is the selection of bargaining teams. The agent, then, presents a list of demands to the institution's representatives, and the negotiation process continues until agreement is reached. If an impasse occurs at any time in the process, mediation, fact finding, or interest arbitration may be used to resolve any differences between the negotiating parties.

The content of the bargaining process is wages, hours, and conditions of employment. Unless restricted by law, virtually anything is negotiable whether it is initiated by the institution or the employees. The initial contract is especially important because it sets precedent. Even though most employees and employers believe they start with the employment conditions they had before bargaining began, all previous policies and agreements, as well as operating procedures, are open for negotiation. This point is significant, for it generally affects management rights and agent's attempts to attract members, which is especially important before bargaining through the legal concept of *past practices.*

Once the contract has been ratified by employees and the institutional governing board, emphasis is placed on the ability of the parties to interact successfully to accomplish institutional objectives within the provisions of the new contract. Because the employment relationship and the contract are new, misunderstandings, conflicts in interpretation, and ambiguous contract language may create the necessity of employing the grievance procedures outlined in most campus contracts. If resolution of the grievance cannot be met through the institutional hearings provided in the grievance procedure, provision usually is made for third party resolution through either advisory or binding grievance arbitration as a final step.

As the initial contract expiration date approaches (most contracts in higher education vary from one year to three years in duration), the two parties meet again to negotiate the next contract. A petition for a recognition election may be filed by any bargaining agent or by the institution. These petitions actually challenge the existing agent's claim that it continue to represent the majority of the bargaining unit membership. The process described for recognition of an exclusive agent is repeated. The process either will replace the agent with another organization, will reaffirm the existing agent's exclusive authority for that bargaining unit, or will discontinue the bargaining process through election of "no union."

A strike may result if at any time during any of these bargaining processes an impasse between the bargaining unit and the institution occurs. Even though strikes are permitted under provisions of the National Labor Relations Act, which regulates private colleges and universities in employee relations, the vast majority of enabling state legislation prohibits strikes by public employees. Because the majority of colleges and universities that have collective bargaining are publicly supported, most strikes in higher education are unlawful. Nonetheless, strikes do occur, and resolution of them can be accomplished through mediation, fact finding, interest arbitration, as well as through various court intervention strategies.

IMPACT ON STUDENT AFFAIRS

The Dilemma

Effects of the collective bargaining process on campus relationships generally indicate the need to change roles and relationships for student affairs professionals and students they serve. Changes in these roles both for students and for student affairs professionals are necessary if campus relationships are to remain effective. If, for example, institutions become more organizationally rigid and if legal contracts define professional roles for faculty and student affairs staff more specifically, will students be served even more effectively? As faculty contracts control curricular and instructional factors, how are student opinions or student affairs concerns to be gathered for consideration? If collective bargaining does lead to higher salaries, what effect does this have on student tuition, on the proportion of the budget provided for student affairs programs and services, and on the institutional mission for colleges and universities—especially for community colleges that have open admission and low tuition?

The significant question for student affairs practitioners is, "are we management, labor, or student advocate?" Unit factors, although varying, usually place chief student affairs administrators and their immediate staff on the management side. Counselors, advisors, and staff members who work with students daily have been determined in many cases to have a commonality of interest with faculty and, therefore, have been placed on the labor side of the table. However, because reports have indicated that students see employee bargaining for economic benefits as a direct threat to their own interests and welfare (Semas, 1977), the role of the student affairs professional in a bargaining unit could be in conflict with the role as advocate for students.

Therein lies the professional dilemma—the integrative and collaborative approach promoted for the student affairs profession currently cannot exist without administrative authority; it also requires affiliation with faculty and other campus personnel, and, therefore, it may lose credibility with students in a collective bargaining environment. Given this dilemma between professional status and needs of students, chief student affairs officers and their immediate staff may be the only advocates for the common interests of students, staff, and institutional mission on campuses experiencing increasing economic and political concerns.

Student Affairs Staff
in the Bargaining Unit

Initial reactions of institutions to the advent of collective bargaining activity may appear to be anti-union or anti-employee. If these reactions are negative, they may lead to unsuccessful institutional strategies that conflict with the educational mission. While employees benefit under collective bargaining provisions, administrators also have advantages such as clarification of authority and specific criteria for accountability of employees. On the other hand, restrictions on administrative authority, while specifically clarified under contract provisions, would have to accommodate intervention by various third parties. The introduction of a formal third party into the communication process provides the possibility for errors and misunderstandings. Although advocates for collective bargaining will state that written contracts will eliminate these misunderstandings, collective bargaining is only one alternative to resolve administrator-staff conflicts. As an adversarial process, bargaining in higher education may be less desirable than a more informal system in which concerns of employees are heard and demonstrable action is taken to address them.

In order to avoid the formal evolution required under collective bargaining, an assertive plan, based on the principle of shared decision making as an alternative to bargaining, may be established. Once a petition for representation has been filed, little can be done, except to make a case for the system that has been in operation. If the positive administrative approach to employee relations, as detailed by Borland (1976b), is adopted, possible changes in policies and procedures can establish the environment in which an institution would like to operate if and when bargaining becomes a reality on campus.

Because of factors used in bargaining unit determination, most student affairs administrators will find themselves in the position of being excluded from a bargaining unit. Demands upon student affairs administrators from the student, the institution, and the profession, therefore, need to be perceived within the context of employee demands from their staff members. The leadership dilemma presented by these demands can be resolved beforehand in that employees may be reluctant to seek collective bargaining, if what they seek through a formal contract is already in effect. The advantage of this situation would be that student needs, which often become neglected at the bargaining table, could remain as the focus of educational colleagues working together to meet the mutual goals necessary for an effective and harmonious educational institution. This mutual decision making is basic to understanding and implementing the changing student affairs administrative role required in contemporary employee relations.

Many individuals believe that positive personnel leadership, before bargaining becomes a reality at a particular campus, would give everything to employees. Others such as Naples (1976) believe that improving working conditions before bargaining costs too much and tends to "raise the floor" for future demands. While these concerns are real, and contemporary personnel leadership does require some risk, the thesis is that student affairs professionals have skills that can move the employment environment from one of conflicting goals, which requires bargaining for resolution, to a process of problem solving where alternatives to reach common goals are established. A potential exists in the profession to control and develop the most positive aspects of bargaining for application to student affairs. This potential will be realized, however, only if positive action begins before bargaining becomes fact on any particular campus.

Just as the *in loco parentis* relationship between student affairs personnel and student has diminished as a matter of student rights, the traditionally autocratic "benevolent administrator" relationship with employees is diminishing as a matter of the assertion of employee rights by staff members. In response to the organizing efforts, for example, student affairs administrators are tempted to say, "Why use collective bargaining—we can give you more than a union can!" A well organized staff will reply, "You've had many years to provide for us, but where did that get us? We're now no longer interested in your 'benevolent gifts': We want our rights." Since student affairs administrators often are not responsible for employee relations and conditions, they are disturbed by such remarks. This shock usually is replaced, then, by anger, rigidity, or fear, which prevent appropriate administrative action. Examples of ineffective administrative behavior at this point would be to commit an unfair labor practice or to fail to encourage staff to vote in the representation election.

An immediate concern to student affairs practitioners is the use of a strike by staff. The potential for a strike by student affairs staff is determined by the bargaining unit composition. If student affairs staff are included with faculty they will have a minority voice in the determination of a strike. If student affairs form their own bargaining unit or, for example, join with other middle management level staff, their collective voice will have more relevance for student affairs administrators. The impact of a strike by student affairs staff, therefore, will be determined by the employment relationships that have existed between these staff members and the student affairs administrative leaders.

The major concern for student affairs staff, either in a unit with other campus staff or in a separate unit, in the decision to call a strike, is whether the student affairs staff has the power to make the weapon of the strike effective. Borland et al. (1979) found that student affairs staff strikes can be effective. While the union claim is true that strike publicity overshadows the fact that a large majority of contracts are negotiated without strikes, preparation for strikes at any one campus is essential.

Once the bargaining process has been implemented for a period of time, administrators begin to adjust and to accept the reality of the new relationship with the staff. This evolving attitude, if the private sector experience is any indication for higher education, will lead to more cooperative staff relationships with administrators over the long term, albeit under differing regulations. Student affairs administrators, who have devoted so much effort and dedication to the effective and comprehensive development of students, must be willing now to devote their concern and efforts equally for the effective and comprehensive development of their staff members as employees in the most facilitative manner.

The Panacea

The process of collective bargaining between an institution and its employees is extremely complex. When collective bargaining is viewed from the perspective of student affairs administrators who are required to mediate the often conflicting needs of the institution, the student, the staff, and the goals of the student affairs profession, the temptation is to feel overwhelmed and to withdraw from active participation in preparing for the process.

In whatever role student affairs staff members may find themselves, however, the negative attitudes and feelings about the bargaining process, which usually exist and which Birmingham and Borland (1980) documented in community colleges, should be overcome. Contrary to popular belief, many contributors to the literature on collective bargaining, such as Kemerer and Baldridge (1975), have noted that under conditions of collective bargaining power will accrue to administrators, albeit a more technical than collegial type of power. Because collective bargaining is a process that attempts to redefine and assign power, the process may provide an opportunity for student affairs professionals to preserve the integrity of their institutional roles.

Therein lies the potential panacea for student affairs in a collective bargaining environment. If the passive role in collective bargaining is forsaken by student affairs for an actively analytical role, goals of the profession may become contract provisions. If the comprehensive development of students is the primary goal of the profession, identification of environmental factors that will facilitate that growth must be expressed formally. These formal expressions can be negotiated into a contract, which becomes a formal commitment by the institution and its constituencies to elements of the professional goals of student affairs. If, for example, the development of students can be facilitated by a reduction in counselor-client ratios, the establishment of a learning center, space for commuter students, budget allocations, or expansion of services through varying office hours, inclusion into a formal contract will insure legal authority for those items. If such formal contracts are to be accomplished at the bargaining table, student affairs professionals must be highly cognizant of the consequences for various campus constituencies with whom they interact. Also, if certain goals are to be included into an employment contract successfully, student affairs must be more active and must become more skilled in the techniques. For example, Teague and Grites (1980) have indicated that in the area of academic advising by faculty, most contracts are silent, and Aaron (1975) indicated that this silence extended virtually to all student affairs concerns. The traditional role in the profession, which tended to avoid such technical and power laden concepts and tended to rely on the informal flexibility that exists in the administration of policy without collective bargaining, must change now to implement this new mechanism. Collective bargaining can facilitate both student and professional growth in the formal atmosphere required under a specific contract. To avoid such a change would be to deny the ethical and pragmatic constructs of the student affairs profession.

CONCLUSION

Whether collective bargaining becomes a dilemma or a panacea for the student affairs profession will be determined by the collective impact of institutional contracts throughout the country. As members of the profession assess the impact of this contemporary issue individually, either through its introduction on their respective campuses or by facing its existence on campuses where they wish to pursue their careers, several factors should be analyzed, as represented by the following questions.

While most of these questions should be analyzed on nonunionized campuses as well, they become either direct legal entities or established past practices within a collective bargaining contract. First, what degree of flexibility is allowed in the working day to meet unpredictable demands of the administration of student affairs? Second, what formal contractual separations or alliances are forbidden between student affairs personnel and faculty, support staff, other administrators, or within the student affairs division itself? Third, how is input about student needs being gathered and formally injected into the negotiating process? Fourth, what incentives does the contract provide personally and professionally that will reinforce implementing student development programs? Finally, is the informal employment atmosphere facilitative of the individual, student, professional, and institutional goals necessary for success in student affairs administration?

Whether attempting to find one's first professional position, a new professional position, or evaluating one's current position, individuals have consulted with colleagues and supervisors in those activities. The advent of collective bargaining gives new emphasis to the employment/personnel aspects of the profession and requires that consultation occur with additional resources, namely union leaders, and the collective bargaining contract as well.

REFERENCES

Aaron, R. M. Accommodating the student personnel worker in faculty collective bargaining: Am empirical overview. *Journal of College Student Personnel,* 1975, *16,* 184-9.

Birmingham, J. C., & Borland, D. T. Collective bargaining in the future: A study of administrator attitudes. *Community/Junior College Research Quarterly,* 1980, *4,* 169-83.

Borland, D. T. Collective bargaining: The road ahead in the South and the West. Paper presented at the Phi Delta Kappa Research and Development Forum, *ERIC Resources in Education,* 1975, ED 119 550.

Borland, D. T. Collective bargaining: Prospectus for the South. *Southern Journal of Educational Research,* 1976(a), *10,* 75-85.

Borland, D. T. Employee relations without collective bargaining. *Journal of the College and University Personnel Association,* 1976(b), *27,* 35-9.

Borland, D. T. Gaining the initiative in collective bargaining. *Community College Frontiers,* 1977, *5,* 10-5.

Borland, D. T. Collective bargaining and student affairs: Guidelines for professional action. *NASPA Journal,* 1979(a), *16*(3), 1-42.

Borland, D. T. Student affairs professionals and collective bargaining: A national exploratory study. *Journal of College Student Personnel,* 1979(b), *20,* 104-12.

Borland, D.T., & Birmingham, J.C. Community college faculty collective bargaining: An attitudinal study in a "right-to-work" environment. *Journal of Collective Negotiations in the Public Sector,* 1981, *10,* 229-45.

Borland, D. T., MacLean, S., White, B. C., & Scott, J. E. Student affairs on strike: A descriptive analysis. *Journal of College Student Personnel,* 1979, *20,* 202-8.

Braun, R. J. *Teachers and power: The story of the American Federation of Teachers.* New York: Simon and Schuster, 1972.

Coe, A. C. A study of the procedures used in collective bargaining with faculty unions in public universities. *Journal of the College and University Personnel Association,* 1973(a), *24,* 1-25.

Coe, A. C. The implications of collective bargaining for students and student personnel administrators. *NASPA Journal,* 1973(b), *11,* 9-18.

Chronicle of Higher Education. Faculty bargaining agents on 681 campuses. July 7, 1980, *20,* 7-8.

Fisher, R. G., & Packwood, W. T. The impact of unit membership for collective negotiations on the role of student personnel workers. *Journal of College Student Personnel,* 1975, *16,* 178-83.

Kellett, R. H. *Collective bargaining and non-teaching professional personnel in higher education.* Washington, DC: American College Personnel Association, 1976.

Kemerer, F. R., & Baldridge, J. V. *Unions on campus.* San Francisco: Jossey-Bass, 1975.

Latta, W. J. Collective bargaining: Issues and implications for the student affairs worker. *Journal of the College and University Personnel Association,* 1979, *30,* 37-46.

Naples, C. J. Management at the bargaining table. In H. B. Means & P. W. Semas (Eds)., *Faculty collective bargaining.* Washington, DC: Editorial Projects for Education, 1976.

Phelan, D. J. Student personnel workers and faculty unionization. *Journal of College Student Personnel,* 1977, *18,* 177-82.

Semas, P.W. Student evaluations of professors limited by many faculty contracts. *Chronicle of Higher Education,* January 24, 1977, *13,* 10.

Sullivan, F. L. The right of a college administrator to speak out during a union organizing drive: How has it been successfully implemented. *Journal of the College and University Personnel Association,* 1974, *25,* 1-17.

Teague, G. V., & Grites, T. J. Faculty contracts and academic advising. *Journal of College Student Personnel,* 1980, *21,* 40-4.

Watkins, B. T. High court calls Yeshiva faculty managers, not subject to National Labor Relations Act. *Chronicle of Higher Education,* February 25, 1980, *19,* 1, 7-9.

SUGGESTED READINGS

Angell, G.W., Kelly, F.P., Jr., & Associates. *Handbook of faculty bargaining.* San Francisco, Jossey-Bass, 1977.

Berlet, C. *Student unionization: Perspectives on estabishing a union of students.* Washington, DC: United States National Student Association, 1975.

Borland, D. T. Collective bargaining and student affairs: Guidelines for professional action. *NASPA Journal,* 1979, *16*(3), 1-42.

Braun, R. J. *Teachers and power: The story of the American Federation of Teachers.* New York: Simon and Schuster, 1972.

Kemerer, F. R., & Baldridge, J. V. *Unions on campus. San Francisco: Jossey-Bass, 1975.*

PART III
STRATEGIES
FOR
ADMINISTRATION
AND
LEADERSHIP

Roger B. Winston, Jr. is Assistant Professor in the Student Personnel in Higher Education Program in the Department of Counseling and Human Development Services and Director of the Student Development Laboratory at the University of Georgia.

For further information please refer to the last section of the book entitled "About the Authors."

William R. Mendenhall currently serves as Associate Vice-President for Student Affairs at the University of Georgia, and he has had seventeen years experience in successive levels of student affairs administration.

For additional information please refer to the last section of the book entitled "About the Authors."

Theodore K. Miller is Professor of Counseling and Human Development Services at the University of Georgia, where he is coordinator of the Student Personnel in Higher Education Preparation Program and Director of the College of Education Center for Student Development.

For additional information please refer to the last section of the book entitled "About the Authors."

Chapter 12

MANAGING HUMAN RESOURCES: STAFFING, SUPERVISION, AND EVALUATION

Roger B. Winston, Jr.
William R. Mendenhall
Theodore K. Miller

Student affairs administration can be conceptualized as designing an institutionally unique formula combining money, physical facilities, ideas, and people to produce programs and services that meet student needs. Of these components, the people ingredient is the most critical because without staff programs cannot exist. Lack of the other elements can limit programs, but will not necessarily preclude them. The human component in student affairs practice including staffing, supervision, and evaluation is examined in this chapter.

THE STUDENT AFFAIRS STAFF

Many assume that "student affairs staff" refers to residence hall directors, counselors, activities advisors, directors of placement, deans, and vice-presidents for student affairs. However, if a student affairs division were composed only of these professional employees, it would function very poorly, if at all. Secretaries, maintenance workers, computer programmers, bookkeepers, receptionists, resident assistants, physicians, paraprofessional counselors, and others are essential to the functioning of an effective student affairs division. When thinking about the personnel of a student affairs division, all those who make contributions toward accomplishment of division goals must be considered a part of the division. A division's personnel can be divided into five categories: professional, allied professional, support, paraprofessional, and volunteer.

Professionals

"Professional staff" are persons who hold at least a master's degree in student personnel, counseling, or higher education administration; who hold membership in and ascribe to the ethical and professional standards of one or more student affairs professional associations; and who have responsibility for outside-the-classroom education of students in post-secondary institutions. This category includes those traditionally thought of as the "staff," ranging from entry level residence hall directors and student activity advisors through middle management department directors to chief student affairs officers. Their formal education, speciality training, and work experiences give them a clear understanding of the purposes of student affairs administration and a firm commitment to the growth and development of college students.

Allied Professionals

Persons responsible for performing or directly supporting outside-the-classroom educational functions but who possess extensive education in specialized professions other than student affairs are allied professionals in student affairs (Delworth & Aulepp, 1976). Personnel in this category come from a wide array of fields. Included are physicians, accountants, computer systems designers, clergy, statisticians, faculty members, editors, and attorneys. Although they bring highly developed skills and expertise, they nevertheless require special training and supervision in the areas of college student development and student affairs administration designed to aid them in applying skills in furthering the goals of the student affairs division. Expecting these kinds of specially trained people to make the maximum contribution to the division's goals without a clear understanding of and commitment to the underlying philosophy of student development is a mistake. Effective allied professionals must appreciate the division's goals and must view themselves as a part of that structure, not as isolated specialists within it.

Support Staff

The third category of staff is support. Support staff members are persons who perform the myriad of activities that enables the professionals and allied professionals to provide essential services and educational opportunities. They are vital to the student affairs division because they complement and supplement divisional goals. "Receptionist," "clerk," "secretary," "keypunch operator," "computer programmer," "security officer," and "printer" are examples of support staff job titles. Generally, these jobs require some specialized training, but seldom a college degree.

Work-study and other part-time student workers who perform tasks such as typing, key punching, duplicating, filing, and maintenance also fit into this category. Although they often need on-the-job training and require more supervision than do full-time support staff, they are important division personnel, especially in an era of limited resources. Employing student workers has an additional payoff: the college is investing in itself because students use much of their earnings to pay tuition and fees. If adequately managed, a part-time employment program can enhance students' educations by providing "hands on" work experience through which marketable skills can be learned.

Support personnel occasionally are referred to as the "nonprofessional staff," an unfortunate selection of words because it reflects a lack of appreciation for the importance of these staff members to the effective functioning of a department. Support staff members are often the first and only contact students have with a particular student affairs office. Frequently, they are the first exposed to disgruntled or troubled students, faculty, parents, and members of the public. How well that contact is negotiated may determine whether a student remains in college and receives the help and services needed or whether potentially emotionally explosive situations are resolved with the skill and diplomacy demanded (Eble, 1979; Williams, 1973).

Paraprofessionals

Paraprofessionals are students who are selected, trained, and supervised in the performance of specific functions that generally would be accomplished by professionals and who are paid compensation in money or kind. Examples of paraprofessionals found on many campuses include resident assistants, peer counselors, peer academic advisors, orientation leaders, and tutors. Graduate assistants may be classifed as paraprofessionals or professionals-in-training (distinguished from professionals primarily by status and pay) depending on the responsibilities assigned them, the nature of their education, and the goals for the position they hold.

Student Volunteers

Finally, students who perform volunteer services are another important source of human resources. Organizationally, these students may function autonomously as recognized student organizations. Such groups may assume responsibility for certain activities such as providing visitors guided tours of the campus, operating nonprofit book exchanges, or serving as ushers and ticket takers for campus cultural events. Students also may provide volunteer services through programs initiated, supervised, and supported by a student affairs department. For example, the admissions office may use volunteer orientation leaders; the counseling center may staff a crises line with volunteers; the international student office may organize volunteer hosts for newly arrived foreign students.

Student affairs administrators must consider many factors when deciding to use student volunteers. First, how critical is the service? Volunteers are using their free time to provide the service. When the amount of their free time is diminished, especially near midterm and final examinations, volunteer activities usually, and rightfully, become secondary. If the service is critical (such as a crisis line), then a backup means of providing services must be planned, or other staff members over whom one has more influence should be utilized. Second, how qualified are the volunteers? Volunteers should be systematically trained before they provide the service and must be supervised thereafter. Simply because one uses student volunteers does not mean that there are no costs. Failure to provide adequate training and supervision is to flirt with disaster and is unfair to and exploitive of the volunteers. Third, what are the legal liabilities? When a college uses volunteers to fulfill a college function, the institution should exercise great care to assure that the student volunteers are qualified to render the services offered, that their work activities are closely monitored, and that their responsibilities do not exceed their level of competence. Volunteers can be a valuable complement to the paid staff, and the experiences can be rewarding for the students involved. However, student affairs administrators should carefully evaluate their use in an objective and critical fashion.

STAFFING THE STUDENT AFFAIRS DIVISION

This section presents considerations and processes involved when staffing the student affairs division with professional, allied professional, and support personnel. Staffing should not be thought of as being synonymous with employment or personnel selection. It "includes all the methods of matching the skills available with the tasks to be performed" (Albright, 1974, p. 4-2), namely organizational analysis, personnel planning, position analysis, recruitment, selection, job/organization restructuring, promotion/demotion, and termination.

Personnel Planning and Forecasting

Whether an institution and its student affairs division are growing, leveling off, or declining, student affairs administrators are under constant pressure to obtain maximum results from the human and financial resources available. Consequently, careful planning, monitoring, and inventorying of personnel needs and changes are essential.

Personnel planning is a systematic process for analyzing an organization's present makeup in terms of categories of people within its work force and its future needs for staff based on both internal and external conditions (Butteriss & Albrecht, 1979).

Forecasting is based on the assumption that, while the future is indeterminable, it will contain extensions of many conditions or forces working in the present and immediate past. In other words, present trends can be projected into the future. Forecasting forms the basis upon which assumptions can be made and, hence, with which uncertainties can be dealt. Personnel forecasting must take into account conditions both internal and external to the college.

Internal Conditions. Internal conditions that need to be considered in personnel forecasting include: (1) the institution's mission as defined by institutional leaders or as assigned by governing bodies; (2) institutional goals, programs, and priorities; (3) present enrollment trends; (4) institutional political issues such as power, authority, and territory (Baldridge, 1971; Barr & Keating, 1979); (5) available funds within existing budget structures; (6) changing demands of internal constituencies such as student groups, faculty governance structures, and collective bargaining units; and (7) career advancement, promotion, and retirement schedules.

Personnel planning must be keyed to fit institutional long-range goals and objectives. For example, if a college plans to emphasize graduate programs as a means of off-setting a projected decline in traditional age undergraduate students, then student affairs staff members will need to be reassigned to programs and services required by such students. However, by custom many assume that graduate students do not need the support provided to traditional age undergraduates. Because of this mistaken idea the student affairs administrator will need to build a data base that can document graduate student needs, begin an educational campaign designed to dispel the conventional (though uninformed) view of graduate students, and initiate staff development activities to prepare staff members for different roles. Also, because most entry-level positions can be expected to be vacated every two to four years as young professionals make their career ladder ascent, the comprehensive personnel planning program must assure that staff with appropriate backgrounds, skills, and experiences are available to meet the changing needs of the division. Just because a vacancy exists in the fraternity advisor's position, for example, does not mean that one automatically seeks another person to perform exactly the same functions. Each position vacancy should be viewed within the overall personnel needs. Without a clear picture of future needs, the division will always be in the position of playing "catch up" or "making do" with inadequately or inappropriately trained staff.

External Conditions. Conditions outside the institution also have an influence on personnel planning and forecasting. Such conditions include (1) governmental funding; (2) changing demographic characteristics of the student population both current and potential; (3) standards and requirements of accrediting agencies; (4) legislative actions such as affirmative action mandates, minimum wage laws, civil service classification systems and regulations, and social security taxes, (5) general economic conditions; and (6) demands and needs of various constituencies such as alumni, trustees, students' parents, the news media, and business and industry.

For example, Deegan (1981) described student affairs practices at a university projecting a 20 percent decline in enrollment. The vice-president "claims" all positions that become vacant. A needs assessment then is conducted of personnel needs within the division; the personnel inventory and forecast are consulted, and only then are decisions made about filling the position. Because of the projected enrollment decline, the student affairs division has adopted a policy of attempting to fill vacancies with existing personnel. If that is possible, then the number of staff members can be gradually reduced through attrition, because the termination process tends to have a deteriorative effect on staff morale and productivity. Only through systematic personnel evaluations and projections can needed reductions be accomplished without adding unnecessary hardships for staff while maintaining high quality services for students. As Sprunger and Bergquist (1978) noted, personnel forecasting in a period of reduction or no growth is critical particularly because it in large measure determines the institution's flexibility in meeting changing needs and circumstances.

Position Analysis

In order to have an effective personnel planning program, gaining a clear understanding of the responsibilities of each position is essential. "The process of position analysis addresses the relatedness of duties and responsibilities to experience, skills, knowledge, and abilities required for the tasks to be performed" (Fortunato & Waddell, 1981, p. 43). Every position in the student affairs division should be reviewed at least once a year (regardless of whether a vacancy is expected).

A number of different schemata has been developed for analyzing positions. The U.S. Training and Employment Service developed a process for analyzing jobs that is related to the *Dictionary of Occupational Titles* known as Functional Job Analysis (FJA) (Fine & Wiley, 1971). Under this approach a position can be divided into three "primitives": data, people, and things (McCormick, 1974). How a worker functions in relation to things (physical manipulation), people (interpersonal relationships), and data (mental processes) can describe a job or position. Each hierarchy under people, data, and things provides two measures: (1) level, a measure of relative complexity, and (2) orientation, a measure of relative involvement with people, data, and things. Data for analyzing a position are obtained from experienced workers or by FJA trained personnel through observations and interviews (Fortunato & Waddell, 1981; McCormick, 1974).

Other commonly used analysis methods include: (1) Job Element Method developed by the U.S. Civil Service Commission, (2) U.S. Department of Labor Method, and (3) Comprehensive Occupational Data Computer Program developed for the Air Force and used primarily by the military (Fortunato & Waddell, 1981; McCormick, 1974). All of these methods require specific training for their use. Depending upon the scope and sophistication of an institution's personnel department, the student affairs administrator may be able to call upon that department for assistance in analyzing the positions within the division. If staff expertise is not available, faculty from the college or department of business may be of assistance.

The position analysis approaches identified previously are most appropriate for support staff positions that typically reflect a relatively high level of standardization and transferability from one campus office to another. The positions assumed by student affairs professionals, however, are often unique in that a campus may have only one or two persons with the same duties. These positions are often extensively influenced by tradition and eccentricities of the institution. Consequently, a less formalized position analysis process that can be performed by one not trained in the technology of position analysis may be more appropriate.

One begins by determining the role definition, that is a description of the outcomes expected from the person filling the position (Sprunger & Bergquist, 1978). For example, a partial role definition for a director of housing might include:

- Do participate with the Vice-President for Student Affairs and other department heads in a team management approach to the campus

- To provide leadership for the area directors and administrative staff by

  (1) building a cohesive team in the department
  (2) calling upon individual expertise to assist in accomplishing objectives
  (3) encouraging participation in division task forces and professional organizations
  (4) promoting and supporting innovation

- To establish mechanisms for the continual development of staff (professional, allied professional, support, and paraprofessional)

- To create residential environments that stimulate and support the intellectual, emotional, and social development of students

- To relate institutional trends, direction, policies, procedures, and problems to the departmental staff

• To direct and monitor business and maintenance operations to assure sound fiscal practices and a safe and healthy environment.

• To create a diversity of living arrangements within the housing facilities to accommodate the full range of student needs.

Once a complete role definition for a position has been developed, an inventory of knowledge, abilities, and skills can be used to identify critical attributes needed. Zion (1977) identified six aspects of administration that may be applied to the role definition in determining the level of skills and abilities needed to be successful: needs assessment, planning, goal setting, selection/training, delineating tasks, and evaluation. Because different roles require different levels of abilities and expertise, identifying them serves as an informal, but effective way to analyze a position. A position's role definition and the profile of requisite skills and abilities should not be viewed as a one-time operation. As institutions change, the requirements of the various positions need to reflect those changes, thus requiring reevaluation at least annually.

Job Specifications and Position Descriptions

Upon completion of the position analysis, job specifications for the position should be formulated. Included in the specifications are (1) an accurate position title, (2) an outline of the scope of activities involved, (3) a description of duties, (4) a statement of responsibilities and authority, (5) a description of expected relationships with others, and (6) the minimum education, experience, and skills required. Job specifications may be different from those of the previous jobholder. Close examination of job specifications when a vacancy occurs is particularly important so as to determine whether a new staff member should have responsibilities different from his/her predecessor.

A position decription may be developed from the position analysis, which includes role definition, survey of skills and abilities, and job specifications. Position descriptions differ from job specifications in that the latter defines and lists desired skills, experiences, and characteristics and is intended to be used as a source document during hiring activities, while the former is (1) based on the job specifications, (2) a public document made available to job candidates, and (3) a part of the contractual documents (Sprunger & Bergquist, 1978).

An adequate position decription should include the following (Fortunato & Waddell, 1981; Sims & Foxley, 1980; Sprunger & Bergquist, 1978):

•Position Title

•Division in which position is located and the title of supervisor for the position

•Goals of the position (why the position exists)

•Work activities and procedures (including duties, responsibilities, scope of authority, materials used, and equipment operated—when appropriate—and a statement such as "performs duties as assigned")

•Position requirements including minimum education, knowledge, and experience needed

•Conditions of employment (wage structure, working hours, permanency of position, and description of benefits).

Position descriptions should be carefully drawn and periodically updated. Berenson and Ruhnke (1966) pointed out that position descriptions have multiple uses, including to (1) reassign or fix functions and responsibilities within an organization, (2) evaluate employee performance, (3) help orient new employees to their positions, (4) delineate lines of authority, and (5) communicate with prospective employees during the selection process.

FILLING POSITION VACANCIES

Professional and
Allied Professional Positions

When a position becomes vacant, a number of predetermined steps should be followed by the chief student affairs officer: (1) consult personnel plan, (2) determine budget availability, (3) consult position analysis and job specification and compare with student needs assessment data, and (4) decide whether to continue the position as is, to restructure, abolish, or transfer it to another department with different duties and responsibilities.

Vertical Staffing. If the plan is to employ a person to fill a position, then a decision must be made either to transfer an existing staff member (vertical staffing) or seek someone from outside the student affairs division (horizontal staffing). Arguments exist on both sides of the issue of promoting from within. On the pro side, divisions that provide in-house staff with promotion opportunities build morale (provided the process is perceived as fair and equitable), commitment and loyalty to the institution, and continuity for programs and services. On the con side, opponents argue that internal promotion (1) retards efforts to increase the representation of minorities and women on the staff, (2) tends to encourage inertia by limiting the input of new ideas, and (3) tends to promote conformity and superficial agreement, while stimulating internecine backbiting. Each division should have a published policy about vertical staffing to which it strictly adheres.

Should a college elect to employ vertical staffing, several procedural rules may lessen the disadvantages. First, announcement of the vacancy should be published in a house organ that all eligible employees receive weekly or biweekly (Fortunato & Waddell, 1981). Second, deadlines for application, as well as specified decision making criteria and procedures, should be communicated to all applicants. Deadlines should be as short as possible, yet ensure reasonable opportunity to apply and sufficient time to evaluate candidate qualifications. If the unit or job classification shows an underutilization of minorities or women, special recruiting efforts may be necessary. The college affirmative action officer can help determine whether external recruiting is necessary. Third, all candidates should be treated the same even if external recruiting is used.

Horizontal Staffing. Following is a model process for recruiting and selecting professional and allied professional staff. Effort has been made to conform to definitions of good practice as specified in Risch (1977), the American College Personnel Association Statement of Ethical and Professional Standards (1981), and equal employment opportunities and affirmative action laws and executive orders.*

1. *Prepare the job specifications and position description.* The chief student affairs officer or department director has responsibility for preparing these documents, ideally in consultation with other staff members.

---

*Five major pieces of legislation and two executive orders are the legal bases for equal employment opportunity and affirmative action: Title VII of the Civil Rights Act of 1964 and a 1971 amendment; Executive Orders 11246 and 11375; Equal Pay Act of 1963 and a 1972 amendment; Age Discrimination in Employment Act of 1967; Rehabilitation Act, Sections 503 and 504; Vietnam-Era Veterans Readjustment Act of 1974. Fortunato & Waddell (1981), Stanton (1977), and Commerce Clearing House (1979) are excellent sources of information on these legal matters.

2. *Appoint and charge a search committee.* A search committee of three to nine persons should be appointed to coordinate the recruitment and selection process. When possible, departments in addition to the one in which the vacancy occurs should be represented. For upper level administrators, care should be exercised to assure broad representation of programs and departments within the student affairs division. Having knowledgeable students and faculty members on the committee is desirable but not essential. Committee members must be well acquainted with the duties and responsibilities of the vacant position if they are to be contributors. To appoint students and faculty is a disservice to all concerned unless they are in a position to be equal partners in the search process.

A written, formal charge of duties, responsibilities, and expectations should be made to the committee. The charge may be to (a) screen applications and accumulate credentials, (b) screen and select a specified number of candidates for in-depth interviews, (c) screen, interview, and recommend either a rank-ordered or unranked list of names, or (d) screen, interview, and offer the position. Confusion and accusations of betrayal have resulted from unclear charges to committees who felt that administrators were manipulating them or withdrawing authority because of displeasure with the committee's decisions. Affirmative action guidelines or preferences for the position should be communicated to the committee at the outset along with the position specifications and description.

3. *Establish working rules of the committee, a detailed description of the selection process, and appropriate deadlines.* The committee should decide the rules under which it will function. Must decisions be unanimous or by a simple majority vote? What constitutes a quorum; how often and when will the committee meet? Will meetings be confidential or considered public?

Deadlines should be established, not only for candidates making application, but also for various stages in the selection process. A clear, concise statement of this process should be formulated and shared with all applicants.

4. *Announce the position and specify application requirements.* Position announcements should include the following: (a) position title, (b) responsibilities and duties, (c) necessary qualifications, specifically education and previous experience, (d) salary range, and (e) application procedure and deadline. Applicants should also be provided information

about the institution, the student affairs division, and any special requirements or restrictions such as live-in requirements, night work, or travel.

A variety of means are needed to communicate the position announcement. Recommended means include advertisements in publications such as *Chronicle of Higher Education, Affirmative Action Register,* and professional association newsletters and placement publications. Letters to university placement offices and preparation programs can be particularly effective for entry level positions. Numerous professional student affairs associations have placement services that provide periodic announcements to their membership and subscribers. The Higher Education Administrative Referral Service (HEARS) is an agency formed by several associations to serve as a year-round liaison for colleges and candidates. Vacancies known in the early spring can find a large applicant pool at the annual conventions of national professional student affairs associations. Preliminary screening can also be done during short interviews at the conventions.

Initial applications should require a resumé or vita only. Requiring letters of recommendation, transcripts, and placement credentials during the initial screening process is unnecessary. Initial screening can be adequately accomplished with the information found in resumés and vitas.

5. *Complete initial screening.* Applicants obviously lacking necessary credentials or the experience specified should be notified immediately that they are no longer being considered. Each committee member should independently evaluate all remaining applications on a predetermined set of criteria. Use of a simple rating scale based on criteria from the job specifications is recommended. After the independent evaluations, each committee member should rank the top 10 candidates to create the short list. The committee as a group can then select its top candidates for further investigation. Candidates eliminated from consideration, as well as those still being considered at this point, should be notified of their status.

6. *Collect and evaluate additional data on the short list candidates.* Each of the candidates on the short list should be contacted by telephone and asked (a) if he/she is still interested in the position, (b) to answer specific questions raised by the committee when reviewing resumés, (c) to submit credentials (and a philosophy statement and/or a portfolio of work samples—if the committee deems that desirable), and (d) for permission to contact identified references *and* other persons not listed as

references. Designated committee representatives should contact by telephone at least one identified reference and one other person on the campus where the candidate is located to solicit evaluations and answers to a short list of questions devised by the committee. References should also be asked to verify and evaluate previous work experiences related to the position. McIntire and Carpenter (1981) in a survey of colleges in the south central United States reported that the primary considerations used in evaluating letters of reference were (a) evidence of ability to fit into a work group, (b) evidence of adaptability, (c) position of reference writer (superior, subordinate, or peer), (d) performance-based (behavioral) statements, and (e) personal knowledge of the writer.

7. *Select candidates from the short list for on-campus interviews.* Once the committee has accumulated and evaluated the data requested, candidates for on-campus interviews should be selected. The number of candidates to be invited to campus may be determined by the amount of travel funds available and by the charge to the search committee. The committee may have been charged to submit a list of five to ten unranked or ranked candidates from which the chief student affairs officer, department director, or president will select, or it may have been charged to invite a specified number of candidates. McIntire and Carpenter (1981) found that the modal number of candidates invited to campus was three, with a tendency to invite five for department heads and chief student affairs officers.

8. *Interview the candidates.* Before candidates arrive on campus, they should be provided written materials to acquaint them with the college, its goals, philosophy, and general mode of operation. Helpful materials include catalogues, student newspapers, student affairs staff manuals, departmental operating manuals, annual report summaries, and maps and descriptive material about the local community. If the candidate would be living off campus, general real estate information should be provided.

The on-campus interview should be planned carefully so that the college can get an accurate picture of the candidate both in terms of skills and knowledge as well as personality and style. Equally important, the candidate should be given opportunity to gain an accurate picture of the college, both strengths and weaknesses. The candidate should have opportunity to meet persons with whom he/she will work, including people outside the division in areas such as business affairs and academic affairs.

The interview process, according to Sprunger and Bergquist (1978), should be designed to determine whether the candidate is able (competency criterion) to perform the job and willing (interest criterion) to do the job. To be qualified is not enough. A useful form that interviewers may use to help systematize the analysis of candidate qualifications is shown in Figure 12.1.

In order to make the interview situation constructive and efficient as a data collection technique that can lead to a satisfactory personnel decision, careful planning and preparation are needed before the candidate arrives for interviews. Sprunger and Bergquist (1978) identified five categories of information that should be sought during the interview process: (a) previous jobs, (b) future career goals, (c) attitude and experience with supervisors, peers, and subordinates, (d) perceptions of colleges at which he/she has worked (were they positive or negative and why), and (e) past compensation record. For student affairs positions, other categories of information to be ascertained during the interview process that generally facilitate making good employment decisions include: (a) knowledge of professional literature, especially student development theory, (b) philosophy of and commitment to the student affairs profession, (c) involvement in professional organizations, and (d) style of relating to students.

Legal limitations exist on the kinds of information that may be sought either on applications or during interviews. Generally speaking, asking questions that do not have a direct and *bona fide* bearing on the performance of the job or asking different questions of applicants based on gender, race, religion, marital status, national origin, age, or status as a Vietnam-era veteran is impermissible. A summary of various antidiscrimination rules and regulations pertaining to employment interviewing is provided in Figure 12.2.

Student affairs professionals can use several guidelines to avoid pitfalls that may be encountered during the interview process.

•Clearly define each interviewer's role and responsibilities. Never ask someone to interview a candidate and then fail to request feedback. If selected personnel are asked only to give the candidate a "feel for the college," and not intended to be involved in the evaluation process, they should be so informed. The candidate also has a right to know who is going to be involved in the decision-making process.

•Establish an interview format that will maximize gaining significant information. A full day of half hour interviews is very fatiguing for the candidate and tends to produce only superficial knowledge.

Candidate's Name_____

Position Applying For_____

There are two critical questions that must be considered in promoting, interviewing, and selection. They are "Can the person perform up to the expected level?" and "Will the person perform?" The first question deals with qualifications, abilities, and experience. The second question deals with motivation and desire. Using the rating scale, indicate your assessment of the candidate on these two factors.

Not Applicable	High Ability and Potential		Average Ability and Potential			Low Ability and Potential	Don't Know
NA	8	7	6	5	4	3	2	1	X
Can Do	Will Do						

_____ _____ 1. Is professionally competent as evidenced by degrees and experience, and will continue to develop professional competence by attending conferences, doing research, writing, etc.

_____ _____ 2. Is intelligent and has academic ability and potential for continued development.

_____ _____ 3. Is physically healthy and is interested in maintaining health.

_____ _____ 4. Shows ability for this position and will grow into it.

_____ _____ 5. Is professionally active in associations and will continue or become more active.

_____ _____ 6. Cooperates with superiors, peers, students.

_____ _____ 7. Is able to motivate students.

_____ _____ 8. Is skilled in organization of subject matter and the teaching/learning process.

_____ _____ 9. Understands the importance of planning, follow-through, and performance of himself and others.

_____ _____ 10. Is and will be positive, empathetic, and fair.

(continued)

Figure 12.1 Selection and analysis form: Used by interviewers to systematize the analysis of candidate's qualifications.

Note. From *Handbook for college administration* by B.E. Sprunger and W.H. Berquist, Washington DC: Council for the Advancement of Small Colleges, 1978, pages 163-4. Reprinted by permission of the publisher.

Figure 12.1 Continued.

————	————	11. Is able to motivate others to high achievement.
————	————	12. Is able to verbalize, write, and illustrate effectively.
————	————	13. Is able to develop rapport with others.
————	————	14. Maintains employment for acceptable length.
————	————	15. Is able and willing to work in excess of minimal demands.
————	————	16. Is able to develop loyalties to institution.
————	————	17. Is self-reliant and perseverant.
————	————	18. Exercises leadership even in difficult situations.
————	————	19. Works with others, but is not dependent.
————	————	20. Is able to make decisions and accept consequences.
————	————	21. Is self-disciplined.
————	————	22. Is unselfish and sharing with others.
————	————	23. For the most part, is free of cynicism and negative attitudes.
————	————	24. Is able and willing to excel and strive for perfection.
————	————	25. Needs status and power.

A cumulative score is less important than matching the responses on the various items with the job specifications and requirements for the position for which the candidate is being considered.

List the candidate's strengths:

List the candidate's weaknesses:

(continued)

Figure 12.1 Continued.

Recommendation to employ: Yes_____ No_____ Reasons:

Rating by _____Date_____

The following list summarizes various antidiscrimination rules and regulations pertaining to employment interviewing. This is not an all-inclusive list of permissible and nonacceptable questions; however, it covers the major areas of questioning relevant to interviewing.

Permissible	Questionable or Prohibited

Name and Address

One may ask the applicant his or her name and address.	One should not ask an applicant whose name has been changed for his or her original name.

(continued)

Figure 12.2 Permissible and impermissible interview questions.

Note. From *Personnel administration in higher education; Handbook of faculty and staff personnel practices* by R.T. Fortunato and D.G. Waddell, San Francisco: Jossey-Bass, 1981, pages 122-5. Reprinted by permission.

Figure 12.2 Continued

Permissible	Questionable or Prohibited

Age

One may ask the applicant if his or her age complies with applicable institutional policies, such as minimum and maximum age for employment, employment certificate, working papers, and the like.

One may ask for proof-of-age card (issued by an applicant's high school) to verify minimum age requirements.

One may not ask to see a birth certificate.

One should not ask questions that imply a preference for a specific age group.

Birthplace

One may not inquire into the birthplace of the applicant, spouse, parents, or other close relatives.

One may not ask the applicant to disclose ancestry or national origin.

Height and Weight

One may ask about an applicant's ability to perform the job requirements.

One should not ask about the height and weight of an applicant, unless they are bona fide job requirements.

Physical Disabilities

One may ask if the applicant has a physical disability that would prevent satisfactory performance on the job.

One may ask about the applicant's general health.

One should not ask about a general physical disability that has no direct bearing on performance of the job in question.

Education and Experience

One may ask about schooling, both academic and vocational.

One may inquire into work experience.

(continued)

Figure 12.2 Continued

| **Permissible** | **Questionable or Prohibited** |

Military Experience

One may inquire into the applicant's experience in the U.S. armed forces or state militia.

One should not inquire into the foreign military experience of the applicant.

One should not require the applicant to produce his or her military discharge papers before employment. (Such papers show birthdate, place of birth, and the like.)

Citizenship

One may ask if the applicant is a U.S. citizen or intends to become one.

One may ask an applicant, who is not a U.S. citizen, about the type of visa possessed.

One should not inqurie whether the applicant or applicant's spouse or parents are naturalized or native-born citizens nor ask for the dates of naturalization.

One should not require the applicant to produce naturalization papers or first papers.

Marital Status

One may not ask about the applicant's marital status. Women should not be asked if their social title is Miss or Mrs.

Family or Relatives

One may ask for the name, address, and relationship of persons to be notified in case of accident or emergency.

One may inquire if the applicant has any relatives employed by the institution. However, such information should be used only to avoid placements in which supervisory lines or the handling of confidential information could influence rates of pay, promotions, or the granting of tenure or if an awkward work situation might result.

One should not inquire into the location outside the U.S. of places of business of the applicant's relatives.

One should not ask about the place of residence of the applicant's spouse, parents, or other close relatives.

One should not ask the applicant about the maiden name of his or her mother. Male applicants should not be asked their wife's maiden name.

(continued)

Figure 12.2 Continued

Permissible	Questionable or Prohibited
	One should not ask the applicant to identify dependent children. If, by chance, this information is volunteered by the applicant, one should not pursue with questions such as, "What plans can you make for childcare, if you are employed?" (Historically, questions regarding dependent children have been shown to have adverse impact on women. Thus, questioning along such lines should be avoided.)

Religion

One may not ask about the applicant's religion, church, parish, or pastor, nor about the religious holidays the applicant observes.

Language

One may ask the language(s) the applicant speaks, reads, or writes, and the degree of fluency.	One should not ask the applicant's native tongue nor the language commonly used at home. One should not ask how the applicant acquired the ability to read, write, or speak a foreign language.

Photographs

One should not require an applicant to submit a photograph before an offer of employment is made.

Memberships

One may ask the applicant about membership in organizations, the nature of which do *not* disclose race, religion, or national origin. One may ask if the applicant belongs to an organization that advocates the violent overthrow of the U.S. government.	One should not ask the applicant to disclose memberships in organizations, the nature of which would indicate religion, race, or national origin.

Arrest and Conviction Record

One may ask if the applicant has been convicted of a crime, and the nature of crime. (In this instance, one may inquire if conviction record is under a different name than the applicant now uses.)	One should not ask the number and kinds of arrests the applicant may have had.

•Allow time in the interview schedule for the candidate to rest or to talk with whomever he/she desires. If there are persons or departments with whom the previous jobholder had difficulty working, make sure the candidate learns of the conflict and meets the antagonist(s). Difficult or unpleasant situations should not come as a surprise *after* the person is on the job.

•Make sure the candidate knows what is changeable or negotiable and what is not. For example, if the present rules about alcoholic beverages on the campus are not open for discussion or if an opportunity to replace certain staff or to hire new staff will not exist, the candidate should be made aware of these factors.

9. Evaluate candidates and make a decision about offering the position. The search committee should collect and organize the data and evaluations on each candidate into a short summary based on the job specifications. The decision on the candidate should be based upon the plan developed when the search committee was appointed and charged.

Once the decision is made, the candidate should be contacted by telephone, offered the position at a specific salary, and given a reasonable period to make a decision (generally two to seven days). The offer should also be made in writing and forwarded to the candidate. The other candidates should be informed by letter that they will be given a decision by a given date (usually two to three weeks). If the first choice candidate accepts, the remaining candidates, both interviewed and uninterviewed, should immediately be notified that the position has been filled. It is highly unprofessional for colleges to fail to notify promptly candidates who are no longer under consideration.

When the applicant accepts the position, she or he should be requested to confirm in writing the acceptance and date of employment, provide transcripts from all degree-granting colleges or universities attended, and complete a formal job application provided by the institution's personnel office.

If the first choice candidate declines the offer, a decision must be made whether to (a) offer the position to another interviewed candidate, (b) interview more candidates from the short list, or (c) reopen the search process beginning again at step 1. Once that decision is made, all parties should be promptly notified.

Support Staff Positions

Many of the same procedures for filling professional positions apply when support staff vacancies occur. However, some differences deserve comment. Steps to be followed in filling support staff positions include: (1) consulting personnel planning and forecasting documents, (2) verifying position analysis, (3) developing job specifications and position description, (4) deciding on vertical or horizontal staffing, (5) announcing the position, (6) receiving applications, (7) screening applications and selecting the list to be interviewed, (8) checking references, (9) interviewing candidates, and (10) offering position.

Consult Personnel Forecast. As with professional and allied professional staff members, the student affairs division should maintain a current inventory of support staff with both short and long range personnel plans. When a vacancy occurs, the forecast should be consulted before making any decision about filling the position.

Verify Position Analysis. If possible every support position in the student affairs division should be analyzed by a personnel management specialist using a method similar to those identified earlier. Ideally, this should be a service provided by the college's personnel office to all divisions of the institution. If this has been accomplished, the student affairs administrator would need to verify that the position still requires the same skills and abilities previously identified. Should changes in duties be desirable, the personnel specialist could assist in ascertaining the levels of skills and knowledge the reconstituted position would require.

Develop Job Specifications and Position Description. After the position analysis has been completed, development of the job specifications and position description is a relatively simple matter. Because of the possibility of legal action, one needs to be especially careful to assure that the job specifications are directly related to the work to be performed. Stanton (1977, p. 40) noted that "in stipulating the requirements of a position, the frame of reference is [often] unduly influenced by the present or last person who happened to have held the particular position. However, such a person may possess qualifications that exceed those actually required." Using systematic position analyses as the basis for job specifications can lessen or eliminate this concern.

Decide on Vertical or Horizontal Staffing. Many of the disadvantages of vertical staffing in filling professional positions are not considerations with support staff. Within the frame of reference of the whole institution it is preferable to promote from within when possible. It allows the college to keep qualified personnel. Internal transfer or promotion is easier when dealing with support staff because the skills needed such as typing, key punching or shorthand are transferable. A secretary in the Office of the Dean of the School of Business needs the same basic skills as a secretary in the Dean of Students' Office.

However, caution should be exercised in making internal promotions. At universities, especially those with large graduate programs, there is often a large pool of highly qualified people who must work at whatever is available to support their family while a spouse earns a graduate degree. Because often these persons are overqualified for the position for which they are hired, positions are sometimes reclassified to administrative or special assistant simply because the persons are talented, intelligent, and capable of assuming responsibility for routine, detailed tasks that professionals once performed. Such reclassifications can become problematic by slowly consuming the personnel budget with support staff when professionals are needed to provide direct service and programs to students.

Announce the Position. Position vacancies should be announced in a wide variety of media. The student affairs administrator either directly, or through the college's personnel department, should make sure position vacancies are listed with the state employment service, local technical or community colleges, and the house organ. In some cases, newspaper advertisements may be necessary.

Receive Applications. Depending upon institutional policy, applications may be received directly by the office with the vacancy or preferably by the personnel office. If the personnel office receives applications, it can also test applicants to determine skill level (typing speed and accuracy, knowledge of spelling and grammar, etc.), and screen candidates who do not possess the requisite skill level. A formal application should be completed by all applicants.

Screen Applications and Select List to be Interviewed. Since reimbursement for travel is not typically involved when interviewing support staff, one has the freedom to interview a large number of applicants. Applications should be rated based on the job specifications with certain criteria serving as cutoff points. For example, if the job requires typing 50 words per minute with 95 percent accuracy, and the applicant has been tested at 35 words per minute, he or she would not have reached the cutoff and would be eliminated from further consideration.

Stanton (1977) has suggested several danger signals that can be spotted on applications. These danger signals should tip one off to investigate further, not to eliminate an applicant.

1. Has the applicant a sketchy and erratic job history, with many periods of unemployment or brief employment?

2. Has the applicant moved frequently from region to region or from one type of work to another, suggesting a lack of personal stability or maturity?

3. Do reasons given for leaving previous positions suggest the applicant has a tendency to be an undesirable or troublesome worker? Did she or he often leave positions over "personality conflicts" or disagreements with supervisors?

A final list of three to ten candidates should be identified for further screening.

Check References. Three types of references exist: (1) personal or character, (2) academic, and (3) work. Several personnel management authorities (Flippo, 1976; Megginson, 1977) maintain that character references seldom produce useful information and are not worth pursuing. Academic references, on the other hand, can be valuable, especially for applicants who have short work histories. Work references are considered the most important because they provide a measure of the applicant's actual accomplishments including productivity and ability to work with others.

Generally, the most efficient and effective means for checking references is by telephone. Ideally, one would wish to interview the applicant's immediate supervisor and others who had daily contact. When calling to check a reference, interviewers should identify themselves and explain the specific reason for calling and assure the person of confidentiality. Briefly describe the job to be filled and ask the referent's opinion of how the applicant would fit. Other questions that often produce useful information include:

How did the applicant get along with others with whom he or she worked?
How did the applicant get along with supervisors?
Did the applicant have any personal habits that you consider to be negative?

How was the applicant's attendance?
Did the applicant meet commitments?
Why did the applicant leave [if that has in fact occurred]?
Would you reemploy the applicant?
What was the nature of the applicant's work with you?
What are the applicant's strengths and weaknesses?
Is there anything else [relevant to the applicant's work] you'd
   like to tell me . . .? (Fortunato & Waddell, 1981, p. 127)

Interview Candidates. Persons who appear to possess the necessary skills, experiences, and personal attributes for the position should be invited for an interview to determine whether the applicant possesses ability for and interest in the position. Especially important for support staff is the determination of whether the applicant will fit in the situation, work well with other employees, and meet the demands of the environment. Because it is often critical that the new employee work closely with other support staff and because support staff are often more familiar with procedures and equipment, it is wise to include support staff in the interview process and decision making.

Offer Position. After receiving impressions and/or evaluations from all who interviewed candidates, a decision to offer the position must be made. If the offer is not accepted, as with professional staffing, a decision must be made to offer it to another candidate or begin the process over. Unsuccessful candidates should be notified promptly.

ROLE OF THE PERSONNEL OFFICE

The role of the college personnel office in staffing varies widely across institutions. It is typical for this office to serve a major role in recruiting a pool of support staff applicants, testing applicants, maintaining employment records, supervising staff benefits, and coordinating support staff evaluations. Its involvement with professional and allied professional staff is usually less extensive.

As a general rule, chief student affairs officers seek the same kind and degree of support and involvement in selecting and evaluating professional and allied professional staff as the personnel department has with faculty selection and evaluation. Specialists in the personnel office can be valuable consultants and sources of technical advice in regard to all levels of staff, and, therefore, a compatible working relationship between student affairs and the personnel office needs to exist.

STAFF SUPERVISION

"Supervision" is viewed with a jaundiced eye by many student affairs practitioners who see it as a negative approach to human relations and deny its validity for their field. To them it is associated with the "scientific management movement" that emphasizes control of workers and assumes that they must be coerced to accomplish organizational goals. As a consequence of this negative attitude, the tendency has been to deny the need for supervision in student affairs. This denial has sometimes led to student affairs divisions that lack direction, provide inadequate or inconsistent services to students, and have poor internal communications. Every student affairs staff member has the right to receive supervision, and most administrators have the responsibility to provide it. Supervision is an integral part of effective organization and of each individual's professional development (see Chapter 14). Supervision includes traditional management functions of organizing, directing, and controlling, within the staffing structure of the institution. The goal of supervision is to facilitate accomplishment of the division's educational mission. Effective supervisors are involved in functions such as (1) establishing organizational structures, defining formal relationships and position responsibilities; (2) selecting, orienting, training, and developing staff; (3) delegating responsibilities; (4) coordinating staff efforts; (5) motivating staff and monitoring morale; (6) managing conflicts; and (7) establishing performance standards, evaluating performance, taking corrective action, and giving rewards.

Organizational Structure

No best way exists of organizing a student affairs division or department. The best structure is one that takes into account the uniqueness and history of the institutions; the structure of other units; and skills, competencies, and weaknesses of the staff. General organizational structure guidelines have been proposed by Dutton and Rickard (1980, pp. 392-3):

• Be consistent with institutional purposes, goals, philosophy, traditions, values, and style

• Facilitate the interaction of human talent, the circulation of ideas and information, and the pooling of human resources in policy development, planning, and other vital organizational tasks

• Take into account the expertise, experience, needs, and attitudes of staff

• Provide for clear and consistent delegation of authority and assignment of duties and provide for line, staff, management, and specialized service roles and functions

• Accommodate a reasonable span of control for line administrators

• Group similar functions together under a middle manager or coordinator, keeping the distance between the chief student . . . [affairs] officer and the the line units as short as possible. . . .

While the organizational structure is important and can influence how effectively a department or division functions, one should not be consumed by a desire to create a perfect structure. For if such exists, it can exist only for a short while because staff and student needs change as do institutional and societal demands. A more profitable activity is making the existing structure work or finding ways to meet both student needs and institutional requirements in spite of the structure.

Several writers (Borland, Chapter 2; Dutton & Rickard, 1980) contended that incorporation of a matrix approach is effective wherein individuals or units have responsibilities in two different areas (housing and student activities, for example) and report to two different administrative units. This approach is preferred because it requires communication and cooperation across units, which overcomes traditions that encourage vertical communication only.

Elements of Effective Supervision

Supervisors are responsible for helping staff members function more effectively and efficiently. Critical elements in effective supervision include style of leadership, approach to decision making, motivation, and morale.

Leadership Style. Blake, Mouton, and Williams (1981) have proposed a grid framework for viewing administrative leadership in higher education (see Chapter 4). The most effective supervisors are classified as 9, 9 on the grid for they are the ones who use a team approach. Team administration is characterized by high concern for both staff welfare and the institution and produces staff commitment to the unit's goals. The supervisor gains this commitment from staff members because they (1) are involved in the planning process, (2) have input into determining individual responsibilities and basic ground rules, within the externally imposed limits, (3) give feedback, (4) share in the problem solving process, and (5) help match tasks to staff capabilities.

Nine general principles guide implementation of the team approach (Blake, Mouton, & Williams, 1981, p. 239):

1. Fulfillment through contribution is the motivation that gives character to human activity and supports productivity.

2. Open communication permits the exercise of self-responsibility.

3. Conflicts are solved by direct confrontation of their causes, with understanding and agreement as the basis of cooperative effort.

4. Being responsible for one's own actions is the highest level of maturity and only possible through widespread delegation of power and authority.

5. Shared participation in problem solving and decision making stimulates active involvement in productivity and creative thinking.

6. Management is by objectives.

7. Merit is the basis of reward.

8. Learning from work experience is through critique.

9. Norms and standards that regulate behavior and performance support personal and organizational excellence.

However, supervisors cannot announce that they will use a team approach and expect the entire staff to "join the team." Hersey and Blanchard (1977) noted that successful supervisors match their leadership styles to each task or assignment (that is, the amount of emphasis on interpersonal relationships with the staff in relation to the amount of emphasis on specifying what the task is and how it is be accomplished) to the maturity levels of the individuals or group. By maturity they mean "the capacity to set high but attainable goals (achievement-motivation), willingness and ability to take responsibility, and education and/or experience of the individual or group" (Hersey & Blanchard, 1977, p. 161). It is appropriate to speak of maturity in relation to a specific task, assignment, or objective, but inappropriate to speak of maturity in a general or total sense. For example, a staff member may be very competent or mature in organizing a student social event, but because of a lack of experience may be very immature if assigned to prepare a budget amendment. A successful supervisor is a good diagnostician who provides appropriate direction and instruction to meet individual or group needs in order to accomplish the goal successfully. Though training, coaching, providing opportunities for continued education, and encouraging staff, the effective supervisor helps individuals and staff as a group mature. The ideal situation is achieved when the staff can function effectively with minimum direct supervision or direction.

Decision Making. Effective supervision requires that staff members be involved in the decision-making process. The axiom "People support that which they have a part in creating" applies to all levels of staff.

While staff members should be involved in decision making—especially as it relates to overall goals, strategies for accomplishing goals, and ground rules for assigning tasks, scope of authority and responsibility—it is unrealistic and undesirable to expect the group to make all decisions. Supervisors should not be perceived as "passing the buck" but should be decisive, making decisions for which the delegated authority provides and standing by them. Supervisors also should delegate decision-making authority to the lowest possible level and stand behind staff members making the decisions. Nothing can destroy trust within an organization faster than a feeling that one's decisions will be second-guessed.

Motivation and Morale. If one assumes that people dislike work, are basically lazy, and require coercion (threat of being fired), or external incentives (money and other economic rewards) to get them to produce, then an authoritarian, materialistic approach to motivation appears logical. From this perspective one promises more money or threatens to cut pay to increase productivity. This approach generally has proven very ineffective.

If one assumes that people basically enjoy work and receive satisfaction from accomplishing organizational goals, then motivation for work is increased when the supervisor provides support. "The human relations approach" is most compatible with the prevailing philosophy of the student affairs profession and the goals of higher education.

Herzberg and Associates (1959) proposed two factors that influence worker motivation—"hygiene" and "motivation." The hygiene factor (work rules, job titles, wages, and fringe benefits) can cause dissatisfaction, but cannot motivate people to work. Once at an acceptable level, the hygiene factor loses force and is taken for granted as a right or entitlement. Motivators, on the other hand, were found to include responsibility, earned recognition, feeling of achievement, and advancement.

Schein (1978) identified several career anchors that can be used as the key to finding effective motivators. Career anchors are patterns of self-perceived talents, motives, and values that serve to guide, constrain, stabilize, and integrate a person's career. By understanding how staff members see themselves and what they find satisfying in work, the supervisor can better tailor tasks and responsibilities both to increase worker satisfaction and improve productivity. *Technical/function competence,* as a career anchor, means that career choices and decisions are made based on the content of work. A person's ultimate goal in student affairs, for example, would be to become a department head in housing, or financial aid, rather than a general administrative position such as dean of students. *Managerial competence,* as an anchor, means that the career goal would be to become a top level administrator. From this perspective a given job is viewed as an interim stage in the acquisition of management skills. *Security,* as an anchor, means that the worker does what is required to maintain a job because a decent income and stable future are the primary goals. *Creativity,* as an anchor, means the individual needs to build or create something that is personally owned or managed. *Institutional identity,* as an anchor, means that job titles and the prestige of the institution are viewed as critical to one's view of career success. *Service to others,* as an anchor, means that career decisions are made based on the ability to exercise interpersonal competence, to be in a helping role.

Using a knowledge of each individual's career anchor or anchors allows a supervisor to structure work assignments better and to provide opportunities for staff to realize their career goals.

STAFF EVALUATION

Staff evaluation has a number of different purposes. The most important are (1) enhancing staff development by giving direct feedback about performance that highlights both strengths and areas that need improvement, (2) making personnel decisions (salary, promotion, or termination), (3) diagnosing areas of weakness within a staff that need attention, and (4) providing data that staff perform effectively and perform essential functions. The most critical function that evaluation serves is to help staff members improve their performance; this should be the guiding principle when designing evaluation systems.

Approaches to Evaluation

Six approaches to staff evaluation—(1) unstructured narration, (2) unstructured documentation, (3) structured narration, (4) rating scales, (5) portfolios, and (6) management by objectives (MBO) (Sprunger & Bergquist, 1978)—have proven effective in higher education.

Unstructured Narration. The staff member is asked to prepare a short summary of work activities and achievements over a specified period of time, usually a year. The primary weakness of this approach is that there is no agreed upon criteria for evaluation and as a consequence weaknessess are usually not identified.

Unstructured Documentation. This requires staff members to document activities in concrete terms, for example, scheduled events, participant evaluations, head counts, and periodic activities logs. Unstructured documentation has the same shortcomings as the first approach, except some objective data are available, albeit selective and somewhat biased.

Structured Narration. Usually completed by the staff member's supervisor, this approach takes the form of short-answer questions. For example, how well did the staff member accomplish the stated objectives? If questions are framed in diagnostic, rather than evaluative form, their answers can provide valuable information to guide improved performance. Without predetermined objectives, however, the evaluation can become highly subjective and provide little useful information.

Rating Scales. Rating scales, usually using a Likert-type response, tend to focus on the areas of (1) knowledge and capability in present position, (2) dependability (meets deadlines, stays on schedule), (3) adaptability (approach to innovation, quality of judgment), (4) interpersonal relationships (ability to manage conflict, tactfulness, verbal and nonverbal communications style), (5) commitment to professional growth (desire for excellence in self and others, involvement in professional associations), (6) resource management (cost awareness, staff supervision, budget management), and (7) institutional loyalty (commitment to service, participation in the community, enthusiasm for institutional goals) (Sprunger & Bergquist, 1978). One primary danger of rating scales is to make the mistake of misplaced precision. Because numbers are generated that may be averaged and plotted, there is the danger that some may assume they have a very precise measure and make unwarranted decisions based on very small numerical differences. Rating scales should be viewed as descriptive, not quantitative.

Portfolios. This form of structured documentation requires compilation of samples of one's work in predetermined categories such as job function, skill area, and performance objectives. A common practice among faculty for promotion or tenure purposes, the portfolio could be effective in student affairs when used in conjunction with other evaluation approaches.

Management-by-Objectives (MBO). If organizations use MBO approach to management, they have built evaluation into the system. This reflects one of the most forceful arguments for its use. MBO also has several shortcomings, especially the amount of time required to acquire and compile data. This approach to management organization requires careful study and preparation prior to its implementation.

Elements of Effective Staff Evaluation

As DeCoster and Brown (Chapter 14) observed, evaluation is an essential component in any effective staff development program. Performance evaluation should observe the following principles to improve worker performance effectively.

1. Evaluation must both be *and* appear to be fair and equitable. If it is viewed as being punitive, staff members will resist and reject it. Acceptance of the evaluation process is more likely when staff members help formulate it.

2. Evaluation criteria must be determined and announced before beginning the process, be directly related to the assigned duties, and stated in a form that can be objectively assessed. It is proven effective for the supervisor and employee to determine jointly three to five objectives to be accomplished by a given time (usually six months or a year). Objectives must be stated in a form that allows for measuring unambiguously their accomplishment.

3. Evaluation should occur frequently enough to allow for corrective action to be taken before matters become severe. If objectives are established for a period of one year, evaluation should be performed at

least every six months, preferably every two months. As Penn (1979, p. 155) noted, "it is best to discuss a staff member's work during the time the work is performed." Praise and critique should both be provided. "To merely criticize without discussing alternatives, identifying attainable goals, or recognizing improved performance may, in fact, lead to additional problems."

4. Evaluation results should both be reported in writing and communicated orally to each staff member in a private conference. Strengths as well as weaknesses should be discussed. A plan of action should be outlined for dealing with areas that require change.

5. When possible, salary review and performance evaluation should be separate processes and accomplished at different times. Performance evaluations deal with staff members' productivity in relation to department goals. Salary review requires a determination about the allocation of budget and overall divisional priorities, as well as the performance of individual staff members (Penn, 1979). It may be necessary, for instance, to give a staff member a smaller raise than would be warranted by the performance evaluation alone because there is a need to employ another staff member in another area.

SUMMARY

Management of human resources is a critical function for the student affairs administrator. To be accomplished effectively and efficiently, staff resources must be objectively evaluated and inventoried and staff needs determined. Armed with a personnel forecast and plan that are consistent with the institution's resources and an appreciation for the relevant legal and ethical parameters, the student affairs administrator can begin the staffing process. The goal of the staffing process is to employ the best people available at all staff levels (professional, allied professional, support, and paraprofessional), and to place them in positions that allow them to make the greatest contribution to the accomplishment of the division's goal.

Once the staff members are employed, they deserve supervision. The student affairs administrator as staff supervisor needs to help establish a workable organization structure; participate in staff selection, orientation, and development; delegate responsibility and authority; monitor morale; facilitate conflict resolution; and establish performance standards and evaluation procedures.

Evaluation processes should be structured in a manner that will help each staff member improve his/her performance. Determination of the form and process of evaluation should be a collaborative process among staff members and their supervisors.

REFERENCES

Albright, L. E. Staffing policies and strategies. In D. Yoder & H. H. Nenaman, Jr. (Eds.), *ASPA handbook of personnel and industrial relations* (Vol. 1): *Staffing policies and strategies.* Washington, DC: Bureau of National Affairs, Inc., 1974.

American College Personnel Association. Statement of ethical and professional standards. *Journal of College Student Personnel,* 1981, *22,* 183-9.

Baldridge, J. V. *Power and conflict in the university.* New York: John Wiley & Sons, 1971.

Barr, M. J., & Keating, L. No program is an island. In M. J. Barr & L. Keating (Eds.), *New directions for student services: Establishing effective programs* (No. 7). San Francisco: Jossey-Bass, 1979.

Berenson, C., & Ruhnke, H. O. Job descriptions: Guidelines for personnel management. *Personnel Journal,* 1966, *45*(1), 14-9.

Blake, R. R., Mouton, J. S., & Williams, M. S. *The academic administrator grid: A guide to developing effective management teams.* San Francisco: Jossey-Bass, 1981.

Butteriss, M., & Albrecht, K. *New management tools: Ideas and techniques to help you as a manager.* Englewood Cliffs, NJ: Prentice-Hall, 1979.

Commerce Clearing House. *Topic law reports.* Chicago: Author, 1979.

Deegan, W.L. *Managing student affairs programs: Methods, models, muddles.* Palm Springs, CA: ETC Publications, 1981.

Delworth, U., & Aulepp, L. *Training manual for paraprofesional and allied professional programs.* Boulder, CO: Western Interstate Commission for Higher Education, 1976.

Dutton, T. B., & Rickard, S.T. Organizing student services. In U. Delworth, G. R. Hanson, & Associates (Eds.), *Student services: A handbook for the profession.* San Francisco: Jossey-Bass, 1980.

Eble, K.E. *The art of administration.* San Francisco: Jossey-Bass, 1979.

Fine, S. A., & Wiley, A. W. *An introduction to functional job analysis: A scaling of selected tasks from the social welfare field.* Kalamazoo, MI: W. E. Upjohn Institute for Employment Research, 1971.

Flippo, E. B. *Principles of personnel management* (4th ed.). New York: McGraw-Hill, 1976.

Fortunato, R. T., & Waddell, D. G. *Personnel administration in higher education: Handbook of faculty and staff personnel practices.* San Francisco: Jossey-Bass, 1981.

Hersey, P., & Blanchard, K.H. *Management of organizational behavior: Utilizing human resources* (3rd ed.). Englewood Cliffs, NJ: Prentice-Hall, 1977.

Herzberg, F., Mausner, B., & Snyderman, B. B. *The motivation to work* (2nd ed.). New York: John Wiley & Sons, 1959.

McCormick, E. J. Job information: Its development and applications. In D. Yoder & H. G. Henaman (Eds.), *ASPA handbook of personnel and industrial relations* (Vol. 1): *Staffing policies and strategies.* Washington: DC: Bureau of National Affairs, Inc., 1974.

McIntire, D. D., & Carpenter, D. S. Employment practices in student affairs. *NASPA Journal,* 1981, *18*(3), 18-24.

Megginson, L. C. *Personnel and human resources administration* (3rd ed.). Homewood, IL: Richard D. Irwin, Inc., 1977.

Penn, J. R. Staff evaluation. In G. D. Kuh (Ed.), *Evaluation in student affairs.* Washington, DC: American College Personnel Association, 1979.

Risch, T. J. (Task Force Chairperson). Placement ethics position statement. *ACPA Developments,* 1977, *4*(4), 12, 16.

Schein, E. H. *Career dynamics: Matching individual and organizational needs.* Reading, MA: Addison-Wesley, 1978.

Sims, J. M., & Foxley, C. H. Job analysis, job descriptions, and performance appraisal systems. In C. H. Foxley (Ed.), *New directions for student services: Applying management techniques* (No. 9). San Francisco: Jossey-Bass 1980.

Sprunger, B. E., & Bergquist, W. H. *Handbook for college administration.* Washington, DC: Council for the Advancement of Small Colleges, 1978.

Stanton, E. S. *Successful personnel recruiting and selection.* New York: AMACOM, 1977.

Williams, W. G. Memo to a college student personnel secretary. *NASPA Journal,* 1972, *10,* 206-10.

Zion, C. Role definition training. *Journal of the College and University Personnel Association,* 1977, *22,* 5-12.

SUGGESTED READINGS

Blake, R. R., Mouton, J. S., & Williams, M. S. *The academic administrator grid: A guide to developing effective management teams.* San Francisco: Jossey-Bass, 1981.

Dutton, T. B., & Rickard, S. T. Organizing student services. In U. Delworth, G. R. Hanson, & Associates, *Student services: A handbook for the profession.* San Francisco: Jossey-Bass, 1980.

Fortunato, R. T., & Waddell, D. G. *Personnel administration in higher education: Handbook of faculty and staff personnel practices.* San Francisco: Jossey-Bass, 1981.

Foxley, C. H. *New directions for student services: Applying management techniques* (No. 9). San Francisco: Jossey-Bass, 1980.

Genova, W. J., Madoff, M. K., Chin, R., & Thomas, G. B. *Mutual benefit evaluation of faculty and administrators in higher education.* Cambridge, MA: Ballinger Publishing, 1976.

Penn, J. R. Staff evalution. In G. D. Kuh (Ed.), *Evaluation in student affairs.* Washington, DC: American College Personnel Association, 1979.

Sprunger, B. E., & Bergquist, W. H. *Handbook for college administration.* Washington, DC: Council for the Advancement of Small Colleges, 1978.

Steven C. Ender received his Ed.D. and M.Ed. from the University of Georgia in counseling and student personnel services and his B.S. from Virginia Commonwealth University in business. He is presently serving as a Counseling Psychologist and Assistant Professor in the Center for Student Development at Kansas State University. Previously he was an assistant professor in the Student Personnel in Higher Education Program, and was the coordinator of Counseling and Tutorial Services in the Division of Developmental Studies, both at the University of Georgia.

His publications include co-authoring *Students Helping Students: A Training Manual for Peer Helpers on the College Campus* and co-editing *New Directions for Student Services: Developmental Approaches to Academic Advising*. He has extensive consultation experience in the areas of student development programming, academic advising, developmental education, and peer helper training and programming.

Chapter **13**

STUDENTS AS PARAPROFESSIONALS

Steven C. Ender

Employment of undergraduates to function as paraprofessionals in student affairs departments and programs is expanding rapidly. Professional literature provides little in the way of definition for the student paraprofessional role. This void may be due to the multiplicity of roles students now perform on college campuses or, perhaps, to the rapidly expanding scope of the paraprofessional movement in higher education.

Delworth and Aulepp (1976) defined the paraprofessional as a person willing to give time and talent to assist others. When this person is identified, selected, and trained to assume tasks usually performed by certain professional staff members, this student becomes a paraprofessional.

Another definition was presented in the American College Personnel Association standards statement on students serving as paraprofessionals recently submitted to the Council for the Advancement of Standards for Student Services/Development Programs. In this statement the student paraprofessional is defined as a student employed by a division of student affairs for purposes of providing direct services to other students on a paid or voluntary basis (Ender & Schuette, 1982). In addition, Ender, McCaffrey, and Miller defined the paraprofessional as "an undergraduate or graduate student who has been trained to assist fellow students in adjusting to, and successfully functioning within, the higher education setting" (1979, p. 12).

In light of these definitions, paraprofessionals are students who have been selected and trained to offer educational services to their peers. These services are intentionally designed to assist in the adjustment, satisfaction, and persistence of students toward attainment of their educational goals. Students performing in paraprofessional roles are compensated for their services and supervised by qualified professionals.

A RATIONALE

A strong rationale for students functioning as paraprofessionals is the powerful impact peers have on one another. Chickering (1969) maintained that relationships with close friends and peer groups are primary forces that influence student development on college campuses. Heath (1968), in research on variables that affect the maturity of college students, concluded that one powerful source of impact is interpersonal relationships with other students. More specifically, Feldman and Newcomb (1970) noted that the peer group assists students in the resolution of many developmental tasks including independence from parental authority, clarification of values, and acceptance of differences in others.

The strong impact students have on peers' growth and development occurs through intrapersonal and interpersonal dynamics of stimulation, psychic dissonance, and the regaining of emotional equilibrium (Chickering, 1969; Heath, 1968). Student growth in intellectual, psychosocial, moral, and ethical areas can be attributed largely to the challenges to ideas and values they experience. These challenges come primarily from other students, forcing reflection and consideration of present behavior. In many instances, reflection results in behavioral change to higher levels of academic, personal, and interpersonal functioning.

Administrators who utilize students in paraprofessional roles are intentionally maximizing the developmental impact students have on each other. Student paraprofessionals serve not only as challengers and supporters in the developmental process but also are role models for others.

Behaviors that student paraprofessionals model are often characteristic of successful, responsible, and self-directed college students. As Miller and Prince (1976) indicated, development can be fostered by creating a developmental milieu whereby students are able to observe and interact with others who effectively model the characteristics, values, and processes that best represent the outcomes to which the environment is committed.

Developmental dynamics created by the implementation of student-staffed programs have a major effect on participating paraprofessionals. Administrators who implement programs should realize that the program itself is a developmental intervention. This is especially true for the training, interviewing, delivery, and evaluating phases of the program. Heath (1980) asserted that personal development of college students can be enhanced through programs that (1) expect and encourage students to take responsibility for growth in others and (2) provide opportunities for students to assume alternative roles. These concepts are underlying principles upon which student paraprofessional programming is based.

Institutional budget restrictions and the conflicting need to offer developmental-based programming to large and divergent populations provide another strong rationale for student paraprofessional programming (Ender & McFadden, 1980). In many instances student affairs administrators may be able to increase student development programming efforts by using student staff, while minimizing budget increases. This is often possible by utilizing already existing institutional resources such as college work-study budgets, room or board waivers, and academic credit for the work experience. Additionally, student volunteers who want work experiences documented in developmental transcripts (Brown, 1980) or for letters of recommendation can be utilized as peer helpers at low cost. (See Chapter 12.)

Not only can more students be reached through paraprofessional programming, but also professional practitioners can be freed to offer services that require higher levels of education and skills (Delworth & Yarris, 1978). For instance, professionals employed in settings that use paraprofessionals can often accomplish more by training, supervising, and evaluating peer helpers than by working directly with students. And, students with more serious concerns can still be referred to the professional. Because most students with personal problems seek help from friends first, through paraprofessional referrals, professionals can likely achieve a wider campus impact than through most traditional approaches. Because paraprofessionals are representatives of many different student subcultures, student affairs practitioners can increase their insight into needs of diverse student groups.

Literature on student paraprofessional effectiveness suggests that peer helpers may be more effective than professionals when dealing with many developmental concerns. For instance, studies concerning the use of undergraduates as study-skills counselors found that freshmen counseled by student paraprofessionals made significantly greater use of the information received during counseling than those counseled by professionals (Zunker & Brown, 1966). Likewise, Carkhuff and Truax (1965) contended that paraprofessionals can be as effective as professionals in facilitating constructive change in people over relatively short periods of time.

In summary, many persuasive arguments have been made in support of employing paraprofessionals in the student affairs division. Paraprofessionals represent a viable method to promote student development.

ROLES, GOALS, AND LIMITATIONS
Roles

In many student affairs programs students currently are employed as paraprofessionals in a variety of roles. The beginnings of this movement perhaps can be traced to residence halls where students have been assisting other students as resident assistants, proctors, hall counselors, or advisors since the turn of the century (Powell, Plyler, Dickerson & McCallan, 1969). Brown's (1972) pioneering study skills counseling model was based on 18 years of testing and counseling research. More recent literature suggests the use of student paraprofessionals in a host of program settings. Smith (1981) reported that students at the University of the Pacific are working in new student orientation; academic advising; learning center; admissions, international services, registrar and financial aid offices, as well as in the Upward Bound and community involvement programs. Other campus roles in which student paraprofessionals are being utilized include peer counselors (Lucian, 1977), peer tutors (Ender & McFadden, 1980; Kelly & Nolan, 1980), student leaders (Duvall & Ender, 1980; Newton, 1980), and assistance in career planning and placement (Johnston & Hansen, 1981).

Goals and Expectations

Even though expectations placed on paraprofessionals change from setting to setting and are somewhat dependent on the particular role the student is being asked to assume, certain guidelines need to be considered as specific paraprofessional expectations are being formulated by the professional staff. Ender and Schuette (1982) proposed six objectives for paraprofessional programs that administrators should consider.

•Provide direct services to college students

•Maximize the potential positive effects of peers interacting with peers

•Provide guidance and developmental support services and programs rather than counseling/therapeutic interventions

•Provide a wide range of developmental services at reduced cost

•Provide positive role models for other students to emulate

•Provide educational and developmental experiences for students serving in the paraprofessional positions.

Blimling and Miltenberger (1981) discussed expectations of the resident assistant that seem equally appropriate for other paraprofessional roles. These expectations include (1) being a role model; (2) serving as a counselor, consultant, or advisor to other students; (3) teaching others; and (4) being a successful student. These expectations were previously endorsed by Ender et al. (1979) as appropriate for all students serving in paraprofessional positions. Other expectations would include serving as ombudsman in regard to campus resources, understanding developmental stage and task theory for particular age groups, and utilizing goal setting and assessment strategies in their own lives as well as in their work with others.

The guiding expectation of students serving in these positions is the developmental nature of the programming thrust. The paraprofessional is expected to perform educational, advising, and preventive services rather than focus on intensive counseling issues or remedial concerns.

Limitations

Several issues affect roles of student paraprofessionals. Administrators need to consider the following in formulating role definitions for paraprofessionals.

Length, degree, and quality of training have a direct bearing on how realistic are the professional's expectations of paraprofessionals. A training program that meets for a weekend cannot teach helping skills one could only realistically expect to master in an intensive semester-long training experience. Also, trainer qualifications must be considered. One cannot expect paraprofessionals to develop helping skills that exceed those of the trainer. Careful consideration of training resources available on campus must be made when considering both expectations and limitations for the paraprofessional position.

Time available and physical proximity of professional staff members for supervision need consideration also. If the supervisor can meet with the paraprofessional only biweekly, the paraprofessional should not be allowed to offer services requiring daily observation and consultation. Likewise, the physical proximity of the supervisor to the paraprofessional work site is important. A rule of thumb is the greater the responsibility of the paraprofessional, the closer and more immediately available must be the supervisor. For example, if the paraprofessional is assisting another student with personal concerns, the supervisor should be within immediate and easy access. Paraprofessionals offering tours of the career library do not need such close supervision. Finally, tasks and duties assigned paraprofessionals must fall within the professional expertise of the supervisor. A paraprofessional working in the tutorial center and supervised by a member of the English faculty should not be asked to be a personal counselor.

The stated goals and objectives of the student affairs division employing paraprofessionals provide guidelines for limitations. A paraprofessional trained to offer services that address one department's goals and objectives should not move to another unit without additional training.

The number of contact hours between the paraprofessional and the target population is an important factor to consider. Paraprofessionals should be able to accomplish their work activities within reasonable or designated work hours. Administrators should be careful not to burden paraprofessionals with unrealistic work expectations.

Developmental or maturity levels of participating paraprofessionals will also govern the limitations of the role to a certain extent. For example, freshmen and sophomore students working in the career counseling center are, in most instances, in a position to help other students with their *career exploration.* On the other hand, they are *not* in a position, developmentally, to assist students who wish to make decisions concerning *career choices,* if they have not themselves mastered this developmental task.

One rather sweeping limitation for all students serving as paraprofessionals is the nature of the target populations. Paraprofessionals should neither be asked to interpret standardized psychological tests, *nor* work with student concerns classified as remedial, requiring therapeutic counseling (e.g., depression, free floating anxiety, sudden or severe weight loss, severe hostility, or paranoia).

A final limitation concerns policies and procedures of the department within which a paraprofessional works. These helpers should *not* be put in the position of having to formulate or interpret policies to other members of the campus community. That responsibility belongs to administrators and other professionals.

IMPLEMENTING PARAPROFESSIONAL PROGRAMS

Three major program phases with corresponding program components need consideration as administrators implement paraprofessional programs. Phase one provides focus and direction for the paraprofessional campus role; phase two identifies recruitment and selection techniques; and phase three attends to training and rewarding the paraprofessional.

Phase One: Focus and Direction

Identification of Campus Role. Role identification is the first step when implementing a paraprofessional program. Careful consideration should be given to such factors as nature of the needs of the population to be served. Factors such as location of paraprofessional work stations, training and supervising new personnel, and acceptance and endorsement of the paraprofessional program by affected professionals all need careful consideration. As these considerations are resolved, the paraprofessional job description can be refined.

Developing Job Descriptions. The job description must be grounded in behavioral language that specifies what the paraprofessional is expected to do (Ostroth, 1981). This attention to actual behaviors assists in all subsequent phases of program development. By having a list of behaviors describing the position, students can assess their abilities to perform as paraprofessionals, and faculty and staff can refer potential paraprofessionals to the program administrator with greater ease. The recruitment process can be enhanced greatly with job descriptions that are written in behavioral language. Additionally, trainers need a definite idea of training areas and helping skills that must be addressed in the training program, and supervisors will be in much better positions to evaluate paraprofessional effectiveness.

Establishing Selection Criteria. Criteria for selection are a natural outgrowth of the behavioral job description and should be disseminated to all recruitment agents (faculty, staff, administrators, and students) on the campus. Ender and Schuette (1982) suggested generic criteria, which include academic records; recommendations from faculty, staff, and employed paraprofessionals; past and present persons in positions of leadership; and desire and willingness of the prospective paraprofessional to assist and help other students. Ostroth (1981) and Smith (1981) suggested that participation in training programs by students interested in the paraprofessional position should be included as one criterion for selection. Some paraprofessional training should take place before selection and employment. By participating in training before selection, students are given the opportunity to make decisions concerning their ability to serve in the position, and professional staff members are able to observe the student functioning in helping interactions before employment.

Phase Two: Identification and Selection

Recruitment Procedures. Student affairs administrators should strive to include as many representatives as possible from the college community in the recruitment process. This representation includes faculty, staff, students, and other administrators. The development and dissemination of behavioral job descriptions and well-defined selection criteria to potential referral agents will aid in the recruitment process and also should result in a pool of well qualified and possibly pretrained students desiring the position, if the selection criteria include participation in training. Administrators need to recruit a heterogeneous group of students who represent the diversity of the population they will be assisting. Factors such as age, gender, race, socioeconomic background, and other demographic characteristics of the target population need to be given careful consideration during the recruitment process. Successful paraprofessionals are able to empathize with concerns of the target population and can model adaptive behaviors that they have learned in overcoming similar concerns.

Selection Procedures. The literature pertaining to selection of paraprofessionals presents a wide range of alternatives for administrators to consider. German (1979) conducted an intensive review of selection procedures used to hire paraprofessional student counselors. The procedures he described included the use of personality inventories (Edwards Personal Preference Schedule and Minnesota Multiphasic Personality Inventory), direct evaluation of actual performance (leaderless group discussion, role plays using rating scales, and sociodrama techniques), and standardized selection interviews.

Ostroth's (1981) discussed techniques used to select resident assistants that also seem appropriate for other types of paraprofessionals. He pointed out that many traditional selection processes, such as resumes, recommendations, and unstructured interviews, have proven to be biased, unreliable, and invalid. Other selection procedures having better utility for selecting paraprofessionals include peer ratings, performance of tasks, role play situations, participation in leaderless group discussions, apprenticeships, and participation in training programs before selection.

Ender and McFadden (1980) suggested initial selection procedures using traditional methods, including application forms, letters of recommendation, and individual interviews. The applicant pool derived from those who completed this process then participated in a training course, followed by group interviews. Paraprofessionals were then selected by a team of staff members.

Phase Three: Training and Rewards

Training Program. A wealth of information exists regarding the training of paraprofessionals for their campus roles. Training can be thought of in two stages. Stage one, pre-service training, occurs before actual employment, and stage two, in-service training, is provided throughout the program.

The training program during the pre-service stage provides opportunities for students to gain information pertaining to the role, participate in personal growth opportunities, and learn specific helping skills. Ender and Schuette (1982) suggested training, at the very minimum, should include such topics as knowledge of the role, awareness of self and power of role modeling behavior, creating and maintaining support groups, student (human) development theory, communciation skills, goal setting strategies and the identification of behavioral objectives, assessment skills and techniques, cross-cultural relations, problems of gender stereotyping, study skills techniques, knowledge of campus and community resources, and referral techniques. The main focuses of the pre-training experience are personal exploration and development of helping skills.

The second stage of training concerns in-service or job-functional training. This stage of training initially concentrates on areas such as divisional goals and objectives; policies and procedures; ethical concerns, such as confidentiality; and job-specific knowledge and skills (Delworth & Yarris, 1978). Other areas of in-service training expand on the skill areas presented earlier in pre-service training and offer additional topics and programs as needed. Several other issues to address include amount of time needed for training, methods of reimbursement for participation in training, and training as a prerequisite for employment.

Training, at its maximum level of effectiveness, should be offered for an academic term for credit. By spreading the experience over several months' duration the trainees have many opportunities to test their abilities to master helping skills and to become better role models. In many cases, training challenges individuals to change their behavior: for example, moving from an advice-giving perspective to a helping frame of reference. Short, intense training experiences, such as the weekend retreat, generally will not result in significant levels of behavioral change on the part of the paraprofessional.

For maximum effectiveness, training needs to be a prerequisite for obtaining the position. Students who choose to participate in this type of experience, with no assurance that they will be employed, are publicly expressing their belief in the importance of learning about themselves in relationship to a helping role. Just as one could not expect competence from a professional staff person who has had no formal preparation, competence cannot be expected from a paraprofessional who has had no training for the paraprofessional role.

Reward System. Administrators and other staff members must understand the necessity for establishing reward systems for students working in paraprofessional positions. Such systems can include pay, fee/tuition waivers, room and board remissions, and course credit. Other reward options include recognition at award ceremonies and documentation of services rendered in the students' permanent records or developmental transcripts.

EVALUATION

Well planned and implemented programs include formative and summative evaluations (Miller & Prince, 1976) throughout each program phase and, in addition, evaluate the strengths and weaknesses of student participants.

Formative Evaluation

Formative evaluation focuses on each phase and component of the program. The evaluation process concludes each phase of the program and is intended to provide immediate feedback to the program administrator and staff so changes can be made to improve the program as it develops (Brown, 1979). This evaluation does not have to be sophisticated. Simple questionnaires and surveys will provide much of the information needed.

Summative Evaluation

Summative evaluation, or evaluation that focuses on the program goals and objectives, should take place at least annually, but preferably more often. From a program perspective this evaluation answers questions pertaining to the accomplishment of program goals and objectives and will typically be reported to administrators who are faced with budgetary decisions (Brown, 1979). The life, depth, and expansion of the program, in many instances, will be influenced strongly by summative evaluation data.

Role of the Supervisor

Quality programs provide both formal and informal evaluation sessions for individual paraprofessionals throughout the academic year.

Typically, informal evaluation sessions are conducted by program supervisors. These evaluations should not be a threat to the paraprofessional's self-esteem, but should focus on the strengths of the individuals as they implement their roles. Additionally, evaluations provide identification of training strategies and programs to offset weaknesses.

These evaluation sessions should be thought of as developmental interviews. This means the primary purpose of the interview is to focus on growth and development of the individual paraprofessional as a person working in a helping position. The interview needs to be highlighted by establishing personal and work-related goals, helping the student assess readiness to complete these goals, developing behavioral objectives for goal accomplishment, and identifying appropriate learning opportunities on campus or in the community.

End of the year evaluations for student paraprofessionals take a different perspective than the developmental procedures previously described. During this evaluation session paraprofessionals receive specific information regarding how they have performed in their roles, and are informed about decisions concerning their continuance on the staff. If the paraprofessional and the supervisor have had good rapport throughout the year, with ample opportunity for participation in additional skill development, this evaluation session should be constructive for both participants.

Supervisors perform three additional functions as they interact with student paraprofessionals. These include consultation, instruction, and mentoring.

Consulting. In a consulting role the supervisor works closely with paraprofessionals reviewing progress of clients in the target population. The supervisor should assist the paraprofessional in identification of appropriate interventions to deal with client problems and serve as a referral agent for client concerns that go beyond the paraprofessional's realm of expertise.

Teaching. In this role the supervisor provides additional training opportunities for the paraprofessional staff. These sessions may address helping skills previously covered in pre-service training, or they may cover new areas that are identified through program assessment and evaluation. Development and implementation of in-service training programs are a primary function of the supervisor in the teaching role.

Mentoring. In the mentoring role the supervisor serves as a confidant and friend to the paraprofessional. The relationship is one in which the paraprofessional feels comfortable sharing and discussing personal, academic, and work-related concerns. In this mentoring role the supervisor models helping skills that are expected of paraprofessionals, in addition to those essential to a helping relationship.

SPECIAL ISSUES

Three special issues concerning paraprofessional staff programs need consideration: (1) the ratio of paraprofessionals to student contacts and professional staff members; (2) staff qualifications for training; and (3) developing professional staff commitment for the program.

Ratios

Student to Paraprofessional. Ender and Schuette (1982) proposed a paraprofessional to student ratio of no greater than 1:35. This ratio would be high if paraprofessionals were expected to have regular sessions with each student weekly, but quite appropriate if they were working in a residence hall or conducting tours of the institution for the admissions office. The ratio is dependent upon the nature of the job description and specific responsibilities of the paraprofessional. This ratio also is predicated on the number of hours per week the paraprofessional works. Given that this person is also a student, 10 to 12 work hours weekly seems an appropriate maximum. If the work required primarily one-to-one interaction, the program administrator could expect each paraprofessional to have no more than 10 to 12 student contacts weekly.

Paraprofessional to Professional. The number of paraprofessionals the professional can supervise is largely dependent on the formal organizational structure of the program. In programs where supervisors are employed full time to coordinate the program and supervise paraprofessionals, they generally can work adequately with a staff of up to 25.

If the supervisor also is performing other responsibilities, (e.g., career counseling or teaching in the learning center), an appropriate ratio for supervision might be one to five. Working in small groups or individually, the professional should plan to spend between two to four hours per week in supervisory sessions with these five paraprofessionals. This is not a sacrifice of professional time considering the fact that each paraprofessional supervised represents between 10 to 35 student contacts weekly.

Staff Qualifications for Training

Guidelines prescribing qualifications are necessary for trainers of paraprofessionals. Possessing an advanced degree may not qualify one to perform the training role adequately. Very few individuals have had formal education in the area of training undergraduate students to function as paraprofessionals. Staff members should seek educational experiences at professional meetings and workshops that address this critical area or pertinent formal training programs.

Minimally, trainers should have an in-depth knowledge of the student affairs division for which the paraprofessional is being trained. Also, professionals should be able to model skills the paraprofessional is expected to learn. Other trainer skills include expertise in student development theory, communication skills, group dynamics, values clarification, and problem solving methodologies. On many campuses co-training approaches could be utilized in order to achieve quality training.

Developing Staff Commitment

Faculty and staff members may be threatened by paraprofessional staffed programs. Administrators must be careful to highlight the many advantages of paraprofessionals, but assure professionals that they are not being replaced by paraprofessionals. Professionals must understand that the paraprofessional is being employed to perform duties that do not require the full expertise of professional training. Also, professionals should be urged to develop training and supervisory skills as part of their professional development. Administrators should support this development through as many channels as possible including attending professional workshops and bringing consultants to campus to provide in-service training for professional staff members. Most professionals will support this type of programming if they understand its purpose and scope and the unique opportunities it offers for their professional development.

SUMMARY

Student paraprofessionals present one vehicle for implementing student development approaches on the college campus. Recent research indicated that students who desire these roles are both mature and self-confident (Ender, 1981). They possess many personal characteristics that will strengthen their role-modeling capabilities. Administrators need to consider the advantages of implementing paraprofessional programs because they represent a powerful strategy that can affect the intellectual and personal development of college students.

REFERENCES

Blimling, S., & Miltenberger, J. *The residence assistant: Working with college students in residence halls.* Dubuque, IA: Kendall/Hunt Publishing, 1981.

Brown, R.D. *Student development in tomorrow's higher education: A return to the academy.* Washington, DC: American College Personnel Association, 1972.

Brown, R. D. Evaluator roles and evaluation strategies: A consumer's introduction. In G. K. Kuh (Ed.), *Evaluation in student affairs.* Washington, DC: American College Personnel Association, 1979.

Brown, R. D. Developmental transcript mentoring: A total approach to integrating student development in the academy. In D. G. Creamer (Ed.), *Student development in higher education: Theories, practices, and future directions.* Washington, DC: American College Personnel Association, 1980.

Brown, W. F. *Student-to-student counseling: An approach to academic achievement* (Rev. ed.). Austin: University of Texas Press, 1977.

Carkhuff, R. R., & Truax, C. B. Lay mental health counseling: The effects of lay group counseling. *Journal of Counseling Psychology,* 1965, *29,* 426-31.

Chickering, A. W. *Education and identity.* San Francisco: Jossey-Bass, 1969.

Delworth, U. (Ed.). *New directions for student services: Training competent staff* (No. 2). San Francisco: Jossey-Bass, 1978.

Delworth, U., & Aulepp, L. *Training manual for paraprofessionals and allied professional programs*. Boulder, CO: Western Interstate Commission for Higher Education, 1976.

Delworth, U., Sherwood, G., & Casaburri, N. *Student paraprofessionals: A working model for higher education*. Washington, DC: American Personnel and Guidance Association, 1974.

Delworth, U., & Yarris, E. Concepts and processes for the new training role. In U. Delworth (Ed.), *New directions for student services: Training competent staff* (No. 2). San Francisco: Jossey-Bass, 1978.

DuVall, W. H., & Ender, K. L. A training model for developing leadership awareness. In F. B. Newton & K. L. Ender (Eds.), *Student development practices: Strategies for making a difference*. Springfield, IL: Charles C. Thomas, 1980.

Ender, S. C. *The impact of a peer helper training program on the maturity and self-confidence of undergraduate students*. Unpublished doctoral dissertation, University of Georgia, 1981.

Ender, S. C., McCaffrey, S. S., & Miller, T. K. *Students helping students: A training manual for peer helpers on the college campus*. Athens, GA: Student Development Associates, 1979.

Ender, S. C., & McFadden, R. B. Training the student paraprofessional helper. In F. B. Newton & K. L. Ender (Eds.), *Student development practices: Strategies for making a difference*. Springfield, IL: Charles C. Thomas, 1980.

Ender, S. C., & Schuette, C. G. *Students serving as paraprofessionals: Employment and utilization*. Washington, DC: American College Personnel Association, Unpublished document, 1982.

Feldman, K. A., & Newcomb, T. M. *The impact of college on students: An analysis of four decades of research* (Vol. 1). San Francisco: Jossey-Bass, 1970.

German, S. C. Selecting undergraduate paraprofessionals on college campuses: A review. *Journal of College Student Personnel*, 1979, *20*, 28-34.

Heath, D. H. *Growing up in college*. San Francisco: Jossey-Bass, 1968.

Heath, D. H. Wanted: A comprehensive model of healthy development. *Personnel and Guidance Journal*, 1980, *58*, 391-9.

Johnston, J. A., & Hansen, R. N. Using paraprofessionals in career development programming. In V. A. Harren, M. H. Daniels, & J. N. Buck (Eds.), *New directions for student services: Facilitating student's career development* (No. 14). San Francisco: Jossey-Bass, 1981.

Kelly, L. P., & Nolan, T. W. Identifying student paraprofessional training needs: An analytical approach. *Journal of College Student Personnel*, 1980, *21*, 431-6.

Lucian, J. Training college peer counselors: A behavior contract model. *Journal of College Student Personnel,* 1977, *18,* 66-7.

Miller, T. K., & Prince, J. S. *The future of student affairs: A guide to student development for tomorrow's higher education.* San Francisco: Jossey-Bass, 1976.

Newcomb, T. M., & Wilson, E. K. *College peer groups.* Chicago: Aldine Publishing, 1966.

Newton, F. B. Community building strategies with student groups. In F. B. Newton & K. L. Ender (Eds.), *Student development practices: Strategies for making a difference.* Springfield, IL: Charles C. Thomas, 1980.

Ostroth, D. D. Selecting competent residence hall staff. In G. S. Blimling & J. H. Schuh (Eds.), *New direction for student services: Increasing the educational role of residence halls* (No. 13). San Francisco: Jossey-Bass, 1981.

Powell, J. R., Pyler, S. A., Dickerson, B. A., & McClellan, S. D. *The personnel assistant in college residence halls.* New York: Houghton Mifflin, 1969.

Smith, B. Orientation aids paraprofessional development. *Orientation Review,* 1981, *11,* 1-7.

Zunker, V. G., & Brown, W. F. Comparative effectiveness of student and professional counselors. *Personnel and Guidance Journal,* 1966, *44,* 738-43.

SUGGESTED READINGS

Blimling, G. S., & Miltenberger, L. J. *The resident assistant: Working with college students in residence halls.* Dubuque, IA: Kendall/Hunt Publishing Co., 1981.

Brown, W. F. *Student-to-student counseling: An approach to academic achievement* (Rev. ed.). Austin: University of Texas Press, 1977.

Delworth, U. (Ed.). *New directions for student services: Training competent staff* (No. 2). San Francisco: Jossey-Bass, 1978.

Ender, S. C., McCaffrey, S. S., & Miller, T. K. *Students helping students: A training manual for peer helpers on the college campus.* Athens, GA: Student Development Associates, 1979.

Sherwood, G. P. Allied and paraprofessionals. In U. Delworth & G. R. Hanson (Eds.), *Student services: A handbook for the professional.* San Francisco: Jossey-Bass, 1980.

David A. DeCoster is currently Dean of Students and Associate Professor of Education with the Department of Educational Psychology and Social Foundations at the University of Nebraska, Lincoln. He has served as an Editorial Board member of three professional journals and presently serves as Associate Editor of the *Journal of College Student Personnel.* His publications include four co-authored books: *Mentoring-Transcript Systems for Promoting Student Growth, Understanding Today's Students, Personal Education and Community Development in College Residence Halls,* and *Student Development and Education in College Residence Halls.* Additional publications include frequent contributions as the author of chapters and articles in a variety of books and professional journals. He makes frequent annual appearances at state, regional, and national professional meetings and serves institutions and agencies involved in postsecondary education as a consultant, speaker, and external evaluator. Before accepting his present responsibilities at the Univerity of Nebraska, he was affiliated with Indiana University, the University of Georgia, the University of Florida, and the University of Michigan in various roles as a student affairs practitioner and faculty member.

Suzanne S. Brown currently serves as Assistant to the Vice Chancellor for Student Affairs at the University of Nebraska-Lincoln where she previously headed the student union program office. She has provided leadership for the Student Affairs division staff development program at UNL for over four years and has made presentations on this topic at numerous regional and national conferences. Holding a B.S. in speech from Northwestern University and a M.A. in English from the University of Arizona, Brown taught English at several colleges before moving into the student affairs field. She is a candidate for the Ph.D. degree in education at the University of Nebraska.

Chapter 14

STAFF DEVELOPMENT: PERSONAL AND PROFESSIONAL EDUCATION

David A. DeCoster
Suzanne S. Brown

Perhaps one reason for the scarcity of research on staff development for student affairs practitioners is that the need for continuous professional growth seems self-evident. Antagonists to this concept are few, and their arguments generally are limited to such subsidiary issues as methodology, cost effectiveness, time requirements, and degree of responsibility that should be assumed by staff members. No one seems to dispute the basic rationale underlying personal and professional developmental efforts.

PHILOSOPHICAL FOUNDATION

Staff development programs are a systematic response to two developmental patterns that occur simultaneously whenever an individual's activities are intertwined with functions of a group, community, or organization. These phenomena—human development and organization development—are not, however, simply parallel processes. For each process to achieve its goals, the two must be integrated. This interdependence assumes many forms as the following analysis of the two basic elements suggests.

Human Development

The student development concept currently incorporated within the educational mission of student affairs was borrowed from the broader body of literature relating to general human development. Briefly summarized, the concept of continuous human growth and maturation contains three major components (DeCoster & Mable, 1980):

Education is Communication. Human beings learn through communication and through interaction. As Dewey (1916) observed long ago, not only are knowledge and values transmitted through community life, but also a society continues to exist only to the extent that common understandings about self and environment are shared and communicated. Open communication and shared understandings are no less important for smaller human groups that function as subunits within a larger society, including institutional, divisional, and departmental organizations.

Learning is a Process. Education is a process, not a product. "Ends" never justify "means," and, in fact, the two cannot be meaningfully separated. Research relating to classroom teaching as well as that based on psychotherapeutic relationships reveals that the quality of the educational process is the important variable in determining the extent of constructive change and meaningful growth in the learner. Student affairs professionals must understand that generally the *way* in which they accomplish a task has greater educational significance than the successful completion of the task itself.

Education Means Total Development. Education is not synonymous with cognitive growth; thus, nonintellectual and affective dimensions must be perceived as not only legitimate but essential ingredients of the learning process. Cultural, spiritual, psychological, physical, and social variables must be addressed along with intellectual growth as human beings move toward increasing levels of personal competence and self-reliance. Thus, the total scope of a staff member's personal and professional life provides the potential agenda for staff development experiences. Moreover, although the study of growth and development was once focused almost exclusively on the earlier stages of the life span, psychological research in recent years has enhanced the understanding of mature adult development and has led to the concept of "lifelong learning." Two bestsellers, *Passages* (Sheehy, 1974) and *The Seasons of a Man's Life* (Levinson et al., 1978), have increased public understanding for viewing human development as continuous and evolutionary throughout an individual's life.

Organization Development

Human organizations are dynamic, fluid systems that not only involve people, but also are characterized by specified goals, procedural frameworks, and operational methods (Kurpius, 1980). Thus, strategies for organization development generally include structural or procedural modifications along with growth-producing experiences. Positive change results from new combinations of human and structural variables that are consistent with goals of both the organization and the individuals within it. Throughout literature, the symbiotic relationships between individual and group needs is stressed (Kurpius, 1980; Mable, Terry, & Duvall, 1980; Tripp, 1977).

For example, Richardson (1975) outlined six stages of organization development beginning with individual and small group learning experiences, but including such processes as analysis and revision of administrative and governance structure and establishing goals and priorities for the institution. Regardless of how lavish the budget or exciting the activities provided for staff development, Richardson insisted that "changed behavior by administrators will not occur unless the institutional environment and its governance procedures support the concept of a community in which everyone grows and learns" (p. 306).

Staff development, then, is not merely a matter of exposing new ideas and experiences to people. Staff development to be effective must be conceived and implemented in terms of the development of the organization. Enhancement of individual performance must be integrated with the institution's needs and goals. According to Nejedlo (1977), the process of organization development ideally culminates in self-directed and continuing "renewal activities" collaboratively designed by organization members.

Staff Development in Student Affairs

Brown (1977) provided an excellent perspective regarding the dimensions of evolutionary change in postsecondary education and the roles of student affairs professionals in this process. He suggested three broad areas of professional development needed for effective performance of these roles. First is the need to confront the basic issues of human existence. On the basis of his analysis of the major issues that have confronted student affairs staff members during the past ten years, Brown concluded that three predominant "universal and timeless" themes have a direct bearing on student affairs practice: (1) tension between personal liberty and social interdependence, (2) conflict between hedonistic needs and altruism, and (3) search for meaning to human existence.

The second area is the need for the knowledge and skills required to influence total student development. Brown warned against the compartmentalization of the organizational structure that may produce some efficiencies but cannot replace personal, individual relationships. And the third area is the need to promote the integration of academic and personal development. This integration involves learning how to work with faculty toward achieving a more humanized learning environment and an integrated curriculum.

In more pragmatic and specific terms, a number of staff development objectives and intended outcomes can be summarized in six categories (Beeler, 1976; Beeler & Penn, 1978; Cox, 1979; Leafgren, 1980; Mable, 1979; Meyerson, 1974, 1975; Miller, 1975, 1980; Stamatakos & Oliaro, 1972; Wanzek & Canon, 1975). As a composite, they represent the curriculum for student affairs staff development.

1. *Facilitating interaction with colleagues and associates:* exchange of ideas; team building and staff interdependence; giving and receiving feedback; promoting positive attitudes and sensitivity toward others; sharing information about the organization; enhancing internal staff communication.

2. *Developing functional skills and specific competencies:* evaluation and analysis; organizational, administrative, and management skills; communication and consultation.

3. *Promoting self-understanding and self-actualization:* helping individuals increase their levels of awareness, autonomy, and self-reliance and refine personal value systems.

4. *Exposure to innovative programs:* encouraging proactive service and program development and active responses to student issues.

5. *Providing opportunities for professional renewal:* developing a professional style; enhancing commitment, accountability, and self-esteem; preventing burn-out; offering new challenges as well as chances for reflection and reassessment.

6. *Conveying theoretical and philosophical knowledge:* enhancing understanding of total student affairs programs through examination of developmental research and literature and discussion of issues in postsecondary education and society.

From many of these same authors, a list of common staff developmental activities and methods is easily abstracted: (1) academic coursework; (2) national, regional, and state convention attendance; (3) on-campus programs utilizing either internal or external consultants; (4) off-campus workshops, seminars, and institutes; (5) staff social functions; (6) organizational newsletters and other written communications; (7) organizational staff meetings, committee and task force participation; and (8) ongoing supervision, performance evaluation, general relationships with colleagues, and administrative fellowships and internships.

In terms of the philosophical foundations for staff development set forth earlier, the problems associated with this list are readily apparent. Many of these frequently mentioned methods, whether on- or off-campus, are structured programs and experiences that tend to emphasize "products" rather then "process." Moreover, the typical cluster of planned events, packages, or programs puts the emphasis primarily on individual development. Only three of the nine methods have an explicit organizational dimension, and, more often than not, these last three categories are not thought of in terms of their developmental potential.

COMPONENTS OF
STAFF DEVELOPMENT

A gap in the literature exists between the understanding of professional development as a process that occurs within the context of organization development and kinds of staff development strategies most often advocated. The latter tend to create the impression for many student affairs administrators that staff development is a "professional agenda" that occurs as a separate, ancillary function to people's organizational roles and daily responsibilities. In the following discussion of five broad components of staff development, the focus shifts back and forth from the needs of the individual to the priorities of the organization; but the underlying principle is that professional development is a continual process that should be anchored in performance expectations and day-to-day, on-the-job behavior. The five strategies that constitute an effective staff development effort are (1) individual motivation and self-assessment, (2) supervision and performance evaluation, (3) mentoring relationships, (4) structured learning opportunities, and (5) professional participation, service, and contributions.

Individual Motivation and Self-Assessment

The ideal framework for professional development is built by interlocking individual initiatives with organizational opportunities, by interfacing individual and organizational goals. But when organizational components are flimsy, the highly-motivated individual is still likely to find or create a means for continuous development. And, conversely, the person who lacks initiative, interest, or self-confidence is unlikely to respond very heartily to even the most systematic efforts initiated by the organization. Individual motivation, then, is the cornerstone of a successful staff development structure.

Long before career planning workshops, self-assessment inventories, and modern systems of goal-setting were commonplace, people were actively engaged in expanding their professional knowledge, sharpening their job-related skills, and cultivating personal qualities needed to succeed in their chosen fields. Often the process was, as it still is for many, largely haphazard and almost unconscious. Some highly motivated people, much like healthy plants, seem to grow naturally without predetermined direction or conscious deliberation and somehow bloom at just the right time and place.

Then others plot their development and advancement with meticulous precision. For centuries, class-based, profession-based, and individual-based prescriptions have guided people through specified sequences of learning followed by certain structured experiences or professional positions to some predetermined pinnacle of expertise, status, or authority. The education of a prince or preparation of a priest in earlier days, the making of a military man or the lockstep climb up the corporate ladder in modern times are examples of this approach to professional development.

Somewhere between risks of undirected growth and rigidity of prescribed patterns of development is the approach best suited to today's rapidly changing world and to the student affairs profession. Self-assessment is a primary method for cultivating a systematic, yet flexible, approach to staff development. It may be employed in many ways: through interest and aptitude inventories, checklists, performance rating forms, discussions with one's supervisor or colleagues, life or career planning workshops, or simply through quiet, but deliberate introspection. The approach suggested might be supplementary to any of the previous activities. Like many similar career "mapping" or self-assessment models, it is simply a tool to help focus analysis and guide thought processes. Because this kind of exercise is rarely easy for the individual, some such form or prefabricated process is often helpful.

As shown in Figure 14.1, the model posits two dimensions: (1) career time frame, and (2) types of personal and professional development needed. Time categories are the present (current position), approximately five years hence (perhaps the next professional position), and, finally, the more distant future or the individual's ultimate career ambition. These time frames readily translate into immediate, short-term, and long-term goals, and the model can help people examine relationships or, perhaps, discrepancies between their self-determined career objectives and level of development that is required to reach them.

Individuals, then, assess areas of knowledge, skills, and personal qualities needed for their present position and for the type of position they plan to attain in each of the other time frames. If a person is considering two or more career paths, then a matrix would be completed for each option and the results compared. It is important to distinguish between competencies and qualities already developed and those requiring further development.

A few words about developmental categories themselves may provide guidance for use of this model and also lay groundwork for examination of other components of staff development that bear some relationship to these developmental areas.

Knowledge, in this context, refers both to theoretical knowledge and to concrete information needed to fulfill various job responsibilities. Generally speaking, the more responsibility an individual assumes within an organizational structure, the broader the scope of knowledge required. For example, entry-level residence hall coordinators or student activity advisors need to know about the policies and procedures of their

Career Time Frame	Types of Personal and Professional Development Needed (List levels of expertise or functioning required to reach each career goal)		
	Knowledge	Skills	Personal Qualities
Current Position (immediate goals)			
Possible Next Position (short-term goals)			
Career Objective (long-term goals)			

Figure 14.1   Self-assessment model for staff development related to career objectives.

agencies and about specific resources available to them. In addition, they would also benefit from a basic knowledge of student development theory and group dynamics.

In order to move into higher positions, beginning student affairs professionals need to become familiar with workings of larger organizational units and develop a foundation of knowledge in such areas as supervision, financial management, and public relations. Through their experience in working with students, they also should have deepened their understanding of developmental principles, student characteristics, and problem-solving strategies.

Increasing professional responsibilities requires still broader knowledge of student affairs objectives, roles, and functions, as well as an in-depth understanding of particular areas—facilities management, food service operations, student financial aid, or political and legal ramifications of student affairs administration, for example. Knowledge of the organization, administration, traditions, and contemporary problems of postsecondary education also becomes increasingly important as one assumes greater responsibility within the profession. In short, as the scope of activity expands, so does the range of knowledge expected and required to be successful.

In terms of skill development, people often speak of sharpening or refining present abilities rather than of broadening or expanding total competencies, though both kinds of development may be required for career advancement. Skills are simply one's ability to do things that must be done—write letters and reports, communicate with a variety of constituent groups (students, colleagues, supervisors, faculty), speak before an audience, lead a committee, organize a publicity campaign, compose a handbook, prepare a questionnaire, interpret statistics, manage time, delegate responsibility, set goals—the list could go on. Skills may be very specific, like bookkeeping or menu-planning, or quite broad, like negotiating, counseling, or supervising. Some skills are used throughout a person's career, though it is to be expected that the quality of skill performance will be enhanced with experience. Other skills may be specific to a given level or type of work and thus be of little benefit in a different position.

Clearly, the first two developmental categories set forth in the model overlap at many points. Knowledge and skills often are so intertwined as to seem inseparable. How does one categorize something like public relations, for example, which involves both knowing and doing? However, because the point of the exercise is *self*-assessment, individuals can make such distinctions in a way that makes sense to them.

The difficulty is compounded by the third category, which is an aggregate of important intangibles. Personal qualities, including a variety of attitudes and values, are affected by one's knowledge and skills. Professionalism, for example, is a most important personal quality, but it is also one of the most difficult to define. It involves a seasoned integration of knowledge, skills, attitudes, values, and personality characteristics. (A comprehensive review of this issue was provided in Chapter 6.)

Equally complex are some of the other qualities likely to be included in this third category: self-confidence, assertiveness, tact, sensitivity to the feelings and intentions of others, loyalty, self-control, motivation, and the ability to work under pressure and manage stress, to integrate personal and professional values, and to achieve a balance between personal and professional goals.

Three observations, then, emerge from this survey of the major developmental categories to be considered in self-assessment. First, just as it is difficult in many instances to distinguish among the three categories, it is also difficult to distinguish between personal and professional development. Indeed, the two are never totally distinct. Improving one's skills in listening to others and in communicating effectively on the job, for example, is bound to have repercussions in one's personal life. Learning to control frustration or anger in personal circumstances will carry over into the way professional problems are negotiated. However specific a bit of knowledge, a skill, or even an attitude might be, the person is the one who integrates the knowledge, develops the skill, or assumes the attitude. Furthermore, the motivation for growth and the direction it takes may derive from relationships with family, friends, organizations, or interests completely apart from the job.

Second, self-assessment is not something to be done once and forgotten. It must be a continual process. The model suggested may provide a starting point leading to other techniques, or it may be reviewed, revised, or totally revamped periodically. Whatever the approach adopted, it must be recognized that few people grow and develop along the neat, tidy lines that models presuppose. Thus, the major prerequisite for self-assessment is self-awareness, keeping up with oneself, with shifts in interests, attitudes, and desires, as well as with growth in knowledge, skills, and experience.

Finally, in spite of efforts to focus on the individual's responsibility to assess strengths and weaknesses and to formulate personal and professional goals, most people need assistance in accomplishing these important tasks. Self-assessment is, in itself, a skill; it is not a capability that people inherit or are likely to acquire in school where assessment has traditionally been the prerogative of teachers. It can be approached in different ways, but the process of self-assessment will be most meaningful when individuals can incorporate information either from others' perceptions of them or when they can count on encouragement and support from others who have an interest in their personal and professional development.

So, again, the joint responsibility of the organization and the individual for professional development is underscored. Even the initial step, individual motivation and self-assessment, depends, to some extent, on the attitudes and actions of the organization. In most instances, the obvious and immediate link between the individual and the organization is the supervisor, the person within a given organizational structure to whom an individual reports.

Supervision and Performance Evaluation

As noted in Chapter 12, the term "supervision" has negative connotations for some student affairs professionals. It suggests monitoring, critiquing, or even disciplining actions often viewed as incongruous with a positive developmental philosophy. Most people generally prefer to think in terms of working *with* colleagues, rather than *for* superiors.

The term "evaluation," as applied to staff performance, is anathema not only among some student affairs administrators, but to managers in many other fields as well. If self-assessment is a skill that must be learned, asssessment of others is an even more sophisticated and demanding skill that few supervisors have been taught or even encouraged to learn. Unless glaring problems occur in staff performance, many people prefer to keep supervision to a minimum and to relegate performance evaluation to a perfunctory annual ritual.

Yet these two managerial functions, supervision and evaluation, are crucial to total professional development. Just as self-assessment is the starting point for the individual, performance evaluation is the most basic contribution of the organization to the development of its staff members. In Fisher's (1978) terms, there is an inherent relationship between personnel evaluation and professional development. While still usually treating them as discrete processes, higher education is beginning to consider both sides of this same coin, realizing that they are concurrent and continuously interacting processes, whether systematic or informal, and whether public or personal. (p. 2)

Perhaps one reason administrators often encounter resistance to performance evaluation is that the emphasis is usually placed on its formal, systematic aspect. Performance evaluation systems, however carefully designed and objectively implemented, can be threatening and counterproductive unless they are introduced into a climate in which assessment and development flourish year round. Supervisors are the key people in the creation of such a climate, and there are a number of strategies they can use for this purpose.

Effective supervision and evaluation require, first of all, awareness of people's strengths, weaknesses, problems, interests, and aspirations. Developing this kind of awareness does not require special interviews or extra supervisory efforts. It can be derived from informal conversation and observation that are part of the daily routine. It does require, however, attention, openness, and a genuine interest in the individuals supervised. In discussing how managers motivate people, Quick (1976) emphasized the importance of being sensitive to implicit as well as explicit needs that employees communicate about their responsibilities, work environment, and professional associates.

Second, by providing frequent informal feedback, both positive and negative, a supervisor can create a climate in which performance evaluation is expected and even welcomed. "Psychologists have found that feedback on performance should be given frequently, and the closer the feedback to the action, the more effective it is" (Glueck, 1978, p. 295). Such feedback should be friendly and genuine, rather than carping or patronizing. Moreover, it should be specific rather than general. Telling people that they are "doing a great job" or that their performance "leaves something to be desired" gives them very little to go on—or to grow on. Praise or constructive criticism focused on specific tasks or actions, on the other hand, shows people that someone notices and cares and thus provides incentive to repeat the positive or improve the negative performance.

Third, the use of staff meetings or special meetings to assess group performance and to establish group goals for a given period of time reinforces the importance of evaluation. If formal or informal assessment is regularly applied to the operation of the office or program as a whole, assessment of individual performance will seem more natural. Moreover, this strategy highlights the relationship between individual performance and the realization of organizational goals.

If a supervisor involves staff members in evaluating the overall performance of the organization, why should these people not also be involved in the evaluation of individual performance, including that of the supervisor? Peer evaluation, the fourth strategy, is highly touted by some and roundly rejected by others, but in a professional setting it is an effective method for obtaining constructive feedback. Indeed, Fisher (1978, p. 5) defined the evaluation process as a review of performance vis-a-vis goal expectations and individual potential through the use of appropriate assessment techniques that involve those persons with whom the individual interacts so as to determine areas of needed and desired professional development. (In addition, Chapter 12 identifies several evaluation formats.)

Inevitably, the perspective of supervisors will be based on the areas of job behavior they directly observe. Performance on important aspects of many student affairs positions may be more accurately assessed by others. Students, for example, can provide valuable feedback regarding the effectiveness of counseling, teaching, or advising functions. Likewise, subordinates can provide relevant information about their supervisors' leadership and delegation skills. Working with professional colleagues is an important part of most student affairs positions, and people can benefit from knowing how their performance is perceived by such colleagues.

A word of caution is in order concerning this strategy. Obviously, such feedback must be obtained through an evaluation process that provides for confidentiality and professionalism. The process works best in an atmosphere characterized by a high level of trust, the absence of staff rivalry, and shared interest in growth and development. With these prerequisites, a peer evaluation process can greatly benefit both supervisors and staff.

Performance evaluation contributes to staff development most directly when the input from both supervisors and peers, along with a person's self-assessment, is used for setting personal and professional goals. Most people perform more effectively when they are working towards specific objectives, a fact that has led to the implementation of elaborate goal-setting systems in both corporate and educational institutions. For most student affairs professionals, however, periodic conferences with supervisors will probably suffice to establish objectives and communicate organizational support. However formal or informal, such individual conferences should include position descriptions, general expectations, evaluation criteria, specific job assignments, working relationships, career aspirations, present job satisfaction, and, ultimately, goals or objectives agreed upon by both parties. A review of professional ethical standards relating to supervision and evaluation, such as those specified by the American College Personnel Association (1981), will yield additional guidance in these regards (See Appendix A).

Organizations and individuals move from goal-setting, to finding a means for achieving goals. Before leaving the role played by supervisors in staff development, some very specific developmental resources are commanded almost exclusively by supervisors. People need not plead that they cannot promote professional development because no resources have been made available for this function. Concern, commitment, and a bit of creativity are all the following techniques require:

1. Shifts in job assignments—trade-offs with other people or simply different emphases for a period of time—can often provide people with an opportunity to practice new skills or learn new functions.

2. Special projects to be accomplished during the summer months or delegation of leadership responsibility for a specific undertaking may expand the scope of a person's knowledge or experience, while providing useful service for the agency.

3. Appointment to an interdepartmental committee or task force may enable staff members to gain new perspectives, contacts, and visibility.

4. Availability of professional journals and current books in the office, coupled with informal discussion of ideas and information in the professional literature, will help people realize the significance of this avenue to development and encourage the habit of reading professional materials.

5. Devoting portions of staff meetings to developmental activities is an easy way to underscore the importance of professional development while, at the same time, imparting useful information and generating ideas regarding specific issues (Shaffer, 1972).

6. Role-modeling of important attitudes, behaviors, and skills by the supervisor is another valuable aid to development. Few supervisors will be expected to exhibit the full range of exemplary professional qualities and skills, but all supervisors should be aware that their staff members are more likely to do as they do than as they say.

7. Release time or rearrangement of schedules to enable people to take a course, attend a workshop, write for publication, or spend some time working in another office can contribute markedly to staff development.

8. Recognition in as many different forms as possible is one of the most effective ways to promote growth. While monetary rewards are not always available, other inexpensive forms of professional recognition may have more meaning. Success breeds success, and for most individuals recognition of achievement spurs further achievement.

Obviously, not all of these approaches are possible or desirable in all situations. The important point, however, is that fostering staff development is a major managerial responsibility for which supervisors at all levels should be held accountable.

Mentoring Relationships

Professional relationships, although seldom recognized as a formal mechanism for staff development, constitute the most powerful source for day-to-day learning and growth. In addition to the supervisory relationship, individual staff members have opportunities to form meaningful relationships with a full constellation of colleagues at various organizational levels. While the present discussion focuses on the impact of mentoring relationships, it is necessary to examine this complicated role in the context of other functions performed by professional colleagues.

In Figure 14.2 is provided a continuum of functional roles, adapted from Shapiro, Haseltine, and Rose (1978). At the left end of the continuum, colleagial relationships with peers in the organization tend to be informal and are characterized by the elements of mutuality and egalitarianism. The traditional roles of counselor, teacher, tutor, and advisor, while generally viewed as "caring relationships," begin to define movement toward associations in which one person in the dyad has greater knowledge or experience than the other. In general terms, the

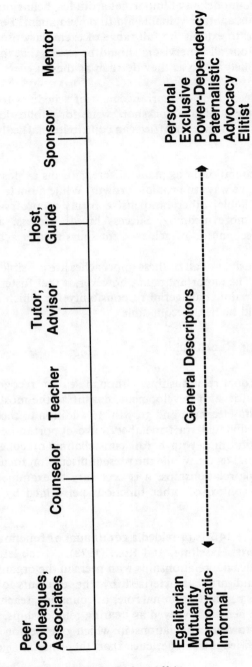

Figure 14.2 Functional roles within professional relationships.

Note. Based on and modified from Shapiro, Haseltine, & Rose, 1978.

shift of power within a relationship becomes increasingly evident as one approaches the right half of the continuum. A "host" or "guide," for example, plays a special role in introducing a new staff member to the traditions, resources, and values of the organization. This process initiates the organizational socialization of a younger, less experienced colleague. The role of sponsor implies an even greater degree of direct power and influence applied on behalf of the initiate. Sponsors will often use their experience and expertise to promote and advance the status of a younger colleague. Finally a mentor-protege relationship is recognized as being more intense, paternalistic, and personal than are the other roles. While this relationship contains mutual admiration, caring, and respect, the mentor is clearly the power figure who usually directs and controls the relationship. Levinson (1978) characterizes the mentor as representing skill, knowledge, virtue, and accomplishment, thereby exemplifying the qualities that the aspiring young professional wants to attain. The mentoring role often becomes so personal and intense that the mentor becomes an "internal figure" who provides a combination of love, admiration, and support while also serving as the novice's advocate and patron. This role, then, encompasses all of the functions on the continuum. Additional terms that have been used in this regard emphasize both the personal and paternalistic nature of the traditional mentoring relationship: coach, godfather, rabbi, mother-figure, or patron *(Business Week,* 1978; Collins & Scott, 1978; Fury, 1980; Hennig & Jardim, 1977; Kanter, 1977; Roche, 1979; Shapiro et al., 1978).

Thus, the traditional mentoring process, as it has evolved in the corporate world as well as within professional groups such as law, medicine, and education, carries some negative political and social implications as well as offers developmental advantages. In order to utilize mentoring relationships to enhance staff development efforts, it is important to recognize the possible liabilities and construct a system that will minimize their impact. Three of these disadvantages are glaring.

Perhaps the most destructive aspect of the traditional mentoring role is identified by Moore (1980) as the unspoken law of homogeneity-homophyly within self-selected relationships. Simply stated, this is the likelihood that individuals will recognize and promote the merits of talented young professionals who reflect values and attitudes acceptable to the mentor and to the current leaders. More often than not, this tendency includes commonality of sex, race, religion, and cultural background. Thus, the phenomenon often referred to as the "old boys' system" generally works to the advantage of people who think, behave, and look alike and to the detriment of people who do not fit the mold—women and ethnic minorities, for example. In discussing opportunities for promotion and career advancement, Scott (1979) advised women and minorities to create support systems for young staff members.

> There are a number of strategies that might be used, but perhaps the first and most important strategy involves finding a mentor or someone who takes a professional interest in your professional growth. (Scott, 1979, p. 37)

A second liability or disadvantage concerns the use of organizational and political power implicit in the traditional mentoring role. The same power that is used to advance a person's career can also become an insidious force that robs a young professional of self-reliance, personal autonomy, and unique personality traits. It is critical that developmental, collaborative relationships be fostered among student affairs colleagues that emphasize mutual learning and diminish the likelihood of dehumanizing partnerships, unhealthy dependencies, or outright manipulation.

A third disadvantage that requires attention is the elitist, undemocratic characteristic of the traditional mentor role. Colleagial relationships that support professional development must be structured on an egalitarian basis. Staff members within an organization must have equal opportunities to contribute to organizational goals.

Personal relationships among professional colleagues offer a dynamic mechanism for staff development, one which will probably operate whether or not it is designed or monitored with this objective in mind. But the benefits are likely to be greater, as well as more evenly distributed, if student affairs organizations deliberately foster helping relationships among individuals for the express purpose of assisting staff members to meet their personal and professional development needs. In short, an organization must minimize favoritism and harness the power inherent in traditional mentor relationships by reinforcing collaboration, sharing, and mutual problem-solving as organizational expectations for staff members.

Structured Learning Opportunities

Structured opportunities for professional development range from academic courses to staff meetings, from week-long workshops to brown bag discussion groups. According to Miller's (1975) survey, student affairs professionals rank off-campus professional development workshops as the most valuable type of structured program and academic courses offered by graduate education programs as the least valuable.

The typical kind of structured staff development program, however, is the short, one-shot session that is utilized for a vast range of organizational and professional topics. Whether as part of a professional conference in a distant city or a session conducted in the local student center, these programs have a number of common characteristics. In length, they range anywhere from an hour to three hours; usually they include a factual presentation or the introduction of new information plus some time for discussion or small group activities.

This more or less standard format for what many people associate almost exclusively with the term "staff development" has some definite advantages, as well as distinct drawbacks. Certainly, it offers people an expedient way to gain background information or new insights regarding a topic of interest. It usually requires no preparation on the part of participants, and they can often remain comfortably passive during the session itself. People seem to enjoy programs of this type both for the change of pace they offer and the knowledge or skill development that may be gleaned from them. Sometimes, of course, such programs lead to lively conversations in conference hotel hallways or at cafeteria tables on campus —and sometimes even to action.

One of the most serious drawbacks to this form of professional development, however, is lack of follow-up. Good intentions may exist, but too often upon returning to the job after a few hours or days of this kind of activity, the good intentions, along with the new ideas and information, begin to evaporate. Given the brevity of such programs and the fact that participants often vary greatly in the amount of prior knowledge they have of the subject, the content tends to be superficial and the impact short-lived.

In some instances, this inherent disadvantage is exacerbated by people's attitudes toward structured professional development programs. Some experienced professionals regard the opportunity to attend such programs (particularly those held at national and regional meetings) as a sort of fringe benefit, rather than as a means of fulfilling their obligation to learn and grow professionally. Others complain that staff development programs are not really relevant to their everyday work situations.

Sometimes, of course, this is not true; but often people fail to make the extra effort required to apply new knowledge, incorporate innovative approaches, or practice new job skills—or organizations fail to encourage and reward such effort.

Academic coursework may be the surest way to overcome some of the drawbacks associated with professional development sessions. Although this approach is stressed for people whose career advancement depends on advanced degrees, it is often overlooked as a means to enhance knowledge and skills for specific jobs. Business writing, accounting, public budgeting and finance, management, marketing, speech communication, personnel administration, and evaluation strategies are just a few of the courses available in most institutions that could contribute significantly to professional development, whether or not they apply to a degree program. Plans that provide for tuition subsidy or remission for staff members, of course, make academic courses an even more attractive option.

On-campus staff development programs, consisting for the most part of workshops and short information sessions, are becoming increasingly common. In their *Handbook on Staff Development in Student Affairs,* Beeler and Penn (1978) summarized a number of different models and provided detailed guidelines for the design, implementation, and evaluation of division-wide staff development programs. Low budget programs generally can be planned by an interdepartmental staff development committee utilizing campus and community resources, rather than external consultants (Brown, 1979) and can have a strong positive impact on staff morale (Wanzek & Canon, 1975). The extent to which they also contribute to genuine professional development depends on a number of individual and organizational variables. Following are a few suggestions for making local, on-campus staff development programs effective.

Integrate Staff Development with Organizational Objectives. Staff development programming should be explicitly linked to student affairs goals and priorities. Stamatakos and Oliaro (1972) maintained that "inservice development is more a *function* of an effective student personnel [sic] program than a service to staff members" (pp. 270-1). Staff development activities should grow directly from current organizational objectives and be integrated with divisional efforts to support the institutional mission and meet the expressed needs of students.

Although this particular suggestion may seem to give higher priority to organizational goals than to the interest of individuals, it can help bring the two together. Moreover, if workshops, coffee hour presentations or short, in-house courses focus on topics of immediate and well-known concern within student affairs (institutional budget, relations with faculty, improving retention of minority students, combatting alcohol abuse among students, affirmative action, and program evaluation), they are likely not only to be relevant to people's jobs, but also to garner the support of administrators. Deliberately planning, publicizing, and presenting staff development programs within the framework of student affairs goals and objectives can enhance both their appeal and their impact.

Relate Staff Development Programs to Self-assessment, Supervision, and Performance Evaluation. One approach to this task is to offer a series of self-assessment workshops at the beginning of the year to help people define their own professional development objectives and examine ways by which they might meet those objectives. A needs assessment form listing a number of possible topics for structured programs could then be completed to guide the staff development committee in program selection. Items on such a form might be derived from student affairs goals or from issues or problem areas identified by supervisors. If cooperation of student affairs managers and supervisors is forthcoming, staff development planning can also be linked to the performance evaluation process. The evaluation form itself, assuming it bears some relevance to actual performance expectations, can even be transformed into a needs assessment instrument on which supervisors and individuals can indicate needs for formal training. Only rarely is the process this explicit, but the principle is important. Additional means for linking the performance evaluation process with the planning of structured staff development programs should be explored.

Emphasize Comprehensive, In-depth Development Experiences. The mini-university format, for example, provides an opportunity to treat areas of knowledge and skill development in greater depth than the more typical one-shot session. This approach involves offering a series of short courses, each consisting of three or four sessions over a period of as many weeks and possibly including some reading assignments as well (Beeler, 1977; Meyerson, 1974; Wanzek & Canon, 1975). Course objectives need to be clearly spelled out in advance and participants need to make a commitment to attend all sessions. Obviously, the cooperation and support of supervisors are critical to the success of this kind of program.

Target Staff Development Programs to the Interests and Needs of Particular Staff Groups. Although some people maintain that staff morale is better served by making all staff development programs open to interested staff members, including clerical staff (Wanzek & Canon, 1975), this approach can result in a watered-down program and lack of participation and support by many professionals. Perhaps a mixed approach—provision of some well-tailored programs targeted to clerical staff, food service personnel, or executive staff, along with other more general programs open to everybody—offers the best solution to this problem.

Use the Retreat Format as an Effective Method for Combining Individual and Organization Development. Generally held off-campus for a period of 24 to 48 hours, retreats offer the advantage of intensity. At one end of a continuum is the task-centered session. A staff group may, for example, take up weekend residence in a resort or camp lodge for the primary purpose of evaluating a year's work, formulating goals, or engaging in long-range planning. Usually, their objective will be to return to campus with a comprehensive plan of action.

At the opposite end of the continuum are retreat formats that focus almost exclusively on process, on team-building and developing awareness of the human relationships that enhance or impede group functioning. A particularly imaginative model for this type of retreat is the "wilderness" or "adventure" program in which participants attempt to solve a physical problem or complete an unusual physical task requiring a high degree of teamwork (Schroeder, 1976). More common methods are those of laboratory education in which, as Reynolds (1980) pointed out, "the involvement level attained through relatively low personal risk required soon leads to intimate communication, cohesive group feelings, and positive feelings about the total experience" (p. 252). Provided a professional facilitator is used and the goals and parameters of the experience are understood in advance by all participants, this kind of retreat can provide invaluable learning.

Harvey, Helzer, and Young (1972) described a model near the midpoint of the continuum, a staff retreat focusing on both tasks and process. During a weekend program, small groups or teams explore specific issues in depth and develop detailed plans. At the same time, throughout the retreat, consultants use facilitative strategies to help participants get a better understanding of individual behavior and of the group process.

Regardless of the purpose or mode of a retreat, thorough planning and carefully designed follow-up are essential if the full potential for staff development is to be realized. In terms of time, energy, and money, retreats require a substantial commitment, but their developmental impact on both individuals and organizations can be dramatic.

Professional Participation, Service, and Contributions

A full range of developmental experiences is available to student affairs professionals through active involvement in state, regional, and national professional associations. Membership and participation in such organizations provide individuals with an identifiable professional community, as well as with opportunities to develop new competencies. Perhaps most importantly, professional associations deliver systematic exposure to the literature, research, and contemporary thought that constitute the body of knowledge that gives meaning and direction to the profession. Many professional development strategies can be created or facilitated through involvement in professional student affairs associations.

Convention, Conference, and Workshop Attendance. Many types of structured learning opportunities are typically available through annual conferences and regional workshops sponsored by professional associations. Conference programs and workshop presentations generally focus on five important areas that contribute to professional development: skill development, innovative programs and services for students, current research findings, the theory and philosophy of human development, and contemporary issues in postsecondary education. Consultants and presenters are identified nationally who have a high level of expertise as well as an experiential base different from that of local colleagues. Additionally, annual attendance at association conferences provides opportunities for interaction with a broad group of professional colleagues. This acquaintance process takes place in the structured learning activities that provide a forum for exchanging ideas and sharing concerns. Dialogue and interaction are also achieved through informal discussions and social gatherings where professional friendships are expanded and solidified. Such relationships create communication networks with colleagues on a national basis and can make a substantial contribution to an individual's professional development. They also contribute to a professional consciousness and a sense of identity with a broad community of colleagues who can provide the same type of supportive relationships that are available with institutional colleagues. In one study, this very experience, "discussions with student affairs colleagues at institutions other than my own," was ranked as the most helpful professional development activity by practicing administrators (Rhatigan & Crawford, 1978).

Individual Reading, Research, and Learning. Professional associations, through journals, learning packages, media aids, research reports, newsletters, and other professional publications, provide individuals with systematic exposure to current literature and research. Unfortunately, some student affairs practitioners rely almost entirely on experiential learning opportunities and fail to enhance their professional growth by implementing a personal program of reading and study. For instance, Rhatigan and Crawford (1978) reported that the six items on their survey involving professional reading received the lowest ratings as staff development activities.

Career Development and Placement. Typically, professional organizations provide a career planning and placement service both for members who are exploring new job opportunities and for those who are seeking candidates for positions at their institutions. Workshops for developing career-related skills such as self-assessment, resume preparation, and interviewing techniques are often also available at annual conferences.

Leadership Development. Since associations provide professional leadership for their constituents, they also challenge members to become involved, to accept leadership roles, and to share reponsibility for the organization's effectiveness. Such opportunities include task force membership, acting as chairperson for a standing committee, and actively seeking election as an executive officer. A large organization offers literally hundreds of possibilities for members to exercise their special talents or simply to devote time and energy on behalf of their colleagues. Such contributions and activities not only generate individual growth and renewal, but also offer a unique personal reward and the feeling of participation in the overall direction and movement of the profession.

Professional Contributions. As individuals mature professionally and develop areas of special expertise, opportunities to share their knowledge or insights become yet another type of professional development. Presenting a program or delivering a paper in the context of a conference or workshop, for example, requires a new set of skills and reflects a still deeper professional commitment. Developing research and writing skills that culminate in professional publications is another method of sharing knowledge that also produces significant professional growth for the individual. Finally, an individual can contribute expertise to colleagues by serving as a consultant or external evaluator for another institution. Each of these activities involves an instructional or sharing process that always creates growth for the teacher as well as for the learner.

Thus, various levels of involvement within the structure of professional associations provide rich sources for individual staff development. These learning experiences touch all of the basic objectives of professional development, and must be recognized as a major component for a total staff development program. Before accepting a position, an individual must clearly understand the institution's posture toward active participation in professional associations, the level of financial support available to attend meetings, and the degree to which professional contributions beyond the institutional structure are encouraged or rewarded.

ISSUES AND IMPLICATIONS FOR THE FUTURE

A number of political, social, economic, and educational issues affect staff development for student affairs professionals. While some of these concerns have been identified in appropriate sections of this chapter, additional issues that transcend specific staff development components are addressed in this section. Five general topics have implications for the future development of student affairs staff members.

Self-Directed Learning

As summarized by Cross (1980), the UNESCO definition of lifelong learning contains three distinct elements: (1) the need to restructure the existing educational system, (2) the utilization of community resources and other agencies in addition to traditional educational institutions, and (3) the concept of education enabling individuals to become self-directed, independent learners and active agents of their own growth and development. The latter concept is closely related to the notion that individual motivation and self-assessment form the cornerstone for staff development. Learning experiences identified with the other four developmental components derive meaning only to the extent that participants are *self-directed* in pursuit of professional growth. With this understanding, student affairs organizations must encourage, facilitate, and reward staff development activities, but resist the temptation to direct or prescribe the developmental experiences of their members.

Professional Standards

The present movement to establish standards for the accreditation of preparation programs, as well as prescribed in-service education requirements, is having an impact on the student affairs profession (American College Personnel Association, 1979; Stamatakos, 1980). Without a full discussion of the merits of such guidelines for the growing profession, it is fair to project that the establishment of preparation and continuing education standards will have a direct influence on staff development efforts. A passage from recent legislation in the State of Nebraska provides an example:

> In order to insure that all nurses have sufficient scientific and practical knowledge to continue to practice nursing, no license to practice nursing shall be renewed after January 1, 1983, unless the nurse has within the preceding five years engaged in the practice of nursing for a minimum of two hundred hours and completed twenty hours of . . . continuing education courses approved by the Board of Nursing. (State of Nebraska, 1980)

Thus, in this instance, twenty hours of Continuing Education Units (CEU) have been mandated as compulsory professional development. While such a requirement does not seem too stringent, this standard means that the individual choosing professional development experiences will feel obligated to enroll for workshops that have been approved by the Board of Nursing and assigned appropriate CEU credits. In practice, then, Nebraska nurses now have a restricted choice of learning opportunities, only approved courses. To some degree, they become a captive audience for particular professional development experiences regardless of their personal goals. The point is that professional standards for student affairs practitioners will have to be carefully considered in relation to self-assessment strategies, the concept of self-directed learning, and the relative merits of institutional opportunities as compared with approved experiences conducted by external agencies.

Institutional Commitment and Resources

As late as 1975, 80 percent of the respondents in a national survey of student affairs staff members reported that their institution had no definitive policy regarding staff development responsibilities or expectations (Miller, 1975). This same sample indicated that an average of 87 percent of their professional development budgets was utilized to underwrite staff attendance at conventions, meetings, and workshops. Somewhat surprisingly, attendance at state, regional, and national conventions received low ratings on relative value and benefit when compared with other types of staff development experience. The conclusion that participation in national conferences is the most visible and obvious activity associated with professional development at many institutions, even though national conferences are recognized as costly and not particularly effective in meeting developmental needs, is difficult to escape. A failure seems to exist among student affairs organizations to identify, assess, and implement systematically full-scale staff development programs that utilize strategies associated with all five components identified. The current norm for institutional efforts relies too heavily on structured learning opportunities and particularly off-campus conference and workshop attendance. The potential "learning power" inherent in the strategies of self-assessment, supervision and evaluation, and mentor relationships remains relatively untapped. Staff development components provide opportunities to integrate individual and organizational objectives and offer great potential to achieve self-directed organizational renewal. Campus student affairs organizations should consciously assess their needs, evaluate the utility of each staff development component to meet established objectives, and deliberately allocate available resources accordingly. No educational evidence exists to suggest that an annual trip to a national conference is the most advantageous use of staff development time and dollars.

Structured Learning Experiences and Contemporary Topics

When asked what type of off-campus workshop they viewed as most advantageous for meeting staff development needs, leaders of one national association who were surveyed produced the following description: a short (one-half to one full day), low-cost (registration fee of approximately $25), drive-in, regional workshop (Ender, 1979). The direct message of this response is (1) maximize the learning experience by providing an extensive, quality program and (2) reduce the expense by minimizing related costs including the need for overnight lodging, extra meals, and social events.

Somewhat contrary to this view is the current practice of various associations, consulting groups, and commercial agencies of planning and expertly marketing week-long workshops often conducted in an attractive city or resort area. Advertisements in the *Chronicle of Higher Education,* for example, and the daily barrage of unsolicited brochures that arrive by mail offer ample testimony that staff development experiences, cassette programs, and written materials are readily available for individuals and organizations with healthy budgets. Without a prolonged discussion, the point must be made that high cost and high quality are not necessarily related. Before committing staff development dollars, student affairs administrators should carefully review and evaluate a given program in terms of its objectives, proposed content, and the reputation of its presenters, as well as examine the comparative cost of similar experiences. It is possible that there are people with equivalent expertise on one's own campus. Perhaps more discriminating decisions could reduce disappointments and provide a broader range of experiences for staff members without additional expenditures.

The same study (Ender, 1979) asked student affairs leaders to identify specific topical areas that should be addressed in professional development workshops. The most frequent topics in each of four areas were as follows:

Management: stress management, time management, confrontation and conflict management, and organizational development.

Student Services: academic advising, career planning, and orientation programs.

Student Development: practical application of developmental theories, assessment strategies, goal setting, and knowledge of student development theory.

General: leadership development, nontraditional students, learning center administration, commuter students, and women's programs.

Many traditional areas within student affairs are absent from these lists. Staff supervision and budgeting, for example, are not priority concerns within the management area. Traditional service and program offices such as student activities, residence education, judicial affairs, and placement are not included among the top choices. Even international student issues, in spite of dramatic worldwide conflicts and concerns, are not identified as major topics for staff development experiences.

A second implication is that a number of these topics relate directly or indirectly to a major contemporary problem for postsecondary education—the satisfaction and, therefore, retention of students—which has been given impetus by declining enrollments. Programs such as academic advising, career planning, orientation, and learning centers are all related to this issue. Specific references to nontraditional, commuting, and women students as target groups also relate to this one overwhelming concern. A final observation is the conspicuous absence of references to ethnic minority students on campus and the important area of cross-cultural communications and relationships.

The Ender (1979) study serves as a reminder regarding the importance of obtaining systematic needs assessments from the constituents to be served through staff development programs. One cannot hope to implement a successful program around traditional topics, what one thinks our colleagues should experience, or a few key buzz-words that happen to be in vogue. Thus, whether the design is for a network of regional workshops or for on-campus experiences at one institution, essential points are to establish current interests and needs, solicit feedback, and provide a mechanism for program evaluation.

Personal and Professional Development

Two trends in society combine to produce a general expectation that job-related benefits and activities should address the total scope of a person's life. First is the growing realization that the pressures of employment have a direct impact upon a person's health, emotional well-being, and family relationships. As Cross (1981) suggested, people feel entitled to a higher quality of life and are "opting for the blended lifeplan which permits learning, work, and leisure to go on concurrently" (p. 9). The second trend is a set of economic and situational dynamics that have created increased stress for some individuals. Underemployment, a lack of career mobility, and the necessity to accept split appointments or positions that demand multiple roles are all examples of job conditions that contribute to feelings of hostility, frustration, and entrapment, all symptomatic of what has been called "burnout." When these conditions prevail, staff development efforts may be perceived by colleagues as one way to address important issues that affect their total lives—personal and professional. Thus, skill development in such areas as stress management, relaxation techniques, and exercise programs should receive some attention. Just as a separation of individual and organizational development can be attempted but is impossible to achieve, the separation of personal and professional issues as distinct entities is most difficult if not impossible.

REFERENCES

American College Personnel Association. Standards for the preparation of counselors and other personnel services specialists at the masters degree level. Mimeographed Report, February 1979.

American College Personnel Association. Statement of ethical and professional standards. *Journal of College Student Personnel,* 1981, *22,* 184-9.

Beeler, K.D. Professional staff development. *Journal of College Student Personnel,* 1976, *17,* 253-4.

Beeler, K.D. Mini-U: A promising model for student affairs staff development. *NASPA Journal,* 1977, *14,* 38-43.

Beeler, K.D., & Penn, J.R. *A handbook on staff development in student affairs.* Corvallis, OR: Oregon State University Book Stores, 1978.

Brown, R.D. Professional development and staff development: The search for a metaphor. In R.P. Wanzek (Ed.), *Staff development.* DeKalb, IL: Northern Illinois University, 1977.

Brown, S.S. Student affairs staff development: A systems approach on a shoestring. Paper presented at National Association of Student Personnel Administrators Conference, Washington, DC, April 9, 1979.

Business Week. Women finally get mentors of their own. October 1978, pp. 74-80.

Collins, E.G.C., & Scott, P. Everyone who makes it has a mentor. *Harvard Business Review,* July-August 1978, pp. 89-101.

Cox, D.W. Professional staff development. Mimeographed course outline. Oxford, MS: University of Mississippi, 1979.

Cross, K.P. Sounding the call for the student personnel profession in the 1980's. Paper presented at the American College Personnel Association Convention, Boston, April 1980.

DeCoster, D.A., & Mable, P. Residence education: Purpose and process. In D.A. DeCoster & P. Mable (Eds.), *Personal education and community development in college residence halls.* Washington, DC: American College Personnel Association, 1980.

Dewey, J. *Democracy and education.* New York: Macmillan, 1916.

Ender, K.L. Interest and planning survey. Mimeographed report for the Professional Development and Consultation Committee, American College Personnel Association, 1979.

Fisher, C.F. The evaluation and development of college and university administrators. In J.A. Shotgren (Ed.), *Administrative development in higher education.* Richmond, VA: Dietz Press, 1978.

Fury, K. Mentor mania. *Savvy,* 1980, pp. 42-7.

Glueck, W.F. *Personnel: A diagnostic approach.* Dallas: Business Publications, 1978.

Harvey, V.P., Helzer, T.A. & Young, J.W. The retreat: Keystone staff development. *NASPA Journal,* 1972, *9,* 274-8.

Hennig, M., & Jardim, A. *The managerial women.* New York: Anchor Press, 1977.

Kanter, R.M. *Men and women of the corporation.* New York: Basic Books, 1977.

Kurpius, D.J. Organization development, systems analysis, and planned change. In C.H. Foxley (Ed.), *New directions for student services: Applying management techniques* (No. 9). San Francisco: Jossey-Bass, 1980.

Leafgren, F. Student development through staff development. In D.A. DeCoster & P. Mable (Eds.), *Personal education and community development in college residence halls.* Washington, DC: American College Personnel Association, 1980.

Levinson, D.J., Darrow, C.N., Klein, E.B., Levinson, M.H., & McKee, B. *The seasons of a man's life.* New York: Ballantine Books, 1978.

Mable, P. A model for staff development: A time for growth. Unpublished manuscript, 1979.

Mable, P., Terry, M.J., & Duvall, W.H. Student development through community development. In D.A. DeCoster & P. Mable (Eds.), *Personal education and community development in college residence halls.* Washington, DC: American College Personnel Association, 1980.

Meyerson, E. Mini-university provides staff training for a big university. *College and University Business,* 1974, *56,* 31-3.

Meyerson, E. Staff development. Paper presented at the Arizona Association of Community College Student Personnel Administrators Conference, Tempe, AZ, November 1975.

Miller, T.K. Staff development activities in student affairs programs. *Journal of College Student Personnel,* 1975, *16,* 258-64.

Miller, T.K. Professional preparation and development of residence educators. In D.A. DeCoster & P. Mable (Eds.), *Personal education and community development in college residence halls.* Washington, DC: American College Personnel Association, 1980.

Moore, K.M. What to do until the mentor arrives. Paper presented at National Association of Women Deans, Administrators, and Counselors Convention, Cincinnati, April 1980.

Nejedlo, R.J. Making staff development happen through organizational renewal. In R.P. Wanzek (Ed.), *Staff development.* DeKalb, IL: Northern Illinois University, 1977.

Quick, T.L. *Understanding people at work.* New York: Executive Enterprises Publications, 1976.

Reynolds, E.L. Laboratory education: Methods for personal development and skill building. In D.A. DeCoster & P. Mable (Eds.), *Personal education and community development in college residence halls.* Washington, DC: American College Personnel Association, 1980.

Rhatigan, J.J., & Crawford, A.E. Professional development preferences of student affairs administrators. *NASPA Journal,* 1978, *15*(3), 45-52.

Richardson, R.C. Staff development: A conceptual framework. *Journal of Higher Education,* 1975, *46,* 303-11.

Roche, G.R. Much ado about mentors. *Harvard Business Review,*   January-February 1979, pp. 14-28.

Schroeder, C.C. Adventure training for residence assistants. *Journal of College Student Personnel,* 1976, *17,* 11-5.

Scott, P.B. Moving up the institutional hierarchy: Some suggestions for young minority and women professionals from the notebook of a novice. *Journal of the National Association for Women Deans, Administrators, and Counselors,* 1979, *43*(2), 34-9.

Shaffer, R.H. Staff development—key to survival. *NASPA Journal,* 1972, *9,* 261-2.

Shapiro, E.D., Haseltine, F.P., & Rose, M.P. Moving up: Role models, mentors, and the patron system. *Sloan Management Review,* 1978, *19*(8), 51-8.

Sheehy, G. *Passages: Predictable crises of adult life.* New York: E.P. Dutton and Co., 1974.

Stamatakos, L.D. Student affairs progress toward professionalism: Recommendations for action. *Journal of College Student Personnel,* 1980, *22,* 105-12, 197-207.

Stamatakos, L.D., & Oliaro, P.M. In-service development: A function of student personnel. *NASPA Journal,* 1972, *9,* 269-73.

State of Nebraska. Laws governing nursing (LB847). Lincoln: Author, 1980.

Tripp, P.A. Student personnel work—whence it came and wither it may be going. In R.P. Wanzek (Ed.), *Staff development.* DeKalb, IL: Northern Illinois University, 1977.

Wanzek, R.P., & Canon, H. Professional growth in student affairs. *Journal of College Student Personnel,* 1975, *16,* 418-20.

SUGGESTED READINGS

Beeler, K.D., & Penn, J.R. *A handbook on staff development in student affairs*. Corvallis, OR: Oregon State University Book Store, 1978.

Leafgren, F. Student development through staff development. In D.A. DeCoster & P. Mable (Eds.), *Personal education and community development in college residence halls*. Washington, DC: American College Personnel Association, 1980.

Miller, T.K. Professional preparation and development of residence educators. In D.A. DeCoster & P. Mable (Eds.), *Personal education and community development in college residence halls*. Washington, DC: American College Personnel Association, 1980.

Reynolds, E.L. Laboratory education: Methods for personal development and skill building. In D.A. DeCoster & P. Mable (Eds.), *Personal education and community development in college residence halls*. Washington, DC: American College Personnel Association, 1980.

Richardson, R.C. Staff development: A conceptual framework. *Journal of Higher Education*, 1975, *46*, 303-11.

Wanzek, R.P. (Ed.). *Staff development*. DeKalb, IL: Northern Illinois University, 1977.

Dwight O. Douglas was born and reared in Mt. Carmel, Illinois. He received the B.S. in education and M.Ed. in guidance and counseling from Eastern Illinois University. His Ed.D. in educational psychology and guidance was earned at the University of Tennessee.

He has had experience in residence hall programs and administration at Eastern Illinois University, University of Tennessee, and University of Georgia, where he also has taught. At the University of Georgia he has served as Director of Housing, Associate Dean of Students, Dean of Students, and Vice-President for Student Affairs, a position he currently holds. He is active in youth work and has held regional office in several community organizations. Dr. Douglas currently serves as chairperson of the University System of Georgia Student Affairs Deans and Vice-Presidents and is the National Association for Student Personnel Administrators State Director for Georgia.

Chapter 15

FISCAL RESOURCE MANAGEMENT: BACKGROUND AND RELEVANCE FOR STUDENT AFFAIRS

Dwight O. Douglas

The ability to manage programs, allocate resources, and justify increased funding is receiving greater attention than ever before. Staff in student affairs need to be knowledgeable of management applications in order to achieve equitable allocations of increasingly scarce institutional resources. As institutions of higher education continue to grow and reevaluate priorities, the cost effectiveness of student affairs programs may be called into question. Success in fiscal management will determine scope and ultimate success of the total student affairs operation.

While competence in the developmental and programmatic aspects of the field is necessary for the student affairs professional, knowledge of management theory and technical fiscal procedures is also required. Because of specialized technical knowledge and managerial skills required for implementing certain services such as housing and food service, some college presidents have placed these areas under business or fiscal affairs in their organizations. On other campuses where the student affairs professionals have evidenced high levels of management skills, they are viewed by campus fiscal officers as partners in campus management. Acceptance is particularly notable in colleges where student affairs has responsibility for the recruiting and admissions program so essential to the institution's survival.

Student affairs professionals, with their understanding of human dynamics and interest in developmental processes of students, link two critical areas of the institution— academic affairs and business affairs. Nevertheless, some misunderstanding of roles of student affairs professionals often occurs.

Berry (1976) and Crookston (1976) both noted that terminology is still a problem in student affairs. Confusion continues as to specific meanings for terms such as student life, student development, student personnel services, and student affairs, because these terms are often not reflective of actual functions performed. Miller and Prince (1976) reflected a view of student affairs practice that emphasized student development and called for facilitating achievment of higher levels of cultural awareness, personal value systems, self-awareness, interpersonal skills, and community responsibility. Management skills are needed by student affairs administrators to enable them to create environments where student development can flourish. Policy formulation, technical knowledge, and fiscal resource management need to be recognized.

Concerning fiscal resource management, the suggestion has been made that the business office's golden rule is "those who have the gold, rule." From a student affairs perspective, effective leadership must marshal resources to accomplish tasks of enhancing cognitive and personality development in students.

The lack of adequate resources for both personnel and operating expenses has been one of the major problems associated with student affairs administration over the years. Although considerable information is available about funding, most of it concerns managing resources. Minimal information, on the other hand, is available to explain the processes that result in determining funding levels, to outline detailed strategies for justifying increased funding, or to show a need that is greater than *other justified needs* in the institution. Current practices of fiscal resources management suggest that management involves a combination of resources and activities so as to produce a desired outcome (Harpel, 1976). Today's successful student affairs administrator also must be able to find ways to increase resources by generating additional income, altering institutional budgets, or using a combination of the two.

Although student affairs units may receive proportional increases similar to other institutional units, the actual cost of doing business may be greater for student affairs units such as financial aid, admissions, and registration because of the rate of inflationary increase involved in these activities. For example, because of increasing expenses for recruitment such as postage, printing, and travel, a reasonable budget fund increment only increases the real financial deficit and requires additional cost cutting measures to maintain past levels of activity.

Harpel (1976) noted that student affairs administrators are particularly vulnerable to criticism concerning management skills because student affairs functions historically have been justified more on idealistic and humanistic grounds than on tangible evidence of impact or results. For years the most *successful* justification for funds, as opposed to the *best* justification, was based on the role of the institution acting in place of the parent, not on the actual needs of students for developmental programs or services.

Often, the relative lack of importance assigned to student development programming by institutional leaders reflects their limited understanding of this important area and limits the likelihood for larger proportions of institutional resources being invested in student affairs. A greater understanding of student affairs functions is needed by the collegiate community. Student affairs professionals have responsibility to the educational process involved. The successful student affairs administrator is one who has a thorough understanding of the institution's budgeting process, has the capacity to inform others of the importance of student affairs, and utilizes technical management skills to acquire resources essential to accomplish its mission.

BUDGETS AS MANAGEMENT TOOLS

One of the best and most effective management tools is a budget representing the placement of funds in categories designed to achieve goals of the institution. Because of institutional systems, state laws, traditions, and types of educational missions, the budgeting process may vary from institution to institution. Budgeting is to be viewed as a continuous activity of allocating funds to meet changing requirements and priorities.

A common method for budgetary change is the budget amendment. This is an institutional form that, when approved, changes categories or amounts of funds as originally allocated. A misconception regarding permanence of budget cycles hinders far-ranging planning. According to Barber,

> budget considerations really begin every time a planning decision is made, or every time a planning decision is altered to respond to the effects of changing social, economic, and other conditions which cannot be anticipated in the development of the original budget.
>
> A change or alteration of a plan requires a budget action to adjust the allocation of resources. Like sights on a rifle, budgeting serves to direct an aim (planning) . . . if the aimer moves, or if external conditions change (such as a windage change), the sights on a rifle have to be adjusted to provide for the unexpected effects or the original aim will not hit the mark. The same is true of the effects of changing circumstances on original budgetary priorities and cost estimates—hence, the need for amendments to an original budget. (1974, p. 1)

The exact definition of *budget* or *budgeting* depends on whether one conceives the term as specific or general. Budgets are established for various types of projects that require specific treatments. But the word *budget* itself also is used in an overall generic sense. The National Association of College and University Business Officers (1974) defined a budget as *a statement of proposed expenditures for a fixed period or for a specific project or program and as a proposed means of financing expenditures.*

For the purposes of this chapter such a definition is accurate in terms of the tangible product. However, this definition does not include prior or established funds or the thought processes leading up to or involving these funds. A budget, therefore, is a tool to be used as a yardstick by which activity toward a goal can be measured. In most instances, this measurement is from a previously justified point rather than a reconsideration of what constituted the original justification. The yearly allocation of new resources into specific budgets represents changing priorities of the institution on a continuing basis. Much of this allocation, however, often is based on annualizing expenses, or prorating increases, rather than resulting from decisions regarding pre-established beginning points or establishing new points of departure.

For budgets to be used as planning tools in an optimal sense, one should view the process as having two parts: the formulation of the budget and the continuous analysis of how the desired results are being achieved. For the first purpose, reviewing recent data at the time of budget preparation is desirable. A routine mechanism in the budget preparation cycle allows the current year's budget and expenses to be available for review as well as the expenses of the immediate previous year. This review provides a logical framework from which to plan. However, this approach has at least three disadvantages. First, the approach is based on the assumption that current expenses and programs need annualizing. Second, budget preparation occurs during the current year, and, therefore, any comparison with the current year is incomplete, thus requiring reliance on the previous year. The third disadvantage is that some atypical expense may have affected the base either up or down, thus making application of percentage on the most recent complete year impractical.

The main purpose for budgeting is to provide financial information about a program or rate of achievement toward a goal. Preparation of the budget from a departmental standpoint involves determining what is needed or desired for the coming year. Additional items of expenditure are reviewed through the administrative hierarchy, evaluated, consolidated, and put into an order of priority at each administrative level and then presented at an institution-wide budget conference. When the spectrum of requests has been heard, decisions for allocations or partial allocations can be made. This process allows the adjustment of funds without annualizing the expense level for those areas thought immediately most important. Specific restrictions or modifications peculiar to a particular budget type should be considered in this process.

FINANCIAL STATEMENTS
AS MANAGEMENT TOOL

A second management tool is the financial statement which helps monitor how the desired results are being utilized toward a given objective. Too often this part of the program simply is subject to the amount of funds originally allocated or made available at a later time.

Once a budget is approved and the fiscal year (FY) progresses, keeping an exact account of how much money is available, how much has been obligated, and how the spending for the current year compares to a previous year is difficult in most budgetary systems. Statements of income and expense are developed to supply this necessary information.

Statements of income and expense reflect accrued income and expenditures and provide current information with which to update plans continuously. Oversimplified, these documents ordinarily are prepared monthly and compare on both a dollar and a percentage basis the relative amount of income and expenses received and expended for that month and for the year up to the date prepared. These totals can be compared with each month of the previous year or with the previous year-to-date totals to capture an overall perspective of the relative relationships of one month or one year to the previous month or year. Knowledge of the sum of expenses, the amount of income, and the cost of planned expenditures allows goals to be adjusted at any time.

The most frequently used statements appear in monthly reports prepared by the chief business officer, and in public institutions are used as part of a system or legislative report. The major value of these reports is that they express the situation in the simplest terms for external agencies and for general internal use. These reports are not as valuable for specific internal planning, however.

For the purposes of illustration, a residence hall budget and a corresponding financial statement can be analyzed. Figure 15.1 provides a sample of a monthly statement of operations for a residence hall. As the residence hall rents are deposited, the appropriate residence hall account is credited. Thus, the August and September monthly financial reports would show an excess of income over expenditures. For the uninformed reader this operating gain would appear to be a large profit, which might suggest that rates were set too high, funds were available for other purposes, or no rent increase would be necessary the following year. Analysis of the same type of financial report in February also could show that a large profit was realized. Reference to Figure 15.1 shows what might appear to be a 30 percent operating gain. Realistically, three income periods—Summer, Fall, and Winter Quarter; or summer, first semester, and second semester—were realized in the income category, but only seven of the twelve monthly expenses were reflected in the expense category. Subsequent monthly statements would show larger increases in expenses than in income until June when income for the year and expenses for the year will even out for a one year budget.

| | YEAR TO DATE | | | | | |
REVENUE	ACTUAL FY '98	%	BUDGET FY '99	%	ACTUAL FY '99	%
Student Rentals	2,253,468.81	92.2	2,483,937.00	93.7	2,445,102.60	93.6
Forfeited Deposits	27,883.75	1.1	29,102.00	1.1	22,319.00	.9
Special Groups	70,391.14	2.9	34,800.00	1.3	44,743.77	1.7
Vending Commissions	34,984.79	1.4	47,912.00	1.8	34,062.35	1.3
Laundry Commissions	8,737.84	.4	54,299.00	2.1	5,545.43	.2
Washer/Dryer Revenue	47,636.64	1.9			60,736.10	2.3
Other	1,452.31	.1			1,064.20	
TOTAL REVENUE	2,444,555.28	100.0	2,650,050.00	100.0	2,613,573.45	100.0
OPERATING EXPENSE						
Salaries	260,686.18	10.7	316,356.00	11.9	303,510.70	11.6
Temporary Wages	445,963.43	18.2	337,867.00	12.7	346,640.11	13.2
Employee Meals	14,039.30	.6	9,406.00	.4	2,178.22	.1
Staff Benefits	36,632.35	1.5	36,938.00	1.4	33,050.37	1.3
Supplies & Printing	56,001.46	2.3	62,284.00	2.3	52,630.80	2.0
Laundry	8,690.30	.4	11,792.00	.5	6,527.15	.2
Maintenance & Repairs	184,726.70	7.6	245,366.00	9.3	225,293.17	8.6
Utilities	287,221.65	11.7	321,363.00	12.1	321,164.94	12.3
Equipment	3,430.80	.1	23,839.00	.9	13,412.00	.5
Telephone	107,083.64	4.4	145,868.00	5.5	143,111.49	5.5
Insurance	14,050.83	.6	31,576.00	1.2	28,108.88	1.1
Travel	1,405.05				122.02	
Debt Service	101,095.00	4.1	101,636.00	3.9	100,365.75	
TOTAL EXPENSE	1,521,026.69	62.2	1,644,291.00	62.0	1,576,115.60	60.3
OPERATING GAIN (LOSS)	923,528.59	37.8	1,005,759.00	38.0	1,037,457.85	39.7

Figure 15.1 Monthly operations statement for a residence hall.

| | MONTH | | | | | |
REVENUE	ACTUAL FY '98	%	BUDGET FY '99	%	ACTUAL FY '99	%
Student Rentals	35,945.85	92.8	50,350.00	95.7	45,269.00	93.7
Forfeited Deposits	424.00	1.0			324.00	.8
Special Groups	502.00	1.3			158.50	.3
Vending Commissions	774.42	2.0	1,240.00	2.4	1,031.67	2.1
Laundry Commissions	155.78	.4	1,020.00	1.9	70.95	.1
Washer/Dryer Revenue	953.60	2.5			1,424.90	2.9
Other	19.55				44.90	.1
TOTAL REVENUE	38,775.19	100.0	52,610.00	100.0	48,323.92	100.0

OPERATING EXPENSES

	ACTUAL FY '98	%	BUDGET FY '99	%	ACTUAL FY '99	%
Salaries	5,365.01	13.8	6,376.00	12.0	6,233.77	12.9
Temporary Wages	6,497.11	16.8	5,048.00	9.6	5,074.66	10.5
Employee Meals	(41.53)	(.1)	100.00	.2		
Staff Benefits	454.18	1.2	545.00	1.0	586.34	1.2
Supplies & Printing	651.63	1.7	1,275.00	2.4	529.68	1.1
Laundry			226.00	.4		
Maintenance & Repairs	2,070.68	5.3	2,826.00	5.4	3,187.85	6.6
Utilities	4,422.90	11.4	5,085.00	9.7	4,636.92	9.6
Equipment						
Telephone	2,533.30	6.5	3,342.00	6.4	3,578.42	7.4
Insurance	298.90	.8	370.00	.7	370.00	.8
Travel						
Miscellaneous						
TOTAL EXPENSES	22,252.18	57.4	25,193.00	47.9	24,197.64	
OPERATING GAIN (LOSS)	16,523.01	42.6	27,417.00	52.1	24,126.28	
Less: Other Expenses						
Administrative Charge	1,600.00	4.1	2,399.00			
Debt Service	2,424.00	6.3	7,574.00			
Sub-Total	4,024.00	10.4				
NET GAIN (LOSS)	12,499.01					

Figure 15.2   Residence hall statement of operations (February FY '99).

	YEAR-TO-DATE					
FY 2000 BUDGET	ACTUAL FY '98	%	BUDGET FY ''99	%	ACTUAL FY '99	%
369,700.00	184,720.20	85.7	229,350.00	92.3	210,150.00	90.4
4,200.00	4,721.00	2.2	3,150.00	1.3	3,144.00	1.4
5,300.00	15,080.00	7.0	4,600.00	1.9	7,228.50	3.1
10,000.00	5,069.97	2.4	6,200.00	2.5	4,513.10	
8,200.00	712.47	.3	5,090.00	2.0	375.87	
	5,066.10				6,856.25	
	107.91				153.04	.1
397,400.00	215,477.65	100.0	248,390.00	100.0	232,420.76	100.0
63,138.00	34,094.07	15.8				
62,931.00	47,608.57	22.1				
1,080.00	2,935.34	1.4				
6,100.00	3,372.85					
12,750.00	6,193.65					
2,260.00	767.82					
29,880.00	13,821.44					
52,512.00						
3,016.00						
33,420.00						
3,700.00						

Some institutions compensate for this disparity by holding the income in a single account and crediting the respective residence hall accounts by a predetermined percentage on a monthly basis. This accrual method does have the merit of allowing checks of insufficient funds to clear and refunds to be processed, but the income accrued is credited to a holding account rather than the account of the originating agency. The elimination of a holding account results in an income being credited sporadically, but actual activity can be compared between financial statements of different months and of the same months of different years.

A desirable use of an accrual statement is to take the budget amount for the year and allocate both in terms of income and expenses in increments reflecting the actual desired income and spending throughout the budget period. The analysis that then can be made of comparable timeframes in terms of actual income and expenses can be used to determine if optional expenses can be incurred. The comparisons are illustrated in Figure 15.2.

Actual revenue for the month of February was greater than the actual revenue for FY '98 but not as great as had been anticipated for FY '99.

The operating gain for the month was greater than FY '98 but not as great as had been anticipated for the budget of FY '99.

On a year to date basis the *revenue* was less than anticipated.

On a year to date basis the *operating expenses* were less than expected.

On a year to date basis the *net gain* was less than expected.

In Figure 15.3 are indicated the same comparisons at the conclusion of the year. Both the income and the expenses were overstated when the budgeted figures and the actual figures were compared. The net operating gain was not what had been anticipated. Although the figures differ between the budgeted amounts and the actual amounts, comparison between the percentages of respective categories reflect the precise differences between categories of income and expenses. For example, it was anticipated that 15.9 percent of the operating expenses would be for salaries. In actuality 15.4 percent was spent for salaries. However, more was spent than had been planned in temporary employee wages.

For the experienced student affairs administrator, much of what has been stated is well understood. Emphasis, then, is placed on refining financial data gathered by the institution into a workable format that can be understood and utilized by all professional staff. The format of financial statements should not take precedent over their use as planning tools. Financial statements are to be designed so that planning can be done with realistic budgetary factors. The first step in this planning is the determination of the fiscal resources.

The fiscal resources used by student affairs units are received on a periodic basis according to a method of allocation. Possibilities for receiving operating resources are numerous and may exist in multiple combinations. The important consideration is the definition or application of the budget as it applies to the institution or program area. Is the budget a commitment toward a direction in an area or for a specific program? Can it be increased or decreased? Is it dependent on external factors? After these questions have been answered, the best budget type can be determined.

TYPES OF BUDGETS

Some budgets are developed on the basis of computation because they derive their identity primarily from a certain cost factor or other mechanisms. Others are formulated according to a base of expenditure (Robins, 1973). A budget is usually labeled as a specific type according to whether a particular fund is referenced from a computational standpoint or from an expenditure standpoint.

Computational Budgets

Line Item Budget. This is a common budget used when overall development of any program or activity initially requires the enumeration of various components. Usually these components are listed by category or sub-category that are represented by respective lines in the calculation. A line can represent a sum of individual expenditures, or individual expenditures may be broken down specifically on additional lines. For example, a line for personal service expenses could be expand-

| | MONTH | | | | | |
REVENUE	ACTUAL FT '98	%	BUDGET FY '99	%	ACTUAL FY '99	%
Student Rentals	6,836.06	44.1	9,320.00	89.2	7,747.00	60.3
Rental Adjustment	7,351.00	47.5			3,138.00	24.4
Forfeited Deposits	166.00	1.0			125.00	1.0
Special Groups	25.00	.2	700.00	6.7	104.00	.8
Vending Commissions	800.49	5.0	240.00	2.3	1,286.90	10.0
Laundry Commissions	(25.04)	(.2)	190.00	1.8	14.35	.1
Washer/Dryer Revenue	393.15	2.4			398.95	3.1
Other	10.01				44.26	.3
TOTAL REVENUE	15,556.67	100.0	10,450.00	100.0	12,858.46	100.0
OPERATING EXPENSES						
Salaries	1,832.90	11.9	5,343.00	51.1	3,286.09	25.6
Temporary Wages	3,980.48	25.8	5,582.00	53.4	4,260.26	33.0
Employee Meals			110.00	1.1	19.67	.1
Staff Benefits	324.33	2.1	508.00	4.9	580.71	4.5
Supplies & Printing	207.10	1.3	1,275.00	12.2	1,241.85	9.7
Laundry	431.37	2.8	226.00	2.2	76.13	.6
Maintenance & Repairs	11,270.13	72.9	2,830.00	27.1	4,203.98	32.7
Utilities	4,421.58	28.6	5,087.00	48.7	4,744.49	36.9
Equipment					910.00	7.1
Telephone	3,437.12	22.3	3,342.00	32.0	3,599.85	28.0
Insurance	298.91	1.9	370.00	3.5	240.63	1.9
Travel						
Miscellaneous	35.00	.2				
TOTAL EXPENSES	26,238.92	169.8	24,673.00	236.1	23,163.66	180.1
OPERATING GAIN (LOSS)	(10,682.25)	(69.8)	(14,223.00)	(136.1)	(10,305.20)	
Less: Other Expenses						
Administrative Charge	1,030.00	6.7	2,399.00	23.0		
Debt Service	2,426.00	15.7	7,573.00			
Sub-Total	3,456.00	22.4	9,972.00			
NET GAIN (LOSS)	(14,138.25)	(92.2)	(24,195.00)	(231.6)		

Figure 15.3 Residential hall Statement of operations (June FY '99).

FY 2000 BUDGET	ACTUAL FY '98	%	BUDGET FY '99	%	ACTUAL FT '99	%
369,700.00	273,688.00	84.5	369,700.00	23.0	329,184.00	89
	7,351.00	2.3			3,138.00	
4,200.00	6,187.00	1.9	4,200.00	1.1	4,619.00	1
5,300.00	19,283.50	6.0	5,300.00	1.3	8,361.00	2
10,000.00	8,321.19	2.6	10,000.00	2.5	8,778.14	
8,200.00	942.73	.3	8,200.00	2.1	516.46	
	7,710.05	2.4			12,026.11	
	154.86				313.82	
397,400.00	323,638.33	100.0	397,400.00	100.0		
63,138.00	51,169.51	15.8	63,138.00	15.9		
62,931.00	68,854.44	21.3	62,931.00	15.8		
1,080.00	3,299.66	1.0				
6,100.00	5,084.18	1.6				
12,750.00	8,554.41	2.6				
2,260.00	1,973.83	.6				
29,880.00						
52,512.00						
3,016.00						
33,420.00						

ed with additional lines listing each position, staff member's name, and source of funds. This approach has the advantage of specifying resources for particular programs, but has a possible disadvantage of limiting flexibility.

Program Budget. When the primary objective is to outline a total program and the cost associated with the various aspects of the program, a program budget could be utilized. This type of budget allows the overall cost associated with various developmental components of a program to be evaluated. Partial allocation might result in accomplishing a predetermined amount or segment of a proposed program. Grant proposals could be considered in this category.

Incremental Budget. Incremental budgets ordinarily take the previous year's total budget or expenses and add some increment or percent increase. The increment may vary from budget to budget based on the perceived value of the program or on the actual cost incurred during the most recent year. This approach works well on budgets that are similar throughout an institution. For instance, if the aggregate of current salaries in a department or larger unit is to be raised by an average amount, this increment may be added to the budget. An extended application of the approach, also based on the previous year expenditure, may result in a more accurate allocation. If during the previous year an additional allocation was received to meet expenses or designated for a particular project, the sum of this allocation prior to the additional increment would need to be analyzed. In the first case the budget might be adjusted upward before figuring an increment, and in the second case the budget might be restored to the previous level. Unless care is exercised, the one-time allocation as well as the additional increment based on this additional sum of money would appear as a routine part of the budget for the following year.

All categories of expense do not rise at the same rate. An incremenal approach across the board may allow expenditures in certain areas to grow at a rapid rate while curtailing efforts in more critically important areas.

Zero Based Budget. This type of budget starts with no assumptions or set priorities according to functions. Although the zero based budget seems ideal in concept, much longitudinal planning can be lost. Flexibility to deal with changing needs is minimized. Zero based budgeting is used to the best advantage in initial planning stages. Zero based budgets also take considerable time and require total institutional commitment if they are to be effective.

Formula Based Budgets. These budgets derive their funding level from a formula that considers predetermined and agreed upon factors (Maw, Richards, & Crosby, 1976). Formula based budgets have the advantage of being flexible. For example, a slight shifting of the formula or formula elements could be made to accommodate a change in appropriations from a state legislature.

Base of Expenditure

Auxiliary Budgets. Auxiliary budgets deal with activities that are self-supporting or largely self-supporting. An auxiliary generates its income by providing sales or services that are different from activities funded from tuition or fees. Auxiliary budgets often include residence halls, food services, bookstores, or many aspects of student centers.

Construction Budgets. Construction budgets are for construction projects. Often these are budgeted separately because of the length of the project or the ability to identify later the cost associated with the project. They may receive resources other than institutional funds such as bonds, grants, and donations. They also may be developed as a category in other budgets.

Student Aid Budgets. These budgets are for very specialized purposes—scholarships, grants, and other student financial aid programs. Funds might come from state and/or federally appropriated monies and are usually augmented by fund drives or contributions. Both public and private institutions also utilize income from endowment funds for student financial assistance.

Education and General Budget. The Education and General budget is for educational programs and general support services. Expenses usually include broad categories such as construction, research, service, and the library.

Lists of budget categories and types of expenditures could be continued. However, the more divisions that are made in the overall expense pattern of an institution, the less the distinction between the budgets. Labels given the budgets outline the type of restrictions that might be present as well as identify some reference point in case a particular item needs review. For example, the overall category of student activity funds might include several types of budget categories. Knowing a student activity fund with generated income was involved would enable budget personnel to determine the precise nature of the account.

LONGITUDINAL FISCAL MANAGEMENT

Once various budgets have been approved, the process of managing and allocating resources according to changing variables begins. Management of functions in umbrella type organizations follows one of two general patterns: (1) allocating the total of available funds to the individual departments involved and requiring some percentage of return for a central support, or (2) maintaining funds centrally and allocating for basic needs of the departments. Depending on the institution, the relative merits of the major type of budget activity involved is one of refinement, stabilization, or program development. The most common approach is a combination of styles in which funds for operational expenses allow some latitude by the unit head, and some of the allocation is retained in a central account for handling emergencies, changes in priority, or cost overruns. This combination approach to budget allocation eliminates the negative aspect of returning funds to a central administrative agency and provides the positive reinforcement for some degree of decision making at the local budget unit level. Regardless of the planning procedures, monthly financial statements need to be monitored by the chief student affairs officer.

Actualization of plans usually does not occur according to schedule or with the anticipated cost. As a result, considerable deviation may be necessary during the course of the fiscal year. Deviations may occur because of changing priorities, new information, different options, or opportunities that later become available. The staff needs to regard any initial allocation as a reflection of the best thinking at the time the budget is established, rather than identifying it as being permanent or resulting from an unalterable ranking of priorities.

Because change frequently is due to different variables interacting throughout the year, several mechanisms exist for dealing with expenses running above or below estimates. If the general budget plan does not allow for an actual change in the budget during the year, savings realized from projects completed for less than the anticipated amount usually are maintained in a central fund, and additional expenses beyond those budgeted items are not allowed. In cases where over expenditures may be approved, funding is provided from a central pool, or an over expense is reimbursed. The advantage to holding to the original budget is that more accurate initial planning may be accomplished with hard decisions on priorities being decided in the original budget. The disadvantages are that plans must be made well in advance, changes of plans are more difficult to accommodate, and the administrator has to make decisions within established priorities.

Another way of accommodating deviations is through a budget amendment process. This process differs from the earlier example in that the allocation of a certain amount of money is thought of more as representing an allocation to meet a total need rather than the sum of precise needs. During the course of the budget year, money may be moved from one category to another to meet changes in expenses or in priorities. So that an accurate account in terms of types of expenses may be maintained, money is placed originally in categories according to anticipated expense. During the year, a desired addition in one category may be accommodated by a corresponding reduction in another. For example, the equipment category may be reduced and the operating supply category raised. If a staff member resigns in midyear, the remaining salary may be amended to any of several categories. Amendment of major sums may require higher administrative approval to insure that continuing obligations are not incurred, such as using salary savings to purchase a computer with no source of funds for paying future operating expenses.

Regardless of the general budget plan utilized, mechanisms for continued decision making must exist. A requirement to operate within a fixed budget is often mandated. If there have been a large number of staff vacancies, a decrease or increase in expenses, or the receipt of additional money, requests need to be submitted through the administrative structure to have these funds evaluated and considered for other uses.

In institutions where changing budget categories are possible, salary savings from vacant positions is likely. These can be accumulated, marked for priority, and expended at a level higher than the departmental level. In student affairs areas, increased costs have made purchase of major pieces of equipment extremely difficult. Accumulating salary savings can amount to large enough sums to purchase a major piece of equipment. Initial reaction to this approach, where it has not been established previously as an institutional policy, is often neutral at best. It is sometimes viewed as "some other department receiving our savings." For the intermediate term, however, this method is an appropriate way to accelerate services and programs offered students beyond those originally provided in the institutional budget.

The previous example illustrates how savings can be accumulated to make major purchases that small individual departments would be unable to purchase. A corollary to this process is the treatment of areas that have the ability to generate needed funds. Each chief student affairs officer is faced with the problem of how best to handle auxiliary income and personnel. For instance, if the housing department requires 25 percent of the administrative time of the dean or vice-president, should one-fourth of the officer's salary be charged against the housing budget? Regardless of the answer, should any housing surplus funds be used to underwrite other campus student services? The initial answer to both questions probably is negative, but the principle is the same as that utilized in the general tuition mechanism for students who elect courses in the humanities as opposed to courses in the sciences. In most operations the solution is a matter of custom, tradition, and degree.

This example indicates consideration of utilizing housing or auxiliary generated funds for the good of the general student body. A converse of this situation would be allowing a housing rate to be charged that would accelerate the expansion of programs in the residence life area at a more rapid rate than similar or corresponding student programs receiving appropriated funds.

BEYOND THE FORMULA, ALLOCATION, OR BUDGET

Just as the budget represents resources allocated for programs, these programs represent decisions that they are worthy of expenditure. Legislative acts and the tone of society during the past 20 years have staunchly supported higher education. Federal programs made resources available for considerable expansion of student financial asistance in higher education. Grant opportunities and other outside income encouraged developing the resource facilities of the institution. Two decades seems like a long period of time, but the change was so gradual that the difference between the beginning and the current complexity of multifaceted institutions was never marked.

For example, 20 years ago the management of residence halls under business officers was a logical arrangement on many campuses. The size of many institutions was such that departments of housing were not necessary. General funds were utilized to cover any deficit, and during periods of financial success profits were used for the good of the institution. This method was logical and worked well. As campuses grew, the scope of the housing and residence life programs on many campuses increased. A decline of the *in loco parentis* concept coupled with the rapid growth in size of institutions accelerated the establishment of separate departments of housing to administer both facilities and programs. The earlier format for administering housing facilities seemed no longer advantageous.

Academic expansion brought about the need to review the best uses for older residence halls. Often located around the perimeter of the old established campus, these buildings were at the core of the emerging campus. At many institutions conversion of housing space to classroom or office space occurred, making newer, cleaner, but also more expensive housing operations. Newer and larger residences often necessitated greater attention to management and business aspects of the operation.

Although departments of housing were established, their authority often was not clear. For example, was the washer and dryer operation a campus auxiliary or a housing operation? If it were an auxiliary operation, should rent be paid to housing for the space utilized? If not, how was the revenue to be replaced? Where was the money from the student housing contracts and the income from vending machines accrued? If institutional income was invested, how was the allocation of interest to be made? The creation of housing departments gave the impression that all of traditional housing functions were incorporated into the new unit. This was not necessarily the case, and these concerns needed attention. In most institutions, no overall plan was adopted. Decisions were made to correct faults brought to the attention of the executive officers of the institution rather than from any studied or long-range plan of action.

The increase in size of many institutions compounded the work load in many areas of campus operations. Many decisions, valid at one time, now needed further review. Using the housing example, does any college area need its own maintenance force? The logical answer would be negative until continued growth resulted in an operation requiring a maintenance staff of a specialized nature. If this concept is considered in terms of duplication of services and applied to the budget process in areas of an instructional nature, the beginning of program conflict is clear. For instance, how many centers for counseling should a campus have? The psychology department, the educational psychology department, the college of education, the mental health unit, the counseling center, and the academic advisement office each might desire to act as the primary counseling service for the campus. In some areas, duplication may be proper; in others, consolidation is better both in terms of quality and economy. Although funds are monitored as expended by an area, monitoring is less effective for funds spent on programs when those programs cross area lines.

For the neophyte in budget management an understanding of the budgeting process in higher education is necessary. Sometimes administrators respond to requests for additional programs by saying no available funds exist. This type of response tends to lead to the theory that if funds can be found, a particular program can be implemented. More realistically, what is meant is that the money that is available has been allocated for something thought to be of a higher priority. Thus no "funds" exist! The question is one of program priority as opposed exclusively to a lack of funds.

In the original budgeting process, legislators have the tendency to take care of particular problems that affect a certain constituency, even though these areas may not be the highest priority of the institution. Funds are allocated, but sometimes not to the area thought most important by the institution. Agreement between all of the parties involved is difficult to achieve, but is necessary.

Allocations and allocation procedures to institutions that are members of a state system of higher education vary. Political processes influence whether allocations are made to a state governing board or an individual institution, whether general allocations are made to a governing body with instructions, or whether allocations are made to an institution for a prescribed purpose.

DETERMINING THE
PLANNING BACKGROUND

In preparation for the various levels of budget conferences, student affairs professionals annually review their allocations and program expenditures. Student affairs administrators preparing budgets must have a complete knowledge of financial needs and priorities not only of student affairs but also of other units of the institution. Because of competition for funds, specific knowledge of needs or selling points of the competition will help shape the best arguments for student affairs.

This preparation often takes a three step form: a review of the institution's budgets, a specific review of areas that have received greater than incremental jumps over the past three years, and an analysis of any historical patterns regarding assignment of new functions and new funds. The consolidated budget of most institutions contains data relative to at least the most recent fiscal year so that any comparison does not require the use of a second document.

The first step, a page by page review of various institutional sub-unit budgets set against the knowledge of the increased funds allocated the institution for the second of the two years, will provide the beginning background regarding funding level and the rate of incremental increases. These yearly comparisons need to be reviewed with full knowledge of the number of students, their full-time equivalency (FTE or EFT), and any other factors that might have affected the allocation.

This review occasionally will indicate functions, departments, schools, or colleges that received larger increases than what has now been recognized as an incremental jump. As a second step these areas should be reviewed closely to determine the specific item or program that received the increase. The completed budget review will indicate these areas, and often the type of pattern or prevailing thought that resulted in the allocation of greater than an incremental increase is apparent.

The third step of preparation is an analysis of historical patterns. In some cases, when a new task is assigned within the institution, funds accompany the assignment. In other areas, an assignment is made without the accompaniment of the appropriate additional funds. Too often, student affairs professionals accept additional responsibility without the corresponding remuneration. This may happen because they have a desire to serve students or the educational community and also because they have not been successful historically in the acquisition of additional funds.

Preparation of student affairs statistical and financial data throughout the course of the year plus information received from the review of budgets, the review of the strategy for above average incremental increases, and the analysis of the historical patterns of assignments, and funding of the institution should result in a more successful allocation procedure.

If an unsatisfactory allocation does occur, the next step would be a refinement of the first three steps, plus an institutional review of particular areas for which funds were requested and a corresponding review of those areas in comparable institutions. Although this review might seem to be a first priority, often more questions are raised than answers obtained by comparing institutional programs. The fact that another institution does things differently does not mean one institution is either over managing or under managing, but rather that the policy is more accurate in terms of particular responsibilities.

RECAPITULATION

Effective resource management in student affairs has been examined. In addition, some of the basic fiscal management functions and types of budgets have been outlined. Budgeting and managing are both continuing and cyclical processes needing constant adjustment and evaluation. Therefore, the successful and effective student affairs administrator recognizes the need for money management skills. Effective fiscal management enhances the credibility of student affairs administrators among institutional decision makers and policy planners. This credibility can be used to promote accomplishment of the central mission of student affairs—student development.

REFERENCES

Barber, A. W. On the budget. *The University of Georgia Community News,* January 1974.

Berry, M. The state of student affairs: A review of the literature. *NASPA Journal,* 1976, *13,* 2-4.

Crookston, B. B. Student personnel: All hail and farewell! *Personnel and Guidance Journal,* 1976, *55,* 26-9.

Harpel, R. L. *Planning, budgeting, and evaluation in student affairs programs: A manual for administrators.* Portland, OR: National Association of Student Personnel Administrators, Division of Research and Program Development, 1976.

Maw, I. I., Richards, N. A., & Crosby, H. J. *Formula budgeting: An application to student affairs.* Washington, DC: American College Personnel Association, 1971.

Miller, T. K., & Prince, J. S. *The future of student affairs: A guide to student development for tomorrow's higher education.* San Francisco: Jossey-Bass, 1976.

National Association of College and University Business Officers. *College and university business administration.* Washington, DC: Author, 1974.

Robins, G. B. *Understanding the college budget.* Athens, GA: University of Georgia Institute of Higher Education, 1973.

SUGGESTED READINGS

Harpel, R. L. *Planning, budgeting, and evaluation in student programs: A manual for administrators.* Portland, OR: National Association of Student Personnel Administrators, Division of Research and Program Development, 1976.

Kaludis, G. (Ed.). *New directions for higher education: Strategies for budgeting* (No. 2). San Francisco: Jossey-Bass, 1973.

Maw, I. I., Richards, N. A., & Crosby, H. J. *Formula budgeting: An application to student affairs.* Washington, DC: American College Personnel Association, 1976.

Robins, G. B. *Understanding the college budget.* Athens, GA: University of Georgia Institute of Higher Education, 1973.

Daniel A. Hallenbeck is currently Director of University Housing at the Univerity of Georgia. His responsibilities include budget, program, personnel, facilities, and maintenance for residence halls and family housing. Previously he held positions as Assistant Director of Residence at Iowa State University and Director of Housing Facilities at the University of Northern Iowa.

His Bachelor of Arts degree is from the University of Northern Iowa. His master's degree is from Michigan State University and Ph.D. from Iowa State University. Throughout his career, Dr. Hallenbeck has been active in the Association of College and University Housing Officers, the American College Personnel Association's Commission III, and the National Association of Student Personnel Administrators. For nine years he served as advisor to the National Association of College and University Residence Halls, a student organization.

Chapter 16

STUDENT AFFAIRS ADMINISTRATOR AS FACILITIES MANAGER

Daniel A. Hallenbeck

The student affairs administrator is charged with the creation of out-of-class learning environments that support the educational mission of the institution and provide for student growth and development. Three facets of this responsibility are creation of environments, management of physical facilities, and structuring of facilities to provide services to students by promoting staff efficiency and interaction.

CREATION OF ENVIRONMENTS

College campuses are dynamic, ever-changing communities. Individuals who inhabit the campuses are constantly in a state of transition—students are arriving, working, studying, growing, and leaving. Faculty and staff work, administer, teach, conduct research, and leave for other opportunities. Even physical components of the campus—landscape and buildings—are forever changing. As needs for the campus change, landscaped "green spaces" become parking lots or sites for new buildings. New buildings are constructed while older facilities are renovated or removed.

Collegial environment is shaped by the people who work, study, and live on campus, the physical facilities, and their interaction. The architectural influence of physical facilities generally will outlast the influence of any particular individual or group. Gerst and Sweetwood (1973) contended that perceptions of the climate or atmosphere, experienced upon entering any situation, are important variables in determining behavior. Messages conveyed through these first impressions demand congruence in behavior. Consequently, being aware of and sensitive to messages the physical environment conveys to prospective students and their parents is important. Students, faculty, and staff who live, work, and interact on that campus experience the impact of the physical facilities on behavior and attitude as well.

Numerous components of the physical environment combine to transmit messages to those who visit, work, and live on campus. One of these components is the spatial relationship of buildings. For instance, what is the focal point of the campus? Are the academic and nonacademic facilities integrated or separated? What is the relative importance of classroom buildings, residence halls, library, student center, bookstore, football stadium, science laboratories, counseling center, intramural facilities, and health center? Answers to these questions are the content of the messages the physical facilities communicate to those who enter campus. Heyck (1978) pointed out if the college teaches through its buildings that ugliness is an acceptable price for efficiency, and that living should be separated from learning, then nothing that is said in the classroom can really counter that message.

Heilweil (1973) contended that physical surroundings impose absolute limits on human behavior. Furthermore, DeYoung, Moos, Van-Dort, and Smail (1974) found that the environmental climate exerts a directional influence on behavior. Because the impact of physical surroundings can be either positive or negative, student affairs adminstrators need to be cognizant of environmental impact and accentuate those components that elicit positive behavior and limit or eliminate those that encourage negative behavior. For instance, if physical surroundings are situated so that they promote a sense of community and provide opportunities for meaningful communication among faculty, students, and staff, this sense of community and flow of communication will be seen as a normal, natural, and positive part of the environment. On the other hand, if classrooms are isolated from student activity centers, such as student center and residence halls, creating a sense of community among participants in the academic enterprise will be difficult.

A component of collegiate environments for which many student affairs administrators have responsibility is the residential environment. Riker (1965) identified the relationship between residential environment and behavior as being significant and important. Gerst and Moos (1972) found that a student's satisfaction with the residential environment influenced self-perception and perception of the college experience so that pursuit of relationships with others and the degree of involvement in intellectually and emotionally significant activities were affected. Moos and Gerst (1974) developed the University Residence Environment Scale (URES) to measure the social-psychological climate of the residential setting. While developing their instrument, they found that student perception of the social climate of the place of residence influenced subjective mood states—for example, depression, alienation, and isolation—and also affected satisfaction with the residential environment.

When a student walks into a campus building an impression is immediately created. The individual either perceives the climate to be one of warmth, caring, and comfort or one that is cold, impersonal, and institutional. Many times this is not a conscious thought, but the feeling is real. This first impression is influenced by color, lighting, floor covering, cleanliness, furnishings, smell, noise level, and furniture arrangement. For instance, everyone has experienced the impact of furniture arrangement. If chairs and sofas in a lounge are in a straight line and the lounge appears unused or has an unlived-in look, feelings that order is more important than function and that ease of cleaning is more important than student need for social interaction are evident. The interaction of the student with the physical environment is particularly important in a residential setting. To have a positive impact, the residential setting must be student-centered, promote interaction, recognize the need for privacy, and facilitate student pursuit of academic goals.

For illustrative purposes in this chapter, residence halls are used as examples primarily because (1) more research is available about them, (2) campuses tend to have numerous such facilities and to view them as "belonging to student affairs," and (3) innovations in facilities management have been numerous in residence halls. However, the basic principles reflected in these examples are applicable to all campus physical facilities.

MANAGEMENT OF PHYSICAL FACILITIES

Student satisfaction, social climate, and perception of the physical environment are highly interrelated (Brandt & Chapman, 1981). Because physical facilities have a strong influence on the level of student satisfaction, the social climate, and the direction and type of behavior exhibited, the student affairs administrator must be an effective facilities manager to maximize the educational and developmental impacts of facilities.

On a residential campus, residence halls are a major source of institutional indebtedness (Williams, 1979). Because the traditional method of financing living facilities of public higher education institutions is through the sale of revenue bonds, retirement of these debts depends on student fees, and requires a consistently high level of occupancy. To maintain a level of occupancy high enough to generate funds to amortize the debt, residential facilities must be attractive and meet the needs of students.

However, Anchors, Schroeder and Jackson (1978) found that most students simply do not feel at home in residence halls. Most residence halls are designed in a highly uniformed, ordered, and regularized fashion. Walls and built-in furniture are usually indestructible and resistant to human imprint. Further, they found that students are often treated as visitors or people passing through. Student complaints about residence hall living include lack of privacy, lack of freedom, and uniformity of rooms and furnishings. According to the report on student housing by the Educational Facilities Laboratory (1972), a double room is used by two people for sleeping, studying, and socializing—all quite different uses for either roommate to have control over the space or schedule.

Although individual differences exist, students are expected to have pretty much the same needs for space, freedom, and privacy in their living unit. Students' inability to control their own space has given rise to the application of the concept of territoriality to help understand the need for and recognition of individual differences in the residential setting (Grant 1974; Schroeder 1976, 1980). *Territoriality is the acquisition, demarcation, and defense of a spatial area with corresponding dimensions of implied ownership, personalization, and maximum control.* This concept is a universally recognized vehicle to maintain desired levels of control, organize behavior, and promote freedom of action. The application of this concept to residence halls has given impetus to room and corridor personalization programs through which students are encouraged to paint their corridors and rooms, to build lofts, room dividers or other structures in order to decorate and deinstitutionalize their immediate surroundings.

Hanson and Altman (1976) found that students who were given the opportunity to personalize and decorate their residence hall rooms were more likely to remain in school than those who were not. A study by Werring, Winston, and McCaffrey (1981) found that residents who were active participants in their living unit's corridor paint projects had a more positive perception of their environment than either residents who elected not to participate in the project or residents who lived in units who chose not to paint. Wichman and Healey (1979) reported that students who were able to build lofts in their rooms generally got along better with their roommates. The literature then supports the contention that students will be satisfied significantly more in an environment over which they exercise some control and which they helped create. As noted by these studies, a variety of ways exists by which students can gain some control over their environment either through building structures, various forms of decoration such as painting, or the addition or deletion of furniture.

Furniture is one of those environmental elements over which students definitely desire control. To students, built-in furniture is equated with built-in frustration because it limits room arrangements and does not contribute to personalization. Room furniture has the joint property of being one of the single most important and least understood factors in the students' immediate environment (Heilweil, 1973). Movable furniture lends itself to the personalization process. As might be expected, the major portion of students' immediate environment consists of the room furniture, and actions in the room are circumscribed by the furniture to a greater degree than by any other element. Because institutional furniture's life expectancy is 20 years, the student affairs administrator must be attuned to the need for selecting residence hall furnishings that will be adaptable, durable, and flexible in meeting student needs through several generations.

Heilweil (1973) pointed out that consequences of having no place to call one's own results in alienation, hostility, ruthlessness, and a sense of transience. On the other hand, those factors that give rise to student complaints about uniformity of surroundings such as identical rooms, long, straight corridors, and group bath facilities also reduce architectural and building costs and, therefore, shorten the length of time required to retire the debt.

Because residence halls traditionally have been built without regard to meeting students' psychosocial needs, they have not lent themselves to being places for self discovery or experimentation with different life styles. Consequently, residence hall staff must work to overcome the architectural obstacles to personal development. Change can occur through various personalization programs, renovation, and refurbishing projects.

STRUCTURING OF FACILITIES

Student affairs administrators must be prepared to play significant roles in planning new facilities and remodeling old facilities. As enrollments decline and the competition for students increases, maintaining institutional facilities in a manner that attracts students will become increasingly important. Individuals with a firm grounding in student developmental theory and a knowledge of the interrelationships between educational programs (both formal and informal) and facilities will be needed to make contributions to campus facility planning and management. Care in designing and building facilities must be exercised because of the long lasting nature of the architecture.

Change has been and will continue to be a constant for higher educational institutions. The Carnegie Council (1980) warned of shifts in enrollment patterns and the resulting adjustment of standards. Their report stated that students will be recruited more actively, admitted more readily, and retained more laboriously. Because the pool of traditional 18-to-24-year-old students will shrink, the competition to recruit and to retain students will become much more intense.

As this competition becomes increasingly acute, a student's impression of the institution upon visiting the campus before enrollment will be even more significant. When a student visits the campus for the first time, an immediate impression is created from the buildings and landscaping. The first impression is lasting—the institution does not have a second chance to make a first impression.

Institutional facilities and furnishings must reflect institutional goals and priorities. The message conveyed by these facilities to the individuals who comprise the institution's many publics will determine the institution's survival and success in the coming decades. That the facilities be attractive and adaptable and that they meet student developmental needs are imperative. Because clientele is changing, new and different demands are put on facilities. An important question facing administrators is how can facilities be adapted.

Interaction of students and staff and the variety of activities that can be accommodated in a residence hall depend on the location of staff rooms, apartments, and hall offices as well as study, meeting lounge, and recreational areas. The hall staff must be located in accessible areas approachable by students. Program and activity spaces must facilitate participation in fulfilling residents' needs and goals.

In the residential setting, Harrie (1968) indicated that a good interior design is flexible and can be converted to meet a variety of needs. The design should be molded to meet the situation at hand instead of molding the student to what is available. Residence hall interiors demand sensitivity to student needs, understanding of and commitment to institutional objectives, and finesse in translating these needs and objectives into furnishings (Walters, 1968). Student affairs administrators must be cognizant of student needs, create environments in which these needs are recognized, and provide needed services for maximum student growth and development throughout the campus community.

PRACTICAL ASPECTS OF FACILITY MANAGEMENT

In the coming decade student affairs practitioners will find it necessary to build new and adapt existing facilities to accommodate programs, activities, and services necessary to respond to a changing clientele. Traditional programs, activities, and services may be modified, or completely discarded to meet needs of the student population, or new ones may be created. In this section the following areas are discussed from the practitioner's point of view: planning, construction, furnishings, and management.

Planning

The planning process employed to construct new or remodel existing facilities should follow seven basic steps: statement of philosophy, needs assessment, statement of space usage, translation of the philosophy into blueprints, cost estimates, methods of financing, and evaluation.

1. Statement of Philosophy. The first step in planning is to state concisely the philosophy of the department building or remodeling the facility. This statement should be in harmony with the institutional mission and should outline the purpose for which the building is intended. Such a statement provides planners with direction in developing plans. The philosophy is helpful particularly to the architect as plans are developed and decisions are made regarding various spaces within the facility and the overall design. Consideration should be given to the relationship of staff to students, students to students, student development theory, the relationship of the facility to programs and people, as well as the interaction between the users and the environment.

2. Needs Assessment. In developing the needs assessment, one must consider the following: Who will use the facility? How will the facility be used? What programs, activities, and services will be offered within the facility? When will the facility be needed? How many students or other participants will be served by the facility? What are the staffing requirements of the facility? What federal regulations must be met in building or remodeling this particular facility? After these questions have been answered, a needs assessment evolves to substantiate the purpose or the reason for building or remodeling the facility.

3. Statement of Space Usage. Consideration of the manner in which spaces within the facility are intended to be used also needs to be delineated. This should coincide with programs, activities, and services identified in the needs assessment. For instance, a student center or residence hall lounge could accommodate music listening, conversation, table games, study, formal receptions, group meetings, and parties; however, the same space would not lend itself to all of these activities. Many times when attention is not given to this phase of the planning process, users find the facility and its furnishings inhibit rather than facilitate intended and actual usage. Furthermore, the relationship of one activity to another needs to be considered when making space designations. For example, locating a study room next to a television or recreation room is unwise.

4. Translation into Blueprints. The fourth step calls for an architect to translate the information from the first three steps into drawings. Spending time with the architect reviewing programs, activities, and services that are intended to be accommodated within the facility is important to ensure thorough understanding. The architect can design the facility appropriately *only after* what is desired and how the facility is intended to be used are understood completely.

5. Cost Estimates. Two methods are used frequently for arriving at a cost of the project: (1) provide the architect with a dollar figure and instructions to design the facility within that amount, and (2) retain the architect to design the facility with the dollar cost to be determined by the design. Although the first method is most common, the actual construction bids still may be over the specified budget ceiling. If construction estimates or bids are above the budget ceiling, revision of plans to bring the project within the budget or allocation of more money is necessary.

6. **Methods of Financing.** The actual method of financing various facilities varies across states and among institutions. At state-supported institutions, self-supporting facilities (residential units, student centers, intramural facilities) are often financed through the sale of revenue bonds. Other facilities such as classrooms are funded from state appropriated or capital expenditure funds. At private institutions, many facilities are funded from gifts earmarked for specific purposes. As an example, a report from the Research and Information Committee of the Association of College and University Housing Officers (ACUHO) indicated the following methods for financing construction or renovation of housing facilities were employed by member institutions: (a) surplus and reserve monies, (b) sale of revenue bonds, (c) state appropriations, (d) gifts, and (e) federal grants and loans (Hallenbeck & Ullom, 1980).

7. **Evaluation.** Before the construction contract is awarded, the final step, an evaluation of the other six planning steps, is in order to ensure that the proposed plans accommodate programs, activities, and services intended for the facility; that enough money is available to complete the project; and that the facility will accomplish the purposes for which it is intended. Assuming everything is satisfactory, the construction phase may begin.

Construction

The construction process is initiated by securing a contractor. At state institutions this commonly is done through a bidding process. Specifications and architectural drawings are provided to interested contractors who submit sealed statements containing their bid to build or remodel the facility. In most instances, the contractor who submits the lowest bid is awarded the contract. Before awarding the contract the institution has the opportunity to evaluate the contractor. Important considerations for this evaluation include the size of the workforce, the probability of meeting the construction deadlines, and the reputation of the firm. The architect's impression of the construction firm and the contractor's willingness to work with the architect are both important. If the low bidder is unsatisfactory, with adequate justification, rejecting the bid is possible. The next lowest bid can then be selected, or plans can be revised and the project rebid.

Once construction has begun, inspection of the project on a regular basis is important. By walking through the project and becoming familiar with the workers, particularly the job foreman and the subcontractors, the institutional representative is able to monitor progress. An additional method of monitoring progress is to attend weekly contractor meetings. Generally the individuals present at these meetings are student affairs administrators, the architect, the contractor, and possibly some subcontractors. At these meetings the progress of the week is reviewed and discussed. Any problems that have arisen are inspected and decisions made as quickly as possible so the contractor can proceed with the project. These regular meetings are vitally important in monitoring the progress of the project and for ensuring that it will be completed on schedule.

A topic usually discussed at the contractor's meeting is *change orders*. Basically a change order is a deviation from original plans and specifications either to do more work or to do something differently than originally planned. Particularly in remodeling jobs contractors find numerous "surprises" as the work progresses. These unexpected conditions usually require additional work, materials, and money. Frequently in new construction an oversight is discovered that needs to be corrected so that the facility can be constructed properly. Change orders have the potential of providing the institution with a much better job than would be the case had they not been submitted and approved. However, an institutional representative must evaluate carefully each change order before it is approved or these changes can cause the cost of the project to exceed significantly the budget ceiling. The student affairs administrator should confer with the architect before approving change orders to determine the necessity of the work being suggested.

As the project nears completion, a formal inspection of the complete work should be undertaken by the institutional representative, the architect, and the contractor. During this inspection a "punch list" should be developed that enumerates the items that still need to be completed or corrected by the contractor before the building is accepted by the institution. Final payment should be withheld until all items on the punch list are completed. When the final punch list has been corrected, the building can be accepted and final payment authorized.

Furnishings

Simultaneously with the construction phase, the student affairs administrator begins work with an interior designer to select the furnishings for the building. Furnishings must facilitate programs, activities, and services that are planned for this space. Review of the needs assessment and space usage statement is important in selecting furnishings. The interior designer provides the administrator choices of various color schemes, types of fabric, and pieces and makes of furniture. The interior designer should assist in the specification writing and bidding process required for the purchase of the furniture. In state institutions the low bidder generally is awarded the contract for furnishings. Starting this project during the early stages of construction enables the arrival of furniture when the building is in the completion stage. The furniture should be inspected carefully upon receipt to ensure that it has not been damaged in the shipping process.

Management

A successful facilities management program (Kaiser, 1980) should

- provide healthy and safe facilities environments
- ensure long life expectancy of facilities
- ensure economy and efficiency of operation
- identify priorities for maintenance
- systematically determine priorities for spending maintenance funds
- support programs
- promote individual student development

Provide Healthy and Safe Facilities Environments. The student affairs administrator must be concerned with housekeeping, routine maintenance, and repair and replacement programs—in addition to various federal regulations and programs, such as handicapped accessibility and environmental safety. Housekeeping, although many times taken for granted, is vital to providing a safe, healthy environment, as well as ensuring the long life of the facility and reflecting the care that the institution has for the facility and the individuals who inhabit the building.

Housekeeping requirements are reflected in a cleaning schedule that outlines the type and frequency of cleaning required, necessary equipment and supplies, and the number of people needed to implement the program. Keys to an effective housekeeping program are a definite cleaning schedule, thorough training in cleaning methods, equipment and supplies, supervision, and evaluation. Housekeeping, the cornerstone of facility upkeep, is a daily need.

Ensure Long Life Expectancy of Facilities. Scheduled routine maintenance ensures that a facility is available when needed and extends its life expectancy. The institution's motto regarding maintenance should be, "do it now, don't wait!" Deferred maintenance is very costly in time, money, and image. The impression created by deteriorating facilities is always negative and long lasting. With spiraling inflation, the cost of repair work will be higher tomorrow than today. A good preventive maintenance program ensures the longest possible life of the facility.

Ensure Economy and Efficiency of Operation. One of the measures of economy and efficiency in the operation of a facility is to hire, train, supervise, evaluate, and to set priorities for housekeeping and maintenance personnel. Having a staff who can respond rapidly to housekeeping and maintenance needs in residence halls, student centers, and health centers is particularly important. Having custodial and maintenance personnel on the student affairs budget is advantageous because it allows for scheduling time and determining the priority in which various tasks and projects are to be completed. The housekeeping and maintenance personnel develop loyalty to and an identification with the facility to which they are assigned, which results in pride of workmanship. Many times loyalty and pride do not develop when the workers come from a centralized campus labor pool with responsibility for the entire campus. For the student affairs administrator to control a particular environment, control of funds and personnel is imperative, particularly as it relates to housekeeping and maintenance. Other arrangements require considerable more negotiation and coordination to gain rapid response to routine maintenance needs.

Identify Priorities for Maintenance. Equipment wears out and becomes obsolete and major repair and renovation projects are necessities. The student affairs administrator needs a planning tool to identify and plan for replacement of equipment and renovation of facilities. One such tool that has proven effective is a five-year repair and replacement program. To establish such a plan, a list is made of all equipment and furnishings, date acquired or date when last maintained, and life expectancy of each item in each facility (Figure 16.1). As an example, in the residential setting mattresses will normally last ten years, desks 20 years, corridor carpet five years, and lounge chairs in public areas five years. Examples of items to be included in the regular repair schedule are painting, roof replacement, and exterior maintenance. From information provided in the equipment and furnishing record (Figure 16.1), a five-year repair and replacement program can be developed (Figure 16.2).

Records such as those illustrated in Figures 16.1 and 16.2 contain information in a concise and sequential outline for the student affairs administrator to gain an overview of replacement and major repair projects for each facility. To be effective, the five-year replacement and renovation schedule should be updated on an annual basis. As unexpected projects surface, they should be added to the plan.

Systematically Determine Priorities for Spending Maintenance Funds. Frequently the student affairs administrator is confronted with replacement and repair items on the five-year plan that exceed funds available. Ranking projects so available resources are spent for the most important or pressing items is necessary. Funds must be allocated or set aside to accomplish those projects that have the highest priority in any particular year. If funds are not available to accomplish all those items on the five-year plan, some projects will need to be moved to another year.

Support Programs. The personalization of student rooms and common areas within residence halls through painting, decorating, and building structures such as lofts or room dividers has become a significant part of housing programs at many colleges. To student affairs administrators this raises the question of whether the value students derive from the program is worth the cost. Does a student-room-painting-program replace the seven-year painting cycle, even though all students will probably not paint their rooms? Does the student-room-painting-program increase the cost for the housing department? In addition, when wooden structures are introduced into student rooms, the facilities manager must be cognizant of the need to meet fire and safety regulations. When does the personalization program infringe on the safety of the occupant of the room and other residents of the building? The student affairs administrator must deal with questions regarding liability, storage of room furniture, damage to the existing structure, use of the room during the summer months, and possible disruptions during summer and during the construction process.

| Hall: Douglas | | | Normal Occupancy | 400 |
| Year Opened: 1966 | | | Expanded Occupancy | 430 |

	Date Acquired	Life Expectancy		Date Maintained	Life Expectancy
Furnishings			**Maintenance**		
Students Rooms:			Painting:		
Mattresses	1976	10 years	Student Rooms	1982	5 years
Beds	1966	20	Corridors	1981	5
Desks	1966	20	Lounges and	1981	5
Desk Chairs	1981	15	Multiuse Areas		
Chest of Drawers	1966	20			
Draperies	1979	10			
Floor Covering:					
Carpet	1980	5	Exterior:		
			Maintenance	1982	2 years
Multiuse Areas:			Repainting	1976	10
Lounge Chairs	1978	5 years			
TV Room Chairs	1979	5	Roof:		
Lounge Drapes	1980	10			
Floor Covering:			Replacement	1966	25 years
Carpet	1980	5			

Figure 16.1 Illustration of a facility equipment and furnishings record that contains date acquired or date when last maintained and life expectancy for each item.

1983	1984	1985	1986	1987
Replace Lounge Chairs	Replace TV Room Chairs Paint Exterior	Replace Lounge and Corridor Carpet Replace Carpet in Student Rooms	Paint Corridors Paint Lounges Replace Matresses Replace Roof	Replace Desks, Chest of Drawers, and Beds (Replacement delayed one year to evenly equalize expenditures) Paint student rooms

Figure 16.2 Five-year replacement and renovation program for Douglas Hall.

These and other questions regarding the value of supporting a particular student program, activity, or service and the resulting maintenance cost constantly confront the student affairs administrator charged with management of a particular facility.

Promoting Individual Student Development. Many facilities for which student affairs administrators are responsible are multiuse-multipurpose facilities. During the planning phase, a particular population was targeted, and various programs, activities, and services were identified to be accommodated. Once the facility is functional, student needs, programs, and services may change requiring flexibility and creativity on the part of the student affairs administrator. Establishing policies and procedures governing use of the facility is essential to provide necessary support for student growth and development. Policies and procedures must facilitate use of the facility by the greatest number of people participating in diverse programs, activities, and services. Various factors to be considered in developing these policies and procedures are reservation of space, responsibility for setup/cleanup, damages that result from above normal wear and tear, vandalism, and priority for usage of space.

Staffing a facility with appropriate personnel significantly contributes to individual student development. In a residence hall, for instance, undergraduate staff, commonly called "resident assistants", custodians, maintenance, clerical staff, and professional staff are all necessary. Placement of resident assistant rooms, reception desk, vending and laundry services, and various activity rooms, such as study, recreation and exercise, will either enhance or impede student development.

A variety of functions must be performed in the residence hall if student growth and development are to be facilitated, and various staff members must work together to accomplish objectives of the residential community. Programs and services performed by hall staff members must be integrated to facilitate student development. Staff must have the appropriate skills to keep the facility in good working order and to accomplish the purpose for which the building was constructed, while maintaining flexibility to accommodate new programs and services as they are introduced.

SUMMARY AND CONCLUSIONS

In preparation for the decades ahead, student affairs administrators must be involved actively in the planning of major renovation and new construction projects. Participation by student affairs administrators ensures that facilities will reflect an understanding of student development philosophy and that facilities accommodate programs, activities, and services required for a changing clientele. This will necessitate active participation of campus planning committees and committees charged with renovation and construction of facilities.

As enrollments decline and money becomes less available, competition for students becomes increasingly acute. The impression created by the facilities that student affairs administrators manage is increasingly important in recruitment and retention. Because facilities reflect the institution's philosophy and attitude toward students, facilities are to be managed and staffed to support programs, activities, and services that are necessary to meet *needs* of those students.

Effective facilities management contributes positively to student development by providing space that facilitates student growth and development through interaction. Physical facilities must contribute to, rather than detract from, programming, program development, and student participation. When student affairs administrators have opportunity to construct or renovate facilities, they must proceed in a systematic manner that includes a planning model consisting of a philosophy statement, needs assessment, program usage, drawings, cost estimates, financing, and evaluation. Futhermore, the student affairs administrator must be sensitive to and aware of the environment that is created by the facilities and the impact that this environment has on student clientele. In the words of Winston Churchill, "we shape our buildings; thereafter they shape us."

REFERENCES

Anchors, S., Schroeder, C. C., & Jackson, S. *Making yourself at home: A practical guide to restructuring and personalizing your residence hall environment.* Washington, DC: American College Personnel Association, 1978.

Brandt, J. A., & Chapman, N. J. Student alteration of residence hall rooms: Social climate. *Journal of College and University Student Housing,* 1981, *11*(1), 37-42.

Carnegie Council on Policy Studies in Higher Education. *Three thousand futures: The next twenty years for higher education.* San Francisco: Jossey-Bass, 1980.

DeYoung, A. J., Moos, R. H., VanDort, B., & Smail, P. M. Expectations, perceptions and changes in university residence climates: Two case studies. *Journal of College and University Student Housing,* 1974, *4*(2), 4-11.

Educational Facilities Laboratory. *Student housing.* New York: Author, 1972.

Gerst, M. S., & Moos, R. H. Social ecology of university student residences. *Journal of Educational Psychology,* 1972, *63,* 513-25.

Gerst, M. S., & Sweetwood, H. Correlates of dormitory social climate. *Environment and Behavior,* 1973, *5,* 440-63.

Grant, W. H. Humanizing the residence hall environment. In D. DeCoster & P. Mable (Eds.), *Student development and education in college residence halls.* Washington, DC: American College Personnel Association, 1974.

Hallenbeck, D. A., & Ullom, M. Survey of new construction, renovation, and/or remodeling. *ACUHO News,* 1980, *19*(4), 18-19.

Hanson, W. B., & Altman, S. Decorating personal places: A descriptive analysis. *Environment and Behavior,* 1976, *8,* 491-504.

Harrie, E. F. The dormitory interior—what the experts think it should be. *American School and University,* 1968, *41,* 40.

Heilweil, M. The influence of dormitory architecture on resident behavior. *Environment and Behavior,* 1973, *5,* 377-412.

Heyck, T. W. Universities, university housing, and national needs. *Journal of College and University Student Housing,* 1978, *7*(2), 8-11.

Kaiser, H. H. Facilities management: A program for the 80's. In H. H. Kaiser (Ed.), *New directions for higher education: Managing facilities more effectively* (No. 30). San Francisco: Jossey Bass, 1980.

Moos, R. H., & Gerst, M. S. *University residence environment scale manual.* Palo Alto, CA: Consulting Psychologists Press, 1974.

Riker, H. C. *College housing as learning centers.* Washington, DC: American College Personnel Association, 1965.

Schroeder, C. C. New strategies for structuring residential environments. *Journal of College Student Personnel,* 1976, *17,* 386-90.

Schroeder, C. C. Designing college environments for students. In F. B. Newton & K. L. Ender (Eds.), *Student development practices: Strategies for making a difference.* Springfield, IL: Charles C. Thomas Publishers, 1980.

Walters, R. R. The dormitory interior—what the experts think it should be. *American School and University,* 1968, *41,* 40.

Werring, C. J., Winston, R. B. Jr., & McCaffrey, R. J. How paint projects affect residents' perceptions of their living environment. *Journal of College and University Student Housing,* 1981, *11*(2), 3-7.

Wichman, H., & Healy, V. In their own spaces: Student built lofts in dormitory rooms. Paper presented at the meeting of the American Psychological Association, New York, September 1979.

Williams, G. D. University enrollments and the battle of retiring the bond. *ACUHO News,* 1979, *18*(5), 5-7.

SUGGESTED READINGS

Anchors, S., Schroeder, C. C., & Jackson, S. *Making yourself at home: A practical guide to restructuring and personalizing your residence hall environment.* Washington, DC: American College Personnel Association, 1978.

Conyne, R. K., & Clack, R. J. *Environmental assessment and design: A new tool for the applied behavioral scientist.* New York: Praeger, 1981.

Frederiksen, C. F. The future is now. *Journal of College and University Student Housing,* 1980, *10*(2), 3-5.

Heilweil, M. The influence of dormitory architecture on resident behavior. *Environment and Behavior,* 1973, *5,* 377-411.

Kaiser, H. H. (Ed.). *New directions for higher education: Managing facilities more effectively* (No. 30). San Francisco: Jossey-Bass, 1980.

Mehrabian, A. *Public places and private spaces.* New York: Basic Books, 1976.

Schroeder, C. C. Student development through environmental management. In G. S. Blimling & J. H. Schuh (Eds.), *New directions for student services: Increasing the educational role of residence halls* (No. 13). San Francisco: Jossey-Bass, 1981.

Wilbur A. Tincher, a native of Frankfort, Kentucky, holds the A.B., M.A., and Ed.D. degrees from the University of Kentucky. He has taught high school English and served as principal of an elementary school.

Upon completion of the doctorate he went to Eastern Kentucky University as Director of Student Personnel and Assistant Professor of Education. He then joined Auburn University as an Assistant Professor and Coordinator of Student Personnel in the School of Education. Subsequently, at Auburn University he became Director of Institutional Research, Director of Educational Services, and then Dean of Student Services which included the offices of High School and Junior College Relations, Admissions, Pre-College Counseling, Student Financial Aid, Registrar, and University Placement Service. During his administrative assignments at Auburn University he held academic rank in the Department of Educational Leadership and was promoted to Professor in 1970. He is a member of the Graduate Faculty and has directed many doctoral dissertations and continues to chair doctoral committees. He recently returned to full-time teaching and research.

Chapter 17

TIME MANAGEMENT AND PLANNING FOR STUDENT AFFAIRS PROFESSIONALS

Wilbur A. Tincher

Student affairs professionals, whether experienced or new to the job, have many responsibilities and consequently many demands on their time. That most people are satisfied with the return they get for the expenditure of time is doubtful. Even so, time is their most precious resource. All persons have the same amount of it: 24 hours a day, 168 hours a week. However time is used, it is expendable, irreplaceable, and irreversible.

While some are concerned about the efficient use of time—getting things done as quickly as possible with the least wasted motion—the student affairs professional must primarily *be concerned about the effective use of time, that is, selecting the most appropriate task and accomplishing it in the most appropriate way.* One may be efficient at performing unimportant tasks, but such efficiency may be ineffective use of one's time. The Greeks use two words for time: *chronos,* which means clock time and *kairos,* which is the time for decision or meaningful time. A major goal of student affairs staff members should be to use time meaningfully.

Planning also is one administrative function that is frequently slighted by student affairs professionals. Simply put, planning means a course of action. Other administrative functions—organizing, staffing, directing, and controlling—are effective only when based upon sound and effective planning. Too few persons recognize the cyclical nature of planning and the importance of time management in the process.

This chapter is designed to assist student affairs professionals in assessing use of their time and, by advance thought and planning, to make its use effective.

EFFECTIVE USE OF TIME

Myths and Misconceptions

All professionals have established patterns for use of time. Those dissatisfied with its use and those wishing to make more effective use probably need to change their behavior. Because behavior is habitual and is, in part, based on conscious and unconscious assumptions about the management of time, one needs to examine his/her assumptions.

The following ten misconceptions or false assumptions regarding time management have been identified and discussed by Douglass (1976).

Myth 1: *If you really look, you can probably find many ways to save time.* Actually no way exists to save time. It cannot be hoarded; neither can it be overspent. Yesterday's 24 hours are spent; all one has is what is at hand now. More benefits will accrue if one stops worrying about "saving" time and focuses on "spending" time.

Myth 2: *Being busy and active is the best way to get the most done.* This is part of the "busyness" syndrome that most adults learned as children, and which has been reinforced in work situations; however, too many student affairs administrators jump into a task before planning and thinking through the value of the task. More thought should be given to each day's activities and questions asked, such as "Does each of my activities contribute to my objectives?" and "Are there other activities that will contribute to my objectives?"

Myth 3: *Time problems can usually be solved by working harder.* Sometimes working harder is the answer; however, working smarter usually beats working harder. Frequently, ways exist to shorten a task or to eliminate some steps. Perhaps ways can even be found to reduce the number of tasks.

Myth 4: *If you want it right, you'd better do it yourself is still the best advice.* New professionals may have to "do it themselves" because no subordinate is available for delegation of tasks. However, help that clerical staff and students can give in accomplishing many tasks should not be overlooked. The experienced professional should delegate when possible, because many tasks can be performed as well, and possibly faster, by subordinates. The delegation of responsibilities is one of the best ways to broaden new professionals' experiences.

Myth 5: *Finding the problems is easy—it's finding the solutions that is difficult.* Administrators may assume they know the problem, but they may need more data to be sure. For example, one may conclude that the telephone is a problem without data regarding the number, source, length, topics, and times of calls. Solutions are more easily discernible once objective data are available.

Myth 6: *Most ordinary day-to-day activities don't need to be planned—and you probably can't plan them anyway.* To control one's time, daily activities need to be planned. While one cannot control the times and nature of meetings, telephone calls, or drop-in visitors, these activities can be organized to make more effective use of time. Flexibility, however, certainly has to be built in.

Myth 7: *Professionals who concentrate on doing tasks efficiently are also the most effective managers.* Efficiency does not necessarily result in effectiveness. If one is efficient, the fewest resources are used to accomplish a given task; to be effective, goals are accomplished. People can be efficient at things that do not need to be done at all, or certainly not by them. Finding the right thing to do determines effectiveness.

Myth 8: *A good way to reduce time waste is to look for short-cuts in managerial functions.* When pressed for time administrators may neglect essential functions in favor of things that may appear more urgent. Such functions as planning and development of new professionals can be delayed, but in the long run the consequences may be costly.

Myth 9: *Managing time better is essentially a matter of reducing the time it takes to accomplish various tasks.* Not so! To manage time better means spending the *appropriate* amount of time on every task. Probably this means spending less time on some things and more time on others. One may want to reduce time spent on meetings, reports, irrelevant conversations, correspondence, and other such activities and spend more time in planning, thinking, developing new professionals, or other important activities. Time added in some areas decreases it in others.

Myth 10: *No one ever has enough time.* Each person has all the time available. Although persons frequently think they have too little time, the problem is not so much the amount of time, but how it is used. People have time to do the things that are important to them; the problem is knowing what is really important.

Those who agree that these statements are false assumptions will have little difficulty in improving their skills in time management. However, those who accept these statements as being accurate may have some blocks to overcome before formulating a time management program. Behavior is, after all, based on assumptions, which when changed, may result in changed behaviors.

Identifying Time Wasters

In reality, little can be done to "manage time." It is expendable, irreplaceable, and irreversible. What is really meant when time management is discussed is management of oneself, and this usually means getting organized. Management of self is not a particularly easy task, however.

Management experts have identified scores of time wasters that apply to personal as well as professional aspects of life. To take the position that one has little control of time is easy; however, an examination of common time wasters reveals that individuals have more control over time, if exerted, than usually realized. The range of things that waste time runs from lack of defined goals and objectives, inability to involve and utilize other persons, to failure to employ practices that make appointments, meetings, and telephone conversations more productive. Mackenzie (1976) has listed 15 leading time wasters encountered by all levels of administrators. These are shown in Table 17.1.

Student affairs practitioners should not be surprised if several of these sound familiar. All administrators have time wasters; however, one person's time wasters may not be another's. All self-management involves habits; and changing of time-wasting habits requires knowing

Table 17.1
The Fifteen Leading Time Wasters

1. Telephone interruptions

2. Drop-in visitors

3. Meetings (both scheduled and unscheduled)

4. Crises

5. Lack of objectives, priorities and deadlines

6. Cluttered desk and personal disorganization

7. Ineffective delegation and involvement in routine and detail

8. Attempting too much at once and unrealistic time estimates

9. Lack of, or unclear communication and instructions

10. Inadequate, inaccurate and delayed information

11. Indecision and procrastination

12. Confused responsibility and authority

13. Inability to say "No"

14. Leaving tasks unfinished

15. Lack of self-discipline

Note. Based on and modified from Mackenzie, 1976, p. 23.

one's present habits, what time management habits are desired, and how one would like to behave.

To have an effective time management plan, controlling time wasters or turning them to time gainers, is critical. To better control time wasters, student affairs professionals need to understand how they waste time. One way of making that discovery is through a weekly log.

To establish a weekly log administrators need to record at hourly intervals how they spent their time during one week. At the end of each day, time can be classified according to the code shown in Figure 17.1. At the end of the week the hours spent on each category of tasks can be counted.

After a time use log for a one-week period has been kept, these questions should be asked:

- What does the analysis tell about the job?
- Where is time being spent?
- Is time being spent where the priorities are?
- What is the administrator doing that others should be doing?
- Is prime time being used for major tasks?
- What is being done that doesn't really need doing at all?
- What is done that wastes the time of others?

(Association of California School Administrators, 1979, p. 17)

If student affairs administrators are like most persons who describe and analyze their use of time for the first time, they may be surprised. Even administrators who consider themselves highly efficient are often shocked at the outcome. According to Halverson (1978) the results of such surveys usually show that (1) the majority of time is spent in crisis resolution instead of planning to prevent crisis situations; (2) frequent interruptions destroy planning incentives or momentum; (3) more time is spent on trivia than on important matters; (4) important objectives receive less time than unimportant objectives; and (5) the most productive time is spent on items that require the least creativity and productivity.

Solutions to Time Wasters

Time wasters for student affairs administrators may be different from those identified by Mackenzie (1969), but assuming they are similar to most peoples, a look at ways time wasters can be turned into time savers is appropriate.

Establish Written Goals and Objectives. An important step in developing a time management system is to ask what one wants from life and commit those goals to paper. All facets of one's life should be included: personal, professional, family, health, community, social, and

Beside each hour of the day, write what you did most of that time. Then, at the end of each working day, classify your time according to this code:

#1—Professional Goal Functions (Program planning with staff and/or student groups, (staff development/evaluation)
#2—Critical/Crisis Functions (Vandalism, accidents, housing emergencies)
#3—Maintenance Functions (Phone calls, correspondence, mail)
P—Personal Activity

	EXAMPLE	MONDAY	TUESDAY	WEDNESDAY	THURSDAY	FRIDAY
8	#3 open mail organize	8	8	8	8	8
9	#2 Dorm bix over weekend	9	9	9	9	9
10	#3 Administrative Council	10	10	10	10	10
11	#3 Answer Corres-pondence	11	11	11	11	11
12	— Lunch	12	12	12	12	12
1	#1 Staff re 5-yr plan	1	1	1	1	1
2	P Dentist	2	2	2	2	2
3	#3 Communication Board meeting	3	3	3	3	3
4	#1 Planning with student groups	4	4	4	4	4

TOTALS: Count the hours you
spend this week on:

#1 _____
#2 _____
#3 _____
P _____

Your goal for
next week:

#1 _____
#2 _____
#3 _____
P _____

Figure 17.1 Time management weekly log.
Note. Based on and modified from Sexton and Switzer, 1978, p. 485.

recreational. While this discussion is concerned with managing professional time, how nonprofessional (personnel) time is spent influences professional effectiveness. A healthy professional does not burn out in any facet of his/her life.

The importance of specific goals and objectives must be recognized. While long-range goals may be idealistic and lofty, specific short-term objectives must be identified clearly. Both long-range and short-term goals and objectives should be listed. Lakein (1973) suggested that the three most important goals in each category should be selected and listed as A-1, A-2, and A-3. Listing goals in order of priority and allocating time to those goals of highest priority is another step in developing a time management system. Monitoring the schedule to make certain that high-priority objectives continue to receive a large amount of high quality time is necessary.

Develop a Plan for Each Role. Most student affairs professionals perform several roles. The *self-service* role involves physical maintenance activities such as eating, sleeping, exercise, and personal care; the *family* role includes that of a parent, spouse, and son or daughter; *social-cultural, recreational* includes activities in which one participates with friends, usually for enjoyment; the *community* role pertains to voluntary, political, or religious activities; the *personal* role involves activities that are done essentially alone such as pleasure reading and hobbies; and the *professional* role is one's work—that which brings in the money to support one's lifestyle (Association of California School Administrators, 1979).

Student affairs staff members assume many functions in fulfilling their professional role, such as administrator, manager, advisor to student groups, speaker to parent and alumni groups, and representative on faculty committees. An area frequently pushed aside because of other demands is one's own professional growth and development. Student affairs professionals need to devote no less than 25 percent of their work week to professional improvement. Assuming an average work week of 48 hours, this means that student affairs professionals should spend 12 hours per week on professional improvement activities such as conferences, journal and book reading, and in-service education.

While important that a plan be developed for each life role, a plan for the professional role is imperative.

Manage Rather Than "Do." Many student affairs administrators feel more comfortable in performing work requiring mostly technical skills, rather than broad administrative skills. This situation is described by Allen (1973) as the "principle of technical priority," which indicates that when required to perform management work and technical work during the same time period, those in management positions will more likely give priority to the technical work.

Student affairs practitioners need to keep in mind that they are managers and obtain results to a great degree from other people. This will help them in not "doing" things and keep them on the track of "managing" the enterprise and the people involved in it.

Schedule Judiciously. While few, if any, persons have complete control over their schedules, several suggestions can be offered to make more effective use of time. The administrator needs to recognize certain "givens" and schedule around them. Little can be done about the weekly meeting of the Administrative Council or regularly scheduled staff meeting; one simply has to schedule around these. Blocks of time of one to two hours are suggested for planning, because a large space of time at one sitting is usually more effective than short spaces scheduled separately.

Most people are most creative in the mornings, and the professional who fits this description should schedule planning time then. Obviously such a schedule varies with environmental conditions. Creative activities need high energy time, while typical telephone calls and letter writing require low energy and should be relegated to later in the day. Provision for daily creative time is highly recommended. At least one-half hour daily to think about who one is, where one is going, and how to solve some of those nagging problems is a very desirable use of time. Every minute of the day should not be scheduled. Scheduling must allow for flexibility in order to handle the unexpected. Allowing a few minutes between activities for breathing time is also a good practice.

Make a Daily To Do List. Lakein (1973) considered the daily *To Do List* a fundamental time planning tool. He suggested making a list daily at a regular time. The list of things one wants or needs to do that day should be made on one piece of paper rather than using scraps.

What should be included on the list? Certainly the list needs to be a realistic one, and routine items may not be included. Items that probably would not be accomplished without special attention should be listed.

Each item on the *To Do List* should be categorized as either an A, B, or C—an A for those that have a high value; a B for those with medium value; and a C for those with low value. A items should be those that yield the most value. Doing the A's first and saving the B's and C's for later will result in getting the most out of one's time.

Consideration should be given to further prioritizing the list by using A1, A2, A3, B1, B2, B3, C1, C2, C3. Some persons color code the entries using black for routine entries and red for top-priority items. An additional suggestion is to place all A and B items on one sheet and the more numerous C's on a separate sheet. The A and B list is kept on top of the C list, and every time that A and B list is raised to do a C, one becomes aware that the best use of time was not made.

Before beginning a day, professionals should determine which tasks can be delegated, and then work should begin on A's, not the C's; usually 80 percent of the items will be C's and 20 percent A's and B's. It is unlikely that all of the items on the *To Do List* will be completed each day. This should not bother administrators; they have tomorrow to make a new list and they shouldn't be surprised if a C item today becomes a B item tomorrow.

Set Deadlines. Realistic firm deadlines should be imposed and met. Staff should recognize that everything usually takes longer than expected, so a 20 percent cushion on the major task deadlines should be built in. Mackenzie (1969) thought one should leave 20 percent of each day unplanned (unscheduled) to compensate for characteristic underestimates. One administrator places due dates on the calendar one week in advance to allow a cushion and to insure prompt task completion.

Placing the due date ahead on the calendar is a good idea unless one tends to procrastinate. A few things one can do to be encouraged and reminded to move toward deadlines include: going public with projects and deadlines (telling others what one intends to do and when); asking help in monitoring progress (a secretary or assistant can help in checking at intervals); use reminders (lists, egg timer, wrist alarm), and rewarding oneself (no coffee until deadline met).

Some deadlines for budgets or reports are set for staff, and although they may sometimes be unrealistic, these require the same, if not more, diligence as deadlines staff set for themselves. While setting deadlines for themselves, student affairs administrators should not be hesitant to set them realistically, but firmly, for others. They, thereby, can help others manage time.

Delegate. Do nothing that can be delegated! This may be hard to do, but administrators might be surprised at the number of tasks on their lists that someone else can do. One's job should be analyzed carefully and tasks or activities delegated that (1) are repetitive, (2) can be done by others more effectively, (3) one does not like to do, and (4) will provide job development opportunities for the staff. If all of a particular task cannot be delegated, a portion of it could be. For example, routine letters of inquiry from parents or prospective students concerning certain aspects of an area can often be responded to by a subordinate or a secretary.

A word of caution may be in order regarding the reverse delegation that occurs if administrators permit subordinates to delegate their problems to them for solution or action. The wise administrator will refuse to make decisions for subordinates; if they need help, and they certainly may, ask the right questions and ask them to bring proposed solutions along with their problems. In-service training should address deficit skill areas and problem solving.

Once a task or activity has been delegated, administrators should not become involved in its details. In delegating, student affairs professionals must recognize the inherent risk being taken—the task may not be done at their level of performance, and mistakes will be made and should be allowed. Fortunately, administrators and subordinates can learn from their mistakes.

To reduce the inherent risk, the student affairs professional should always delegate authority commensurate with the responsibility assigned. In addition, concise, complete, unambiguous instructions should be given. And progress should be checked in time to take corrective action if required. The person should be held accountable for the end result, not procedures.

Once everything that can be delegated has been delegated, administrators have more time for those A items on their *To Do Lists*. And delegating effectively is an important contribution to an administrator's professional growth as well as to the growth of the staff.

Establish Proper Working Conditions. Student affairs professionals should analyze their activity areas to determine if conditions are ideal for working. They should start in their offices. How long has it been since desks were cleared? Some persons claim they work well and effectively at a cluttered desk, but management experts assert that a reasonably ordered work area is an asset to productivity. At least, they say, time spent looking for letters, documents, and other papers can be reduced if the desk is organized. Rogers (1973) suggested four hints to organize a work area: (1) separate items by importance, (2) separate reading material to be done later, (3) separate work that can be done at odd moments, and (4) set aside a place for messages.

Before trying to use Rogers' hints, it might be advisable to take everything from the top of one's desk and from every desk drawer and place the things on a table. These items should be sorted into A's, B's, and C's. It may be advisable to obtain folders or file boxes for the A's and B's and place them on the desk. The C's should be placed in a bottom drawer that should be examined weekly or less often, and it is possible that many of the C items can be discarded periodically.

One student affairs dean asks that the mail be pre-sorted into three piles: that needing attention, items of information, and publications. This pre-sorting, while not always accurate, assists the dean in deciding which are A's, B's, and C's. The A's and B's are treated as such; the C's are placed in the bottom drawer.

An important general principle to follow is that a paper should be handled only once. It is possible to pen a response at the bottom of a letter; the secretary can prepare a response for the administrator; the salient points of a report can be highlighted and disseminated. If the administrator is unable to handle the paper only once before disposing of it, at least something should be done to move toward its final disposition. For instance, an assistant may be asked for additional information. The practitioner should write on it, file it, send it on, or whatever; however, it should not be put down just to be picked up or shuffled through later.

A key factor in good working conditions is the secretary, who can be of immeasurable assistance in achieving goals. The student affairs professional and the secretary are a team. Each is essential to effective management, but teamwork develops only through care and nurturing. It is important to keep the secretary informed, including what the goals are and any changes in them. The secretary's role should be well defined, and those responsibilities should be accompanied with commensurate authority. An alert and effective secretary can help keep the administrator's desk clear, meet deadlines, screen junk mail, retrieve information, reduce interruptions (telephone calls, drop-in visitors), and generally make office life pleasant. Administrators should remember a few minutes spent each day planning with their secretaries will be time well spent.

Avoid Unnecessary Interruptions. High on everyone's list of time wasters are telephone calls and visitors. How to eliminate unnecessary calls and visits and to reduce necessary ones to reasonable lengths of time is a problem for all administrators. This is particularly true of student affairs administrators because most were trained in the principle that student affairs professionals should always be available to students; most of them subscribe to the open door policy, which is applied not only to students but also to staff, faculty, and others. This issue is not easy to resolve, and student affairs administrators need to recognize the difficulty involved in dealing with it.

Perhaps a more realistic principle to subscribe to is that the student affairs office has an open door policy, which means that students, staff, faculty, and others always have access to *a* professional staff member, but that not *all* professionals need to be available to everybody all the time. If the administrator can accept this idea, several suggestions for controlling the telephone and visitors' interruptions may be useful.

A time log of phone calls showing the origin, extent, and reasons for calls is advisable. A plan should then be developed to screen, refer, and consolidate calls. The secretary can be instructed to take and divert calls. The secretary could give the administrator telephone messages periodically during the day and calls could be returned two or three times a day. The establishment of a "call-back" time in one's schedule is important. Of course, when the secretary takes the call, the caller should be advised of the approximate time the call will be returned.

Should the secretary interrupt the conference with a student when a telephone call is received? It is most important that the secretary be provided with a definite procedure. For example, a list of those persons (such as the president or immediate supervisor) for whose calls the administrator expects to be interrupted should be given to the receptionist.

On calls initiated by the administrator, it is wise to group the calls and make them only at specified times during the day, if at all possible. Some find an agenda saves time. Be brief and terminate lengthy conversations with an announcement that "I have another call. I'm sorry." Calls also can be shortened by socializing elsewhere, not on the telephone.

If the amount of time occupied by drop-in visitors is unknown, the student affairs staff member would do well to take (or have the secretary take) a time log of visits, both business and personal; internal and external; the scheduled and unscheduled. Visitors are a great part of student affairs business, and the object here is not to exclude them but to provide a modicum of control over visits so that necessary verbal communication is provided for, and yet time required to accomplish other tasks and obligations is available.

Again, the secretary can play a key role by screening visitors without offending them. The secretary can assist additionally by interrupting when it is time to conclude a visit—scheduled or otherwise. For example, the administrator can pre-arrange to be reminded by the secretary (by intercom) of another appointment or impending meeting after a ten-to-fifteen minute period of time. Many administrators have felt for years that they just had to see whoever comes to their offices; however, it is possible that they may have overestimated the importance of their immediate availability to others. The secretary may be able to divert the visitor to another staff member or to schedule an appointment at a later time.

A modification of the open door policy may be in order. Rather than maintaining an open door throughout the day, the administrator could restrict such practice to limited times during the day or week. If staff and students are made aware of this practice, they will probably accept it after an adjustment period.

Again socializing may need to be curtailed and restricted to lunch or more appropriate times. Sometimes visits can be shortened by guiding the discussion toward objectives of the visit; administrators should not feel guilty about monitoring the visitor's time because it is their time being used. A visit that exceeds one's time expectations can be terminated by a direct but courteous comment "Let's get together later. I have another commitment now."

Make the Most of Meetings. Meetings, meetings, meetings plus inefficient agendas or lack of closure are familiar to many. Everyone spends more time than necessary in meetings. For the administrator who is in a position to call meetings or to chair them, several suggestions can be offered.

"Is this meeting necessary?" should be asked before one is scheduled. A meeting should not be held if the same objectives can be achieved through individual contacts, a memo, a telephone message, or some other communications device. If it is determined that the meeting is necessary, who should attend? Only those who are needed should be invited, and if administrators have been invited to a meeting over which they have no control, they may want to consider sending a representative if they decide it proper to do so. Remember, the administrator may delegate a member of the staff to be the representative for certain committees that often meet on a regular basis.

A chairperson should always be named and the location of the meeting should be planned for expediency and convenience. An agenda for each meeting that lists the items for discussion and the estimated length of the meeting is desirable, and it should be circulated before the meeting if possible. The student affairs professional, as chairperson or as a participant, can help facilitate the meeting by encouraging that items not on the agenda be tabled for future sessions.

Few things are more irritating than for a meeting not to start on time. By delaying for late arrivals, the chairperson penalizes those who arrive on time and rewards those who come late. The continuance of a meeting past the anticipated ending time may be reason for administrators to excuse themselves, unless, of course, the meeting was called by the boss and it would be unwise to leave.

Circulation of minutes of the meeting or a summary of actions taken, if either is appropriate, within 48 hours to those in attendance and to others who need to know about the meeting is recommended.

If it is impossible to control or restrict meetings to one's satisfaction, they could be called at one hour before lunch or quitting time. Socializing is better left to other times.

Ask the question: "What is the best use of my time right now?" This question, proposed by Lakein (1973) can be a valuable tool. He said that statements of goals, *To Do Lists,* and schedules are "musts" to develop an effective time management system and are excellent planning tools; however, those tools simply are not the best to use 10-15 times a day in making what sometimes becomes minute-by-minute decisions on the use of time. Lakein suggested that the time to ask the question is after one has been interrupted by a necessary visitor or telephone call; when there is an intuitive feeling that one is not making the best use of time; when distracted; or when torn between two or more projects.

An administrator may have had a particularly hard time getting started on a high-value task and discovers there are 10 minutes before the next appointment or 15 minutes before lunch. It is surprising how beneficial it may be to spend those 10 to 15 minutes doing something about that task. If it is making a budget, to do no more than to read or re-read the mandated guidelines, or to get last year's budget papers from the file and review them will at least make a start on that project. It may be easier the next time to do more.

Another appropriate time to ask "What is the best use of my time right now?" is when one has waiting time, commuting time, or other transition time. While commuting, one can catch up on news and thus save some time in newspaper reading; listen to cassette tapes to improve skills and knowledge; or dictate letters, notes, or ideas on a tape. While standing in line or waiting for a doctor who is late or running behind schedule, use reading material that was stuck in a pocket before leaving the office or just think through a particularly sticky problem. And a note pad or note cards on which to record an idea or a reminder should be carried at all times. Jogging, if done alone, is an excellent time to review goals and solve all kinds of problems.

Measuring Effectiveness

Any endeavor should include an evaluation procedure that affords an assessment of achievement. A time management system is no exception. It is important to look at the program and the process to determine if changes need to be made.

Brechin (1979) suggested that a review procedure be planned at least twice a year. Six months, she feels, is ample time to allow for goals and actual time expenditure to be tested, and an examination of them after that time permits an assessment of success or failure of efforts. It is unlikely that one will experience success with every goal or technique employed. Some goals may have been unrealistic and some techniques may not work given the constraints of a particular work environment.

Several questions to be asked at six-months' intervals are posed by Brechin (1979) (Table 17.2). In effect, they require one to look at how time is currently spent; the extent to which professional and personal goals have been met and if not, why not; what the problem areas are; and how the time management system can be altered to achieve professional and personal goals in the next six months.

Table 17.2
Six-month Review Questions

—How is my time spent now?	—Are my personal goals being met?
—Have I met my professional and career goals?	—If not, why not?
—If not, why not?	—How can I alter my time management system to increase my personal growth and happiness?
—How can I alter my time management system to increase my effectiveness in the organization for the next 6 months?	

Note. Based on and modified from Brechin, 1979, p. 20.

Successes and failure will result. Credit should be given for successes, but failures should not be dwelled upon. They should be used as learning experiences. Most persons will be trying to change habits of long standing, and it may take a long time—a year or two—to get control of one's time.

DECIDING WHAT NEEDS TO BE DONE

Management Functions

All student affairs professionals, new and experienced, have some management responsibilities. Some activities done may not be recognized as management functions; nevertheless, practitioners perform them at one time or another in some manner. The basic elements with which a manager deals are ideas, things, and people. Do not student affairs deal with all three? Management of these basic elements is very closely related, according to Mackenzie (1969, p. 80), "to conceptual thinking (of which planning is an essential part), administration, and leadership." While each administrator may have more strength in one of these tasks—conceptual thinking, administration, or leadership—than the others, all administrators are probably required to perform all of these tasks, and in reality, it may be hard at times to differentiate between them.

Some of the most popular management models include Planning, Programming, and Budgeting Systems (PPBS), Management by Objectives (MBO), Organization Development (OD), and Management Information Systems (MIS) (Foxley, 1980). All models contain the planning function in one form or another. One of the most standard models is that of Mackenzie (1969), who listed as sequential functions of the management process: planning, organizing, staffing, directing, and controlling. A detailed description of the planning part of the process is shown in Table 17.3.

Need for Planning

All organizations accomplish their goals and objectives through people who use ideas and things in the process. If members of a student affairs organization were at liberty to develop independently their ideas, goals and objectives, strategies, programs, and action patterns, it is unlikely that overall goals and objectives of the student affairs unit would be realized. Organization goals and objectives would more likely be achieved if a predetermined course of action—a plan—was developed.

The need for planning—that is a conscious choice of ideas, goals, objectives, program structure, and action patterns designed to coordinate efforts of people for some period of time toward chosen broad goals—becomes obvious. Planning pervades and is the underpinning of other management functions; it has been labeled the "primary function." Only when all members of an organization understand all they need to know about a plan is the organization likely to acieve its goals successfully.

Each member does not need to understand fully all details of the plan, but each must comprehend how his/her responsibilities fit into the overall general plan and understand the member's contributions to be

Table 17.3
Planning as a Management Function

SEQUENTIAL FUNCTION: PLAN	
Definition:	**Predetermine a course of action**
Activities	**Definitions**
Forecast	Establish where present course will lead
Set objectives	Determine desired end results
Develop strategies	Decide how and when to achieve goals
Program	Establish priority, sequence, and timing of steps
Budget	Allocate resources
Set procedures	Standardize methods
Develop policies	Make standing decisions on important recurring matters

Note. Based on and modified from Mackenzie, 1969, pp. 81-82.

made to it. For example, an institution may establish a goal of constructing of a new student center. The student programming staff should be directly involved in the planning of space requirements or types of meeting rooms for organizations, but they should not be involved in procurement of architects, methods of financing, and such.

Planning, then, is an activity that should be employed regularly at all levels of student affairs administration. Planning may be long-range—20 years, 5 years—or short-range—six months, one month, one week, or one day; division-wide—for the entire student affairs division or by units (counseling, housing, placement, financial aid); programmatic (financial assistance program, career and vocational counseling program); and individual—in professional and personal development (time management, for instance).

Planning Cycle

Process of planning may begin with a vague hunch or an element of intuition on the part of an individual or a group. The alert student affairs professional will set into action planning procedures as quickly as possible after the hunch or intuition surfaces. Planning consists of several sensible and logical steps that are familiar to professionals already. The process may be formal or informal, may involve many or few persons, may be time consuming or accomplished in short order. In most instances it is advisable to formalize the process, making it systematic and explicit.

Harpel (1978, p. 21), in discussing the evaluation of student services from a time management perspective, presents a model, all elements of which should be covered in the planning process. These elements should be considered in the planning process:

•Identifying the problem (assessing needs)
•Assessing environmental constraints
•Stating goals and objectives
•Defining program structure (selecting programs and activities)
•Budgeting
•Assessing outcomes

Harpel (1978) described these elements as being cyclical, a process that provides for periodic review, feedback, and repetition. The elements listed by Harpel are similar to a list provided in Chapter 16 for successful facilities management.

Identifying the Problem. One of the primary purposes of higher education institutions is to meet the needs of its constituents. For student affairs divisions, this means the goal is to serve students of the institution. Student affairs professionals should continuously be attuned to student needs and the several standardized instruments available to assist in this endeavor. For illustration purposes, suppose that the dean of students or a member of the staff has a hunch that older returning students on the campus have unmet concerns and problems. The dean, a member of the staff, or an interested group of staff members and/or older returning students could seek information about the number of older returning students on the campus and what concerns or problems they have. The intent is to obtain objective information about these students. When the data are collected, the dean may find students have needs and problems previously unidentified.

Assessing Environmental Constraints. Students have many needs, and it is not possible or desirable that institutions attempt to meet all of them. Administrators need to recognize that there are some things institutions of higher education cannot do for students and thereby plan accordingly. Limiting factors include social, economic, political, and legal constraints.

Stating Goals and Objectives. The basic stage of any planning is the conscious and explicit statement of goals and objectives. Goals are generally broad and less explicit than objectives, are usually hard to measure; should be derived from the assessment of needs, and should give direction to the program and activities of the unit or project. Goals should answer the questions "What is it we really want to do?" and "What are our aims? Goals of a program for older returning students might include (1) "facilitating assimilation of these persons as students" and (2) "providing effective career and vocational counseling."

Objectives, which are expected outcomes, should be derived from goal statements and be explicit, practical, and realistic. They may be short-range and should describe an outcome that can be measured at the end of a specified time period. Objectives should answer the question "How will we know when we get there? Objectives for this project could include (1) "to reduce the feeling of being outsiders in the classroom" and (2) "to develop realistic career goals."

In short, defining goals and objectives simply means determining desired results. If desired results can be established, the unit, program, or project has direction.

Selecting Programs and Activities. Who is going to do what, how, and when? When that question has been answered, a program structure will exist. A program is a definite and explicit statement of steps to be taken to achieve an objective. Stated another way a program is a group of activities and resources focused on a common objective.

An important concept to be remembered is that the structure of a program may not resemble or be represented by a typical organizational chart. A program to achieve a particular objective may be a temporary arrangement of people and resources drawn from several different units within an organization, each making its unique contribution to the accomplishment of the particular objective. Upon completion of the project or a portion thereof, the group is dissolved. The program for older returning students would most likely involve resources from placement, counseling, student housing, as well as some academic units.

Budgeting. Budgeting is the process of allocating resources to activities of the program. This is the point that planners say "These are activities that will make a difference and will help achieve goals and objectives."

Possibly an administrator may be in a position to ask for funds above the normal operating budget. Most find it necessary to set priorities within the normal operating budget, which means allocating portions of staff members' time and salaries, travel costs, supplies and expenses, and possibly even space. The fraction or percentage of staff time and amount of operational dollars to be contributed by respective units should then be combined under each of the various activities. These combined resources represent the amount of money needed to conduct program activities.

This process may help the administrator decide that the program is worthwhile and its costs within the budget or that because of scarcity of funds, something must be cut because the proposed program will be too costly.

Assessing Outcomes. Attention to assessing outcomes or evaluation too often is not addressed as part of the planning function. Often a program or project is well underway when someone decides that something should be done about evaluation of outcome. Evaluation should be an integral part of the planning process and evaluation activities should be as explicitly stated as objectives and program. Theoretically if measurable objectives were written in an earlier planning step, several instruments for evaluating changes or achievement should already have been identified.

Harpel (1978) identified two types of measures that should be included in evaluations: (1) activity or output (such as the number of students served or applications processed), and (2) impact or outcome (increased skills, reduction in attrition, or increased satisfaction, for instance).

Data of both types are important and means of collecting them should be planned when objectives are drafted.

In summary, planning is the basic element on which management functions depend. Planning is cyclical and plans should have built-in flexibility because any number of unforeseen things can happen; Murphy's law "if anything can go wrong, it will" should be remembered.

If planning has been done well, the completion of the program or project should enable student affairs practitioners to have answers to the following questions as related to each step in the planning cycle:

•*Needs assessment:* Were the true needs of students identified?

•*Environmental constraints:* Did the assessment reveal some constraints that were not expected?

•*Goals and objectives:* Were sights set too high or too low?

•*Programs and activities:* Were the right things done to produce change?

•*Budget:* Were the right combination of resources available to achieve goals?

•*Evaluation:* Were evaluation measures chosen: Was design adequate? (Harpel, 1978, p. 32)

Planning Generalizations

In this section management functions, the need for planning, and the planning cycle have been discussed; a reiteration of several of the major points that have been made are included in Massie (1979, pp. 89-90).

1. A plan should be directed toward well-defined *objectives.*

2. Plans made by different [student affairs] specialists should be *coordinated* through adequate communications among specialists.

3. Planning is a *prerequisite* to other functions of management.

4. Adaptation of plans to current actions demands continual *redrafting* of plans.

5. Planning pervades the hierarchy of an organization. [Planning at lower levels tends to be detailed and for short periods in the future; planning at higher levels tends to be general and for long periods of time.]

6. A manager [administrator] should relate the degree of *commitment* of his resources to the need for definite plans.

7. Plans should retain *flexibility*.

Planning should not be ignored whether planning for management of time, a new student residential program, or an older returning student program.

A RECAPITULATION

The effective use of time by student affairs administrators and the importance of planning student affairs programs have been discussed. Because of many demands made on student affairs staff members, they must maintain a time management system that permits them to achieve its effective and meaningful use. The development of a time management system requires a look at basic beliefs and assumptions about time and its control; an examination of current use of time, commitment to and application of techniques and strategies to effect changes and honest assessment of results.

Planning, pre-determining a course of action, frequently receives a low priority by student affairs staff members because of the multitude of duties, activities, and tasks for which they are responsible and that have a way of consuming an inordinate amount of time. Time management and planning are inextricably interwoven: an effective time management system would permit time for critical planning functions.

One must plan for planning; however, sound planning occurs, even when time is available, only when logical steps are followed. These steps include recognizing the need for planning and implementing a time planning cycle that encompasses identifying the problem, assessing environmental constraints, stating goals and objectives, defining program structure, budgeting, and assessing outcomes.

REFERENCES

Allen, L. A. *Professional management: New concepts and proven practices.* New York: McGraw-Hill, 1973.

Association of California School Administrators. *An update on time management* (Operations Notebook 8), February 1979. (Eric Document Reproduction Service No. ED 172 426).

Brechin, J. D. Time management. *Management of student affairs in the 1980's.* Portland, OR: NASPA, 1979.

Douglass, M. E. Test your assumptions about time management. *The Personnel Administrator,* November, 1976, pp. 12-5.

Foxley, C. H. (Ed.). *New directions for student services: Applying management techniques* (No. 9). San Francisco: Jossey-Bass, 1980.

Halverson, D. E. *Time management* (Rev. ed.). Redwood City, CA: San Mateo County Board of Education, April 1978. (ERIC Document Reproduction Service No. ED 154 476).

Harpel, R. I. Evaluating from a management perspective. In G. R. Hanson (Ed.), *New directions for student services: Evaluating program effectiveness* (No. 1). San Francisco: Jossey-Bass, 1978.

Lakein, A. *How to get control of your time and your life.* New York: Signet, 1973.

Mackenzie, R. A. The management process in 3-D. *Harvard Business Review,* November-December 1969, pp. 80-7.

Mackenzie, R. A. *Time management notebook,* 1976. (Mimeographed manuscript.) Source: Author.

Massie, J. L. *Essentials of management* (3rd ed.). Englewood Cliffs, NJ: Prentice-Hall, Inc., 1979.

Rogers, J. M. *Time management.* San Jose: Lansford Publishing Co, 1973.

Sexton, M. J., & Switzer, K. The time management ladder. *Educational Leadership,* 1978, *35,* 482-6.

SUGGESTED READINGS

Born, W. M. Time management for the harried campus administrator. *Educational Record,* 1979, *60,* 227-33.

Brechin, J. D. Time management. *Management of student affairs in the 1980's.* Portland, OR: NASPA, 1979.

Brown, S. An evaluation process for student affairs agencies. *NASPA Journal,* 1981, *18*(1), 2-13.

Hanson, G. R. (Ed.). *New directions for student services: Evaluating program effectiveness* (No. 1). San Francisco: Jossey-Bass, 1978.

Lakein, A. *How to get control of your time and life.* New York: Signet, 1973.

Pillinger, B. B., & Kraack, T. A. Planning for student affairs. *Management of student affairs in the 1980's.* Portland, OR: NASPA, 1979.

Margaret J. Barr is Vice-President for Student Affairs at Northern Illinois University. She has served in a variety of student affairs positions at the State University of New York at Binghamton, the Trenton State College, and the University of Texas at Austin. Her master's degree is from Southern Illinois University, and her Ph.D. was earned at the University of Texas at Austin. She has been highly involved in the American College Personnel Association serving as a Directorate Body member for Commissions II and III, Chair of Commission II, Vice President for Commissions and Program Chair for the 1980 Convention. Currently, she is President-Elect of ACPA and will assume the presidency in July 1983. She is the author of over fifteen publications in professional journals, books, and the Jossey-Bass New Directions for Student Services monograph series.

Michael J. Cuyjet is Director of Programming and Activities at Northern Illinois University, where he has served for several years as Administrative Associate to the Vice President for Student Affairs. He holds a bachelor's degree in speech communication from Bradley University, a master's degree in counseling from Northern Illinois University, and is currently completing his doctoral dissertation in counseling education at NIU.

Among his professional activities, he has held several regional and national offices in the National Association for Campus Activities (NACA). He has just completed a three year term as a member of the association's national Board of Directors including one year at Vice-Chairman for Program Services.

Chapter 18

PROGRAM DEVELOPMENT AND IMPLEMENTATION

Margaret J. Barr
Michael J. Cuyjet

Agreement on a clear, precise definition of the term *program* by student affairs professionals is difficult to achieve. Depending on the philosophy of the individual practitioner, the institutional mission and history, and the philosophy of the student affairs division, program can mean entirely different things to different people (Barr & Keating, 1979). For purposes of this chapter, *program* is used to encompass three distinct definitions.

First, the term applies to *administrative units organized to deliver specific activities or services that meet either institutional or student needs.* Examples of this first category of programs include placement services, residence hall programs, and new student orientation.

The second definition is perhaps the one most commonly used in student affairs: *a series of planned interventions by student affairs practitioners to meet a specific goal for a defined target population.* Such programs are characterized by a clear definition of the desired outcomes, a specific time frame for implementation, and an identified target group. Illustrative programs of this definition include: fine art series, assertiveness training groups, seminars for returning adult students, and career exploration courses.

The third definition covers *programs that are planned as a one-time activity with a planned target and purpose.* Programs that adhere to this definition include one-time workshops for student leaders on motivation and group morale, orientation programs for parents, the presentation of a concert, lecture or film, or a staff development program on dealing with angry students. All three definitions are useful and helpful to student affairs professionals as they deal with what programs should be planned and implemented in their respective institutional settings. No matter what definition is used, there is, however, a logical and systematic approach that can be used to assess the viability and usefulness of programs.

Five-step Model

A five-step model for program development that can be implemented or modified for any institutional setting is presented. Step one focuses on assessment of student needs, environment, and resources. In Step two, a planning approach for program implementation is devised. Step three involves the implementation of the program, including evaluation. In Step four, attention is given to post-assessment procedures and practices. Step five focuses on the need for a clear administrative decision about program continuance and support.

The five-step model proposed is predicated on a strong foundation by the practitioner in student development and organization theory. Without the ability to relate theory to practice, the practitioner cannot design programs that are congruent with the goals and mission of student affairs.

THEORY AND PRACTICE IN PROGRAM DEVELOPMENT

In earlier chapters of this book, theoretical constructs of organizational and student development were discussed. Programming is the logical extension of such theoretical constructs into the actual practice of providing services for students. Although a student affairs practitioner may be able to organize successful programs without a strong theoretical foundation, a deficit in this area of preparation is keenly felt at the evaluation stage of the program. Theory provides the basis for understanding a situation and permits the student affairs staff member to analyze critically both successes and failures in program endeavors.

The theoretical orientation of the practitioner has an important influence on program design, implementation, and the ultimate outcome of the program. Use of one theoretical base to the exclusion of others may narrow the vision of the program planner and ultimately have a serious negative effect on the program. Reliance on one theoretical base without understanding an application of other theories is not enough for successful program development. Student development theory provides a practical basis for analysis of the student population, the target of most student affairs programming endeavors. Familiarity with the work of Brown (1972), Crookston (1972), Erikson (1963), Maslow (1970), and Chickering (1969) provides a strong foundation for program development. Programs, however, must relate to the broader institutional environment. Thus, the program planner also must have knowledge about organizations and how they work.

If programs are based only on student development theory, the chance is that they may fail. To illustrate, a program planner is interested in designing a series of interventions to assist academically underprepared students in gaining critical skills for success in college. This program series is thus designed and is soundly grounded in student development theory. The idea, however, is never supported within the larger institutional environment because the policy of the institution is being reshaped on an organizational level to raise admissions standards and deny admission to under-prepared students. These program planners, therefore, must use their knowledge of how organizations work and how decisions are made within highly structured organizations to avoid such pitfalls. A foundation in organizational theory including Weber (1947), Katz and Kahn (1966), Merton (1956), and Bennis (1962) provides such knowledge. A student affairs program cannot exist in a vacuum, and proposed efforts must relate to the larger organizational structure and goals and mission of the institution.

Morrill, Oetting, and Hurst (1974) and Moore and Delworth (1976) have provided models of program development that bridge the gap from theory to practice.

The Cube

Originally designed as a classification system for counselor outreach programs, "The Cube" has evolved into a useful tool for the general student affairs programmer (Morrill, Oetting, & Hurst, 1974; Morrill & Hurst, 1980). The three dimensions of the cube include: (1) the target of the intervention, (2) the purpose of the intervention, and (3) the method of the intervention. Because programs by definition are interventions, the use of the cube to analyze program activities can be both useful and helpful. The target group(s) range from the individual to the whole institution. The purpose of the intervention may be classified as direct, indirect, or media. Analysis of a program plan through use of this classification enables the practitioner to define all three dimensions. To illustrate, in developing a plan for an administrative program unit to serve handicapped students, the program planner has clear choices. Although often these administrative units concentrate on individual remedial and direct services, the use of the cube permits the program planner to become aware of other possibilities. It is possible to make institutional, developmental, or indirect interventions with regard to handicapped students with the goal of changing the environment and thus reducing some of the need for direct services. Choices are clarified and can be then incorporated into a program plan. Through their work with the Western Interstate Commission on Higher Education, Moore and Delworth (1976) have developed an extensive model for program development based on the work of Morrill et al. (1974). Their approach to program development is linear, with each step of the model leading to and supporting the work of the following stages. The first stage of the model focuses on extensive use of a planning team in the analysis of a program idea according to the "Cube" classification system (Figure 18.1). Only after the target and the purpose of the program are clearly defined are decisions made about the method of intervention. The model focuses in the initial stages on resource and institutional assessment to assure that the original program idea is viable within the context of the institution, is not a duplication of other efforts, and is useful to the proposed target population. Stage two in the model focuses on explicit program goals, training of personnel, evaluation and research decisions and the need to pilot test the proposed program. Stage three involves the practical problems of pilot testing a program idea and evaluation of the pilot effort. The fourth stage involves actual program implementation and additional training needs. In the last stage consideration is given to the use of evaluation data to make decisions with regard to program maintenance, continuance, and redecision. Throughout the model, emphasis is given to the need to develop a broad-based, highly-involved program planning team and the necessity for constant evaluation and monitoring of the program plan.

The model proposed in this chapter draws heavily on Morrill and Hurst (1980), but places emphasis on different steps in the planning pro-

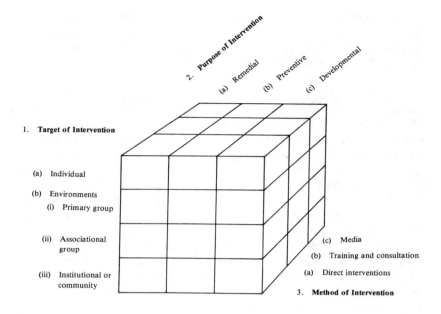

1. **Target of Intervention**

(a) Individual

(b) Environments
   (i) Primary group

    (ii) Associational group

    (iii) Institutional or community

2. **Purpose of Intervention**
  (a) Remedial
  (b) Preventive
  (c) Developmental

(c) Media
(b) Training and consultation
(a) Direct interventions
3. **Method of Intervention**

Figure 18.1. Dimensions of intervention for student development.

Note. From "Dimensions of counselor functioning" by W. H. Morrill, E. R. Oetting, and J. C. Hurst, Personnel and Guidance Journal, 1972.
Copyright 1974 by Morrill, Oetting, and Hurst. Reprinted by permission.

cess. Often the student affairs practitioner is asked to produce a program under less than optimal conditions of professional and institutional support. Under such conditions, a step-by-step approach to program planning can provide a useful tool for the practitioner.

A MODEL FOR PROGRAM PLANNING
Step One: Assessment

A detailed assessment of the current institutional environment needs to be made as the first phase of the assessment process. Unfortunately, the need for careful pre-assessment in program development is often overlooked. Although the ideal method to carry out assessment is through the use of a broad based planning team, the program planner may carry out many assessment procedures on an independent basis. A word of caution, however: if necessity dictates independent assessment, then it is essential that the conclusions drawn from such procedures be tested with other knowledgeable persons in the institution and the community. To do less invites program failure.

To illustrate, a staff member becomes concerned with women students who are experiencing adjustment difficulties after a divorce. Three students were seen by the staff member on an individual basis within the last month. Based on this limited sample, the staff member moved toward developing a program solution to what was viewed as a larger problem. The reasoning process by the staff member involved a quantum leap from the few students seen in the last month to a conclusion that many students are having problems with divorce. In isolation, the staff member proceeded to plan a meeting for divorced students, sent out publicity for a divorced women's support group, reserved the room, and waited for it to fill up. All too often not one student comes. What went wrong? An analysis of this common approach to program planning reveals that careful assessment of needs was forgotten in the rush to produce a program. Other than the limited sample seen by the staff member, no other sources of information were checked. Therefore, the first step in successful program development and implementation is the need to assess carefully three critical elements: student needs, the institutional environment, and available resources.

Student Needs. At least three methods are available to assess student needs for program interventions: a study of the demographic characteristics of the student body, unobtrusive measures, and obtrusive measures. All are valuable, and the needs assessment phase of program development should probably consider using a combination of these approaches to assure that an accurate measurement is made of real needs of students.

A careful analysis of demographic characteristics of the student population can provide useful and valuable information for programming activities. Knowledge of the number of students who are in particular age classifications, ethnic groups, and academic majors can assist in understanding whether some programs are actually needed on a campus. In addition, such demographic data provide an overview of the entire student population and can perhaps uncover new student populations whose unique needs and concerns should be addressed via formal program interventions. A sophisticated student data base provides a great amount of useful data for programming purposes. If, however, such a data base is not available, other sources of demographic data can be useful and helpful. A careful search of the institutional environment can uncover many data sources with regard to the student population. Checks should be made about enrollment figures by college and major, residence hall information, or admissions data. An analysis of all of these sources can provide a composite picture of who students are and focus attention of the program staff on identifiable student subgroups that may need service.

Unobtrusive measures of student needs provide much of the foundation for program ideas. Observations by staff members of student participation in current activities and programs provide valuable information for assessing the viability of a new program. Such observations should be guided by questions such as:

1. How many students are attending programs on particular topics?

2. Are students staying for the entire program and are they involved in the program activity?

3. Are there specific times of the year when program interventions are most successful?

4. What are the demographic characteristics of participants in current programs?

Observational data can provide important information for program planners. In addition, other student affairs staff members and faculty colleagues can provide a wealth of information through both their formal and informal contacts with students. Are there common characteristics among students who fail, students in disciplinary trouble, and those students who are involved with alcohol abuse? The careful program planner needs to ask questions of others in the environment on a regular basis to gain insight into potential students needs.

Finally, if resources permit, obtrusive measures such as questionnaires, entrance and exit interviews, and standardized environmental assessment instruments can provide solid information for program planners. The work of Astin (1968, 1977), Conyne (1975), Feldman (1971), and Pace (1969) are sources for methodology review that can be used to assess student needs and the institutional environment. If the program planner is not familiar with obtrusive data collection approaches, then assistance can be sought from faculty members with specialized knowledge in research and evaluation. The key variable is the ability of staff members engaged in program planning to sort data and ascertain what needs are critical for students within the context of a particular institution. The astute programmer attempts to use all information sources that are available to assess student needs. To do so, of course, requires attention to needs and concerns of other units and agencies within the institution and intentional efforts to increase communication with others engaged in providing services and programs to students.

Institutional Environment. Assessment of the institutional environment as an entity can be a more difficult task than that of assessing student needs. Programs that are well planned and meet student needs may also fail because of a mismatch between the program goal and that of the institution.

To succeed, programs must be compatible with the overall goal and mission of the institution. To illustrate, a program focusing on abortion as an alternative to pregnancy may never succeed in an institution with a high identification with conservative religious values. However, a program that focuses on the ethical and moral choices associated with sexual behavior may well be both supported and encouraged in such an institution.

Assessment of the institutional environment requires the student affairs practitioner to attend carefully to four variables: the goal and mission of the institution, the institutional history, current activities and programs, and political considerations. Each institution is a unique entity and attention to these variables assists those charged with program responsibility to develop program interventions that are compatible within the context of the institution. In order to conduct an institutional assessment, it is critical that the student affairs practitioner read, listen, question, and conduct research.

Lofty institutional mission statements provide little direct guidance to the student affairs practitioner. The program planner must fill in the data and use all available resources to understand the institutional environment. Use of historical records is an important first step to find out what activities and programs have been conducted in the past. Talking to individuals who have experienced a span of institutional history to find out why some programs were successful and to gain perspective on why others failed can be helpful. One must listen carefully in order to identify the idiosyncratic views of the institution held by those consulted.

Part of the assessment of the institutional environment is merely to find out what activities and programs are already in progress on the campus. Often a number of programs concerned with the same topics exist, but lack shared information and intentional links between them. For example, at a larger multiuniversity a charge was given to a staff member to recommend an institutional direction for health education efforts. Through careful assessment of current activities on the campus over forty distinct program efforts were discovered ranging from research projects to individual programs in birth control. None of these efforts were, however, intentionally linked together. In this instance, the recommendation of the staff member wisely was not to create a new administrative entity but instead to develop a coordinating function for already established programs. Evaluation showed that better health education information was available for students, but the method chosen to meet that goal involved only modest resource reallocation. Assessment showed that a new program unit was just not needed.

Political realities also must be considered in the institutional assessment phase of program development. Issues of territoriality, power, and current program responsibilities must be assessed early in the planning process. Questions regarding current perceived territories for program development also must be analyzed before the development of a program plan. Campus politics are a critical part of the assessment process.

Methods to accomplish the difficult task of assessment of the total institutional environment are very diverse. Questionnaires provide a relatively standard method to collect data and can be used both for structured interviews and survey instruments. Berdie and Anderson (1974) presented an approach to questionnaire design and use that should be useful to the program planner. Struening and Guttentag's (1975) handbook on evaluation is also a useful reference on approaches and strategies in assessment. Moos (1979) developed a framework for evaluating educational environments that provides a useful perspective on assessment issues. Finally, the assessment process is best served by the adoption of a theoretical basis for analysis of the college environment. Assessment of the institutional environment requires care in both data collection and data analysis. Ultimately, however, understanding the institutional environment rests on the ability of the program planner to synthesize data from many sources and translate it into sound programs.

Resource Assessment. The real strength of a program lies in the resources that are available to develop, implement, and sustain the idea.

Three sources must be assessed for strong program development: staff, money, and physical resources.

Assessment of staff really means getting to know people and learning something about them to develop an inventory of the skills and abilities available for the proposed program. Examination of the educational background of staff members including fields of study, specific training, and thesis topics or special research interests is needed.

One needs to review staff member strengths in daily interactions as an assessment of interpersonal skills. Individuals can be polled concerning their interests and ideas. The creativity of others is an extremely important resource and knowing others interests permits a match to be made between people and programs. Determine staff members' management abilities and administrative skills because any successful program requires leadership at a variety of levels. Knowledge of staff abilities is critical to program success.

Staff as a resource is not limited to individuals within the department or the office planning the program or to those only in closest proximity to that unit. Use of this assessment process for anyone, even on the periphery of the work environment, could be helpful in developing the proposed program. This is especially critical if the assessment indicates that those with immediate responsibility for the program do not have necessary skills for program implementation.

The biggest problem in assessing fiscal resources is a failure to identify all of the fiscal needs of the program. How many times has a program failed because after initial funding something unexpected developed for which money was not available? No one can be expected to be prepared for every possible eventuality. Yet a careful, comprehensive review of all costs associated with the program is a first step in determining how much money is needed to assure program implementation. Ask for assistance in this initial assessment phase as it is often easier for someone not directly associated with the program idea to identify hidden costs.

Several sources, in addition to Douglas (Chapter 15), are particularly useful in assisting the program planner with fiscal planning. Maw, Richards, and Crosby (1976) provided a cogent explanation of formula budgeting techniques and specifically applied it to student affairs. Deegan and Fritz (1975), focusing on a management by objectives approach, provided practical applications of fiscal planning to higher education. Baldridge and Tierney (1979), Budig (1972), Coombs (1972), and Weathersby (1977) all provided broad views of fiscal planning. Each of these authors enhance the program planner's perspective. The question then becomes one of applying these principles within an individual institutional setting.

Sources of funds vary from institution to institution; however, the most stable form of fiscal support is the central or general revenue budget of the institution. Acquiring resources from this source, however, requires advanced planning because institutional budgets are generally built on a two to three year time frame. Central budget funds also are carefully monitored, and sound justification usually must be shown to acquire new program funds from this source.

Other fiscal sources include sponsoring organizations, fee-allocating bodies, and grants. On-campus clubs or groups that are organized for a purpose analogous to the intended goal of the program as well as off-campus groups or the private sector are possible sources of funds. Some programs might appeal similarly to existing offices or administrative units that would be willing co-sponsors. Every fee collected at the institution needs to be determined, and the body that determines the allocation of those dollars should be identified. Fees that can be used to fund programs need to be investigated and criteria for their use determined. Grants from government agencies or private enterprises are often overlooked by program developers in student affairs largely because of the mystique that surrounds the grant application processes. Publications and colleagues with grantsmanship skills can help cut through this obscurity.

The program itself can be a fiscal resource. If it is a service for which a user fee may be charged, or if it consists of revenue-generating events, the program could be totally or partially self-supported.

Space and potential physical resources must also be considered as part of the initial assessment. An analysis should be made to determine what kinds of resources are necessary to assure program success. Physical needs include furnishings, equipment, commodities, and some services. Yet, the primary physical resource for any program is the appropriate configuration of rooms. Adequate space is needed to accommodate comfortably all the activities included in the program. The space selected should provide an environment with comfortable temperature and adequate lighting.

Physical resources also include equipment and supplies. Assess each function in a potential program to furnishings required for the particular activity. Meetings or sessions require chairs and possibly desks arranged in a specified manner. Registration areas or clerical functions require a table or desk, a typewriter, and typing supplies. Ticket-takers need stub collection boxes. Ushers need flashlights. Group leaders need chalkboards, chalk, erasers, or flipcharts and marking pens. Other supplies could be listed. The important thing to remember is to think through all functions of the program beforehand in order to generate a list of equipment needs. Many items, especially audio-visual equipment and printed supplies, must be ordered well in advance.

Services such as telephones, postal service, clerical assistance, and a print shop are generally available at the institution. Obtain a listing of all such services which includes how to access them and their costs. The assessment of needed resources continues throughout the planning process. Early identification of needs, costs, and constraints does provide useful guidance for all subsequent steps in program development.

Step Two: Planning

After a comprehensive assessment is made of student needs, the institutional environment, resources, and potential costs, specific planning for a program is ready to begin. The question becomes one of determining the best method to respond to needs within the constraints identified in the assessment process.

Developing a Planning Team. Selecting the planning team is an outcome of the staff resource assessment process. Program development activities, at their best, are open to new data, new information, and new ideas throughout the process. Program planning cannot be isolated from the constantly changing larger environment, but instead should provide for interaction and feedback from that environment. Development of a broad-based planning team helps assure that this will occur. A broad-based planning team provides the best opportunity to capture all information for a successful program plan. At minimum, the planning team should be composed of those individuals who will be directly affected by the program effort. The planning group can then seek consultation from experts such as those in food services or data processing as needs arise.

The key to a successful planning team is to establish a small but effective working group. Others can be involved in the actual development and implementation of the program. A planning team is designed to set attainable goals and objectives, based on the assessment process, and then monitor all stages of program development.

Goals, Objectives, and Evaluation. The first task of the planning team is to determine what specific outcomes should occur for whom and under what conditions. Too often objectives for student affairs programs are of the "mom, dad, and apple pie" variety. Such objectives are certainly hard to be against, but they are difficult to be *for.* More importantly, broad-based objectives for any type of program are difficult to evaluate. Thus, time spent by the planning team to ascertain what differences they expect the program to make is time well spent. As a result, program success or failure is easier to determine, and decisions about program continuance are more systematic.

Specific goals and objectives also help determine the actual target population to be served. By focusing on the population early in the planning process, a diffuse program with no measureable impact is less likely to be the result.

At this stage of program development, the program planner must consider how determination will be made of program success. In other words, will evaluation be possible to determine how effective the program is? If the answer is no, then redefine the objectives before making final program plans.

Selecting an Approach. A wide variety of approaches to successful program implementation always exists. The key is to choose the best approach for a particular institution at a specific time. Thus, encouragement should be given to the planning group to think as divergently as possible with regard to program configurations. "The Cube" (Morrill & Hurst, 1980) is a useful construct at this stage of program planning. Questions should be raised about the use of media, technology (including computer support), and integration of the proposed program with already established courses and programs. Every alternative has strengths and weaknesses. None should be rejected out of hand and all should be evaluated. For example, if the assessment phase shows that alcohol abuse is increasing on the campus, several program responses are possible: spot announcements on cable television, training of student staff, an alcohol awareness day, the development of printed materials, in-service training for front-line staff on recognizing alcohol problems, provision of alternative programs that do not use alcohol, an alcohol hotline, and so forth. Each has validity, and by exploration and evaluation of all the alternatives, a combination of the best alternatives can be used for the actual program plan.

Convergent thinking, on the part of the planning group, limits alternatives and restricts the planning group to consideration of alternatives that are solely within their span of control. This process of choosing an approach provides the best method of assuring workable program options.

How to Begin. Two questions need to be asked by the planning team once an approach is selected. What should be the initial scope of the program, and is it necessary to pilot the proposed program? Three alternatives exist at this phase of planning: moving forward with the total program package, starting on a small level and adding preplanned program components when resources are available, and pilot testing the program. Each of the alternatives has strengths and weaknesses and needs to be assessed in terms of the institutional climate and the resources available.

To advocate only full program implementation may result in a negative response if the assessment phase was not complete. An "all or nothing" approach carries with it the risk that nothing may happen. The advantage of an incremental approach to program development is that a program can be started on a modest level without major resource reallocation. If the program is a success at this initial level, then the way is paved for additional support in the future. There is a danger, however, when resources are limited that program development will cease at the initial funding level and never gain support for total development.

Pilot programs also have both positive and negative aspects. On the positive side, a pilot program provides opportunity to gain further insight into program alternatives at low risk to students, the agency, and the administrative decision maker. To use the example of an alcohol abuse program, one intervention for one population on a controlled level with evaluation built-in, provides an opportunity to test the feasibility of the program within the institutional setting. Data that are gathered through the pilot program can identify defects in program design not anticipated during planning. The only negative aspect to pilot programs is that they may not work. If that is true, then the entire program idea needs to be re-examined.

Training. Any new program idea also must include some type of training so that personnel associated with the program understand responsibilities and expectations. In some instances extensive training is needed for students and staff members associated with program implementation. Training needs must be considered early in the planning process. Assumptions should not be made regarding the skills, abilities, and knowledge of those charged with program implementation. A well-trained, competent staff is the single most critical variable to program success (Baier, 1979).

Budget. A final step in initial program planning is determining the actual fiscal resources necessary for program completion. The budget should include all costs associated with the program, including personnel, materials, space, postage, food, and equipment. When the budget is completely developed, it serves as another checklist at the program implementation step. The information gathered in the assessment step can now be used for final budget preparation.

Establishing a Time-line. Successful program implementation is dependent on an accurate estimate of the time needed to complete the project. One useful method for establishing a time-line is to plan backwards from the program implementation date. Working from the target date, the planners can establish a week-by-week activity scheme outlining decisions that must be made in order to meet the target date. Problems or unexpected events will inevitably occur, and a realistic time-line allows for such circumstances and helps program planners anticipate the unexpected.

Step Three: Implementation

Planning should lead to a product: a specific program. If the elements in steps one and two are thoroughly considered, then actual program implementation should be relatively trouble free. A number of issues must be attended to, however, in order to assure program success.

Defining Responsibilities. Concise directions must be given with regard to expectations for those associated with the program. In the assessment step, an inventory of skills and abilities in relation to the program was proposed. At this step, a match needs to be made between those skills and abilities and the tasks that must be done. Accountability lines should be clearly drawn and reporting relationships defined. It is only through careful, thorough assessment of abilities and assignment of responsibilities for implementation that program success can be assured. The successful program planner should never hear the plaintive cry, "I didn't know I was responsible for that."

Delivery. Three key elements are important for successful program delivery: publicity, location, and timing. All three must be carefully addressed to assure success.

Publicity is often the most essential element in a successful program. If the target population is not aware of the opportunity, then poor participation will be the inevitable outcome. The best publicity catches people's attention so they can receive the message being sent. The publicity that best catches people's attention is creative and imaginative. As in many other phases of program development outlined, people are the best resource for an effective publicity campaign both for ideas and promotion. Word-of-mouth can often be the best promotional medium. Determine what effect publicity ideally should have on people and try to focus the entire publicity campaign on that effect. One effective method is to develop a list of free publicity (e.g., public service announcements on radio or cable television) and use brainstorming to identify creative approaches to program promotion. One must not waste resources; but one also should not sacrifice effect for the sake of economy. Remember these two elements of human nature: curiosity and "what's in it for me?" Publicity should make people want to seek more information and should make them feel it is worth their effort to attempt to do so.

The physical location of the program can either enhance or partially diminish the positive effects of the publicity. Despite all the wonderful things they have heard or read, if people feel the program is inaccessible, they generally do not attend. For this reason every effort should be made to locate the program in the most accessible location available. Often the needs of the program limit choices of suitable space; however, where a choice is possible, another should be considered. If there is a location that has proven to be very popular at the institution because of aesthetics or decor or merely because of accessibility, advantage should be taken of this built-in attraction. If numbers of students attending the program will likely drive, consider parking spaces in selecting the location. For an ongoing program, consider locations adjacent to related activities or other established programs that may complement it. For programs consisting of a series of meetings or events, try to hold each session in the same location at a consistent time and date or day as well. Consider, also, that visibility is self-fulfilling; the program in a highly visible location serves as its own promoter.

The timing of the program can have either positive or negative effects. First, select a date for the program that allows sufficient time to develop a quality program. Unrealistic deadlines that do not permit adequate preparation as outlined should be avoided.

Programs aimed at specific populations must accommodate the clients' schedules. A workshop for freshmen on coping with test anxiety does little good after midterm exams. A series of classes to teach Cardio-Pulmonary-Resuscitation (CPR) to residence hall staff members is much more useful in September than in May. Timing also means coordination with other programs. CPR classes might be even more appropriate during "health week," or a session on resumé writing would fit nicely with a big "career day" program. A comprehensive listing of upcoming events from the office on campus that is responsible for scheduling programs is an invaluable tool.

Probably the most critical aspect of timing is to avoid conflict with other events. When making the decision about when to schedule the program a listing of campus events, a calendar that indicates all national, state, and religious holidays, and a list of civic events from the city or town should be prepared. Enlisting the help of a colleague who is a sports enthusiast is important, also. Testimony as to the importance of checking sports schedules can be given by anyone who had inadvertently held a workshop on Superbowl Sunday or planned a weeklong seminar during the World Series. All factors must be considered in the timing of an effective program.

Evaluation. An evaluation plan and procedure must be considered as an integral part of the planning process. Too often, however, evaluation procedures are overlooked or are the last elements considered in program planning. This is a mistake. Unless program planners can assess the effectiveness of the program, decisions may be made on a political or other basis rather than on the needs met by the program.

Two types of evaluation data need to be considered: process and product. Process evaluation concentrates on how well all phases of the planning and implementation steps are proceeding. The focus is on how well the program is progressing and analysis is made of problems in the system during planning and implementation. Careful records should be kept and open dialogue maintained during the planning and implementation phase. Process problems can then be identified and analysis made of their causes. Such data are also useful beyond the specific program that is being evaluated. A process evaluation provides valuable guidance for future program planning endeavors.

Process evaluation is usually best done by an outside, objective evaluator. The addition of an outside evaluator to the program planning team proves the best assurance for objectivity in the process. An outside evaluator can often be obtained through academic departments that are seeking substantive out-of-class experiences for graduate and undergraduate students. If an outside evaluator cannot be obtained, then a member of the planning team should assume responsibility for this important planning activity.

Product evaluation permits program planners to assess whether the activity met goals and objectives that were defined early in the planning process. Most product evaluations concentrate on paper and pencil responses from program participants. Such probes, however, must be designed to gather data that can measure goal and objective attainment. Instrumentation is a costly evaluation item and must be planned as an integral part of the program budget. In addition, evaluation procedures must be developed in a manner that does not interfere with program activity. Therefore, the evaluation scheme must be a joint enterprise between program planners and the evaluator. Attention must be paid to issues both of content and process, if the choice is to use instrumentation for evaluation of the program.

Alternatives to paper and pencil are available for evaluations. The range includes guided group discussion, structured telephone interviews, and face-to-face interviews. Decisions on alternate techniques have a greater potential for extra personnel and special training. Use of one of the alternate methods for evaluation also has a greater potential to effect directly the organization and structure of the program than do paper and pencil. Thus, it is essential to decide on technical aspects of evaluation and integrate evaluation into the total program plan.

The goal of evaluation is to provide accurate, useful data to enable decision makers to assess the effectiveness of the program. The timing of the collection of the evaluation data potentially can alter the usefulness of the procedure. A "halo" effect can occur and thus diminish the usefulness of the data for program decisions. Evaluation as a tool for program planning should not be entered into without forethought and planning. If all aspects of the evaluation plan are not carefully considered, then data produced are virtually useless in the next step.

Step Four: Post-assessment

The development of programs is a task that consumes both agency and personal resources. Therefore, it is not surprising when a program has been established that a tendency develops on the part of the program planner to devote less time, energy, and attention to the program. New programs are, however, extremely vulnerable to being cut back when fiscal and personnel resources are restricted. Established programs also need assessment to assure that the proper allocation of resources to the program is being maintained. Program development and implementation must, therefore, include the fourth critical step of post-program assessment. Methods must be used to assure that a highly structured review of the program is conducted and the recommendations are developed with regard to the future of the program activity. To do less cedes the complete decision of the future of the program to other levels in the administrative hierarchy.

Use of Evaluation Data. Step three included evaluation as part of the program implementation and planning process. An evaluation is of no value, however, unless it is used to make decisions about programs or activities. Too often, student affairs programs include elaborate evaluations producing comprehensive reports that are read but never used in the decision-making process about programs. Program planners should relate evaluation data to program goals and then be prepared to make recommendations regarding the future of the program or activity. In order to accomplish this goal, evaluation data must be carefully analyzed by program planners.

Several questions need to be answered in the analysis:

1. Did the program actually attract the target population for which it was originally intended?

2. If not, why not?

3. Did the program serve another population?

4. If so, what are the characteristics of that group?

5. How well did the program accomplish the stated objectives?

6. How did participants react to the program?

7. Can identification be made of the causes of participant reaction? Process? Content? Both?

8. What suggestions did the program participants have to improve or modify the program?

9. What suggestions do the program staff have regarding program improvements?

Analysis of evaluation data through the use of these or other guided questions can have a significant effect on future directions of the program. At a large multiuniversity, for example, a tutoring program was established to serve the needs of a group of economically disadvantaged students. The program was originally established under federal funding and students seeking tutoring had to meet financial eligibility for participation. As the program became established on campus and became known to students who were not in the original target group, many of these other students came to the tutoring office to seek assistance. Although the program as originally funded could not accommodate their needs, the program staff allowed these students to contact the tutoring staff and pay them directly for their services. Program planners did not view this as a new program effort but merely as an alternate method to fund needed services for students. Careful attention was paid to data collection before and after the alternate structure was established. At the end of the fiscal year of operation, the data were analyzed by the program staff. The results were interesting. Not only did the original program successfully serve the original target population, but the alternate structure provided tutoring services to as many students as did the original program. In addition, many students had to be turned away, although they were willing and able to pay for services, because the size of the tutoring staff was limited. These data changed the future direction of the tutoring program on the campus. Not only was there a need for tutoring for economically disadvantaged students, but a university-wide response for all students was needed. After the initial year the program was redesigned as a university tutoring program providing the same services to economically disadvantaged students, but also providing a method to provide tutoring services for all students. Evaluation data and careful post-assessment by program staff provided an opportunity to serve the needs of another student sub-population, which may not have been responded to if data had not been available.

Program Modification. Post-assessment also has another goal, that of program modification. The best plans can sometimes go awry because of circumstances not under the control of the planning team. Post-assessment that focuses on suggestions for change and modification of the program can assist in "fine-tuning" efforts to approximate more closely goals and objectives of the program. Small changes such as hours of availability of services, location of the program, and publicity can all make a difference in the success or failure of the program for the institution and ultimately for students. Unless there is, however, a structured means to gather these suggestions both from program participants and program staff, they may be lost. A number of methods can be used to gather data including: open-ended questionnaires, a suggestion box in the program office, or merely paying careful attention to the questions and concerns of the support staff attached to the program. The point is, however, to create an opportunity for program planners to listen and to analyze these suggestions toward the goal of program improvement.

Obviously, post-assessment for one-time programs will occur after the completion of the event. However, for programs consisting of a series of events or for ongoing programs, post-assessment occurs at periodic intervals during the course of the program. This allows for immediate use of evaluations for program modification and refining.

In addition, the program planning teams should be asked to give their holistic assessment of the program. How do they feel about what was accomplished? Was it worth the effort? Would they be involved in such a project again? Such subjective evaluation data provide great insight for making a decision about program continuance.

Fiscal Accountability. While the post-assessment phase often focuses on the reactions of people to the program, another assessment needs to be made concurrently that confronts program costs. Cost-effectiveness has become the byword of fiscal managers in recent years, yet student affairs practitioners have yet to use effectively the language and the process to the advantage of establishing successful student affairs programs (Maw et al., 1976). Program planners need to be able to ascertain the cost per student for a particular program activity, the cost per transaction within a particular service, and the cost to the institution for providing support for a program or activity. Two uses can be made of such data. First, these data can provide a strong sense of support for cost avoidance in the institution. For instance, if the counseling center has provided in-service training for the residence hall staff and the number of problems associated with first year freshmen has been reduced on the campus, then the intervention may be one that is costly initially, but avoids more expensive costs for the institution in the future. Second, it can be used as a yardstick to see if alternate methods of delivery that are less expensive are available. Either is legitimate and helpful to the program planners and their administrative superiors. Unfortunately, too often student affairs practitioners do not look at these variables in the post-assessment phase and are, therefore, unprepared to defend costly program innovations when resources are scarce.

Institutionalization of student services programs occurs very quickly in student affairs. Once a program is offered, an assumption is often formed that it is a permanent part of an array of student services. Unfortunately, some programs fail or need extensive modification or redesign in order to be a viable component of student affairs (Thomas, 1979). Structured post-assessment can help the program planner deal with the consequences of program failure and can provide the needed data for step five of the program planning cycle.

Step Five: Administrative Decision

The final step in program planning and implementation involves a decision about the future of the program effort. If the first four steps of the program planning cycle have been carefully followed, then the decision for program continuance is a fairly easy process. However, implications exist with regard to any decision to continue, to modify, or to abandon a student affairs program (Thomas, 1979). Inclusion of this fifth step as an identifiable part of the process for students and staff members to give input to and react to the final decision about the program's future is imperative.

Some states are engaged in a statewide effort to monitor and evaluate noninstructional programs in institutions of higher education. Often fiscal constraints are causing similar monitoring efforts to occur at the institutional level on many campuses. The five-step model proposed equips the student affairs practitioner to respond to both external and internal review efforts from an active rather than a passive or reactive stance. Control of the future of program efforts can then be more firmly controlled by student affairs practitioners because the entire process of planning and evaluating programs has been integrated into the program planning cycle.

Three decisions can be made about any program: continuation, modification, or abandonment. Continuation should be decided for an identifiable time period, and program planners should be required to follow the five-step approach to program planning promulgated in this chapter. Then careful cyclical review can be made of all student affairs programs on a routine basis, providing needed data to respond to changing institutional and student needs.

Decisions for modification mandate complete reentry into the program planning model. Specific goals and objectives should be established for the modified program and careful analysis made of the potential effects of modification on the implementation and evaluation plan. Again, modification requires that redecision be made about the modified program at some future date.

Abandonment of a program is perhaps the most difficult decision of all. Abandonment carries with it an overtone of failure. However, many other causes for abandonment exist. Perhaps the program adequately fulfilled its original objectives and is, therefore, no longer needed. Alternatively, the needs of students may not be the same, and the program is no longer the most effective means to respond to changing needs. Finally, the program, though excellent in theory or concept, may be mismatched with the institutional environment. Fiscal and political realities also change, and programs must respond to them or risk failure. Finally, the program may be good, may have met its objectives, but is simply not reaching enough people to justify continuation. Other resources and methods must be found to meet the needs formerly met by the program.

The decision for program continuance is both a rational and emotional process for program planners. It may indeed be difficult to modify, abandon, or limit the continuation of programs that have taken considerable time and effort to create. Program planners must, however, assume this responsibility; otherwise, it will occur without their input.

SUMMARY AND IMPLICATIONS

Practical Applications. In this chapter a five step model for program development that has practical application in a wide range of institutional settings has been presented. Each of the steps is an interlocking component of the entire model; yet attention must be paid to the individual steps so that the program planner can begin to identify some of the practical applications of this process.

Assessment of student needs is vital enough almost to qualify as a program in itself. Administrative units such as the placement service or the counseling center could be guilty of wasting their valuable resources in personnel and material if they fail to set viable goals based on real needs of their constituents. Planned programs such as a series of assertiveness training groups or seminars for reentering students are useless if the student population possesses adequate assertiveness training skills or consists entirely of recent high school graduates. One-time activities like a chamber music concert or a financial aid information session are likewise wasteful if the population to which they are aimed has no need or no interest.

The practical need for resource assessment is just as strong. Regardless of the demand, attempting to set up a health center is folly if medical personnel and proper facilities are not available. A seminar series on mid-life crises cannot be conducted by staff who do not fully comprehend the implications of such events, nor can a large dance troupe be programmed in a facility designed for solo coffeehouse performers. To begin the planning and implementation of any program without proper assessment wastes resources and cultivates failure.

The establishment of a planning team has an effect beyond the singular program for which the team is brought together. The group dynamics, cooperation, and goal setting that take place within such a team are an important staff development, which transcends the specific program being planned. One additional result from the planning model is the development of a useful process for asking important questions about goals, objectives, training, budget, and evaluation at appropriate times before the program is fully implemented.

The post-assessment step has a double application. This procedure serves primarily to evaluate the product and the process of the program. The process itself of conducting a post-assessment can develop a pattern of good, comprehensive recordkeeping. If done properly, post-assessment, even from a program that fails to meet the original expectations, teaches a lesson about the process of program development and implementation that can be employed in all future programming endeavors.

Because programs are, after all, interventions, procedures described in this chapter can be viewed as practical applications of the theoretical model of defining and targeting interventions (Morrill & Hurst, 1980). Moreover, this model of program development and implementation is designed to augment the "development milieu" (Miller & Prince, 1976). Campuses should strive to provide not just academic experience, but the comprehensive human development of all students (Brown, 1972). Student development theory advocates not only attention to the developmental needs of students, but also the provision of interventions to help them reach their potential. Effective program development and planning skills are essential if the student affairs practitioner is truly going to be successful in translating theory to effective practice.

To assist the practitioner with the program planning process, a checklist has been developed as a practical guide to program planning:

Program Development Checklist

I. Assessment

_____identify and analyze the demographic characteristics of the student body

_____solicit unobtrusive observations by colleagues about student needs

_____analyze obtrusive measures of student needs—questionnaires, interviews, standardized instruments, structured research

_____develop a clear understanding of the stated institutional mission and goals

_____review the institution's historical records

_____review current and recent past campus activities

_____learn campus politics as they may affect program development

_____learn the background, interests, and skills of all staff personnel who may contribute

_____identify all possible sources of fiscal support

_____know the physical needs of the program and identify the space, equipment, and supplies necessary

II. Planning

_____select a small, effective planning team to develop the program

_____identify expected outcomes by listing clear, specific goals and objectives define the specific outcomes(s) that will indicate the program's success

_____identify the target population

_____select the approach to developing the program and identify the resources it will include

_____identify methods to evaluate all components of the program—the process employed as well as the product delivered

_____decide whether or not an initial pilot program is necessary or desirable _____determine what training the planning team or other staff involved may need

_____develop a complete budget

_____establish a realistic time line

III. Implementation

_____assign specific responsibilities to each staff member

_____identify and employ the most effective publicity and promotion

_____select the physical location most conducive to successful attendance

_____list and identify the source of all equipment, supplies, and other physical resources necessary

_____schedule the program at a time that will be the most comfortable for participants and conflicts least with other campus/community events

_____collect evaluation data on both the process and the content of the program

IV. Post-assessment

_____apply evaluation data to stated goals and identify both unmet goals and any outcomes that were not identified in the original goal statement

_____include staff reactions in evaluation analysis

_____make recommendations for modifications in program process or content

_____make recommendations for program cost efficiency

V. Administrative Decision

_____decide the future of the program: continuation, modification, or abandonment

REFERENCES

Astin, A.W. *The college environment.* Washington, DC: American Council on Education, 1968.

Astin, A.W. *Four critical years: Effects of college on beliefs, attitudes and knowledge.* San Francisco: Jossey-Bass, 1977.

Baier, J.L. Competent staff: The critical variable. In M.J. Barr & F.L. Keating (Eds.), *New directions for student services: Establishing effective programs* (No. 7). San Francisco: Jossey-Bass. 1979.

Baldridge, J.V., & Tierney, M.L. *New approaches to management: Creating practical systems of management information and management by objective.* San Francisco: Jossey-Bass, 1979.

Barr, M. J., & Keating, L. (Eds.). *New directions for student services: Establishing effective programs* (No. 7). San Francisco: Jossey-Bass, 1979.

Bennis, C., Benne, K.D., & Chin, R. *The planning of change.* New York: Holt, Rinehart, and Winston, 1962.

Berdie, D., & Anderson, J. *Questionnaire: Design and use.* Metuchen, NJ: Scarecrow Press, 1974.

Brown, R.D. *Student development in tomorrow's higher education: A return to the academy.* Washington, DC: American College Personnel Association, 1972.

Budig, G.A. *Dollars and sense: Budgeting for today's campus.* Chicago: College and University Business Press, 1972.

Chickering, A.W. *Education and identity.* San Francisco: Jossey-Bass, 1969.

Conyne, R. Environmental assessment: Mapping for counselor action. *Personnel and Guidance Journal,* 1975, *54,* 150-5.

Coombs, P.H., & Hallak, J. *Managing educational costs.* New York: Oxford University Press, 1972.

Crookston, B.B. An organizational model for student development. *NASPA Journal,* 1972, *10,* 3-13.

Deegan, A.X., & Fritz, R. *MBO goes to college.* Boulder, CO: Division of Continuing Education, Bureau of Independent Study, 1975.

Erikson, E.H. *Childhood and society* (2nd ed.). New York: Norton, 1963.

Feldman, K.A. Measuring college environments: Some uses for path analysis. *American Educational Research Journal,* 1971, *8,* 51-70.

Hoy, W.I., & Miskal, C.G. *Educational administration: Theory, research and practice.* New York: Random House, 1978.

Katz, D., & Kahn, R.L. *The social psychology of organizations.* New York: John Wiley and Sons, 1966.

Maslow, A.H. *Motivation and personality* (2nd ed.). New York: Harper and Row, 1970.

Maw, I., Richards, N.A., & Crosby, H.J. *Formula budgeting: An application to student affairs.* Washington, DC: American College Personnel Association, 1976.

Merton, R.H. *Social theory and social structure.* New York: Free Press, 1956.

Miller, T.K., & Prince, J.S. *The future of student affairs: A guide to student development for tomorrow's higher education.* San Francisco: Jossey-Bass, 1976.

Moore, M., & Delworth, U. *Training manual for student services program development.* Boulder, CO: Western Interstate Commission for Higher Education, 1976.

Moos, R. *Evaluating educational environments.* San Francisco: Jossey-Bass, 1979.

Morrill, W.H., & Hurst, J.C. (Eds.). *Dimensions of intervention for student development.* New York: John Wiley and Sons, 1980.

Morrill, W.H., Oetting, E.R., & Hurst, J.C. Dimensions of counselor functioning. *Personnel and Guidance Journal,* 1974, *52,* 354-9.

Pace, C.R. *College and university environment scale technical manual* (2nd ed.). Princeton: NJ: Educational Testing Service, 1969.

Struening, E. L., & Guttentag, M. *Handbook of evaluation research* (2 vols.). Beverly Hills, CA: Sage Publications, Inc., 1975.

Thomas, W.A. Exit valor, enter veracity. In M.J. Barr & L. Keating (Eds.), *New directions for student services: Establishing effective programs* (No. 7). San Francisco: Jossey-Bass, 1979.

Weathersby, G.B., & Jacobs, F. *Institutional goals and student costs.* Washington, DC: American Association for Higher Education, 1977.

Weber, M. *The theory of social and economic organization.* New York: Free Press, 1947.

SUGGESTED READINGS

Astin, A.W. *Four critical years: Effects of college on beliefs, attitudes and knowledge.* San Francisco: Jossey-Bass, 1977.

Barr, M. J., & Keating, L. (Eds.). *New directions for student services: Establishing effective programs* (No. 7). San Francisco: Jossey-Bass, 1979.

Brown, R.D. *Student development in tomorrow's higher education: A return to the academy.* Washington, DC: American College Personnel Association, 1972.

Chickering, A.W. *Education and identity.* San Francisco: Jossey-Bass, 1969.

Hoy, W.K., & Miskal, C.G. *Educational administration: Theory, research and practice.* New York: Random House, 1978.

Moore, M., & Delworth, U. *Training manual for student services program development.* Boulder, CO: Western Interstate Commission for Higher Education, 1976.

Packwood, W.T. (Ed.). *College student personnel services.* Springfield, IL: Charles C. Thomas, 1977.

Louis C. (Lou) Stamatakos is Professor of Higher Education at Michigan State University. He holds three degrees from Indiana University, including the doctorate, and has served the profession for seventeen years as an administrator (residence halls, student activities, Dean of Men, Dean of Students) in five collegiate institutions prior to assuming full-time teaching, research, and advising responsibilities at Michigan State University in 1967.

As an active member of the professional associations, he has served as President of the Wisconsin Association of Deans, President of the Michigan College Personnel Association, three terms at Member-at-Large in the American College Personnel Association, six years on the Association's Monograph Board, two terms as ACPA's Senator to the American Personnel and Guidance Association, and was its first Editor of Commissions Publications. He has served as consultant for over thirty institutions in the United States, and for institutions and Ministries of Education in Brazil, Mexico, and Greece, and has taught at Cambridge, London, and Oxford.

Chapter **19**

MAXIMIZING OPPORTUNITIES FOR SUCCESS

Louis C. Stamatakos

This chapter is intended to aid persons entering the field of student affairs in examining the fundamental issues and activities that affect the nature and quality of both professional preparation and initial years of practice.

PROFESSIONAL PREPARATION

Student affairs has long been staffed with paraprofessionals and allied professionals, faculty selected to serve as administrators because of their skills and interests in working with students outside the formal classroom. Contemporary demands and expectations in student affairs require more sophisticated professional preparation and performance. This increased demand for professionally prepared student affairs practitioners has resulted in over 100 colleges and universities offering professional preparation programs enrolling about 2,700 students annually (Rockey, 1977).

Of the approximately 30,000 currently employed student affairs practitioners, it is unknown how many have received specialized graduate-level preparation. What is known, however, is that each year over 1,000 graduates of these programs actively seek entry level positions (Greer, Blaesser, Herron, & Horle, 1978). The wide variance in their application skills and the quality of their preparation heightens the competition for positions and for survival and success within the profession (Stamatakos, 1980). Rodgers (1977) reported that preparation programs tend to be characterized by either an emphasis upon organization and administration (institution-centered objectives, administrative processes, and how-to-get-it-done application skills) or counseling (development of counseling skills and achievement of therapeutic outcomes). Although the majority are characterized by an emphasis on counseling, some were found to emphasize student and organization development.

Student affairs is characterized by constant change, which demands new knowledge and understanding and requires both practitioner and program adaptations. Preparation programs in student affairs vary widely in admissions, content, supervision of practice, duration, and qualifications of faculty. Taking these factors into account, one can readily understand the tremendous ecumenicalism and inconsistency of philosophies and practices that characterize the profession (Mueller, 1961; Stamatakos, 1980).

Whatever the setting and emphasis, individuals enrolling in student affairs preparation programs need to assume a professional role at the onset. This role demands commitment to a lifetime of intense and constant preparation and self-improvement. Such dedication requires both intellectual and affective skill development of the highest order, no less than that expected of a scientist, artist, or philosopher. The true professional must exercise self-determination to keep growing and developing.

Each generation of new student affairs professionals has profound impact upon the nature, direction, and quality of practice. The more professionally oriented students are, the more they will demand of and benefit from graduate professional education; professional practice, thereby, will be positively affected.

Expectations for improvement of professional practice are a fundamental responsibility of faculty members. Incumbent upon faculty members is the need to be aware of the profession's strengths, weaknesses, directions, and needs. Similarly, they must possess the knowledge, understanding, skills, and competencies needed by new professionals to insure quality performance and improve practice. Further, the faculty must have the capacity to serve as role models for appropriate and successful instructional, advising, and mentoring activities. All professional faculty and staff members interacting with students need to assume a scholar-doer orientation similar to that expected of their students. Such congruence maximizes achievement.

Formal Courses and Scholarly Activity

Students and Scholars. Faculty are responsible for introducing students to the philosophical and theoretical constructs that underlie the profession. These include studying publications such as the *Student Personnel Point of View* (ACE, 1949), and "Student Development Services in Post Secondary Education" (COSPA, 1975), and gaining an understanding of human development theories (Chickering, 1969; Erikson, 1963; Heath, 1968; Kohlberg, 1969; Maslow, 1968; Perry, 1970) so as to assist students in establishing a firm and substantive foundation for the profession. It is precisely this foundation that is being addressed in the professional preparation standards included in Appendix C of this book. Those responsible for professional preparation programs will wish to examine Appendix C closely.

Some students coast along doing mediocre work and appear to be qualified during the process, while others pursue each concept, theory, and construct until they are internalized into well-formed, highly skilled, and definitely articulated statements and behaviors. The contrast between these approaches is glaringly obvious to instructors, supervisors, and peers alike. Further, differences are not attributable to superior intellect but, rather, recognition by the latter group of their personal responsibilities. The degree to which students integrate basic tenets and theories of the profession into their own professional style distinguishes them from functionaries and "hacks" who associate themselves with the profession.

An unfounded notion is that the profession of student affairs attracts doers and not scholars. Many bright students are definitely attracted to the profession, but are not sufficiently challenged by faculty members and supervisors or by the content in the program of study to become serious thinkers and scholars as well as doers. Demand for proficiency in communication, for exhibiting essential knowledge and skills, for integrating and synthesizing philosophical and theoretical concepts in practical ways, for active participation in well-designed and monitored practicum and assistantship activities, all coupled with frequent, rigorous assessment and grading practices, will reasonably ensure that scholar-practitioners enter the profession in greater numbers. These students, because they have met such high level expectations, in most instances transfer their learning directly to their professional work as well.

Transfer of Learning. Because of tradition and lack of specialized faculty and programs, many students are exposed to courses designed for those who work in elementary-secondary educational settings. Courses such as educational research, tests and measurements, learning theory, and philosophy of education all too often are taught with no attempt made to help students transfer their learning into higher education settings. Instead of berating the course content or instructors for emphasizing the K-12 setting, students are obligated to relate that knowledge and skill directly to the higher education setting through assistantships or practica. The learner has the responsibility to identify and activate ways to make classroom education relevant to the work setting. This suggests that competent student affairs professionals are self-directed people.

Behavioral Science as a Foundation. Student affairs practice is applied behavioral science. Yet only a minority of graduate students enter professional preparation programs with substantive backgrounds in psychology, sociology, or anthropology. In addition, few preparation programs require formalized study of behavioral sciences within core courses or as a required minor or cognate (Rockey, 1977).

As an aspiring professional, the student has an obligation to be well versed in theories of human development, human learning, and group dynamics as well as to apply this knowledge to program planning, development, and implementation. Just as critical is the ability to lead and instruct subordinate staff members in these areas. Most students have elective courses within their programs of study. Electives should be used to overcome any deficiencies in the behavioral sciences. If such options do not exist, students should study these disciplines on their own. Students should not be permitted to graduate and practice with deficiencies in the basic behavioral sciences.

Faculty are Human Beings Too. Many faculty members actively engaged in preparation programs were educated as guidance counselors, psychologists, sociologists, historians, and athletic coaches. Some practicing student affairs administrators are products of another era with different orientations and emphases from those currently prevalent. These differences in background preparation and in experiences may produce differences among faculty members in perceptions and methods as they work to make the student's preparation program dynamic, strong, and appropriate to the profession's needs and expectations.

The faculty must engage in many different activities in order that they keep striving, productive, and current. One activity is an exchange and interaction with students and graduates. Thus, the faculty needs current students' input and former students' feedback if the faculty are to maintain a high level of quality and consistency in their work. Improved professionalism on the part of both student and faculty members is contingent upon the student's willingness to be an active partner in the teaching-learning process.

When the faculty are failing the student in any way—as instructors, role models, advisors, colleagues—they should be so informed. Students should be responsible to give thoughtful, constructive recommendations for change. The applicability, quality, and credibility of one's preparation and academic degree are greatly dependent upon the level of personal involvement in the learning process. Openly shared positive collegial responsibility of this nature is critical to the improvement of both professional preparation and practice and is the responsibility of both faculty members *and* students.

Maximizing the Learning Process. Most courses require students to read, understand and be well-versed in the professional literature. Many courses in student affairs also ask students to put this knowledge into practice. If students are to profit from the learning of others, they must absorb and utilize knowledge effectively as a natural part of their professional behavior. To achieve this objective students must cite and utilize information from their reading in assistantships, practica, and classes.

As many students know from their undergraduate experiences, the formal classroom can be either a relatively bland, passive place, or it can be an environment of stimulation, intense involvement with risk, change, and growth. The extent to which students experience and benefit from the active classroom is directly proportionate to their willingness to become active contributors to, and partners in, the learning process.

The classroom should be a place in which the student is unafraid to question and probe, to challenge assumptions and beliefs, to reexamine personal attitudes, values, and assumptions, and to grow. Faculty members are responsible for creating an environment in which such growth occurs naturally, effectively, and efficiently. In consort with the instructor's efforts, the student's responsibility is to take advantage of opportunities for growth. This learning partnership requires advance preparation as well as a mutual commitment on the parts of both faculty and students. Assuming such preparation and mutual intent exist, the tinder awaits ignition by informed and intense faculty-to-student and student-to-student interaction. Ultimately, students control the dynamics that fuel the fire of learning, and students bear the greatest responsibility for their own learning and growth.

In professional preparation "not all learning takes place in the confines of the formal classroom." A careful study of out-of-class learning opportunities related to professional preparation will reveal that students learn and grow by writing, editing, and publishing newsletters and journals, by sponsoring speakers' series, by involvement in graduate student professional societies, by participating in volunteer activities with human services centers and campus student groups, by conducting or assisting in research and preparation program evaluations, and by preparing and presenting papers and programs at conferences and conventions. Activities designed both to aid the professional development of students and to strengthen the quality of preparation are essential components of a graduate course of study in student affairs.

Applying Classroom Learning

A former president of Indiana University once suggested that a person could live on that campus for several years and, although not enrolling in a single class, obtain a tremendous education by simply taking advantage of the free lectures, concerts, performances, open meetings, and libraries, and by talking to faculty members. Analogously, the campus environment in which professional preparation programs exist are steeped with learning resources and enriching opportunities for graduate students. These resources should be carefully considered when developing a program of professional study. Failure to consider seriously volunteer involvement as important to the learning process is to ignore the third curriculum (Fredrick, 1965) and the wealth of opportunity it provides.

Practica Make Perfect. In most preparation programs, students are required to enroll in one or more practica for the purpose of obtaining firsthand experience in various organizational units and settings. Disappointingly, some practica expose students to questionable practices and procedures, to functionaries who manage programs with little forethought to or understanding of the program's potential for developmental impact, or to a limited perspective of the potential relationships that could be established between a given office and other agencies (Stamatakos, 1980).

Obviously, the practicum student is not in a position to criticize openly or change others' behaviors, but is in an excellent position to develop an understanding of the potential for the office becoming more effective in the service and the delivery of developmental activities. As a professional in training, the student is expected to learn to differentiate between the ideal, the potential, and the real. More importantly, the student is urged to examine each activity, each experience, each office, and each staff member within the context of what ought to be and what could be if the student were responsible. As one who knows why and how the profession's practice could become more effective, the student has both an opportunity and an obligation to work actively for its improvement. A practitioner is better for having been fired from a position for trying to achieve the goals of the profession, than for having lived a lifetime of safe but frustrating and unfulfilling mediocrity.

A wide variety of practica assignments should be made, including, where possible, off-campus or other college campus opportunities. The practicum should be conceived broadly and with the objective of providing each student with the most appropriate, stimulating, and growth-producing experience possible, while assuring a high standard of student preparation and performance and of supervisor instruction and direction.

Practica should be initiated only after students have had sufficient exposure to the field of study and possess sufficient knowledge and understanding of the basic philosophical and theoretical underpinnings of the profession. Without such knowledge and some professional skill students are ill-equipped to perform effectively or learn from the practicum experience. The assumption is that all practica entail active and contributing performance by students involved and that a practicum consisting only of observation and listening is undeserving of either the title or the sponsorship of a professional preparation program.

The Graduate Assistantship. Historically, graduate assistantships have been sponsored by collegiate institutions in order to encourage and attract bright and able students to pursue graduate studies. Coupled with financial support, students are given an opportunity to learn research and teaching skills appropriate to their disciplines. In student affairs, graduate assistantships are usually geared toward financial assistance for services rendered in a student affairs office, such as admissions, financial aid, student activities, or residence halls. Through this arrangement the institution secures bright, energetic, and capable paraprofessional and professional part-time staff who contribute significantly to the maintenance and improvement of operational units. Intentional use of "living laboratories" such as student activities and residence hall programs offer graduate students excellent opportunities to develop skills in working with undergraduate students as a systematic part of professional preparation experiences.

When properly orchestrated, theoretical and philosophical concepts and principles can have a tremendous impact upon students when intentionally applied within assistantships. If such arrangements are not evident, students should seek to rectify the situation in cooperation with faculty and supervisory staff. If professional practice is to be congruent with philosophy and theories advocated by authorities, practitioners, faculty, and students alike can capitalize upon assistantships, which are some of the best opportunities available within the learning environment.

If congruence between learning and practice is to be realized, supervisors must model behaviors and skills appropriate to preparation program emphasis. Likewise, collaboration between academic faculty and practice supervisors likely results in mutually beneficial activities such as team teaching, integrated program planning, and staff development projects. Such instructional partnerships lend credence to the profession.

Institutional Governance as a Resource. The institution's governance structure promotes collegiality through the process of guiding its organization and programs. Although professionals are expected to perform within an institutionally governed framework throughout their careers, governance issues are often overlooked during preparation.

Graduate students are encouraged to become involved in the governance structure either as student representatives or by attending meetings of faculty governing bodies and committees in order to gain firsthand experience. Such experiences aid understanding of the unique relationship that exists between faculty and administrators. If student affairs is to "return to the academy," as Brown (1972) suggested, such exposure and experience should enhance that return. Similarly, attending meetings of student government and boards of trustees can provide knowledge. To study Corson's *Governance of Colleges and Universities* (1960) is one thing, but altogether different insights and revelations result with actual observation of interactions that occur when administrators, faculty members, students, and trustees meet to deliberate and decide policy matters.

In-service Staff Development. The best student affairs divisions invariably sponsor continuous in-service staff development programs. Too often, graduate students tend to be excluded from such activities, although exposure to professionals involved in developing new skills presents a propitious educational climate for the budding professional.

Faculty and student affairs staff members must arrange for regular and systematic inclusion of graduate students in staff development activities. Such an approach results in students learning from practitioners. Practitioners, in turn, profit from the freshness and candor of student contributions. This is an excellent way for practitioners to model professional behavior and to contribute to the learning and growth of future leaders.

Taking Professional Responsibility

Two excellent opportunities within the larger profession are available to students when they apply their classroom education: professional associations and publications. Graduate students should be encouraged to take full advantage of both as integral parts of their professional education.

Professional Associations. A responsibility of every professional is active involvement in appropriate professional associations. Most of these organizations encourage student membership by offering regular member benefits at reduced costs. Often, student members can serve on executive boards, committees, and commissions. Student members also receive journals, newsletters, and other association publications.

Paraphrasing Mueller's (1961) excellent chapter on professionalism, the following listing highlights some personal and professional reasons for membership in professional associations:

•To meet other professionals in the field

•To discover new ideas for programs and services

•To develop new skills through workshops

•To receive publications sponsored by associations

- To attend conferences sponsored by associations

- To have access to association job listings and placement activities

- To serve one's colleagues through association membership

- To attain status among peers

- To influence policy and direction in professional practice

- To gain and exercise power

- To achieve a sense of identity within the profession

- To use the association as an aid to the achievement of other personal or professional goals

Significant experiences come about through professional association related activities such as committee work, program development and administration, holding office, presenting papers and programs, testing ideas in the open forum of professional peers, and reviewing work of colleagues. Often, the most able, respected, and active members of the profession are leaders in its associations as well. Many of them began their association activities early in their graduate studies or soon after.

One's lifelong professionalism usually begins with graduate studies and continues long thereafter through active, contributing involvement in professional associations. Commitment to and involvement in associations provide continuity, depth, and breadth of varying and wide-ranging professional interests and perspectives rarely found on a single campus or within a single program of studies. As noted in Chapter 6, professional associations are essential to the existence of a profession.

Where and how does the student start? Most faculty members are actively involved in state and national associations; they can make membership forms available and know whom to contact to make a recommendation for the student's initial involvement. The following six steps can be used as a guide by students who wish to become responsibly involved:

1. Start by selecting an appropriate association and taking out a membership.

2. Become thoroughly knowledgeable of the association's committees, commissions, officers, and general structure.

3. Volunteer for any kind of work for which one has talent. (Continue to work for others through the association, and the opportunity for recognition and increased responsibility will naturally follow.)

4. Plan, propose, and participate in programs at annual conferences and workshops in areas of expertise and interest.

5. Follow through on commitments and promises made to the association and do not accept assignments that cannot or will not be accomplished.

6. Plan to devote many working hours to demands made upon active members of the association.

Publication Opportunities. To a great extent, one's professional career development is contingent upon the quality of oral and written expression. In light of this, it is incumbent upon students to develop these skills during the time they are under the tutorage of faculty who share their concerns. During their graduate studies, students are often called upon to prepare written materials of publication quality. Many institutions sponsor student affairs publications that solicit student written articles. In addition, local, state, regional, and national associations sponsor journals and newsletters that welcome student written papers on a variety of topics. If the profession is to nurture quality thinking and writing, students should be encouraged to be active contributors to the professional literature. Benefits to be derived from writing for publication are many and include sharpening of both ideas and writing skills, testing of one's thinking in the professional marketplace, enhancement of professional credentials, and satisfaction and confidence derived from being published.

ENTERING THE PROFESSIONAL WORKWORLD

Usually with trepidation and anxiety students begin preparations for obtaining their first full-time professional position. A period of relatively non-directional activity may occur or perhaps even a total paralysis. Neither of these responses is necessary when students have prepared for what can be a stimulating, exciting, and positive new learning experience.

Preparing the Resumé

Although professional preparation expands one's education and sophistication, many graduating students may still wonder what they have to offer a prospective employer. An effective vehicle that can help answer these questions is the professional resumé. Simply stated, the resumé is a summary of preparation and practical experiences that reflects one's professional career qualifications. Most resumés are presented on quality paper with the express purpose to entice prospective employers to offer the applicant an employment interview. Its purpose is clear, although the specific content to be included often has been a source of disagreement among professionals.

Content of the Resumé. The resumé often follows some acceptable form agreed upon by students and their advisors, and contains demographic information such as full name, mailing address, and telephone numbers. Gender, age, race, religion, handicap, marital status, and photographs, although generally prohibited factors in determining employability, may be included as the student chooses. A brief statement regarding the nature of positions sought and types of institutions in which employment is desired may also be included, although some professionals maintain that such statements are too restrictive during periods of low employment opportunities. Others argue that specificity of this sort implies firmness and conviction and is well accepted in the hands of the right people. Compromisers suggest that students prepare two resumes, one with and one without the statement, then use them judiciously.

Information on earned degrees, granting institutions, years in attendance, along with academic majors, minors, and honors are presented briefly in descending (most recent first) chronological order. Professional experience usually follows, again in reverse chronological order, and is elaborated upon with titles, promotions, responsibilities, committee assignments, and special accomplishments. Beginning professionals usually include all positions held, including those part-time in nature. More experienced people may exclude positions that no longer appear germane to the employment being sought. Students may wish to include also in this section practica, volunteer experiences, and internships that relate to special abilities, skills, and interests. Professional associations, honorary societies, and special honors and awards usually follow, along with professional organization memberships, offices held, years of appointment, and special assignments.

Participation in professional association conferences as a presenter or panelist is usually noted along with reference to dates, location, and nature of involvement. Also, a complete bibliographic reference for any publications should be provided at this point with care taken to distinguish between publications in refereed journals and non-refereed publications and books. Internal reports, papers, and "house organ" publications should *not* be included under the publications section, because they are not "publications" in the professional sense of the word no matter how significant they may be. The student might wish to conclude the resumé with additional information under separate headings such as undergraduate college activities or miscellaneous.

After finishing the resumé, one often begins to sense a personal integration or completeness not heretofore experienced. In effect, the physical process of organizing one's experiences and education in written form aids in the self-awareness process. Questions that need to be addressed at this point are: "Have I included everything of importance? Have I included information that is immaterial or irrelevant to the resumé's purpose? Have I been completely honest and forthright in the manner in which things have been stated? Is this the best format, content, and writing style for expressing the real me?" Consultation with a faculty member or peer may be helpful at this point. Obtaining an objective and critical review of the resumé from others is considered essential, if one is to put the best foot forward in the job-seeking process.

Final copy should pass through at least three proofings by others for form, style, content, grammar, spelling, unintended inferences, and overall impression. Its printing should be done professionally using a quality grade of paper. Care should be taken to assure that color, typeface, or artwork do not cheapen the effect of the resumé. When one considers that the resumé is a direct reflection and extension of oneself, the importance for care and caution can be easily understood.

Planning Strategies
for Convention Placement

Although individuals are seldom hired at professional association conventions or placement activities, employment contacts and interview opportunities for persons seeking employment sufficiently warrant careful planning and preparation in advance of attendance. Convention placement listings range from a few to several hundred positions, from entry level jobs such as residence life coordinator and admissions counselors to chief student affairs officers. Whether the job-seeking practitioner is new or a seasoned "old pro," a certain amount of homework is mandatory if employment is to result.

Psyching Out the System. This part of the process entails determining in advance physical location and layout of the conference placement operation, method of operation, message exchange system, forms to be completed, fees to be paid, types and number of credentials to be filed, advanced position listings, and opportunities available for volunteering to serve as an aid in the convention's placement program. Faculty and staff members are usually able to assist students in securing this information in advance of the conference and should be asked without hesitation.

Effective Time Utilization. Often, students nearing graduation, involved in time-consuming practica or concerned with graduate assistantship responsibilities, are prone to approach the job search in less than the professional manner it requires. Students should begin planning several months before entering actively into the job search.

Sufficient time should be provided for drafting the resumé, determining the kind of position and type of institution for which one is best suited, estimating the amount of professional on-the-job supervision necessary, and establishing the level of personal needs for professional development and upward mobility. Once these factors have been identified, the student must sift through the many possible employment options to establish the best match. Again, assistance should be available from qualified faculty and staff members to advise, counsel, and recommend.

Another pre-convention strategy involves correspondence with selected individuals at institutions where employment is being sought. A short, well-written letter accompanied by a resumé requesting an opportunity to meet with an institutional representative during the upcoming conference can open many doors. Note that letters addressed to "Dear Dean" or "To Whom It May Concern" are not only poor form, but *rarely* elicit a positive response from the recipient. Also, poorly composed letters with misspellings and grammatical errors almost invariably result in criticism of the applicant as well as the preparation program and faculty.

In addition, letters to student affairs associates and former graduate student colleagues now employed in other institutions can be useful; they may be knowledgeable of positions opening on their campuses or elsewhere. They also might be able to make introductions to others during conventions, which may lead to additional employment opportunities. Many excellent employment leads have been discovered during informal conversations with professional friends.

Planning the Interview. Both a thoughtful set of questions the candidate will wish to ask and considered responses to probable questions from interviewers should be prepared in advance. Responses to be considered should include substantive, thoughtful answers to questions such as "Why do you want to work at our college?"; and "Why do you think you are qualified for the position?" These are not easy questions to answer effectively without advance preparation; role rehearsal can help. Practice with peers or faculty members followed by critique sessions can promote naturalness in presenting oneself in the best possible light as well as improving the good timing of questions and the appropriate responses to the interviewer's questions.

The Interview. In many ways the initial interview is the pivotal point in the convention job placement process. Proper attire for an interview is business dress. One's apparel is an important part of the initial impression made on a prospective employer. Even more important are the first few minutes of the interview, for they often determine the impression the interviewer will carry thereafter. Questions asked should be direct and relevant. Similarly, the candidate's responses to questions should be concise and direct without appearing to be either brash or blase. Unless specifically asked, the candidate should avoid repeating information already contained in the resumé, for judicious use of time is critical. A wise candidate concentrates the interview on the institution's needs and how he/she can benefit the institution rather than upon why the job is being sought. Keeping the accent on the positive is a good strategy to follow even when candidates are asked to "describe their weaknesses." Keep in mind that no employer wants to employ a loser, especially one who is obvious about it.

If the candidate and interviewer seem to be compatible and if the interviewer appears to be favorably impressed, the candidate may wish to indicate an interest in making a campus visit and attempt to make preliminary arrangements for that visit before concluding the interview. Conversely, if the candidate discovers that the position is not desirable or that the interviewer is not positively impressed with or enthusiastic about the candidate, the candidate can properly initiate termination of the interview and conclude with an expression of appreciation.

Some behaviors to avoid during the interview include the failure to see that the interviewer receives the resumé before the interview, chewing gum, smoking without securing approval, responding to the interviewer's questions before they are completed, appearing disorganized or confused, appearing overly effervescent, wildly enthusiastic, or bored, indulging in trivia, and asking inappropriate questions.

Interview Follow-up. Post-interview action is nearly as important as the interview itself. If possible, a thank-you letter containing facts learned about the organization and indicating that the interview confirmed interest in the position should be written to the interviewer. Use information learned in the interview about problems, needs, and growth plans to reiterate contributions to the organization's goals one can make. This is a bread and butter letter that sometimes may be a deciding factor in obtaining a campus interview.

Making On-site Visits

An invitation to visit a campus is initiated by the prospective employer and indicates serious interest in the applicant as a future employee. In most instances employers offer to pay the expenses incurred to make a campus visit. For some entry level positions, however, some or all of the cost may have to be borne by the candidate. Whatever the case, the terms should be established and agreed upon at the onset of negotiating an on-site visit so that misunderstandings are avoided. If the applicant cannot afford the visit, yet is truly interested in the position, consideration might well be given to borrowing the necessary funds against future earnings. Occasionally, employers are receptive to negotiating some expenses. In some instances the candidate may be forced to take the risk and invest the money in travel and lodging.

On-campus Visitations. The following strategies should be seriously considered when making a campus visit:

•Learn as much as possible about all aspects of the institution before the visit.

•Dress appropriately and anticipate weather changes.

•Plan the itinerary carefully and inform hosts about travel arrangements. Leave some time for browsing around campus and town.

•Be punctual for all appointments. Tardiness is invariably viewed with disfavor.

•Take along extra resumés and work samples.

•Visit with students and staff of one's own choosing. Hosts will seek to impress and sometimes may fail to provide exposure to some of the institution's less positive aspects.

•Recognize the virtue in consistency, so pursue campus interviews in the same style used during the original interview.

•Realize that interviews are like two-way streets, both parties are interviewers and have a right to ask questions and probe. Questions should address opportunities for professional development as well as working conditions, reward systems, and opportunities for applying knowledge and skills on the job.

•Indicate interest in the position but withhold a decision. If an offer is made during the visit, wait until opportunity is available to weigh objectively all advantages and disadvantages involved.

•Send a letter following the on-site visit that demonstrates understanding of the position, personal strengths, and appropriateness for the position as well as showing appreciation for the hospitality received.

•Review with care any position offer received to make sure that conditions of employment are spelled out, including a specific job description as well as the staff benefits to which entitled. Some institutions also may pay moving expenses.

Upon Accepting the New Position

Once a position has been accepted, the professional notifies the hiring official in writing, verifying the acceptance and the date that employment begins. Subsequent correspondence regarding housing and other personal matters should be directed to those persons designated by the employee's supervisor. At this point one should notify one's current employer that a new position has been accepted. Letters also should be sent to all others with whom one has been negotiating, indicating withdrawal from candidacy. To pursue other employment opportunities after a position has been accepted is professionally unethical.

Getting Started. Beginning work in the new position requires advance planning as did the job search itself. Answers to the following employment concerns should be sought from appropriate sources:

•Is there congruity between the stated policy and the actual behavior of the staff?

•What behaviors, skills, procedures, and results are rewarded by salary increases and promotions; who makes such judgments, how and when?

•What should be reported to one's supervisor, under what conditions, and in what form?

•How does change in programming, procedures, policies, and job descriptions occur, and how can one influence that change?

•In what ways can a staff member make needed and significant contributions to the improvement of the unit's program?

Questions such as these need to be addressed by new staff members because the answers may greatly influence their work styles, job functions, and professional growth. Employers expect new employees to be motivated and enthusiastic about their work and to be active learners as well as contributors to the institution. The assumption is that an employee's professional preparation, skills, and administrative leadership abilities will benefit the employing agency and those they serve.

BEING PROFESSIONAL

The concept of professionalism implies that practitioners adopt excellence as their goal along with the responsibility that accompanies it. Although excellence is a subjective concept, it is intrinsic to the concept of professionalism and reflects a compelling mind set of the practitioner toward constant renewal and expansion of skills and understandings. Coupled with a mature awareness of one's personal limitations and those of the field, the professional constantly seeks new knowledge and new understanding to aid in serving others in an effective, efficient, and human manner.

A more detailed and in-depth treatment of professionalism is presented in Chapters 6 and 20. The following discussion, therefore, is concerned with specific ways that both beginning and advanced practitioners manifest professionalism in their work.

On and Off the Job Behavior

Attitude, demeanor, deportment, values, and general work style of a staff member communicate to others a message about the degree of professionalism present, and subtly guide the practitioner's behavior in accordance with this message. Practitioners who strive for professionalism seek professional role models to emulate in regard to skills, attitudes, and values that are held to be ideal. Advanced professionals have the responsibility for seeking effective ways to model and teach those who are less advanced. Part of being a professional includes being generative, as noted by Carpenter in Chapter 6.

Professional decorum requires that staff members maintain preeminent moral and ethical standards of conduct. Failure to do so is demeaning in the eyes of colleagues and students alike and erodes one's stature, authority, and degree of achieved professionalism. Staff members must familiarize themselves with the ethical and professional standards that guide student affairs practitioners and act accordingly. In Chapter 7, Winston and McCaffrey discussed the role and function of such standards in some detail. It is strongly recommended that the "American College Personnel Association Statement of Ethical and Professional Standards" (Appendix A) be kept close at hand and used as a reference when ethical questions arise.

Both on and off-the-job environments are potentially conducive to the physical, spiritual, emotional, and intellectual improvement. Ample time for recreation, contemplation, and structured self-improvement should be built into one's schedule. New professional literature needs to be read, theories and applications need to be examined and conceptualized in light of new learning, and additional professional skills need to be acquired and strengthened for the purpose of increasing one's depth and breadth of responsibility and service. Self-renewal and continued growth are essential to the existence of any student affairs professional.

Developing Expertise

Basically, expertise reflects *know-how* in a particular field of endeavor. Too often the assumption is that, once graduated from a quality preparation program, a staff member has the expertise to achieve the employing unit's goals and objectives. This expectation is largely unreasonable given the wide variance in both people and their educational experiences. Thus, practitioners must continue their professional development in preparation for advanced assignments and increased responsibilities.

Development of expertise occurs in various ways, most of which involve some degree of planning and systematic study. A common form is in-service staff development, which should be a basic function of the employing agency. If such activities are not available, every effort should be expended to create them (Beeler, 1978; Stamatakos & Oliaro, 1972). Formats for staff development programs are virtually limitless but should always be purposeful, directional, well conceived, and thoroughly planned. In-service programs should always emerge from assessed staff needs and involve all affected staff members (see Chapter 14).

Advanced graduate study is another mode for increasing expertise and may be initially entered on a non-degree or continuing education basis to permit ease of entry and flexibility. As professional needs are recognized, courses in management, behavioral sciences, helping skills, or higher education administration, among others, can enhance one's expertise. Subsequently, one may wish to apply these courses to an advanced degree program. Also, most professional student affairs associations sponsor workshops and conferences that focus on relatively specific areas and are designed to increase practitioner expertise.

Skill development also can take place in the confines of one's home or office through reading, self-study projects, cassette lessons, and discussion sessions with peers and advanced professionals. The nature and extent of professional skill development are contingent upon the amount of time purposely given it. The attainment of professional expertise is not accomplished like reading a novel where one can start and stop on impulse. Rather, skill development is intentionally planned, nurtured, and implemented as an essential component of one's life as a professional.

Network Building and Maintenance

Both professionals and those seeking to achieve that status have ample opportunity to develop personal and collegial relationships that deserve nurturing, cultivation, and maintenance in that they are enjoyable, positive, supportive, and professionally helpful. Each relationship possesses the potential for providing one with both joy and professional sustenance.

During one's professional life, from entrance into graduate school through advancement up the ladder of increasing responsibility, one can gain an advantage by maintaining contact with respected colleagues whom one would assist when called upon and who would assist one in return. Establishing a network of professional contacts, developed and maintained over an entire professional lifetime, reaps rich rewards.

Many advanced professionals make commitments for helping younger professionals by developing and maintaining networks of current and former students and staff members that encourage professional loyalties and ties. Through frequent correspondence, publication of newsletters, sponsorship of hospitality hours at conferences, and nomination and support of qualified candidates for employment and association positions, professionals pay some of their "dues" to the profession.

Assuming reasonably similar career paths and interests, network members think of each other when opportunities for jobs, consultations, and conference presentations occur. To make the point more emphatic, when letters of recommendation and reference need to be written, one does not call upon Professor X, Administrator Y, and Colleague Z after a three to ten year silence and expect them to write very effectively and enthusiastically about a person they may no longer know. One's professional network, in many ways, enhances one's enjoyment and effectiveness in being a professional.

THE IMPORTANCE OF A MENTOR

In the initial stages of professional development, especially during preparation and early years of professional employment, establishing and maintaining a close, professionally intimate relationship with a more advanced professional has great utility. Such a person, herein referred to as a mentor, serves to bridge the transition from direct dependence on others to self-sufficiency and interdependence. A mentor is a mature professional with whom a protégé forms a close, collegial relationship and who provides guidance, support, and opportunities during an extended period of time. The mentor is the one from whom the beginning professional seeks advice, counsel, and sponsorship in professional and sometimes personal matters. Few student affairs practitioners have achieved full professional status without assistance from one or more mentors.

Establishing Relationships
with a Mentor

The relationship between a prospective professional and a mentor usually begins with the recognition of mutually shared values, professional objectives, achievement aspirations, and standards of performance. Oftentimes, individual efforts toward achieving mutual objectives signal beginnings of a mentor relationship. As this interaction grows, the younger professional begins to emulate many of the mentor's attitudes, values, behaviors, and, sometimes, personality characteristics. Simultaneously, the mentor manifests an increasing interest in the student's personal as well as professional development and begins to assume an active role in its content, form, and direction. Thus, the relationship, whether intentionally established by mutual consent or less deliberately on the basis of felt needs, develops slowly and unfolds gradually taking on breadth over time until it blossoms into an intense and directional interaction.

Mentor Benefits

Professional skills, depth of understanding, and level of performance exhibited by the mentor along with personal maturity, knowledge of the profession, and recognition as a leader enhance the beginning professional's development, competence, and confidence by association alone. When the mentor recommends resources, introduces the beginner to organizations and individuals advantageous to his/her career development, and makes recommendations to officials for placement purposes or for involvement in professional association activities, the young practitioner is even more blessed.

Note that not all the benefits accrue to the younger professionals alone, for the mentor profits from such relationships as well. As noted in Chapter 6, being generative is an advanced stage of professional development, and the education of future leaders assures professional improvement. The mentor also gains professional status through identification as a mentor to bright, talented future leaders. Just as important, both parties profit from the constant and challenging intellectual interaction that is created. Interestingly, mentor relationships may well develop into strong, rich personal friendships of deep respect, love, and affection that can last a lifetime. At the very least, they are essential to the early development of student affairs professionals.

Becoming a Mentor

Just as one has matured through and benefited from a mentor relationship, the opportunity will ultimately present itself to serve as a mentor to other young professionals. In many ways, survival of the profession requires that mature professionals accept such opportunities as a professional responsibility. In order to meet this responsibility when the time comes, one should become fully aware of the characteristics of those who have served as personal mentors and the delicate nature and weighty responsibilities attendant to carrying out the mentor role. Some characteristics to consider include the following:

•Knowledge of the profession and the ability to transmit its essence to others

•Enthusiasm for the profession and its importance to academe

•A genuine interest in both the professional and personal development of new professionals

•Warmth and understanding in relating to students and staff members in both formal and informal settings

•High, yet achievable, standards of performance for both oneself and others

•Active involvement in and support of professional associations

•Being a trusted friend and counselor who exhibits honest emotional rapport with others

•Willingness to commit substantial time and energy to others

•Willingness to share personal insights and acuity with others

•Encourages others to commit high levels of involvement to professional matters

•Gently stimulates others to extend themselves intellectually, emotionally, and professionally

•Exposes others to a select but broad based network of professionals who can help

•Seeks to guard the young professional from taking on responsibilities beyond that which the present level of experience warrants

Perpetuating mentor relationships assures the profession of the early identification of talent and provides it with the stimulation, challenge, youthful vigor, and enthusiasm the profession requires for continual growth.

REFERENCES

American Council on Education. *The student personnel point of view* (Rev. Ed.). American Council on Education Studies, (Series 6, Vol. 13, No. 13). Washington, DC: Author, 1949.

Beeler, K., & Penn, J. *A handbook on staff development in student affairs.* Corvallis, OR: Oregon State University Book Stores, 1978.

Brown, R.D. *Student development in tomorrow's higher education: A return to the academy.* Washington, DC: American College Personnel Association, 1972.

Chickering, A.W. *Education and identity.* San Francisco: Jossey-Bass, 1969.

Corson, J.J. *Governance of colleges and universities.* New York: McGraw-Hill, 1960.

Council of Student Personnel Associations in Higher Education. Student development services in post secondary education. *Journal of College Student Personnel,* 1975, *16,* 524-8.

Erikson, E.H. *Childhood and society* (2nd ed.). New York: Norton, 1963.

Fredrick, R.W. *Student activities in American education.* New York: Center for Applied Research in Education, Inc., 1965.

Greer, R.M., Blaesser, W.W., Herron, R.D., & Horle, R.F. College student personnel graduate placement. *Journal of College Student Personnel,* 1978, *19,* 342-8.

Heath, D.H. *Growing up in college: Liberal education and maturity.* San Francisco: Jossey-Bass, 1968.

Kohlberg, L. *Stage and sequence: The cognitive-developmental approach to socialization theory and research.* New York: Rand McNally, 1969.

Maslow, A. *Toward a psychology of being* (Rev. ed.). New York: Van Norstrand Reinhold, 1968.

Mueller, K. H. *Student personnel work in higher education.* Boston: McGraw-Hill, 1961.

Perry, W.G., Jr. *Forms of intellectual and ethical development in the college years.* New York: Holt, Rinehart and Winston, 1970.

Rockey, M.D. (Ed.). *Directory of preparation programs in college student personnel.* Washington, DC: American College Personnel Association, 1977.

Rodgers, R.F. Student personnel work as social intervention. In G.H. Knock (Ed.), *Perspectives on the preparation of student affairs professionals.* Washington: DC: American College Personnel Association, 1977.

Stamatakos, L.C., & Oliaro, P.M. In-service staff development: A function of student personnel. *NASPA Journal,* 1972, *9*(4), 269-73.

Stamatakos, L.C. Pre-professional and professional obstacles to student development. In D.G. Creamer (Ed.), *Student development in higher education: Theories, practices, and future directions.* Washington, DC: American College Personnel Association, 1980.

SUGGESTED READINGS

Fisher, M. B., & Smith, M. R. *Writing as a professional activity.* Washington, DC: National Association for Women Deans, Administrators, and Counselors, 1976.

Hedlund, D. E. Preparation for student personnel: Implications of humanistic education. *Journal of College Student Personnel,* 1971, *12,* 324-8.

Knock, G. H. (Ed.). *Perspectives on the preparation of student affairs professionals.* Washington, DC: American College Personnel Association, 1977.

McGovern, T. V., & Tinsley, H. E. A. A longitudinal investigation of the graduate assistant work-training experience. *Journal of College Student Personnel,* March 1976, *17,* 130-3.

Ostroth, D. D. Master's level preparation for student work. *Journal of College Student Personnel,* 1975, *16,* 319-22.

Penn, J. R. Professional accreditation: A key to excellence. *Journal of College Student Personnel,* 1974, *15,* 257-9.

Stamatakos, L. C. Student affairs progress toward professionalism: Recommendations for action. *Journal of College Student Personnel,* 1981, *22*(2), 105-12, 197-207.

Wallenfeldt, E. C., & Bigelow, G. S. Status of the internship in student personnel studies. *Journal of the National Association of Women Deans and Counselors,* 1971, *34,* 180-4.

Winston, R. B. Jr., & McCaffrey, S. S. Development of ACPA ethical and professional standards. *Journal of College Student Personnel,* 1981, *22,* 183-9.

William R. Mendenhall currently serves as Associate Vice-President for Student Affairs at the University of Georgia, and he has had seventeen years experience in successive levels of student affairs administration.

For additional information please refer to the last section of the book entitled "About the Authors."

Theodore K. Miller is Professor of Counseling and Human Development Services at the University of Georgia, where he is coordinator of the Student Personnel in Higher Education Preparation Program and Director of the College of Education Center for Student Development.

For additional information please refer to the last section of the book entitled "About the Authors."

Roger B. Winston, Jr. is Assistant Professor in the Student Personnel in Higher Education Program in the Department of Counseling and Human Development Services and Director of the Student Development Laboratory at the University of Georgia.

For further information please refer to the last section of the book entitled "About the Authors."

Chapter 20

ROLES AND FUNCTIONS OF STUDENT AFFAIRS PROFESSIONALS

William R. Mendenhall
Theodore K. Miller
Roger B. Winston, Jr.

Crucial to the identity of a profession is the use of general models for practice or unique role orientations. Often the literature and preparation programs in student affairs imprecisely define roles. Practitioners, however, hold at least a vague sense of role as defined by the various activities that occupy their work days. Delworth and Hanson (1980) stated that role orientation can be conceptualized as "the glue that holds context, theory, and skills together in a model of practice" (p. 156). Role orientations provide general direction and self-definition for work in colleges and universities.

A role is defined as the carrying out of the duties and responsibilities expected of one assigned a certain status. Status refers to the rank or position of an individual in a group or of a group in relation to other groups. Historically, student affairs administration has exhibited a changing role and status as a constantly evolving profession (Mueller, 1961). With roots in the vocational counseling and testing movements, student affairs practitioners later became concerned with student activities and student behavior. As detailed in Chapter 1, the emphasis returned, as in colonial America, to include the education of the total person. This foundation supported research on human development and led to the application of intentional student development concepts. Student affairs is currently in an era that emphasizes management, especially as it relates to creating and maintaining effective learning environments where the goals of student development can be realized.

VIEWS OF MANAGEMENT IN HIGHER EDUCATION

Unfortunately management has not been a highly regarded term in higher education. The terms *administration, governance, leadership,* and *management* have often been used interchangeably. In many organizations administration is viewed as the orderly distribution and implementation of resources and policies that have already been determined. Faculty members often use the word governance to refer to their authority to make institutional policy decisions and view administrators as only implementors of the collective will. Leadership can mean anything from supervision to inspiration. It is subjective in nature and focuses on individuals rather than on institutions or organizations.

Management, however, involves the organization and conduct of human affairs toward the accomplishment of particular goals (Park, 1980). Focusing on specific purposes, management can be either collective or individual. Drucker (1964) emphasized that the role of management is not so much the doing of right things, but finding the right things to do and then concentrating resources and efforts on them.

Many people in higher education believe that management is an infringement upon the teaching, research, and service functions and view it as a drain on resources. In reality, management is a human endeavor—developing people and resources, not directing things.

Cohen and March (1974) stated that the role of the manager in a higher education setting is particularly difficult because it is often either ambiguous or restrictive. Conflicting expectations from various constituencies, personal and individual expectations of the campus community, pull of the organization, and sometimes unpleasant tasks to be performed all combine to make management of educational institutions a complex balancing act.

Many college administrators do not rest easily in a clearly defined role, nor can they easily exert leadership in the role they do occupy. They are frequently caught in the uncomfortable position of being held accountable for programs and resources while the authority for policy formation and decision making is vested with others. (Sprunger & Bergquist, 1978, p. 5)

If management is viewed as a theory base for *how* to do what is to be done and connected with student development theory as the rationale for *why* to do it, operationally student affairs practice is grounded in two distinct bodies of knowledge that are complementary and run in tandem. Student affairs practitioners cannot be effective in managing organizations, programs, and services if they do not understand both of these bodies of knowledge—the *how* (management and administration) and the *why* (student development) of their work. Successful practice, therefore, needs an integration of the two; unique roles and functions essential to professional practice must take this into account. The student affairs administrator is a person who combines theory and research about the management of organizations with theory and research about human development to create practical strategies for accomplishing goals of higher education.

ROLES

Student affairs practice has often been equated with the many functions performed in divisions of student affairs. Unfortunately, this tendency to define the whole by attending only to some of the more obvious parts has created confusion in the academic community and beyond. Too frequently, for instance, false dichotomies are drawn that appear to reflect adversarial relationships between counseling and administration. While such distinctions are convenient, they are inaccurate and tend to promote a kind of astigmatism in the perceptions of all involved.

Administration is not just a science, human relations, or an art—rather, all of these are involved. It must be viewed in light of one's personal and professional experience. Effective administration, regardless of the specific tasks to be performed, includes at least eight characteristics: (1) open communication, (2) teamwork, (3) participation in decision making, (4) encouragement of initiative, (5) mutual support, (6) high standards, (7) use of objectives, and (8) performance evaluation (Park, 1980). Student affairs practice should be viewed as a process embracing these principles.

Four roles identified as being especially important to student affairs practice include the administrator, the counselor/consultant, the student development educator, and the environmental designer. While none of these roles is discreet or compartmentalized, each reflects essential functions for the effective initiation and operation of student affairs programs.

Administrator

The primary role for many student affairs professionals is administrative. The rationale for the administrative role is grounded in five assumptions that reflect both the historical roots of student affairs practice and the current realities faced by higher education.

1. The basis of the profession rests on the effective development and delivery of programs to accomplish educational goals for students.

2. Administrative procedures and educational/developmental goals are not dichotomous.

3. Student affairs must be effectively managed and integrated with academic affairs to achieve desired educational outcomes.

4. A visable structure for the delivery of student progams is necessary for policy formulation and resource allocation.

5. Flexibility for responding to student and institutional needs is enhanced within an administrative structure (Ambler, 1980).

Administration is an essential component of effective management of student affairs programs. Many authorities agree that among the several approaches to administration the operational approach organized around generally recognized managerial functions is the most desirable (Haiman & Scott, 1974; Koontz & O'Donnell, 1978; Sprunger & Bergquist, 1978). The modified classification of administrative functions presented parallels closely the Sprunger and Bergquist six function model: planning, organizing, staffing, leading, evaluating, and developing. These functions are interrelated and operate in an open systems environment as parts of a whole. The open systems concept holds that change in any one function of a system causes changes in others (Katz & Kahn, 1966). More importantly, however, neglect in one area weakens the entire system.

Planning. Planning is a cyclical process that includes several activities. In existing organizations it should precede the implementation of new programs, procedures, or policies. Planning activities include assessing internal and external conditions that may affect positions, budgets, or resources to be allocated; establishing, reviewing, or modifying goals and objectives; identifying, testing, and implementing strategies for program development or maintenance; and monitoring programs, procedures, and plans to make needed adjustments. As Tincher outlined in Chapter 17, the effective and efficient use of time is critical to the planning aspect of administration.

A plan is viable only when a decision is made to commit human and fiscal resources to it. Otherwise, the exercise becomes moot. The planning process is complete when decisions have been made to allocate resources for implementing the plan or significant portions of it.

Organizing. This process involves the assignment of specific tasks, a division of labor in the organization, and defining relationships to show how each component or subgroup fits into the total effort. Delegation of authority and responsibility is critical in this process. Organizing can be viewed as creating the internal structure to carry out a plan or to meet objectives.

Staffing. Administrators are responsible for providing adequate and competent staff to achieve desired objectives. As detailed in Chapter 12, persons with appropriate skills and a concern for the mission of the institution must be appropriately identified, selected, trained, and encouraged in accordance with an overall plan or direction. The responsibility for forecasting staff needs and maintaining policies and practices that ensure both institutional flexibility and stability falls to the administrator. Flexibility is essential in dealing with changing student needs and institutional resources while ensuring equitable and non-discriminatory treatment of personnel.

Leading. Leadership, as discussed in Chapter 4, is essential to effective administration. Relying heavily on communication and motivational skills, the effective leader actively participates in achieving institutional goals. Leadership, perhaps more than any other function of administration, is a matter of what others perceive. Miles and Steiner (1982) stated that no objective reality exists in leadership—only perception because effective leadership requires others to follow. People follow those who they believe will enable them to achieve their own personal goals. The responsibility of a student affairs professional is to help create an environment that others find satisfying and challenging. Communication and motivation are essential in helping others accept change while also maintaining stability in the organization.

Evaluating. Monitoring progress is critical in determining whether organizations and personnel meet desired objectives. If evaluating and controlling activities are absent, necessary adjustments cannot be made, nor can scarce resources be utilized effectively to assure achievement of long-range plans. Evaluation is the primary process through which an institution can learn from both mistakes and achievements and assist staff members to do likewise.

Developing. Student affairs practitioners have a responsibility to assist with the professional growth and development of staff members. As DeCoster and Brown point out in Chapter 14, staff development is important in all organizations and should be viewed as a continuing educational process. The application of human development theory to practice is important not only to the growth of students, but also has equal importance for professional staff. Assisting staff members in assuming new responsibilities, providing access to developmental programs for personal and professional enrichment, and retraining staff members when their personal and organizational needs change are all essential functions of development. Often given only minimal attention in higher education, staff development is becoming increasingly important as enrollments and economic resources stabilize or decline.

Mackenzie (1969) noted that management deals with three basic elements: people, ideas, and things—probably in that order. The three central functions of problem analysis, decision making, and communication permeate all aspects of management and are central to all functions of administration. The degree to which any of these functions becomes important is largely dependent on the stage of project completion and the personal characteristics and positions held by leaders within an organization. Higher education administrators face a complex set of managerial tasks and responsibilities in a continually changing environment making it necessary for student affairs administrators to engage regularly in professional development activities.

Because administration is a process and not an end in itself, basic functions in organizations are integrative. The interplay of management theory and administrative practice becomes the backdrop for actualizing student development in higher education. The personal and academic growth of students is still the focal point for all administrative activity. A dynamic student affairs administrative model keeps the student emphasis uppermost in any delivery system. Although student affairs practice has traditionally been viewed as an administrative function providing services complementary to instruction, it is actually much more. The administrative structure serves as an effective vehicle for directly contributing to student growth and development.

Counselor/Consultant

The counseling and consultation role of student affairs practice is an outgrowth of training and practice in the disciplines of counseling and educational psychology which have historically provided much of the conceptual basis for training (Betz, 1980). As early as 1939, Williamson stated that counseling, as the basis for work with individual students, served to coordinate and focus the findings and efforts of all areas of student affairs. Williamson believed that counseling was universally applicable to all of the functions of the profession and served as a core approach from which all other student affairs functions are derived. Williamson (1961) outlined a set of rational procedures for counselors to use with students: analysis, synthesis, diagnosis, prognosis, counseling, and follow-up. Components of this directive counseling process for individuals closely resemble the administrative components oulined by Sprunger and Bergquist for organizations. The emphasis or target for action is the major difference between the administrative role and the counselor role, the former targeting the organization and the latter focusing upon the individual.

The counseling approach assumes that human beings are essentially good, desire to contribute to society, and want to develop their potential. This confidence in human potential underlies the belief that an important purpose of education is the development of the whole person and the recognition and acceptance of individual differences.

Many writers have emphasized the centrality of counseling processes to effective student affairs practice. Prior to Williamson's elaboration of counseling as the central component of student affairs practice, Patterson (1925) made significant contributions to the area of counseling. He viewed research as fundamental to a sound program of student affairs. With a background in educational measurement, Patterson maintained that many student problems in higher education could be approached from a scientific perspective. His major contribution included studies in individual differences and the development of tests and methods for evaluating student aptitudes and interests.

Berdie (1944) applied counseling concepts to student affairs practice through his studies of college student variables. He investigated students' satisfaction with college as part of a series of studies about college student characteristics (Berdie, 1944; Berdie & Layton, 1952). Later, Parker (1966) elaborated upon Williamson's belief that education as a counselor is extremely important to preparation for student affairs practice. He noted the concepts of human dignity and independence as essential bases for effective student affairs practice. Parker stressed that student affairs practitioners need not only skills pertinent to their areas of specialization but also counseling training to develop sensitivity to others, skills in interpersonal relationships, interviewing skills, ability to analyze objectively individual strengths and weaknesses, an awareness of individual differences, ability to identify learning difficulties, and knowledge of how people learn. In addition, Parker (1978) emphasized the developmental concerns of college students that may be addressed through the personalization and individualization of classroom instruction. Rogers (1942, 1961) also contributed to the counseling role, emphasizing a client-centered, non-directive approach to assisting students.

The counseling approach currently emphasized in most student affairs practice contains contributions from many disciplines. The role is supported by a set of beliefs about people and life and assumes an active position relative to human growth and development. Counselor training is grounded in the behavioral sciences and should produce individuals with interpersonal skills and knowledge regarding human behavior and dynamics. The major components of counseling as outlined by Betz (1980) include knowledge of human learning, theories of career and life planning, skills in using test and psychometric data, and skills in communication and perception.

Of particular importance among these components for student affairs practice is the knowledge of how people learn. Knowing the many ways in which people learn gives student affairs practitioners a distinct advantage in planning and evaluating their tasks. It provides alternative strategies for achieving the ultimate goal of higher education—the education and development of students. The counseling approach also involves knowledge and skills for helping students to learn to manage career and life planning.

Many counseling skills have direct application to general student affairs practice. The student affairs practitioner is a critical link for aiding and assisting students in using campus services and resources. The referral function is a daily activity that most student affairs practitioners perform. Providing support and encouragement to students is a primary function of the counseling role. Student affairs practitioners have many opportunities for providing service to students. Working in varied settings, practitioners can often observe relationships and personalities of students that might be shielded from them if they adhered strictly to formal client-centered contacts.

The counseling role is not necessarily limited to direct service to students. Relationships with colleagues and associates are enhanced and developed through utilization of counseling skills. These skills do not guarantee success, however, in interpersonal relationships, staff development, supervision, or conflict management, but practitioners with knowledge and competence in these areas can make significant contributions to staff relationships and group problem solving.

Student affairs practitioners also function as consultants, whether working directly with students, staff members, faculty, or community members. The practitioner trained in counseling skills can facilitate the flow of technical information and assist in the development and evaluation of programs through clarifying issues and suggesting various alternatives to problems. The counselor/consultant role must be viewed as much a way of thinking and synthesizing as a set of prescribed role behaviors. The counselor/consultant is one who has learned to listen, has developed skills in assisting others, and can provide assistance and direction through interpreting and clarifying various points of view. An attitude of openness and respect for the worth and dignity of others is a foundation of the counselor/consultant role.

This role has a direct effect on a person's understanding of and beliefs about self and others. The tools provided can be used to help others develop skills in self-management. The counseling role, in addition to providing a philosophical base for practice, can be extended to impact the total campus environment. Skills of the counselor form a "basis for effective, informed, and comfortable functioning" as a student affairs practitioner (Betz, 1980, p. 188).

Student Development Educator

The role of the student development educator reflects knowledge about both theories and practices of learning and human development that relate to the intellectual, cultural, emotional, physical, moral, and interpersonal aspects of life (Brown, 1980). While the education of the whole student has long been regarded as desirable in higher education, only in the past few years has the concept of intentional student development taken on primary significance. Institutions historically have not systematically and intentionally fostered the personal growth of students. The availability of human development theory and principles has heightened and expanded the dimensions of student affairs practice, and their applications have been refined to produce a role for the student development educator (Brown, 1972; Chickering, 1969; Chickering & Associates, 1981; Miller & Prince, 1976, Sanford, 1962, 1967).

One of the most important historical expressions of the aims of higher education and the foundations of student development was expressed by the American Council on Education in 1937 and redefined in 1949 as *The Student Personnel Point of View*. As noted in Chapter 1, this philosophical position called for students to be considered as whole persons, viewed as being unique, and responsible for their own personal and social development. Sanford (1967) advocated a broad general education to help students see productive roles and perspectives, develop values that can withstand organizational pressure, and lead meaningful lives apart from their occupations. He defines a program where institutions consciously promote identity formation based on qualities of flexibility, creativity, openness, and responsibility. This blending of cognitive and affective development was later articulated by Brown (1972) and Miller and Prince (1976) in the Tomorrow's Higher Education Project of the American College Personnel Association.

With the publication of *Student Development in Tomorrow's Higher Education: A Return to the Academy* (Brown, 1972), considerable discussion was focused on the specific content of student development. Miller and Prince (1976) presented a process model designed to apply student development concepts to higher education and student affairs practice. While the role of the student development educator in student affairs practice originally focused on interpersonal skills, the concept has been elaborated and expanded to include five major activities: (1) assessing developmental status, (2) establishing goals with students, (3) program planning and instruction, (4) evaluating and recycling, and (5) recording student progress (Brown, 1980).

In developing this flow of activities, Brown maintained that human development should be considered a required part of the college curriculum. While perhaps ambitious, such a curriculum should be viewed as a distinct possibility for student affairs practitioners. As elaborated throughout this book, components of the student development educator role have existed for some time in one form or another. Functions grounded in human development theory do not contradict or conflict with the other roles required of student affairs practitioners. Rather, they are complementary. The role of the student development educator is one of attitude and belief as well as one requiring specific skills.

Interest in using instructional concepts involving assessment, goal setting, and evaluation or actualizing and fostering intentional student development has recently gained momentum. If the student development educator is to have impact, models must be developed to analyze and measure developmental stages of students. Such a role assumes that human growth and development is an integral part of the collegiate experience.

Using Brown's (1980) five-phase approach for student development education, the student development educator builds a profile of a student's relative strengths and weaknesses as based on formal data and informal information and provides structure and guidelines for the selection of developmental goals. These goals may be academic, professional, or personal. The role for the student development educator, then, becomes one of assistance in exploring the student's wants and needs and the institution's options available for meeting them. Once these steps have been achieved, new goals are established, and the cyclical nature of the developmental process continues. In this incremental and step-by-step way students learn to actualize their potential.

According to Brown (1980), each institution should have at least four program paths for students to develop their potential: (1) academic course offerings, (2) specific courses (credit or non-credit) in human growth and development, (3) experiential learning activities such as fieldwork, co-operative education, or internships, and (4) significant and varied informal campus opportunities of both a group and individual nature for growth and exploration.

Traditionally the first and last of these four avenues have received the most attention on campuses. Both formal instruction in the classroom and "extracurricular" activities have long been a part of the campus experience. Unfortunately, this dichotomy between formalized coursework and structured out-of-class experience leads to a false distinction between the natures of academic affairs and student affairs. Academic affairs and student affairs must be viewed as two aspects of the same whole. The integration and merger of these two thrusts is the current challenge if higher education is to have a significant effect on students. Strengthening the human developmental aspects of all instruction, along with the expansion and strengthening of experiential education programs as the worlds of learning and earning are merged, holds the key to the success of the student development educator.

In facilitating the integration of academic affairs and student affairs toward the development of the whole person, the student development educator serves as a vital link. Primary contributions from practitioners emphasizing this role orientation include at least four essential functions:

• Basic research on human growth and development

• Translation of research findings into models

• Development of technologies and intervention strategies for use with individuals, groups, and organizations

• Instruction and training of students, staff, and paraprofessionals to help facilitate intentional development

The effective student development educator serves as the catalyst for translating theory to practice in student affairs.

Environmental Designer

A relatively new role for the student affairs practitioner is that of environmental designer or campus ecology manager. Crookston (1975) defined milieu management as "the systematic coordination and integration of the total campus environment—the organization, the structures, the space, the functions, the people and the relationships of each to all others and to the whole—toward growth and development . . ." (p. 46). In other words, the campus must be viewed as an interrelated ecology or system.

Perspective. Banning (1980a) has identified four different perspectives that those in student affairs have taken for viewing students and their college: (1) unenlightened, (2) counseling or adjustment, (3) developmental, and (4) ecological.

The unenlightened view of the relationship between students and institution holds that if students do not fit into the established structure of the college, then they must be encouraged or forced to terminate the relationship. The primary function for student affairs in this view is to maintain the *status quo* and to remove threats when they are identified.

The counseling or adjustment perspective sees poor interaction between the student and the college environment as an adjustment problem. Students are encouraged and assisted in changing their behavior or attitudes to be consistent with the expectations and demands of the institution. This approach is exemplified by viewing students as clients. While this approach may be quite beneficial for the students, to view them as only clients makes it a simple step to also see them as ill or deficient in some skill, behavior, or characteristic. When students are thought of as clients, the tendency is for the counseling function to become passive, dealing with students only when they have a problem, seek out help, or cause a disturbance in the environment (Banning & McKinley, 1980).

The developmental perspective takes a view of the student-environment interaction similar to the counseling perspective—change falls on the shoulders of students, not the institution—but the nature of the change is based on the idea that students are "in a growth period where new skills need to be gained in order to better arrange the fit between themselves and their environment" (Banning, 1980a, p. 130).

Finally, the ecological perspective has a concern both for individual change or growth and for modifying the college environment to meet student needs and concerns more effectively. The focus of the concern is on the transactional relationship between students and their environment.

Banning and Kaiser (1974) are quick to point out, however, that a need exists for all four types of interventions. Counseling is a valuable intervention for students when they are unable to manage their behavior in desired ways or when they have emotional disturbances. Likewise, there is a definite need to provide students with programs that are designed to help them develop life skills or accomplish developmental tasks. All of these perspectives fit within the larger ecological perspective.

Impact. Two different, but related, aspects of the environment (physical and psychosocial) influence the inhabitant's behavior, attitudes, and feelings (Moos, 1976). Three general principles are important in understanding the relationship of individuals to their environment.

The first is a *congruence* between the person's needs, attitudes, goals, and expectations and the environmental press, demands, supports, and the characteristics of others in the setting. Congruence promotes satisfaction, productivity, performance, achievement, and personal growth. Incongruence produces stress that may lead to physical illness or antisocial behavior. There needs to be a balance between congruence and incongruence, however, because a perfect fit produces none of the challenge needed to stimulate growth or acquisition of new behaviors (Huebner, 1980).

The second general principle is that the *interaction* between the individual and the environment needs a balance between stability and change. Students need to feel secure that the rules of the game are not changing every day, while feeling that the rules allow enough flexibility to meet their perceived needs and desires if they are willing to exert reasonable effort.

The third principle is that a *balance* is necessary between the idiosyncratic needs of the individual and the collective needs of the group. Students need an environment that is permissive enough to allow them to experiment with new behaviors, but one where the group has enough influence on individuals to moderate their behavior and provide psychological support (Hurst, Morrill, & Oetting, 1980).

Probably the most effective use of the concepts of environmental management has been in residence halls. Using the idea of territoriality borrowed from animal behavior research, residence hall staff have instituted programs designed to encourage students to have a sense of ownership of their building, personalize it, and assume responsibility for what occurs within its walls.

Many features of traditional residence halls impede healthy interaction and promote dissatisfaction. For example (Schroeder 1980, 1981):

•Corridor arrangements that require heavy sharing of public spaces and communal baths increase residents' feeling of crowding.

•Residence halls with long corridors and poor insulation against noise increase students' arousal levels. Long periods of sustained high arousal lead to stress. Students often attempt to reduce the environmental load by leaving the immediate environment.

•Small cell-like rooms produce contradictory effects: they isolate students from each other and force prolonged undesired interaction with others (especially roommates).

•Double occupancy rooms often create stress by destroying the sense of privacy many students had at home in their own rooms. Students are forced to use their individual rooms for sleeping, studying, and entertaining; when at home they had different spaces set aside for each of these activities.

•Uniform furnishings, bland wall color, and redundancy of design often cause students to feel restricted, submissive, and powerless. (Schroder 1980, 1981.)

Research on attempts to modify the physical setting has substantiated that such changes do influence social relationships as well as other behaviors. For example, Schroeder (1976) reported that following a personalization project in a men's residence hall, retention increased 40 percent and damages declined 82 percent. However, Werring, Winston, and McCaffrey (1981) found that simply painting public spaces in residence halls is not enough, that only residents who were active participants in the personalization project came to view the environment more positively. It had little effect on non-participants' perceptions of the environment. These findings can serve as a reminder that environmental design is neither mechanical nor simple to implement.

Besides altering the architecture or painting and personalizing buildings, attempts have been made to create communities or social groups with specified goals. Mable, Terry, and Duvall (1980, p. 103) described a community building approach that "concentrated on the involvement and growth of students who consciously assume responsibility for self-development and for collaboration with other individuals by sharing goals, responsibilities, and communication." Crookston (1974) helped establish the Intentional Democratic Community as an approach to developing a supportive social environment. Winston, Hutson, and McCaffrey (1980) found that fraternities stressing academic achievement in their living environments achieved higher grade point averages than those who did not, even though ability levels were approximately the same. A social climate with an emphasis on academics reinforces those behaviors of group members and applies sanctions against those who do not value academic achievement.

Function. Environmental management can be used to encourage the growth and development of students or to control their behavior and maintain the *status quo*. Like administration, the environmental design function is an empty technology unless coupled with a worthy purpose. Banning (1980b) proposed incorporating student development concepts with the technology and conceptualization of environmental design in order to have a complete picture of student affairs practice. "Developmental processes are not automatic but must be purposefully triggered and carefully nurtured by the environment if full growth and development is to be reached" (Banning, 1980b, p. 217). He suggested viewing student affairs programs and services from Blocher's (1974) framework or structure system—opportunity, support, and reward.

The opportunity structures are the sets of tasks, activities, or situations within which people deal or participate in order to exert mastery or control and ultimately to gain competence. The support structure encompasses the resources in the environment available to help people cope or reach their goals. The reward structure includes those properties and contingencies in the environment that reward effort. The environment designer's role, then, is to design and manage environments that offer opportunities, resources, and rewards for accomplishing important developmental tasks. For instance, if the developmental task is to achieve instrumental autonomy, then opportunities must be available to students to face the various components of this task: for example, locate academic resources, take responsibility for maintenance of living areas, and use the library. Support might be in the form of guided tours of the library and learning resource centers, introduction to programmed study skills material, or a program in a residence hall in which students provide routine maintenance of their living unit. Rewards might include reduced residence hall rents, grades, internal rewards (satisfaction, feeling of accomplishment), and recognition from the institution (such as letters or certificates).

Environmental design often requires performing also as administrators, counselor/consultants, and student developmental educators. If the purpose of student affairs is to enhance growth, development, and functioning of individual students then the total environment must be addressed. The ecological or environmental perspective allows one to examine and influence the college from a systems approach. Physical structures, social climates, rules, policies, procedures, and individual personalities interact to produce an environment in which members of the college community live. It is essential that each of these elements be examined and that the effect of their interaction be assessed. The student affairs professional must participate both in designing growth-producing environments and in communicating assessment data about students to others in the college.

Integration of Roles

This section has explored four primary roles for the student affairs practitioner of the 1980's. None of the roles is exclusive, each is complementary to the others. Various positions within an institution necessitate a greater or lesser emphasis on certain of the four roles. But all are essential to actualize student development in higher education. All student affairs professionals need knowledge and skills for performing all four roles. While administrative responsibilities are varied and diffuse, the uniqueness of each position enhances the totality of the student affairs program.

Veteran chief student affairs officer Chet Peters (Appleton, Briggs, & Rhatigan, 1978) may have summed up the multi-faceted nature of student affairs practice best when he said, "You should look for staff who offset weaknesses in your organization or in yourself. It is not a crime to be unable to do things; it is a crime not to find someone who can" (p. 72). An eclectic and diversified staff is essential to accomplish the varied and complementary roles of modern student affairs practice.

ACCOUNTABILITY FOR ROLES AND FUNCTIONS

The performance of the chief student affairs officer is subjected to continued scrutiny by a variety of constituents. The manner in which major administrative and programmatic functions are enacted and perceived in a given situation is often evaluated differently. Practitioners need to know the philosophical and operational bases for their actions and to institute formal systems of evaluation and accountability. Evaluation of individual performance, of course, is a continuous process. A structure for the process, however, can provide a concrete and objective base in documenting performance for the various publics with whom the practitioner deals.

Shaffer (1979) suggested four areas for accountability and evaluation regardless of the size or scope of the student affairs operation: (1) staff development and leadership, (2) administrative competencies, (3) institutional contributions, and (4) student concerns and relationships. These categories of accountability closely parallel the four major operational components for effective student affairs and institutional management outlined earlier. Shaffer (1979) proposed that the first step toward accountability in any of these areas is self-evaluation and self-assessment by the individual practitioner.

Good evaluation is central to the continued development of student affairs practice. According to Hanson (1978) effective evaluation is comprised of five critical characteristics: (1) is theory based, (2) is decision-oriented, (3) is both effective and efficient, (4) uses sound research methods, and (5) requires effective communication.

Accountability means being a good steward. Those who have been entrusted with the physical and financial resources as well as with the responsibility for the growth and development of students should periodically and routinely be called to account. Harpel (1976) developed a set of eight guidelines for student affairs practice that can assist greatly in establishing a framework for accountability.

•Identification and definition of a specific need or problem for a target population

•Assessment of the environmental constraints in the planning to address the problem

•Stating goals in long-range and abstract terms by describing ideal results and including as many members of the organization as possible in the process

•Stating measureable objectives with specific criteria for behavior and acceptable performance

•Developing an action plan of activities bearing a direct relationship to the goals of the organization

•Describing the program structure in organizational terms showing clusters of activities to be performed

•Budgeting and allocating resources with priority related to outcome

•Evaluation in terms of both activity and impact as related to objectives and costs

Harpel's (1976) outline is a rational system. One step follows naturally from the previous one, and the process is cyclical. While this eight-step approach may suggest that administration is a science, it must be remembered that it is also an art. Student affairs staff may often find themselves relying solely on rational systems when sometimes functioning in an irrational environment. Baldridge (1973) noted that political skills are also a necessary component of the management process when functioning in a predictable but often less than logical operational environment.

Stake (1975) developed a responsive evaluation approach designed to assist in the identification of issues important in program decisions and to provide useful information related to issues and decisions. His twelve events are not necessarily sequential in nature and emphasize determining what the real issues are in the decision making process and in gathering related information. They are, however, another approach toward achieving the same end.

•Identification of program boundaries

•Discussion of program with clients, program staff, and various audiences

•Observing the program for an overview

•Discovering rationale, intents, standards, hopes, and fears

•Conceptualizing issues and problems

•Identifying data needs for issues and problems

•Observing designated antecedents, transactions, and outcomes

•Recording observations

•Keeping records and finding contingencies with similar themes

•Choosing reportable issues

•Preparing a format for reporting and discussing

•Issuing formal reports if needed

Regardless of the particular approach taken in evaluation, the concept of accountability is applicable to all fundamental elements of institutional existence and to characteristics of individual professional practice. Institutional characteristics for accountability include mission, accreditation and standards, resource management, leadership, job performance, delivery and outcome of services, legality, and the effective communication of institutional roles and responsibilities. Individual practitioners must also be accountable for their training, effectiveness, research and development, and commitment to the service ideal. All aspects of both individual and institutional operations must meet the test of evaluation if student affairs practice is to be an effective and respected endeavor.

Accountability can be described in terms of the various roles outlined as well as in terms of expectations of appropriate authorities, constituencies, associations, or agencies. These significant others include, first and foremost, students, but also include parents, governing boards, governmental agencies, employees, professional associations, and society at large. The list may seem endless, but it is only illustrative of the need for evaluation and accountability. No perfect system of evaluation exists and methods must be adapted to fit individuals, specific institutions, and particular constituencies. Recognizing the need for accountability through a continuing process of evaluation is a necessary first step.

PROFESSIONALS IN ORGANIZATIONS

Student affairs practitioners, of course, work only in the higher education setting. As such, they are examples of a growing number of professionally trained persons who function within complex organizations. Viewed from an operational standpoint, student affairs staff are trained to perform professional services but are not free or able to control totally the institutional environments in which these services are delivered and performed.

The involvement of professionally trained personnel in organizations has existed for some time. Increasingly, technically trained specialists from many disciplines are employed in the labor force and are generally recognized by society at large as being professionals. Pressure from organizational interests increases as more professionals are employed by formal organizations (Goode, 1957; Pavalko, 1971, 1972). Carpenter elaborated upon this concept as applied to student affairs in

Chapter 6. Traditionally, the professional existed apart from the formal organization and was involved in independent practice with occupational allegiances only. Mid-twentieth century America has changed that traditional role for the professional.

Two decades ago Hughes (1963) asserted that professions were changing the way in which their work was organized, becoming increasingly dependent upon organizations to carry out their activities. This shift created a professional-organizational conflict between the principles of the profession and those of the organization. Student affairs administrators, by virtue of their unique tasks, have always worked in the context of an organization. This role conflict, therefore, assumes an even greater significance as one moves closer to meeting the traditional criteria of a profession.

As a profession, student affairs is young. Both the formal curriculum and the professional associations have begun relatively recently (Nunn, 1964). The field is broadly diversified, not completely recognized by the general public, and often ranked low in the hierarchy of the academic community. Some student affairs staff members actually identify more closely with academic disciplines or specialties than they do with student affairs.

Williamson (1961) noted that professionals sometimes enter institutional duties with ideas that are functionally inappropriate for the interests of the organization. New professionals may not be prepared to perform organizational services that are vital in an effectively coordinated institutional program of student affairs. Institutional needs and goals are a part of the work of the student affairs professional. The discrepancies between the expectations of the professional and the needs of the employing organization are a possible source of conflict. The greater the understanding of the functional role performance and expectations within organizational constraints, the greater the likelihood for effective management of the student affairs unit.

Increasing numbers of professionals working in bureaucratic organizations may cause difficulties for professions, professionals, and organizations. The difficulties for the profession take the form of decreased influence upon the professional (Mendenhall, 1975). Goode (1957) noted that the professional community becomes less important for career advancement when the professional works within a complex organizational structure. Assessment by the organization of the professional's ability and success becomes paramount and the role of assessment by colleagues is lessened, thus providing less impact for sanctions from the community outside of the organization. The concept of public recognition for professionals is also diluted within the organization. When one is employed within an organization that is not aware of the professional attitude of the employee, or does not recognize claims of the staff member to being a professional, conflict is assured (Vaughan, 1970).

A basic difficulty for both the professional and the organization arises from the conflict that develops when the two operate together. There may be a contradiction between the principles of the profession and the principles or priorities of the organization (Gouldner, 1957, 1958; Reissman, 1949; Thornton 1968).

Caplow and McGee (1958) examined the organizational and professional orientation of the faculties of several universities in their classic, *The Academic Marketplace*. They pointed out that the orientation of scholars to their institutions may disorient them from their disciplines and unfavorably affect their professional prestige. Likewise, a strong identification with the discipline may disorient them from the organizations in which they are employed.

Scott (1966) outlined four major areas of conflict between professionals and organizations: (1) resistance to prescribed regulations, (2) rejection of bureaucratic standards, (3) resistance to highly structured supervision (often by one outside of the profession), and (4) conditional loyalty to the organization. However, Clark (1966) illustrated how universities try to adapt their organizational structure to the needs of professionals, rather than requiring strict adaptation to pre-existing requirements. These organizational trends influence the authority of the faculty and other collegiate professional groups in a multitude of ways.

Higher education is only one example of institutions under fire from society. External forces continue to complicate the role of professionals in complex organizations. The paradoxes and conflicts that emerge are somewhat predictable given the operational environment, but, nevertheless, tend to be ignored by most practitioners until a strong dose of reality takes hold. Vaughan (1970) noted that at least three areas of conflict arise for the student affairs practitioner within higher education: (1) autonomy versus colleague control, (2) the service ideal versus the organization, and (3) professional versus organizational loyalty.

Student affairs professionals often view themselves as facilitators, change agents, or educators seeing group leadership with students as their main focus. If, however, the organization were to define the same role, it would probably place greater emphasis on supervision of personnel and the effective implementation of institutional policy. The perceived necessity for procedure and detail on the part of a bureaucratic structure may run counter to the concept that professionals should know their jobs and be allowed to do them on their own. Regulation may cause resentment and a feeling that self-determination of work demands and priorities is not permissible within the organization.

The service ideal instilled in professionals may be one of the first casualties when student affairs practitioners begin their work in the bureaucracy, unless they have a realistic set of expectations. Often feelings of inability to perform activities felt to be important and for which trained may occur. Staff may resent the routine or the seemingly endless meetings syndrome suggesting that they should be out helping students change the educational system. This ideal for change probably will not find the same level of priority with the power structure of the institution. Regardless of how an individual staff member may feel personally or professionally, the pressure is always there to conform to the institutional position.

The student affairs professional may be called upon to uphold outdated or even unwise policies or to defend administrative colleagues in the institution. They may find themselves in conflicting role relationships with professional clients. The institutional expectation for administrative performance goes beyond the professional-client relationship. When higher-level directives or policies interfere with obligations to students and the profession, conflict is inevitable.

An increase in professionalization may also tend to produce less loyalty to the employing institution. As practitioners identify more with preparation programs, academic disciplines, or professional associations, the degree to which organizations wish to rely on them as organizational stalwarts lessens. If a professional does not like the style or intensity of institutional control or policy direction, then a move to another work setting can be pursued. The fact that student affairs practice is limited to an organizational context (as opposed to private practice) coupled with steady state enrollments and a stagnate economy may produce a feeling of being trapped. When the expectations for professional practice and advancement are not met by the organization, staff may increasingly turn to colleagues at other institutions and to professional associations for support and fulfillment. The organization in this instance becomes the long-term loser.

Institutions of higher education are unusually vulnerable when compared to other bureaucratic organizations for at least four reasons: (1) They are client serving, people organizations; they do not make things, they help to change people. (2) They are goal diffuse and as a result anyone can justify almost anything. (3) They have unclear technology and are, therefore, technologically diffuse. (4) They are highly susceptible to outside influences and are extremely permeable in the sense that the outside has access to colleges and universities most of the time (Baldridge, 1973).

Baldridge maintained that the failures of both the purely bureaucratic model of organization and the collegial model within colleges and universities have given rise to the increased vulnerability of higher education. He proposed a political model approach to bring about closer consensus between professional ideals and organizational expectations. If the college or university is in fact a political institution, then political tactics are needed to bring about institutional change. Balridge's seven step model includes

Never fight an issue you can't win. It will probably return to be fought again tomorrow anyway.

Never fight without a goal in mind.

Concentrate your efforts on certain people within the organization and on their characteristics.

Learn the history of an issue because most places have very short institutional memories.

Build a coalition. Never be a loner.

Get on a committee where the real work is done. Go to the source of power and use the formal structure to your advantage.

Follow through. Policies are never made; they are always in the process of being made. They are never finished, always being refined. (Baldridge, 1973, np)

Baldridge (1973) suggested then, that to be successful professionally in an organizational setting, one must have a broad vision and understand the political nature of higher educational institutions. Approaching institutions as miniature political systems with fluid participation, unclear goals and technology, and extremely fluid decision-making structures will not only enhance the probability of institutional success but also of professional reward as well.

The role of the student affairs professional within the institution may be illustrated using the force field concept developed by Lewin (1936). A force field analysis is a methodological approach depicting the driving and restraining forces that may affect any future event. The *drivers* are those conditions or characteristics that increase the likelihood of events occurring. The *restrainers,* conversely, are the forces, conditions, or characteristics that decrease the likelihood of an event's occurring.

Force field analysis provides a systematic method of visualizing conditions in the institutional/organizational environment that affect a particular event or situation. Drivers and restrainers can be identified by brainstorming, observation, professional literature, surveys, interviews, expert consultation, personal experience, or similar approaches. Regardless of the identifying technique employed for assessment, the concept of counterveiling forces within an open systems environment provides a convenient model for illustrating the competing roles of conflict and accommodation for the professional in the organization (Miller, Carpenter, McCaffrey, & Thompson, 1980).

The administration of student affairs programs requires a broad knowledge base and a repetoire of skills. All student affairs professionals need background experience that will allow them to be administrators, counselor/counsultants, student development educators, and environmental designers as the need arises. Each position in a student affairs division requires different levels of emphasis on particular roles, but all four roles must be filled if the student affairs division is to fulfill its institutional mission effectively. Only when theory and professional practice, management and human development concepts, student development philosophy and institutional policy are integrated can student affairs hope to actualize the goals of student development in higher education.

REFERENCES

Ambler, D. A. The administrator role. In U. Delworth, G. R. Hanson, & Associates (Eds.), *Student services: A handbook for the profession.* San Francisco: Jossey-Bass, 1980.

American Council on Education. *The student personnel point of view.* American Council on Education Studies, (Series 1, Vol. 1, No. 3). Washington, DC: Author, 1937.

American Council on Education. *The student personnel point of view.* (Rev. ed.). American Council on Education Studies, (Series 6, Vol. 13, No. 13). Washington, DC: Author, 1949.

Appleton, J. R., Briggs, C. M., & Rhatigan, J. J. *Pieces of eight: The rites, roles, and styles of the dean by eight who have been there.* Portland, OR: NASPA Institute of Research and Development, 1978.

Baldridge, J. V. Organizational change processes: A political systems approach. In J. R. Appleton (Ed.), *Selected major speeches and excerpts from NASPA's 55th annual conference.* NASPA (Monograph No. 4), October 1973.

Banning, J. H. Campus ecology: Its impact on college student personnel work. In D. G. Creamer (Ed.), *Student development in higher education: Theories, practices, and future directions.* Washington, DC: American College Personnel Association, 1980(a).

Banning, J. H. The campus ecology manager role. In U. Delworth, G. R. Hanson & Associates, *Student services: A handbook for the profession.* San Francisco: Jossey-Bass, 1980(b).

Banning, J. H., & Kaiser, L. An ecological perspective and model for campus design. *Personnel and Guidance Journal,* 1974, *52,* 370-5.

Banning, J. H., & McKinley, D. L. Concepts of the campus environment. In W. H. Morrill & J. C. Hurst (Eds.), *Dimensions of intervention for student development.* New York: Wiley, 1980.

Berdie, R. F. The prediction of college achievement and satisfaction. *Journal of Applied Psychology,* 1944, *28,* 239-45.

Berdie, R. F., & Layton, W. L. Predicting success in law school. *Journal of Applied Psychology,* 1952, *36,* 257-60.

Betz, E. The counselor role. In U. Delworth, G. R. Hanson, & Associates (Eds.), *Student services: A handbook for the profession.* San Francisco: Jossey-Bass, 1980.

Blocher, D. H. Toward an ecology of student development. *Personnel and Guidance Journal,* 1974, *52,* 360-5.

Brown, R. D. *Student development in tomorrow's higher education: A return to the academy.* Washington, DC: American College Personnel Association, 1972.

Brown, R. D. The student development educator role. In U. Delworth, G. R. Hanson, & Associates, *Student services: A handbook for the profession.* San Francisco: Jossey-Bass, 1980.

Caplow, T., & McGee, R. J. *The academic marketplace*. New York: Basic Books, 1958.

Chickering, A. W. *Education and identity*. San Francisco: Jossey-Bass, 1969.

Chickering, A. W., & Associates. *The modern American college: Responding to the new realities of diverse students and a changing society*. San Francisco: Jossey-Bass, 1981.

Clark, B. R. Organizational adaptation to professionals. In H. M. Vollmer & D. C. Mills (Eds.), *Professionalization*. Englewood Cliffs, NJ: Prentice Hall, 1966.

Cohen, M. D., & March, J. G. *Leadership and ambiguity: The American college president*. New York: McGraw-Hill, 1974.

Crookston, B. B. A design for an intentional democratic community. In D. A. DeCoster & P. Mable (Eds.), *Student development and education in college residence halls*. Washington, DC: American College Personnel Association, 1974.

Crookston, B. B. Milieu management. *NASPA Journal,* 1975, *13*(1), 45-55.

Delworth, U., Hanson, G. R., & Associates. *Student services: A handbook for the profession*. San Francisco: Jossey-Bass, 1980.

Drucker, P. A. *Managing for results*. New York: Harper & Row, 1964.

Goode, W. J. Community within a community: The professions. *American Sociological Review,* 1957, *22,* 194-200.

Gouldner, A. Cosmopolitans and locals: Toward an analysis of latent social roles—I. *Adminstrative Science Quarterly,* 1957, *2,* 281-307.

Gouldner, A. Cosmopolitans and locals: Toward an analysis of latent social roles—II. *Administrative Science Quarterly,* 1958, *2,* 444-80.

Haimann, T., & Scott, W. G. *Management in the modern organization*. Boston: Houghton Mifflin, 1974.

Hanson, G. R. (Ed.). *New directions for student services: Evaluating program effectiveness* (No. 1). San Francisco: Jossey-Bass, 1978.

Harpel, R. L. Planning, budgeting, and evaluation in student affairs programs: A manual for administrators. *NASPA Journal,* 1976, *14*(1).

Huebner, L. A. Interaction of student and campus. In U. Delworth, G. R. Hanson, & Associates (Eds.), *Student services: A handbook for the profession*. San Francisco: Jossey-Bass, 1980.

Hughes, E. C. Professions. In K. S. Lynn and Editors of *Daedalus* (Eds.). *The professions in America*. Boston: Beacon Press, 1963.

Hurst, J. C., Morrill, W. H., & Oetting, E. R. The target of intervention. In W. H. Morrill, & J. C. Hurst (Eds.). *Dimensions of intervention for student development*. New York: Wiley-Interscience, 1980.

Katz, D., & Kahn, R. L. *The social psychology of organizations.* New York: Wiley, 1966.

Koontz, H., & O'Donnell, C.*n ssentials of management* (2nd ed.). New York: McGraw-Hill, 1978.

Lewin, K. *Principles of topological psychology.* New York: McGraw-Hill, 1936.

Mable, P., Terry, M. J., & Duvall, W. H. Student development through community development. In D. A. DeCoster & P. Mable (Eds.), *Personal education and community development in college residence halls.* Washington, DC: American College Personnel Association, 1980.

Mackenzie, R. A. The management process in 3-D. *Harvard Business Review.* 1969, *47,* 80-7.

Mendenhall, W. R. *A Case Study of the American College Personnel Assocation: Its contributions to the professionalization process of student personnel work.* Doctoral dissertation, Florida State University, 1975.

Miles, A., & Steiner, P. *Winners, losers, and hired hands: Leadership theories applied for student affairs officers.* Tuscaloosa, AL: Randall Publishing, 1982.

Miller, T. K., Carpenter, D. S., McCaffrey, S. S., & Thompson, M. J. Developmental programming: An action-planning model. In F. B. Newton & K. L. Ender (Eds.). *Student development practices: Strategies for making a difference.* Springfield, IL: Charles C. Thomas, 1980.

Miller, T. K., & Prince, J. S. *The future of student affairs: A guide to student development for tomorrow's higher education.* San Francisco: Jossey-Bass, 1976.

Moos, R. H. *The human context: Environmental determinants of behavior.* New York: Wiley-Interscience, 1976.

Mueller, K. H. *Student personnel work in higher education.* Boston: Houghton Mifflin, 1961.

Nunn, N. L. *Student personnel work in American higher education: Its evolution as an organized movement.* Doctoral dissertation, Florida State University, 1964.

Park, D. What management is and isn't. *Educational Record,* 1980, *61*(4), 72-5.

Parker, C. A. The place of counseling in the preparation of student personnel workers. *Personnel and Guidance Journal,* 1966, *45,* 254-61.

Parker, C. A. (Ed.). *Encouraging development in college students.* Minneapolis: University of Minnesota Press, 1978.

Patterson, D. G. Student personnel service at the University of Minnesota. *Journal of Personnel Research,* 1925, *3,* 449-53.

Pavalko, R. M. *Sociology of occupations and professions.* Itasca, IL: F. E. Peacock, 1971.

Pavalko, R. M. (Ed.). *Sociological perspectives on work.* Itasca, IL: F. E. Peacock, 1972.

Reissman, L. A study of role conceptions in bureaucracy. *Social Forces,* 1949, *22,* 305-10.

Rogers, C. R. *Counseling and psychotherapy.* Boston: Houghton Mifflin, 1942.

Rogers, C. R. *On becoming a person.* Boston: Houghton Mifflin, 1961.

Sanford, N. (Ed.). *The American college: A psychological and social interpretation of the higher learning.* New York: Wiley, 1962.

Sanford, N. *Where colleges fail: A study of the student as a person.* San Francisco: Jossey-Bass, 1967.

Schroeder, C. C. New strategies for structuring residential environments. *Journal of College Student Personnel,* 1976, *17,* 386-90.

Schroeder, C. C. Territoriality: An imperative for personal development and residence education. In D. A. DeCoster & P. Mable (Eds.), *Personal education and community development in college residence halls.* Washington, DC: American College Personnel Association, 1980.

Schroeder, C. C. Student development through environmental management. In G. S. Blimling & J. H. Schuh (Eds.), *New directions for student services: Increasing the educational role of residence halls* (No. 13). San Francisco: Jossey-Bass, 1981.

Scott, R. Professionalism in bureaucracy: Areas of conflict in professionalization. In H. M. Vollmer & D. L. Mills (Eds.), *Professionalization.* Englewood Cliffs, NJ: Prentice-Hall, 1966.

Shaffer, R. H. The chief student affairs administrator. In G. D. Kuh (Ed.), *Evaluation in student affairs.* Washington, DC: American College Personnel Association, 1979.

Sprunger, B. E., & Bergquist, W. H. *Handbook for college administration.* Washington, DC: Council for the Advancement of Small Colleges, 1978.

Stake, R. E. *Evaluating the arts in education.* Columbus, OH: Merrill, 1975.

Thornton, R. G. *The involvement of professionals in organizations: Conflict or accommodation?* Doctoral dissertation, Florida State University, 1968.

Vaughan, C.E. A case study of student personnel workers. *National Catholic Guidance Conference Journal,* 1970, *14*(4), 237-47.

Werring, C. J., Winston, R. B., Jr., & McCaffrey, R. J. How paint projects affect residents' perceptions of their living environment. *Journal of College and University Student Housing,* 1981, *11*(2), 3-7.

Williamson, E. G. *How to counsel students.* New York: McGraw-Hill, 1939.

Williamson, E. G. *Student personnel services in colleges and universties.* New York: McGraw-Hill, 1961.

Winston, R. B., Jr., Hutson, G. S., & McCaffrey, S. S. Environmental influences on fraternity academic achievement. *Journal of College Student Personnel,* 1980, *21,* 449-55.

SUGGESTED READINGS

Appleton, J. R., Briggs, C. M., & Rhatigan, J. J. *Pieces of eight: The rites, roles, and styles of the dean by eight who have been there.* Portland, OR: NASPA Institute of Research and Development, 1978.

Chickering, A. W., & Associates. *The modern American college: Responding to the new realities of diverse students and a changing society.* San Francisco: Jossey-Bass, 1981.

Delworth, U., Hanson, G. R., & Associates. *Student services: A handbook for the profession.* San Francisco: Jossey-Bass, 1980.

Miller, T. K., & Prince, J. S. *The future of student affairs: A guide to student development for tomorrow's higher education.* San Francisco: Jossey-Bass, 1976.

Miles, A., & Steiner, P. *Winners, losers, and hired hands: Leadership theories applied for student affairs officers.* Tuscaloosa, AL: Randall Publishing, 1982.

Owens, H. F., Witten, C. H., & Bailey, W. R. (Eds.). *College student personnel adminstration: An anthology.* Springfield, IL: Charles C. Thomas, 1982.

Sandeen, C. A. Student services in the 80's: A decade of decisions. *NASPA Journal,* 1982, *19*(3), 3-9.

Sprunger, B. E., & Bergquist, W. H. *Handbook for college administration.* Washington, DC: Council for the Advancement of Small Colleges, 1978.

Vollmer, H. M., & Mills, D. L. (Eds.). *Professionalization.* Englewood Cliffs, NJ: Prentice-Hall, 1966.

APPENDICES

APPENDIX A

American College Personnel Association Statement of Ethical and Professional Standards

PREAMBLE

The American College Personnel Association, a Division of the American Personnel and Guidance Association, is an educational, scientific, and professional organization whose members are dedicated to enhancing the worth, dignity, potential, and uniqueness of each individual and thus to the service of society. Although members work in various post-secondary educational settings, they are committed to protecting individual human rights, advancing knowledge of college student growth and development, and promoting effectiveness in student affairs organizations and operations. As a means of supporting these commitments, members of the American College Personnel Association subscribe to the following standards of ethical and professional conduct.

These standards are designed to provide a guide for ethical and professional behavior in general student affairs practice and to complement the existing "Ethical Standards" of the American Personnel and Guidance Association. Members in specialized student affairs settings are also encouraged to consult ethical standards specific to their settings.

A. Relationships With Students

1. Members treat students as individuals who possess dignity, worth, and the ability to be self-directed and assist students in becoming productive, responsible citizens and members of society. Members are concerned for the welfare of *all* students and work for constructive change on behalf of students.

2. Members respect the student's right of self-determination. The student's freedom of choice should be limited only when the individual's decisions or actions may result in significant damage to self, to others, or to the institution.

3. Members explicitly inform students of the nature and/or limits of confidentiality in non-counseling, as well as in counseling relationships.

4. Members respect the student's right to privacy and share information about individuals only in accordance with institutional policies, or when given permission by the student, or when required to prevent personal harm.

5. Members confront students in a professional manner with issues and behaviors that have ethical implications.

B. General Responsibilities

1. Members contribute to the development of the profession through sharing skills and program ideas, serving professional organizations, educating emerging professionals, improving professional practices, keeping abreast of contemporary theories and applications, and conducting and reporting research.

2. Members realize professional growth is continuous and cumulative and is characterized by a well-defined philosophy that explains why and how members function in the student affairs profession. Members base this philosophy upon sound theoretical principles and an explicitly examined personal value system (assuming congruence with the basic assumptions from the Stu-

Note. From *Journal of College Student Personnel*, 1981, *22*, 184-9. Copyright 1981 by American Personnel and Guidance Association. Used with permission. No further reproduction authorized without APGA permission.

dent Personnel Point of View and the Student Development Point of View).

3. Members model ethically responsible behavior for students and colleagues and expect ethical behavior among members and nonmembers at all times. When information is possessed which raises serious doubt as to the ethical behavior of professional colleagues, whether Association members or not, members are encouraged to take action to rectify such a condition. Possible actions include (a) confronting the individual in question, (b) utilizing institutional channels, and/or (c) using available Association mechanisms.

4. Members do not seek self-enhancement or self-aggrandizement through evaluations or comparisons that are damaging to others.

5. Members perform in a fashion that is not discriminatory on the basis of race, sex, national origin, affectional/sexual preference, handicap, age or creed, and they work actively to modify discriminatory practices when encountered.

6. Members maintain and enhance professional effectiveness by improving skills and acquiring new knowledge through systematic continuing education and assure the same opportunity for persons under their supervision.

7. Members monitor their personal functioning and effectiveness and when needed seek assistance from appropriate professionals (e.g., colleague, physician, counselor, attorney).

8. Members accurately represent their professional credentials, competencies, and limitations to all concerned and are responsible for correcting any misrepresentations of these qualifications by others.

9. Members have a clear responsibility to ensure that information provided to the public or to subordinates, peers and supervisors is factual, accurate, and unbiased.

10. Members establish fees for professional services after consideration of fees charged by other professionals delivering comparable services and the ability of the recipient to pay. Members provide some services for which they receive little or no remuneration.

11. Members demonstrate sensible regard for the social codes and moral expectations of the communities in which they live and work. They recognize that violations of accepted moral and legal standards may involve their clients, students, or colleagues in damaging personal conflicts and may impugn their own reputations, the integrity of the profession, and the reputation of the employing institution.

12. Members maintain ethical relationships with colleagues and students and refrain from relationships which impinge on the dignity, moral code, self-worth, professional functioning, and/or personal growth of these individuals. Specifically, members are aware that sexual relationships hold great potential for exploitation. Consequently, members refrain from having sexual relationships with anyone to whom they act as counselors or therapists. Sexual relationships with staff members or students for whom one has supervisory or evaluative responsibilities have high potential for causing personal damage and for limiting the exercise of professional responsibilities and are therefore unprofessional and unethical.

C. Professional and Collegial Relationships

1. Members seek to collaborate and to share expertise with other student affairs staff members, faculty members, administrators, and students.

2. Members contribute periodically to the professional development of colleagues with no compensation other than for immediate expenses.

3. Members accurately acknowledge contributions to program development, program implementation, evaluations, and reports made by others.

4. Members support the appropriate efforts of fellow student affairs professionals and institutional programs. Constructive criticism and professional disagreements are shared (in private when possible) with those individuals concerned and in a manner that is not demeaning.

5. Members establish working agreements with subordinates and supervisors that clearly define accountability procedures, mutual expectations, evaluation criteria, position duties, and decision-making procedures.

6. Members conduct themselves in such a

manner that their positions are not used to seek unjustified personal gains, sexual favors, or unfair advantages, including goods and services not normally accorded those in such positions.

7. Members regularly evaluate the professional development and job performance of direct line subordinate staff members and recommend appropriate actions to enhance professional development and improve job performance.

8. Members seek regular evaluations of their job performance and professional development from colleagues, supervisors, and clientele.

9. Members are fair and unbiased in judgments they render about persons with whom they work. Members have a right to expect that colleagues and supervisors will strive to render fair and unbiased judgments about them. Members respect the rights of others to differ in the judgments and evaluations they render so long as these judgments are not intended to do harm or disservice.

10. Members have the right to request and to receive support from the Association in matters of ethical practice and standards as defined herein.

D. Institutional Relationships

1. Members make contributions to their employing institution in support of its goals, missions, and policies.

2. Members ensure that accurate presentation of institutional goals, services, programs, and policies are made to the public, students, prospective students, colleagues, and subordinates.

3. Members inform appropriate officials of conditions that may be potentially disruptive or damaging to the institution's mission, personnel, and property.

4. Members inform employers of conditions which may limit or curtail the members' effectiveness.

5. Members have responsibilities both to the individuals served and to the institution within which the service is performed. The acceptance of employment in an institution implies that members are in general agreement with the mission of the institution. Therefore, the professional activities of

members are expected to be in accord with the mission of the institution.

6. When the member and the institution encounter substantial disagreements or conflicts concerning professional or personal values, the member has the responsibility to directly and constructively seek resolution of the conflicts. Resolution of such conflicts may result either in sustained efforts to modify institutional policies and practices or in a decision by the member to terminate the institutional affiliation.

7. Members regularly and systematically evaluate those programs, services, and courses for which they are responsible in accord with sound evaluation principles and make these evaluation results available to appropriate institutional personnel.

E. Employment and Hiring Practices

1. Employers disseminate widely advertisements and notices which accurately and clearly describe: (a) responsibilities of the position; (b) information about the institution; (c) necessary qualifications, such as education, skills, and experiences; (d) salary range and benefits; (e) special restrictions, if any (e.g., live-in requirements, night work expectations, travel requirements, positions of a temporary nature).

2. Employers clearly specify in writing the interview and selection process to the applicant and strictly follow that process. Applicants are periodically notified of the status of their applications during the selection process.

3. Employers do not discriminate against applicants on the basis of race, color, creed, sex, national origin, affectional/sexual preference, age, or handicap.

4. Employers hire only individuals for professional positions who have received educational preparation experiences appropriate for the requirements of the positions.

5. Employers provide opportunities during the interviewing process for the applicant to gain accurate information about institutional colleagues, policies, philosophy, and about position requirements and responsibilities.

6. Employers notify employees within a minimum of thirty days when terminating or changing the status of their employment,

specifying reasons and providing full due process rights.

7. Applicants accurately represent their education, skills, and experiences.

8. Applicants respond to job offers without undue delay. Applicants accept only those professional positions they intend to assume. Both applicants and employers honor mutually derived contracts.

9. Applicants advise all institutions at which applications are pending immediately when they have signed a contract and are withdrawing from the applicant pool.

10. Members inform their employers a minimum of thirty days before leaving their positions.

F. Research, Publication, and Written Communication

1. Members are aware of and responsive to all pertinent ethical principles when planning any research activity dealing with human subjects (see *Ethical Principles in the Conduct of Research with Human Participants* [1973], Washington, D.C.: American Psychological Association).

2. Members who serve as principal researchers are ultimately responsible for assuring that all research activities conform to ethical standards. Others involved in the research activities share full and equal responsibility.

3. Members are responsible for the welfare of their research subjects throughout the study and take precautions to prevent injurious psychological, physical, or social effects:

    a. When control groups are used care is exercised to assure that they are not deprived of services to which they are entitled.

    b. When withholding information or providing misinformation to subjects is essential to the investigation (provided the conditions above are met), members fully inform subjects about the nature of the research and take corrective action as soon as possible following data collection.

    c. Participation in research is expected to be voluntary.

4. Members disguise the identity of the subjects when supplying data or when reporting research results unless specific authorization to do otherwise has been given by such subjects.

5. Members conduct and report investigations in a manner that minimizes the possibility that results will be misleading.

6. Members become familiar with and give recognition to previous work on the topic (both published and unpublished), observe all copyright laws, and give full credit to all to whom credit is due when conducting and reporting research.

7. Members who agree to cooperate with another individual in research and/or publication must cooperate as promised in terms of punctuality of performance and with equal regard for the completeness and accuracy of the information provided.

8. Members acknowledge major contributions to research projects and professional writings through joint authorships, listing the author who made the principal contribution first. Minor contributions of a professional or technical nature are acknowledged in footnotes or introductory statements.

9. Members do not demand co-authorship of publications when their involvement has been ancillary. Teachers and/or supervisors exercise caution when working with students and/or subordinate staff so as not to unduly pressure them for joint authorship.

10. Members make sufficient original research data available to qualified others who may wish to replicate the study.

11. Members communicate to other professionals the results of any research judged to be of professional or scientific value. Results reflecting unfavorably on specific institutions, programs, services, or vested interests should not be withheld for such reasons.

12. Members submit manuscripts to only one journal when seeking publication of an article. If not accepted by that journal the manuscript may then be submitted to another journal. Members do not seek publication of the same material in more than one publication without receiving consent from the editors and/or publishers involved. Slightly altered, previously published manuscripts or manuscripts under review are not submitted without first informing the editors of both publications.

G. Professional Preparation and Development

Members who are responsible for teaching others should be guided by statements on professional preparation issued by the Association and relevant accrediting agencies. Members who function as faculty members assume unique ethical responsibilities that frequently go beyond that of members who do not function in this capacity.

1. Members inform prospective students of program expectations, basic skills needed for successful completion, and employment prospects prior to admission to the program. Information about programs based on a particular theoretical position is clearly communicated to students upon application.

2. Members ensure that experiences focusing on self-understanding or growth are voluntary or, if required as part of the program, are made known to prospective students prior to entering the program. When the program offers a growth experience with an emphasis on self-disclosure or other relatively intimate or personal involvement, members should have no administrative, supervisory, or evaluative authority regarding the participant.

3. Members support preparation program efforts by providing practicum settings, field placements, and consultation to students and/or faculty members.

4. Members in charge of preparation programs ensure that such programs integrate both academic study and supervised practice.

5. Members develop and implement clear policies within their institution regarding field placement and the roles of the student and the supervisor in such placements.

6. Members present thoroughly varied theoretical positions or make provision for their study so that students may develop a broad base of knowledge.

7. Members establish programs directed toward developing students' skills, knowledge, and self-understanding, stated whenever possible in terms of competency or performance.

8. Members identify the level of competence of the student during and at the end of the programs and communicate these assessments to the student.

9. Members, through continual student evaluation and appraisal, are aware of any personal limitations of the students that might impede future performance. Members not only assist students in securing remedial assistance but also screen from the program those students who are judged unabled to perform as competent professionals.

11. Members provide programs that include research components commensurate with the levels of expected functioning. Paraprofessional and technician-level personnel should be trained as consumers of research and should learn how to evaluate their own and their program's effectiveness. Advanced graduate education, especially at the doctoral level, includes preparation for conducting original research.

11. Members make students aware of the ethical responsibilities and standards of the profession by distributing and discussing this document and other relevant documents.

12. Members conduct professional preparation in keeping with the most current guidelines of the American Personnel and Guidance Association and the American College Personnel Association.

13. Members who serve as preparation program faculty members and/or practitioners aid in providing in-service development programs and educational experiences to one another.

H. Counseling and Testing

This section constitutes general guidelines for counseling and testing experiences frequently encountered by student affairs professionals. Those professionals who are engaged in intensive counseling and/or testing activities are urged to consult the American Personnel and Guidance Association's Ethical Standards for more specific standards.

To the extent that the student's choice of action is not imminently self- or other-destructive, the student must retain freedom of choice.

1. The counseling relationship and information resulting therefrom must be kept

confidential, consistent with the obligations of the member as a professional person.

2. Members who learn from counseling relationships of conditions that are likely to harm the client or others, immediately report the condition to a responsible authority in order to preclude harm.

3. Members inform students of the conditions and/or limitations under which they may receive counseling assistance at or before the time when the counseling relationship is entered. This is particularly so when conditions exist of which the student could be unaware.

4. Records of the counseling relationship, including interview notes, test data, correspondence, tape recordings, and other documents, are to be considered professional information for use in counseling and they are not part of the public or official records of the institution or agency in which the counselor is employed. Revelation to others of counseling records shall occur only upon the expressed consent of the client or upon court order.

5. Members avoid initiating a counseling relationship or terminate an existing relationship if they are unable to be of professional assistance to the student. In either event, members refer the student to an appropriate specialist. (Members must be knowledgeable about referral resources so that a satisfactory referral can be initiated.) In the event the student declines the suggested referral, members are not obliged to continue the relationship.

6. Members adhere to the American College Personnel Association standards established in "The Use of Group Procedures in Higher Education: A Position Statement by ACPA." *Journal of College Student Personnel*, 1976, *17*, 161–168.

7. Members provide adequate orientation or information to students prior to and following any test administration so that the results of testing may be placed in proper perspective with other relevant factors. In so doing, members recognize the effects of socioeconomic, ethnic and cultural factors on test scores.

8. Members inform students about the purpose of testing and make explicit the planned use of the results prior to testing. Members ensure that instrument limitations are not exceeded and that periodic review and/or retesting are made to prevent stereotyping.

9. Members recognize the limits of their competence in the administration, scoring, and interpretation of tests and perform only those functions for which they are qualified.

10. Members ensure strict test security because the meaningfulness of test results used in personnel, guidance, and counseling functions generally depends on students' unfamiliarity with the specific items on the test.

11. Members do not permit the appropriation, reproduction, or modification of published tests or parts thereof without the expressed permission and adequate recognition of the original author or publisher.

12. Members refer to the following sources in the preparation, publication, and distribution of tests:

  a. *Standards for Educational and Psychological Tests and Manuals* (1974), revised edition, published by the American Psychological Association on behalf of itself, the American Educational Research Association, and the National Council on Measurement in Education.

  b. "The Responsible Use of Standardized Tests" the position statement of the American Personnel and Guidance Association, published in *Guidepost*, October 5, 1978.

*Adopted by the
American College Personnel
Association Executive Council
November 6, 1980*

AN INTRODUCTION TO LEGAL RESEARCH

Donald D. Gehring

HOW TO BEGIN LEGAL STUDY

Reading Chapters 9 and 10 in this book is a good place to begin legal study of higher education but it is only a beginning. Entire books have been published that lay good foundation for practitioners interested in the legal aspects of college administration. There are also some excellent subscription services that can be used to keep informed. Many of these books and services are written for the lay reader. All student affairs professionals should have at least one basic text and an updating service as part of their library.

Reading texts and subscription services is an excellent way to develop a basic understanding and keep abreast of current case law. Sometimes, however, more in-depth knowledge is required, and the administrator may want to read the entire case referred to by an author or examine a specific statute or regulation. One need not be an attorney to read the law.

RESOURCES AND HOW TO FIND THE LAW

The law affecting student affairs administration can generally be found in three sources: federal and state statutes, federal regulations, and case law.

Statutes

All federal statutes (laws passed by the Congress) are codified in the *United States Code (U.S.C.)*. Commercial printers also publish versions of the Code that contain useful cross indexes and annotations. Many volumes make up the Code, and each volume contains laws related to a specific topic. In some instances several volumes may be devoted to one topic. Each topic is referred to as an Arabic numeral title. For example, Title 42 refers to public health and welfare laws while Title 20 contains the laws related to education. References to Arabic numeral titles should not be confused with references to Roman numeral titles such as Title VI.

Title VI, which prohibits discrimination on the basis of race in federally assisted programs, is a part of the Civil Rights Act of 1964. Once that Act was passed by the Congress and signed by the President it became a law and was codified as a specific section of Title 42 (which contains all the federal civil rights laws). Citations to federal statutes will be written with the title number first, the name of the publication *(U.S.C., U.S.C.A. or U.S.C.S.)* and the section. For example, 42 U.S.C. 2000d refers to Title 42 of the United States Code, Section 2000d. The symbol § is sometimes used and simply means "section." More popular sections such as section 1983 of the Civil Rights Law of 1871 may be referred to simply as § 1983. Each of the published codes will also have index volumes filed at the end of volumes containing the statutes.

State statutes are also codified in several volumes. There are usually one or more index volumes filed at the end of the state code. State statutes are generally cited with an Arabic number representing the chapter or section of the code following an abbreviation for the name of the state statutes. For example *KRS 164.891* refers to Kentucky Revised Statutes Chapter 164 (Colleges and Universities), Section 891 (defines "agents" for purposes of malpractice insurance at the University of Louisville). Administrators who wish to become familiar with their state laws may want to peruse the index volumes for such topics as "Colleges and Universities," "Students," "Education," "Alcoholic Beverages," "Open Public Records Law," or other topics of interest.

The reference room of most college and university libraries will have copies of the *United States Code* and state statutes. These basic references can also be found in most county court houses, attorneys' offices, and public libraries.

Regulations

Often when a federal law is enacted, it will call for executive agencies (i.e., Department of Education) to issue rules to effectuate the law. For example, when Title IX of the Higher Education Amendment of 1972 was made law, it required federal agencies to make rules to implement the law. Those rules or regulations have significant impact on the daily administration of programs in postsecondary education.

Proposed regulations are first published in the *Federal Register (F.R.),* and the public is encouraged to comment on them. Once the comment period has ended, the regulations are again published in the *F.R.*

in their final form and then incorporated in the *Code of Federal Regulations (C.F.R.).* Both the *F.R.* and *C.F.R.* usually may be found in the federal documents section or reference room of most college or university libraries. They also will be in the library of a U.S. Attorney or Federal Court House.

References to federal regulations normally will cite the *C.F.R.* Like the *U.S. Code,* the *C.F.R.* is codified by title with each title covering a specific topic and designated by an Arabic numeral. For example, Title 34 refers to education while Title 29 contains regulations pertaining to labor. The title number appears first followed by *C.F.R.* (designating the publication) and the specific part to which referred . Thus, 34 *C.F.R.* 99 refers to Title 34 (education topic) of the *Code of Federal Regulations,* part 99 (The Buckley Amendment or Family Educational Rights and Privacy Act).

Case Law

Another primary source of law affecting the administration of student affairs programs is case law. Statutes are enacted by the legislative branch of government; regulations are one of the ways the executive branch of government effectuates the law, and when a controversy is settled in court, a judicial interpretation attaches to the constitution, statute, or regulation. The latter is referred to as case law.

Case law becomes very important. For instance, Title VI (part of the Civil Rights Act of 1964 passed by Congress) in essence prohibits discrimination on the basis of race in programs receiving federal financial assistance. However, the case law related to that title has held that an institution may under certain circumstances use race as one of several factors in evaluating candidates for admission without violating Title VI. However, courts also have held that the institution may not operate a quota system in which a specific number of places in an entering class are reserved for members of a particular race. Such a quota system in admissions programs would violate the intent of Title VI.

Cases decided by state courts appear in reports as indicated by the following:

N.E. 2d.   Northeastern Reporter, Second Series. Cases decided in the state courts of Massachusetts, Rhode Island, Ohio, Indiana, and Illinois.

A. 2d. Atlantic Reporter, Second Series. Cases decided in the state courts of Maine, New Hampshire, Vermont, Connecticut, New Jersey, Pennsylvania, Delaware, and Maryland.

So. 2d. Southern Reporter, Second Series. Cases decided in state courts of Florida, Alabama, Mississippi, and Louisiana.

S.E. 2d. Southeastern Reporter, Second Series. Cases decided in the state courts of Virginia, West Virginia, North Carolina, South Carolina, and Georgia.

S.W. 2d. Southwestern Reporter, Second Series. Cases decided in the state courts of Kentucky, Tennessee, Missouri, Arkansas, and Texas.

P. 2d. Pacific Reporter, Second Series, Cases decided in the state courts of Montana, Wyoming, Idaho, Kansas, Colorado, Oklahoma, New Mexico, Utah, Arizona, Nevada, Washington, Oregon, and California.

N.W. 2d Northwestern Reporter, Second Series. Cases decided in the state courts of Michigan, Wisconsin, Iowa, Minnesota, North Dakota, South Dakota, and Nebraska.

N.Y.S. 2d. New York Supplement, Second Series. Cases decided in certain New York state courts. Some of these cases also may be reported in N.E. 2d.

Cal. Rptr. California Reporter. Cases decided in the state courts of California. Some of these cases also will appear in P. 2d. The California Reporter was started in 1960 and California cases decided prior to 1960 can be found in P. 2d.

The 2d appearing after the names of the publication simply means second series.

Cases decided by United States District Courts are primarily reported in the *Federal Supplement (F. Supp.)* although some are also reported in the *Federal Rules Decisions (F.R.D.)*. There are many District Courts, and they exercise jurisdiction over a geographic area (e.g., Western District of Michigan).

Only 12 Federal United States Courts of Appeals exist and they have jurisdiction over geographic areas as listed in the following:

CIRCUIT	GEOGRAPHIC AREA COVERED
First	Rhode Island, Massachusetts, New Hampshire, Maine, Puerto Rico
Second	Vermont, Connecticut, New York
Third	Pennsylvania, New Jersey, Delaware, Virgin Islands
Fourth	Maryland, Virginia, West Virginia, North Carolina, South Carolina
Fifth	Mississippi, Louisiana, Texas, Canal Zone
Sixth	Ohio, Michigan, Kentucky, Tennessee
Seventh	Indiana, Illinois, Wisconsin
Eighth	Minnesota, North Dakota, South Dakota, Iowa, Nebraska, Missouri, Arkansas
Ninth	California, Oregon, Nevada, Washington, Idaho, Montana, Hawaii, Alaska, Arizona, Guam
Tenth	Colorado, Wyoming, Utah, Kansas, Oklahoma, New Mexico
Eleventh	Alabama, Florida, Georgia

The District of Columbia is a separate judicial circuit.

Appeals Court decisions are currently reported in the second series of the Federal Reporter *(F. 2d.)*

The United States Supreme Court is the highest court in the land and its opinions are of great significance. Thus, U.S. Supreme Court opinions are reported in several sources. The government publishes decisions of the Supreme Court in *United States Reports (U.S.).* Several commercial companies also publish the Court's opinions—*Supreme Court Reporter (S.Ct.); Lawyers Edition 2d (L.Ed.2d);* and *United States Law Week (L.W.).*

How to Read a Citation

All published opinions are cited in a similar fashion. The first name generally refers to the person initiating the suit or action, the plaintiff. The second name is the individual defending against the action, the defendant. Next there will be a series of numerals preceding and following the abbreviation for the reporter in which the case appears. The first numbers refer to the volume of the reporter while the following numbers refer to the page on which the case may be found. Finally the court (if necessary) and the year of the decision are given.

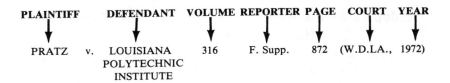

PLAINTIFF		DEFENDANT	VOLUME	REPORTER	PAGE	COURT	YEAR
PRATZ	v.	LOUISIANA POLYTECHNIC INSTITUTE	316	F. Supp.	872	(W.D.LA.,	1972)

Thus, in this citation Pratz brought an action against Louisiana Polytechnic Institute. The opinion in that case was given by the United States District Court (only U.S. district court cases are reported in *F. Supp.)* for the Western District of Louisiana (W.D.LA.) in 1972. The opinion of the court may be found in volume 316 of the *Federal Supplement* on page 872.

Citations in U.S., S.Ct. or L. Ed., list only the year in parentheses since the United States Supreme Court is assumed as court.

Nyquist v. *Mauchlet,* 97 S. Ct. 2120 (1977)

Citations of Regional Reporters for State Supreme Courts list only the name of the state and the year in parentheses.

Melton v. *Bow* 274 S.E. 2d 100 (GA., 1978)

State reporters can be found in attorneys' offices, county court houses and law school libraries. Federal reporters will generally be maintained by U.S. Attorneys, U.S. Court House libraries, and law school libraries. They will normally not be kept by local attorneys or, except possibly for Supreme Court cases, by college or university libraries.

AMERICAN COLLEGE PERSONNEL ASSOCIATION

STANDARDS FOR THE PROFESSIONAL PREPARATION OF STUDENT AFFAIRS SPECIALISTS AT THE MASTER'S DEGREE LEVEL

Adopted by the ACPA Executive Council March 1979 (Revised Draft April 1982)

These professional Preparation Standards are currently in the process of being revised and should be viewed as a working document. These Standards are published with permission of The American College Personnel Association and may be reproduced with the stipulation that appropriate credit be given to ACPA.

SECTION II.

Program of Studies*

1. *Common core for student personnel education with DEVELOPMENTAL emphasis: This common core is composed of general areas considered to be necessary in the preparation of human and organizational development oriented student personnel educators.*

    a. Human development theory and practice: Includes studies of theories of human development from age 17 through adulthood and models and principles for translating theory into practice. Socio-cultural foundations, psychosocial, cognitive-developmental, person-environment, humanistic, and behavior theories are emphasized, along with instruments for individual, group and environmental assessment. Student development program designs in various student affairs areas also are emphasized.

---

*Select one from among 1, 2, or 3.

b. Organization behavior and development: Includes study in areas such as organizational behavior, leadership, formal organizational theory, naturalistic research methods, organizational diagnosis, data-based feedback, process consultation, the consulting relationship, organizational design, and the planning and management of such notions as organizational change, decision making, conflict resolution. Offerings from areas such as higher education administration, business administration and industrial psychology may supplement program offerings.

c. The consulting relationship and group interventions for human and organizational development: Includes studies in theories and types of group interventions which could be used for organizational or human development. Group processes and structured group laboratories are emphasized. The consulting relationship is examined. Supervised practice is provided both in organizational and human developmental areas.

d. American college student and college environment: Includes study in areas such as impact of college environment on different kinds of students, attitudes and characteristics of students, sub-cultures, uses of leisure time, traditional compared with adult students and needs analysis and environmental assessment techniques.

e. The helping relationship and career development: Includes counseling theory and research, development of counseling skills and self-awareness through pre-practicum labs, theories of career development, changing roles and life patterns for men and women, career exploration techniques, and supervised practicum with clients.

f. Higher education and student personnel functions: Includes study of history, philosophy, research forms, and current and future problems and issues in higher education and in student personnel functions within higher education. Supervised practica in student personnel offices are included.

g. Administration: Includes study in areas such as legal aspects of higher education, personnel evaluation and supervision, unionization and collective bargaining, budget and finance, governance and policy making, human resource development and management information systems. Such areas as higher education administration, public administration and business administration may supplement program offerings.

h. Research and evaluation: Includes study in research design, beginning statistics, computer literacy, proposal writing and evaluation models and methodologies.

2. Common core for student personnel education with AD-MINISTRATIVE emphasis: This common core is composed of general areas considered to be necessary in the preparation of administratively oriented student personnel educators.

a. Higher education and student personnel functions: Includes study of history, philosophy, research forms and current and future problems and issues in higher education and in student personnel functions within higher education. Supervised practica in student personnel offices are included.

b. Administration: Includes study in areas such as legal aspects of higher education, personnel evaluation and supervision, unionization and collective bargaining, budget and finance, governance and policy making, human resource development, and management information systems. Such areas as higher educational administration, public administration and business administration may supplement program offerings.

c. Organization behavior and development: Includes study in areas such as organizational behavior, leadership, formal organizational theory, naturalistic research methods, organizational diagnosis, data based feedback, process consultation, the consulting relationship, organizational design and the planning and management of such notions as organizational change, decision making, conflict management. Offerings from areas such as higher education administration, business administration and industrial psychology may supplement program offerings.

d. Group interventions for leadership and organizational development: Includes theories and types of group interventions which could be used in leadership training and organizational development interventions. Group process and structured group laboratories are emphasized. Design and facilitation skills are emphasized as well as supervised practice.

e. American college student and college environment: Includes study in areas such as impact of college environment on different kinds of students, attitudes and characteristics of students, sub-cultures, uses of leisure time, traditional compared with adult students, and needs analysis and environmental assessment techniques. An overview of developmental theory of college students also is included.

f. Research and evaluation: Includes study in research design beginning statistics, computer literacy, proposal writing, and evaluation models and methodologies.

3. *Common core for student personnel education with COUNSELING emphasis: This common core is composed of general areas considered to be necessary in the preparation of counseling oriented student personnel workers.*

a. The helping relationship: Includes (1) philosophic bases of the helping relationship; (2) counseling theory, skill-building labs; supervised practice and application; (3) consultation theory, supervised practice and application; and (4) an emphasis upon development of counselor and client (or consultee) self-awareness and self-understanding.

b. Groups: Includes theory and types of group counseling, as well as descriptions of other group practices, methods, dynamics and facilitative skills. It also includes supervised practice in group counseling. Practice in other types of group work are provided as electives.

c. Life style and career development: Includes such areas as theories of vocational choice and development, relationships between career choice and life style, sources of occupational and educational information, approaches to career decision-making processes and career development exploration techniques.

d. Research and evaluation: Includes study in research design, beginning statistics, computer literacy, proposal writing and evaluation models and methodologies.

e. Appraisal of the individual: Includes the development of a framework for understanding the individual including methods of data gathering and interpretation, individual and group testing, case study approaches, and the study of individual differences. Ethnic, cultural, sex and physical disabling factors are also considered.

f. Higher education and student personnel functions: Includes study of history, philosophy, research forms and current and future problems and issues in higher education and student personnel functions within higher education. Supervised practica in student personnel offices are included.

g. American college student and the college environment: Includes study in areas such as impact of college environment on different kinds of students, attitudes and characteristics of students, sub-cultures, uses of leisure time, traditional compared to adult students, and needs analysis and environmental assessment techniques. An overview of developmental theory of college students also is included.

4. *Specialized studies: The student personnel professional preparation program includes those specialized studies necessary for practice in different work settings.*

a. Specialized studies: Includes the specialized knowledge, skills and experience needed to work effectively in different professional work settings. For example, students preparing to work in an international students or financial aids office might need opportunities for learning through seminars, assistantships, practica or field experience in these areas.

Supervised Experiences

1. *Appropriate supervised experiences provide for the integration and application of knowledge and skills from didactic study.*

a. Students' supervised experiences are in settings which are compatible with their career goals.

b. Supervised experiences include observation and direct work with individuals and groups within the appropriate work settings.

c. Opportunities are provided for professional relationships with staff members in the work settings.

2. Supervised experiences include laboratory, practicum, and/or internship.

a. Counseling and career laboratories: Counseling laboratory experiences, providing both observation and participation in specific activities, are offered in the counseling and developmentally oriented programs. These labs might include role playing, listening to tapes, viewing videotape playbacks, testing, organizing and using personnel records, interviews with field practitioners, preparing and examining case studies and using career information materials.

b. Supervised practicums: Counseling, student affairs, organizational development, human development.

(1) Supervised counseling practicum experiences provide interaction with individuals and groups actually seeking services from counselors. Some of these individuals and groups should come from the environments and represent sub-groups with whom the student is preparing to work.

(a) a minimum of one counseling practicum with individuals is required for student personnel education programs with a counseling emphasis. A counseling practicum with individuals is recommended for student personnel education programs with a developmental emphasis.

(b) the minimum recommended amount of actual counseling contact with individuals or groups for students preparing for careers in college student personnel work in programs with a counseling, developmental or administrative (if taken as an elective for administrative majors) emphasis is 12 clock hours extending over a single quarter or 18 clock hours over a single semester of supervised practicum.

(c) the supervisor's role is clearly identified and sufficient time for supervision is allocated. The recommended weekly minimum of counseling supervision is one hour of individual supervision and one hour of supervision in a group for each week in which clients are seen. Supervisory responsibilities include critiquing of counseling, either observed or recorded on audio or video tape.

(2) Supervised student affairs practicum experiences provide the student with understandings of and experience in the central mission of various student affairs offices. An array of practica in various student affairs offices are provided in different types of postsecondary institutions. The student selected student affairs practicum areas consistent with career goals.

(a) at least *two different* student affairs practica are minimum requirements for all three types of student personnel professional preparation programs. A minimum of 8 hours per week for an entire semester or quarter is the minimum required for each practicum.

(b) assistantship or internship experiences not used to meet the internship requirement (see 2 c which follows) can be used in place of student services practica. Students should be encouraged to take practica in order to broaden their experiential understanding of the scope of student personnel, however, even if assistantships or internships are used to meet the student affairs practicum requirement.

(c) the supervisor is selected from the host student services office. The supervisor's role is clearly identified and sufficient time for supervision is allocated. The recommended weekly minimum of student affairs supervision is one hour of individual supervision.

(3) Supervised organizational development practicum experiences provide students with understanding and practice in negotiating a relationship with the client group, diagnosis/needs analysis, formulation of goals

and objectives, intervention design, facilitation of an intervention and evaluation.

    (a) at least one organizational development practicum is required for student personnel education programs with a developmental or administrative emphasis.

    (b) the supervisor's role is clearly identified and sufficient time for supervision is allocated. The minimum of supervision should consist of critiquing each phase of the project before it is initiated (i.e., the contract, the diagnosis/needs analysis, goals and objectives, design, facilitation and evaluation).

    (4) Supervised human development practicum experiences provide students with understanding and practice in negotiating a relationship with client (individual or group), diagnosis/needs analysis, formulation of goals and objectives, intervention design, facilitation of an intervention and evaluation.

    (a) at least one human development practicum is required for student personnel education programs with a developmental emphasis and is recommended for those with a counseling emphasis.

    (b) the supervisor's role is clearly identified and sufficient time for supervison is allocated. The minimum of superivision should consist of critiquing each phase of the project before it is inititated (i.e., the contract, diagnosis/needs analysis, goals and objectives, design, facilitation and evaluation).

    c. Internships: An internship is an actual in-depth, on-the-job experience. At least one internship is required.

    (1) the internship placement is selected on the basis of the student's career goals.

(2) the internship includes activities that a regularly employed staff member would expect to perform. In the work setting, the intern is expected to behave as a professional and should be treated like one.

(3) the intern spend a minimum of 20 hours per week on the job within a term (semester or quarter). It is desirable that the internship be a paid experience.

(4) graduate assistantships not used to meet student services practicum requirements qualify for this experience.

(5) supervision is performed by appropriate staff in the field placement setting who have designated time allocated for these duties.

(6) the faculty provides these field supervisors with opportunities for in-service education in supervision.

(7) there should be close cooperative working relationships between staff in field placement settings and the faculty.

3. Faculty and staff with adequate time allocated to supervision are provided for laboratory, practica and internship experiences.

a. Members of the on-campus faculty responsible for supervision include those who:

(1) have earned doctoral degrees from accredited institutions; and

(2) have had experience and are competent in the type of experience being offered.

b. Doctoral students serving as supervisors of practicum experiences are themselves supervised by qualified faculty as defined above.

c. The practicum and internship experiences of all types described above are tutorial forms of instruction; therefore, supervision of six students is considered equivalent to the teaching of one three-hour course per term. This ratio is considered maximum for faculty, Ph.D. students or field supervisors.

4. Facilities, equipment and materials are provided for supervised experiences in both on and off-campus settings (see also Section IV).

Preparation Program Outreach

1. The faculty encourage individual efforts and student affairs offices to use the faculty of the preparation program in planning and conducting in-service education and in designing program improvement models.

a. The faculty is provided a teaching-work load recognition for their part in in-service and program development activities in cooperating offices or agencies.

b. The faculty involves advanced graduate students in outreach programs of in-service education and in program development planning and implementation when and where appropriate.

INDICES

NAME INDEX

A

Aaron, R 270, 271, 279, 281
Albrecht, K 91, 106, 289, 320
Albright, L 289, 319
Alderfer, C 70, 77, 80
Alexander, K 237
Alinsky, S 46, 49, 51
Allen, L 427, 444
Altman, S 403, 416
Ambler, D 506, 528
Anchors, S 402, 416, 417
Anderson, G 209, 455, 473
Angell, G 282
Appenzeller, H 237
Appenzeller, T 237
Appleton, J 19, 20, 25, 148, 149, 164,
    165, 175, 176, 189, 519, 528
Argyris, C 59, 65, 77, 87, 106
Astin, A 23, 25, 70, 77, 140, 200, 453,
    473, 475
Aulepp, L 14, 25, 140, 286, 320, 323, 338
Axelrod, J 12, 28
Ayers, A 9, 26

B

Baca, M 191, 245, 246, 261
Baier, J 461, 473
Baird, L 142
Baker, F 73, 77
Baldridge, J 45, 49, 279, 282, 289, 319,
    457, 473, 521, 526, 528
Banet, A 127, 128, 141
Banning, J 12, 26, 120, 140, 514, 515,
    517, 518, 528
Barber, A 378, 397
Barclay, J 177, 189
Barker, R 140
Barr, M 289, 319, 447, 473, 475
Beckhard, R 66, 77
Beeler, K 344, 360, 361, 370, 373, 496, 500
Bell, C 54, 62, 67, 78, 80
Bender, L 237
Benne, K 62, 78, 473
Bennis, C 449, 473
Bennis, W 69, 77
Berdie, D 455, 473, 510, 528
Berenson, C 294, 319
Berezet, L 99, 108
Berger, R 76, 78, 79

Bergquist, W 291, 292, 293, 299, 316,
    321, 504, 506
Berlet, C 282
Berry, M 376, 397
Betz, E 509, 510, 511, 528
Bickel, R 237, 261
Birenbaum, W 51
Birmingham, J 265, 279, 281
Blaesser, W 478, 500
Blake, A 94, 106, 108
Blake, R 62, 77, 312, 313, 320, 321
Blanchard, K 51, 93, 94, 106, 108, 313,
    320
Blimling, G 327, 337, 339
Blocher, D 140, 518, 528
Bloland, P 151, 164
Bolton, C 75, 77
Borland, D 42, 46, 47, 49, 53, 69, 70, 77,
    80 264, 265, 270, 271, 272, 276, 278,
    279, 281, 282, 312
Born, W 445
Boswell, L 195, 209
Bowditch, J 54, 79
Bowers, D 65, 66, 77
Boyer, R 69, 70, 75, 77, 78, 80
Bradford, L 62, 78
Brandt, J 401, 416
Braun, R 271, 281, 282
Brechin, J 434, 444, 445
Brechner, J 237, 261
Briggs, C 19, 20, 25, 148, 149, 164, 165,
    175, 176, 189, 519, 528
Brown, R 15, 26, 29, 44, 49, 140, 175,
    177, 189, 317, 325, 326, 333, 337, 343,
    370, 449 , 470, 473, 475, 484, 500, 508,
    511, 512, 513, 528
Brown, S 360, 370, 445
Brown, W 326, 337, 339
Brubacher, J 3, 5, 6, 7, 26, 29
Bruening, W 169, 189
Bryer, J 136, 143
Budig, G 457, 473
Burns, D 85, 92, 93, 96, 97, 106, 108
Butteriss, M 91, 106, 289, 320

C

Canon, H 344, 360, 361, 362, 372
Caplow, T 51, 524, 529

Carkhuff, R 326, 337
Carpenter, D 152 154, 155, 164, 165, 167,
   173, 189, 190, 298, 320, 522, 527, 530
Carroll, C 73, 79
Casaburri, N 338
Chamberlain, P 48, 49
Chambers, C 172, 174, 190
Chapman, N 401, 416
Chickering, A 12, 13, 23, 26, 29, 113, 115,
   118, 127, 128, 129, 130, 132, 133, 141,
   324, 337, 449, 473, 475, 479, 500, 512,
   529
Chin, R 321, 473
Citrin, R 140
Clack, R 417
Clark, B 141, 524, 529
Clark, D 59, 78
Coe, A 268, 273, 281
Cohen, M 504, 529
Cohen, S 73, 79
Collier, J 59, 78
Collins, E 357, 370
Comstock, C 70, 77
Conyne, R 74, 76, 78, 79, 417, 453, 473
Coombs, P 457, 473
Cooper, A 15, 26, 122, 141
Corazzini, J 141
Corey, S 59, 78
Corson, J 484, 500
Cowley, W 9, 26, 149, 164
Cox, D 344, 370
Crawford, A 364, 372
Creamer, D 29
Crockett, C 69, 70, 78, 80
Crookston, B 141 151, 164, 165, 376, 397,
   449, 473, 514, 517, 529
Crosby, H 389, 397, 456, 474
Cross, K 365, 369, 370
Cyert, R 22, 26

D

Darley, J 167
Darrow, C 142
DeCoster, D 317, 342, 370, 508
Deegan, A 456, 473
Deegan, W 290, 320
Delworth, U 14, 25, 28, 29, 140, 286, 320,
   323, 325, 332, 338, 339, 449, 450, 474,
   475, 503, 529
Deutsch, M 127, 141
Dewey, J 342, 370

DeYoung, A 400, 416
Dickerson, B 326, 339
Dickson, W 34, 50
Donnelly, J 32, 49, 51
Douglass, M 420, 444
Drucker, D 89, 106, 504, 529
Drum 14, 26, 117, 141
Dutton, T 311, 312, 320, 321
Duvall, W 326, 338, 343, 371, 517, 530

E

Eble, K 287, 320
Edwards, T 237
Eiseman, J 127, 128, 141
El-Khawas, E 174, 190
Emery, F 56, 78
Ender, K 29, 326, 338, 367, 368, 369, 370
Ender, S 175 190, 323, 325, 326, 327, 330,
   332, 335, 337, 338, 339
Epperson, D 70, 77
Erikson, E 12, 26, 96, 106, 141, 449, 473,
   479, 500
Etzioni, A 35, 49, 51

F

Fargo, J 174, 190
Fayol, H 34, 49
Feldman, K 200, 209, 324, 338, 453, 473
Ferguson, M 84, 106
Fiedler, F 92, 93, 94, 106
Fine, S 291, 320
Fisch, P 99, 108
Fisher, C 351, 353, 370
Fisher, M 501
Fisher, R 270, 281
Flacks, R 142
Flippo, E 309, 320
Fordyce, J 72, 78
Fortunato, R 291, 293, 295, 310, 320, 321
Fowler, J 141
Foxley, C 293, 321, 436, 444
Franklin, J 65, 66, 77
Frederickson, C 417
Fredrick, R 482, 500
French, W 54, 62, 67, 78, 80
Fritz, R 456, 473
Frohman, M 59, 60, 78
Fury, K 357, 370

G

Gantt, H 33, 49
Gehring, D 237, 261
Genova, W 321
German, S 331, 338
Gerst, M 400, 401, 416
Gibb, J 62, 78
Gibson, J 32, 49, 51
Gilbreth, F 33, 49
Glidewell, J 127, 143
Glueck, W 352, 371
Golightly, C 169, 190, 191
Goode, W 522, 523, 529
Gordon, W 104, 106
Gould, R 141
Gouldner, A 524, 529
Grambsch, P 42, 49
Grant, W 402, 416
Greeley, A 70, 77
Greenwood, E 173, 190, 209, 211
Greer, R 478, 500
Grites, T 279, 282
Gross, E 42, 49
Guba, E 59, 78
Guttentag, M 455, 474

H

Haimann, T 506, 529
Hallak, J 473
Hallenbeck, D 407, 416
Halverson, P 424, 444
Hammond, E 237
Hansen, R 326, 338
Hanson, G 28, 29, 445, 503, 520, 529
Hanson, W 403, 416
Harpel, R 376, 377, 397, 438, 441, 444, 520, 529
Harrie, E 405, 416
Harrison, R 63, 78
Harvey, O 141
Harvey, V 362, 371
Haseltine, F 355, 372
Hausser, D 62, 65, 66, 78
Havelock, R 59, 78
Havighurst, R 12, 26, 141
Healey, V 403, 417
Heath, D 13, 26, 141, 324, 325, 338, 479, 500
Hedlund, D 501
Heilweil, M 400, 403, 416, 417

Helzer, T 362, 371
Hennig, M 357, 371
Herbst, J 5, 26
Herron, R 478, 500
Hersey, P 51, 93, 94, 106, 108, 313, 320
Herzberg, F 94, 106, 314, 320
Heubner, L 12
Heyck, T 400, 416
Higgin, G 36, 50
Holland, J 12, 26, 141
Hollander, P 237, 244, 261
Hollingsworth, R 136, 143
Homans, G 36, 49
Hopkins, L 9, 27
Horle, R 478, 500
Hospers, J 169, 190
House, J 94, 106
Hoy, W 473, 475
Huebner, L 27, 141, 143, 516, 529
Hughes, E 523, 529
Hull, R 90, 107
Hullfish, H 209
Hunt, D 141
Hurst, J 14, 19, 20, 27, 29, 142, 449, 450, 459, 470, 474, 516, 529
Huse, E 54, 59, 62, 79, 80
Hutson, G 517

I

Ivancevich, J 32, 49, 51

J

Jackson, S 402, 416, 417
Jacobs, F 474
Jantsch, E 98, 106, 108
Jardim, A 357, 371
Joenig, K 142
Johnson, W 101, 106
Johnston, J 326, 338
Jones, J 62, 64, 66, 79, 127, 128, 141, 142, 143

K

Kahn, R 36, 49, 54, 56, 79, 80, 98, 106, 449, 474, 506, 530
Kaiser, H 416, 417
Kaiser, L 515, 528
Kaludis, G 397
Kanter, R 103, 104, 107, 357, 371
Kaplin, W 237
Kast, F 54, 79

Katz, D 36, 49, 54, 56, 79, 80, 98, 106, 449, 474, 506, 530
Katz, J. 70, 77, 99, 108
Kauffman, J 70, 77
Kavanagh, M 59, 60, 78
Keagan, R 142
Keating, L 289, 319, 447, 473, 475
Kellett, R 270, 282
Kelley, P 282
Kelly, L 326, 338
Kemerer, F 279, 282
Keniston, K 142
King, P 142
Kirn, A 62, 79
Kirn, M 62, 79
Kitchener, R 142
Klein, E 142
Knefelkamp, L 14, 21, 27, 28, 29, 119, 127, 128, 142, 144
Knock, G 151, 164, 501
Kohlberg, L 11, 13, 27, 96, 107, 142, 479, 500
Koile, E 150, 164
Koontz, H 506, 530
Kottler, J 177, 180, 191
Kraack, T 445
Kuhn, T 84, 107
Kurpius, D 343, 371
Kurtz, R 127, 142

L

Lakein, A 426, 427, 433, 444, 445
Lanning, W 17, 27
Larson, N 111, 142, 209
Latta, W 266, 282
Lawrence, P 36, 49, 56, 62, 79, 80
Layton, W 510, 528
Leafgren, F 344, 371, 373
Leonard, E 6, 27, 148, 164, 165, 193, 209
Levine, A 84, 107
Levinson, D 142, 343, 357, 371
Levinson, M 142
Lewin, K 12, 27, 34, 49, 59, 60, 79, 142, 527, 530
Likert, R 92, 107
Lippitt, G 4, 9, 27
Lippitt, R 59, 60, 79, 93, 108
Lloyd-Jones, E 149, 164
Loevinger, J 142
Lorentz, E 73, 79
Lorsch, J 36, 49, 56, 62, 79, 80

Lowell, C 237
Lucian, J 326, 339
Lynch, M 99, 107

M

Mable, P 342, 343, 344, 370, 371, 517, 530
Mackenzie, R 422, 424, 428, 436, 444, 508, 530
MacLean, S 271, 281
Madoff, M 321
March, J 504, 529
Maslow, A 87, 96, 107, 449, 474, 479, 501
Massie, J 441, 444
Maton, K 73, 79
Mausner, B 320
Maverick, L 9, 27
Maw, I 389, 397, 456, 467, 474
Mayo, E 34, 50
McCaffrey, R 403, 417, 517
McCaffrey, S 323, 338, 339, 495, 501, 527, 530
McCallan, S 326
McClellan, S 339
McCormick, E 291, 320
McFadden, R 325, 326, 331, 338
McGovern, T 501
McGowan, J 171, 190
McGregor, D 86, 87, 107
McIntire, D 298, 320
McKee, B 142
McKinley, D 120, 140, 515, 528
Megginson, L 309, 320
Mehrabian, A 417
Mendenhall, W 523, 530
Merton, R 39, 50, 449, 474
Meyerson, E 344, 361, 371
Miles, A 507, 530
Miller, J 195, 209
Miller, T 9, 14, 15, 21, 27, 28, 29, 70, 72, 73, 75, 79, 151, 152, 153, 154, 155, 164, 165, 167, 173, 175, 189, 190, 323, 325, 333, 338, 339, 344, 359, 366, 371, 373, 376, 397, 470, 474, 512, 527, 530
Miltenberger, L 327, 337, 339
Mintzberg, H 90, 107
Miskal, C 473, 475
Mitchell, T 94, 106
Montagu, A 14, 27
Mooney, J 34, 50
Moore, K 357, 371

Moore, M 449, 450, 474, 475
Moos, R 12, 27, 142, 144, 400, 401, 416,
  455, 474, 515, 530
Morrill, W 14, 27, 29, 142, 449, 450, 459,
  470, 474, 516, 529
Mosher, R 142
Mouton, J 62, 77, 94, 106, 108, 312, 313,
  320, 321
Moyers, B 85, 107
Mueller, K 478, 485, 501, 503, 530
Murray, H 36, 50

N

Naples, C 277, 282
Nejedlo, R 343, 371
Neugarten, B 142
Newcomb, T 142, 200, 209, 324, 338, 339
Newton, F 29, 326
Nolan, T 326, 338
Nordin, V 237
Nunn, N 523, 530
Nygreen, G 151, 164, 165

O

O'Donnell, C 506, 530
Odiorne, G 89, 102, 107, 108
Oetting, E 449, 474, 516, 529
Oliaro, P 344, 360, 372, 496, 501
Ostrander, S 104, 107
Ostroth, D 330, 331, 339, 501
Ouchi, W 108

P

Pace, C 12, 27, 142, 453, 474
Packwood, W 153, 165, 270, 281, 475
Paradise, L 178, 191
Park, D 504, 505, 530
Parker, C 2l, 28, 29, 119, 127, 142, 144,
  510, 530
Patterson, D 509, 530
Patton, M 59, 79
Paul, S 120, 142, 143
Pavalko, R 147, 154, 165, 209, 522, 530
Pecorella, P 62, 65, 66, 78
Penn, J 151, 165, 210, 211, 318, 320, 321,
  344, 360, 370, 373, 450, 501
Penney, J 150, 165, 210
Perrow, C 42, 50
Perry, W 11, 14, 28, 119, 127, 128, 129,
  130, 132, 143, 479, 501
Pervin, L 143

Peter, L 90, 107
Peterson, J 175, 190
Pfeiffer, J 127, 143
Phelan, D 270, 282
Piaget, J 11, 28, 143
Pillinger, B 445
Plyler, S 326
Pollack, A 36, 50
Porter, L 127, 143
Powell, J 326, 339
Prince, J 9, 14, 15, 21, 27, 28, 29, 70, 72,
  73, 75, 79, 151, 164, 175, 190, 325, 333,
  339, 376, 397, 470, 474, 512, 530
Pyler, S 339

Q

Quick, T 352, 371

R

Rapin, L 76, 78, 79
Reece, J 524, 529
Reiley, A 34, 50, 62, 66, 79
Reissman, L 524, 531
Reynolds, E 362, 371, 373
Rhatigan, J 19, 20, 25, 148, 149, 164, 165,
  175, 176, 189, 364, 372, 519, 528
Richards, N 389, 397, 456, 474
Richardson, R 343, 372, 373
Rickard, S 311, 312, 320, 321
Riker, H 20, 28, 401, 416
Rippey, D 14, 28
Risch, T 295, 320
Robins, G 385, 397
Roche, G 357, 372
Rockey, M 477, 480, 501
Rodgers, R 14, 21, 28, 117, 120, 125, 136,
  143, 144, 200, 203, 210, 478, 501
Roethlisberger, F 34, 50
Rogers, C 510, 530
Rogers, J 430, 444
Rose, M 355, 372
Rosenzweig, J 54, 79
Rudoloph, F 5, 6, 7, 28, 148, 165 210
Rudy, W 3, 5, 6, 7, 26, 29
Ruhnke, H 294, 319
Russel, J 9, 26

S

Saddlemire, G 175, 176, 190
Samples, B 104, 107
Sanford, N 12, 13, 28, 120, 143, 512, 531
Sarason, C 73, 79

Sashkin, M 59, 60, 78
Schein, E 37, 50, 51, 62, 67, 68, 79, 80, 315, 321
Schlesinger, L 75, 79
Schmidt, L 171, 190
Schmidt, W 4, 9, 27, 107
Schneider, L 8, 28
Schroeder, C 362, 372, 402, 417, 516, 517, 531
Schroeder, H 141
Schroeder, L 104, 107
Schuette, C 323, 327, 330, 332, 335, 338
Schulberg, H 73, 77
Scott, E 506
Scott, J 271, 281
Scott, P 357, 358, 370, 372
Scott, R 524
Seashore, C 75, 79
Seiler, J 54, 79
Selman, R 143
Semas, P 275, 282
Sexton, M 444
Shaffer, R 25, 28, 237, 354, 372, 519
Shaffer, W 140
Shanteau, W 99, 108
Shapiro, E 355, 357, 372
Sheehy, G 143, 343, 372
Sherwood, G 338, 339
Sherwood, J 127, 143
Shoben, E 150, 165
Shroeder, C 416
Sikes, W 75, 76, 79
Simon, N 100, 107
Sims, J 293, 321
Smail, P 400, 416
Smith, B 326, 330, 339
Smith, M 501
Snyderman, B 320
Solomon, E 237
Sprinthall, N 142, 143
Sprunger, B 291, 292, 293, 299, 316, 321, 505, 506
Stake, R 521
Stamatakos, L 167, 190, 200, 207, 208, 210, 344, 360, 366, 372, 478, 483, 496, 501
Stanton, E 307, 309, 321
Steele, F 62, 79
Stein, B 103, 104, 107
Stein, R 191, 245, 246, 261
Steiner, P 507, 530

Stern, G 12, 28, 143
Stoner, J 85, 87, 107
Struening, E 455, 474
Sullivan, E 141
Sullivan, F 272, 282
Sweetwood, H 400, 416
Switzer, K 444

T

Tannebaum, R 94, 107
Taylor, F 33, 50, 85, 108
Teague, G 279, 282
Terry, M 343, 371, 517, 530
Thomas, G 321
Thomas, K 127, 143
Thomas, R 46, 49
Thomas, W 468, 474
Thompson, M 527, 530
Thornton, R 524
Thrash, P 197, 210, 211
Tierney, M 457, 473
Tilley, D 99, 108
Tinsley, H 501
Toffler, A 83, 101, 108
Tripp, P 9, 26, 343, 372
Trist, E 36, 50, 56, 78
Trow, M 141
Truax, C 326, 337
Trueblood, D 151, 165, 167, 191
Turk, H 73, 80

U

Ullom, M 407, 416
Urick, L 34, 50

V

Vaillant, G 143
Van Hoose, W 177, 178, 180, 191
VanDort, B 400, 416
Vaughan, C 524
Vickers, G 105, 108
VonBertalanffy, L 97, 108

W

Waddell, D 291, 293, 295, 310, 320, 321
Wallenfeldt, E 501
Walters, R 405, 417
Walton, R 127, 134, 143, 144
Wanzek, R 344, 360, 361, 362, 372, 373
Warwick, D 142

Watkins, B 265, 282
Watson, J 59, 60, 79
Watzlawick, P 99, 108
Weakland, J 99, 108
Weathersby, G 457, 474
Weber, M 38, 39, 50, 449, 474
Weil, R 72, 78
Weisbord, M 54, 56, 57, 58, 64, 65, 80
Weistart, J 237
Werring, C 403, 417, 517
Westley, B 59, 60, 79
White, B 271, 281
White, R 93, 108, 144
Whyte, W 89, 108
Wichman, H 403,, 417
Widick, C 14, 21, 28, 29, 119, 125, 127,
   142, 143, 144
Wilensky, H 173, 191
Wiley, A 291, 320
Wiley, G 129, 144
Williams, G 402, 417

Williams, M 94, 106, 108, 312, 313, 320,
   321
Williams, W 287, 321
Williamson, E 151, 165, 210, 509, 523
Wilson, E 339
Winston, R 14, 28, 152, 164, 167, 173,
   175, 189, 190, 403, 417, 495, 501, 517
Wissler, A 62, 65, 66, 78
Wrenn, C 10, 28, 150, 165, 167, 178, 191

Y

Yarris, E 325, 332, 338
Young, D 237, 261
Young, J 362, 371
Young, K 200, 207, 208, 210

Z

Zawacki, R 54, 62, 78, 80
Zion, C 293, 321
Zunker, V 326, 339

SUBJECT INDEX

A

ACPA
  American College Personnel
    Assoc 15, 26, 27, 28, 29, 47,
    77, 80, 107, 141, 143, 153, 162,
    164, 165, 168, 177, 189, 190,
    199, 202, 209, 210, 236, 282,
    319, 320, 321, 323, 337, 338,
    354, 366, 370, 371, 372, 397,
    416, 473, 474, 475, 500, 501,
    528, 529, 530, 531, **Appendix A**
ACSPA
  American College Students
    Personnel Assoc 47
ACUHO
  Assoc of College and University
    Housing Officers 202
ACUHO News 416
ACU-I
  Assoc of College
    Unions-International 202
AFA
  Assoc of Fraternity Advisors
    202
AHSSPE
  Assoc of Handicapped Student
    Services Programs in
    Postsecondary Education 202
APGA
  American Personnel and Guidance
    Assoc 49, 167, 189, 191, 338
A Return to the Academy 15
ASCUS
  Assoc for School, College, and
    University Staffing 202
Accreditation 201-2
  definition 194
  foundations 197
  nongovernmental agencies 198
  practice 198-9
  preparation programs 198-9
  standards 195, 201
Action Research
  organization development 58-62
Administrative Science Quarterly
    529

Administrators
  definition 19-20
  developing 508-9
  leading 507-8
  organizing 507
  planning 507
  role 506-9
  staffing 507
American Assoc of Collegiate
    Registrars and Admissions
    Officers 168, 189
American Assoc of Higher Education
    236, 474
American College Health Assoc
    198, 209
American College Personnel Assoc
    ACPA 15, 26, 27, 28, 29, 47,
    77, 80, 107, 141, 143, 153,
    162, 164, 165, 168, 177, 189,
    190, 199, 202, 209, 210, 236,
    282, 319, 320, 321, 323, 337,
    338, 354, 366, 370, 371, 372,
    397, 416, 473, 474, 475, 500,
    501, 528, 529, 530, 531,
    Appendix A
American College Personnel Assoc
    Statement of Ethical and
    Professional Standards 178,
    182, 183, 184, **Appendix A**
American College Students
    Personnel Assoc ACSP 15, 27, 28,
    29, 47, 77, 107, 141, 143
American Council on Education 9,
    25, 49, 140, 150, 163, 176,
    189, 473, 500, 528

*American Education Research
    Journal* 473
American Journal of Sociology 191

American Personnel and Guidance
    Assoc APGA 49, 167, 189, 191, 338
American Scholar 142

American School and University
    416, 417

American Sociological Review 150
    80, 529
Annual Review of Psychology 80

Assessment
  function 16-7
  resources 455-8
Assoc of College and University
  Housing Officers ACUHO 168, 202
Assoc of College
  Unions-International ACU-I 168,
  202
Assoc of Fraternity Advisors
  AFA 202
Assoc on Handicapped Student
  Services Programs in Postsecondary
  Education AHSSPPE 202
Assoc of Independent Colleges and
  Schools 195
Assoc for School, College, and
  University Staffing ASCUS 202

B

Behavioral theory
  organizations 32, 34-5
Budgets
  auxiliary 389
  categories 389-90
  construction 389
  education 389
  formula based 389
  general 389
  incremental 388
  line item 385, 388
  planning 394-5
  program 388
  student aid 389
  types 385-90
  zero based 388
Bureaucratic theory
  organizations
    characteristics 38-9
Business Week 357, 370

C

CACREP
  Council for Accreditation of
  Counseling and Related
  Educational Programs 199,
  203

CAS
  Council for the Advancement of
  Standards for Student
  Services/Development Programs
  153, 201, 202, 203, 209, 210, 323
COPA
  Council on Postsecondary
  Accreditation 194, 203, 209
COSPA
  Council of Student Personnel
  Assoc 15, 26, 141, 175, 176,
  190, 210
CPC
  College Placement Council 168,
  202
Carnegie Council 168, 189, 191,
  404, 416
Case Studies 125-144
  data, student 129
  evaluate 137
  goals 133-4
  resident advisor data 130,
  Table 131
Certification 196
Chronicle of Higher Education 265
  273, 281, 282, 368
Collective Bargaining
  impact 263, 274
  initiation 268-9
  private sector 264-5
  process 268-75
    elections 269
    unit determination 269-75
  public sector 265-6
College Entrance Examination Bd
  168, 189
College Entrance Examination of
  Collegiate Registrars and
  Admissions Officers 168, 189
College Placement Council CPC 168-202
College and University Business 371

Colleges, land-grant 8
Commission on Colleges 205, 209
Commission on Colleges of
Southern Assoc of Schools and
Colleges 195
Commission on Professional
  Development 26
*Community/Junior College Research
  Quarterly* 28
Consultation

THE strategy 16-7
Council for Accreditation of
    Counseling and Related Educational
    Programs CACREP 199, 203
Council for the Advancement of
    Small Colleges 321
Council for the Advancement of
    Standards for Student Services/
    Development Programs CAS 152, 201,
    202, 203, 209, 210, 323
Council on Postsecondary
    Educ COPA 194, 203, 209
Council of Student Personnel
    Assoc COSPA 15, 26, 141, 175, 176,
    190, 210
Counseling bureaus 9
Counseling Psychologist 142
Counselor/consultant
    role 509-11
Counselor Educ and Superv 144
Court Cases Cited
    American Future Systems, Inc.
        v. Penn State 221, 233
    Americans United v. Rogers
        217, 233
    Assoc Stu, Inc. v. NCAA 225, 233
    Barnes v. Converse Col 230, 233
    Bayless v. Martine 220, 233
    Behrend v. State 228, 233
    Berrios v. Inter American
        Univ 215, 233
    Blackburn v. Fisk Univ 215, 233
    Blanton v. State Univ of New
        York 223, 233
    Bd of Curators v. Horowitz 222,
        233
    Bd of Regents v. Roth 244, 260
    Browns v. Mitchell 215, 233
    Brush v. Penn State Univ 221,
        233
    Buckton v. NCAA 225, 233
    Bundy v. Jackson 250, 260
    Burton v. Wilmington Parking
        Authority 215, 233
    Bynes v. Toll 224, 233
    Cannon v. University of Chicago
        229, 233
    Carey v. Piphus 256, 260
    Chess v. Widmar 217, 233
    Cooper v. Nix 226, 233
    Corning Glass Works v. Brennan
        250, 260

Court Cases Cited
    Counts v. Voorhees Col 215, 233
    Crawford v. Univ of N Carolina
        230, 233
    DeRonde v. Regents of Univ of
        Calif 229, 233
    Dickson v. Sitterson 233
    Dixon v. Alabama St Bd of
        Education 215, 221, 222, 223,
        229, 233
    Eisele v. Ayers 227, 234
    Eisen v. Regents 219, 234
    Esteban v. Central MO St Col
        222, 234
    Esteban v. Central MO 220, 222,
        234
    Ferguson v. Thomas 244, 260
    Fisher v. Flynn 249, 250, 260
    Fitzpatrick v. Bitzer 257, 260
    French v. Bashful 223, 234
    Fullilove v. Klutznick 253, 260
    Furnco Construction Company v.
        Waters 249, 260
    Gardenhire v. Chalmers 223, 234
    Girardier v. Webster College
        230, 234
    Good v. Associated Students
        219, 234
    Griggs v. Duke Power Company
        249, 260
    Grossner v. Trustees of
        Columbia University 215, 234
    Hammond v. Tampa 216, 234
    Handsome v. Rutgers 230, 234
    Healy v. James 219, 234
    Hutchinson v. Proxmire 256,
        260

    Jones v. Illinois Dept of Rehab
        Serv 230, 234
    Jones v. Vassar 227, 234
    Keene v. Rodgers 220, 234
    Lemon v. Kurtzman 217, 234
    Mahavongsana v. Hall 227, 234
    Maher v. Gagne 257, 260
    Maine v. Thiboutot 257, 260
    Marston v. Gainesville Sun
        230, 234
    Maryland Public Interest
        Research Group v. Elkins
        219, 234
    Mauclet v. Nyquist 224, 234

Court Cases Cited

McDonald v. Hogness 229, 234
McDonnell Douglas Corp v.
  Green 249, 260
Merkey v. Bd of Regents 219, 234
Mollere v. Southeastern
  Louisiana College 226, 234
Moore v. Troy State 220, 235
Morale v. Grigel 220, 235
Mt. Healthy City School
  Dist Bd of Educ v. Doyle 247, 260
National Movement v. Regents
  221, 235
National Strike Information
  Center v. Brandeis 219, 235
Nzuve v. Castleton State College
  224, 235
Papish v. Board of Curators of
  Univ of Missouri 218, 235
People v. Lanthier 221, 235
Perry v. Sindermann 244, 26
Piazzola v. Watkins 221, 235
Pickering v. Bd of Educ 247, 260
Powe v. Miles 215, 235
Pratz v. Louisiana Polytechnic
  Institute 226, 235
Pride v. Howard 227, 235
Purdie v. University of Utah
  224, 226, 235
Regents v. Bakke 229, 235
Robinson v. Davis 215, 235
Robinson v. Eastern Kentucky
  University 228, 235
Roemer v. Board of Public Works
  217, 235
Rowe v. Chandler 215, 235
Schick v. Kent St Univ 226, 235
Shamloo v. Mississippi St Bd of
  Trustees 220, 235
Shelly v. Kraemer 215, 235
Siegel v. Regents of the
  University of California
  218, 235
Smythe & Smith v. Lubbers 221,
  235
Soglin v. Kauffman 222, 235
Solid Rock Foundation v. Ohio
  State University 217, 235
Southeastern Community College
  v. Davis 230, 235
State v. Kappes 221, 236

Court Cases Cited

Steinberg v. Chicago Medical
  School 227, 236
Student Coalition v. Austin
  Peay State University 218,
  236
Sweeney v. Board of Trustees of
  Keene State College 249, 260
Sword v. Fox 220, 236
Tanner v. Board of Trustees
  228, 236
Tilton v. Richardson 217, 236
Tinker v. Des Moines 215, 218,
  236
Torres v. Puerto Rico Junior
  College 215, 236
United States v. Coles 220,
  236
University of Delaware v.
  Keegan 217, 236
Uzzel v. Friday 229, 236
Veed v. Schwartzkoph 219, 236
Weber v. Kaiser Aluminum
  Company 253, 260
Wood v. Strickland 256. 260
Wright v. Texas Southern
  University 222, 236
Credentialing 195-7

D

Dictionary of Occ Titles 291

E

Education amendments of 1972
  (PL92-318) 174
Educ Facilities Laboratory 402
Educational Leadership 444
*Educational and Psychological
  Measurement* 209
Educational Record 25, 26, 445,
  530
Educational Record Supplements 27
Employment practices
  advertising 242-3
  affirmative action 252-3
  authority, delegating 241
  civil rights liability 256-7
  contracts 243-4
  contracts, nonrenewal 244

Subject Index 569

due process 244-5
equal pay 250-1
evaluation 245-6, 258 **Appendix A**
financial exigency 248
job qualifications 242-3
legal considerations 240-62
legal issues 239-262
positions, classifying 241-2
private/public distinction
240-62
selection 243-5
separation 246-7
tort liability 240-1
Endorsement, peer 197
Environment assessment
methods 455-8
Environment and Behavior 416
Environmental resources 10
management
THE model strategies 16-7
Ethical code 171-4
functions 171
Ethical conduct
recommendations 186-7
Ethical decision-making
model 178-80
principles 182-4
Ethical decision-making process
application cases 182-91
Ethical orientation model 178-9
Ethics 169, **Table** 170
definition 168-9
general process model 179
Figure 181
statements 168, 178, 183, 184,
Appendix A
student affairs 167-91
Evaluation 285-322
functions 17-8
process 16

F

Facilities
construction 407-8
financing 407
furnishings 409
individual student development
413-4
life expectancy 410-11
maintenance 410-11

maintenance funds priorities
411
management 409-11
needs assessment 406
planning 405-6
philosophy 405-6
repair schedule 411, **Figure** 412
replacement program 411
Figure 413
space usage 406
structuring 404-5
Family Educational Rights and
Privacy Act 230
Fraternities 7,8
Functions
accountability 519-22
professionals 503-31
Future of Student Affairs 15

G

*General Order on Judicial
Standards of Procedure and
Substance in Review of Student
Discipline in Tax Supported
Institutions of Higher
Education* 222, 234
Grounded formal theory 129, 133,
137

H

Harvard 5
Harvard Business Review 27, 77,
106, 107, 370, 372, 444, 530
Hawthorne study 34
Human relations theory
organizations 34-5

I

Institute for Educ
Mgmt 26
Instruction
THE strategy 16-7
Integrated theory
organizations 32, 33-9
International Assoc of Counseling
Services 198, 209

J

Job application
  accepting job 493-4
  convention 489-90
  interviews 491-2
  on-site-visits 492-3
  resume 488-9
Joint Statement on Principles of
  Good Practice in College
  Admissions and Recruitment 168
Journal of American College
  Health Assoc 209
Journal of Applied Behavioral
  Science 78, 107, 141
Journal of Applied Developmental
  Psychology 142
Journal of Applied Psychology 528
Journal of Collective Negotiations
  in the Public Sector 281
Journal of College Student
  Personnel 27, 47,, 49, 78, 140,
  163, 164, 165, 189, 190, 210,
  211, 281, 282, 319, 338, 339,
  370, 371, 372, 417, 500, 501
Journal of the College and
  University Personnel Assoc
  281, 282, 321, 416
Journal of Contemporary Bus 106
Journal of Counseling Psych 337
Journal of Educ Psych 141, 416
Journal of Higher Education 77,
  78, 79, 80, 209, 210, 211, 372
Journal of the National Assoc of
  Women Deans and Counselors 501
Journal of Personality 143
Journal of Personnel Research 530
  531
Journal of Social Issues 79, 141

L

Leadership
  characteristics 93-4
  contingency model 93-4
  definition 85
  grid 94, **Figure** 95
  life cycle theory 94
  motivation theory 96
  systems theory 97-8
  transactional leader 96
  transforming leader 97-8

Leadership development 364-5
  contributions, professional
  364-5
Leadership theory 92-7
  "Great Man" 93
Leadership, managerial 83-109
Legal issues 213-38
  activity fees 219
  Buckley Amendment 230-2
  civil rights liability 253-7
  constitutional parameters
  216-7
  contractual relationships
  226-7
  due process 223-4
  hearings 222-3
  notice 222
  employment practices 239-62
  First Amendment 216-7, 247-8
  Fourteenth Amendment
  due process 221-1
  equal protection 224-6
  Fourth Amendment 220-1
  nondiscrimination statutes
  248-52
  private colleges contracts
  215-6
  private/public institutions
  214-5
  regulatory relationships
  228-231
  separation church/st 216-7
  speech and expression 217-8
  student organizations 218-9
  tort liability 253-6
  defamation 255-6
  proprietary practices 254
Legal responsibilities 213-4
Licensure 196
Literary societies 6-7

M

Management
  behavior theory 86-7
  budget 440
  classical theory 85-6, 91-2
  definitiion 85
  delegate 429
  evaluation 434-5, **Figure** 435
  facilities 399-417

facilities, physical 401-4
functions 87, 435-42
function, controlling 90
function, directing 90-1
function, organizing 89
function, planning 89, 90,
    436-42, **Table** 437
function, staffing 89-90
higher education 504-5
interruptions 431-2
longitudinal 390-2
meetings 432-3
outcomes 440
planning 419-45
process theory 87, 89, **Figure** 88
quantitative theory 90-1
residential environment 401
resources 375-97
scientific management 33-4
secretary 430-1
theory X 86-7
theory Y 86-7
time 419-45
    effective use 420-34
    set deadlines 428-9
time usage log 424, **Figure** 425
time wasters 422-4, **Table**_423_
tools
    budgets 377-9
    statements, financial
    379-385 **Figure** 381, 382-3,386-7
    universal principles 34
vignette
    change 103-4
    financial exigency 100-1
    moral leadership 104-5
    raison d'etre 102-3
working conditions 429-30
Management functions
planning 98-9
Management practices
flexible staffing 101
flexible time 92
human resource
    accountability system 92
job enlargement 91
job enrichment 91
job rotation 91
Mentors, professional 161,
    497-500
Morrill Act 8

N

NACA   National Assoc of Campus
    Activities 202
NACAC
    National Assoc of College
    Admission Counselors 168, 189,
    202
NASPA
    National Assoc of Student
    Personnel Administrators 26, 167,
    189, 190, 202
NASPA Journal 49, 164, 189, 281,
    283, 320, 321, 372, 397, 445,
    473, 501, 529
NAWDAC
    National Assoc for Women Deans,
    Administrators, and Counselors
    202
NCATE
    National Council for
    Accreditation of Teacher Education
    199, 203
NCCP
    National Clearinghouse for
    Commuter Programs 202
NCSD
    National Council on Student
    Development 202
NIRSA
    National Intramuara-Recreational
    Sports Assoc 202
NLRB
    National Labor Relations Board
    264, 265
NODA
    National Orientation Directors
    Assoc 202
NUCEA
    National University Continuing
    Education Assoc 202
National Academic Advising Assoc
    NACADA 202
National Assoc of Campus Activities
    NACA 168, 202
National Assoc of College
    Admissions Counselors NACAC 168,
    189, 202
National Assoc of Foreign Student
    Advisors 168
National Assoc of Secondary
    School Principals 168, 189

National Assoc of Student
Personnel Administrators NASPA 26,
167, 189, 190, 202
National Assoc for Women Deans,
Administrators, and Counselors
NAWDAC 202
National Clearinghouse for
Commuter Programs NCCP 202
National Council for Accreditation
of Teacher Education NCATE 199,
203
National Council on Student
Development NCSD 202
National Intramural-Recreational
Sports Assoc NIRSA 202
National Labor Relations Board
NLRB 264, 265
National Orientation Directors
Assoc NODA 202
National University Continuing
Education Assoc NUCEA 202
Nebraska, State 366
Northwest Assoc of Schools and
Colleges 195

O

OD
organization development 53-81
Oberlin College 7
Organization
characteristics, healthy 72
Organization development (OD)
53-81
action research phases 60-2
data collection phase 60
data feedback phase 61
diagnosis phase 61
entry phase 60
evaluation phase 61
planning phase 61
scouting phase 60
campus community
examples, levels OD 75
definition 54, **Table** 55
dimensions 54
higher education 69-71
student affairs
responsibilities 71
interventions
agenda-setting 68

classifying 62-3
consultation process
facilitators 67-8
depth 63
environment 62-3
feedback 65
goal setting 65-7
individual-group phenomena
63
process consultation 67-8
sensing interview 64-5
structured suggestions 68
target groups 63-4
task-process 63
team building 66-7
open systems 54-8
open system model 57
resource exchange model 73-4
student affairs division-wide 73
Organization developmental stages
birth 4-7
maturity 4, 8-10
youth 4, 7-8
Organization theories
integrated 35-6
Organizational analyses 39-44
goals 41-2
goals analysis 43-4
goals, classification 42-4,
Figure 43
goals, derived 43
goals, official 42-3
goals, operative 42-3
goals, output 42-3
goals, product 42-3
goals, societal 42-3
goals, system 42-3
Organizational analyses components
40-4
administrative structure 40
individual characteristics 40
informal structure 40-1
physical environment 40
role position 40

Organizational analyses emphases
39-44
goals 39, 41-44
interdependence 39-41
structures 39-40
Organizational assessment model
53, **Figure** 57

Organizational structures, **Figure** 47
  bureaucratic model 45-6
  closed system 56
  formal 45-6
  informal 45
  matrix pyramid 46-8
  open system 56, **Figure** 56
  political models 45-6
Organizations
  balance 36-7
  behavioral theory 32, 34-5
  bureaucracy theory 36, 38-9
  economic theory 32-3
  human relations theory 34-5
  integrated theory 32, 33-9
    systems 36
  macroorganizational factors 31-48
  scientific management theory 35-6
  theories 32-9
  work behavior perspectives 32-9
Orientation Review 339

P

Paraprofessionals
  criteria, selection 330
  evaluation 333
    formative 333
    summative 333
    supervisor role 333-4
  goals 327
  job descriptions 330
  limitations 328-9
  procedures, recruitment 330-1
  programs 329-30
    focus 329-30
    special issues 335-6
  rationale 324-6
  roles 326
  students 323-9
  supervisor consultation 334
  supervisor instruction 334
  supervisor mentoring 334-5
  training 331-2
Personnel and Guidance Journal 78, 164, 165, 189, 190, 191, 210, 338, 339, 397, 473, 474, 528, 530
Personnel Administrator 444
Personnel Journal 319
Philosophy
  holism 175
  humanism 175
  individualism 175-7
  pragmatism 175-6
Policy Studies in Higher Education 168
Process model
  THE 16
  Tomorrow's Higher Education THE process model 16-7
Process models
  developmental 18
Profession criteria 111-2
Professional assoc 162-4
Professional community
  definition 152
Professional development
  factors 155-9
  mentor 497-500
  model 154-5, 159-60
  resources 366-7
  topics 368-9
Professional ethics 171, **Figure** 172
Professional learning
  application 482-3
Professional organizations 522-7
Professional practice 125-6, 161, 193-211
Professional preparation 477-500
  formal courses 479-60
  graduate assistantship 483-4
  programs 187-8
  stages 154-9, **Figure** 156-7
    additive 154, 158-9
    application 154, 158-9
    formative 154, 157-8
    generative 154, 159
Professionalism 494-7
Professionals
  functions 503-3
  responsibilities 185-6
  roles 503-31, 505-19
Programs
  classification
    cube 459-60

definitions 447-8
development 447-75
implementation 461-2, 447-75
Program assessment
institutional environment
454-5
Program classification system
cube 449-51, **Figure** 451
Program development
accountability 461-78
checklist 471-2
modification 466-7
post-assessment 464-5
practice 448-51
theory 448-51
Program development process
decisions 468-9
Program planning 458-61
assessment 451-4
budget 461
delivery system 462-3
evaluation 459, 463-4
initiating 460-1
model 451-69
objectives 459
responsibilities defined 461-2
team 458-9
time-line 461
training 460-1

R

Registry 196
Resolution conflict model 134,
Table 135
Rockford College 7
Role
administrators 506-9
counselor/consultant 509-11
environmental designer 514-8
student development educators
511-4
Roles
accountability 519-22
professionals 503-31, 505-19

S

SACSA
Southern Assoc of College
Student Affairs 202, 209

School Counselor 143
School and Society 165, 210
Scientific management theory
organizations 35-6
Sloan Management Review 372
Social Forces 531
Social Research 78
Social Work 190, 209, 211
Southern Assoc of College Student
Affairs 202, 209
*Southern Journal of Educational
Research* 281
Staff
evaluation 315-9
approaches 316-9
effective 317-8
management-by-objectives
317-8
portfolios 317
rating scales 316-7
structured narration 316
unstructured documentation
316-7
unstructured narration 316
leadership style 312-3
motivation and morale 314-5
organizatinal structure 311-2
paraprofessionals 287-8
professionals 286-7
student voluneers 288
supervision, effective 312-3
supervisors 311

Staff development, **Figure** 348
academic course work 360
components 345-65
discussing groups 359
mentoring 355-8
motivation 346-51
performance evaluation 351-5
self-assessment 346-51
structured learning 358-60
supervision evaluation 351-5
in-service 485
issues 365-73
standards, professional 366
objectives 344-5
organizational 360
personal 369
personal education 341-73
personal professional reading
364

philosophical foundations
341-3
professional 369
professional education 341-73
professional participation
363
professional responsibilities
485-7
programs
human development 342-5
self-assessment 361-2
publication opportunities 487
retreat format 362-3
roles 355 **Figure** 356
self-directed learning 365-6
structured learning experiences
367
Staffing 285-322
horizontal 295, 307-8
interviews 310-11
interviewing candidates 298-9,
Figure 300-2, **Figure** 303-5
personnel forecasting 289-91
personnel planning 289-91
position analysis 291-4
references 309
support positions 207-8
vacancies 294-310
vertical 295-6, 307-8
Standards
impact 206
implications 207-8
professional preparation ACPA
153, **Appendix C**
using 207-8
Standards components 204-6
activities 205
ethics 206-7
evaluation 206-7
financial and physical resources
204-5
human resources 204
programs 205
relationships 205-6
services 205
Standards, professional 200-1
Standards rationale
practice 199-200
preparation 199-200
Student affairs
definition 3

ethics 153, 167-191, **Appendix A**
factors 22-4
endowments 22
functions 22
location 22
sex 22
size 22-4
type 23-4
historical perspective 4-10
mission 18
preparation, professional 160-1
profession controversy 150
professional development 147-165
rationale 10
theories and practices 111-44
values 175-6
Student affairs administrator
responsibilities 186-7
Student development
definition 20-1
process model 14, 15
cube 14
ecosystem 14
education 14
grounded formal 14
seven-dimensional 14
responsibilities 24
theory-to-practice approaches
116
Tomorrow's Higher Education
functions 15
educators role 511-4
services postsecondary
education 175
*Student Development in Tomorrow's
Higher Education* 15
Student Developmental Task
Inventory 14
Student health programs 8
Student housing 8
Student needs 452-4
Student Personnel Point of View
THE 9, 150, 175, 176
Student service functions 9
Supervision 285-322
System characteristics 37-8

T

Theories 111-44 **Figure** 117
cognitive 11

developmental 10-1, 13
  phases, definition 14
  stages, definition 14
life cycle 12
organizations bureaucratic 38-9
person-environment interaction
  11-2
psychological 11
psychosocial 12
Theory
  cognitive 119
  depth 113-5, **Figure** 114
    Figure 116
  locations 1-4, 113-115
  formal 117-8
  grounded formal 129
    phases 125-6
  person-environment interaction
    119-20, **Figure** 121
  process model 122-3, **Table** 124
  psychosocial 118
Theory to practice
  case study 125-44
    resident advisor data 130,
      Table 131
  case study data, student 129,
    Table 130
Tomorrow's Higher Education, THE
  15
  process model 16-7
    assessment function 16
    goal setting function 15-6
THE Tomorrow's Higher Education
  15
THE process model 17
  strategies
    consultation 16-8
    environmental resource
      management 16-7
    instruction 16-7

U

Unionization
  factors, contributing 267-8
    security 267
  process
    election results 272-5
    negotiations 273-5
    organizing 271
    petition 272-3
    reactions 276-80
Unionization factors
  economics 267
  structural complexity 267
  United States National Student
    Assoc 283

V

Vectors 115, 118, **Figure** 116

W

Wesleyan Female College 7
Western Interstate Commission on
  Higher Education 25, 28, 140,
  320, 338, 474, 475
William and Mary, College 5
Work behavior perspectives
  organizations 32-9
Workshop 137 **Table** 138-9

Y

Yale University 5

ABOUT THE AUTHOR

Theodore K. Miller is Professor of Counseling and Human Development Services at the University of Georgia, where he is coordinator of the Student Personnel in Higher Education Preparation Program and Director of the College of Education Center for Student Development. Born in Iowa and reared in Indiana, he was awarded the B.S. degree in business and English and the M.A. degree in counseling and guidance from Ball State University. He received the Ed.D. degree in counseling and student personnel services from the University of Florida.

Dr. Miller is co-author of *The Future of Student Affairs, Students Helping Students,* and the *Student Developmental Task Inventory.* He also co-edited *New Directions for Student Services: Developmental Approaches to Academic Advising.* He has been active in professional association activities and was President of the American College Personnel Association (1975-76) and Chairperson of the ACPA Tomorrow's Higher Education Project (1974-75). He is a member of the Board of Directors of the American Personnel and Guidance Association (APGA), a member of the Executive Council of the American College Personnel Association (ACPA), and is President of the Council for the Advancement of Standards for Student Services/Development Programs (CAS). He is currently a member of the Board of Directors of the Council for Accreditation of Counseling and Related Education Programs (CACREP).

ABOUT THE AUTHOR

Roger B. Winston, Jr., is Assistant Professor in the Student Personnel in Higher Education Program in the Department of Counseling and Human Development Services and Director of the Student Development Laboratory at the University of Georgia. He received an A.B. in history and philosophy from Auburn University, and the M.A. in philosophy and the Ph.D. in counseling and student personnel services from the University of Georgia. Prior to his assuming a teaching position, he was Dean of Men and Associate Dean of Students at Georgia Southwestern College. He is co-author of the *Student Developmental Task Inventory,* co-editor of *New Directions for Student Services: Developmental Approaches to Academic Advising,* and author of numerous journal articles.

Professionally, he has been active in the American College Personnel Association, serving as the first editor of *ACPA Developments,* a senator and executive council member, chairperson of the task force that developed the ethical and professional standards adopted in 1980, member of the standing committee on ethical and professional conduct, and a member of the directorate of Commission XII (preparation of student personnel professionals). In the Southern Association for College Student Affairs, he has served as chairperson of the professional standards committee and associate editor of the *College Student Affairs Journal.*

ABOUT THE AUTHOR

William R. Mendenhall currently serves as Associate Vice-President for Student Affairs at the University of Georgia, and he has had seventeen years experience in successive levels of student affairs administration. The initial five years was served in housing and residence hall programs at Indiana State University and Illinois State University. Later, he served in several specialized administrative roles including Greek affairs adviser, new student orientation director, staff development specialist, and budgetary officer at the University of Florida after working on the staff of the Florida Board of Regents. His current duties at the University of Georgia include supervision and coordination of seven of the twelve units in the Student Affairs Division and responsibility for continuing staff education and graduate teaching.

Dr. Mendenhall received his B.S. degree in social science education and his M.S. degree in sociology, both from Indiana State University. He received the Ph.D. from Florida State University in higher education administration and sociology. He has had both undergraduate and graduate teaching experience in sociology, higher education, and student development at the Illinois State University, the University of Florida, and the University of Georgia. He has served as NASPA State Director for Georgia and as a member of Commissions III and XII of the American College Personnel Association.